W9-AZU-706

Promoting Literacy in Grades 4–9

A Handbook for Teachers and Administrators

Edited by

Karen D. Wood

University of North Carolina at Charlotte

Thomas S. Dickinson

Indiana State University

Allyn and Bacon

Boston ■ London ■ Toronto ■ Sydney ■ Tokyo ■ Singapore

This book is dedicated with love to my children:
Eric, Ryan, Lauren, and Kevin
K.D.W.

And to Kathleen Sheehan Dickinson,
who taught me how to read.
T.S.D.

Series editor: *Arnis E. Burvikovs*
Series editorial assistant: *Bridget Keane*
Marketing manager: *Stephen Smith*
Manufacturing buyer: *Suzanne Lareau*

 Copyright © 2000 by Allyn & Bacon
A Pearson Education Company
Needham Heights, MA 02494

Internet: www.abacon.com

All rights reserved. No part of the material protected by this copyright
notice may be reproduced or utilized in any form or by any means, electronic
or mechanical, including photocopying, recording, or by any information
storage and retrieval system, without written permission from the
copyright owner.

Library of Congress Cataloging-in-Publication Data

Promoting literacy in grades 4–9 : a handbook for teachers and administrators /
edited by Karen D. Wood and Thomas S. Dickinson.
    p. cm.
    Includes bibliographical references and index.
    ISBN 0-205-28314-4
    1. Language arts (Elementary)—Handbooks, manuals, etc. 2. Language arts
(Middle school)—Handbooks, manuals, etc. 3. Literacy programs—United States.
I. Wood, Karen D. II. Dickinson, Thomas S.

LB1576.P76 2000
372.6—dc21   99-055413

Printed in the United States of America

10 9 8 7 6 5 4 3 2 1   04 03 02 01 00

CONTENTS

PREFACE AND ACKNOWLEDGMENTS

As the editors of this book, *Promoting Literacy in Grades 4–9: A Handbook for Teachers and Administrators,* we have had numerous experiences working with teachers, administrators, curriculum coordinators, undergraduates, and graduate students, and we have found that the questions and concerns across the nation appear to be the same. We typically hear questions such as: Which book will give the necessary information for improving schoolwide literacy? Is there one resource to which I can refer that addresses the literacy needs of both the teacher and the administrator? How should I teach literacy in the intermediate grades? and the middle grades? These questions and more prompted us to put together this handbook. We use the term *handbook* because this book is more than just a textbook; it is a reference guide. It can be read cover to cover or can be referred to by chapter or topic when more detailed and specific information is needed. Like a reference handbook, it is comprehensive and covers everything from the role of the principal and the characteristics of the learners to teaching the gifted and motivating the reluctant learner. Like a textbook, it can be used at either the undergraduate or graduate level to provider learners with a thorough examination of current literacy issues, research, and practices at these grade levels.

Each chapter in this handbook is written in a "reader friendly" style, with an array of examples of student work, classroom vignettes, sample lessons, and step-by-step descriptions of instructional strategies. In most instances and whenever it is relevant, the chapters are presented in a "research into practice" format, with a research synthesis that represents the current thinking in the field. We also offer "voices"; that is, the chapters are written by a variety of professional educators, leaders in the field, who have firsthand experience of these literacy issues in the classroom.

This book is divided into three sections. The first section, Part One, The Literacy Program in the Intermediate and Middle Grades, takes a global view of the school, community, teachers, administrators, and parents and the role of each in promoting literacy. The first three chapters define the role of the teacher (Nancy Farnan), the principal (Dana L. Grisham, Diane Lapp, and James Flood), and the literacy specialist (K. Denise Muth and Shawn M. Glynn) using actual case studies, scenarios, and current research. Then, in Chapter 4, David W. Moore examines both administrative and classroom settings and how they affect schoolwide literacy. Timothy Rasinksi, known for his extensive work in parent education and family literacy, is joined in Chapter 5 by Director of Curriculum and Instruction, Gay Fawcett, to offer numerous classroom-tested ways to involve parents in the literacy program. Next, Laurie Stowell describes the different dimensions of community and how literacy can be used to build community alliances. Finally, Sharon O'Neal, reading director in the Texas Education Agency, teams up with Barbara Kapinus of the National Education Association to give us a practical view of how national and state standards can help students move "beyond the basics" into more critical and creative thinking and application.

Part Two, Literacy and the Intermediate and Middle School Learner, examines the developmental, cognitive, and instructional variations common to this age group.

The opening chapter by Judith L. Irvin and Susan E. Strauss demonstrates how understanding young adolescent development can help in the vision for a schoolwide program of literacy. Then, drawing on her extensive expertise in this area, Linda B. Gambrell and coauthors Ann J. Dromsky and Susan Anders Mazzoni provide a number of suggestions for increasing student motivation to learn. Tom Liner and Deborah Butler show how grouping for literacy can be used to give students a "voice" in their learning. Recognized leader in special education Bob Algozzine and coauthors John Beattie, Bob Audette, and Monica Lambert share their expertise in Chapter 11. Next, Josefina Villamil Tinajero and Sandra Hurley keep us informed about the best practices for students acquiring English. The last chapter in this part, by Shelagh A. Gallagher, gives us numerous ways to fit literacy to linguistically gifted learners.

The last and largest section, Part Three, Promoting Literacy in the Classroom, is devoted solely to instruction. Here we find not only the "why," the basis in research and theory, but also the "how": how to teach students in grades 4 through 9 to write, to study, to think, and to read. Jeanneine P. Jones introduces us to classroom-tested ways to integrate the curriculum through interdisciplinary units, and Karen Bromley offers specific suggestions for integrating language arts with the content areas. Chapter 16 by Karen D. Wood and William Dee Nichols provides sample lessons and examples of student work actually used in classrooms. Known for their extensive work with children's literature, Miriam Martinez, Nancy L. Roser, and Susan Strecker show how picture books can be used with older children. Charles Temple shares his special interest, knowledge, and expertise in spelling in Chapter 18. Patricia M. Cunningham, known nationally and internationally for her work in phonics and word study, extends her familiar theories to the upper grades in Chapter 19. Roser, Strecker, and Martinez expand on their work with children's literature in Chapter 20, Literature Circles, Book Clubs, and Literature Discussion. Former editor of the technology column for *The Reading Teacher,* Robert J. Rickleman, and teacher Robert M. Caplan team up to take us to a possible classroom scenario in the year 2010 in Chapter 21. Extending their landmark work in the visual and communicative arts as well as their current *Reading Teacher* column, Diane Lapp and James Flood, accompanied by Wendy Ranck-Buhr, give us practical ways for promoting visual literacy in tomorrow's classrooms. Paul Cantú Valerio is joined by John E. Readence, known for his expertise in content area literacy, in Chapter 23. Dera Weaver along with Donna Alvermann, well recognized for her research in comprehension, tell us the why and how of improving students' critical thinking and discussion. Writing is the focus of Chapter 25 by Debra Bayles Martin and James V. Hoffman, as they show us how concerns theory can be used to help students focus their thinking and improve their writing performance. Patricia Douville and Janet Finke provide student examples and vignettes to show us the power of creative drama such as readers' theater, puppetry, and improvisational drama in Chapter 26. Realizing that the ability to read and understand documents constitutes the majority of society's reading time, Cathleen M. Rafferty gives specific examples of how to prepare intermediate and middle grades students to become document literate. Jeanne R. Paratore, drawing on her extensive work in flexible grouping, and Rachel L. McCormack's practical classroom applications and adaptations of this work give us numerous ways to incorporate grouping in the intermediate and middle grades. Chapter 29, the final chapter, is on assessing the intermediate and middle grades learner, and who better to make this contribution than Roger Farr, whose expertise in literacy assessment is recognized nationally and internationally.

Acknowledgments

Our appreciation goes to the following reviewers for their comments on the manuscript: Elaine Charkonas, Dominican University; Cheryl L. Cooke, University of Minnesota; Lauren Freedman, Western Michigan University; and Susan McIntyre, University of Wisconsin, Eau Claire.

   Whether you journey through this book from start to finish or visit and revisit destinations as needed, we trust you will enjoy the trip!

K.D.W.
T.S.D.

PART ONE

The Literacy Program in the Intermediate and Middle Grades

1

The Role of the Teacher in the Literacy Program

NANCY FARNAN

San Diego State University

Who is your most memorable teacher, and why does this person come to mind? For me, it was Mrs. Barber, who seemed ancient at the time, but who was probably only in her fifties when I was in fifth grade. Her white hair was short, and I remember that it was tucked behind her ears and lay close to her head. She was tall and projected a no-nonsense image of strength and dignity, mixed with a wink and a wide smile outlined with bright red lipstick. She read Milne's *House at Pooh Corner* to our class and breathed life into Eyeore, Tigger, Christopher Robin, and, of course, Pooh. I remember watching the deeply etched lines in her face as they worked with her voice to create the different characters. I was a reader long before Mrs. Barber's class, but *House at Pooh Corner* remains on my top ten list these many years later. I read it to each of my children, laughed again, maybe in different places this time, and have a complete set of Milne's books in a prominently placed bookcase in my home.

Today, as a teacher and teacher educator, and well beyond my fifth-grade year, I can reflect on Mrs. Barber's expertise through filters of my own experience as a professional educator. Although Mrs. Barber did not read Trelease's *The Read-Aloud Handbook* (1995), she was, as I remember it, a captivating reader whose eyes, gestures, and voice modulation created rich images in concert with the words on a page. She was a teacher with an expert's grasp of what Shulman (1987) referred to as pedagogical content knowledge, the knowledge and expertise required to bring content and pedagogy together to engage learners and promote learning.

Research on Teachers' Necessary Knowledge and Skills

I know now that what was a delight to me in fifth grade was actually the result of a complex interaction of teacher skill and knowledge. Not surprisingly, however, research on the views of individuals just entering the teaching profession reveals a somewhat simplistic perspective on teaching and learning. In a review of this research,

Brookhart and Freeman (1992) found that two themes emerged. First, preservice teachers entering their teacher preparation programs tended to see their primary role as nurturing and ensuring positive interpersonal relations with their students. Second, they tended to see teaching as the dissemination of information, with learning occurring through the transfer of information from themselves to the students in their classes.

In contrast, research on the knowledge and skills required of beginning teachers (Reynolds, 1992) revealed quite a different picture. In her synthesis of research, Reynolds concluded that preservice teachers should enter their first year of teaching with the following:

- Subject matter knowledge
- An interest in their students and the school and the ability to gather relevant information
- Knowledge of strategies, techniques, and the skills to use them to create an effective learning environment
- Knowledge of effective pedagogy that relates directly to the content being taught
- The ability to function as reflective practitioners to continually improve their teaching

In addition to these abilities, Reynolds concluded that during the first year of teaching, teachers should:

- Plan lessons that tie new learning to students' prior knowledge and experience
- Establish and maintain positive rapport and personal interactions with students
- Manage the physical organization of the classroom so that it always represents a learning environment most effective for the task
- Help students develop metacognitive awareness of the task and of their own learning
- Use a variety of assessment processes and be able to use the results to inform subsequent instruction
- Reflect not only on their own teaching, but also on students' responses in the learning environment

When Darling-Hammond (1996) discussed what teachers need to know and be able to do, she included many of the things that Reynolds described, such as in-depth subject matter knowledge and an ability to tie new learnings to students' prior knowledge and everyday life. Teachers must be able to address students' misconceptions; create opportunities for interdisciplinary connections; understand child and adolescent development and how to support young learners' cognitive, social, emotional, and physical growth; and design strategies, activities, and plans that ensure learning for a student population that is increasingly linguistically and culturally diverse. In addition, teachers must design environments in which learning is supported by positive rapport and caring, where students are motivated to engage in academic tasks and reflect on their own learning, where assessment informs instruction, and where multiple strategies are tailored to the learner and the task demands. Finally, teachers must be able to reflect on both their teaching and students' learning for the purpose of continually improving curriculum and instruction.

Ruddell (1997) offered a research-based look at what he called a "portrait of the influential teacher" (p. 39), defined as a teacher who has been recognized, either by student or peer nomination, for outstanding teaching effectiveness. What the research on traits of highly effective teachers tells us has implications for understanding the roles of the literacy educator. These teachers were judged to be among the most influential for the following characteristics and abilities:

- They are aware of and sensitive to individual students' needs, abilities, and motivations.
- They are aware of students—who they are and what they know—and are able to help learners relate their prior knowledge to new learning.
- They make content personally relevant to students.
- They are skillful at using strategies for learning and "are masters at orchestrating their instruction" (p. 50).
- They promote active participation and give students useful feedback to support learning.
- They are masterful at running classrooms where students share responsibility and take ownership of their learning.
- They help students self-assess and monitor their own learning.
- They have high expectations for themselves as well as their students.

The research on teacher knowledge and effective teaching highlights the magnitude of teacher responsibilities, skills, and competencies. The role of the teacher is a daunting one from the very beginning.

Teachers at the Center of Literacy Teaching and Learning

At the heart of this chapter is the assumption that the teacher is the sine qua non in a setting where the objective is to work expertly in the complex processes of teaching and learning to ensure the literacy development of all children. Said simply, the teacher's role is a powerful one. Darling-Hammond (1996) spoke unambiguously of the importance and power of the teacher's role, stating that "regulations cannot transform schools; only teachers, in collaboration with parents and administrators, can do that" (p. 5).

She described a "quiet revolution" that has resulted in the setting of rigorous standards for teaching and learning, a revolution in which schools participate through reform agendas that include organizational changes in the form of interdisciplinary teams and site-based management, school–university partnerships that involve a joint commitment to preservice teacher education, and an increased emphasis on professional development. Many of today's reforms focus on teacher development, highlighting the teacher's central role in education.

The remainder of this chapter looks at four roles of the teacher in a literacy program. Based on the extensive research on teacher knowledge and skills and characteristics of effective teachers, each role is grounded in the premise that the very best teachers, those who are expert in the application of up-to-date literacy issues and practices, are committed to career-long professional growth and leadership. Kagan (1992), in her review of research on the professional growth of preservice and beginning teachers, defined professional growth as "changes over time in the behavior, knowledge, images, beliefs, or perceptions of novice teachers" (p. 131). Although it is reasonable to define professional growth as beginning when teachers enter the field of education as novices, in this chapter the definition of professional growth and development shifts to include an emphasis not only on novice teachers, but also on midcareer and veteran teachers. Professional growth, then, is career-long growth and development that leads to ever-increasing expertise and to an ability to assume leadership roles both inside and outside the classroom.

As they all relate in a significant way to teachers' ongoing professional growth, each of the four roles described in this chapter has import for highly effective teachers and is, therefore, critical to the literacy development of students. It is problematic, however, that as soon as the roles are identified and written down, reduced to descriptors or labels, they suddenly seem insufficient to do what is intended: to delineate the various roles of teachers in the literacy program. This sense of insufficiency may exist because attempting to capture complex ideas with words is difficult; the labeling itself implies a simplicity and discreteness of ideas, a concreteness rather than flexibility of thought. In reality, the roles, as described in this chapter, are complex and overlapping, and it is obvious that the lines between them quickly begin to blur. Nevertheless, for the sake of discussion, this chapter identifies four roles, albeit related and overlapping, that are central to being an effective literacy educator.

Teacher as Reflective Practitioner

In 1987, Schön wrote about *Educating the Reflective Practitioner.* His concept of the reflective practitioner focused on the roles of the teacher as problem solver and decision maker. Avery (1993), whose professional life as an English teacher, librarian, and first-grade teacher has been grounded in literacy learning, wrote about these roles as a teacher in her first-grade classroom. She commented that "effective teaching is based on continuous decision making by a professional in response to the current context of the classroom," where "thoughtful decisions are made in response to individual children in particular settings at given moments in time" (p. 16).

Nowhere is this as true as it is in literacy development. Without reflection, it is impossible to know whether young readers understand the alphabetic principle, have mastered basic concepts about print, and understand that reading is a meaning-making process. It is impossible to know whether adolescent readers mobilize their prior knowledge as it relates to a reading, have appropriate strategies to guide them when they do not understand what they read, or realize that a history text is not read in the same way that they read *Seventeen* magazine or the novel *The Education of Little Tree* (Carter, 1976).

Clearly, reflection is closely tied to inquiry and assessment, and the thinking and evaluating that represent reflection lead directly to adjustments and change. For example, teachers often express concern that students do not seem motivated to read, a concern that shows up in research (O'Flahavan, Gambrell, Guthrie, Stahl, & Alvermann, 1992; Veenman, 1984). In fact, the term *aliteracy* was coined specifically to refer to capable readers who choose, for whatever reason, not to read (Harris & Hodges, 1995). The question is, How do teachers know whether, for a particular student, a lack of motivation to read represents the primary obstacle to reading? To problem solve around the issue of a student's disinclination to read, a teacher may decide to assess students' motivation to read by administering the Motivation to Read Profile (MRP) (Gambrell, Palmer, Codling, & Mazzoni, 1996), which combines a group survey with individual interviews so as to assess two major determinants of reading motivation: a student's self-concept as a reader and the value he or she places on reading. Tested for both validity and reliability, this instrument helps teachers make decisions about subsequent instruction based on the finding that a low level of motivation might be interfering with student engagement.

Using results of the MRP, the teacher can create an action plan to adjust classroom practice. For instance, if a child self-reports that reading is hard or boring, the teacher can offer books or other materials that might be at the child's independent reading level and be of specific interest to the child. For students whose scores on the MRP indicate a low self-concept as a reader, the teacher can, again, introduce the child to interesting reading materials at his or her independent reading level, where the child could experience success and potency as a reader. Another motivational activity is encouraging the child to practice reading a book in preparation for reading it to a younger student (Gambrell et al., 1996).

Because action research relates to a specific teacher and his or her own classroom, the opportunity to reflect is directly relevant and focused. At the heart of a teacher's responsibility lies the need to have a dynamic classroom that meets the continuously changing needs of students. Therefore, an important role of the literacy educator is to be a reflective practitioner, an informed problem solver and decision maker who strives to answer essential questions regarding students' literacy development: If we are teaching students to read, how do we know they are learning? If our students are not reading, what do they need? Where do the problems lie? Action research may, in fact, be one of the best models of the reflective practitioner.

The next section of this chapter looks at the role of *teacher as collaborator*. It begins with a focus on collaborative action research, highlighting that boundaries between the concepts of *teacher as reflective practitioner* and *teacher as collaborator* quickly blur. Often in action research we work collabortively with others, and we are spurred on by one another's practices and creativity.

Teacher as Collaborator

Darling-Hammond (1996) highlighted the natural connection between teacher research and teacher collaboration: "Teachers learn best by studying, doing, and reflecting; by collaborating with other teachers; by looking closely at students and their work; and by sharing what they see" (p. 8). Sagor (1991, 1992) reported on findings of an extensive collaborative action research project involving Washington State University and over 50 schools. From this project, Project LEARN (League of Educational Action Researchers in the Northwest), lessons were learned about the power of collaborative action research. Teachers gathered concrete evidence of improved student learning, improved their own practices, were aware of increasing their professional expertise, and felt connected to and supported by a professional community. They became adept at collecting a variety of data, including students' journals and other writings, projects, observation checklists, and results of both formal and informal assessments, to address their questions.

Sagor (1992) described the steps of action research as those associated with inquiry and problem solving: data collection, data analysis, reporting of results, and developing an action plan based on findings. The action plan is the critical component of action research. In Project LEARN, those plans included presentation of data to others and pilot programs designed to substantiate effective practice. Participants in the project concluded that collaborative action research removes the traditional isolation felt by teachers in their classrooms, offers support for new learnings and professional development, gives teachers a voice in decision making, and contributes to an overall knowledge base.

Another example of extensive collaborative action research includes the work of Santa, who has provided extensive leadership and support for teachers engaging in action research. Underlying her work in a collaborative teacher–researcher community is the idea that teachers "can make decisions closest to the point of delivery by observing their own teaching and analyzing the performance of their students" (1990, p. 64). As curriculum director of her school district, instead of spending time writing notebooks full of curriculum materials, she worked with teachers to become a "community of researchers."

Collaboration was at the heart of their work as teacher researchers. They reported that the collaboration allowed them to "create opportunities to talk about new instructional ideas and to formulate questions for our own research. We conduct research in our classrooms and talk about it with students and colleagues" (Santa, 1990, p. 66).

Although these collaborative groups began at the high school level, teachers with similar concerns at intermediate and middle grades gradually became involved in the teacher–researcher community. The initial concern that caused teachers to search for change was students' lack of ability to read and learn from assigned texts. Together, teachers read articles and books on such things as helping students understand text organization, the role of prior knowledge in reading and learning, metacognition, and active learning strategies. Readings and discussions led teachers to examine whether what they were learning would work in their classrooms. In the project, a math teacher explored the effects of prior knowledge and prediction on students' reading and learning in one of her geometry classes. She shared with her students not only the new strategies she was bringing to the classroom but also what effect those strategies might have on their learning. She talked informally with her colleagues about her procedures and the data she collected along the way. Finally, when she collected data to substantiate that her experimental group had outperformed the control class, she made a more formal presentation at a faculty meeting and summarized her results for distribution in a districtwide newsletter.

Participating history and science teachers conducted action research on the effect of two-column notes on student reading and learning. Teachers in two sixth-grade classrooms formed a study team and researched the efficacy of round robin reading as a strategy for content reading. One class was the experimental group, whereas the other did round robin reading, both using the same amount of time to read and study a chapter in the social studies text. The teachers then reversed the treatments for the two classes. In each case, they found that the class that used round robin reading as a content reading strategy learned less content than the other class. At the end of their research project, they asked for students' reflections. They discussed why they had learned more from the experimental procedure than from the round robin reading, providing further evidence for the power of the experimental strategy. The teachers then disseminated their results at staff meetings and in newsletters. Their action plan was clear. Round robin reading would be replaced by new strategies to help youngsters read and learn from content.

More recently, Harris and Drake (1997) reported on schoolwide action research teams that were formed in a large urban school of 1,400 students in southern Ontario. The objective was "to develop teacher leaders, teachers as change agents, and a collaborative reflective culture" (p. 15). Unfortunately, the project was not an unqualified success. After three years of working on the project, they concluded that teachers learned to work better together. Clear goals for the research teams were never clarified, however. Another problem was that there may not have been enough time for teachers to become familiar with the role of research in their professional growth and development. Participation in the study teams was mandated by the principal, and many teachers, already overburdened with responsibilities and commitments, were reluctant to participate in one more activity. The top-down nature of the study team project may have usurped teachers' own motivations for participating in action research. In addition, because time is always a critical commodity for teachers, teachers' inquiry and their research must become an integral part of their classroom needs and agendas. In other words, motivation must come from the teacher researchers themselves.

Grisham (1998), a university teacher educator working with teachers in a professional development school (PDS), developed teacher study groups (TSG) specifically around teachers' interests and concerns. Teachers volunteered to participate in TSGs, which centered on three themes of interest expressed by the teachers: literature response circles, spelling, and reluctant writers. These groups met monthly throughout the academic year. Two of the groups evolved into action research teams for the purpose of investigating their own practices and their effect on students' literacy development. In the action research teams, teachers read and studied professional books and journals to inform them about the subject of their inquiry. They discussed what they were currently doing and adjusted their practices to meet the needs of the children in their individual classes.

In the second year of the project, teachers in the study groups, which they officially renamed action research/study groups, attended five workshop sessions associated with Project LEARN (Sagor, 1992) to refine their developing expertise in conducting collaborative action research. At the end of that second year, teachers presented the results of their action research projects at a one-day conference held for teachers in their own and surrounding districts. The action research had not only resulted in action plans for curriculum and instruction in the teachers' classrooms: The teachers also planned to present their research results to the school board as input to decisions regarding the district's cycle of spelling adoptions.

Assessment of the TSG project showed that the role of *teacher as collaborator,* combined with the role *of teacher as reflective practitioner* through action research, offered considerable support to teachers' growth in knowledge and expertise as literacy educators. Three elements judged critical to the success of the endeavor were the project's foundation in teachers' interests, a focus on classroom practice, and support of the school administrator who was committed to school reform and children's literacy achievement. Teachers in the project reported on the direct impact their participation in the collaborative action research team had on their practices and, thus, on their students' learning. Teachers and the principal commented that the entire faculty was more united around issues of effective practice. To illustrate the impact of the TSG project on the entire school, following the project's second year, the entire faculty of the PDS elected to form study groups around shared topics of interest. The original literature study and spelling study groups continued, adding new members, and additional groups formed around such topics as guided reading and multiple intelligences.

It seems clear that in the role of *teacher as collaborator,* teachers have opportunities to become responsible and informed leaders who have control over outcomes. In LeBlanc and Shelton's research (1997), in which they attempted to describe characteristics of as well as the needs of teachers in leadership positions, the five teacher leaders involved reported that collaboration was an integral component of leadership and that it was through committee work and projects that they made their greatest contributions as professional leaders. In addition, they reported that their collaborations and participation in decision-making processes contributed to their professional development. These teacher leaders reported being motivated by a desire for lifelong learning and by a realization of the importance of their relationships with other professionals in a collaborative environment. These individuals had a high need for achievement and recognition, as well as for affiliations with their peers, which represented a potential conflict because affiliation and individual recognition are often seen as exclusive of one another. It seems that a key to effective collaboration is balancing the need for personal achievement with the need to work closely with others. They also acknowledged that the amount of time available represented either support for collaboration or an obstacle, when there was a dearth of time, that hindered effective collaboration.

Clearly, there are many positive literacy outcomes associated with the role of *teacher as collaborator,* including increased teacher expertise and professionalism, enhanced student achievement, and an increasing focus on effective classroom practice. A first-grade teacher, a member of the 1998–1999 California Reading and Literature Project's Literacy Research Cohort, commented on the power of her role as a participant in the cohort study group: "It has helped me think in a more focused way on what I want to accomplish." Collaboration can occur, as it does for this first-grade teacher, in the context of a formally structured literacy project in which teachers work together to share information, in teacher study teams formed around shared questions and concerns, or informally in teachers' lounges and lunchrooms. It can involve a variety of purposes, including action research and preservice and new teacher development. Of course, as with the other categories describing the critical roles of literacy educators, this role is intertwined with the role of *teacher as active professional and leader,* described next.

Teacher as Active Professional and Leader

It could be argued that the most important role of the literacy educator is to be an informed professional and leader—in the classroom, school or university, and the larger community. It is a role that is supported by both the roles of *teacher as reflective practitioner* and *teacher as collaborator.* Active professionals are career-long learners. They surround themselves with other educators who have like passions and concerns. They attend conferences; read professional journals and books; participate in collegial forums in which ideas, concerns, and insights are exchanged; disseminate information from their action research projects; and participate in graduate programs at both certificate and master's degree levels. They are active problem solvers who seek collegial environments in which others are engaging in inquiry and who enthusiastically share what they discover and learn about becoming increasingly effective literacy educators.

As discussed earlier, teaching is a challenging profession, one that perhaps is not for the fainthearted. For the exemplary teacher, however, teaching gives more energy than it takes, and although much of that energy comes from being a catalyst for children's learning, much comes from experiencing one's own developing expertise as it is fueled by reading, study, and collaboration, knowing, of course, that one's increasing expertise has explicit impact on the literacy learning of children and adolescents. That may be a partial explanation for why approximately 12,000 literacy educators converge yearly at the International Reading Association's conference. It may explain why the exhibit halls of professional conferences are filled with educators perusing the latest professional books and materials. It may explain why a relatively new forum, the listserv, such as CATEnet sponsored by the California Association of Teachers of English, attracts over 500 literacy educators around the United States to participate through e-mail in open-ended, collegial exchanges on theory, research, policy, and practice. Another forum, NCTE-talk, is a national listserv sponsored by the National Council of Teachers of English. This electronic network consists of English and language arts educators who participate in online conversations about such things as language learning, literature, literacy, research, standards, and policy. The conversations include K–12 teachers, preservice teachers, graduate students, and university teacher educators who ask questions, provide resources for one another, offer suggestions for practice, and share successes and joys (as well as frustrations).

To this point, this discussion has focused primarily on reflection, collaboration, and leadership within the profession. Effective literacy educators, however, must be active professionals and leaders in the larger community of parents, families, and policy makers. Morrow (1995) unequivocally made the point that "family literacy should be viewed by schools and community agencies as one of *the* most important elements in literacy development" (p. 6). Although the concept of "family literacy" is complex and, therefore, not amenable to succinct and simple definition, Morrow discussed basic principles that apply. These principles, developed by the International Reading Association's Family Literacy Commission, emphasize the following as elements in family literacy:

- The various ways literacy is used at home and in communities
- Literacy that functions in life to accomplish day-to-day activities
- Literacy activities that may be initiated by parents, but may also occur spontaneously during everyday living
- Literacy activities that reflect a family's cultural, racial, or ethnic heritage

In research on many existing family literacy programs, Auerbach (1995) and her colleagues found that programs often followed a transmission model and were designed to give parents and families information about literacy practices, materials to promote literacy development, effective ways of interacting and communicating, and effective parenting practices. Assumptions underlying such programs are that literacy skills transfer from school to home, that the home offers little or no opportunity for literacy development, that literacy activities must be schoollike activities, that home factors determine who will succeed, and that parents' problems interfere with having positive home literacy experiences. Auerbach (1995) provided substantial evidence to counter each assumption and concluded that, given the principles associated with family literacy, teachers and schools must look within homes and communities for literacy activities that center on community and family, activities that bring relevant social issues and cultural forms and practices into the school, rather than attempting to overlay school practices and procedures directly onto families and communities.

Teachers who are active professionals will make it a part of their ongoing professional development to be informed about the basic principles associated with family literacy. They will take leadership roles in designing practical applications for building school–community relationships (Fuller & Olsen, 1998) and literacy partnerships. Many models exist: programs that use grant funding to create liaisons that connect families to schools (Halford, 1996), programs that build upon intergenerational connections (Conyers, 1996), and programs that create full-service schools that function as community hubs of activity and where community and family members feel welcome and comfortable (Dryfoos, 1996). It is the *teacher as active professional and leader* who is integral to helping parents, schools, and communities work together to support young learners in their literacy learning.

It is the also the role of the active professional to provide leadership that informs policy to support the very best of teaching and learning. As only one example, recall the earlier description of teacher study groups. As a result of their collaborative work, teachers in one of these groups gave input to school district policy regarding adoption of spelling curriculum. An important role of the literacy teacher is to have a voice in the implementation of best practices and be able to explain to noneducators, and perhaps other educators, why certain policies make sound educational sense whereas others might not. The voice of the teacher as leader must be heard at local, state, and national levels, offering an informed perspective that advocates for practices that will support the literacy development of all children and adolescents.

The fourth role of the literacy educator is as a mentor for other professionals, particularly novice teachers, who often feel unprepared to meet all the demands they face in their early years of teaching. This is a role closely tied to the roles of active professional, leader, and collaborator.

Teacher as Mentor

Halford (1998) used an interesting phrase to describe the teaching profession. She called it "the profession that eats its young" (p. 33). She cited research on the staggeringly high teacher attrition rates of 30% within the first five years of teaching, a number that often includes those who seem to have the most potential for success. She also made the point that although the profession as a whole suffers, particularly when it attempts sustained reform, from the high rates of attrition, it is students who suffer most from a revolving door of novice teachers who have not received sufficient support to learn and develop expertise within the profession.

There are many models of teacher preparation, from five-year integrated programs to four-year undergraduate programs to fifth-year postbaccalaureate credential programs. Many of these programs do an exemplary job of preparing novice teachers, and reports of effective teacher preparation programs are plentiful in publications such as the *Middle School Journal* (see the May 1995 themed issue on reforming teacher preparation), *Educational Leadership, Action in Teacher Education,* and *Journal of Teacher Education.*

Nevertheless, when preservice teachers exit teacher preparation programs, they are still novices. Halford (1998) reminded readers that although all teachers should have opportunities for ongoing learning, it is especially crucial that new teachers be viewed as learners. McGreal, when being interviewed by Ron Brandt, executive editor of *Educational Leadership* (Brandt, 1996), stated that "it's evident that probationary or non-tenured teachers have some special needs" (p. 31), needs that require "intensive involvement with alternative sources of data such as multiple observations, journal writing, and artifact collections" (p. 31). He also stressed that these activities need to be accompanied by a strong mentoring program.

Although mentoring programs take many forms, key ingredients contribute to their success (Halford, 1998). One is a committed administration that places high priority on the support of beginning teachers. Another is specialized professional development for the mentors themselves. This professional development should focus on such things as how to provide appropriate feedback to the new teacher. For example, it is important to know that mentoring is most productive when feedback is not evaluative and judgmental, but rather when it emphasizes the role of mentor as a knowledgeable friend and support provider.

One example of a comprehensive mentoring program is California's Beginning Teacher Support and Assessment Program (BTSA) and its precursor, the California New Teacher Project. The BTSA program has been instrumental in reducing teacher attrition, thus reducing the costly expenses, both monetarily and in human capital, of high attrition and subsequent recruitment and hiring (California Commission on Teacher Credentialing, 1992). In addition, teachers in the BTSA program tend to give students more complex academic tasks than most novices attempt and to use a variety of instructional processes for the purpose of engaging students of diverse cultural and linguistic backgrounds in learning. Not surprisingly, as the project teachers' sense of confidence and expertise grew, so did their inclination to engage in inquiry and reflect on their teaching practices. The mentoring has also benefited the veteran mentor teachers, who learned new approaches that helped them reflect on and refine their own teaching practices.

Dayton, Ohio, public schools implemented a program that used video case studies as a focus for reflective practice and for mentoring new teachers (Rowley & Hart, 1996). The Becoming a Star Urban Teacher project used videos of exemplary teachers in problem-solving settings to promote discussion of how the exemplary (star) teacher functioned. For example, one video, titled *What to Do about Raymond,* took a look at behaviors of a nonengaged student in a classroom and at the teacher's attempts to work with him and problem solve his behaviors. Mentors, functioning as coaches and facilitators of discussion, helped new teachers analyze and reflect on what they were seeing in the video and together discussed the implications for their own classrooms.

Mentoring can occur in many forms. One is the formal, structured mentoring program such as BTSA, which serves approximately 6% of first- and second-year teachers in California, or programs such as the Peer Assistance and Review (PAR) mentoring program established in 1986 the Columbus, Ohio, public schools (Stedman & Stroot, 1998). In the PAR program, new teachers participate for one year with mentor teachers who visit their classrooms weekly and, in addition, give feedback and problem solve with the new teachers through conferences, e-mail, and telephone conversations. Mentoring can also occur in more informal situations where novice teachers are invited to collaborate in planning and problem-solving sessions with one or more experienced teachers. These sessions, in which teachers share ideas and materials with new teachers and offer collegial input to help a new teacher negotiate what can seem like a maze of policies, expectations, and concerns, can even occur over lunch or coffee. Yet another form of mentoring occurs in school–university partnerships in which teachers participate as master or collaborative teachers for those in the midst of their credential programs. Whether serving as a mentor in a formal or informal capacity, the role of *teacher as mentor* is a critical one because of its potential for direct impact on both new and experienced teachers, specifically on what they know and are able to do, and, consequently, on the quality of classroom literacy practices.

Conclusion

Going back to the idea expressed earlier that the teacher is at the heart of literacy teaching and learning, Darling-Hammond (1996) commented that "reforms that invest time in teacher learning and give teachers greater autonomy are our best hope for improving America's schools" (p. 4). This goal is certainly something for which we should strive diligently, even relentlessly, because the stakes are so high—the learning of children and young adults. For the literacy teacher, the stakes are especially high because literacy skills represent a foundation of skill and knowledge necessary for learning not only in the fourth, sixth, and eighth grades, but also in the subsequent years of an individual's life. The four roles discussed in this chapter—*teacher as reflective practitioner, teacher as collaborator, teacher as active professional and leader,* and *teacher as mentor*—require that teachers continuously consider the impact of curriculum and instruction on student learning; commit to a career in which professional development regularly informs theories and practice; participate professionally as a learner but also as a disseminator of information for colleagues, parents, and the larger community; and offer compassionate support for those less experienced or expert in the world of teaching and learning. Central to each role is the question, What can each of us do to ensure our professional strength and vitality, and the strength and vitality of our colleagues, for the purpose of ensuring the success of all children?

REFERENCES

Auerbach, E.R. (1995). Which way for family literacy: Intervention or empowerment? In L.M. Morrow (Ed.), *Family literacy: Connections in schools and communities* (pp. 11–27). Newark, DE: International Reading Association.

Avery, C. (1993). *. . . and with a light touch: Learning about reading, writing, and teaching with first graders.* Portsmouth, NH: Heinemann.

Brandt, R. (1996). On a new direction for teacher evaluation: A conversation with Tom McGreal. *Educational Leadership, 53,* 30–33.

Brookhart, S.M., & Freeman, D.J. (1992). Characteristics of entering teacher candidates. *Review of Educational Research, 62,* 37–60.

California Commission on Teacher Credentialing. (1992). *Success for beginning teachers: The California New Teacher Project.* Sacramento: California Department of Education.

Carter, F. (1976). *The education of Little Tree.* Albuquerque: University of New Mexico Press.

Conyers, J.G. (1996). Building bridges between generations. *Educational Leadership, 53,* 14–16.

Darling-Hammond, L. (1996). The quiet revolution: Rethinking teacher development. *Educational Leadership, 53,* 4–10.

Dryfoos, J.G. (1996). Full-service schools. *Educational Leadership, 53,* 18–23.

Fuller, M.L., & Olsen, G. (1998). *Home-school relations: Working successfully with parents and families.* Boston: Allyn and Bacon.

Gambrell, L.B., Palmer, B.M., Codling, R.M., & Mazzoni, S.A. (1996). Assessing motivation to read. *The Reading Teacher, 49,* 518–532.

Grisham, D.L. (1998, April). *The impact of teacher study groups on a community of practice.* Paper presented at the annual meeting of the American Educational Research Association, San Diego, CA.

Halford, J.M. (1996). How parent liaisons connect families to school. *Educational Leadership, 53,* 34–36.

————. (1998). Easing the way for new teachers. *Educational Leadership, 55,* 33–36.

Harris, B., & Drake, S.M. (1997). Implementing high school reform through schoolwide action research teams: A three year case study. *Action in Teacher Education, 19,* 15–31.

Harris, T.L., & Hodges, R.E. (Eds.). (1995). *The literacy dictionary: The vocabulary of reading and writing.* Newark, DE: International Reading Association.

Kagan, D.M. (1992). Professional growth among preservice and beginning teachers. *Review of Educational Research, 62,* 129–169.

LeBlanc, P.R., & Shelton, M.M. (1997). Teacher leadership: The needs of teachers. *Action in Teacher Education, 19,* 32–48.

Morrow, L.M. (1995). Family literacy: New perspectives, new practices. In L.M. Morrow (Ed.), *Family literacy: Connections in schools and community* (pp. 5–10). Newark, DE: International Reading Association.

O'Flahavan, J., Gambrell, L.B., Guthrie, J., Stahl, S., & Alvermann, D. (1992). Poll results guide activities of research center. *Reading Today, 10,* 12.

Reynolds, A. (1992). What is competent beginning teaching? A review of the literature. *Review of Educational Research, 62,* 1–35.

Rowley, J.B., & Hart, P.M. (1996). How video case studies can promote reflective dialogue. *Educational Leadership, 53,* 28–29.

Ruddell, R.B. (1997). Researching the influential literacy teacher: Characteristics, beliefs, strategies, and new research directions. In C.K. Kinzer, K.A. Hinchman, & D.J. Leu (Eds.), *Inquiries in literacy theory and practice* (pp. 37–53). Forty-sixth yearbook of the National Reading Conference. Chicago: National Reading Conference.

Sagor, R. (1991). What Project LEARN reveals about collaborative action research. *Educational Leadership, 48,* 6–7, 9–10.

————. (1992). *How to conduct collaborative action research.* Alexandria, VA: Association for Supervision and Curriculum Development.

Santa, C.M. (1990). Teaching as research. In M.W. Olson (Ed.), *Opening the door to classroom research* (pp. 64–76). Newark, DE: International Reading Association.

Schön, D. (1987). *Educating the reflective practitioner.* San Francisco: Jossey-Bass.

Shulman, L. (1987). Knowledge and teaching: Foundations of the new reform. *Harvard Educational Review, 57,* 1–22.

Stedman, P., & Stroot, S.A. (1998). Teachers helping teachers. *Educational Leadership, 55,* 37–38.

Trelease, J. (1995). *The read-aloud handbook,* 4th ed. New York: Penguin Books.

Veenman, S. (1984). Perceived problems of beginning teachers. *Review of Educational Research, 54,* 143–178.

2 The Role of the Principal in the Literacy Program

DANA L. GRISHAM

DIANE LAPP

JAMES FLOOD

San Diego State University

What does it take for a site administrator to become an effective instructional leader in literacy? Although the answer to this question is quite complex, research in the 1970s, 1980s, and 1990s clearly defines the role of the "effective" principal in the "effective" school as one of *instructional leadership* (see, for example, Northwest Regional Educational Laboratory, 1984). Wepner and Seminoff (1995) stated, "In effective schools, principals have five broad instructional and leadership areas: working with teachers, working with students, creating a school atmosphere, providing policy leadership, and building community support" (p. 31). In this role, we believe the instructional leader has the responsibility to create a "reading climate" in which he or she

1. Shares mutual concerns with teachers about the school's reading programs.
2. Provides needed staff development.
3. Gets involved with students' literacy activities.
4. Promotes awareness of the school's reading program in the community.

In this chapter, we chronicle the efforts of four effective principals as they create literate learning communities in their schools. The chapter is organized into sections that examine (1) a brief review of the research literature on what we know about the principal's role in literacy development from research since the 1970s; (2) an exploration of the work of four school principals selected because they are exemplars who have implemented the research findings at their school sites; and (3) a synthesis of the findings from the interviews with these principals about *how* they implement the findings from research in the contexts of their schools, including recommendations for practice and for future research.

Important Elements in Literacy Learning

Literacy theory in the elementary and middle school is in the midst of change and uncertainty due to a deepening conflict between qualitative and quantitative "paradigms" of research (see, for example, Hill & Patterson, 1997). Although the majority of this debate concerns the beginning stages of literacy learning, the conflict has far-reaching implications for all research on reading and language arts learning and practice. For a review of the epistemological elements of the two paradigms, see Cunningham and Fitzgerald (1996). At the present time, principals and teachers may be confused by the various claims of educational research on literacy. We believe that there are multiple ways of looking at the classroom and that principals who are knowledgeable about research into literacy provide a more theoretically consistent leadership for their schools than other principals. Thus, we provide the following brief overview of the types of research with which principals need to acquaint themselves.

One View

Qualitative or naturalistic research studies are those that take place within the context of the classroom and often attempt to capture the *emic* perspective; that is, What do the participants (the insiders) believe is occurring? In addition, naturalistic studies provide an *etic* (or observer) perspective into the context to answer Wolcott's (1988) classic question, What's going on here? In qualitative studies, research questions are proposed and refined as the study unfolds. Since 1980, naturalistic studies have provided many valuable insights into the workings of classrooms around the country and, indeed, the world. Classic studies include Erickson's anthropological perspectives; Sarason's organization and structural studies, and Cazden's analyses of classroom discourse (see, for example, Cazden, 1988; Erickson, 1993; Sarason, 1972).

Naturalistic inquiry provides educators with new windows into a world that we think we know well and provides us with richly contextualized studies that describe and interpret events based on anthropological and linguistic theories of research. At its best, naturalistic studies assist in the building of theory through the accretion of concrete universals (Erickson, 1986). Many teachers (and principals) are finding their voices and are providing additional research into classroom operations through action research (Lytle & Cochran-Smith, 1990).

Another View

The older methodology of educational research is quantitative research, based on cognitivist principles that emanate from the hard sciences and that are based on psychometric guidelines. These principles include testing hypotheses through interventions (or "experiments") with random assignment of subjects to treatment and control groups, carefully controlled collections of quantitative and/or behavioral data, both descriptive and multivariate statistical manipulations of variables that provide for statistical "significance" to prove or disprove the hypothesis, and reports of the research that deal exclusively with the questions posed. Such studies have contributed greatly to educational theory, and examples of such research abound. In literacy, a classic study is Bond and Dykstra's first-grade studies (Bond & Dykstra, 1967), which found that teachers, more than curriculum, were instrumental in the successful literacy learning of children.

Our View

Although we feel that both types of research are essential to the educational process, the recent emphasis on national standards and accountability has strengthened the arguments of cognitivist (and quantitative) researchers for validity, generalizability, and reliability as criteria for "valid" scientific research. Nevertheless, we have reviewed research studies from both "paradigms."

Literacy

One result of research is the use of the term *literacy* instead of reading, writing, listening, and speaking. Literacy suggests that a constellation of concepts undergirds the individual's communication with others. The term *literacy* strongly suggests the integration and interdependency of the language arts (California State Department of Education, 1987).

At the upper elementary grades and in middle school, the focus shifts from learning the skills and concepts of literacy (e.g., "learning to read and write") to comprehension (e.g., "reading and writing to learn"). Anderson and Pearson (1984) rediscovered the work of Bartlett (1932), and many studies ensued that focused on schema theory. Thus, "background knowledge"—both activation of existing and building of new—has become a major focus of literacy instruction.

An important element of literacy instruction at the upper grades and middle school is content area literacy. In 1992, Langer and Allington reported that only occasional mention of reading (literacy) in content area classes had been addressed by the many blue-ribbon commissions on the state of reading in the United States. Recent research on content area literacy reveals that students construct meaning across the curriculum by having authentic experiences within the content areas (Cooper, 1997). These experiences involve and integrate all aspects of the language arts and involve the activation or construction of background knowledge for the student. Construction of meaning occurs when students build relationships between old and new knowledge and between curricular areas. Finally, students need "scaffolded support" from the teacher and their peers to help them build understanding of concepts. Because reading and writing in the content areas are significantly different from reading and writing narratives, principals need to understand these differences and the instructional strategies that support student learning in the content areas.

Certain notions about what matters most in literacy are provided by award-winning elementary and middle school principals in *Best Ideas from America's Blue*

Ribbon Schools (National Association of Elementary School Principals, 1994; 1995). Ideas from sample issues include integration of curriculum, inquiry-based and hands-on learning, cooperative learning, authentic assessment, academic excellence, and literature discussion groups.

What Research Says about the Principal's Role in Literacy Leadership

As defined by Hughes and Ubben (1994), a principal, or site administrator, may be said to have five major functions: curriculum development, instructional improvement, pupil services, financial and facility management, and community relations. The principal's managerial and leadership behaviors are the variables that cut across the five major functions. Indeed, Hughes and Ubben made the case that the principal is "the most significant individual in the creation of an effective school" (p. 5).

Curriculum development has gained in importance as one of the principal's premier functions, primarily due to the instantiation of site-based management. Site-based management usually leads to a decentralization in curriculum development and an accompanying autonomy for each school faculty to adapt programs to fit the needs of its particular learning community.

Radencich (1995) outlined the historical changes to the role of the principal that have occurred in the twentieth century. Radencich characterized the most recent time frame, from 1960 to the present, as an era of research orientation from which two themes emerge: (1) the research focus and (2) the principal as organizational change agent. Burg, Kaufman, Korngold, and Kovner (1978) quite accurately predicted that this period would see the following concerns in supervision: demands for greater accountability and effectiveness, constraints stemming from growing teacher professionalism and independence, collective bargaining, inequities in school financing, public attitudes toward education, changing career patterns, and the provision of services to students with special needs. In addition, concern for democracy has given way to concerns for effectiveness in an era of rapid change.

Visions for the future roles of school-based administrators in the reading and writing program are predicted by numerous researchers:

1. Pajak (1992) stated that schools are "teaching" institutions, but they are not necessarily "learning" organizations. In the 1990s and beyond, educational reforms must help schools learn better.
2. Senge (1990) recommended that our image of an educational leader be transformed into that of designer, who has a systemic approach to vision and core values. The educational leader would be viewed as a steward, with its implied commitment of service to people, to the organization, and to the teacher. The role of the educational leader would be one of assisting in the restructuring of views of reality to deal with underlying problems and their causes.
3. Glickman (1992) suggested that restructuring schools means doing away with supervision and replacing it with the idea of shared governance, shared leader-

ship, and collegiality. Glickman argued that hierarchical models left over from the industrial revolution must be replaced with risk-taking practitioners. The term *supervisor* would be replaced by *instructional leader.*

4. The National Board for Professional Teaching Standards has developed certification standards (Darling-Hammond with Sclan, 1992). Elements affected might include forms of self-evaluation, peer review, portfolio development, and the development of various forms of career ladders.

5. Harris (1986) anticipated that social reconstruction will expand teachers' job requirements to encompass many of the former supervision functions.

6. The International Reading Association (1992) defines a coordinator/supervisor as having seven mandates:

   ■ The improvement of curriculum methodology and management of districtwide reading and language arts programs
   ■ The application of research and theory in the refinement of reading and language arts instruction
   ■ The coordination and implementation of collaborative reading research
   ■ Attainment of resources through budget processes and grant applications
   ■ Development of community support for the reading and language arts program
   ■ Supervision and evaluation of the classroom teacher, specialists, and consultants
   ■ Support of professional development through provision for attendance at workshops, conferences, and conventions

Researchers appear to enjoy compiling profiles and checklists of those attributes desirable in instructional leaders in literacy (Dungan, 1994; Lickteig, 1995; Sanacore, 1996). Quite a lot of research has been done on the principal as the instructional leader, but when the subject area is literacy, several studies are worth mentioning. Potter (1994) cataloged several approaches principals may use to put reading first in the middle school. Chance (1991) found that Tennessee principals' perceptions of themselves as instructional leaders in literacy varied with the reality. She found that principals were more involved in the management and evaluation of reading programs than in their planning and operation. She also found that female principals were more involved with reading than male principals and that principal involvement in reading was linked to increased training in reading. Murphy (1994) documents the effect of a new principal on improved instruction in an accelerated reading program of a small, rural elementary school. Hallinger (1996) found that there was no direct effect from a principal's instructional leadership in reading on reading achievement scores; there was, however, a direct influence on overall school effectiveness through actions that shaped the school's learning environment. Scharer and Rogers (1994) found similarly in a longitudinal study, which also included the finding that teachers and students were shielded from the tensions of high-stake testing by the principal acting as mediator.

As the principal's role grows more complex, preparation for the position requires additional professional development. Daresh and Playko (1992) studied the entry-level programs for principals and determined that new principals need structured and formal mentoring in addition to their more comprehensive professional development.

Principals may not start out as "experts" in literacy, but they should educate themselves quickly about what constitutes effective reading programs in their schools. According to Wepner and Seminoff (1995), "An enriched reading program has administrators, reading specialists, classroom teachers (both elementary and content area), parents, librarians, auxiliary personnel, school board members, community members, and students working closely together to develop and implement a cohesive, systemwide program at the elementary and secondary level" (p. 25). Principals may, for example, learn much from the exchanges that take place with more knowledgeable literacy teachers at their sites. In fact, Radencich (1995) recommended that principals may find more support for literacy projects requested by a committee than by an individual. Thus, the principal must be able to work with a committee composed of the members suggested earlier as well as union representatives, special education representatives, and students. Among other recommendations, Radencich suggested that three are key to successful literacy programs: (1) opportunity for all students, (2) a high degree of organization, and (3) keeping enthusiasm sky high (Radencich, 1995, p. 149).

The management styles of principals may not be critical to an effective literacy climate in schools. A study by Hallinger and Murphy (1987) reviewed two schools whose administrators used very different approaches to involvement in their respective reading programs. One principal interacted closely with the details of the program, whereas the other managed the program from a distance. Both programs espoused similar goals and schoolwide policies and practices. Despite the difference in management style, reading scores improved for students from both programs.

What may be more important than the management style of the principal is his or her commitment to the systematic development of the literate community in the school. Sparks and Hirsch (1997) documented a paradigm shift in staff development resulting from three powerful ideas. First, reform in education is "results driven" in that educators are increasingly being asked to examine the end results of their efforts. That is, what have students learned to do as a result of teaching? For teachers to decide at the beginning of the planning process what learning outcomes students must demonstrate moves the focus from what the teacher does (e.g., teaching) to what the student does (e.g., learning). Throughout the United States, the impetus toward accountability in education is a powerful idea that is transforming school culture (Sparks & Hirsch, 1997).

A second powerful idea driving school reform is "systems thinking." As our world grows more complex, we must conceptualize change and learning as systemic—part of a system—rather than as the piecemeal and fragmented parts of the old paradigm. Change occurs continuously within a system, even when its results are not immediately obvious. Disconnectedness occurs when piecemeal changes are wrought without thought for their unintended consequences. Disconnectedness has been endemic in school change for that very reason; educators need to focus instead on "leverage" or points in the system where small changes can have big consequences. The individual cannot change without concomitant change in the system; thus, educators must learn to think more systemically and must focus on structural as well as individual changes. Moreover, educators must think systemically to avoid "oscillation," which occurs when people think they make a change, but the change is temporary and individuals return to the original behaviors and structures. When we apply systems thinking to education it means that we must approach reform both systematically and systemically for the purpose of producing fundamental change (Holzman, 1993).

Constructivism is the third powerful idea contributing to educational change. Constructivists believe that learning occurs when the learner creates knowledge, rather than having it passed down by transmission. Constructivist thinkers (Vygotsky, Piaget, Dewey, Elkind, and Gardner, for example) believe that the individuals use existing knowledge structures to engage actively with new experiences to modify or create new knowledge structures. This inquiry orientation to learning requires the learner to be actively engaged and in charge of the learning process. For teachers to create constructivist classrooms, they must have had constructivist learning experiences themselves (Sparks & Hirsch, 1997).

When these three powerful ideas work together, the result is a school in which planning processes "more often begin by determining the things students need to know and be able to do and then working backward to the knowledge, skills, and attitudes required of educators if those student outcomes are to be realized" (Sparks & Hirsch, 1997, p. 41).

The Actions of Four Effective Principals

Interviews with four exemplary principals named as effective literacy leaders in their schools shed light on what principals can do to promote a "reading climate" in their schools. These principals were selected because of their reputations as excellent literacy leaders. In addition, they are very familiar to us because of their partnership with San Diego State University's Teacher Education faculty and programs. These four principals, two at the elementary level, one at the middle school level, and one at the high school level, all acknowledged instructional leaders in literacy, contributed their insights into the literacy programs in their schools. This chapter's appendix contains the interview protocol used.

Jamacha Elementary School

Principal Jeanne Koelln has a focused and systematic plan for literacy at her school. She began by assessing the existing literacy program and then comparing it with a "model" program to be adopted. She initially set an implementation time line of three to five years, but she continues to push the program beyond the time lines because the need for student literacy is critical.

Ms. Koelln educates herself about literacy by extensive reading in the field, but she feels that she owes a great deal to the knowledgeable teachers of literacy within her school. Jamacha school in El Cajon, California, a city east of San Diego, enjoys a site-based approach to literacy (Timar, 1989).

Jamacha Elementary School has a population of 617 students in kindergarten through grade 5. The school was built six years ago and began its life as a professional development school as part of the Model Education Center, a partnership of the Cajon Valley School District and San Diego State University that has been in operation for 15 years. School demographics reflect a predominantly Caucasian American, middle-class population, although 20% of the students are ethnic minorities in the following order of representation: Arabic, Chaldean, Hispanic, and African American. The school is the bilingual magnet school for the northwest region of the district. Parent participation in the school is extremely active. For example, the parent organization raises about $50,000 per year for the school, doubling the principal's budget and providing for many extra programs. Only 20% of the population is on free or reduced lunch.

Using a continuous improvement model, Jeanne and her staff adopted a published literacy program whose author was engaged to provide ongoing professional development to the teachers. This "balanced" program of literacy spans all five grade levels at Jeanne's school and provides for a coaching model in which teachers may observe lessons and give each other feedback. Ms. Koelln herself embarked on an action research project for her school: She personally tracked a high, a medium, and a low student in each of her grade 3, 4, and 5 classrooms to assess the effectiveness of the program and the literacy teaching.

Jeanne reports an increased dialogue about literacy learning among the educators at her school, which she attributes to the administrator's "blessing" of the literacy program. What she means is that teachers engage more with the literacy program now that it has been "blessed" by principal recommendation. In addition, students will read and discuss literature that has been introduced and "blessed" by the teacher more often than if those same books had not been blessed.

Jeanne's theoretical stance toward literacy has been formed "from my teachers," many of whom went to New Zealand for their "training" in whole language. Routman's books, as well as the numerous professional articles she reads, such as those that appear in *Educational Leadership,* have been a major influence on Jeanne's thinking. Jeanne also named the early literacy instruction (ELI) workshops she attended as influential in her thinking about literacy.

For Jeanne, the key to literacy is in understanding the emergent reader. She maintains that no child can access the curriculum without skill in reading and, therefore, students should be taught strategies to read to gain knowledge. Jeanne reads publications such as *Schools That Work* and follows recommendations made therein. One example she cited of a strategy that her school favors is the need for students to reread materials.

In response to how literacy is made a priority in her school, Jeanne starts with the California State Framework (California State Department of Education, 1987). She participated in the implementation of the framework as a teacher. When she became principal at Jamacha, she made sure that all her K–2 teachers received training in teaching using quality literature. She implemented a "sacred time" for language arts instruction that everyone works hard to make inviolable. Jeanne views accountability as essential to making literacy a priority in her school, and established benchmarks for the grades at her school. These are flexible or "moving" benchmarks based on a continual assessment through running records as provided for by the ELI.

Ms. Koelln also worked to educate the parents at her school. Each year they pledge to read to and with their students daily.

In the second year of Jeanne's plan for literacy, she concentrated on the upper grades (grades 3 to 5). The adopted program provided for all grades in the school. In addition, a schoolwide literacy event was established to make literacy a priority, and family homework was instituted. Another innovation Jeanne implemented was a volunteer teaching expert program. Teachers at each grade level were selected as literacy coaches for the other teachers. These are voluntary positions without additional remuneration, and Jeanne frankly states that the quality of the program depends upon the extraordinary efforts of caring and committed teachers. Goals for the present year include improvement in teaching using quality literature, phonics, and spelling.

Jeanne sees technology as "the great equalizer" for students, and she works hard to provide access to technology for all her students. In addition, she started a literacy club—a tutorial administered by instructional aides in the school—for students. Students who are in Literacy Club are tutored twice a week for an eight-week period.

The media center or library is somewhat problematic at Jeanne's school. Although they are lucky to have a certificated teacher in charge, rather than an instructional aide, the media center director is somewhat traditional in her approach. Jeanne is working on making the library more accessible to more students for greater periods of time. Of particular importance is more creative scheduling for students in grades 4 and 5, because there is no public library in the school's locale. Recently, Jamacha applied for and received a $5,000 library improvement grant.

With regard to professional development practices at the school, Jeanne talks about the goals for the year. This year there will be a program quality review in writing and spelling. The accelerated literacy program (Walker, 1995) as well as the role of phonics in beginning reading instruction and spelling for all grade levels are areas on which teachers will focus. For the teachers at Jamacha, Jeanne feels that much professional development work can be done at faculty meetings. For example, sometimes the faculty will read and jigsaw a professional book and discuss it. Other professional development opportunities are more formally structured workshops. Teachers are guaranteed three off-site professional development experiences that they may choose. In fact, part of their evaluation depends on their participation in these professional development experiences. Jeanne tries to list all opportunities in the local area for the teachers. When requested, she is often able to offer more than the minimum of three. The district offers a summer academy for teachers where coaches provide support for a given mission.

For Ms. Koelln, success in professional development and success in providing a quality literacy program at Jamacha is a cooperative rather than a top-down enterprise and depends on the hard work and dedication of many people. Jeanne's expectations, however, are made up front and form part of her evaluation of her teachers. When necessary, she uses her power as principal to persuade her staff to comply with the literacy plan.

Oak Park Elementary Music Conservatory with Enriched Studies

Principal Juel Moore is a nationally recognized principal at Oak Park Elementary School in San Diego. Oak Park principal and faculty have made literacy learning throughout all content areas a primary focus. Oak Park is an elementary school within the Crawford High School Cluster. Schools in the San Diego Unified School District are grouped together into 16 geographically related clusters. Each cluster is named after the high school it represents. Oak Park is located on the periphery of an inner city community and is classified as a Title I school because 64% of the students receive free lunches. Because Oak Park is a music conservatory with enriched studies magnet school, it is necessary to integrate all areas of the curriculum. This year Dr. Moore honored teachers' requests with two hours of uninterrupted language arts time. The music teachers developed their schedules around this time. The music teachers also confer with classroom teachers to enrich the language arts program by using a thematic approach. For example, when the teachers are reading about zoo animals, the music program enriches the theme with music and songs. The principal supports this approach.

Most recently, Dr. Moore, the faculty, staff, and parents started to address accountability issues. Three critical questions are being asked: (1) Why is our performance the way it is? (2) What is the whole picture? (3) What is the school doing to ensure student success? School data revealed an achievement gap between white and nonwhite students. Specifically, the Hispanic and African American students were low achievers. This principal's motto is, "If it's not working, why are we doing it?" To address these issues, Juel is using classroom observations, holding meeting and discussions with key personnel and parent groups, coaching, and providing mentors for new teachers to enhance student literacy. She also insists that teachers research the cultural background of children assigned to their classrooms. She believes that it is important that teachers really know each child and the role of the family and community.

Oak Park is a school of approximately 800 students with more than 150 nonresident white students coming in from outside the neighborhood to participate in a music and enriched studies magnet program. Oak Park has a diverse student body, and the faculty and principal recognize that every effort needs to be made to respect diversity and encourage participation of all ethnic groups. They do this by sending home communication in the family's primary language and by continuing to provide opportunities for two-way communication. Their bilingual advisory committee meets on a regular basis to address their students' needs and improve the instructional program for English language learners. Annually, a home–school compact is developed and is available for parents at the first parent conference of the school year. This compact delineates roles and responsibilities of parents, teachers, students, and administrators working as a team so that all children will reach their highest potential. In addition, a site discipline plan, including a dress code, is sent home for parent review.

The primary goal at Oak Park is not to do old jobs better but, rather, to use **assessment** and **evaluation** to guide literacy learning. The focus of the school is literacy in all content areas. Teachers are involved in the integration of instruction with assessment and accountability. One modified day a month and eight staff development days a year are used for staff development purposes. The faculty continually focuses on refining a K–5 literacy system.

Like Jeanne Koelln, Juel establishes a focus on literacy at the start of each school year. Juel begins with the very first staff meeting, governance team, and parent meetings each year. In these meetings, she uses a model to show how literacy must be the center of all subjects taught in the school. In addition, she discusses how standards, portfolios, and evaluations will all emphasize literacy learning. In fact, she ensures that the entire physical plant of the school displays their literacy focus.

Juel believes that literacy is developmental and sees that student maturation, life experiences, and social interactions have much to do with the way in which students gain the knowledge necessary for literacy learning. Meaning is constructed by the way a child interacts with the environment. Homes that encourage an appreciation of books help to create a love for reading.

Through Dr. Moore's example, Oak Park faculty recognizes the importance of having parent involvement to support school success and academic achievement. In addition, the faculty believes that parent involvement also promotes a warm and inviting environment for the school as well as a positive effect on the overall high performance of the site. To ensure a successful collaboration of parents, community, and the school, this school is committed to

- Involving parents as active participants in meaningful, shared decision making groups such as governance team and school site council as well as on other committees
- Encouraging a broad parent volunteer program that includes classroom and schoolwide activities on a regular basis and for special events
- Attracting parent participation in family-oriented activities that encourage academic achievement, such as family kindergarten, family math, and family reading programs
- Connecting parents on a referral basis to Crawford Community Connection for agency referral and community support
- Developing parent education activities that enhance parent skills and effectively connect parents with the school
- Encouraging direct and frequent communication between teachers and parents via meetings, telephone calls, and notes home
- Planning home learning activities that encourage direct parent involvement with a child in the daily learning process at home
- Communicating the parent involvement policy to the entire Oak Park Community

Oak Park uses staff development days (nonstudent days) for the purpose of teacher training. The school attempts to accommodate parents who would like to attend by scheduling some activities late in the day.

For Juel, a study of the research literature is necessary to becoming a leader in literacy, but it is also her passion. She is interested in the academic achievement of her students and the professional development of her faculty. She has pursued knowledge in literacy through attending numerous workshops and conferences. Juel often presents at research and instructional conferences. She models and supports professional development for her faculty. From research reports made at conventions such as the National Reading Conference to workshops on Early Literacy Inservice Course, Total Reading, Success for All, and Reading Recovery to the many research articles she has read and co-authored, Juel has formed a well-reasoned position on literacy learning. Juel sees the development of literacy as a continuum and seeks to understand the development from its earliest stages. This view enriches her understanding of the literacy development of her students. Juel encourages her staff to collect classroom data to answer their instructional questions.

At Oak Park, teachers are currently using a basal program as the core curriculum. They supplement this program with materials from the Wright Group, Total Reading, Scholastic (Eagle Reading), and a variety of core literature. The teachers at Oak Park have become more structured in their approach to literacy instruction since the mid-1990s. There has been a "back to phonics" movement in the state and less use of whole language. Juel supports her teachers, but encourages the use of literature in what she calls a "balanced curriculum."

Parents are encouraged to go into classrooms at Oak Park as volunteers, act as rolling readers, and take care of the "books and beyond" program.

Self-selected reading time varies in each classroom. Juel estimates that an average of one hour per day is used for such reading. Writing is part of the integrated language arts, and all teachers teach the writing process.

Teachers use various assessment processes to report student progress. Standardized tests and portfolios are used, and teachers are now using a pre/post form of assessment they developed that they feel provides a more objective basis for monitoring student progress than other assessment methods.

Surveys, discussions, meetings, and retreats are tools used to assess needs. Surveys conducted by the district and school indicated overall satisfaction. The report cards and standardized tests were seen as adequate reflections of a student's progress.

Literacy is made a priority at Oak Park because everyone at the school insists on it. Every part of the school is involved in literacy efforts. For example, the student support team assists by developing intervention strategies.

Teachers decide on what they need to learn to be professionally successful at their craft. If the cluster or the district offers special trainings, teachers are encouraged to attend, and Juel finds money for substitutes. At grade-level meetings, at student study team meetings, and during one-on-one conversations, Juel and her teachers discuss literacy issues. Juel models, encourages, and supports conversation and study of literacy-related issues.

Monroe Clark Middle School

Monroe Clark Middle School may be one of the newest schools in the San Diego Unified School District, but principal Frank Peterson has been around for many years and has definite ideas about what role he must undertake as instructional leader and the critical importance of literacy at the middle school level. Monroe Clark Middle School opened in September 1998 with 1,300 students enrolled. The ethnic composition is

65% Hispanic, 19% African American, and 5% Vietnamese, and the other 11% in descending order are Somali, Cambodian, Laotian, and European American. Ninety-six percent of the students qualify for free or reduced lunch. Monroe Clark is a part of the Hoover Cluster, which means that Hoover High School is the high school the students will attend.

Before the school opened, it was estimated that approximately 300 students would require English language services. More than half of the students (approximately 700), however, need English language services and are now placed appropriately.

Mr. Peterson emphasizes the importance of literacy by always making it the focus at staff and faculty meetings. Teachers know that he thinks it is the most important job they have: to teach kids how to be better speakers, readers, writers, and listeners.

Frank supports the modeling of reading by everyone at the school. Teachers routinely share books, and as principal, he models book sharing for both his faculty and the students. He also believes that providing a structure for reading practice during the day is vital. A reading component in advisory has been added to the schedule, when all school participants are involved in reading for pleasure during sustained silent reading. Every day, Frank talks to students to emphasize the importance and benefits of literacy development.

As principal, Mr. Peterson's theoretical stance is "balanced," but he is "more in the whole language camp." In a high-quality whole language program, the phonics piece is both present and based on the needs of the individual student. Literacy is the acquisition of the skills of being literate based on a developmental process, the early stages of which mean acquiring the "literacy big picture." This understanding to the meaning of literacy must be in place before students can progress to the next developmental stage. These developmental stages can be monitored, assessed, and enhanced through good teaching. The school has adopted a set of tools called First Steps Literacy from Australia. Frank states that it is the best resource he has ever encountered for teaching literacy.

Frank's theoretical orientation and commitment to First Steps did not come easily. He learned to read (and teach) with the phonics model. He came to embrace whole language because it allows teachers to be an "educational parent" in the sense that they create an educational "home" for the student that is print rich. This print-rich environment is not easily established in a classroom that is skills, phonics, and worksheet based. This environment is especially important for the early stages of literacy. Frank asks, What good is competence in reading if kids hate reading? He sees much of this "aliteracy" when it shows up as students get older. If students never choose to read, Frank maintains, they might as well be illiterate. With whole language, teachers get the chance to excite kids about good literature. Frank cites a recent article from *Educational Leadership* as stating that in Beverly Hills the average house has 900 books. Across town, in Compton, the average house has 2.5 books, whereas in Watts, the average number of books in each house is 0.5. Children who do not have a print-rich environment at home need one in school; they may already be up to five years behind their more fortunate age-mates. Schools must commit themselves to assisting these students to catch up.

Reading to learn is the literacy gatekeeper in middle school. Mr. Peterson's commitment to a schoolwide implementation of First Steps addresses that issue. He notes that whatever subject area a teacher teaches, he or she has an important role in teaching children to be more literate. A cadre of teachers who have been trained as First Steps tutors, including himself, are enthusiastically committed to its schoolwide efficacy. He cautions, however, that people must understand the developmental nature of literacy. It is not realistic to expect students to catch up overnight, but they can improve in both their literacy development and their love of literacy through a cohesive systemwide application of the First Steps program.

At the time of our interview, the school had been in operation for only 12 weeks, yet plans were progressing for implementing the First Steps program throughout the entire school. The first stage of implementation involved assessment to get students placed along the developmental continuum. Once placed, instruction is focused on what the child needs to move along the continuum. Although the school will be evaluated on the degree to which students are able to meet new state academic standards, Frank feels that his students are better served if instruction is individualized and appealing to them. The First Steps instructional program aims to improve both reading and writing as well as encourage the positive view of literacy needed for increased student motivation. An emphasis on students in grades 6 and 7 for the first year should see the improvement of test scores in subsequent years. Next year, the school plans to provide students with an extra period in the day for reading in which First Steps would form the curriculum. The plan is to provide each cluster of students with a reading teacher, and the neediest students would receive additional reading assistance through a computer application of literature reading. Accelerated Reader is one program the school is investigating for this purpose, because Frank believes that rewarding students in the right way is a positive motivator for them. Accelerated Reader is self-pacing, so this program seems to be an appropriate use of the five computers present in each classroom. He believes the challenge is to ensure that the school possesses a sufficient number of books at all the different levels. The school librarian has directed her efforts in this direction.

Professional development in content area reading is provided by teachers the district selected to develop content strategies to use with students. At Monroe Clark Middle School, the First Steps program content is relevant and helps students with content area reading strategies. Teachers originally selected First Steps because they wanted something to help their lower achieving students to do better, but they found the program to be good for all students.

Parents are involved in First Steps as well. Prior to the opening of the new school, Mr. Peterson shared the program planning through letters and invited parents to workshops. Although he sees that as a positive beginning for a new school, he also sees a need to do more to get parents involved. A parent component has been developed for each grade level. This packet goes home to advise parents what they can do to help their child. Additional outreach projects are in the planning stages. For example, Frank plans to emphasize to both parents and teachers that a substantial portion of homework should involve reading for pleasure.

Frank would like to see teachers emphasizing reading for pleasure when classwork is done. To this end, all classes, no matter what the subject area, have been provided with their own libraries in addition to those found in the central library. The beautiful central library will eventually house $75 million in books, and each class-room library will contain 55 to 60 titles.

In addition, Frank plans to start a weekly book club with struggling students. He would like to make it highly visible, where students and their parents sign a contract to join. He envisions the book club as an opportunity for students to talk about the book in engaging ways. Rather than writing book reports or performing in-depth character analyses, he sees students who will learn to love reading by discussing books with oth-ers. In this respect, Frank sees making the middle school more like the elementary school than the high school. For him, reading is the number one job and the most important area of the curriculum. He is busy convincing his teachers. He meets with them individually and in small groups, and he listens to them as much as he talks. He frequently distributes articles that he thinks can create the "uneasiness" necessary for conceptual change.

Hoover High School

Dr. Doris Alvarez, the National Principal of the Year, is the principal of Hoover High School in San Diego. Nineteen hundred students attend Hoover High. Hoover is com-posed of students from diverse cultures and languages, with the primary ethnic group currently Hispanic (51%).

The instructional leadership of the principal is critical for a school's instructional efforts and positive outcomes. Since Dr. Alvarez became Hoover High's principal 11 years ago, improvement of literacy has been a priority, so much so that it has guided and directed much of the school reforms in teaching and learning. The faculty is so committed to the goal that they believe it would be negligence on their part if they did not focus on issues of language learning and reading improvement. For example, only one quarter of the students are native English speakers. Hoover High School has the highest poverty rate of any high school in the city. Moreover, the community is one of high transience and crime. All these factors contribute to a situation in which there are many students who, because of life's circumstances, have the potential to be or become academically at risk.

Early in Dr. Alvarez's tenure, she realized that she could influence literacy learn-ing by setting up situations for teachers to discuss and learn together. Through a unique staff development arrangement with San Diego State University and two reading pro-fessors, teachers received an after-school course that focused on strategies for promot-ing reading across the content areas. This arrangement allowed teachers to try a strategy presented in the course and return the next week to discuss it. Not only did teachers receive the benefit of the instruction and the discussion and interaction with each other, but they also received college credit for salary advancement. In addition, the two professors and Dr. Alvarez set up multicultural reading groups in which every-one read and discussed literature of third-world authors. These groups introduced teachers to literature that would give them different perspectives and different ways of looking at the world. Since then, they have used this model of staff development exten-sively. Doris credits the success of this arrangement with providing an approach that she would use and adapt for many years to come.

Another important way Doris has found to influence literacy learning is to be a role model for reading and speaking. She shares book titles with the faculty and communicates the importance of reading whenever she is given the chance, in speeches to parents, and in the newsletter that she sends to students' homes each month. Dr. Alvarez also speaks to students in classes and shares books with them that she has read and enjoyed.

Dr. Alvarez believes that her "greatest influence of literacy learning has occurred in the context of the reforms that have been made in the high school." She explains that Thomas Newkirk, in a chapter on the language development in the high school years, stated that "language development is not a natural unfolding but rather reflects and gains direction from the culture of the school" (Newkirk, 1991, p. 335). "Likewise, the reforms that I have influenced at the school have directly impacted how language is developed and taught. Teachers are with students for longer periods so they have less students. Because they have fewer students and are working together in teams, they plan interdisciplinary problem-oriented units that cause more than the mere acquisition of facts and figures. The result is a move toward the constructivist classroom in most of our humanities classes."

Dr. Alvarez believes that she has been influenced by the work of Vygotsky, who maintained that language learning is social and interactive. She states that "students learn from each other in meaningful interactions. They learn from others responding to them and providing them with models. This is a picture of students as active learners rather than as passive recipients of teacher presentations." For this reason, Doris believes that the Hoover High teachers use structured cooperative learning groups, Socratic seminars, and a focus on students working and learning in the community in which they live. Teachers at Hoover High also connect the curriculum with the experience of their students. "In schools such as ours with such diverse learners, they use these connections to not only engage students in meaningful ways but to have students build on their prior knowledge as they expand their learning," Dr. Alvarez said.

She recently read *The Right to Learn* (Darling-Hammond, 1997). "In this book Darling-Hammond describes learner-centered schools that are working for students in many communities. Her focus is on good teaching in constructivist classrooms, and staff development programs that are ongoing and meaningful for the teacher. As it pertains to literacy learning, she identifies features that result in deep understanding for students: (a) the use of higher order cognitive functions beyond recall and reproduction of information; (b) having students apply skills and ideas to meaningful contexts and activities; (c) building on student prior knowledge and pressing them to go beyond this knowledge. I believe this exemplifies what we are doing at Hoover High," stated Dr. Alvarez.

"I belong to many professional groups . . . that focus on instruction and literacy. The professional journals I receive are important for not only my own but my staff's growth. I frequently share articles with them on literacy," she said. "About five years ago as chair of the professional development committee of the San Diego Administrators Association, I began an administrative reading group that continued for about four years. In this group, we read books that helped us to see divergent points of view and varying perspectives. It was an extremely positive step toward acknowledging our own literacy needs as professionals. I network frequently with local and national groups in the area of literacy learning and reform agendas. This networking has positively affected what we do as a school as well as enriching our repertoire of strategies," she said.

Because Hoover High's instructional priorities center on issues of second language learning and reading improvement, the faculty has placed literacy learning—reading, writing, speaking, and thinking—as the underpinning of all they do. Thus, they have clustered into academic teams for promoting literacy schoolwide. Many programs at Hoover High address literacy, and every student keeps a portfolio of his or her work. The portfolio is divided into six sections that represent the schoolwide learner outcomes. Students place their work from all classes into the portfolio and write a reflection piece that details their learnings. Because teams plan units together, they have exit requirements for each team. Each academic team requires students to read and produce reader responses for a set number of books. Each team requires students to develop in-depth research papers on thematic team-developed topics. All seniors are required to present the results of four years of work to a panel of businesspersons and community leaders in 45-minute presentations. All academic teams have two major exhibitions of student work each semester. Papers and projects are judged by community representatives. There is tremendous parent involvement in these exhibitions. This program has been the primary means of promoting parent involvement.

The portfolio assessment at Hoover High is unique in that it is schoolwide. All students know the language of Hoover Learner Outcomes and all students understand that they are accountable for student work in their portfolios. Students at Hoover High are writing more, reading more, and are much more active learners in the process than they used to be. Beginning in February 1999, the school issued a portfolio report card to parents to show parents and students that students and faculty value the work in the portfolio so highly that it should be reported officially. Because portfolio scores are being reported to University of California and California State University Admission officers in a pilot project, it makes sense to include parents in the process.

Teachers at Hoover High do consensus assessment of student work in their academic teams. The result is that assessment is improving instruction. It is tied to the work that students are doing. This is unlike standardized tests that have no relationship to what goes on in the classroom.

In addition to the schoolwide emphasis on portfolios, Hoover High has a sustained silent reading period in which most teachers have students do some form of reader response. Most teachers follow through well and consider silent reading a priority because Dr. Alvarez insisted that she would like it to be a priority. Each year she and the faculty continue to build classroom libraries. When they received extra funds from the governor, they poured thousands of dollars into upgrading the library.

In addition to Dr. Alvarez's gentle prodding of each teacher to stress reading in his or her classroom, she requires that each teacher being evaluated do an objective in the area of reading. She said, "This is my opportunity to help them evaluate their strengths and weaknesses in this area. Some very unique and creative strategies have emerged from this exercise, and I have asked those teachers to share their ideas with the faculty."

Doris has also developed a unique professional development program that releases teachers for a portion of each day for an extended period. Teachers can do personalized research on an issue of choice, develop a teaching unit, or participate in seminar discussions with other teachers. In addition, the teachers share readings and discuss them. In the past, Dr. Alvarez has brought in experts to help on various strategies for the teaching of reading and writing: graphic organizers, reciprocal teaching, and so forth. But in addition to the personalized professional growth seminars (PPGS), she has developed weekly team meetings that allow the faculty to discuss student work and strategies for teaching.

"We are in the process of revising our literacy plan to address the issue of having more second-language learners in all of our classrooms. Over the years, many changes have taken place and we have not regrouped recently to bring it all together," said Dr. Alvarez. "Also, many issues will have to be decided with the advent of state standards. Will a student graduate if he does not meet the standard? How will we assess whether he has met the standard? Will the Governor's Test do it? What leeway will we have with the new STAR program for second language learners? I know they will be tested, but to what avail?"

The principal sets the stage for instructional leadership. Dr. Alvarez believes that her most potent force for creating change is staff development. But, she cautions, "Staff development will not be the answer if you have not set up structures for staff development to take place in meaningful ways. Thus, at Hoover, we have teams, the personalized professional growth seminars, the practice of examination of student work, and a schoolwide focus on what students should be able to do when they graduate. All these practices and structures drive any plan that addresses school issues and student needs."

Dr. Alvarez emphasized that the literacy development of all Hoover High students is what the faculty believes to be their primary responsibility. Dr. Alvarez sees her role as supporting, promoting, and applauding these efforts.

Recommendations for Practice and Future Research

Although the principals we interviewed operated at different levels, possessed differing theoretical viewpoints, and espoused different programs in the differing contexts of their respective schools, there were many points on which they were in basic agreement. Each principal uses the recommendations from research in appropriate ways. Table 2.1 on page 35 compares the principals' stances on various issues.

Radencich (1995) provided counsel for the district leadership as follows. District leadership should

1. Stay well informed.
   - Join organizations such as the International Reading Association.
   - Collect an extensive professional library.
   - Know your school and its personnel well.
2. Serve as a role model for the behaviors you want.

TABLE 2.1   Principal Comparison Chart

Principal/School	**Jeanne Koelln** *Jamacha Elementary School*	**Juel Moore** *Oak Park Music Conservatory with Enriched Studies*	**Frank Peterson** *Monroe Clark Middle School*	**Doris Alvarez** *Hoover High School*
Theoretical Stance	Balanced, developmental, based upon inquiry and accountability, New Zealand Model, literature	Developmental, meaning construction, research-based, culture and home influence, balanced curriculum	Developmental, cueing systems, whole language, literature, aesthetic stance	Integrated content-related literacy, diagnostic assessment and instruction
Literacy Program	Accelerated literacy, accountability through benchmarks, special interventions	Basal core literature, extended literature, special interventions, integrated curriculum, assessment	First Steps (Australia); assessment, literature, discussion, special interventions	Language arts strategies integrated throughout curriculum areas
Literacy as a Priority in the School	Focused, systematic plan, educate and involve parents, sacred time, set benchmarks, establish teaching experts, remedial tutoring	Involve whole school, establish focus, use a model, establish standards, expand accountability, incentive reading programs	Literacy as focus for all teachers, stress importance, continual emphasis, extra reading time, class libraries, book club	Literacy development of L1 and L2* is a priority of all teachers; multicultural book clubs enhance literacy
Professional Development	Goals each year, Program Quality Review, faculty meetings, structured workshops, off-site workshops, summer academics, cooperative process	Teacher's choice, workshops to answer critical questions about student learning, collaboration, cluster (K–12) workshops on current research, mentor observations	First Steps training, teacher's choice of workshops, district in-services	Professional conferences, mini-sabbaticals, in-service educational journal readings, and collegial interactions promote continuous professional development

*L1 and L2 refer, respectively, to the first and second languages spoken by the student.

3. Provide direction and support.
   - Formulate a workable plan of action for literacy.
   - Make effective presentations about your program.
   - Select and nurture reading teachers.
   - Respond promptly and effectively to requests.
   - Visit schools.
   - Provide unsolicited support (be a cheerleader and sell your program).
4. Start, carry out, support, and evaluate programs (e.g., teacher study groups).
5. Support reading resource teachers.
   - Provide opportunities for networking.
   - Provide for formal and informal gatherings.
6. Work effectively with district consultants.
7. Work effectively with the community.
8. Work effectively with publishing companies.
9. Assess program effectiveness.
   - Assess faculty.
   - Assess schools.
   - Assess the district.

Although Radencich's recommendations are intended for "district" leadership, most of them also apply to the site administrator and are represented in our exemplars' work.

When we look at our exemplars' instructional leadership, it becomes apparent that each meets most of the characteristics for outstanding reading programs set forth by Radencich and the findings from the review of research.

Patty, Maschoff, and Ransom (1996) set forth the characteristics of outstanding reading programs as follows: (1) the program is based on strong instructional leadership; (2) the literature-based curriculum is focused on text understanding, and reading across the curriculum is endorsed; (3) a strong library or media center with a capable librarian is a program foundation; (4) time is set aside during the school day to read for fulfillment; (5) program and learner assessments are based on multiple measures of reading; (6) writing helps reading and reading supports writing, and writing across the curriculum is nurtured; (7) accelerated word knowledge is based on metacognitive processes; and (8) active parental participation and support of reading exists through volunteerism and home activities (p. 3).

The principals interviewed were all involved in site-based management attended by a decentralization in curriculum. Although this state of events is changing, in California, at least, it has provided an unparalleled laboratory for innovation in curriculum and instructional approaches. Principals who find themselves in contexts in which this flexibility is provided have a much increased responsibility for keeping themselves and their teachers informed and responsive to student learning.

Two of the four principals stressed the importance of the library/media center to their instructional programs. All the principals tried to involve parents more actively in support of their reading programs. The interrelatedness of reading and writing was noted by all the principals, as was the use of multiple measures to assess learners' progress. All the principals made arrangements for a "sacred" time for self-selected reading; two of the four endorsed the notion of reading in all subject areas. All the principals saw reading as a developmental process that could be enhanced through appropriate instruction using literature.

These principals were involved, well-informed, inquiring individuals who interacted positively with their faculty, often exposing their own struggles with literacy issues and often giving credit to talented teachers for leaps in their own thinking. Keeping literacy as a focus for their faculty was a major goal for each literacy leader. The notion that the principal was a "lifelong learner" was unstated but very easy to infer, and studies from both paradigms of research informed their thinking.

The principals confirmed the Sparks and Hirsch (1997) argument for three powerful ideas. First, each principal was concerned with accountability issues, confirming the need to provide "results" for time, effort, and expenditure in education. Second, the concern for systematic change at the school level was readily apparent. The elementary and middle school principals were particularly insistent on the coherence and systemic nature of programs to be put into place. The third powerful idea, constructivism, is again readily discernible in the interviews. Concern that students are provided with experiences that enable them to "construct meaning" and to become actively involved in their own learning are valued by these principals. The use of benchmarks and outcomes as measures of success and the change from "inputs" or teaching to "outputs" or learning are all hallmarks of the changes that principals are encouraging as instructional leaders. The effective literacy instructional leader possesses a vision for the literacy program, involves the major constituents (parents, staff, students) in the process, provides curricular and instructional support for teachers, models the importance of literacy, supervises and monitors the reading program and its assessment features, provides professional development opportunities, creates the climate for literacy (and diversity) in the school, and participates in identifying and delivering interventions for special needs students.

To get started in revising your literacy program, begin with a knowledge of the context in which you work. What kind of community is the school located in? What do parents expect? Second, find out what is currently going on in your school. What materials and programs are being used? How do the teachers feel about this? Which beliefs and practices are entrenched? Which can be changed?

Once you know what is going on in literacy at your school, you can begin to frame the changes you would like to make. A teacher study group formed to examine theory and practice in literacy can present findings to the faculty and make recommendations for programs to be adopted.

When a program has been chosen, it is time to begin a three-part process for change:

1. Assess your current program.
2. Compare your current program to the model chosen.
3. Plan to implement the changes recommended.

As program implementation proceeds, plan for changes based on a "continuous improvement model" that allows for course corrections based on the input of teachers, parents, and students.

Conclusion

The complexity of rapidly changing school landscapes makes the principal's role a demanding and dynamic one. Although the principals we interviewed made it look easy, to become an instructional leader in literacy in your school means a constant search for understanding and consensus among the participants—students, teachers, parents, and other district administrators—as well as accountability to these audiences and the school board. Constant self-study and strong communications skills are required.

R E F E R E N C E S

Anderson, R.C., & Pearson, P.D. (1984). A schema-theoretic view of basic processes in reading. In P.D. Pearson (Ed.), *Handbook of reading research* (pp. 255–292). White Plains, NY: Longman.

Bartlett, F.C. (1932). *Remembering.* Cambridge, MA: Cambridge University Press.

Bond, G.L. & Dykstra, R. (1967). The cooperative research program in first-grade reading instruction. *Reading Research Quarterly, 2* (4), 5–142.

Burg, L.A., Kaufman, M., Korngold, B., & Kovner, A. (1978). *The complete reading supervisor—tasks and roles.* Columbus, OH: Merrill.

California State Department of Education. (1987). English/language arts framework for California public schools, K–12. Sacramento: California State Department of Education.

Cazden, C.B. (1988). *Classroom discourse.* Portsmouth, NH: Heinemann.

Chance, C. (1991). Principals' perceptions of their involvement in the elementary school reading program. *Reading Improvement, 28* (1), 26–34.

Cooper, J.D. (1997). *Literacy: Helping children construct meaning* (3rd ed.). Boston: Houghton Mifflin.

Cunningham, J.W., & Fitzgerald, J. (1996). Epistemology and reading. *Reading research quarterly, 31*(1), 36–60.

Daresh, J.C., & Playko, M.A. (1992). Entry year programs for principals: Mentoring and other forms of professional development. *Catalyst for Change, 21*(2), 24–29.

Darling-Hammond, L. (1997). *The right to learn: A blueprint for creating schools that work.* San Francisco: Jossey-Bass.

Darling-Hammond, L., with Sclan, E. (1992). Policy and supervision. In C.D. Glickman (Ed.), *Supervision in transition,* Yearbook of the Association for Supervision and Curriculum Development (pp. 7–29). Alexandria, VA: Association for Supervision and Curriculum Development.

Dungan, F. (1994). Teachers say administrators can make a difference in the school's reading program. *State of Reading, 1*(1), 46–48.

Erickson, F. (1986). Qualitative methods in research on teaching. In M.C. Wittrock (Ed.), *Handbook of research on teaching* (3rd ed., pp. 119–161). New York: Macmillan.

———. (1993). Transformation and school success: The politics and culture of educational achievement. In E. Jacob & C. Jordan (Eds.), *Minority education: Anthropological perspectives* (pp. 27–51). Norwood, NJ: Ablex.

Glickman, C.D. (1992). Introduction: Postmodernism and supervision. In C.D. Glickman (Ed.), *Supervision in transition,* Yearbook of the Association for Supervision and Curriculum Development. Alexandria, VA: Association for Supervision and Curriculum Development.

Hallinger, P. (1996). School context, principal leadership, and student reading achievement. *Elementary School Journal, 96* (5), 527–549.

Hallinger, P., & Murphy, J. (1987). Schools show improvement in reading skills. *AARSIC Abstracts 2*(4), 2–4.

Hammond, Linda D. (1997). *The right to learn.* San Francisco: Jossey-Bass.

Harris, B.M. (1986, March). *Leadership for quality instruction: Looking toward the twenty-first century.* Paper presented at the Annual Meeting of the Association for Supervision and Curriculum Development, San Francisco.

Hill, M., & Patterson, L. (Eds.). (1997). Critical connections: Research on early reading instruction. In *Reading Online,* ISSN 1096–1232, May.

Holzman, M. (1993). What is systemic change? *Educational Leadership, 51,* 1–18.

Hughes, L.W., & Ubben, G.C. (1994). *The elementary principal's handbook* (4th ed.). Boston: Allyn and Bacon.

International Reading Association. (1992). *Standards for reading professionals.* Newark, DE: International Reading Association.

Langer, J.A., & Allington, R.L. (1992). Curriculum research in writing and reading. In P.W. Jackson (Ed.), *Handbook of research on curriculum* (pp. 687–725). New York: Macmillan.

Lickteig, M.J. (1995). Ways elementary administrators support literacy education. *Reading Horizons, 35*(4), 299–309.

Lytle, S L., & Cochran-Smith, M. (1990). Learning from teacher research: A working typology. *Teachers College Record, 92*(1), 83–103.

Murphy, T.A. (1994). Power teaching: A key to quality education. *Reading Improvement, 31*(4), 211–213.

National Association of Elementary School Principals. (1994). *Best ideas from America's blue ribbon schools* (Vol. 2). Thousand Oaks, CA: Corwin Press.

———. (1995). *Best ideas from America's blue ribbon schools* (Vol. 2). Thousand Oaks, CA: Corwin Press.

Newkirk, T. (1991). The learner develops: "The high school years." In J. Flood, J.M. Jensen, D. Lapp, and J. Squire (Eds.), *Handbook of research on teaching the English language arts* (pp. 331–342). New York: Macmillan.

Northwest Regional Educational Laboratory. (1984). *Effective schooling practices: A research synthesis.* Portland OR: The Laboratory.

Pajak, E. (1992). A view from the central office. In C.D. Glickman (Ed.), *Supervision in transition,* Yearbook of the Association for Supervision and Curriculum Development (pp. 126–138). Alexandria, VA: Association for Supervision and Curriculum Development.

Patty, D., Maschoff, J.D., & Ransom, P.E. (1996). *The reading resource handbook for school leaders.* Norwood, MA: Christopher-Gordon Publishers.

Potter, L. (1994). Putting reading first in the middle school: The principal's responsibility. *Reading Improvement, 31*(4) 243–245.

Radencich, M.C. (1995). *Administration and supervision of the reading/writing program.* Boston: Allyn and Bacon.

Sanacore, J. (1996). Guidelines for successful reading leaders. *Research in Education.* (ERIC Document Reproduction Service No. ED393 063)

Sarason, S.B. (1972). *The culture of the school and the problem of change* (2nd ed.). Boston: Allyn and Bacon.

Scharer, P.L., & Rogers, T. (1994). *Assessment and decision-making in two schools: The Ohio site* (Technical Report #596). Urbana, IL: Center for the Study of Reading.

Senge, P.M. (1990). *The fifth discipline: The art and practice of the learning organization.* New York: Doubleday/Currency.

Sparks, D., & Hirsch, S. (1997). *A new vision for staff development.* Alexandria, VA: Association for Supervision and Curriculum Development.

Walker, R. (1995). *Accelerating literacy: A handbook to assist educators in creating balanced literacy instruction.* San Diego, CA: Walker Enterprises.

Wepner, S.B., & Seminoff, N.E. (1995). Evolving roles and responsibilities of reading personnel. In S.B. Wepner, J.T. Feeley, & D.S. Strickland (Eds.), *The administration and supervision of reading programs* (2nd ed., pp. 22–38). New York: Teachers College Press and International Reading Association.

Wolcott, H.F. (1988). Ethnographic research in education. In R.M. Jaeger (Ed.), *Complementary methods for research in education.* Washington, DC: American Educational Research Association.

Vygtosky, L.S. (1978). *Mind in society.* Cambridge, MA: Harvard University Press.

Interview Protocol for the
Instructional Leader in Literacy

1. It is generally acknowledged that the principal of the school sets the pace for all instructional efforts. How do you see your role as instructional leader in literacy, and how do you act to influence literacy learning in your school?

   Probes: Can you say more about your role as instructional leader?

   Can you say more about how you influence literacy learning in your school?

2. What is your basic theoretical stance toward literacy? What have you read or what conferences have you attended that have helped to form your leadership position in literacy?

   Probes: What influences formed your knowledge base about literacy?

   What is the latest thing you have read about literacy learning?

   Are you involved in professional groups (e.g., International Reading Association) about literacy issues?

   Do you network with other professionals? Please describe.

3. Can you describe the literacy program(s) in place at your school? How have they evolved over the past five years?

   Probes: What changes have occurred in the past five years?

   What role have you played in the changes?

   Have parents been involved? If so, how?

   How much time is devoted to self-selected reading?

   How does your writing program figure into the overall literacy effort?

   What kinds of assessment are used? How do they fit into your overall literacy program?

4. How is literacy made a priority in your school?

   Probes: How is this different from what might be going on elsewhere?

   What is unique about literacy in your school?

   How is the library or media center involved in your literacy efforts?

5. How does your school handle professional development opportunities for teachers in literacy? How does this differ from other professional development opportunities in other content areas?

   Probes: Can you describe for me what professional development opportunities you have tried to make available to teachers?

   Do you have a unified plan to address literacy issues?

   How has your faculty responded to this?

6. What else would you like to add about your role as instructional leader in literacy learning?

3 The Role of the Literacy Specialist

K. DENISE MUTH

SHAWN M. GLYNN

The University of Georgia

The literacy specialist plays a critical role in the education of young adolescents. It is during the middle-grade years that young adolescents form attitudes about education and its relevance to their future. During these years, they also make decisions about how long to remain in school and whether to prepare for higher education. More often than not, young adolescents make these decisions based on their ability to read and write about what they are learning as well their ability to contribute constructively to classroom discussions and conversations. In this chapter, we discuss the role that literacy specialists play in helping young adolescents acquire a good education and prepare for the future.

The remainder of this chapter is divided into six sections. In the first section, we list the qualifications of literacy specialists and highlight some of the key reasons they are needed in the middle grades. In the second section, the goals of an ideal middle-grades literacy program are identified and described. In the third, fourth, and fifth sections, we outline specific ways that literacy specialists can work with teams of teachers, with at-risk students, and with parents, respectively. In the final section, we provide literacy specialists with guidelines for coordinating a middle-grades literacy program.

Need for Middle-Grades Literacy Specialists

What exactly are literacy specialists, and why are they needed in the middle grades? Literacy specialists are teachers who have received advanced training and certification in reading and the English language arts. Ideally, these teachers have undergraduate middle-grades degrees with an emphasis in language arts. They also have extensive classroom experience as middle-grades reading or language arts teachers and K–12 master's, specialist, or doctoral degrees in reading and literacy.

Why is there a need for literacy specialists in the middle grades? Early adolescence is a time of great change. Students at this age are experiencing the physical, cognitive, social, and personal changes associated with moving from childhood into adolescence. Many of these students are also experiencing the changes associated with moving from elementary schools to middle schools or junior high schools. In addition, due to a variety of social transformations such as changes in the family structure and a world dominated by the media, the sociocultural context in which young adolescents are growing up today is significantly different from that of only a few years ago (Carnegie Council on Adolescent Development, 1995).

For many young adolescents, the changes associated with early adolescence occur quite smoothly, but for others, the impact of these changes can have negative effects, such as declining grades, decreased interest in school, poor attendance, and low self-esteem (Wigfield, Eccles, & Pintrich, 1996). New research, however, suggests that middle-grades schools can help make this time of change a positive experience for young adolescents (Mullins, 1997; Warren & Muth, 1995). The school should have a well-run literacy program with a literacy specialist who works not only with students but with teachers and parents as well.

Literacy specialists are crucial to the teaching–learning process that occurs in the middle grades for several reasons. First, the early middle grades are usually the point at which young adolescents begin to move from narrative to expository text, a process that places increasing demands on the students' literacy skills. Despite these increasing demands on their literacy skills, however, formal reading instruction ends for many young adolescents once they enter middle school.

Second, recent research has shown that about 50% of middle-grades teachers do not receive training in the teaching of reading at the middle level during their teacher preparation programs (Scales & McEwin, 1996); even fewer receive preparation in using writing across the curriculum. Consequently, these teachers are unprepared to teach content area literacy strategies to their students.

Third, given the emphasis on an integrated curriculum, all middle-grades teachers, regardless of the subjects they teach, are being called on to integrate the language arts into their curriculum. Many are not prepared to do so. Research has shown that requiring preservice teachers to take a single course in content area literacy is just a beginning, and practicing teachers still need on-site follow-up with experienced teachers, such as literacy specialists (Romine, McKenna, & Robinson, 1996, p. 197).

Goals of a Middle-Grades Literacy Program

Literacy specialists are responsible for coordinating schoolwide literacy programs that are developed around the needs of young adolescents. What should such literacy programs look like? Irvin (1997) maintains that successful middle-grades literacy programs should aim to accomplish five goals: (1) focus on the learning process, (2) facilitate language development, (3) provide strategy-based instruction across the curriculum, (4) integrate the language arts, and (5) encourage recreational reading and reading aloud to students.

Focus on the Learning Process.   Literacy specialists should help teachers focus on student understanding, problem solving, and connections across disciplines rather than equating student learning with memorization of facts. Teaching should occur in a manner that facilitates student learning as an active, constructive process rather than as a passive, reproductive process. That is, students should be active participants in their own learning so that they can learn new material in meaningful ways.

Facilitation of Language Development.   Literacy specialists should assist teachers in promoting the language development of young adolescents. This goal implies that communication, dialogue, discussion, and interaction between the teacher and the students, and between the students themselves, are crucial if meaningful learning is to occur. Activities in which students interact in meaningful ways with the teacher and with each other should become commonplace in middle-grades classrooms. Listening and speaking in all content areas should receive more emphasis in the middle-grades curriculum. Granted, students frequently engage in these two activities, but they receive little formal instruction in effective listening and speaking skills. As Weaver (1997) reminded us, "Good conversation that does not degenerate into dogmatic pronouncements or heated argument is a life skill that many adults have yet to master" (p. 40).

Strategy-Based Instruction.   Literacy specialists should help teachers identify the most appropriate strategies for presenting the content. The strategy continuum in Table 3.1

TABLE 3.1   Strategy Continuum with Example Strategies

Teacher-Centered Strategies	Teacher-Assisted Strategies	Peer-Assisted Strategies	Student-Centered Strategies
Lecture	Drill and practice	Role playing	**Rehearsal strategies**
Direct instruction	Discovery learning	Peer tutoring	repeated reading
Demonstration	Brainstorming	Reciprocal teaching	selective underlining
Recitation	Discussion	Cooperative learning	two-column notes
			Elaboration strategies
			mental imagery
			guided imagery
			creating analogies
			Organizational strategies
			clustering
			graphic organizers
			outlining
			Comprehension monitoring strategies
			K-W-L
			Motivational strategies
			time management
			effort management

depicts the range of teacher and student involvement in a variety of strategies that are used in middle-grades classrooms. Strategies range from teacher-centered at one end of the continuum to student-centered at the other end. In between are strategies in which the teacher assists the students and strategies in which students interact with and receive assistance from one another. Thus, moving from left to right along the continuum, the role of the teacher becomes less dominant and the role of the student becomes more dominant, until students are learning autonomously. Peer-assisted and student-centered strategies should be used to help students move toward independent learning.

Integration of the Language Arts.   The concept of an integrated curriculum is the focus of several chapters later in this book. Given that a primary goal of an integrated curriculum is to have students play active roles in their learning, literacy specialists should help teachers focus their classrooms as much as possible around peer-assisted and student-centered strategies. Students who have learned to read, write, listen, and speak should use these skills to extend their learning. Lessons that integrate reading, writing, listening, and speaking with content area material should play a key role in middle-grades classrooms. Activities such as play writing and performances, role playing, improvisation, poetry readings, journal writing, and peer editing are excellent devices not only for integrating language arts into the curriculum but also for capitalizing on the social nature of young adolescents.

Recreational and Reading-Aloud Reading.   One of the goals of any literacy program should be for students to enjoy and engage in reading and writing, for learning purposes as well as enjoyment. Accordingly, opportunities should be provided for students to read and write for recreational purposes in all content areas and on a variety of topics. Recreational reading should allow middle-grades students to read, at their own pace, from sources of their own choosing. Similarly, recreational writing should provide students with opportunities to write, on any topic, without having to concentrate on form, punctuation, and spelling and without worrying about sharing their writing with others. Similarly, reading aloud to middle-grades students provides them with informal opportunities to respond and react to what they are hearing. In addition, they can use the information in future activities and projects. Reading aloud to students also establishes a common starting point for class discussions and other activities.

Coordinating a middle-grades literacy program such as the one just described involves three specific tasks on the part of the literacy specialist: working with teams of teachers, working with at-risk students, and working with parents. Because many of the topics (e.g., teaching and learning strategies, assessment methods) discussed in the next three sections are described in detail in other chapters in this book, here we identify some of the ways that literacy specialists can work with teams of teachers, at-risk students, and parents and provide some very general guidelines about how they can do so.

Working with Teams of Teachers

In this section, we highlight five ways that a literacy specialist and teams of teachers can work together to achieve the schoolwide literacy goals just described. Although the focus is on the literacy specialist's work with teams, all the ideas in this section can be applied to individual teachers as well.

1. Plan with Teams

Many middle-grades schools are organized around interdisciplinary teams of teachers. These teams typically include two to four teachers who plan the language arts, mathematics, science, and social studies curriculum together during a common planning time. Literacy specialists should meet on a regular basis with all teams to help them plan ways to integrate the language arts into the curriculum. Ideally, these meetings should occur when the teams are in the beginning stages of planning integrated units and themes. Specific sessions should be scheduled to help teams brainstorm activities and assignments that involve integrating reading, writing, listening, and speaking into the content. Literacy specialists should also help teachers learn and use strategies that will help them move, as much as possible, from a teacher-centered to a student-centered curriculum. When working with teams, literacy specialists should also include media specialists, guidance counselors, and special education teachers when appropriate.

2. Help Teams Assess Students' Literacy Achievement

In addition to helping teams plan for instruction, literacy specialists should work with teams to help them integrate authentic assessment into the teaching–learning process. Unfortunately, it appears that many teachers receive little training in sound assessment practices in general, let alone in authentic types of assessment such as portfolio and performance assessment that link instruction and assessment (Cizek, Fitzgerald, & Rachor, 1995–1996; Stiggins, 1995). In addition, among teachers who are familiar with current assessment practices, many are reluctant to use them because of the time involved. Literacy specialists should work with teams, from the ground up, to design and implement these types of assessment on a teamwide basis. Literacy specialists should also meet with teams to explain and discuss their students' performance on criterion- and norm-referenced tests that they take.

3. Give Demonstration Lessons

Teachers are more likely to use new strategies and integrate authentic assessment methods into those strategies if they have seen them in practice. Literacy specialists should routinely give demonstration lessons for teams. These lessons should be videotaped for other teachers in the school and should be used for simulated recall sessions with groups of teachers. This practice is especially helpful when a team is using a new strategy or activity for the first time and they want to see it modeled by someone who is familiar with its use. The team members should be involved in helping to plan the lesson that will be demonstrated, and the lesson should be taught to the students on the team.

4. Observe Teachers and Give Feedback

When teachers incorporate new strategies into their teaching, feedback from a trained observer can help them master the strategy. Literacy specialists should observe teachers only when the teachers specifically request it. Ideally, the lesson should be videotaped so that the teacher, the literacy specialist, and perhaps even the teacher's teammates can discuss the lesson in a nonthreatening way. If all teachers on a team are routinely observed as a type of formative evaluation, the process becomes an integral part of the team's routines. If the team has recently met with the literacy specialist to discuss the progress of at-risk students on the team, as discussed later in this chapter, then the teachers should be observed soon afterward and provided feedback on how they are interacting with and helping these students.

5. Engage Teams in Action Research

Recent perspectives on the changing roles of teachers in literacy instruction highlight the notion of teachers as researchers (Hiebert & Raphael, 1996). Many classroom teachers, however, have neither the training nor the time to carry out research projects to evaluate their ideas and practices in their classrooms. Literacy specialists, on the other hand, who have training in research methods, can help teams design and carry out action research projects. Ideas for such projects should be generated by team members and should center around questions and concerns they have about their own practices. Literacy specialists should then serve as consultants to help the teams carry out the projects. Literacy specialists should also encourage and help teachers publish their results in practitioner-oriented journals. An excellent example of such a collaboration is Santa, Isaacson, and Manning's (1987) action research project designed to introduce content area teachers to strategies other than oral reading to help their students learn from text.

Working with At-Risk Students

A major portion of a literacy specialist's time is spent working with at-risk students, either individually or in small groups, outside of the regular classroom. Many middle-grades schools have resource rooms where this type of instruction takes place. Students who participate in such a program have usually been identified by test scores or referred by their classroom teachers or parents. In this section, we review five major tasks of a literacy specialist when working with at-risk students.

1. Reinforce Skills and Strategies Taught by Classroom Teachers

When working individually or in small groups with at-risk students, a literacy special-ist should, first and foremost, reinforce the reading, writing, listening, and speaking skills and strategies on which the students' teachers are focusing in their classrooms. Additional practice in these skills and strategies in the way of developmentally appro-priate activities, projects, and assignments will increase the likelihood that at-risk stu-dents will apply these skills and strategies when needed. Ideally, a literacy specialist should strive, just as classroom teachers do, to integrate the language arts with each other as well as with the content. For example, if a team has just taught Ogle's (1986) K-W-L strategy to students, the literacy specialist should provide at-risk students with additional practice applying the strategy to sections from their English, mathematics, science, and social studies textbooks.

2. Teach Study, Metacognitive, and Time-Management Strategies

A primary goal of a literacy specialist should be to help at-risk students become stra-tegic, independent learners. Unfortunately, for many at-risk students, literacy seems to have no relevance to their lives. Many of these students have been placed at risk because they appear to have neither the motivation nor the ability to study and apply themselves in an organized and efficient manner. Thus, strategies at the right-hand side of Table 3.1 need to be constantly stressed with at-risk learners. Modeling, during which the literacy specialist clearly demonstrates the particular strat-egy while thinking aloud through each step, is a critical component of helping at-risk students learn and apply these skills. Perhaps more than anything else, literacy spe-cialists need to provide at-risk students with adequate time to become proficient in the use of a particular strategy and frequent opportunities to practice it in a risk-free environment.

3. Administer Individual Literacy Assessments

A literacy specialist is responsible for assessing the strengths and weaknesses of at-risk students. For example, assessment devices such as the Individual Reading Inventory (IRI) and the Test of Written Language (TWL) are excellent mechanisms for identify-ing at-risk students' specific reading and writing difficulties, respectively. Perhaps even more important than assessing these students' strengths and weaknesses, however, is assessing their interests and attitudes toward literacy. Because many at-risk students see no use for literacy in their lives, a critical factor in their success is finding some way to connect the school literacy program to their personal interests and experiences. A literacy specialist should also design systems for tracking at-risk students' progress in specific literacy areas and should have that information readily available for class-room teachers and parents. An excellent source of information on the various types of assessment procedures available to the literacy specialist is Harp's (1996) *Handbook of Literacy Assessment and Evaluation*.

4. Observe Students in Their Regular Classrooms

A literacy specialist should observe at-risk students in a variety of situations in a variety of their classes. By observing how these students apply learning strategies, organize and monitor their time, participate in discussions, and interact with their peers and teachers, the literacy specialist will have an ideal opportunity not only to assess student progress but also to identify strengths on which to build. These observations also provide the literacy specialist with an opportunity to see if the at-risk student exhibits consistent behaviors across subjects. Observations should be discussed ahead of time with team members to determine the days, times, and specific classes in which to conduct the observations. The literacy specialists should work to ensure that classroom teachers do not feel threatened by these observations. The literacy specialist should take time to cultivate the support of these teachers so that a collaborative and collegial relationship can be established.

5. Communicate with Classroom Teachers

All the individual and small-group work that is done with at-risk students will be for naught unless literacy specialists regularly communicate with these students' classroom teachers. As discussed earlier, literacy specialists meet regularly with teams for a variety of reasons. Some of these meetings should be devoted exclusively to discussing the strengths, weaknesses, and progress of the at-risk students on the team. Literacy specialists need time to discuss the work they have been doing with these students, and classroom teachers need time to ask questions about the ways they work with these students in their classrooms. Team meetings can also be used to plan for parent conferences, which are discussed in the next section. Only by establishing clear avenues of communication can classroom teachers and literacy specialists work together to help at-risk students succeed.

Working with Parents

All too often, parents are left out of the schoolwide literacy program. Granted, they are expected to attend parent–teacher conferences and they are contacted when their children are not doing well, but they are frequently overlooked as important partners with teachers in their children's literacy success. In this section, we identify three ways that literacy specialists can work with parents to get them involved in the schoolwide literacy program. These strategies apply equally well to grandparents, guardians, and even older siblings who may be in positions to help the young adolescents in their families.

1. Communicate with All Parents

The literacy specialist is responsible for communicating schoolwide literacy goals and objectives to all parents. It is also a good idea to have parents work with teachers to identify these goals and objectives and revise them as needed. Establishing a schoolwide parent literacy committee is an excellent way to get and keep parents involved in the school's literacy program. In addition, literacy newsletters that highlight current projects, commend students for their successes, recognize teacher accomplishments such as publications and presentations at literacy conferences, and perhaps even give tips for helping students prepare for standardized tests are much appreciated by parents.

2. Conduct Workshops

Another excellent way for the literacy specialist to keep parents involved in the literacy program is to conduct workshops specifically designed for parents. The parent literacy committee can help solicit ideas from parents and teachers on topics that might be appropriate for such workshops. Workshops should be scheduled at times that are convenient for parents and may even be repeated on different days. The workshops can be announced in the literacy newsletter, and, when appropriate, students should attend with their parents. Topics such as books for young adolescents, getting your children involved in writing at home, dinnertime discussions, television and videos for young adolescents, helping your children with their portfolios, and the ins and outs of standardized testing should be of interest to many parents.

3. Attend Team Parent–Teacher Conferences

Interdisciplinary teams frequently meet with parents, particularly those of at-risk students, to discuss their childrens' strengths, weaknesses, and progress. These conferences are excellent opportunities for the literacy specialist to support the teachers on the team while providing parents ideas for working at home with their children. Prior to the conference, the literacy specialist should meet with the teachers on the team to plan the specifics of the conference. For example, decisions about who will run the meeting, areas to be discussed, which samples of the students' work should be brought to the conference, and what recommendations to make to the parents all need to be planned ahead of time.

Coordinating a Schoolwide Literacy Program

Above and beyond all the work they do with teachers, students, and parents, literacy specialists are responsible for coordinating the schoolwide literacy program. In this section, we describe five major responsibilities of literacy specialists to ensure that the literacy programs in their schools are successful.

1. Develop Schoolwide Goals and Objectives

Perhaps the most important responsibility of literacy specialists is to "achieve faculty . . . consensus on what graduating students should be able to do in the areas of reading and writing (as well as speaking and listening)" (Miller, 1994, p. 26). Without agreement among teachers on what is important, literacy programs too often end up focusing primarily on improving standardized test scores. Although good scores on tests are important, they should not be an end in and of themselves. Equally important, without goals and objectives that are specific to individual schools, teachers have little sense of how to build on what has been taught previously and how to prepare students for what will be taught in the future. Progress toward goals should be measured at the end of every year and revised when needed.

2. Conduct Schoolwide Workshops

Unfortunately, research indicates that teachers are less than enthusiastic about workshops and in-service programs. For example, when Hosking and Teberg (1998) asked middle-grades teachers about the types of support they need to meet the expectations of their literacy programs, the teachers reported that they needed more time for planning and more support from district personnel. They expressed little interest in attending workshops. We believe, however, that if literacy specialists and teachers work cooperatively, workshops can be designed that will meet teachers' needs. The first step is to find out what topics the teachers would like to learn more about, which can be done in a variety of ways, from surveys and questionnaires to anonymous suggestion boxes. Workshops should be held at times convenient for teachers, preferably not after school, and attendance should always be voluntary. If at all possible, teachers should be released from classes and substitutes hired. Workshops can be videotaped so that other teams can watch them and so that individual teachers can watch them at home at their convenience.

3. Maintain a Professional Library for Teachers and Parents

Keeping current with advances and research in literacy is critical for literacy specialists. Equally important, however, is helping classroom teachers stay abreast of changes in the field. An ideal way for literacy specialists to do this is to maintain a literacy library someplace in the school so that all teachers have access to it. The library should include current books, journals, reports, conference programs, instructional videotapes, and newsletters and newspapers from professional literacy organizations. Literacy specialists should be familiar enough with the materials in the school library to help teachers locate what they need and even make suggestions to them. Ideally, the library should have a computer so that teachers can access the electronic journals that are available through the World Wide Web. Anderson-Inman (1998) provides detailed information about literacy-related information that is available through the Web as well as excellent directions on how to access it.

4. Coordinate the Literacy Assessment Program

Literacy specialists are responsible for coordinating the standardized, state criterion-referenced, and classroom literacy tests at the school level. At the state and district level, this coordination involves helping officials choose and develop assessments that are appropriate for young adolescents. For example, literacy specialists can serve on state and district literacy assessment committees and provide input on the types of assessments that the students in their schools will be required to take. On the more local level, as discussed earlier in this chapter, literacy specialists are responsible for working with classroom teachers to help them administer these tests, interpret the results, and communicate these results to students and parents. Finally, literacy specialists are responsible for working with classroom teachers to help them design their own classroom assessments and use the results to make instructional decisions as well as decisions about individual students.

5. Assess the Literacy Program

Even the most successful literacy programs must be assessed routinely, and all stakeholders must be involved in the process. Coordinating this effort, which may be the most important responsibility of literacy specialists, involves three specific tasks. First, schoolwide literacy goals and objectives should be annually reviewed, revised, and even eliminated if necessary. For example, just because all students are achieving a certain objective does not mean that the objective should remain part of the curriculum. Second, literacy specialists should use assessment data to measure student progress toward goals and objectives. This information can then be used by literacy specialists to make systematic revisions in their schoolwide efforts and help teachers make revisions in their classroom practice. Third, teachers, students, and parents should be surveyed annually to get their input on the overall strengths and weaknesses of the program as well as on individual components of the program.

Conclusion

Literacy specialists are playing an increasingly important role in middle-grades literacy programs. Their work is exciting and rewarding, but also complex and demanding. Literacy specialists are teachers who have advanced training in reading and English language arts; the talent to communicate and collaborate effectively with teachers, students, and parents; and the organizational skills to coordinate the efforts of all those interested in the literacy development of young adolescents in schools.

REFERENCES

Anderson-Inman, L. (1998). Electronic journals in technology and literacy: Professional development online. *Journal of Adolescent and Adult Literacy, 41,* 400–405.

Carnegie Council on Adolescent Development. (1995). *Great transitions: Preparing adolescents for a new century.* New York: Carnegie Council of New York.

Cizek, G.J., Fitzgerald, S.M., & Rachor, R.E. (1995–1996). Teachers' assessment practices: Preparation, isolation, and the kitchen sink. *Educational Assessment, 3,* 159–179.

Harp, B. (1996). *The handbook of literacy assessment and evaluation.* Norwood, MA: Christopher-Gordon.

Hiebert, E.H., & Raphael, T.E. (1996). Psychological perspectives on literacy and extensions to educational practice. In D.C. Berliner & R.C. Calfee (Eds.), *Handbook of educational psychology* (pp. 550–602). New York: Simon & Schuster/Macmillan.

Hosking, N.J., & Teberg, A.S. (1998). Bridging the gap: Aligning current practice and evolving expectations for middle years literacy programs. *Journal of Adolescent and Adult Literacy, 41,* 332–340.

Irvin, J.L. (1997). Building sound literacy learning programs for young adolescents. *Middle School Journal, 28*(3), 4–9.

Miller, T. (1994). Improving the schoolwide language arts program: A priority for all middle school teachers. *Middle School Journal, 25*(4), 26–29.

Mullins, E.R. (1997). *Changes in young adolescents' self-perceptions across the transition from elementary to middle school.* Unpublished doctoral dissertation, University of Georgia, Athens.

Ogle, D.M. (1986). K-W-L: A teaching model that develops active reading of expository text. *The Reading Teacher, 39,* 564–570.

Romine, B.G.C., McKenna, M.C., & Robinson, R.D. (1996). Reading coursework requirements for middle and high school content area teachers: A U.S. survey. *Journal of Adolescent and Adult Literacy, 40,* 194–198.

Santa, C.M., Isaacson, L., & Manning, G. (1987). Changing content instruction through action research. *The Reading Teacher, 40*(4), 434–438.

Scales, P.C., & McEwin, K. (1996). *Growing pains: The making of America's middle school teachers.* Columbus, OH: National Middle School Association.

Stiggins, R.J. (1995). Assessment literacy for the 21st century. *Phi Delta Kappan, 77*(3), 238–245.

Warren, L.L., & Muth, K.D. (1995). The impact of common planning time on middle grades students and teachers. *Research in Middle Level Education, 18,* 41–58.

Weaver, D. (1997). Stepping back, listening, and letting students talk about poetry. *Middle School Journal, 29*(2), 40–45.

Wigfield, A., Eccles, J.S., & Pintrich, P.R. (1996). Development between the ages of 11 and 25. In D.C. Berliner & R.C. Calfee (Eds.), *Handbook of educational psychology* (pp. 148–185). New York: Simon & Schuster/Macmillan.

4 Settings for School Literacy Programs

DAVID W. MOORE

Arizona State University West

Take a few seconds and think of the Grand Canyon. Did you glimpse the different ways that you can think of the canyon's 1-mile depth, 10-mile width, and 275-mile length? You can view the canyon from the perspective of air tours, rim overlooks, mule expeditions, hiking and backpacking, and river rafting. You can concentrate on its geological features, physical challenges, and aesthetics. The canyon as a land formation, fitness exercise, tourist destination, laboratory of climate variation, and site of human settlement are some possible dimensions to consider.

Like examinations of the Grand Canyon, you can consider many dimensions of school literacy programs. No single dimension offers a complete sense because programs are multifaceted and multilayered. They are bound up in issues regarding funding, staffing, equity, curriculum, technology, community, and so on. You can perceive literacy programs through the eyes of national educational policy makers, community business leaders, parents, teachers, and students.

In this chapter, I call attention to grade 4–8 school literacy programs' administrative and classroom settings. Administrative and classroom settings are highlighted because they play a large role in shaping what occurs. Programs always play out in the context of a specific social and historical situation. Indeed, educators searching for programs that work or that reflect best practice are shortsighted if they ignore contextual issues such as administrative support, resource availability, classroom order, and parental participation. I also call attention to administrative and classroom settings because educators have many opportunities to affect them. These settings are within the purview of school and school district personnel.

In the sections that follow, aspects of administrative and classroom settings that favorably affect school literacy programs are presented. After describing noteworthy aspects or each setting, ecology as a metaphor for thinking about relationships among them is discussed.

Administrative Settings

Literacy programs pivot about decisions made by school district personnel, principals, and leadership teams. These decisions mainly constitute programs' administrative settings. At least three aspects deserve consideration: direction, professional development and evaluation cycles, and resources.

Direction

Clarity about common purposes, expectations, and definitions characterize effective school programs for early adolescents (Lipsitz, 1983). Practically all members of the schools' administrative and teaching staff reach consensus about a direction for the program, and they articulate this consensus readily. Direction provides a unifying identity that helps people band together in a special community, working for and with something bigger than themselves.

Effective literacy programs' directions are evident in language and in action. Mission statements and other formal documents are well defined, people in the community and the school use the same terms when describing the program, teachers plan and implement instructional practices consistent with the direction, and students realize that they are part of an ongoing purposeful enterprise. The reality and the rhetoric match.

Program directions are expressed multiple ways. Districts often present them through succeeding statements of vision, mission, values, goals, benchmarks, and performance indicators. Rather than trying to disentangle one level from another, I simply offer here some examples of general statements of shared directions. The following statements address overall program directions that embed literacy:

- To empower learners for the choices and challenges of the twenty-first century
- To develop independent lifelong learners
- To promote personal fulfillment and responsible citizenship
- To develop critical thinking and creative problem solving
- To provide the knowledge, skills, and attitudes that enable success in a changing world

The next two statements address overall directions, although they speak to literacy somewhat more directly:

- To foster strategic readers and writers
- To develop students who can read and write and who will read and write

These statements address learners' outcomes; they suggest program directions based on what learners generally are expected to be able to do. Other statements of direction focus on instructional approaches and practices. They express desired means of instruction while only implying learners' outcomes. Some key words associated with middle level approaches and practices that embed literacy include

- Developmentally appropriate instruction
- Curriculum integration
- Interdisciplinary teaming
- Partnerships

- Cooperative learning
- Inclusive accommodations and adaptations
- Heterogeneous grouping
- Authentic assessment

Like the terms just presented, the following terms address overall approaches and practices, although these speak more specifically to literacy:

- Guided reading and writing
- Explicit strategy instruction
- Responding to literature
- Reading aloud

- Inquiry projects
- Intensive word study
- Reading self-selected materials
- Language arts integration

Finally, effective middle-level literacy programs often concentrate on systematically designed and named instructional approaches and practices. Educators might implement Reading Across Disciplines to achieve curriculum and language arts integration in a middle school (Rathjen, 1998). They might institute Just Read to increase students' reading of self-selected materials (Wolf, 1998). They might have commercially published comprehensive literature-based literacy programs. Or, they might move in the direction of well-accepted practices such as book clubs (McMahon & Raphael, 1994) or reciprocal teaching (Palincsar, 1994).

People in effective middle-level literacy programs can articulate where they are going and how they intend to get there, and their actions support their words. I suspect a program has some direction when I hear from several people something like, "We promote students' lifelong learning by teaching them strategies so they can complete real world tasks. We do this mainly by designing assessments that culminate each unit of instruction. The assessment calls for students to produce a spoken or written response, and it relates to the world outside the classroom. Then we examine the assessment to determine what new reading and writing skills students require to complete it." When I visit corresponding classrooms and observe teaching–learning strategies occur alongside real world, authentic literacy tasks over time, I then accept the existence of a shared direction in at least one part of a school literacy program.

I consider direction part of the administrative setting because school or school district leaders typically establish and maintain literacy program purposes, expectations, and definitions. Leaders come from the ranks of administrators, teachers, and community members. School district curriculum supervisors, principals, teacher team leaders, school board members, and campus improvement team members set program directions. Of course, these leaders now are aligning program directions with state and professional organization standards established during the 1990s. Effective leaders include all the program's stakeholders when deciding on any substantive changes.

Professional Development and Evaluation Cycles

Professional development and evaluation cycles help people move collectively in a common direction. These cycles influence—and are influenced by—teachers' and administrators' knowledge, expertise, and commitment relative to school literacy programs. Numerous means of professional development and evaluation are possible.

Many districts provide workshops or course work for staff new to teaching or new to the district. These courses are often quite clear about the way things are done in the district, expressing expectations, responsibilities, and techniques. In addition, first-year teachers typically have mentors or peers available for collaborative problem solving. These development opportunities readily encompass literacy program issues.

Experienced teachers have available many staff development avenues to focus on their literacy program. Experienced teachers often participate in study groups to refine practices currently in place and to examine new ideas. Classroom inquiry projects are vehicles for systematically examining classroom dynamics. Teachers and administrators might explore a literacy-related topic such as collaborative writing, gender bias during class discussions of text, or pretesting vocabulary knowledge for information about their future instructional decisions. They might coach each other about new ways of teaching through collaborative planning, scheduled observations, and debriefing sessions. Distance learning events are becoming more common as individuals hook up electronically with widespread authorities and participants.

Many conventional ways to address school literacy programs are available. School leaders address literacy programs during district- and school-level meetings. Grade-level, interdisciplinary team, or departmental meetings provide another forum. In addition, summer course work is a time-honored means of professional development.

Many districts explicitly connect staff development with teacher and student evaluations. Teachers, teacher leaders, and administrators observe ongoing practices such as writing conferences or literature discussion groups and offer feedback. They examine student outcomes to determine whether the program and the teachers' actions are benefiting the learners. When limitations are noted, teachers might visit other classes, consult appropriate professional readings, record and reflect on their performances, or collaborate with someone. Some districts now have experienced teachers produce goals to stretch their current levels of functioning, and the teacher and administrator later review progress in accomplishing them.

Staff development and evaluation cycles are part of the administrative settings that embed school literacy programs. Looking at the cycles of upgrading and assessing staff competencies relative to literacy instruction helps one see an important determinant of literacy program success.

Resources

Here, *resources* refers to some tangible aspects of administrative settings. One highly visible administrative resource enmeshed with school literacy programs is the organization of course offerings. Schools that provide self-contained, interdisciplinary, and departmentalized structures provide different challenges and opportunities to literacy programs. Whether reading is offered as a distinct subject and whether it is offered as a required or elective subject also deserve consideration. To illustrate, most middle-grade schools require reading as a subject that is separate from English language arts (Valentine, Clark, Irvin, Keefe, & Melton, 1993); schools requiring separate reading courses, however, decrease as students move from grades 5 (82%) through 9 (57%).

In schools with interdisciplinary teaming, 51% presented reading as a teamed subject, but the amount, nature, and quality of literacy instruction presented during this interdisciplinary teaching were not reported. Separate literacy instruction often occurred in these schools as a remedial offering, an exploratory course, and as part of a study skills elective.

Administrative decisions about resources other than course offerings also are enmeshed with literacy programs. Hiring practices influence the quality of literacy instruction. For instance, is there a proper balance among teachers with elementary, middle school, or secondary certification in middle-level schools? What about teachers from historically underserved groups? Partnerships with universities, businesses, community agencies, service centers, volunteer groups, and senior high and primary-grade schools also shape literacy learning opportunities. Print resources available through the school library, the Internet, and the classroom certainly warrant attention, too.

Classroom Settings

Two middle-level classes with the identical title and grade might be taught during the same time of day, have the same reading and writing materials, address the same topics on a course outline, and have lesson plans calling for the same literacy practices. They could be part of the same administrative setting. Despite such similarities, students might exhibit fundamental differences in how they experience the literacy program and in how they develop literacy proficiencies. The differences could be due to classroom settings.

Like administrative settings, classroom settings embed literacy programs. Five aspects of these settings deserve consideration. literacy engagement, meaningfulness, active participation, academic challenge and support, and social support (Moore, Moore, Cunningham, & Cunningham, 1998).

Literacy Engagement

Students who are engaged readers and writers use print frequently for long periods of time. They read and write to learn, to do things, and for pleasure. Individually and in groups, engaged readers acquire new ideas, perform tasks, and experience literary worlds. The satisfaction they obtain through reading and writing motivates them to read and write even more. They are taught strategies appropriate for particular types of materials and tasks, and they draw on these strategies to succeed in new situations.

Literacy programs characterized by engagement offer print-rich classrooms and regular attention to reading and writing. Students have access to multiple reading materials through public and school libraries, computer technology, book dubs and fairs, subscriptions, and school supplies. They read primary historical documents, science reports, and literary works. They encounter multiple genres of writing and multiple perspectives on topics. Students frequently refer to what they read during discussions with classmates and teachers. Engaged readers learn about the world and about the written word as teachers enable them to learn with texts and about texts. Classroom interactions often center about print, teachers and students talk about how to go about making sense of it, and classroom success depends on reading and writing.

Meaningfulness

Meaningful classroom settings involve students in a range of thinking operations that are goal directed. Learners in meaningful situations use their minds fully to address problems and construct significant ideas. They are involved in higher-order thinking about worthwhile ideas, encountering facts in action. For instance, in social studies, students might be studying the decades of the early 1900s. Given the guiding question, "In which decade were people better off?" students learn about particular inventions, wars, and social movements for reasons larger than passing a test. Students might learn about DNA to interpret parents' chances of genetic disorders, about bacteria to explain sanitary conditions, and about poetry to justify favorite song lyrics.

Rather than participate in rote recitations about the contents of a textbook, students in meaningful classroom settings think like historians, scientists, or artists involved in purposeful work. Students in these settings can explain why they are completing reading and writing tasks. They might say something like, "We are explaining the main character's actions so we can decide if we agree with them or not. If we learn to do this with this character, we can do it with others." Or they might say, "We're creating a time line of events so we can better understand this era. Then we'll be able to create other time lines of other time periods on our own." Sometimes these explanations refer to the literacy program's shared direction, such as when students say, "We're summarizing this passage because it's a strategy that will help us later in life."

Meaningful literacy settings are characterized by authentic compositions. In the case of meaningful letter writing, students would work on an entire letter that they have good reason to mail rather than on isolated worksheets stressing salutations, opening paragraphs, and so on. When students have a sense that what they are producing has integrity in its own right, they are on their way toward participating in a meaningful setting.

Another feature of meaningful literacy settings is a sense of connectedness. This sense comes when learners perceive clear relationships among the ideas they encounter. Connections are made among ideas from outside and inside the classroom. For instance, middle-grade teachers often promote connectedness by linking instructional activities to a topic that cuts across the curriculum. For instance, the disciplines of language arts, social studies, science, mathematics, and fine arts could be readily connected to the theme of tobacco smoking. Students could critique and produce cigarette advertisements for language arts, research smoke-free legislation for social studies, examine the physical effects of smoking for science, determine the percentage of full-page magazine ads devoted to cigarettes for mathematics, and produce a musical or visual statement related to smoking for fine arts.

Linking learning activities to the world beyond the school is another way to foster connections in literacy settings. When students' personal, community, and occupational worlds are connected to the academic world, schooling can be seen as a relevant, coherent enterprise. To return to the topic of smoking, because it is an issue that young people face daily, it has an intrinsic appeal that more academic topics such as propaganda techniques and government controls lack. Deciding whether or not to smoke is a personal value-based decision that individuals need to make.

Programs that embed literacy practices in meaningful activities allow students to make sense of reading and writing as purposeful and useful endeavors. They provide opportunities for students to acquire reading and writing strategies on their own and apply strategies that have been presented.

Active Participation

Active participation is another aspect of classroom literacy settings deserving attention. Learners who are active participants energetically respond to situations, interacting with teachers and each other while manipulating print and nonprint resources.

Classrooms with active participation exhibit flexible grouping practices. Students meet as a whole class for teachers to introduce new learning and directions, build common experiences, and review what has been presented. Students meet in small groups to collaborate on projects and share ideas. They work on their own to pursue individual goals, read silently, and draft and revise their writing.

Teachers with much active participation in class explicitly teach class expectations and routines early in the year, and they persist with these guidelines. If you visit such classrooms late in the year, you see learners participating in reading and writing activities with little overt teacher control. For instance, quick writes are a somewhat common class routine. If you were reviewing the major aspects of communicable diseases, you might have students quickly write in their notebooks three things they remember about communicable diseases and then have a few students share what they wrote. Presenting this quick write routine the first week of class would go far in promoting active participation throughout the year.

Student choice is a defining feature of classrooms with active participation. Teachers might begin by offering alternatives regarding which learning activities to perform and the order in which to complete them. Given two possible writing assignments, students pick the one they are most interested in completing. Given a set of short stories, students decide which ones to read, the sequence in which to read them, and the response activities they will accomplish. Eventually, students decide some of their own learning goals, topics, and experiences. They have a voice in classroom decision making.

Academic Challenge and Support

I have played racquetball for many years, and I mark my greatest gain in enjoyment and skill during a two-year span when I had a weekly game with Dean, a one-time state-level doubles champion. Dean's love for the game led him to play anyone just so he could be on the court.

The first time we played, I scored only a few points, but Dean commented on my potential and suggested ways I could improve my backhand. I walked away from that game believing that I could do better. Sometimes Dean gave me an advantage by hitting only straight drives to my backhand or by serving only at half speed, and he often demonstrated stroke and court positioning techniques. After a few months of this, my racquetball improved so much that I actually began winning a few matches against Dean.

As with racquetball, literacy improves in situations with appropriate challenges, ones that stretch students' abilities without becoming frustrating. Appropriate challenges call for special effort, but they are not defeating. They are at the cutting edge of students' abilities, neither too easy nor too demanding. Appropriate challenges are tasks that students are unable to accomplish at first but are able to accomplish with the help of others or with reasonable individual effort. Such levels of challenge allow students the pleasure of exerting themselves and experiencing success. They strengthen wills to succeed by keeping higher levels of accomplishment always within sight.

For challenging learning environments to be most effective, learners require support. My racquetball would have improved little if Dean had left me in a sink-or-swim situation; fortunately, we entered into something like a master–apprentice relationship. In the context of stimulating and complex games, Dean taught me how to get to the next level, encouraged me, and offered occasional criticisms. He supported my development.

Academic supports bridge gaps between learners' current abilities and their successful completion of complex activities. In racquetball, Dean supported my early development by not exploiting a weak backhand, by slowing his serve, and by explaining what to do in certain situations. In school, teachers support complex writing strategies by displaying model papers previous students completed; explaining how to complete such papers; providing checklists, cue sheets, and rubrics; orchestrating whole class, small group, and individual activities; and regulating the level of sophistication expected for the papers.

Social Support

A fifth classroom setting important for literacy programs, social support, calls attention to interpersonal relations. It involves a class's emotional and attitudinal climate. Social supports are as necessary in a literacy program as the academic supports presented earlier.

Classroom order is an important social support. Even the floor of the New York Stock Exchange, which appears chaotic to newcomers, has a well-developed underlying system for face-to-face interactions. Traders know how to make sense of the messages presented on the floor and how to express themselves efficiently. Similarly, students need a structured social system that allows them to make sense of their classrooms and to access literacy fully. They need to have social structures for participating with each other appropriately and effectively.

Positive expectations are another social support. Learners do best when they and their teachers expect their efforts to result in high-quality accomplishments. To return to the racquetball story, Dean seemed convinced that my racquetball game would improve. I came to believe it, too, and in self-fulfilling fashion, my game improved.

Projecting enthusiasm is another way to support learners. You project enthusiasm when you convey an intense eagerness to develop reading and writing, when you are passionate and sincere about literacy. As with positive expectations, enthusiasm is contagious. Students learn to value what their teachers do (and do not!) value.

Perhaps the key social supports are respect and care. Among other things, respectful, caring relationships are apparent when teachers and students treat one another like longtime members of a cohesive club. Each person is an insider; there is a sense of community and rapport. Favoritism and cliquishness are not evident because everyone enjoys the same privileges. Social divisions such as achievement level, ethnicity, gender, or peer affiliation do not affect classroom interactions. Efforts are made to enfranchise those who feel alienated. When students struggle academically or misbehave, teachers intervene quickly out of concern for the individual's well-being.

Assessing Classroom Settings

The classroom settings that embed literacy programs are only partially visible in classroom designs, lesson plans, and observations. Teachers certainly should promote these settings in class, but they are difficult to see because they depend on participants' interpretations. "You need to talk with students to determine the extent to which they experience literacy engagement, meaningfulness, active participation, academic challenge and support, and social support. You might ground questions about these settings in actual events. For instance, you could instruct a respondent, "Think of a time when you talked about a passage read in this class. Describe it for me." One student might report the talk as an academic debate over flaws in classmates' interpretations, and another might report seeing it as a meaningful conversation about the passage's central message. Or you could say, "Tell me about the amount of reading and writing you did last week for this class." Students' responses to such questions suggest how meaningful the class is to them and how much they actually engage in the literacy called for by literacy programs.

An Ecological Metaphor for Literacy Programs

Metaphors are conceptual and linguistic tools for representing the world; they are vehicles of thought as well as of communication. Metaphors represent conceptual domains by crossing phenomena, allowing us to understand and experience "one kind of thing in terms of another" (Lakoff & Johnson, 1980, p. 5). A generative view of metaphors treats them as "central to the task of accounting for our perspectives on the world: how we think about things, make sense of reality, and set the problems we later try to solve" (Schön, 1993, p. 137). I find ecology to be a productive metaphor for thinking about school literacy programs' administrative and classroom settings.

The noted environmentalist John Muir was an early proponent of ecological thinking. While leading hikes in the Sierra Nevada, Muir occasionally highlighted small plants in the ground and proclaimed how they connected to all other parts of the forest. He called attention to ways the soil, water, air, plant life, and wildlife affected—

and were affected by—the single plant. He promoted thinking about ecology, the relations among organisms and their environment. And, as the 1998 El Niño phenomenon reminded us, an ocean current in the western Pacific can influence weather conditions around the globe.

Comparing literacy programs to ecological systems contrasts with static metaphors such as onion skins or rings of concentric circles. Thinking about school literacy programs in terms of ecology stresses the notion of interdependence. In school literacy programs, teachers, students, administrators, parents, and community members act in mutually dependent webs. For instance, the resources available for buying books affects students' reading of self-selected materials. Schoolwide contests that reward students with free pizzas for reading the most books can challenge program goals of students reflectively reading and responding to complex books. High-stakes standardized assessments affect the meaningfulness of classroom settings and the explicit strategy instruction that is provided.

Ecology also calls attention to the mutual relationships among systems' parts. For instance, an ecological view enmeshes school principals' and teachers' actions in each other. Principals' decisions about hiring new faculty embed their beliefs about the current staff's needs, competencies, and predicted reactions. Decisions, then, are not made in a vacuum; they implicate various aspects of the system in numerous, frequently invisible ways.

Ecology provides a tool for thinking about the separate entities of literacy programs by foregrounding the fluid, flexible, and responsive nature of programs. It calls attention to the ways energy moves through programs. Knowing that systems involve transformative processes means that looking at school literacy programs involves looking at parts as well as the settings enmeshed with the parts.

REFERENCES

Lakoff, G., & Johnson, M. (1980). *Metaphors we live by.* Chicago: University of Chicago Press.

Lipsitz, J. (1983). *Successful schools for young adolescents.* New Brunswick, NJ: Transaction.

McMahon, S.I., & Raphael, T.E. (1994). Book club: An alternative framework for reading instruction. *The Reading Teacher, 48,* 102–117.

Moore, D.W., Moore, S.A., Cunningham, P.M., & Cunningham, J.W. (1998). *Developing readers and writers in the content areas* (3rd ed.). New York: Longman.

Palincsar, A. (1994). Reciprocal teaching. In A.C. Purves (Ed.), *Encyclopedia of English studies and language arts* (Vol. 2, pp. 1021–1022). New York: Scholastic.

Rathjen, N. (1998). Reading across disciplines program. In J.L. Irvin, *Reading and the middle school student* (2nd ed., pp. 247–253). Boston: Allyn and Bacon.

Schön, D. (1993). Generative metaphor: A perspective on problem solving in social policy. In A. Ortony (Ed.), *Metaphor and thought* (2nd ed., pp. 137–163). New York: Cambridge University Press.

Valentine, J.W., Clark, D.C., Irvin, J.L., Keefe, J.W., & Melton, G. (1993). *Leadership in middle level education: Vol. 1. A national survey of middle level leaders and schools.* Reston, VA: National Association of Secondary School Principals.

Wolf, J. (1998). Just read. *Educational Leadership, 55*(8), 61–63.

5 Encouraging Family Involvement in the Intermediate and Middle Grades

TIMOTHY RASINSKI
Kent State University

GAY FAWCETT
Summit County (Ohio) Educational Service Center

"**F**amilies, children, and literacy learning." Ah, the words just roll off the tongue as if they were meant to go together. Say the phrase to yourself, silently first, then out loud. It almost sounds poetic, doesn't it! For many teachers, particularly those in the intermediate and middle grades, however, poetry is the last thing that comes to mind when they think of families, children, and literacy learning. And for many families of intermediate and middle school children, literacy learning, if thought about at all, is thought of as a dreaded time of nagging to do reading and language arts home-work. Although it may make intuitive sense to encourage reading and writing at home by appealing to and involving families, many teachers will say that it simply is not worth the effort. Getting parents involved in their children's literacy learning just does not work.

In this chapter, the contrary view is argued. We would like to provide evidence that family involvement can work. We recognize that many children today do not have traditional families and that suggestions for "parent involvement" may seem out of date. We do know, however, that when children receive support—whether "family" is defined as parents, guardians, siblings, or other relatives or caretakers—literacy learn-ing improves. In this chapter, when the term *parent* is used, it can usually be expanded to include families. We provide some guidelines for developing effective parent involvement programs in the intermediate and middle grades, and we conclude the chapter with some examples of possible parent involvement literacy programs that can work in grades 4 through 8.

Does Parent Involvement in
Literacy Learning Work?

To answer this question, we first want to examine a study of fifth-grade students' reading outside of school. In this study (Anderson, Wilson, & Fielding, 1988), fifth-graders were trained to keep track of the amount of reading they did between the end of one school day and the beginning of the next. One initial finding of the study was that the amount of reading students did outside of school was directly related to their reading achievement. Students who read the most outside of school had the highest levels of achievement in reading. In addition, as the amount of time spent reading outside school decreased, reading achievement of students decreased correspondingly. Students who read the most outside of school were the best readers and those who read least struggled the most.

Now, a close reading of the above might lead one to ask, Which causes which? Does reading outside of school lead to higher levels of achievement? Or, does higher achievement in reading make reading easy and enjoyable for students, which, in turn, leads students to read more at home? Of course, it is not possible to determine which possibility is correct. We suspect, however, that both are. The more students read at home, the better readers they become. The better they become in reading, the more likely they are to read voluntarily at home. At the very least, it is extremely difficult for us to imagine how most children can become proficient readers if they do not spend a significant amount of their time engaging in the very act itself.

Other studies have also hinted at the connection between reading at home and reading achievement. In a large-scale (nearly 100,000 students and over 4,000 schools) international study of literacy learning, Postlethwaite and Ross (1992) identified a set of variables that appeared to differentiate more effective schools in literacy teaching and learning from less effective schools. Of the 56 significant variables found, what was, overall, the second most potent? None other than voluntary reading at home! Teachers and schools that promoted voluntary reading outside of school were more likely to have students who had high levels of achievement in reading.

Just how do teachers and school promote voluntary reading at home? One way is certainly through the action and intervention of parents. One of the easiest ways to get parents involved in their children's literacy growth is to encourage parents to have their children read at home. Again, there is some proof to this assertion. In the Postlethwaite and Ross study, the most powerful factor differentiating more and less effective schools in the teaching of reading was parent involvement. Teachers who endeavored to involve parents in their children's literacy learning (we suspect in many cases by nothing more than encouraging voluntary reading at home) were most successful in helping children attain high levels of achievement in reading.

Thus, it is difficult to dismiss the connection between parent involvement, student reading at home, and student growth in reading. Many other studies have consistently shown that when parents are involved, children's learning improves (e.g., Durkin, 1966; Henderson, 1988; Rasinski, 1995; Topping, 1987). Indeed, Epstein (1984, 1987), as a result of her review of research on parent involvement, has noted that the greatest positive effects for the most students comes from teachers involving parents in helping their children learn.

But just what is the present state of affairs with children reading at home and family involvement? Unfortunately, it is, in general, not good. Anderson, Wilson, and Fielding (1988) found that fifth graders who achieved at the 50th percentile (students who we would say are achieving in the middle of the pack) read, on average, fewer than 15 minutes per day outside of school. Fifteen minutes per day! This pales in comparison to the several hours per day that students spend watching television, playing video games, or playing and practicing organized sports.

Despite the great potential for improving children's literacy growth through family involvement, children actually do little outside of school to improve their literacy growth, and sometimes families perpetuate this situation. Many times, adults do not realize the power of modeling literate behaviors, so their children never see them read a book, pick up a newspaper or magazine, or write a letter. Families want their children to be readers, but often they do not know how they might effectively help them. Our own research (Fawcett, Rasinski, & Linek, 1997) suggests that teachers themselves may also be part of the problem when they do not offer the suggestions and information that families need to help their children. If no support comes from the children's school, many families may do little or nothing or sometimes even do the wrong things such as punishing children when they do not exhibit desired literate behaviors, which, then, reinforces teachers' original perceptions of parents and families that "parents just don't give a damn" (Walde & Baker, 1990). *Newsweek* columnist Robert Samuelson (1995) summarized this vicious cycle when he wrote:

> The true "inputs" to education are students' hard work, quality teaching, rigorous standards, and parental engagement. When these are missing, money and reorganization can't compensate. In some ways, public opinion is the biggest obstacle to better schools. Our delusion is that "the schools" are solely responsible for educating our children, and that asks too much of schools.
>
> . . . My main gripe with our local school is that it doesn't tell parents what's expected of students, or how, exactly, parents can help. But this failing is widespread and reflects a silent compact between schools and parents. Schools find engaging parents too hard and threatening. Harried parents don't want more demands on their time, and also want to blame schools if children don't do well. The compact encourages mediocrity. (p. 61)

Principles of Parent Involvement in the Intermediate and Middle Grades

Parent involvement in students' literacy is important regardless of the age or grade level of the student. But just how do teachers and schools get started in developing parent involvement programs that work? To help guide professionals in developing and implementing such programs, we offer the following guiding principles based on our own work with and observations of teachers, schools, and parents collaborating to help students read better.

Attitude

In our estimation, the most important entering characteristic of parent involvement programs that work is the attitudes held by the participants, particularly the teachers. Teachers need to believe that parents can help their children in literacy and are willing to invest time and effort to that goal. In an earlier study, we surveyed teachers about parent involvement in reading (Fawcett, Rasinski, & Linek, 1997). We were surprised to find that a significant number of teachers had negative attitudes about parents working with their children in reading. Although teachers felt that parents had the capabilities to help, many teachers felt that parents are not really interested in working with and helping their children. This attitude, in most cases, was based on the frustration of previous attempts to involve parents.

Getting parents and families involved in their children's education is, to be certain, a difficult and challenging task. It is made even more difficult when teachers themselves feel that getting parents involved is a waste of time and effort. We have seen enough successful school–home programs to know that even the most reluctant parents are interested in their children's learning and are willing to work with their children. Many of the most reluctant parents themselves had poor experiences in schools and come to their children's school with lots of negative baggage about schools based on their own frustrations and poor experiences as students. Many parents, too, do not have the training, materials, time, organization skills, or support from others to engage in ongoing work with their children. This situation is particularly true in the upper grades, where the curriculum content is more challenging for parents as well as students.

Certainly, these factors are impediments to parent involvement, but they can certainly be overcome with consistent and persistent efforts by teachers, principals, and other school personnel. We need to address these needs and obstacles, rather than become overwhelmed and frustrated by them and develop an attitude that parent involvement is futile. Negative attitudes by teachers almost certainly will spell doom for parent involvement initiatives. On the other hand, teachers who are enthusiastic about parent involvement, committed to the long term, and willing to support one another in their parent involvement efforts are much more likely to meet success in their efforts, and such success will lead to improved student achievement and more positive attitudes toward schools and teachers by parents. This consequence is certainly not trivial in these days where public perceptions of schools and teachers are not always good.

Communication and Support

Home–school connections and teacher–parent collaboration imply that communication will exist between the school and home. Clearly, communication is essential to the success of any home–school literacy initiative. Parents need to be made aware of the program, its goals, its activities, the time frame involved, and the materials involved. Teachers need to communicate to parents their expectations for the home literacy project. As mentioned earlier, parents usually do not have the appropriate knowledge, training, and materials to provide optimal support for their children. Through a well-designed communication program, teachers can meet these needs for parents and even help to encourage enthusiasm among parents for helping their children.

Communication can take a variety of forms. The written newsletter is an excellent tool for sharing information with parents. Not only does it provide teachers with opportunities to share important information with parents, but it also provides information in the mode of communication that teachers want students themselves to use. Newsletters or other forms of written communication for parents need to be written in language easy for parents to read; many parents themselves may have difficulty in reading as well as limitations in the time they have available to peruse a school newsletter. To make the newsletter more inviting for parents (and children), teachers can include written compositions by students as well as news about students' accomplishments. Still, the intent of a classroom literacy newsletter, from the point of view of the teacher, is to provide parents with information that will allow them to become better able to help their children in reading and writing.

Direct personal contact with parents is another form of communication for teachers who wish to involve parents in their children's literacy learning. Having parents come to the classroom is a great way to explain the reading program, and the home–school literacy initiative and to answer questions that parents themselves may have. If you intend to embark on a particular form of parent–child literacy activity at home, the classroom meeting with parents is a superb opportunity to train them in the program.

Although home visits can carry a whole set of problems that teachers may wish they could avoid, some families will only be reached in this way. There may simply be no other way to connect with adults who lack the literacy skills to read the newsletters, who do not have telephones or transportation, or who are intimidated at the thought of going to school, a place that, for many, carries memories of failure, frustration, and anger. Some teachers visit each student's home at the beginning of the year to establish rapport with families. Other teachers concentrate on those adult caregivers who could not be reached in any other way.

Phone or e-mail communications are a bit more personal than a classroom newsletter, but a bit less personal than actually meeting with parents. Teachers can update parents on what is going on in the reading program via these resources, and parents can also ask questions or provide other information that may be requested.

Up to this point, we have been discussing communication as a one-way street, teacher to parent. Ideal communications are reciprocal: teachers communicating with parents and parents communicating with teachers. Parents have a wealth of information about their children that would be very helpful for the teachers who work with their children. Teachers need to build into their communication program some provision for allowing parents to communicate with them. In some schools, teachers regularly send home advisement sheets in which they ask parents to provide information on how the parents feel their children are doing in reading and how they are responding to the instruction they are receiving, and to inform teachers about current issues in their children's lives that may affect their learning. Teachers are very appreciative of such information, and parents, too, are appreciative and empowered by teachers who ask parents their opinions about education matters.

Communication is essential, but it is not enough! Communication must result in support, but teacher–family collaboration can be a risky venture for both teachers and families. The anxiety that may be generated from such close encounters can be mollified with provisions for mutual support. Teachers who are willing to try family involvement in literacy may wish to collaborate with other teachers in their school or with all the teachers from a particular grade level, or they may attempt to make the program a schoolwide project. The more teachers involved, the more opportunities teachers will have to support and share with one another.

Teachers should also think of ways of providing support for families. One way is to invite parents or other caregivers to belong to a classroom advisory committee. Parents who attend the regularly scheduled meetings of such a group will definitely feel empowered as they help set the agenda for parent involvement in their child's classroom. Moreover, parents will have the opportunity to ask questions about the program and to get answers not only from the teacher, but also from other parents. The connections that parents make among themselves will eventually work for the benefit of students and the school if teachers make note of those parents who work in a positive direction and who work well with one another.

Authentic Reading and Writing

We have all heard that the best way to become a good reader is to read a lot and the best way to become a writer is to write a lot. Although this statement is a cliché, we feel it is also true. Enough studies have demonstrated that reading achievement is related to the amount of reading done. In their study of fifth-grade students, Anderson and colleagues (1988) found that the amount of reading done at home was closely related to the achievement of students; students who read the most were the best readers, and those who read the least were the students who had the most difficulty in reading. Similarly, Postlethwaite and Ross's (1992) international study found that the amount of reading done at home and at school were the number two and three variables most strongly associated with achievement in reading.

These and other studies convince us of the primacy of authentic reading and writing experiences in promoting students' growth in literacy. It is not the number of workbook or skill sheets complete or the time spent learning about phonics and phonics rules or the number of reading and writing tests taken or the number of individual subskills goals attained that promote reading growth as much as it is the time students spend with their collective noses in front of a book or other form of text. This is true for school, and it is equally true for the home.

Encouraging families to engage in authentic literacy activities at home may require that teachers stretch their definitions of literacy. Most U.S. teachers come from a white, middle-class background that equates *literacy* with bedtime stories, thank-you letters to grandma, and Madeline L'Engle novels. Teachers must recognize that learning to read the city bus schedule, making a grocery list, or filling out a job application is just as legitimate a literacy activity as reading a book for 30 minutes each evening. In addition, many of today's students spend time on the Internet reading from their favorite rock star's Web site or communicating with others via e-mail. These are legitimate literacy activities that will help students become better readers and writers, and they should be encouraged just as we encourage families to "read to your child" or "provide books and magazines for your child at home."

Thus, our third guideline is that any parent involvement program in literacy learning should have as its main activity students, and parents, reading and writing for real purposes: to enjoy a story, to learn about the world, to communicate with others, to refine thinking through note taking and organizing information, to compose a personal story. Occasionally, it may be acceptable to ask parents and children to work on a skill related to reading, or to practice for a test, but the majority of the time teachers ask parents and children to spend together on literacy activities should be for reading and writing with real-world purposes. Indeed, not only should such activities be motivating and authentic, but they should also make connections to the lives of the families. When parents and families see literacy activities as actually enriching their personal and family lives, they will be much more willing to engage in such activities with their children.

When reading and writing are authentic, when they serve a real purpose, students are more likely to value and find enjoyment in the literacy experience. When something has value and enjoyment for students, students are more likely to engage in it in the future. And, the more students engage in reading and writing over time, the more likely it is that their achievement and advancement in reading will occur.

Make It Manageable

It is not an exaggeration to say that life today is busier than it has ever been. Parents work around the clock, take their children from one activity to another after school, and have so many other responsibilities that many are utterly exhausted at the end of each day. Many parents who do not participate consistently in home–school reading programs often say that they simply do not have the time or the energy after a hard day of work to help their children in reading. "It's the school's job anyway," they may be prone to say.

Again, this situation presents a challenge to those of us who are interested in family involvement in literacy learning. Whatever we ask parents to do with their children in the name of literacy needs to be something that can be accomplished in a matter of minutes at home. If we want parents to be involved consistently, then the activity needs to be quick. Because parents work on such activities with the undivided attention of their children, a short time together can go a long way. Topping's (1987) very successful paired reading project asks parents to work with their children for as little as 5 to 10 minutes each evening.

These four guidelines may seem simple and make intuitive sense, but they usually are easier to understand than they are to implement. Next we present actual ways in which families and children have worked together, under the auspices of the local school community, to develop the literacy skills of their children. This sampler shows the variety and potential available for those teachers willing to make parent involvement an integral part of their classroom literacy curriculum.

Parent Involvement Programs

Parents and families can be engaged in helping their children in literacy in several ways. Simple programs involve communicating with parents and informing them of their children's work and how they can assist their children at home. More complex programs actively attempt to engage parents in working with their children consistently and intensively in systematic ways over extended periods of time. In this section, we provide examples of both approaches.

Communication Programs

It may seem simple and easy to most readers to develop communication programs for parents to help their children in literacy. In truth, though, how many individual teachers or schools actually go to the trouble of communicating with parents and families about literacy development, one of the fundamentals of all subsequent learning? Our experience has been that the answer is few indeed.

In Johnston Middle School, the sixth-grade language arts teachers have been publishing a monthly newsletter on literacy that they call *Literacy Links* for parents and families for the past five years. The newsletter has three major purposes. First, teachers use the four- to six-page paper to inform parents of what is going on in the sixth-grade language arts curriculum. Parents are always kept abreast of what the classes are studying and reading and what assignments or major projects are coming up. Second, *Literacy Links* is an opportunity for teachers to share ideas with parents on reinforcing students' school learning at home. Third, brief individual articles on developing study skills and study environments in the home, good books for gifts, key vocabulary for sixth graders, keeping family journals, reading and writing over spring break and summer vacation, and using family rituals as opportunities for reading have all been covered in past issues. Finally, teachers use the newsletter to highlight student work. The best of student poetry and sections from student prose are often shared.

Although we cannot say that all parents read *Literacy Links,* many do, and those who do find it very helpful. "I find it very nice to get a monthly update about my child's reading instruction," said Marge Lucas. "The first thing I do is read through the students' work that is published. I usually hope to find Tom's work included, but even when it isn't, I enjoy reading the excellent pieces by students. Sometimes it's hard to believe that students are capable of such good writing and reading. After that I browse through the class updates and the hints for helping your child. While I may not use every suggestion made by the teachers, I do try out many and I share them with my neighbors."

Such testimonials are gratifying to teachers. "It's not that big a thing for us," Janet Faber said. "It only takes a few hours every month for us to put this newsletter together. In fact, the students themselves contribute to the development of the newsletter. In a way it's their publication. But the feedback we get from parents is great. They like to know what is going on, they like to be in touch with their children's teacher, even if it is this once-a-month sort of thing. For many parents, I think, they feel comfortable hearing from their children's teachers, but they also want to keep some distance from the school, particularly as their children get into middle and high school. This newsletter fits very nicely with their own needs and levels of comfort."

Other teachers take a slightly different tack to communication with parents. Peggy uses a workshop approach in her seventh-grade reading class. Students come to her class and read. They often discuss what they are reading or respond to what they are reading in their response journals that the teacher or other students read, but the main activity of Peggy's class is to choose good reading material and then to read.

Peggy's approach to parental communication is workshop oriented as well. "I used to have monthly open meetings for any parents who would like to attend," she said. "I would cover general information to strategies for helping students become better and more avid readers at home. As my reading workshop has matured, my open parent meetings have emerged as well. Now, I will usually send home a brief one-page summary of a professional article that I have read from *The Reading Teacher, Language Arts, The Journal of Adolescent and Adult Literacy,* or some other professional journal and ask parents to read it in anticipation for the meeting. I will also provide parents with the article when they come to the meeting and spend the first five minutes or so asking them to read or skim the article. I usually try to pick an article or articles dealing with some issue of relevance to reading with middle-grade students such as motivation for reading, choosing appropriate materials, developing solid study routines, or helping children who struggle in reading. After they read my summary of the article, I ask them to respond to the article by writing down their thoughts on paper. I will give a brief presentation, and then I will open up the group for discussion. Usually it connects to the reading and to some aspect of their children's reading achievement. We have had some absolutely wonderful discussions. The nice thing about the short summary reading is that it gives all of us a starting place and some common ground on which to base our discussion. And the discussions are very, very productive."

The primary direction for these communication models has been teachers to parents. Certainly parents have the opportunity to speak with teachers in either model, but that sort of communication is not directly fostered or invited in these models. Linda and Stacey are two eighth-grade teachers who have strived to make communication work for them by encouraging parents to enter into the dialogue.

In Linda and Stacey's language arts program, parents get regular newsletters from the teachers. Linda and Stacey also call parents at least twice each year to let them know how their children are doing in reading and the language arts. Built specifically into these types of communications are encouragements for parents to inform teachers about their child's learning. Attached to four of the newsletters is a response sheet in which the teachers ask parents to give feedback about how their children are responding to the instruction they are receiving. Questions include, Is the reading/language arts homework too long or short?, Does your child like what she or he is reading in my class?, What is happening in your child's life that may affect the way that he or she reads or his or her confidence about reading?, and What can I do to make reading more enjoyable and meaningful for your child?

When talking on the phone, these questions will also find their way into the conversation. Teachers make it a point to ask parents. Teachers tell parents that they are a team with the parents and that they value what parents have to say about their children.

Stacey says that parents really appreciate not only being included in conversation, but being included as a valued partner. "I can't tell you what a difference it makes to parents to learn that we really want to know how their children are doing at home. Parents do feel more like they are appreciated by us, the teachers, and when we do ask them to engage in some sort of reading with their children, they are much more willing to do it," she said.

Every year just before school starts, Joyce visits the home of each student in her sixth-grade class. She calls ahead and tells the parents that her only purpose for coming is to get to know the child and his or her family before school begins. During the visit, she asks questions about the child's interests, the family's activities, and the family's best hopes for the child for the school year. Sometimes the conversations will move into issues of literacy, but Joyce does not force it. She said, "Once the family sees that I am genuinely interested in their child, when I request literacy involvement at home it's a piece of cake." Joyce admits that the visits are time consuming and sometimes difficult. When parents do not respond to her letter requesting a time to visit, she telephones. Sometimes families simply refuse. Then Joyce waits for the parents of other children in her class to talk, and usually the parents will eventually call back and set up a time. Joyce's school is in a low-income, blue-collar area, and occasionally she enters dangerous situations. One time she sat talking to a mother while the live-in boyfriend sat across the room with a shotgun across his lap. Joyce is a feisty and fearless woman, but she recognizes the danger and often recommends that teachers make visits in teams. Joyce swears that the progress she makes with her students as a result of getting families involved from before day one is worth the effort.

Literacy Activity Models

No matter how good literacy communication programs can get, and they can get very good, they can only go so far. Achievement in reading and writing will improve only when students engage in reading and writing extensively, consistently, and for real reasons. Communication can give parents ideas for getting their children reading at home, but specific activities assigned by the school to be done at home, under the support and supervision of parents, is the best way to ensure that students will read and write at home.

In Laketon Middle School, the school staff has worked together over several years to develop home–school literacy activities. One activity is woven into the sixth-, seventh-, and eighth-grade curriculum fabric. During the first few weeks of January of every school year, students spend time in their reading and language arts classes learning about their families and themselves.

In sixth grade, students learn about their extended families. During this period, the teacher reads literature that deals with generations of families. Students may also be asked to read and discuss a core book that tells the story of families over multiple generations. Students interview their grandparents, aunts, uncles, and other relatives to learn the history of their families. They learn about the countries and states of their ancestors. They learn what it was like to live two or three generations in the past. They find out, in a very personal sense, what it was like to live through wars and times of economic uncertainty. Then, they write about what they learned; they write about their family's history in the world. They write down the many short stories and vignettes they heard as children about different members of their family. They try to create a family tree. When they have completed this task, they have a fairly complete history of their family, something that many family members in the past probably had wanted, but never got around to doing. A class celebration to which all family members are invited brings this portion of the extended project to an end.

Although students are allowed to take the histories home to share with family members, they are asked to return them to the school because they will become part of a larger document over the next two years. If students leave the school prior to the end of eighth grade, the unfinished report is given to the students.

In the seventh-grade year, the focus shifts to each child's immediate family. Now the students interview their parents, siblings, and other close members of their family. They find out what it was like for their parents when they were growing up. They learn about their parents' hopes and ambitions as children, their school stories, and stories of their first jobs. They learn how their parents met and dated. They explore what life was like when their parents were first married and how their lives changed when they had children. They find out from their brothers and sisters details about their lives that they may not have known. They also read stories and expository articles about families and the issues and concerns that many families face.

Students spend a considerable amount of time preparing for these interviews. They develop questions to ask their family members. They share their questions and concerns with their classmates. They practice interviewing one another. They develop codes and shorthand methods for recording information from the interviews. Finally, they are ready to schedule interviews with their parents and siblings and begin their in-depth interviews.

As in the previous year, the interviews and other data and artifacts are distilled into writing. These immediate family stories and reports are shared, read, and reread in the classroom. Parents and family members are invited to attend an after-school celebration of families. The writing becomes the second chapter in the stories of their family's history. Again, this second contribution to a larger document is held by the teachers for completion during the eighth-grade year.

For those few students without families or whose family circumstances do not allow for such an extended exploration of their own families, teachers can usually match students with adults who have previously volunteered to participate in the project. In many instances, students are paired with other teachers from their school or with teachers from their elementary school. This helps students (and teachers) view the school as a community or family in itself.

During the eighth-grade year, a considerable amount of time is spent by students exploring their own lives: where they have been, where they are now, where they hope to be heading in the future. This assignment involves writing a personal history that requires fairly extensive involvement of parents. Again, time is spent in the classroom exploring issues of "who I am" and "where I am going." Students discuss and share their dreams and ambitions with one another and their plans for achieving those goals. During this time, students read books in which adolescent characters explore these very same issues.

Eventually, students craft this information into a written report that itself becomes the third chapter of their life's story. Students work with parent volunteers in the school to bind the three chapters and ancillary material into an impressive book that for most of the students will become a family treasure to be read and reread by generations of family members. A final celebration when all the books are bound and placed on display before going home culminates the three-year experience.

Although the project only takes up two or three weeks of the school curriculum each year, a lot of authentic and motivating reading, writing, talking, interviewing, and discovery is taking place. Students not only learn about themselves and their families, but they learn about their classmates and their families, and they learn about what family life is all about, whether seen through the eyes of a child, a parent, a sibling, a friend, a classmate, an author, or an expert who studies family life. As eighth-grade lead teacher, Monica said, "These students really learn a lot . . . about themselves and others, particularly about their families. There have been just so many students in our classes whose outlook on their families have changed drastically because of this project. And the reading and writing skills that the students develop . . . well, let me just say that these students are really engaged in reading and writing and you can see the improvement when they are asked to [do] something that is meaningful to them. Now things such as topic sentences, noun–verb agreement, proper punctuation, good spelling, and much more become very important to them."

The project just described is involved and takes several years to complete. It does require the cooperation of several teachers and the school administration. In most respects, however, it is truly not that difficult to implement. When several teachers collaborate on the planning and implementation of a project such as this one, doing the project is not very difficult for any one teacher and can actually lead to a greater sense of comraderie among faculty members.

As mentioned earlier, simply the students' contextual reading, including and especially at home, is highly correlated with their reading achievement (U.S. Department of Education, 1996). Yet sadly, the picture developed by the research demonstrates that many students, especially those in the middle grades, do little reading at home for pleasure (Smith, Young, Bae, Choy, & Alsalam, 1997). One way the Talridge Middle School has attempted to combat this lack of interest and engagement in reading has been through its yearly schoolwide reading incentive program. At the beginning of the year, the teachers at Talridge calculate the total number of minutes that would have to be spent reading if every student in the building read 20 minutes per day every day from October through May. This figure then becomes the schoolwide goal in the reading marathon program.

Each year, the marathon begins with a schoolwide assembly near the end of September. Teachers and the principal explain to students what the marathon is about. Students are asked to read at least 20 minutes each night and to track their reading on record forms.

At the end of each month, students return their reading logs and pick up new ones. Teachers use a spreadsheet program to determine the school's progress toward its ultimate goal as well as the number of minutes read by grade levels and individual classrooms.

Introductory sessions are also made for parents. These sessions emphasize the importance of the students' reading on their own at home as well as strategies for parents to help their children. Update sessions as well as a monthly newsletter are mailed to update parents on the progress of their children and to provide further information on helping their children in reading at home.

Throughout the year, students and teachers make bulletin boards, wall displays, and posters to keep students' interest in the marathon high. A large cardboard thermometer is cut out and displayed near the entrance to the school to show visitors and students alike the kind of progress being made. Also, school and grade-level assemblies are held throughout the year to update students on the progress of the program and to keep spirits up.

Students are asked to read two or three books written by an assigned author during this period. All other books are chosen by the students. Students demonstrate that they have read the books by completing a short form after each book is read.

At the end of the program, in May, a reading festival day is held. The author of the assigned books is brought to the school to speak to students and faculty. Throughout the day, small group sessions are held on topics ranging from language and literature games to newspaper writing. These breakout sessions are run by individual teachers, parents, and faculty and students from a nearby state university who have volunteered to assist in the project.

Parents are essential to the success of the marathon, and they participate in the reading marathon program in many ways. They attend informational sessions on how to help their children at home in reading. A core group of parents has taken over the administration of the program from the teachers. This group makes building displays and secures funding for an honorarium for the speaker, develops and sends the newsletters, runs a significant portion of the reading festival activities, and provides core books to students and teachers.

Although one could say that the program "is just reading," it does have an impact on students. If reading is what helps students become better and more engaged readers, then anything to promote reading outside of school is highly desirable. Tom notes that most students love the program. "It has something for everyone . . . choice reading, enthusiastic rallies, a celebration at the end of the year, and weekly updates on the ultimate school goal of reading over a million minutes every year," he said. "I think every student in this school reads more than he or she normally would because of the reading marathon. For some kids it's just a minor increase, but for others we see a major increase in the amount of reading they do and in their reading achievement."

Parents and families are, or should be, indispensable elements of a school reading program, even in the middle grades. Most parents are very interested in their children's learning, especially in reading and language arts, and we have found that those parents are willing to put in the time and effort to helping their children.

It simply takes teachers of good will and creativity to plan and implement programs that connect students, their families, and the school in mutually supportive literacy activities. Using the principles outlined earlier, along with some dogged determination and persistence, middle-grade teachers can develop programs that make parents part of the literacy team and that lead to better and more satisfying reading for students.

REFERENCES

Anderson, R., Wilson, P., & Fielding, L. (1988). Growth in reading and how children spend their time outside of school. *Reading Research Quarterly, 23,* 285–303.

Durkin, D. (1966). *Children who read early.* New York: Teachers College Press.

Epstein, J. (1984). School policy and parent involvement: Research results. *Educational Horizons, 62,* 70–72.

———. (1987). Parent involvement: What research says to administrators. *Education and Urban Society, 19,* 119–133.

Fawcett, G., Rasinski, T., & Linek, W. (1997). Family literacy: A new concept. *Principal, 76,* 34–37.

Henderson, A. (1988). Parents are a school's best friend. *Phi Delta Kappan, 70,* 148–153.

Postlethwaite, T.N., & Ross, K.N. (1992). *Effective schools in reading.* The Hague, Netherlands: International Association for the Evaluation of Educational Achievement.

Rasinski, T. (1995). Fast Start: A parental involvement reading program for primary grade students. In W. Linek & E. Sturtevant (Eds.), *Generations of literacy: The 17th yearbook of the College Reading Association* (pp. 301–312). Harrisonburg, VA: College Reading Association.

Samuelson, R. (1995, December 4). Three cheers for schools? *Newsweek,* 61.

Smith, T.M., Young, B.A., Bae, Y., Choy, S.P., & Alsalam, N. (1997). *The condition of education 1997.* Washington, DC: U.S. Department of Education, National Center for Education Statistics.

Topping, K. (1987). Paired reading: A powerful technique for parent use. *The Reading Teacher, 40,* 608–614.

U.S. Department of Education. (1996). *NAEP 1994 reading report card for the nation and the states.* Washington, DC: U.S. Department of Education, National Center for Education Statistics.

Walde, A.C., & Baker, K. (1990). How teachers view parents' role in education. *Phi Delta Kappan, 72,* 319–321.

6 Building Alliances, Building Community, Building Bridges through Literacy

LAURIE STOWELL
California State University, San Marcos

The idea of an education that simply gives individuals the methods and skills they need to get ahead in the world is almost certainly inadequate, even as "job preparation," in an advanced technical economy, which requires morally and socially sensitive people capable of responsible interaction. It is even more inadequate in preparing citizens for active participation in a complex world.

—Bellah, Madsen, Sullivan, Swidler, and Tipton, 1991, p. 170

What endures? What do students take with them when they leave middle school literacy classrooms? What tools are at teachers' disposal that can ensure students will take with them things that matter? Building community within the classroom and then building bridges to the community outside of the classroom have the potential to do just that. "Encouraging students' quests for their place and their gift and their role in the larger society must be central to all of our teaching" (Kohl, 1994, pp. 86–87).

Everyone needs to feel part of some group, especially in middle-level classrooms. It is easier for students to learn from people who they feel care about them and whom they care about than those who do not. Students also see more easily how they and their education are connected to the smaller groups that they participate in than how they connect to the larger society. Not only are they part of society, but they are functioning, efficacious, empowered people who have something important to contribute. Connectedness is part of the support system students need to succeed in education. "Of all the riches denied to disadvantaged children, perhaps the most important is a network that would allow them to thrive in school and give them a sense of belonging. . . . They have not become part of the networks that add to the intellectual enrichment of children (Maeroff, 1998, p. 426). Human rights activist Jane Addams said, "The good we secure for ourselves is precarious and uncertain until it is secured for all of us and incorporated into our common life."

To teach all kids, the teacher must have a connection with all kids. Learning that stays with a student is tied to a relationship and emotion. Building alliances among students and teachers and then building a classroom community reinforces for students and adults the importance of the affective domain of learning. Young adolescents are not just academic beings. In fact, at this time in their lives, they are primarily social beings. In *A Place Called School,* Goodlad (1984) found that junior high students value their school friendships and social relationships far more than they value school subjects and teachers. When asked, "What is the one best thing about this school?" well over a third of the students in Goodlad's study responded "my friends," and 15 percent named sports activities. About two-thirds of what students appreciated about school was the opportunity to meet and mix with their peers. In fact, at 8 percent, "nothing" outranked "classes I am taking" (7 percent) and teachers (5 percent). Goodlad also found that junior high students' satisfaction with school stemmed from their perceived success in peer group relationships rather than from characteristics of the school itself (p. 254). Rather than bemoaning these facts, educators can capitalize on students' natural tendencies to be social and use it to the students' advantage. "Successful schools for young adolescents choose to become environments that promote social development" (Perisco, 1996, p. 39).

Literacy is the most natural means to discover and embrace these connections. Literacy connects us as humans. It is an important way that we develop and maintain community. "The primacy of being human is how we use language in social contexts to make meaning" (Wink, 1997, p. 83). We invent (and reinvent) ourselves and our relationship to others through language. Therefore, literacy can be the most powerful tool teachers have for building alliances, building communities, and building bridges. The basic aim of language arts teachers is to help students become more effective communicators. The more literacy is used for a variety of purposes, with a variety of forms and in a variety of contexts, the stronger it becomes. Literacy learning within and across communities may be our best hope for preparing responsible, caring, empowered citizens who will lead lives that matter.

Sociocultural Nature of Literacy Learning

Building community is an especially important notion for literacy educators. It is built on the very solid theoretical and research foundations of Vygotsky (1978, 1986), Smith (1978), Goodman (1996), Freire and Macedo (1987), Moll (1990), Fish (1980), and others. In short, these experts tell us that literacy is socially constructed. Children learn how to speak to get things done and to communicate with the people in their lives. By the same token, adults read and write to get real things done and to be part of the local and global community. Humans read to learn how to put something together, fix a broken appliance, keep up with current events, gossip about a celebrity, or enjoy a letter from a loved one. Similarly, any piece of writing originates in some real social purpose and, after it is composed it is sent to some audience in the real social world to accomplish its purpose (Zemelman & Daniels, 1988, p. 48).

One of Vygotsky's important concepts is sociocultural learning. All the meaning we make out of this world is socially and culturally grounded. We make meaning according to the social and cultural groups of which we are members. No literacy event occurs in a vacuum. Any literacy event (listening, speaking, reading, or writing) is influenced by the environment from which it came and in which it is received. Freire and Macedo (1987) extended this notion by saying that we must be able to read the world and the word. Reading the word is obvious: making meaning out of print, connecting it to our own lives, experiences, culture, and knowledge. But young children learn to read the world first: stop signs, McDonald's, a favorite toy store, the expression on the face of a loved one, and so forth. Freire said that reading the world is all those things, reading the people and the community around us as well as the visible and invisible messages of the world. Reading is understanding the implicit power structures of society: how power is constructed and by whom it is held. Research shows that children of many cultures know a great deal about reading and writing before they get to school, and they very quickly learn the value of that knowledge in school settings. Are their ideas really valued if they are different from those in power—that is, the teacher? Is their cultural knowledge and experience valued when sharing and in making connections in class, or is only one kind of background experience valued? Is everyone's language or dialect valued? Is everyone's voice valued? Children learn to read the world of their school by how well it is taken care of, how safe it is, what groups they are put into, and how much power they are given over their education. Most young adolescents are especially good at reading the power structure of peer and social groups: what gets you in and what is "out."

Vygotsky's second important concept is the zone of proximal development (ZOPD)—that is, "the distance between the actual developmental level determined by independent problem solving and the level of potential development as determined through problem solving under adult guidance or in collaboration with more capable peers" (Vygotsky, 1978, p. 86). What children can do with help today, they can do alone tomorrow. Trade apprenticeships are a good model of the ZOPD. A young person works side by side with a master carpenter or painter and learns and makes mistakes in a safe environment with lots of support until he or she is able to accomplish the craft on his or her own. In literacy, we read to children and with children before they are ever expected to read on their own. Even as a child approximates reading and continues to read, teachers support that reading in many ways. In middle schools, teachers often teach a new concept and have students practice it in pairs or in a small group setting before they are expected to accomplish it on their own. Vygotksy's theory is one of the bedrocks of our educational philosophy: We (in Dewey's words) accept the child where he is and support his learning, all the while tugging him to the next cognitive level.

Smith, a more contemporary literacy educator, said the same things with different words. He said, "I can sum up all learning in seven words: You learn from the company you keep." Learning is an intellectual and a social activity, it is a result of engagement, being a "member of the club." It is not strictly a technical, systematic process. Students differ so much in what they know because of the informal learning experiences they have. "Children learn to read and write effectively only if they are admitted into a community of written language users, which I shall call the 'literacy club,' starting before they are able to read or write a single word for themselves. . . . Admission to the club rapidly results in becoming like established members in spoken language, in literacy and in many other ways as well" (Smith, 1978, p. 2). The literacy club functions like any other club. When we join, we want to be like the members of the club, behave the way they do, talk their talk, and have the members support our learning how to be good members of their club. Smith uses the example of when he learned to sail. He joined a sailing club and dressed like a sailor, talked like a sailor, learned to tie knots like a sailor, and sailed with more experienced sailors until he could sail on his own (ZOPD). The same happens with reading and writing when we join the literacy club. When we read, we join the company of the author and other readers, and when we write, the reader joins us.

Fish (1980) took Smith's ideas a step further with the idea of the interpretive community. He argued that meaning is not inherent in the text, but rather that we all read in much the same manner because of the culture of our interpretive community (largely schools). Each of us is socially constructed; therefore, all text is socially constructed. Understanding a book is specific to the community in which it is read and interpreted. Before the reader steps up to the book, he or she is the socially constructed sum of the communities in which he or she has been a part. It is those experiences that the reader brings to the book and that enable him or her to construct its meaning. Therefore, there are not incorrect interpretations of texts necessarily, but rather different constructions based on social and cultural experiences and knowledge. Fish gives a wonderful example of this interpretive community in action. He taught two classes back to back in the same classroom: linguistics and literary theory, and religious poetry. During the first class, he wrote the names of various linguists and theorists on the blackboard as he spoke about them. When the religious poetry students came in for class, he drew a box around the names, wrote "p. 43," told them it was a poem, and asked them to interpret it. They did! Interpreting text, in this case a poem, is the act of constructing, and that construction is largely based on the communities the reader comes from and is a part of when the constructing takes place (Fish, 1987).

Building Alliances

There is an extensive body of research about group formation and group dynamics. Like individuals, groups develop through a series of identifiable stages. Knowledge of how groups form can help a teacher work with the process, rather than against it, from the beginning. Schmuck and Schmuck (1983) identify the first stage as psychological membership. Classroom activities that help students develop strong feelings of membership, being recognized, known and valued within the group, can be devised. Nurturing group development then helps to teach reading and writing. It takes time for students to feel comfortable sharing ideas about a piece of literature, offering and accepting feedback on a piece of writing, and speaking in front of the class.

Building Alliances within the Classroom

In the nineteenth and early twentieth centuries, most students were educated in communities—that is, in one-room schoolhouses. They learned from and taught one another. They learned by example and through collaboration. When schools found it more efficient to group students by age, students became more concerned with keeping up than helping one another out. Teachers became managers rather than collaborators. Building community in larger schools does not happen as naturally as in small schools. Understanding how to form a community and be a functioning member is as important as any content discipline. If classrooms are not safe, democratic spaces, learning may not take place. Similarly, if students do not learn how to get along with one another and operate reasonably and responsibly in the classroom, how can we expect them to behave that way outside of the classroom? A true community classroom means more than caring and cooperative learning. Being part of a community means being needed as well as needful. It means believing that you have something to contribute. There is an inherent need to be useful and helpful to others. Community expectations are balanced by respect for individual needs.

In the beginning of the academic year, it is important for all members of the community to be explicit about their expectations. No matter the age of the students I teach, I begin a school year with an activity that facilitates this. I ask students to get in pairs and to discuss and write their responses (on big paper so that it can be seen by everyone) to the following:

1. What do you expect/hope/need from the members of this class to have a successful year?
2. What will/can you do to make this year run smoothly for everyone? (What will you contribute?)
3. What expectations do you have of the teacher?

Following the discussion of their expectations and contributions, the students number off in pairs and then face a partner by forming an inside circle and an outside circle with the partners facing each other. Each partner has one minute to answer a question (be sure both share their answer); the outside circle then moves two people to the left and asks another question; the inside circle then moves four people to the right; and so forth. The questions can be any kind of icebreakers for the students to get to know one another: "A book I'd recommend is . . ." or "My favorite place is. . . ." The last question asked is, What does it mean to you to be part of a community? Students then go back to their seats and we discuss their answers. I end this first class session by reading a book—such as *Swimmy* (Lionni, 1963)—about forming communities and asking students to write a letter to me explaining what I need to know about them as a learner and how I can help them be successful. I have gotten answers such as "I don't like to speak out in class but I am listening" and "My parents are getting a divorce."

They usually share their academic as well as personal needs. I keep the letters and periodically ask the students to write an updated version. Understanding students, their needs, and their expectations as well as students understanding a teacher's expectations are important first steps to building community.

What Is Community, and What Does It Mean to Be Part of a Community?

We all become members of whatever communities we belong to through literacy. By the same token, learning what communities we are a part of, building community, and contributing to various communities will also build literacy skills. It gives students a real reason for using literacy.

What does it mean to become a community? A first step for members of the potential community is to know one another and trust one another—that is, to build alliances. Customarily, community is applied to virtually any group—a neighborhood, town or city, school, church, or social club—even when the members may be total strangers. But community requires quality communication, not the mere exchange of words. "Community is a way of being together with both individual authenticity and interpersonal harmony so that people become able to function with a collective energy even greater than the sum of their individual energies" (Peck, 1993, p. 272). Christensen (1994) said that "to become community, students must learn to live in someone else's skin, understand the parallels of hurt, struggle and joy across class and culture lines and work for change. For that to happen, students need more than an upbeat, supportive teacher; they need a curriculum that teaches them how to empathize with others" (p. 50).

Community does not happen in a day, nor does it come easily. It has to be constantly nurtured and built. Stormy periods are normal on the way to developing an authentic community. The bedrock of community is commitment, a willingness to hang in there when the going gets tough.

> In genuine community there are no sides. It is not always easy, but by the time they reach community the members have learned how to give up cliques and factions. They have learned how to listen to each other and how not to reject each other. . . . Just because it is a safe place does not mean community is a place without conflict. It is, however, a place where conflict can be resolved without physical or emotional bloodshed and with wisdom as well as grace. A community is a group that can fight gracefully. (Peck, 1987, p. 71)

Building Community

> *In the first place, the school must itself be a community life in all which that implies.*
>
> —Dewey, 1916, p. 358

Building alliances is the foundation of building community. People who know and trust one another are more likely to form a community. But building a community is much more than knowing its members. The real work is developing and maintaining a true community.

What Communities Are We Part Of?

It is important for students to recognize and for the teacher to know what communities they consider themselves a part of and to tell the stories of their communities. That, in turn, becomes a part of the story and history of the community built within a classroom. How does membership in particular communities impact their participation in this community? I ask students to draw a graphic representation of the communities they are a part of and show the relationship of these communities to one another. This exercise gives rise to a class discussion about the communities in which students spend the most time, that have the most influence, and those in which they would like to spend more time. This information gives the students and the teacher a great deal of important background information about the social and cultural influences that students will bring to bear in class. An ensuing discussion can serve as a starting point about the nature and norms of a classroom community, and then the class can enter into community-building activities.

There are a multitude of resource books on activities that build community within a classroom. Examples are: *The Community as Classroom* (Gillis 1992), *Personalizing Education* (Howe & Howe, 1975), *Values Clarification* (Simon, Howe, & Kirschenbaum, 1972), and advisement activities handbooks usually put together by district teachers. A key factor is ongoing community building that supports these principles:

- Build on student strengths and interests.
- Know everyone's names (and use them), interests, and feelings.
- Help everyone feel connected to someone or something.
- Share space, the center of attention, our materials, ourselves, all of us.
- Create a climate where people are willing to take risks.
- Struggle toward a common goal.
- Collaborate and cooperate on projects.
- Make room in the circle for latecomers and people who are not best friends.
- Be friendly to everyone.
- Building community takes time.
- Do things together for fun (not always academics).
- Do things together for other people.
- Building community does not occur in a straight line.
- Solve conflicts together.
- Respect everyone's opinion and the right to have it.
- Demonstrate that we care about the people in our community.

Due to the social nature of literacy learning, community building in language arts classrooms is especially facilitated through methodology such as the reading and writing workshop (Atwell, 1987) and literature circles (Daniels, 1994). Because writing and discussing literature are opportunities for students to share themselves, language arts classrooms must be safe spaces in which students have built alliances. In fact, it is through the sharing of reading and writing that alliances are built. Teachers also enhance opportunities for building community by showing vulnerability and sharing their own stories.

When Students Deconstruct Community: Getting Back on Track

Too often, we as teachers read accounts of wonderfully productive classrooms that do not match the chaos we all meet, and we end up feeling inadequate because we have not created smoothly running communities of learners. "Each September I have this optimistic misconception that I'm going to create a compassionate, warm, safe place for students in their first days of class because my recollection is based on the final quarter of the previous year. In the past, that atmosphere did emerge in a shorter time span. But the students were more homogenous and we were living in somewhat more secure and less violent times" (Christensen, 1994, p. 50).

Many theorists who have studied groups and community formation predict a stage of chaos. For a community to form authentically, there will probably be times when all is not going well. It is not always warmth and harmony, and politeness can often mask resentment or unspoken thoughts and feelings. If the community is committed to forming community and stays with it, everyone will come out better on the other side.

To form community with a class takes more than get-acquainted activities. It takes a lot of listening to who the students are, what they are interested in and what will engage them. It then requires being responsive to the students. Those interests need to be taken seriously, as exhibited by bringing literature and writing into the classroom that speaks to them and that has real meaning and purpose for them. Literature should operate as windows and mirrors. It can be a window on the world to be learned about and a mirror of the reader's own life experience. Freire and Macedo (1987) said that reading a book and never seeing yourself is like looking in a mirror and seeing nothing reflected back. Again, as Dewey said, it is accepting the student where he is. A question that often comes up is, How do we do that and teach the required curriculum? One response is, How do you teach the curriculum with a group of unengaged, resistant learners? Are they really going to learn a teacher's objectives? Students learn best when they are in a positive relationship with the person from whom they are learning.

Allowing students to bring their stories into the classroom can become the foundation of any curriculum. Micere Mungo, a Kenyan poet, said, "Writing can be a lifeline, especially when your existence has been denied, especially when you have been left on the margins, especially when your life and process of growth have been subjected to attempts at strangulation" (Christensen, 1994, p. 53). The word *story* can be traced to the Greek *eidenai,* which means "to know" (Atwell, 1998). Students can understand themselves and others better through reading and writing their stories. "For many students, their stories have been silenced in school. Their histories have been marginalized to make room for 'important' people, their interests and worries passed over so I can teach Oregon history or *The Scarlet Letter*" (Christensen, 1994, p. 53). When given the opportunity, students will share amazing stories, and when those stories are moved from the margins, they no longer feel the need to put someone else down.

Community can also be difficult to form when rival schools are asked to merge.

One middle school principal describes how a "community of friends" was formed when two rival middle schools in Chicago, one predominantly black and one predominantly white, were merged into one school in 1987 (Bullard, 1995, p. 26). Since then, Crete-Montee Middle School has won two national awards for excellence in education and has become a model of multicultural and cooperative learning. The principal credits his school's success to three things: shared leadership, an emphasis on community building, and inclusive academics (heterogeneously grouped classes).

These two schools had been rivals in everything from academics to band to athletics. When the two school faculties got together, one of the counselors suggested, "If you're gonna get kids to learn together, they gotta be friends first" (Bullard, 1995, p. 26). The community of friends was born. It was more than a slogan, it was a commitment to change student behavior. During orientation sessions, students engaged in community-building simulations and activities within groups composed of both schools. These efforts continued throughout the academic year. Teachers were given a "building a community of friends" handbook filled with suggestions for discussions and activities that promote harmony. More important, time was set aside to practice these skills throughout the school year, and community building was incorporated into the curriculum.

One of these activities they use is called "four of a kind." Students are grouped by fours and sit around the four sides of a large sheet of paper that has a large square drawn on it. Each member of the group writes his or her name on one outside edge of the square. The group identifies four things they all like or dislike and writes them in the center of the square. For example, they may all share a common interest in rap music or a common dislike for brussel sprouts. Then all individuals in the group identify four things about themselves that are different from the other members of the group and write them down in their section of the square under their name. For example, one person may be the only one who wears glasses or who has five brothers. Students may use words, symbols, or drawings. At the end of the exercise, each group may share their square and a discussion ensues about what they discovered (Bullard, 1995, p. 31).

Problem Solving through Class Meetings

What should a student do when he or she thinks that another student copied answers on a test? What if items are missing in the classroom? What happens when students exhibit racial bias or homophobic behavior? How can a community be safe for everyone? Big and small issues will arise to challenge a community that has been built. Establishing the routine of class meetings when things go astray can be an important means of getting the community back on track. Well-run class meetings that place the responsibility for problem solving on the students are the most effective. This process communicates to the students a sense of shared power and decision making. Students can determine the rules of operation for class meetings, but basic rules would be to meet regularly or as the need arises, meet in a circle so all can see, keep time, do not put down others, listen to each other without interrupting, and let the teacher serve as gatekeeper and keep the group focused on the topic and the rules. A different student can volunteer or be designated to run each meeting. Charney (1992, p. 80) suggests the following steps:

1. Introduce the problem and review the rules. (If a student chooses not to follow the rules, he or she leaves the circle, but later usually returns.)
2. Gather information through personal observation and feelings using "I messages."
3. Begin the discussion with, "What do you need to . . . ?" (What do you think you would need to be more friendly and stop picking on people?)
4. The class proposes solutions (avoid "shoulds").
5. The initiator of the problem chooses the solution that he or she will execute (they should be workable, realistic, and within school rules).
6. Choose a consequence if necessary—what happens if the solution does not work.
7. Close the meeting by complimenting the class.

The possibility for topics is endless and need not only apply to specific individual problems. The teacher could start with questions such as, What makes you want to turn in your work? What makes you want to do your best work? What do you need to feel good about your work in this class? How much power should the teacher share in regard to curriculum decisions? and Why are you afraid to say no to peers when they ask you to do something that makes you uncomfortable? Talking about issues in a class meeting before they arise may give students tools to act appropriately when they encounter difficult situations. Students may also make links between the problems they discuss and those outside the classroom doors: how a fight waiting for the bus can lead to a discussion about the Civil War or more current events such as conflict in the Middle East. Reading good adolescent literature can serve as a springboard for discussing problems the students have. Such titles include Soto's *Taking Sides* (moving to a more upscale neighborhood and trying to keep old friends), Martinez's *Parrot in the Oven* (gangs and an alcoholic father), Leeper Buss's *Journey of the Sparrows* (harsh realities of legal and illegal immigration), Garland's *Shadow of the Dragon* (Asian gangs), Arrick's *Chernowitz!* (anti-Semitism), Lorbiecki's *Just One Flick of a Finger* (gun violence), Alicea's *The Air Down Here* (many issues a Puerto Rican American teen in the Bronx faces), Mathis's *Teacup Full of Roses* (drugs), Oneal's *The Language of Goldfish* (not wanting to grow up too quickly), Slepian's *The Alfred Summer* (coping with disabilities), Bridgers's *Notes for Another Life* (contemplating suicide), Lionni's *Swimmy* (working together to overcome difficulty), Pfeffer's *The Year without Michael* (missing a younger brother), Klein's *Mom, the Wolfman and Me* (divorce), Philbrick's *Freak the Mighty* (standing up for a unique friend and the power of sticking together), Arkin's *The Lemming Condition* (the dangers of following the crowd), Garden's *Annie on My Mind* (exploring homosexuality), Betancourt's *My Name Is Brain Brian* (learning disabilities), Bang's *Common Ground* (using up Earth's resources), Hahn's *December Stillness* (homelessness), Hamilton's *Plain City* (homelessness), Voight's *Izzy Willy Nilly* (girl loses her leg because of a date's drunk driving), and Bunting's *The Terrible Things* (standing up and speaking out).

Beginning a class meeting with a poem such as "Honeybees" from Fleischman's (1988) *Joyful Noises: Poems for Two Voices* can be a reminder that there are multiple ways of looking at a situation. Each person has an important and valid point of view.

All can learn from one another, and respectful dialogue is a key component of building a democratic community.

Class meetings can also be a forum for problem solving much larger issues. Often, the unique problems that students bring into the classroom can be linked to factors or problems in society. Learning to solve their individual and collective problems can serve as models for how these problems can be solved within society. Social justice issues such as the unequal distribution of resources within and among school districts (why does the middle school across town have better sports equipment and uniforms?) can prompt thematic curriculum that might take a year to explore adequately. Students may wish to discuss what their shared vision of a just society is and how the class can work toward that both within the classroom and without. Literacy is power: Listening, speaking, reading, and writing gives language users power over their environment. The more opportunities students have to engage in the use of literacy with one another and their communities, the more empowered they will be. Students may learn that they are not passive recipients of an education designed to make them fit into society, but rather that they can remake society to fit them (Wood, 1984, p. 220).

Building Bridges

What good is academic learning if young people don't learn to become contributing members of society?
—Nelson, 1987

A time of rapid personal change and natural self-centeredness characterizes young adolescents. They need to balance this view by connecting to larger communities. Young adolescents do not look at school as primarily a place to *get ready* for what matters in life. What matters is what is happening to them *right now* (Atwell, 1987). Therefore, there is no time better than now to work within the community outside of the classroom. "The world outside the classroom is a limitless resource of diverse people, purposeful activity and the innumerable artifacts of a culture—cars, buildings, bridges, art. Our children grow out of and into this world. They are its products as well as its architects" (Gillis, 1992, p. 130). Bringing young adolescents and the community together rewards both.

The ancient Greeks understood this well: A person who is completely private is lost to civic life. The Greek concept of Paideia is essentially the "interplay between the development of mature, enlightened individuals and maximum cultural development. The community optimally educates. . . . Education is no more confined exclusively to schools than is religion confined to churches, mosques and synagogues" (Goodlad, 1984, p. 349). Gillis (1992) suggested three goals for integrating classroom and community: (1) help students live harmoniously within their environments by knowing them better, (2) help students see themselves as capable of shaping and changing their worlds, and (3) enable them to understand language as a powerful means of interacting with one's community.

Goodlad (1984) suggested an ecological perspective of school, in concert with Dewey's (1916) notions that the learning in school must be continuous with that out of school. "There should be a free interplay between the two. This is possible only when there are numerous points of contact between the social interests of the one and the other" (Dewey, 1916, p. 358). John Adams said, "It takes the whole of the people to educate the whole of the people." An ecology of education is one in which there is give and take between the school and the institutions, agencies, and people of the community. It is more than the cliché, "It takes a village to raise a child." Rather, the child is an active member of that village, one who has something to give back and who plays a role in shaping that village as well.

The metaphor of the bridge may be more appropriate than the village. A bridge makes links, enables parties from both sides to enter and exit at will, and requires action on the part of the builder, the bridge walker, and the maintainer of the bridge. A poem is one way to introduce these notions to students. One poem that works well is a Silverstein (1981) poem which begins, "This bridge will only take you half way there / To those mysterious lands you long to see." The poem ends by saying, "The last few steps you have to take alone." If teachers expect students to carry what they have learned beyond the classroom walls, then we have to build the bridge with them to those "mysterious lands" they long to see.

Dialoguing with Other Communities

One way that middle school students can connect with another community is through dialogue journals. In a survey about students' interests, Lynn, a middle school teacher, found that in her diverse class of seventh-graders from a small urban community in southern California, 80% said that they wanted to go to college. Listening and respecting this interest, she wanted to expose them to the realities of college and college students. Lynn, a former student of mine, contacted me and asked if I would come speak to her class about what college was like. I visited the class a couple of times and got to know the students, and then Lynn and I devised a plan that would benefit our students, accomplish some of our literacy objectives, and connect both groups to another community.

As a professor of middle-level preservice teachers, I want my students to understand young adolescents, their interests in life and reading, and view their writing more closely. Lynn wanted her students to have a better understanding of college and college students and to have authentic purposes for writing for an authentic audience. We decided to trade dialogue journals. Lynn provided journals to each of her students to be used specifically for this purpose. Her students began by writing a letter about themselves; many included a picture and questions they had for my students, which tended to be more personal than academic. My students wrote back telling about themselves, answering questions, and asking others. And so it went. We both read "My Journals" from *Hey World, Here I Am!* (Little, 1986) to our classes, and read about various other writers' use of journals and excerpts from writers' journals. Several pieces of children's literature such as *Pedro's Journal, Catherine Called Birdy, Zlata's Diary, Amelia's Notebook* (Moss, 1995), *The Secret Diary of Adrian Mole Aged 13-3/4* (Townsend, 1982), and *The Green Book* (Walsh, 1982) are written in journal form.

What surprised Lynn and me was the extent and depth of what they revealed. We thought that the seventh-graders would be guarded and obtuse and would only ask questions about college. Instead, they had a very different agenda. They wanted to know their audience, they wanted to know the person who went to college, and most of all they wanted someone to really know them. The students found it much easier to reveal themselves in writing to one single person who would respond back. One boy wrote about his nervousness about asking a girl out, one wrote about his fear that his brother would run away, some shared fights their parents had, and many asked advice.

My preservice teachers were equally surprised by the personal sharing and nervous about their responsibility not only to respond back to their student, but also to face a whole class of students with these interests, concerns, fears, and hopes. Responding to one seventh-grade student at a time, however, was manageable. They viewed it as a wonderful opportunity to get an inside perspective on middle school and middle school students. When student teachers begin, they tend to see a sea of faces and worry about how to manage the group, and they often lose sight of the 33 individuals who make up that group. The dialogue journals also gave the preservice teachers an opportunity to see middle school students in the most favorable light: They were not rude, disrespectful, or complaining. They shared themselves, and they really let us inside their heads and inside their lives.

About halfway into the academic year, we decided to have two meetings, one at each of our respective locales. The preservice teachers visited the classroom to meet their students and to watch literature circles (Daniels, 1994) in action. Before our arrival, we read "Blackmail," a short story from *Local News* (Soto, 1993), that the seventh-grade students would be discussing on that day. The preservice teachers sat in the literature circle groups with their partner seventh-grade student. The students led the discussions and were the experts. They taught their partners how to work in a group, how to lead the discussion, and how to perform the various roles within the literature circle. As befits any gathering of this nature, after the discussion we ate together. The seventh-grade students had suggested bringing food, and one girl and her mother baked a cake. She said it was like having guests in her home and she wanted to make it a special visit.

Reciprocally, the preservice teachers hosted a visit by the seventh-grade students to our campus. We began with a welcome by our dean, a snack, and a reacquainting. The preservice teachers planned a campus tour via a scavenger hunt in small groups of two and three partners. The hunt encompassed the financial aid office, an empty classroom and active classroom, the math and writing lab, student recreational centers, and so forth. The seventh-grade students had also prepared questions prior to their arrival that they wanted answered during their visit. We finished with lunch together and then escorted the seventh-grade students to their bus.

Beyond journal writing, the seventh-grade students also had a built-in authentic audience or reader who gave feedback about a draft of a piece of writing. A couple of times during the school year, Lynn asked the preservice teachers to read the students' papers and give them feedback about how well they were communicating their ideas.

Real people who are interested in what students have to say and who give valuable feedback can only serve to strengthen students' writing.

Building community among various populations is possible and vital. This experience is very adaptable to many domains. Students can exchange journals with any number of groups who have a real purpose for interacting and learning from one another. Pen pals have been a popular activity for decades, but they are largely between children and classes of the same age. Students can (and do) write to senior citizens in residential homes or to juveniles and other incarcerated individuals (with parental permission and using only the address of the school; in this case, students have to be cautioned about not revealing too much personal information). In this technologically accessible society, with appropriate hardware and software, it is very easy to dialogue online. One class of eighth-grade students discusses the books they are reading with a group of college students. Both classes have learned from the other's perspectives.

Gathering Information
and Challenging Assumptions

Language shapes and expresses our views and values. All our attitudes about our communities are learned. What a culture values is reflected in its words, such as the use of the pronoun *he* to refer to doctors, scientists, and athletes and *she* to refer to teachers and nurses. *Immigrant, illegal alien, undocumented worker,* and *new American* are all words to describe a person not born in this country, yet all reflect different social and political dimensions. Gillis (1992) suggested using language in all its forms to explore the sources of our ideas about our communities. A reciprocal relationship is then engaged in which language is used to understand culture and society and the language itself is strengthened.

One simple exercise to have students examine their assumptions and stereotypes is a kind of word association. First, the students list all the nouns and adjectives they identify with immigration, old people, homelessness, or whatever the topic of study is. Then they categorize the words by whether they think the word has a positive connotation, a negative connotation, or no connotation. A discussion follows about the kinds of images their words conjure for them. Telling or writing about people described by these terms is a good way to discover the meaning of them and a possible source of stereotypes. A similar activity is to give students pictures from magazines and cut-out words and ask them to match the pictures with the words and then write a story about the person using those words. Or, students can be given the same pictures and different words and asked to write a story about their picture. When they read their stories about the same people using different words, the class can discuss the impact that language has on how we view people (Gillis, 1992).

Students can explore their ideas about a particular population or issue before engaging with that community through writing. Before a group of eighth-grade students visited a homeless shelter, soup kitchen, and food bank, they wrote about what they thought they would see and why. After the visit, the same group wrote about their reactions and what they thought could be done to serve those populations. Because a newspaper reporter covered the trip and printed their before-and-after writing, some students decided that letters to the editor, letters to local and state politicians, and letters of request for needed resources would be the most effective way to serve the homeless and hungry. They saw not only the power of print, but of their own voices.

One university professor points out a necessary caution: It is very easy to assign journals and reaction papers and let it go at that (Herzberg, 1994). "A colleague reported overhearing a conversation between two students: 'We're going to a homeless shelter tomorrow and we have to write about it.' 'No sweat. Write that before you went, you had no sympathy for the homeless, but the visit opened your eyes. Easy A'" (p. 309). Writing is an important part of processing any experience, but it alone is not sufficient, nor is a one-time reflective journal assignment enough to understand the social forces that sustain poverty, discrimination, and injustice.

Through literature, writing, and drama, students can also pursue questions regarding how neighborhoods, locales in a community (parks, beaches, a local store), and the people in the community are perceived as safe/unsafe or inviting/uninviting. Literature (such as that mentioned previously) can be read and pictures examined for how communities are represented. Bunting's *Smoky Night* (1995) is a beautiful picture book relating the civil disobedience in Los Angeles following the Rodney King verdict from a child's perspective. Students can compare the book's explanation and images with that of the media and print reports of the same events. What words are used to describe the people portrayed? How are the streets and neighborhoods described? How would you feel about these portrayals if you lived there? Students can engage in letter-writing campaigns to publishers, authors, television personnel, and sponsors who perpetuate stereotypical, demeaning, and negative images. Students can seek out and publish their own more accurate images in stories, books, and films about their neighborhoods and the people in them.

> Images that are false, stereotypical or even absent may contribute to students' preconceptions or misconceptions about their communities. . . . Only when we have accurate information are we free from the kind of fear and prejudice that can limit our relationships with people and restrict our opportunities in life. The more students learn about their communities, the more comfortable they are in them, the less likely they are to behave in destructive ways and the more able they will be to participate actively. (Gillis, 1992, pp. 137–138)

Service Learning

> If our education is to have any meaning for life, it must pass through an equally complete transformation. . . . When the school introduces and trains each child of society into membership within such a little community, saturating him with the spirit of service and providing him with the instruments of effective self-direction, we shall have the deepest and best guaranty of a larger society which is worthy, lovely and harmonious. (Dewey, 1899, pp. 24–25)

Service learning is not new. It is grounded in the writings of Dewey, experiential education, Toqueville's notion of service as citizenship, Ivy League schools' preparation for future leaders, citizenship education, participatory democracy, and social justice. *Turning Points* (Carnegie Council on Adolescent Development, 1989) advocates not only connecting schools with communities but also providing opportunities for youth service by 10- to 14-year-old students: "Youth service in the community should be part of the core program in middle school education" (p. 70).

> Service learning connects students to the community, placing them in challenging situations where they associate with adults and gain experience and knowledge that can strengthen and extend their school studies. Service learning helps to make classroom study relevant, since young people discover connections between their actions and the world that exists beyond the school's walls and the content they study in the curriculum. (Fertman, White, & White, 1996, p. 3)

People for the American Way (Fowler, 1990) surveyed more than 1,000 15- to 24-year-old young people. One question asked them to rate seven possible goals. They rated career and financial success as number one, a happy family life as number two, and enjoying yourself and having a good time as number three. Being involved in helping your community be a better place ranked seventh. When asked to describe (in their own words) what constitutes a good citizen, most equated being a good citizen with being a good person. A typical description was, "Honest, a good friend, trustworthy." Rarely did their notion of a good citizen hold a social or political dimension, and only 12% believed that voting was an important part of citizenship. When asked how schools could improve teaching about citizenship, students called for a more active, hands-on approach. Fifty-one percent favored making community service a requirement for high school graduation. They said that the barriers to getting involved were pressures to do well in school and get a good job (68%), lack of parental encouragement (45%), and that no one asks young people to get involved or shows them how (42%). More recently, Hodgkinson and Weitzman (1992) found that 61% of teenagers (between the ages of 12 and 17) volunteered an average of 3.2 hours per week. Of these, only 25% reported that their service was school related.

Increasingly, service learning is becoming a powerful tool for learning about content, increasing reading and writing skills, and linking students with their communities. Most service learning advocates agree that a good program has five components:

1. Those being served control the service provided. The needs of the host community, rather than the academic program come first in defining the work of the students placed there and the community defines those needs.
2. Those being served become better able to serve and be served by their own actions. The aim of the students' service should be the collaborative development and empowerment of those served.
3. Those who serve are also learners and have significant control over what is learned.
4. There are many opportunities for reflection.
5. There is a celebration of the service or a means for making it public beyond the classroom.

Literacy can play an important and powerful role in each part of the service learning process. Literature such as *Seedfolks* (Fleischman, 1997) can operate as a springboard for discussion and investigation. *Seedfolks* is the story of a young girl, Kim, who by her example inspires a neighborhood to turn the local vacant lot into a garden, and the book "records through the garden's progress the growth of its most precious crop—the tendrillike sense of community" (book jacket). *Almost a Hero* (Neufeld, 1995) is a novel about how involved a seventh-grade boy, Ben, becomes in his service learning project volunteering in a day-care center for children of the homeless His journey of discovery of working for children within and without the system is a good introduction to the pitfalls and possibilities of engaging in service learning.

To allow the host community to define its own needs, students can develop an interview or survey protocol. The needs assessment can include questions such as, Are there people in this community who could be served in some way? Are there physical facilities that could be serviced (cleanup, upkeep, building)? Are there other living things (plants, animals) that could be serviced? Is there some political action or advocacy that could be done to service this community (letter writing, informational fliers)? Is there some product or performance that would help this community (a pamphlet of information on bike safety, a play about drug prevention, a song about taking care of our environment)? and Is there anything we could teach to members of this community that would be valuable to them? The surveys can be completed individually and compiled as a class. Students then have an opportunity to see what the needs are and, depending on their availability and comfort level, how they may best serve them.

Needs are plentiful, and the possibilities for service learning projects are endless. Middle school students have tended gardens and donated the fresh produce to local soup kitchens; taken animal shelter pets to local nursing homes to visit patients; painted over graffiti in their local park; written picture books and put on plays about local environmental issues; made toys in industrial arts and clothes in home arts for homeless children at the holidays; studied a local lagoon and become docents and advocates for saving it; read books on tape for young children and blind persons; and been zoo volunteers, child-care aids, library aids, special Olympics volunteers, recycling volunteers, envelope stuffers, museum guides, and hospital volunteers.

Processing the service experience and helping students make links to literacy and other curricular areas through reflection can take a variety of forms: small and large group discussion, one-on-one conferences with the teacher, talks or slide presentations to other audiences, journal writing, case study writing, research papers, painting, drawing, music, or drama. Using varied forms may be beneficial to appeal to a larger number of participants. Ongoing reflection is key to maximum gains in awareness and understanding of the service and the issues related to it.

Celebration and recognition reinforce and nurture a culture of caring. "They teach youth to care about others in their community and foster a community that values its youth. . . . Students celebrate learning and achievement. They are recognized for their demonstration of learning in real life situations that address community needs" (Fertman et al., 1996, p. 37). Making presentations to families, peers, and community members, highlighting service projects in the school and local newspaper, and noting the number of service hours on report cards are just a few examples. My university is currently developing a student profile that will accompany a student's transcripts. The profile includes extracurricular, leadership, and service activities that students engage in during their college careers. The message to students and potential employers is that these experiences are equally as valuable as those inside classrooms.

Conclusion

Literacy and community study have no end. Building alliances and building community within a classroom support and empower students to act beyond the classroom. The classroom is a very appropriate place for students to become adept not only at academic literacy, but at reading and writing about our communities as well. Middle school classrooms may be the best opportunity to provide students with a vision of what is possible for their future lives in this global community: a more just society than the one we live in now. Our classrooms are a bridge to their communities, but we can only take them halfway there. The last few steps they have to take alone.

REFERENCES

Atwell, N. (1987). *In the middle.* Portsmouth, NH: Heinemann.

———. (1998). *In the middle* (2nd. ed.). Portsmouth, NH: Heinemann.

Bellah, R., R. Madsen, W. Sullivan, A. Swidler, & S. Tipton. (1985). *Habits of the heart: Individualism and commitment in American life.* Berkeley: University of California Press.

———. (1991). *The good society.* New York: Knopf.

Beyer, L. (1996). *Creating democratic classrooms: The struggle to integrate theory and practice.* New York: Teachers College Press.

Bullard, S. (1995). Past rivalry: When bitter school rivals merged, a community of friends was born. *Teaching Tolerance, 4*(2), pp. 26–31.

Carnegie Council on Adolescent Development (1989). *Turning points: Preparing American youth for the 21st century.* New York: Carnegie Corporation of New York.

Charney, R.S. (1992). *Teaching children to care.* MA: Northeast Foundation for Children.

Christensen, L. (1994). Building community from chaos. In *Rethinking our classrooms* (pp. 50–55), Milwaukee, WI: Rethinking Schools.

Daniels, H. (1994). *Literature circles: Voice and choice in student centered classrooms.* York, ME: Stenhouse.

Dewey, J. (1899). *The school and society.* Chicago: Chicago University Press.

Etzioni, E. (1993). *The spirit of community: Rights, responsibilities, and the communitarian agenda.* New York: Crown.

Fertman, C., White, G., & White, L. (1996). *Service learning in the middle school: Building a culture of service.* Columbus, OH: National Middle School Association.

Fish, S.E. (1980). *Is there a text in this class? The authority of interpretive communities.* Cambridge, MA: Harvard University Press.

———. (1987). How to recognize a poem when you see one. In D. Bartholomae and A. Petrosky (Eds.), *Ways of reading* (pp. 222–234). New York: St. Martin's Press.

Fowler, K. (1990). Democracy's next generation. *Educational Leadership, 48*(3), pp. 10–15.

Freire, P., & Macedo, D. (1987). *Literacy: Reading the word and reading the world.* South Hadley, MA: Bergin and Garvey.

Gillis, C. (1992). *The community as classroom.* Portsmouth, NH: Heinemann.

Goodlad, J. (1984). *A place called school.* New York: McGraw-Hill.

Goodman, K. (1996). *On reading.* Portsmouth, NH: Heinemann.

Herzberg, B. (1994). Community service and critical teaching. *College composition and communication, 45*(3), pp. 307–319.

Hodgkinson, V.A., & Weitzman, M.S. (1992). *Giving and volunteering 1992: Findings from a national survey.* Washington, DC: Gallup Organization.

Howe, L., & Howe, M.M. (1975). *Personalizing education.* New York: Hart.

Kohl, H. (1994). *I won't learn from you and other thougths on creative maladjustment.* New York: New Press.

Lewis, B. A., & Espeland, P. (1995). *The kid's guide to service projects: Over 500 service ideas for young* people who want to make a difference. Minneapolis, MN: Free Spirit.

Maeroff, G. (1998). Altered destinities: Making life better for schoolchildren in need. *Kappan, 79*, pp. 424–434.

McCaleb, S.P. (1994). *Building communities of learners: A collaboration among teachers, students, families, and community.* New York: St. Martin's Press.

Moll, L. (Ed.). (1990). *Vygotsky in eduation: Instructional implications and applications of sociohistorical psychology.* New York: Cambridge University Press.

Nelson, J. (1987). *Positive discipline.* New York: Ballantine Books.

Peck, M.S. (1987). *The different drum: Community and making peace.* New York: Simon and Schuster.

———. (1993). *A world waiting to be born: Civility rediscovered.* New York: Bantam Books.

Persico, M. (1996). Our responsibility is teaching responsibility. *Middle School Journal, 28*(2), pp. 39–42.

Schmuck, R., & Schmuck, P. (1983). *Group processses in the classroom.* Dubuque, IA: William C. Brown.

Simon, S., Howe, L., & Kirschenbaum, H. (1972). *Values clarification.* New York: Hart.

Smith, F. (1978). *Joining the literacy club.* Portsmouth, NH: Heinemann.

———. (1990, August 7) Speech presented at the Upper Arlington Summer Institute, Upper Arlington, OH.

Vygtosky, L. (1978). *Mind in society.* Cambridge, MA: Harvard University Press.

———. (1986). *Thought and language.* Cambridge, MA: The MIT Press.

Walberg, H.J., & Greenberg, R.C. (1997). Using the learning environment inventory. *Educational Leadership, 55,* pp. 45–47.

Wink, J. (1997). *Critical pedagogy: Notes from the real world.* New York: Longman.

Wood, G.H. (1984). Schooling in a democracy: Transformation or reproduction? *Educational Theory, 34*(3), pp. 219–239.

Zemelman, S., & Daniels, H. (1988). *A community of writers.* Portsmouth, NH: Heinemann.

CHILDREN'S AND ADOLESCENTS' LITERATURE

Alicea, G., with DeSena, C. (1995). *The air down here.* San Francisco: Chronicle Books.

Arkin, A. (1976). *The lemming condition.* New York: Harper and Row.

Arrick, F. (1981). *Chernowitz!* New York: Signet.

Bang, M. (1997). *Common ground: The water, earth and air we share.* New York: Blue Sky Press.

Betancourt, J. (1993). *My name is Brain Brian.* New York: Scholastic.

Bridgers, S.E. (1981). *Notes for another life.* Toronto, Canada: Bantam.

Bunting, E. (1980). *The terrible things: An allegory of the Holocaust.* Philadelphia: Edward Nelson.

———. (1995). *Smokey night.* San Diego, CA: Harcourt Brace.

Carlson, L. (Ed.). (1994). *Cool salsa: Bilingual poems on growing up Latino in the United States.* New York: Henry Holt and Company.

Cohn, J., D.S.W. (1995). *The Christmas menorahs: How a town fought hate.* Morton Grove, IL: Albert Whitman.

Feinman Moss, E. (1997). *Helping out is cool.* New York: Scholastic.

Fleischman, P. (1997). *Seedfolks.* New York: HarperCollins.

———. (1988). *Joyful noises: Poems for two voices.* New York: Harper and Row.

Fox, M. (1985). *Wilfred Gordon McDonald Partridge.* New York: Kane/Miller Books.

Garden, N. (1982). *Annie on my mind.* New York: HarperCollins.

Garland, S. (1993). *Shadow of the dragon.* San Diego, CA: Harcourt Brace.

Hahn, M.D. (1988). *December stillness.* New York: Clarion.

Hamilton, V. (1993). *Plain city.* New York: Scholastic.

Klein, N. (1972). *Mom, the wolfman and me.* NewYork: Avon.

Lasky, K. (1995). *She's wearing a dead bird on her head.* New York: Hyperion Books.

Leeper Buss, F. (1991). *Journey of the sparrows.* New York: Dell.

Levine, E. (1995). *The tree that would not die.* New York: Scholastic.

Lionni, L. (1963). *Swimmy.* New York: Dragonfly Books.

Little, J. (1986). *Hey world, here I am!* New York: Harper and Row.

Lorbiecki, M. (1996). *Just one flick of a finger.* New York: Dial Books.

Martinez, V. (1996). *Parrot in the oven.* New York: HarperCollins.

Mathis, S.B. (1972). *Teacup full of roses.* New York: Puffin.

Moore Gray, L. (1993). *Miss Tizzy.* New York: Simon and Schuster.

Moss, M. (1995). *Amelia's notebook.* Berkeley, CA: Tricycle Press.

Neufeld, J. (1995). *Almost a hero.* New York: Antheneum.

Oneal, Z. (1980). *The language of goldfish.* New York: Fawcett Juniper.

Pfeffer, S.B. (1988). *The year without Michael.* Toronto, Canada: Bantam.

Philbrick, F. (1993). *Freak the mighty.* New York: Scholastic.

Silverstein, S. (1981). *A light in the attic.* New York: Harper and Row.

Slepian, J. (1982). *The Alfred Summer.* New York: Scholastic.

Soto, G. (1991). *Taking sides.* San Diego, CA: Harcourt Brace.

———. (1993). *Local news.* New York: Scholastic.

Townsend, S. (1982). *The secret diary of Adrian Mole aged 13-3/4.* London: Methuen.

Voight, C. (1986). *Izzy Willy nilly.* New York: Antheneum.

Walsh, J.P. (1982). *The green book.* New York: Farrar, Straus, and Giroux.

7 Standards in the Middle

Moving Beyond the Basics

SHARON O'NEAL

Texas Education Agency, Austin

BARBARA KAPINUS

Senior Policy Analyst and Program Consultant,
National Education Association

Before Standards: One Story

It was late June 1975, in Birmingham, Alabama. A summer school class had been convened at an inner-city kindergarten-through-eighth-grade campus. The summer school teacher, Mrs. Stone,[1] usually taught students in grades 6, 7, and 8, but this assignment would be different. She was to instruct all students who had, as the children called it, "flunked." This group included students just completing a year in first grade all the way to students who had just completed a year (or two) in grade 8. Alphonso was one of those eighth-grade students. At 16 years old, he towered over his summer school teacher. He had a reputation for taking the best teacher and reducing that person to tears after a mere 45 minutes in a classroom. Clearly, this would be a challenge for her.

The first day of summer school arrived. The classroom was filled with color and encouraging words and places ready to display all manner of student work. Mrs. Stone was prepared for her students, but she was not prepared for the preschool brothers and sisters who accompanied them. It seemed that when mama or grandma went to work in the summertime, the school-age sibling was to care for the younger children. Suddenly this mixed-age class included six-month-old babies to adolescents the size and age of Alphonso. Surprisingly, the class went well. Students who had been difficult behavior problems during the school year seemed to blossom in this mixed-age setting. Older

---

[1] The name "Stone" is an alias. The story, however, is true.

students took responsibility for younger ones, and the younger ones looked up to the "Alphonsos" of the world. Mrs. Stone's problem was not organization or student behavior. Mrs. Stone's problem was not even instructional for most of the class. She could find enough books that fit each student's ability level. Each child seemed to be able to find interesting topics to read and write about. In fact, many stayed long after the ending bell to discuss books or papers or even to help straighten the room. It seemed that summer school, without the demands of grades and changing classes and multiple teachers, was the perfect place for these youngsters. Mrs. Stone's problem was Alphonso.

He was wonderful with the younger children. He was well behaved. But he had one problem. As Mrs. Stone reported, "He couldn't read a lick." Perhaps he could recognize his name, but even that was not certain. In desperation, this teacher tried to think of purposeful tasks for Alphonso. He became her assistant with the younger children. He helped her line them up for dismissal and breakfast and helped with the classroom arrangements. Mrs. Stone knew she would be doing him no favors, however, if she did not quickly find something academic that he could do. In a brief diagnostic session, she realized that he did know the alphabet. She began with an alphabetizing task. He loved it and asked for more. As a teacher with a bachelor of science in secondary education and a major in history and speech, Mrs. Stone was ill-prepared to teach a nonreader. She was embarrassed to confess that, during the brief summer session, she never found another academic task for Alphonso.

One day, Alphonso did not come to school. He had had perfect attendance up to that point, and his teacher was worried. A million things ran through her mind. Was he all right? Had he grown tired of the "baby work" she was giving him? Was he finally so bored that he could not take another minute of the alphabet? At that minute, she thought she had failed. Later that morning, she looked up and there was Alphonso, holding the hand of a fragile, elderly woman. Alphonso volunteered, "Miss, I brought my grandma to see my work."

As Mrs. Stone later learned, this was the grandmother with whom Alphonso lived, the grandmother who had received countless notes from countless teachers about Alphonso's inappropriate behavior and to whom had been delivered countless bad report cards. She was so very proud of those simple little alphabetizing tasks.

The instruction given Alphonso that summer was far from adequate. Alphonso was, however, provided with work at which he could succeed, work that for him required some teacher direction but not constant supervision. Alphonso may have finally been operating, albeit briefly, in his "zone of proximal development" (Vygotsky, 1978). Alphonso deserved more than low-level alphabetizing tasks that summer. Students like Alphonso are capable of much more.

How do teachers provide students of all abilities with challenging instruction yet work within that grasp of understanding that allows them to move to a more difficult task with expediency and efficiency? How do teachers know what should be expected of students in each subject area, especially in the middle grades as they are prepared to move successfully to high school? How could Mrs. Stone have better prepared Alphonso?

A vision that has been an integral part of the standards movement is the idea of all students having access to challenging curriculum. Thus, if students come to school poor, with a different language or cultural background, or with fewer readiness experiences, they will still be offered a chance to learn challenging, complex, and engaging concepts and skills. Some students might need extra help, but the days of educators simply throwing up their hands and saying, "Well, that child just isn't going far, so we will provide less in the way of instruction," are over. If Alfonso's previous teachers had been in a standards-driven context, would he have been as far behind? In a standards-driven summer program, would he have been placed not only in the nurturing environment Mrs. Stone provided, but also in an academic environment that would have efficiently and expediently improved his literacy skills?

Where We Are

Currently, teachers and scholars in most content areas are struggling with the development and implementation of content standards to answer that question of expectations. With these standards efforts being mounted across multiple disciplines, however, it may be difficult for individual teachers, especially those responsible for more than one content area, to address all these rigorous academic expectations for students.

This chapter assists in the effort to understand standards by summarizing selected national work in the foundation areas and discussing those skills and strategies that seem to cross all standards documents. This chapter also examines the literacy needs of students across content areas and provides examples of classroom work at the middle school level that serve to clarify these common skills and strategies.

Content Standards

A standards glossary provided by *Education Week* (Wolk, Edwards, & Olson, 1995), stated that "content standards" spell out the subject-specific knowledge and skills that schools are expected to teach and students are expected to learn. The term *performance standard* indicates the degree to which students have met the content standards. Other standards terms exist, including *delivery standards, evaluation standards,* and *instructional standards,* but content and performance seem to be at the heart of the major efforts taking place at both state and national levels. Currently, 38 states have adopted content standards in the core subjects. Iowa is the only state not working on statewide academic standards (Jerald, Curran, & Olson, 1998).

At a national level, standards exist in multiple forms and in multiple documents. For example, within the area of social studies, one can select from documents published by the National Council for the Social Studies, the Geography Education Standards Project, the National Center for History in the Schools, and the Center for Civic Education. Math and the English language arts have national standards published by their professional organizations, whereas science educators worked in collaboration with the National Science Foundation, the Department of Education, and other institutions to produce an array of standards documents. The National Council of Teachers of Mathematics established their Commission on Standards for School Mathematics in the 1980s and thus set the stage for the development of content standards in many content areas. A brief summary of selected national standards in four core content areas at the middle grades follows.

Math Standards

Across all grades, the *Curriculum and Evaluation Standards for Mathematics* (National Council of Teachers of Mathematics, 1989) tells us that students must not only "know" mathematics, but they should be constantly engaged in applying mathematics in useful and purposeful situations. These standards ascertain that mathematics knowledge will grow in direct proportion to its usefulness. Therefore, students are asked to apply mathematics across all disciplines. Specifically, at the middle grades, students are asked to (1) engage in problem solving, (2) communicate mathematical ideas, (3) engage in reasoning, (4) make connections between and among mathematical concepts and the world outside of school, (5) develop number and operation sense and engage in computation, (6) understand patterns and their functions, (7) work in the area of algebra, (8) understand and apply statistics, (9) use probability to solve problems, (10) understand geometry and its relationship to problem solving, and, finally, (11) estimate and use measurement.

The math standards go on to include a twelfth standard, directed to the teacher rather than the students. This final standard asks teachers to facilitate learning by engaging their students in the exploration and application of mathematics using technology and concrete materials and by assessing their students' needs regularly.

Underlying the national standards for mathematics is the goal that all students will develop "mathematical power," which "denotes an individual's abilities to explore, conjecture, and reason logically, as well as the ability to use a variety of mathematical methods effectively to solve non-routine problems" (National Council of Teachers of Mathematics, 1989, p. 5).

Science Standards

Like mathematics, themes of inquiry and problem solving run throughout the science standards. *The National Science Education Standards* (National Research Council, 1996) focuses attention at all grades in six areas: (1) science as inquiry, (2) physical science, (3) life science, (4) earth and space science, (5) science in personal and social perspectives, and (6) the history and nature of science. At the middle grades, students are asked to continue their focus on the inquiry in which they engaged at earlier grades, but students' reports of findings from these inquiries are expected to become more formalized. Students are asked to use the language of science to communicate their explanations and to continue to refine their work based on the evaluation of others as well as self-evaluation. In the area of physical science, students address the more complicated properties of the materials from which objects are made. Students in these middle grades question how motion and force can assist in the understanding of matter and its properties. In the area of life science, students examine multiple aspects of the structure, functions, and characteristics of living systems, from organisms to populations to ecosystems. Middle grade students study our planet's systems and its history as a part of earth and space science. With regard to science and technology, students begin to understand how technology provides the tools for investigation, analysis, and inquiry.

Science is also examined in light of personal needs. Students are challenged to see how science relates to their personal health and to the population as a whole. The relationship between humans and the environment is studied. Finally, middle grade students begin to understand the place of science in the modern world as well as in history. Throughout all aspects of study, students inquire, analyze, and synthesize findings, and communicate these new understandings to others.

Social Studies Standards

Communication is a key part of the Curriculum Standards for the Social Studies (National Council for the Social Studies, 1994) as well. At all grades, the national standards for social studies ask students to communicate their understandings about (1) culture and cultural diversity; (2) how human beings view themselves in and over time; (3) the people, places, and environments throughout our world; and (4) their own individual development and identity. Students are also asked to (5) explore interactions among individuals, groups, and institutions; (6) take note of how people create and change the structures of power, authority, and governance; (7) study how people organize for the production, distribution, and consumption of goods and services; (8) identify, describe, and come to understand the relationships among science, technology, and society; (9) discover the global connections and interdependence of people, nations, and causes; and, finally, (10) come to a deepened understanding of the ideals, principles, and practices of citizenship in a democratic republic.

English Language Arts Standards

Like the social studies, Standards for the English Language Arts (National Council of Teachers of English/International Reading Association, 1996) are sensitive to diversity. The theme that continually runs through the national English language arts standards is understanding and communicating with a variety of audiences. Students are repeatedly asked to use the language arts effectively to communicate for varied purposes, in a variety of situations to a variety of audiences. One standard asks that students read a wide range of texts for both personal and academic purposes. Next, students are asked to focus on a variety of literature in order to better understand the human experience. Students are also expected to use and apply a variety of comprehension strategies and to adjust those strategies as needed. In addition, students are asked to adjust their language according to the purpose so that they might better communicate with a wide variety of audiences. Just as with reading, students in writing are also expected to use a range of strategies when engaging in written communication and to vary those strategies according to different audiences and a variety of purposes. Students are asked to create, critique, and discuss print and nonprint communications using their knowledge of language and media. As with the other content areas, students are expected to conduct research and communicate findings in ways that suit both the purpose of the investigation and the audience to whom the information is given. Students are also asked to use technological and other resources to gather and synthesize information.

Diversity of language is highlighted, and students are asked to understand and respect language diversity. Students whose first language is not English are asked to make use of their first language to develop competency in English. Students participate in a variety of literacy communities and use language effectively for their own purposes.

Connecting Themes

Certain themes are constant across all these carefully crafted content standards. In all content areas, students are asked to (1) explore and make inquiries; (2) analyze and synthesize information; (3) make connections within and across disciplines; (4) evaluate their tasks and products and those of others; (5) identify and know the critical facts and tenets of each content area; and (6) express themselves through writing, talk, and products.

In the area of inquiry, students across all content areas are asked to be active learners who ask genuine questions related to each discipline. For each of the four disciplines reviewed in this chapter, inquiry and investigation is not only a piece of the content area standards but is at the heart of the study of the discipline. Inquiry serves as the foundation and the rationale for the study. To answer questions posed in each discipline, middle school students are asked to summarize information and issues through analysis. Through this process, students extract the essence of the discipline and describe the critical elements found in the content. Such analysis often calls for students to make connections both within and across areas of study and to connect their own personal experiences, previous investigations, and knowledge to the material at hand. Threaded throughout the content standards is the critical skill of evaluation. To evaluate, students are continually required to use criteria to judge the effectiveness and quality of their own speaking, writing, and products. In addition, students are expected to use self-generated criteria and established criteria to judge their work and the work of others.

Putting It All Together:
Science and English Language Arts

But how might teachers provide opportunities for students to engage in these common areas of inquiry, synthesis, connection, evaluation, knowing, and expression? In their quest to provide their students with experiences that will prepare them for study at the high school, middle school teachers have often worked in purposeful interdisciplinary units of study. This method often results in bringing the content standards' common themes of exploration and inquiry, analysis and synthesis, connection, evaluation, identification, and expression together in one or more units of study.

The Council of Chief State School Officers asked content experts and teachers to prepare examples that demonstrated how standards can be "rolled out" as instructional activities (Council of Chief State School Officers, 1997). In an example from science, students studied photosynthesis in the larger context of tropical rain forests, exploring the complex series of relationships and processes that take place as a result of photosynthesis. Students researched historical discoveries related to photosynthesis and presented their research findings in small groups to the class. They had to use both knowledge about science and knowledge and skills in reading, writing, listening, and speaking. They also had to use their skills as contributing members of a work group. As a culminating activity, after several other lessons and activities, students were asked to "creatively explain" photosynthesis as a process and tell why photosynthesis was important to the jaguar found in the rain forest.

But how is such a task graded? Using carefully crafted rubrics, or guidelines, for scoring, teachers were able to score several aspects of this project. The scoring for the scientific aspects of the task included the need for scientific detail and clear explanation. The scoring for the writing task focused on organization, a voice appropriate for the task, mechanics, and clarity. Such grading is a substantive endeavor that calls for a realistic integration of knowledge and skills that should be developed in both science and language arts.

Putting It All Together:
Social Studies and English Language Arts

In a seventh-grade English language arts class in Texas, the topic of slavery involved not only the students but parents in the unit of study. The unit focused on composing historical fiction by asking students to chronicle the journey of African slaves from capture, through their journey to America, and to their escape to freedom via the Underground Railroad. Prior to beginning their fictitious diaries, students were asked to research slavery in the United States. Textbooks as well as trade books served as resources. Students assisted the teacher in gathering these multiple information sources and, with teacher guidance, prepared an inquiry chart (Figure 7.1).

Once students had gathered sufficient information on the period, they began to compose first drafts of their "slave diaries" around the assigned topics. At the beginning of each week, students met with partners in class for peer editing and conferencing and met with parents or another adult midweek to further identify strengths and weaknesses in their writing. Parents and peers were provided with comment sheets and rubrics (see Figures 7.2 through 7.4) to guide their remarks. Students were graded on the content, grammar, mechanics, and spelling of the final draft submitted at the end of each week and on the collection of feedback from peers and parents (see Figures 7.5 and 7.6). In addition to the composition assignment, students read books related to the Civil War and slavery and studied maps that indicated routes taken in the Underground Railroad and that identified confederate, slave, and border states. Students left this unit with a unique understanding of that period of American history, an understanding of

FIGURE 7.1   Inquiry Chart

Resources and Questions	What I Already Know	Textbook	Her Stories: African American Folk Tales, Fairy Tales, and True Tales, by Virginia Hamilton	Escape from Slavery: The Boyhood of Frederick Douglass in His Own Words, edited by Michael McCurdy	Conclusions
How were slaves brought to America? How were they sold and traded?	Slaves were captured in Africa and brought to America on boats. Once here, they were sold.	Africans were forced into slavery. They were placed in chains and did not come willingly.			
What was it like to live as a slave?	Slaves had no rights. They had to do whatever their masters said. Sometimes families would be split up.	Slaves helped clear thousands of acres of land. They planted and harvested cotton, tobacco, coffee, and sugar.	Slaves were often treated like animals. Slaves were property to be worked, fed, and driven.	F. D. educated himself so that he could escape to freedom. He changed his name and ran away to Massachusetts. He worked to end slavery.	Each slave's story is different. Yet whether they were treated well by their master or mistreated, their lives were harsh. They were always treated as the property of another.
Did any slaves gain their freedom? If so, how?		Many slaves escaped through the Underground Railroad. The Underground Railroad was made up of the barns, attics, and cellars of White people. They would hide and protect slaves and help them escape.	Some slaves were afriad to be free and did not try to escape. Even after the Civil War ended, some stayed with their masters. Some slave owners did not understand what the end of the Civil War meant and kept their slaves.		Escape was dangerous. Many lost their lives, and others endured harsh conditions in order to gain freedom.

FIGURE 7.2   Parent Directions and Rubrics for Comments on Student Essays

Dear Parents:

As you know, your child is currently working on the process of writing to write an original, creative, historical narrative that chronicles the journey of an African slave from his/her capture to America and his/her escape to freedom via the Underground Railroad. Your child has written several journal topics relating to this theme. At the beginning of each week, students will write their first drafts and participate in peer editing these drafts. We would like your involvement in your child's process of writing each weekly composition. We would like you to help your child identify challenges within his/her writing. Some of these challenges may include the following:

- spelling errors
- punctuation errors
- capitalization errors
- correct paragraphing
- avoiding run-on sentences
- avoiding fragments

We would also like your help to encourage your child to create his/her own style of expression, appealing to the senses and using figurative language. Please remind your child to use a thesaurus, to seek out new words to enrich and expand his/her vocabulary. Additionally, have your child share with you his/her examples of similes, metaphors, and personification in the compositions.

This project will last the entire six weeks. Each new composition begins on Monday and is due at the end of the week. The topics are as follows:

- "My Capture"
- "Journey on a Slave Ship"
- "On the Auction Block"
- "Life on the Plantation"
- "Escape to Freedom" (via the Underground Railroad)

Ideally, we would like your participation in this process each Wednesday evening so that your child may make revisions on Thursday. We feel confident that this process will help your child understand and appreciate the time, energy, and diligence it takes to create a quality composition. We truly appreciate your involvement in helping your child strive for academic quality.

Sincerely,

Amie Lowenthal
Amie Lowenthal

Terri Machias
Terri Machias

FIGURE 7.3 Parent Comment Sheet, English Language Arts

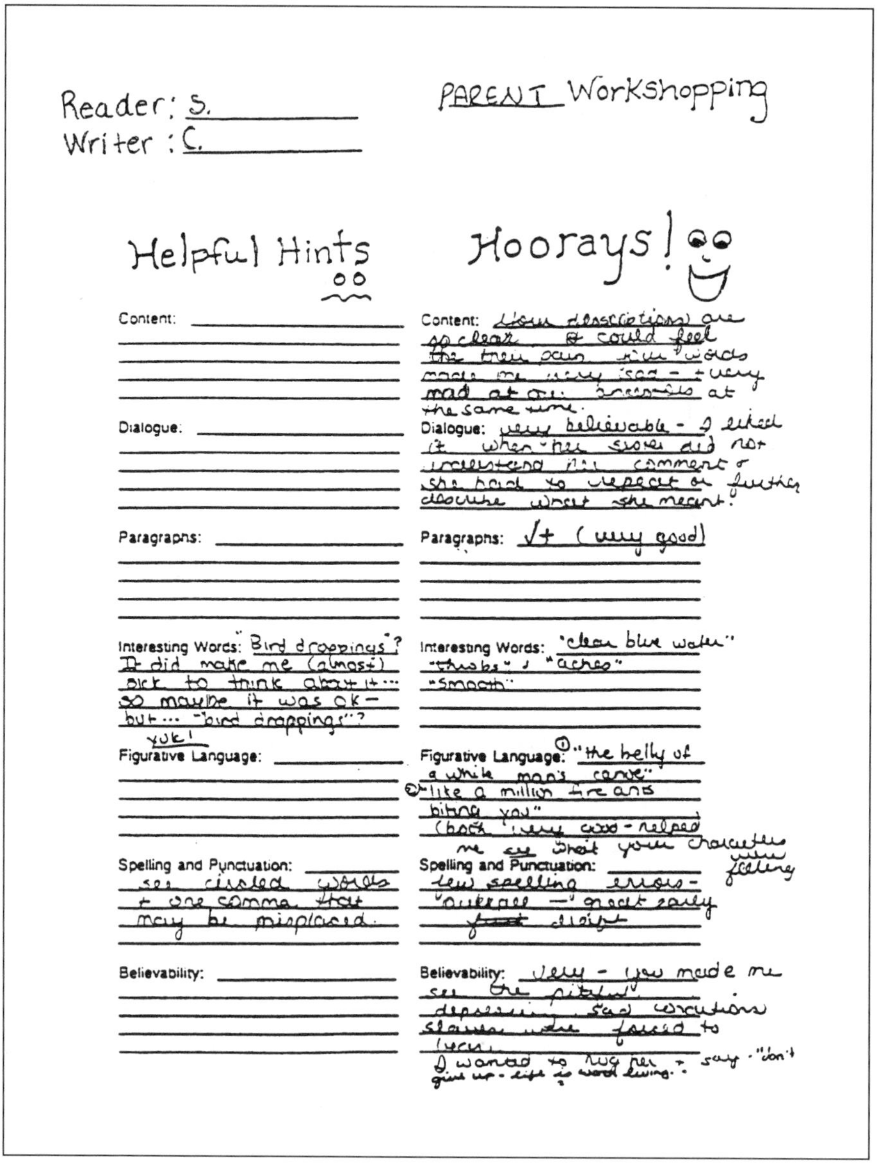

FIGURE 7.4 **Peer Comment Sheet, English Language Arts**

C. _____'s paper

Grader – B.

Very Good	Needs Work
Content: ~~_____~~	Content: _____
I like the way you explained everything so clearly.	
Dialogue: _____	Dialogue: You could add some dialogue when you and your sisters' are playing
Paragraphs: You tried to make 7 paragraphs! (I had 1 big one.)	Paragraphs: Try dividing the 2nd paragraph in both between when you are in the river and being captured.
Interesting Words: You explained things with good adjectives	Interesting Words: You could describe more about the mad and river with interesting words like cool, gurey and swampy.
Figurative Language: _____	Figurative Language: You didn't use any! Try adding some where you get captured.
Spelling and Punctuation: You're a great speller!	Spelling and Punctuation: I don't think I saw the correct punctuation on same parts. You got one word misspelled! Uncarthous.
Believability: Your story is very believable. I like the names you used.	Believability: _____

FIGURE 7.5   Writing Rubric for English Language Arts

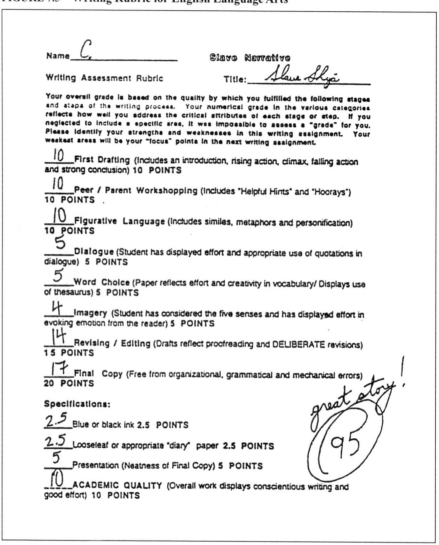

Name *C.* _____   Slave Narrative

Writing Assessment Rubric   Title: _*Slave Slya*_

Your overall grade is based on the quality by which you fulfilled the following stages and steps of the writing process. Your numerical grade in the various categories reflects how well you address the critical attributes of each stage or step. If you neglected to include a specific area, it was impossible to assess a "grade" for you. Please identify your strengths and weaknesses in this writing assignment. Your weakest areas will be your "focus" points in the next writing assignment.

__*10*__First Drafting (Includes an introduction, rising action, climax, falling action and strong conclusion) 10 POINTS

__*10*__Peer / Parent Workshopping (Includes "Helpful Hints" and "Hoorays") 10 POINTS .

__*10*__Figurative Language (Includes similes, metaphors and personification) 10 POINTS

__*5*__Dialogue (Student has displayed effort and appropriate use of quotations in dialogue) 5 POINTS

__*5*__Word Choice (Paper reflects effort and creativity in vocabulary/ Displays use of thesaurus) 5 POINTS

__*4*__Imagery (Student has considered the five senses and has displayed effort in evoking emotion from the reader) 5 POINTS

__*14*__Revising / Editing (Drafts reflect proofreading and DELIBERATE revisions) 15 POINTS

__*17*__Final Copy (Free from organizational, grammatical and mechanical errors) 20 POINTS

great story!

Specifications:

__*2.5*__Blue or black ink 2.5 POINTS

__*2.5*__Looseleaf or appropriate "diary" paper 2.5 POINTS

__*5*__Presentation (Neatness of Final Copy) 5 POINTS

__*10*__ACADEMIC QUALITY (Overall work displays conscientious writing and good effort) 10 POINTS

(95)

historical fiction, and the ability to secure factual information through multiple sources. Students analyzed the information they found and pared the information down to the data most critical to the perspective they took in their journal writing. Clear connections across social studies and language arts were made as students discovered the knowledge required to write historical fiction. Through the rubrics and focused comment sheets, students engaged in a sophisticated evaluation of their tasks and products and those of others.

FIGURE 7.6   Example of Seventh-Grade Student's Historical Narrative

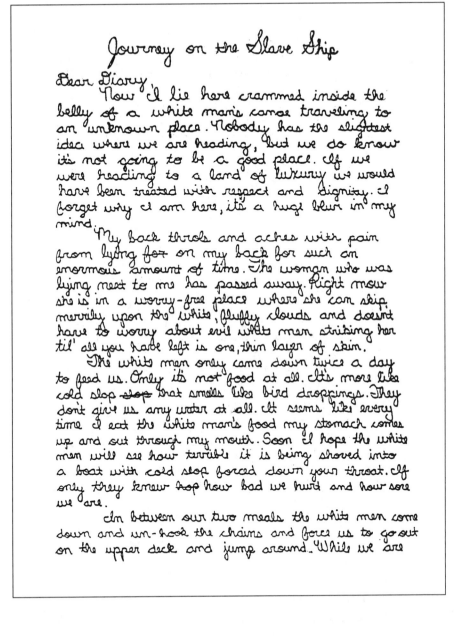

Journey on the Slave Ship

Dear Diary,
Now I lie here crammed inside the belly of a white man's canoe traveling to an unknown place. Nobody has the slightest idea where we are heading, but we do know it's not going to be a good place. If we were heading to a land of luxury we would have been treated with respect and dignity. I forget why I am here, it's a huge blur in my mind.

My back throbs and aches with pain from lying for on my back for such an enormous amount of time. The woman who was lying next to me has passed away. Right now she is in a worry-free place where she can skip merrily upon the white, fluffy, clouds and doesn't have to worry about evil white man striking her til' all you have left is one, thin layer of skin.

The white men only come down twice a day to feed us. Only it's not food at all. It's more like cold slop stop that smells like bird droppings. They don't give us any water at all. It seems like every time I eat the white man's food my stomach comes up and out through my mouth. Soon I hope the white men will see how terrible it is being shoved into a boat with cold slop forced down your throat. If only they knew top how bad we hurt and how sore we are.

In between our two meals the white men come down and un-hook the chains and force us to go out on the upper deck and jump around. While we are

FIGURE 7.6   *(continued)*

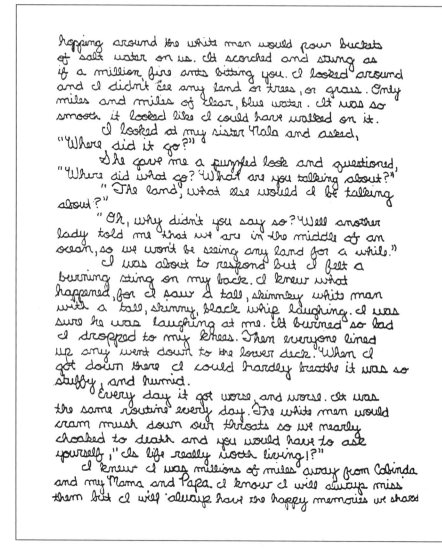

hopping around the white men would pour buckets of salt water on us. It scorched and stung as if a million fire ants biting you. I looked around and I didn't see any land or trees, or grass. Only miles and miles of clear, blue water. It was so smooth it looked like I could have walked on it.

I looked at my sister Nala and asked, "Where did it go?"

She gave me a puzzled look and questioned, "Where did what go? What are you talking about?"

"The land, what else would I be talking about?"

"Oh, why didn't you say so? Well another lady told me that we are in the middle of an ocean, so we won't be seeing any land for a while."

I was about to respond but I felt a burning sting on my back. I knew what happened, for I saw a tall, skinny white man with a tall, skinny, black whip laughing. I was sure he was laughing at me. It burned so bad I dropped to my knees. Then everyone lined up any went down to the lower deck. When I got down there I could hardly breathe it was so stuffy, and humid.

Every day it got worse, and worse. It was the same routine every day. The white men would cram mush down our throats so we nearly choaked to death and you would have to ask yourself, "Is life really worth living!?"

I knew I was millions of miles away from Cabinda and my Mama and Papa. I know I will always miss them but I will always have the happy memories we shared

Making Connections:
The Key to Middle-Grade Education

For students in middle school, the content and skills to be learned are highly complex. Teachers are challenged by the effort to make sense of the standards in one content area, let alone all those that a student must master. For the sake of the students, however, it is important to make connections and integrate learning tasks and activities; in the real world, we do not only do science. Steven Hawking, the famous scientist, did not make his contributions by working in a lab. He used his abilities to read, write, think, and do mathematics to develop and explain theories of the universe. That is authentic integration and authentic science.

If middle school teachers are going to address standards effectively, an essential approach is planning together. Only by working as a community of educators, supporting the teaching and learning of one another, can middle school teachers hope to integrate and relate learning across domains in ways that increase the likelihood of increased student success and achievement. The science teacher, for example, needs to talk to English and math teachers about how to address mutual goals.

A word of caution, however. In the writing assignment for science described above, students were required to apply a substantial understanding of complex scientific processes to the task. The content was challenging. Would students grow in their understanding of content if they were given tasks that looked like integration of content but in actuality offered little possibility for the demonstration of deep understanding of content or complex skills? Probably not. Think of how much richer the photosynthesis writing assignment was than a task that asked students to "write about a day in the life of a leaf." The latter assignment can be a vehicle for creative writing, but it does not afford the same type of opportunity for demonstrating a deep understanding of complex content knowledge.

Conclusion

There is no denying that standards, at the national and even at the state level, are challenging teachers and students to accomplish more. For teachers, whether new or seasoned, it will be necessary to explore more content and new pedagogy. Most standards call for a deeper understanding of basics as well as learning more challenging skills and concepts. To help all students, including those previously passed up as incapable, to meet the standards, teachers will need to have a better understanding of the content and skills themselves and will need to stretch their instructional abilities. Although such complexity may be possible by a single teacher, the opportunities for student success may be multiplied through collaboration with colleagues. Teachers can do this if they help one another. If they do approach the challenge as a community of educators who are also learners themselves, it is likely that they will not only help their students learn more, but they will find a deeper engagement and reward in their own tasks and learning. They will be modeling the very authentic aspect of being a scientist, a mathematician, or a writer. That is, the teachers themselves will be lifelong learners in their own content areas and will also be seeking learning in other domains. Such is the primary goal for students and teachers across all standards, across all grades.

REFERENCES

Council of Chief State School Officers. (1997). *Toolkit: Evaluating the development and implementation of standards.* Washington, DC: Author.

Jerald, C.D., Curran, B.K., & Olson, L. (1998, January 8). The state of the states. *Education Week,* pp. 76–77.

National Council for the Social Studies. (1994). *Curriculum standards for social studies.* Washington, DC: Author.

National Council of Teachers of English/International Reading Association. (1996). *Standards for the English language arts.* Urbana, IL: Author.

National Council of Teachers of Mathematics. (1989). *Curriculum and evaluation standards for school mathematics.* Reston, VA: Author.

National Research Council. (1996). *National science education standards.* Washington, DC: National Academy Press.

Olson, L. (1995, April 12). The view from the classroom. *Education Week,* pp. 47–48.

Vygotsky, L.S. (1978). *Mind in society.* Cambridge, MA: Harvard University Press.

Wolk, R.A., Edwards, V.B., & Olson, L. (Eds.). (1995, April 12). On assignment special pull out report: Struggling for standards [Special issue]. *Education Week,* pp. 4–20.

PART TWO

Literacy and the Intermediate and Middle School Learner

Developmental Tasks of Early Adolescence

The Foundation of an Effective Literacy Learning Program

JUDITH L. IRVIN

SUSAN E. STRAUSS

Florida State University

Edward walked the crowded halls between classes, joking and laughing as he planned activities with this friends. He eagerly reported results of the weekend soccer game and touted his accomplishments on a video game. Because he is an excellent cartoonist, his friends often asked for a sketch. Edward was obviously engaged in communication. During the next class, however, this verbally proficient young man sat in the last seat of the farthest row away from the teacher. He rarely read or wrote anything; consequently, he was failing all his classes that required reading and writing.

Hallways filled with young adolescents teem with language. Young adolescents read, write, speak, listen, think, and solve problems enthusiastically and for a good reason: They wish to communicate. The challenge of every middle-grades teacher is to connect this heartbeat of the hallway filled with the relevance of communication to classroom instruction.

Literacy programs for middle-grades students are often driven by the frustration of teachers, parents, and administrators over low-performing readers and writers. Parent teacher organization or school advisory council meetings seem to avow each year a new commitment to a focus on reading. Educators, of course, yearn to help the less able reader become more successful; it is right and good that programs be designed to help struggling readers and writers. It is also appropriate to provide the opportunity for all middle-grades students to increase their ability to become more literate. Even if students *can* read, many of them *do not* read. Even proficient readers should be challenged by more difficult, longer, and a wider variety of text and learn to think critically about it. In additon, all middle-grades students should learn strategies for studying and continue to increase their vocabulary knowledge. This literacy learning does not occur without a deliberate, planned, sequenced literacy learning program.

"Students in the middle years face increasingly complex literacy challenges as they move from a curriculum where acquiring initial literacy knowledge and competencies permeates the school day, to a time when their literacy skills and interests are prerequisites for success across the school curriculum" (Hosking & Teberg, 1998, p. 332). Concurrent to the difficulty young adolescents may have in dealing with increasingly complex literacy challenges is the rapidly changing nature of the physical, socio-emotional, cognitive, and moral growth they experience during early adolescence.

Literacy learning can facilitate young adolescents' progress through these essential stages; conversely, as young adolescents work through these developmental tasks, they become more adept at literacy. Language development parallels growth in socio-emotional and cognitive growth for middle-grades students (Vygotsky, 1962). Literacy learning is not only essential for success in later school experiences and everyday life, but it facilitates necessary transition through the developmental tasks of early adolescence.

The National Assessment of Educational Progress defines literacy as "using printed and written information to function in society, to achieve goals, and to develop knowledge and potential" (Keller-Cohen, 1993, p. 294). Using this definition, we describe the overall status of current literacy programs in the United States and provide suggestions for the design of a comprehensive literacy program for young adolescents. In addition, we present a brief overview of the developmental tasks that challenge young adolescents and developmentally effective approaches that serve as a foundation to a dynamic literacy learning program.

Status of Current Literacy Programs

Operating under the assumption that only those students who are less proficient readers and writers need any type of systematic reading instruction, some middle-level educators offer only remedial reading instruction, whereas others offer no systematic instruction at all. "Almost half of the middle schools offer no systematic reading instruction . . . [and] approximately one-third of middle schools offer a semester-long remedial reading course at all grade levels" (Irvin & Connors, 1989, p. 306). Remedial courses generally consist of skill instruction and vocabulary development and are based on the reading of (primarily) narrative text. Consequently, the reading instruction students receive in remedial classes is quite different from the reading demands placed on them in their content area classes.

Developmental reading classes are offered in about 60% of middle schools (Irvin & Connors, 1989). Typically, these classes are offered as elective classes and most often to sixth-grade students as part of a "wheel" of exploratory classes such as computer classes or art. Developmental reading classes usually include the development of comprehension, vocabulary, flexible reading rates, and study strategies (Irvin, 1997). This type of reading class is sometimes taught in relative isolation to the students' content area reading requirements, but reading teachers who communicate with content area teachers about the types of reading required of students and who incorporate reading strategies and appropriate vocabulary development into developmental reading classes help to integrate and facilitate students' more complex reading needs.

Teaching reading through the content areas has been a recommended approach to reading instruction for secondary students since the early 1900s (Moore, Readence, & Rickelman, 1983). Using this approach, content area teachers teach reading strategies that enable students to comprehend the expository text used in the class better; ideally, a reading specialist is available to help the content area teacher with resources and individual student concerns. Content area teachers, however, are often pressed by the demands of the discipline in which they teach and do not see themselves as teachers of reading. Therefore, although it is often offered as a theoretical option for a reading program, the integration of reading and content instruction does not seem to be widely applied across the country (Gee & Forester, 1988; Irvin & Connors, 1989; Witte & Otto, 1981).

Some middle-level educators seek to include reading instruction within the language arts class or classes. By using an integrated language arts approach, teachers more and more are using some form of a reading and writing workshop, first introduced by Atwell (1987) in her book *In the Middle: Writing, Reading, and Learning with Adolescents*. This type of approach includes student choices of books and writing topics, talking to one another about their writing and reading, and direct instruction focused on the reading and writing needs of individual students. An integrated language arts approach is difficult to implement in a typical class period; those who successfully use this approach to reading instruction usually allocate longer blocks of time during the school day for the language arts.

All these approaches can be designed to help middle-grades students become more literate. In fact, a multifaceted schoolwide approach is desirable. The starting point in planning a literacy learning program, however, is the nature and needs of the young adolescent learner.

The Developmental Tasks of Early Adolescence

Anyone who has walked the halls of a middle-level school has probably encountered flying arms and legs, changing voices, and behavior that ranges from childish to mature. Within any middle-grades classroom, it is common to find students varying in height from 6 to 8 inches and in weight as much as 40 to 60 pounds. More extreme differences are not uncommon. This variety in physical growth is further compounded by a wide range of emotional maturity, intellectual ability, attentiveness, and interest. To make life still more interesting, individual students, reacting to changes in their bodies, may not even display the same behavior from day to day. All these factors make the middle-level school a fascinating place in which to teach.

Knowledge of the rapid and profound changes that young adolescents experience can help teachers understand, if not fully endorse, the behavior they display. With the onset of puberty, students undergo a series of swift and dramatic physical changes. Along with these physical changes are changes in intellectual capacity and emotional stability. Many students begin to develop the ability to think abstractly. Well known to most middle-level teachers is that students' emotions tend to run high at this age and are often unpredictable. This period of life is also characterized by a new sense of social awareness in which students move from the security of the family to an added dependence on relationships with their peers. Coping with and adapting to all these new experiences is often difficult for young adolescents. A developmentally appropriate literacy program can facilitate a successful transition to young adulthood.

Physical Development

The most dramatic and obvious changes are, of course, those associated with rapid physical growth and development. Puberty is preceded by a growth spurt in which there is a marked increase in height, weight, heart rate, lung capacity, and muscular strength. Bone grows faster than muscle, which may leave bones unprotected by muscles and tendons. Middle-level students often have problems with coordination as a result of this rapid growth; thus, they are often characterized as awkward. Although all young adolescents experience this growth spurt, girls tend to undergo these changes approximately two years earlier than boys.

Sexual maturation is the other obvious physical change to which young adolescents must adjust. The average age at onset of puberty shows a trend toward earlier occurrence due to improvements in nutrition and general health care (Brooks-Gunn & Reiter, 1990). Physical changes are viewed as a cultural event that marks a transition clearly visible to peers and adults. Whenever young people experience these changes, the appearance of secondary sex characteristics often makes them self-conscious about their bodies. Being "off time" with respect to maturation—maturing physically either earlier or later than most of one's peers—is what generally causes concern in young adolescents.

Whether on or off time, most educators agree that, at this age, physical differences between students should be minimized by adults and in the school setting. Group showers and competitive sports, for example, merely accentuate the differences in physical ability and development. Information about the variability of growth spurts can be used to provide some reassurance for these students. Also, reading stories and novels about other young adolescents dealing with life changes helps students realize that their development, whether early or late, is normal. Reflective journals or letters to friends about these issues decrease their isolation and feeling of self-consciousness.

Socioemotional Development

Those who live and work with young adolescents know that peers and social relationships are of extreme importance. Friendships are vital at this age, especially same-sex relationships. Feeling comfortable and secure with peers of the same sex at ages 10 to 12 helps young adolescents progress toward opposite-sex relationships, which come later. Because rejection by peers represents a major crisis, students at this age spend much of their time trying to figure out ways to win acceptance by their peers. "Friends allow us to compare families, contrast values, and take risks. Their reactions to our dress, our jokes, our athletic ability, and our appearance allow us to measure our ability in these areas" (Milgram, 1992, p. 19). Socialization is a developmental task of early adolescence.

Social validation is important for young adolescents to build and to maintain a positive self-concept (Lipka, 1997; Milgram, 1985). It is, therefore, imperative that educators recognize the developmental needs of young adolescents and provide opportunities for appropriate socialization. Middle-level schools that accommodate rather than deny this socialization facilitate growth in this important developmental task.

Emotions, both happy and sad, run high at this age. A teacher may observe the same girl happy and giggling at one minute and sad and tearful the next minute. These extremes in emotion, probably caused by hormonal activity, are normal experiences and are heightened by the young adolescents' feelings of confusion about the changes within themselves and about their place within the social group.

Changes in intellectual functioning may be the partial cause of emotional changes. "The advent of formal operational thought is considered by most to be a prerequisite for adolescent self-reflection. The very ability to think about one's thinking, to reflect on internal events, does not become fully developed until this period" (Harter, 1990, p. 362). Sometime during the middle years, young adolescents recognize that they are the potential focus of another's attention. For the first time in their development, they are able to take the other person's perspective. This new perspective leads to an egocentrism in which they "assume themselves to be a focus of most other people's perspectives much of the time" (Steinberg, 1990, p. 271).

The development of a personal identity is really not possible until children move beyond concrete levels of thinking, which enables them to be self-conscious and introspective. The development of a positive self-esteem takes reflection, introspection, comparisons with others, and a sensitivity to the opinions of other people. These processes only become possible with the advent of formal thinking.

In a thorough review of relevant literature on self-esteem, Kohn (1994) questioned the value of "programs" designed to enhance self-esteem. Educators would do better to treat students with "respect [rather] than shower them with praise" (p. 282). "When members of a class meet to make decisions and solve problems, they get the self-esteem building message that their voices count, they experience a sense of belonging to a community, and they hone their ability to reason and analyze" (p. 279). A meaningful curriculum (Beane & Lipka, 1986), a safe and intellectual challenge (Wigfield & Eccles, 1994), and meaningful success experiences (Kohn, 1994) lead to the long lasting development of positive self-esteem.

The onset of formal thinking triggers a host of emotional tasks to be completed, not the least of which is the development of a positive self-esteem and some degree of autonomy from parents and teachers. New cognitive capacities often lead to difficulty in controlling and applying them. The by-products of this difficulty are emotional turmoil, erratic behavior, and egocentrism. Although these characteristics are troublesome for adults and students alike, they are a natural part of the transition to adulthood.

Time to talk about events in novels or information in a textbook is essential so that students can understand, internalize, and benefit from new insights. Not only does guided discussion help students learn social skills, but this discussion helps them respond to reading and writing in a more authentic context. During these success-oriented, nonthreatening discussions, students receive validation for their ideas and opinions and have the opportunity to consider the viewpoints of others. They participate in real literacy discussions and have the opportunity to form a positive self-esteem and make positive progress toward autonomy.

Cognitive Development

An understanding of the cognitive changes that take place in students is of paramount importance in planning a meaningful literacy program and establishing appropriate classroom practices. This age is characterized by a new capacity for thought. Students are moving from the "concrete" stage (able to think logically about real experiences) to the "formal" stage (able to consider "what ifs," think reflectively, and reason abstractly). This intellectual change is gradual and may occur at different times for different students, but it generally begins at age 12 and is not firmly established until about age 15 or 16. Students may even shift back and forth from the concrete to the abstract, although it is important to remember that not all young adolescents, and not even all adults, achieve this capacity.

Cognitive growth is intricately linked to social and emotional development. In fact, this new capacity for abstract thinking helps young adolescents make sense of new social demands, new feelings, and an emerging self-concept. Social and emotional growth and cognitive functioning work hand in hand to facilitate the developmental of all areas. Abstract thinking is developed as young people struggle to make sense of their feelings, the behavior of others, and their place within a social context.

The cognitive activity called metacognition actually regulates and controls social and emotional activity. Metacognition is "the ability to monitor one's own cognitive activity for consistency, [and] for gaps in information that need to be filled" (Keating, 1990, p. 75). It is important to remember, however, that these new metacognitive abilities for young adolescents represent "potential accomplishments rather than typical everyday thinking" (p. 65). During early adolescence, students are practicing this new ability. Like any new skill, formal reasoning must be practiced repeatedly in a safe, encouraging environment.

Young adolescents often have difficulty with such tasks as analyzing political cartoons and understanding metaphors. Students do, however, need to personalize the abstract. This practice helps students make the transition to consistent formal reasoning. Inferential leaps should be small, and sometimes minuscule, for young adolescents to "get" to the level of abstract thinking. Strahan and Toepfer (1984) hypothesized that "latent formal thinkers" can solve problems if given a second try and a moderate amount of prompting. Cooperative learning, guided discussion groups, and reflective journals allow the potential "latent formal thinkers" a chance to explore abstract thought in a success-oriented way.

The young adolescent is egocentric, but the emerging formal thinker is, for the first time, able to consider the thoughts of others. Discussion and debate help students consider issues that are important to them and resolve conflicting viewpoints; they are forced to reexamine their own views in light of the views of others. Students can, for the first time, conceive of what might be possible or what might occur rather than merely what is. This process of social interaction enables young adolescents to mature both socially and intellectually.

Moral Development

The development of character is intricately linked to socioemotional and cognitive growth. A new capacity for abstract thinking allows the "what ifs," but social and emotional growth provides the context for the answers. "Character develops within a social web or environment" (Leming, 1993, p. 69). Reference groups such as families, peer groups, and television are particularly important as students seek to understand their place in the world (Rice, 1990). Young adolescents form lifelong self-concepts and identities. "Middle school students can be helped to think about who they are and who they want to be, to form identities as self-respecting, career minded persons" (Davis, 1993, p. 32). Events in history, new technologies, the ethics of science, or characters in novels are worthy of value analysis.

Young adolescents will acquire a value system with or without the help of parents and teachers. At a stage of development when students are emerging as reflective citizens, educators can still help students to be consciously aware of constructive values, to think logically about consequences, to empathize with others, and to make personal commitments to constructive values and behavior (Davis, 1993).

The onset of adolescence brings with it a profound set of physical, social, emotional, and intellectual changes. More than at any other stage of life, the young adolescent is in a state of flux. Rapid physical growth is accompanied by sexual maturation and changes in basal metabolism. An increased social awareness gives rise to an increased emphasis on peer relations. Emotions, stirred by hormonal and psychological changes, run high, and many young adolescents begin to experiment with abstract thinking.

Those who make decisions regarding literacy learning during the middle grades must understand and accommodate the physical and psychological needs of young adolescents. Middle-level students need to move and change activities frequently, to engage in positive social interaction with peers, to move slowly and successfully from the concrete to the abstract, and to gain confidence and emotional stability through success and the development of self-worth.

Effective Approaches to Literacy Learning

Brian was a bright student; he managed to pass most of his classes even though he spent a fair amount of his time at school involved in some type of disciplinary "incident." He had a hair-triggered temper and a flair for inciting others. If there was an altercation of any sort at school, Brian was most certainly involved. He seemed, more and more, to become caught up in a cycle of fighting and subsequent discipline.

When presented with the opportunity to choose a young adult novel to read and then present to the class, the media specialist suggested to Brian that he read *Fallen Angels* (Myers, 1993). Although his teacher showed some concern about the length of the book (over 300 pages), Brian quickly became caught up in this story about a small group of young marines trying to survive their tours of duty in the Vietnam War. He read quietly during times provided in class and wrote reflective entries about the book in his journal. When the time came for him to give his presentation to the class, he brought in a collage of pictures that depicted themes of war and personal choices. He spoke knowledgeably about the book and compassionately about its subject. *Fallen Angels* had obviously been an important book to Brian, and his classmates were surprised by his involvement in this project. Brian later told his teacher that it was the best book he had ever read.

What were the components of this "literacy event" that enabled a somewhat troubled young adolescent (along with the rest of his classmates) to succeed and flourish in the classroom? First, each student could choose the book he or she would read from a list of young adult novels the teacher had compiled from respected resources and personal experience. Sometimes, teachers and media specialists can recommend books that they think students would like, or book talks and sharing student favorites can help students make book choices. Second, students were given time in school to read and respond in personal journals. As they finished reading, the teacher conducted individual conferences that were guided in part by these entries. A third component was student choice in the final project. Some students wrote scenes that could have occurred (but did not) in the book; some put together sample "newspapers" that included articles about characters in the books; yet others dressed as a character and gave a monologue or acted out a scene from the book. Fourth, the students had opportunities to write and talk about their books from their own perspectives, thus communicating orally and in writing the way real readers do. "Engaging students in literacy events requires shifts in the control teachers give to students, the models teachers provide, the tasks they assign and schedule, and the literacy materials they use" (Roe, 1997, p. 38).

Students need to be engaged in literacy events, but they must also be enabled (Roe, 1997). To enable students means that individual students' reading and writing development are regularly assessed and that student needs, not curricular demands, drive classroom instruction. To meet the increasing demands for the reading and comprehension of expository text in the middle grades, students need to be taught reading strategies. Direct instruction of reading strategies that help students activate prior knowledge and organize expository text can help students deal successfully with the more challenging types of reading expected of them in the middle grades (Dole, Brown, & Trathen, 1996; Irvin, 1998; Roe, 1997).

To enable students as critical thinkers, teachers can provide them with opportunities to discuss text that is relevant and thought-provoking. Teaching students to ask questions of text, to base opinions on text, and to discuss disparate opinions in an objective manner all contribute to the young adolescent's socioemotional, cognitive, and moral development. The ever-present media can also be a tool used in the teaching of critical and analytical thinking.

The use of the Socratic seminar is another way to engage students in active, critical dialogue. After reading a text, students ask questions about the reading and in response to other student comments. They are engaged in "disciplined conversation"; the seminar is designed so that students will develop abilities such as discussing ideas and values, solving abstract problems, making more mature decisions, resolving conflicts between people and ideas, and applying knowledge and skills to new situations (Chesser, Gellatly, & Hale, 1997, p. 41). As students become proficient in forming thoughtful ideas and making meaning from abstract concepts, feelings of self-worth grow. Students who feel competent feel good about themselves (Tredway, 1995).

Developmentally appropriate classroom approaches are essential to helping students develop their literacy abilities and make a graceful transition to adulthood. These classroom approaches alone, however, fall short of maximizing student potential. Implementing a schoolwide literacy program provides a literate environment in which learning is planned, sequenced, and reinforced across the curriculum and throughout the school day.

Components of a Schoolwide Literacy Program

"High performing schools for young adolescents are developmentally responsive. They act on the knowledge that the imperatives of early adolescent development are too compelling to be denied. They adapt school practices to this knowledge" (Lipsitz, Jackson, & Austin, 1997, p. 535). Components of a successful schoolwide literacy program include:

A Schoolwide Vision and Commitment to Literacy Learning.   Creating a literate environment cannot be successful if implemented by only a few "key people." All teachers, administrators, parents, and staff of the middle-level school must endorse and participate in the literacy program. School advisory groups that include literacy learning as a goal for the entire school are more likely to address schoolwide concerns and goals for literacy learning in a comprehensive and integrated fashion than other groups. Administrator support for this focus on literacy is imperative.

A Reading/Literacy Committee.   Made up of the school media specialist, reading specialist, teachers from various (not just language arts) content areas, administrators, and parent and student volunteers, this committee can direct, revitalize, and sustain the focus on literacy learning. The tasks of this committee include planning, coordinating, and evaluating schoolwide literacy events, administering and interpreting tests, working with content area teachers to reinforce learning strategies, planning staff development, and locating resources from the community.

A Vision of the School Media Center as the "Hub" of the School.   Through the use of programs designed to grab the attention of students, motivating contests, tutoring and homework programs, and consistent classroom use of technical tools and reference materials, the media center becomes an integral part of the school community. The media specialist can also work with classroom teachers to provide fresh collections of high-interest books for students. These collections can be integrated to support themes taught in the content areas or arranged by genre. Rotating and maintaining classroom collections exposes students to new titles and new authors and piques their interest in reading and responding to books.

Reading/Writing in the Content Areas.   Students in the middle grades must make the transition from reading and writing primarily narrative text in a (typically) self-contained elementary classroom to reading and writing text that is largely expository within various content areas. Young adolescents often need strategy instruction to comprehend expository text that may contain unfamiliar vocabulary and structure. Students particularly benefit from coordinating this instruction across the content areas. For example, students map information from a chapter in social studies and write from the mapped information to create a summary in language arts. Or, students complete a K-W-L+ (Carr & Ogle, 1987) chart in science and use that information in art or music to create a project. Eighty percent of the reading for middle-grades students is expository; the more students receive direct, sequenced, and reinforced instruction in learning strategies, the better equipped they will be to understand the demands of expository text.

A School Reading/Learning Specialist.   Essential to an effective schoolwide literacy program is a trained professional with a rich academic background in literacy learning. The reading/learning specialist should aid classroom teachers with materials and strategies for reading instruction, contribute to staff development that focuses on literacy, structure a reading program that meets the needs of a diverse group of students, and be actively involved with school decision making as it affects the culture of literacy in the school.

Ongoing Staff Development.   Providing teachers and administrators with the opportunity to learn about strategies for expository text, integrating of reading and writing activities in the subject areas, and student-centered classroom activities help them become more adept at creating literate environments for young adolescents. An essential starting point for all educators is learning the fundamentals of learning theory, including the concepts of schema and metacognition. Understanding how to build background information, activate prior knowledge, and evaluate understanding is essential in developing skill as a reader and writer. Tying these concepts to the developmental tasks of early adolescence provides the foundation of a middle school literacy program.

A Read-aloud Program.   Too often, reading aloud declines or stops altogether when students reach the middle grades. Older children and young adolescents still benefit from hearing interesting stories or information from an informational text read to them. Read-aloud sessions give them access to text they are not able to read themselves, expose them to a genre or author previously unknown or unappreciated, increase vocabulary development, aid in critical thinking, and encourage reading for sheer enjoyment.

All the benefits of reading aloud to students can be obtained in a language arts class, but reading aloud can also reinforce learning in other content areas as well.

Adults Who Model Engagement in Literacy Events. When students see teachers, coaches, principals, and parents engaged in reading or writing activities, they are more likely to view those activities as valuable. Sustained silent reading time is the perfect opportunity to invite guest readers to school from the community and expose students to opportunities to talk to adults about good books they have read.

A School Culture That Supports, Facilitates, and Celebrates Literacy Learning. Reward systems, the attitude of the media specialists, or the student work displayed in the halls (or lack thereof) can enhance or destroy efforts to maximize literacy learning. Schools that hold special assemblies, awards, and contests heighten engagement and remind members of the school community about what is considered important. Highlighting the literacy successes of students, teachers, and other members of the school community and telling stories about those who have experienced success in the areas of reading, writing, and speaking help to instill literacy as a valued aspect of the school culture (Irvin, 1997). A periodic "culture audit" (Champy, 1995; Fierson, 1997) of the school may eliminate the potential threat of sabotage to the literacy learning program.

Ongoing Assessment and Evaluation. Assessment of student achievement, teacher competence, and administrator support is necessary to guide decisions and changes in the program. In addition, ongoing evaluation of the program is necessary for success. Action research on classroom practices or schoolwide initiatives help direct decisions about the program.

Implementation of a successful schoolwide literacy program hinges on the support of faculty, parents, and school administrators. The majority of stakeholders in the school have to enthusiastically support a schoolwide program that serves the needs of the entire student body. When the goal of a schoolwide program is to meet the literacy needs of all students, not just those who are less proficient readers, a vision and commitment to literacy learning is likely. Adults who participate in and model literacy learning themselves help to create a rich environment for literacy learning, fostering a school culture in which literacy is valued. As teachers, parents, and school administrators work to maintain and improve the school culture of literacy, all students benefit.

Conclusion

Planning a schoolwide literacy program should begin with consideration of the developmental nature and needs of the young adolescent. The rapid and profound changes in physical, social, emotional, cognitive, and moral development affect the 10- to 14-year-old student in a plethora of ways. The young adolescent's behavior, feelings about self and others, thinking processes, socialization, and value system are all influenced by these developmental tasks.

When plans for instruction are guided by the developmental growth of the young adolescent, classrooms naturally become student centered. Students in the throes of early adolescence have varied and changing learning needs; instruction that allows for some student choice and independent learning will facilitate individual growth. Class time allotted for real "literacy events" such as reading engaging text, writing for authentic reasons, or participating in dynamic discussions communicates to students that teachers value literacy learning. Furthermore, teaching strategies that enable students to comprehend expository text enables them to meet the increased demands of a secondary school. Not only must educators understand young adolescent development, but they must also connect this understanding with a vision for a schoolwide program of literacy learning. The two are intricately linked. Consideration of the developmental tasks of early adolescence is the foundation of an effective literacy learning program in a middle-level school.

REFERENCES

Atwell, N.A. (1987). *In the middle: Writing, reading, and learning with adolescents.* Upper Montclair, NJ: Boynton/Cook.

Beane, J.A., & Lipka, R.P. (1986). *Self-concept, self-esteem, and the curriculum.* New York: Teachers College Press.

Brooks-Gunn, J., & Reiter, E.O. (1990). The role of pubertal processes. In S.S. Feldman & G.R. Elliott (Eds.), *At the threshold: The developing adolescent* (pp. 16–53). Cambridge, MA: Harvard University Press.

Carr, E., & Ogle, D. (1987). K-W-L Plus: A strategy for comprehension and summarization. *Journal of Reading, 30*(7), 626–631.

Champy, J. (1995). *Reengineering management: The mandate for new leadership.* New York: Harper-Collins.

Chesser, W.D., Gellatly, G.B., & Hale, M.S. (1997). Do Padeia seminars explain higher writing scores? *Middle School Journal, 29*(1), 40–45.

Davis, G.A. (1993). Creative teaching of moral thinking: Fostering awareness and commitment. *Middle School Journal, 24*(4), 32–33.

Dole, J.A., Brown, K.J., & Trathen, W. (1996). The effects of strategy instruction on the comprehension performance of at-risk students. *Reading Research Quarterly, 31*(1), 62–88.

Fierson, R. (1997). Creating a middle school culture of literacy. *Middle School Journal, 28*(3), 10–15.

Gee, T.C., & Forester, N. (1988). Moving reading instruction beyond the reading classroom. *Journal of Reading, 31*(6), 505–511.

Harter, S. (1990). Self and identity development. In S.S. Feldman & G.R. Elliott (Eds.), *At the threshold:*
The developing adolescent (pp. 352–387). Cambridge, MA: Harvard University Press.

Hosking, N.J., & Teberg, A.S. (1998). Bridging the gap: Aligning current practice and evolving expectations for middle years literacy programs. *Journal of Adolescent and Adult Literacy, 41*(5), 332–340.

Irvin, J.L. (1997). Building sound literacy programs for young adolescents. *Middle School Journal, 28*(3) 4–9.

———. (1998). *Reading and the middle school student: Strategies to enhance literacy* (2nd ed.). Boston: Allyn and Bacon.

Irvin, J.L., & Connors, N.A. (1989). Reading instruction in middle level schools: Results of a U.S. survey. *Journal of Reading, 32*(4), 306–311.

Keating, D. (1990). Adolescent thinking. In S.S. Feldman and G.R. Elliott (Eds.), *At the threshold: The developing adolescent* (pp. 54–89). Cambridge, MA: Harvard University Press.

Keller-Cohen, D. (1993). Rethinking literacy: Comparing colonial and contemporary America. *Anthropology and Education Quarterly, 24*(4), 288–307.

Kohn, A. (1994). The truth about self-esteem. *Phi Delta Kappan, 75*(1), 272–283.

Leming, J. S. (1993). In search of effective character education. *Educational Leadership, 51*(3), 63–71.

Lipka, R. (1997). Enhancing self-concept/self-esteem in young adolescents. In J. L. Irvin (Ed.), *What current research says to the middle level practitioner* (pp. 31–40). Columbus, OH: National Middle School Association.

Lipsitz, J., Jackson, A.W., & Austin, L.M. (1997). What works in middle-grades school reform. *Phi Delta Kappan, 7*(7), 517–556.

Milgram, J. (1985). The ninth grader: A profile. In J.H. Johnston (Ed.), *How fares the ninth grade?* (pp. 5–9). Reston, VA: National Association of Secondary School Principals.

———. (1992). A portrait of diversity: The middle level student. In J.L. Irvin (Ed.), *Transforming middle level education: Perspectives and possibilities* (pp. 16–27). Boston: Allyn and Bacon.

Moore, D.W., Readence, J.E., & Rickelman, R.J. (1983). An historical exploration of content area reading instruction. *Reading Research Quarterly, 18*(4), 421–438.

Myers, W.D. (1993). *Fallen angels.* New York: Scholastic.

Rice, F.P. (1990). *The adolescent: Development, relationships, and culture* (6th ed.). Boston: Allyn and Bacon.

Roe, M.F. (1997). Combining enablement and engagement to assist students who do not read and write well. *Middle School Journal, 28*(3), 35–41.

Steinberg, L. (1990). Autonomy, conflict, and harmony in the family relationship. In S.S. Feldman & G.R. Elliott (Eds.), *At the threshold: The developing adolescent* (pp. 255–276). Cambridge, MA: Harvard University Press.

Strahan, D., & Toepfer, C.J. (1984). The impact of brain research on education: Agents of change. In M. Frank (Ed.), *A child's brain.* New York: Haworth Press.

Tredway, L. (1995). Socratic seminars: Engaging students in intellectual discourse. *Educational Leadership, 53*(1), 26–29.

Vygotsky, L.S. (1962). *Thought and language.* Cambridge, MA: MIT Press.

Wigfield, A., & Eccles, J.S. (1994). Children's competence beliefs, achievement values, and general self-esteem: Change across elementary and middle school. *Journal of Early Adolescence, 14*(2), 102–106.

Witte, P.L., & Otto, W. (1981). Reading instruction at the postelementary level: Review and comments. *Journal of Educational Research, 74*(3), 148–158.

9 Motivation Matters

Fostering Full Access to Literacy

LINDA B. GAMBRELL
Clemson University

ANN J. DROMSKY
University of Maryland

SUSAN ANDERS MAZZONI
University of Maryland

Teachers and administrators who work with children in the intermediate grades recognize that motivation is at the heart of many of the pervasive problems faced in educating today's youth. There are far too many students in classrooms who seem unmotivated to learn. Research indicates that teachers rank *motivating* students as one of their primary and overriding concerns (O'Flahavan, Gambrell, Guthrie, Stahl, & Alvermann, 1992; Veenman, 1984). There is also converging evidence to suggest that motivation plays an important role in learning (Deci & Ryan, 1985; Dweck & Elliott, 1983; McCombs, 1989). There is an almost universal consensus that motivation makes the difference between learning that is superficial and shallow and learning that is deep and internalized (Gambrell & Codling, 1997). Clearly, we need to understand more fully how intermediate grade students acquire the motivation to develop into active, engaged readers and writers (Gambrell, 1996; Guthrie, Schafer, Wang, & Afflerbach, 1993; Oldfather, 1993).

Why is literacy motivation important? First, students who are motivated and who spend more time reading than other students are better readers (Anderson, Wilson, & Fielding, 1988; Taylor, Frye, & Maruyama, 1990). Second, some students, particularly those who have had more experiences with books and book language and those who have strong home support for literacy development, are better prepared for success at reading than others (Allington, 1991). Third, supporting and nurturing reading motivation and achievement is crucial to improving educational prospects for students who find learning to read difficult (Allington, 1986; Smith-Burke, 1989).

There is particular concern about reading motivation during the intermediate-grade years. Research reveals that students' intrinsic motivation for literacy learning may diminish as they make the transition from elementary to intermediate grades (Old-father, 1995). By fourth grade, some students begin to lose self-confidence, become anxious about school, and consequently engage in activities that inhibit rather than facilitate literacy learning. At this stage of development, motivational problems are often expressed in terms of low-effort expenditure, poor attention, high anxiety, or act-ing out (Stipek, 1988). Also, beginning in fourth grade, there is a shift in emphasis toward reading and gaining information from content area trade books and textbooks as well as extended expectations for independent learning from text and for indepen-dently producing written text. For some children, these texts and tasks can present significant difficulty and may result in high levels of anxiety and frustration. Unfortu-nately, there are also a considerable number of students in grades 4 through 8 who are at risk of reading failure. We know that many of these students are at a pivotal stage of academic achievement as they enter the intermediate grades and that attention to moti-vational factors related to literacy learning can make the difference between success and failure. According to Wilson (1995), past failure with reading typically results in low levels of motivation. It is students who have a history of low achievement in read-ing who are of particular concern in this chapter.

Clearly, intermediate-grade students must be supported and nurtured in both affective and cognitive aspects of literacy learning (Gambrell, 1995; Oldfather, 1993). In this chapter, we draw on motivational theory and research and provide suggestions for creating classroom cultures that foster literacy motivation.

What Does Learning Theory Tell Us about Creating Motivating Classroom Contexts for Literacy Learning?

In the 1990s, motivation gained prominence in numerous models of learning. Because depth and breadth of literacy learning are influenced by motivational factors (Ford, 1992; McCombs, 1991; Oldfather, 1993), researchers have attempted to explain *why* different students expend different amounts of time and effort on literacy tasks (Borkowski, Carr, Rellinger, & Pressley, 1990; Gambrell, 1996; Iran-Nejad, 1990; Pin-trich & DeGroot, 1990). Understanding motivational orientations can provide insight on how to create classroom contexts that foster literacy learning.

Learning theorists and educational researchers have put forth a vast number of ideas in their attempts to explain human motivation. Generally speaking, motivation involves processes that occur as students initiate and sustain goal-directed actions (Pin-trich & Schunk, 1996). Students who are motivated to engage in literacy tasks are interested in reading and writing, feel competent about their abilities, expend effort to be successful at literacy tasks, are persistent at these tasks, and use effective task and cognitive strategies in pursuit of their literacy goals. Because motivation is a pro-cess rather than a product (Pintrich & Schunk, 1996), we cannot observe motivation directly. We infer motivation from specific behaviors such as choice of tasks, effort expended on a task, persistence at completing a task, and verbal (e.g., "I really like this story!") or nonverbal (e.g., frowns, grimaces, avoidance) behaviors.

Although there are varying perspectives on motivation, the ideas are not necessarily incompatible. Theories related to intrinsic and extrinsic motivation, value-expectancy theory, and self-determination theory provide insights for literacy instruction that are particularly relevant to students in the intermediate grades.

Supporting the Development of Intrinsic Literacy Motivation

Motivation theorists make a distinction between extrinsic and intrinsic motivation. Extrinsic motivation refers to forces that are external to an individual that influence their inclination to engage in a particular behavior such as reading or writing. For instance, offering students candy or free time in exchange for a specified behavior is considered a form of extrinsic motivation. On the other hand, behavior that is motivated by internal needs, desires, or feelings is considered intrinsic. Students who behave appropriately in a classroom setting out of a sense of pride are considered intrinsically motivated. The concepts of intrinsic and extrinsic motivation are very broad and can be applied to many aspects of literacy behavior. Specifically, research indicates that a student's perception of the intrinsic or extrinsic value associated with literacy tasks is an important aspect of literacy motivation (Cameron & Pierce, 1994; Gambrell, 1996; Gambrell & Marinak, 1997; Palmer, Codling, & Gambrell, 1994).

Intrinsic motivation appears to be based on two components, both of which seem important to an individual's engagement in literacy activities and events (Spaulding, 1992). The first component, competence, involves the student's knowledge that he or she is capable of successfully engaging in the literacy task at hand. The second component, self-determination, is the ingredient that makes the student feel as if he or she has some degree of control over the task. Deci, Vallerand, Pelletier, and Ryan (1991) developed a theory of self-determination that expands on the concepts of intrinsic and extrinsic motivation. They pointed out that student actions are "self-determined," or intrinsically motivated, to the extent that the student is engaged volitionally. Research by Deci et al. (1991) found that intermediate-grade students who were self-determined, or intrinsically motivated, displayed greater conceptual understanding and better memory than students who were extrinsically motivated. On the other hand, student actions are "controlled," or extrinsically motivated, if students are compelled to engage in the actions as a result of some interpersonal (i.e., a bribe) or intrapsychic (i.e., guilt) force.

In a demonstration of the effects of extrinsic motivation on learning, Deci et al. (1991) conducted an experiment in which they informed some students that learning text material would help them on an upcoming test (a bribe), whereas other students were simply instructed about the importance and relevance of the text material. They found that the students who were told that learning the text material would help them on an upcoming test did more poorly than students who were not told about the test. This line of research suggests that emphasizing the relevance and value of learning to students is a more powerful motivational force than external forces such as getting a better grade on a test. In this study, intrinsically motivated students had higher achievement and reported more positive classroom attitudes and greater enjoyment of school work than did the extrinsically motivated students.

Reward and recognition systems such as honor rolls and achievement awards are usually implemented to motivate students in their academic endeavors. The ultimate goal of most reward and recognition systems is to motivate the unmotivated. The use of extrinsic rewards can, however, under certain conditions, undermine the development of instrinsic motivation (Cameron & Pierce, 1994; Lepper & Hodell, 1989). These reward systems give students the message that *demonstrating* ability rather than *increasing* ability is the goal. These methods of recognition do not take into consideration students' entering aptitudes. Midgley and Urdan (1992) described research- and theory-based principles of recognition that can be used to provide recognition to a wide range of students for their intellectual contributions. The following suggestions, adapted from Midgley and Urdan (1992, p. 252), focus on important considerations for fostering intrinsic motivation in all students, particularly the lower achieving, less motivated student:

1. Recognize individual student effort, accomplishment, and improvement (examples: rising star awards when a student increases his or her score by a certain number of points; personal best awards when a student reaches a score that represents a new high for him or her).
2. Give all students opportunities to be recognized.
3. Give recognition privately whenever possible.
4. Avoid using *most* or *best* for recognizing student work, as in "best project" or "most improved." These words usually convey comparisons with others.
5. Avoid using the same criteria for all students. For example, avoid giving an award to "all students who get an A on the test," or "all students who read 10 books."
6. Recognize students for doing challenging work or for stretching their own abilities, even if they make mistakes. This recognition gives a strong and important message about what is valued in the classroom.
7. Recognize students for coming up with different and unusual interpretations, new ways to solve a problem, or a novel approach to a task.
8. Recognize the quality rather than the quantity of students' work. For example, recognizing students for reading a lot of books might only encourage them to read easier and shorter books.
9. Avoid recognizing and stressing grades and test scores, which diminish the emphasis on learning and problem solving.
10. Recognition must be honest and based on reality. For example, do not recognize students for improving if they have not improved or for trying hard if that is not the case. Trust will be diminished if recognition is not based on real accomplishment. The important factor is communicating to students that they have the opportunity to be recognized in these areas.

Taken together, research studies support the notion that self-determination and intrinsic motivation are fostered in classrooms in which the relevance, value, and importance of learning are made explicit to students. The basic premise behind self-determination theory is that intrinsic motivation is a desirable goal that supports three inherent human needs that are of critical importance during the intermediate grade years: competence, relatedness, and autonomy (Deci & Ryan, 1991). A classroom climate that enhances opportunities for meeting the needs of competence, relatedness, and autonomy will foster self-determination.

Supporting the Need for Competence in Literacy Learning

Competence relates to the student's feelings of capability for accomplishing tasks. In the intermediate grades, students are in a developmental period characterized by rapid and varied physical, cognitive, and emotional growth that often causes them to feel unsure of themselves and to lack self-confidence (Wilson, 1995). Literacy tasks and events that focus on what students *can* do well and that are challenging help them develop feelings of literacy competence.

Important changes occur in children's conceptions of ability and intelligence during early adolescence. Very young children tend to believe that they can learn anything if they just try hard enough. They interpret lack of ability as the failure to try hard enough. During early adolescence, however, children begin to view ability as capacity relative to that of their peers (Harari & Covington, 1981; Nicholls, 1986). These beliefs are critical in determining whether learning is pursued or abandoned. Children who believe that ability is "fixed," or determined by intelligence, are more likely to have maladaptive patterns of learning. Those who believe that ability is "modifiable," or related to effort, display more adaptive and effective patterns of learning. Midgley (1993) pointed out that it is important to recognize that the classroom context can create strong tendencies for students to adopt one conception of ability over another. For example, in a study by Bempechat, London, and Dweck (1991), children who were told that the acquisition of a new ability depended on effort displayed more adaptive learning patterns than those who were told that the new ability was something with which people were endowed.

Although conventional wisdom suggests that tasks that are very easy and result in success will result in increased motivation to learn, Colvin and Schlosser's (1997/1998) research suggested that the opposite may be closer to the mark. Their work revealed that students' perceptions of themselves as less capable learners are often reinforced when they are given literacy tasks that are "easy" and less challenging than those assigned to their peers. Colvin and Schlosser (1997/1998) found that students responded positively to learning tasks that challenged them and required them to make an investment of time and effort. They suggested that teachers think in terms of Vygotsky's (1986) zone of proximal development and provide students with reading material that is slightly beyond their level to complete when working alone, but that they can successfully read when they receive assistance from the teacher. In general, research suggests that feelings of competence and increased motivation result from completing tasks that require effort and investment of time and energy, rather than tasks that are easily and quickly completed (Colvin & Schlosser, 1997/1998; Gambrell, 1996; Oldfather, 1993).

Value-expectancy theory emphasizes the importance of self-perceptions about literacy competence (Eccles & Midgley, 1989). This theory suggests that we need to help students realize the critical link between effort and success. Helping students to reexamine their attributions for success and failure may help them change negative perceptions they have of themselves as learners and readers. This aid may be especially important for students who have experienced repeated past failure and have developed negative attitudes toward reading and writing.

We know that feelings of competence increase when students experience success at reading tasks that are challenging and require effort on their part. Such experiences reinforce a positive self-concept as a reader and increase the likelihood that the student will be intrinsically motivated to engage in subsequent reading tasks. Pintrich, Roeser, and DeGroot (1994) suggested that teachers employ literacy tasks that promote deep cognitive engagement, such as higher-level questions and requesting written work that requires this type of thinking. "By considering both student motivation and cognition and how they are influenced by the nature of classroom instruction and tasks, teachers will be able to create classrooms that are both motivating and thoughtful, a context that can only benefit the development of young adolescents" (Pintrich, Roeser, & DeGroot, p. 159).

Supporting the Need for Relatedness in Literacy Learning

Students in the intermediate grades are at a developmental stage that is characterized by an increasing need to feel related, especially with respect to their peer group. This strong desire for relatedness refers to the development of relationships with others in the social context in which the activity occurs. One of the most robust findings in the research literature is the positive effect of social interaction on learning (Gambrell, 1996; Johnson & Johnson, 1985; Slavin, 1984). Opportunities for social interaction with peers foster feelings of relatedness. When creating literacy events for intermediate-grade students, we need to keep in mind the importance of having students engage in book-sharing activities, discussion groups, and small group sharing of student-authored text.

Guthrie, Alao, and Rinehart (1997) emphasized the need for students to engage in collaborative literacy learning activities. They suggested that balance is appropriate, with some work being completed individually and some work being completed in groups. Many opportunities can be provided during literacy instruction for students to work together to formulate questions, conduct observations and experiments, and find answers to their questions. Groups can then present their findings to their class or other groups. Collaboration fosters feelings of relatedness, and according to Guthrie et al. (1997) and Heath (1991), participation in collaborative social groups contributes to increased literacy engagement.

Supporting the Need for Autonomy in Literacy Learning

Autonomy refers to the student's ability to initiate actions and regulate those actions independently (Deci & Ryan, 1991). As students enter the intermediate-grade years, they begin to want more control over their own lives and learning. Three areas of importance in creating a classroom climate that fosters literacy motivation and autonomy are choice, materials, and time.

Choice.   There is some evidence that teachers who provide opportunities for students to make choices and decisions about their learning are more effective in facilitating intrinsic motivation in their students than teachers who do not provide such opportunities. Furthermore, a number of studies have shown that, compared to elementary teachers, teachers in the intermediate grades believe that they must control students more and trust them less (Midgley, Feldlaufer, & Eccles, 1989; Moos, 1979; Sweeting, Willower, & Helsel, 1978; Willower & Lawrence, 1979). More specifically, research based on both student and teacher reports revealed that intermediate-grade teachers were more oriented to control than elementary teachers (Sweeting, Willower, & Helsel, 1978; Willower & Lawrence, 1979). Other researchers have documented that a warm, supportive environment in which students are given opportunities to make learning choices and decisions is associated with positive motivational outcomes (Feldlaufer, Midgley, & Eccles, 1988; Fraser & Fisher, 1982; Moos, 1979).

Research indicates that students exhibit more positive motivational patterns when their teachers provide them with opportunities to make choices about their learning (deCharms, 1980; Ryan & Grolnick, 1986). Furthermore, the work of Oldfather (1995) suggested that intermediate-grade students want to feel as if they have some authority or voice in their learning. Research by Gambrell, Dromsky, and Mazzoni (1998), Midgley (1993), and Mizelle (1997) suggested that choice is positively related to motivation to read. Across all these studies, students were more motivated to read when they chose their own reading materials.

In studies conducted by Gambrell and colleagues (Gambrell, 1996; Gambrell et al., 1998), fifth- and eighth-grade students were asked to tell about the "most interesting" narrative and informational text they had read recently. The overwhelming majority of both the fifth- and eighth-grade readers reported that they had self-selected these materials. Students frequently commented that they had selected a book because a teacher or friend had recommended it or told them about it. The responses of these fifth- and eighth-grade students suggest an important relationship between choice and social interactions with others about text. Choice allows students to voice preferences for engagement in reading and writing activities and to experience some control over their learning environment. Students need to play an important role in suggesting and selecting reading materials and topics for writing.

Letting students choose what they read, and even when and where they read, increases intrinsic motivation and supports the development of autonomy. Younger and less mature students can be supported in making good choices through the use of "bounded choice." The concept of bounded choice is simple but very useful. For example, some readers have difficulty choosing texts that are appropriate for independent reading, often choosing books that are far too difficult or far too easy. For those students who have difficulty selecting books that are appropriate, the teacher might employ bounded choice by selecting several books that are appropriate and allowing the students to choose from among these texts. In other words, the students are still making the final selection, but it is within the bounds of a range of appropriate texts. Bounded choice could also be provided by giving students different options for completing a task.

Evidence from a number of studies suggests a strong correlation between choice and the development of intrinsic motivation (Paris & Oka, 1986; Rodin, Rennert, & Solomon, 1980; Spaulding, 1992). In addition, research related to self-selection of reading material supports the notion that the books and stories that students find "most interesting" are those they have selected for their own reasons and purposes. In a study conducted by Schiefele (1991), students who were allowed and encouraged to choose their own reading material expended more effort in learning and understanding the material. It seems clear that providing students with opportunities to select their own reading materials and writing topics increases task engagement and intrinsic literacy motivation.

Materials. Classrooms should have an abundance of print materials representing a broad range of genres, including literary, informational, and documentary text. Literary texts include reading materials such as novels, poetry, short stories, letters, diaries, folktales, fables, speeches, plays, autobiographies, legends, personal essays, and biographies. Informational texts include reading materials such as trade books, textbooks, reference materials, government documents, historical documents, manuals, pamphlets, and editorials. Documentary texts include reading materials such as illustrations, photographs, diagrams, tables, cartoons, graphs, time lines, schedules, and reference access systems such as indexes.

Two factors that affect students' use of materials are access and level of difficulty. Research reveals that students are more motivated to select books when they can view the cover (Gambrell & Codling, 1997). Face-front displays of books draw the readers' attention to titles, favorite authors, and interesting topics. Rich classroom libraries also offer students the opportunity to read books at their independent and instructional level as well as time to engage with challenging texts (Farnan, 1996; Heathington, 1979). Wordless picture books, content textbooks, novels, and short fiction help students experience reading texts at different levels for different purposes.

Time. Studies conducted by Heathington (1979), Midgley (1993), and Mizelle (1997) found that time was a primary factor in motivational literacy environments. Across observations and student interviews, the amount of time devoted to actually reading and writing was related to students' level of motivation. Clearly, when the only time available for free reading and writing is when all other work has been completed, the struggling learner is at a disadvantage. In such a situation, the students who are more able, and generally already more motivated, are the ones who then have additional time to engage in reading and writing activities. The time allotted to reading and writing influences students' perceptions of the value of literacy. A primary goal for creating a classroom culture that fosters literacy motivation should be to ensure that all students have opportunities to engage in sustained reading and writing events. To send the message that reading and writing are valued, appropriate periods of time must be provided for students to engage in sustained literacy activities.

Classrooms that foster literacy motivation are filled with the noise of collaborative inquiry; allow for attention to individual learning styles; encourage the use of language for meaningful purposes; and give attention to the needs of adolescent learners for competence, relatedness, and autonomy (Carroll, 1998). According to Foster

(1994, p. 12), a classroom culture that fosters literacy motivation is student centered and allows students both the freedom and impetus to do the following:

- Search for themselves, seeking answers to problems and issues that perplex them through reading, writing, seeing, and listening experiences that make sense to them
- Use language to communicate thoughts and feelings that are important for them to express
- Debate and ponder issues important to the community as well as the individual
- Grow as language users, becoming strong readers, writers, listeners, and viewers
- Empathize with the different ways groups use language and grow to understand how audiences and situations shape the nature of the language

In Montaigne's essays, written in 1590 and first published in 1925, he succinctly makes the case for the critical importance of motivation in learning: "In the education of children, there is nothing like alluring their interest and affection; Otherwise you create only so many mules laden with books" (p. 236).

REFERENCES

Allington, R.L. (1986). Policy constraints and effective compensatoy reading instruction: A review. In J. Hoffman (Ed.), *Effective teaching of reading: Research and practice* (pp. 261–289). Newark, DE: International Reading Association.

———. (1991). The legacy of "slow it down and make it more concrete." In J. Zutell and S. McCormick (Eds.), *Learner factors/teacher factors: Issues in literacy research and instruction* (pp. 19–30). Chicago: National Reading Conference.

Anderson, R C., Wilson, P.T., & Fielding, L.G. (1988). Growth in reading and how children spend their time outside of school. *Reading Research Quarterly, 23,* 285–303.

Bempechat, J., London, P., & Dweck, C.S. (1991). Children's conceptions of ability: An interview and experimental study. *Child Study Journal, 21,* 11–36.

Borkowski, J.G., Carr, M., Rellinger, E., & Pressley, M. (1990). Self-regulated strategy use: Interdependence of metacognition, attributions, and self-esteem. In B.F. Jones & L. Idol (Eds.), *Dimensions of thinking: Review of research* (pp. 2–60). Hillsdale, NJ: Erlbaum.

Cameron, J., & Pierce, W.D. (1994). Reinforcement, reward, and intrinsic motivation: A meta-analysis. *Review of Educational Research, 64,* 363–423.

Carroll, P.S. (1998). A (w)hole in the middle: Language study for transformed middle schools. In J.S. Sim-mons & L. Baines (Eds.), *Language study in middle school, high school, and beyond: Views on enhancing the study of language* (pp. 20–40). Newark, DE: International Reading Association.

Colvin, C., & Schlosser, L.K. (1997/1998). Developing academic confidence to build literacy: What teachers can do. *Journal of Adolescent and Adult Literacy, 41,* 272–281.

deCharms, R. (1980). The origins of competence and achievement motivation in personal causation. In L.J. Fyans, Jr. (Ed.), *Achievement motivation: Recent trends in theory and research* (pp. 22–33). New York: Plenum.

Deci, E.L., & Ryan, R.M. (1985). *Intrinsic motivation and self-determination in human behavior.* San Diego, CA: Academic Press.

———. (1991). A motivational approach to self: Integration in personality. In R. Dienstbier (Ed.), *Nebraska symposium on motivation: Vol. 38. Perspectives on motivation* (pp. 237–288). Lincoln: University of Nebraska Press.

Deci, E.L., Vallerand, R.J., Pelletier, L.G., & Ryan, R.M. (1991). Motivation and education: The self-determination perspective. *Educational Psychologist, 26,* 325–346.

Dweck, C.S., & Elliot, E.S. (1983). Achievement motivation. In E. M. Hetherington (Ed.), *Socialization, personality, and social development* (pp. 643–681). New York: Wiley.

Eccles, J.S., & Midgley, C. (1989). Stage-environment fit: Developmentally appropriate classrooms for young adolescents. In C. Ames & R. Ames (Eds.), *Research on motivation in education* (Vol. 3, pp. 139–186). San Diego, CA: Academic Press.

Farnan, N. (1996). Connecting adolescents and reading: Goals at the middle level. *Journal of Adolescent and Adult Literacy, 39,* 436–445.

Feldlaufer, H., Midgley, C., & Eccles, J.S. (1988). Student, teacher, and observer perceptions of the classroom environment before and after the transition to junior high school. *Journal of Early Adolescence, 8,* 133–156.

Ford, M.E. (1992). *Motivating humans.* Newbury Park, CA: Sage.

Foster, H.M. (1994). *Crossing over: Whole language for secondary English teachers.* Fort Worth, TX: Harcourt Brace.

Fraser, B.J., & Fisher, D.L. (1982). Predicting students' outcomes from their perceptions of classroom psychosocial environment. *American Educational Research Journal, 85,* 567–580.

Gambrell, L.B. (1995). Motivation matters. In W.M. Linek and E.G. Sturtevant (Eds.), *Generations of literacy: Seventeenth yearbook of the College Reading Association* (pp. 2–24). East Texas, TX: College Reading Association.

———. (1996). Creating classroom cultures that foster reading motivation [Distinguished Educator Series]. *The Reading Teacher, 50,* 14–25.

Gambrell, L.B., & Codling, R.M. (1997). Fostering reading motivation: Insights from theory and research. In K. Camperell, B.L. Hayes, and R. Telfer (Eds.), *Yearbook of the American Reading Forum* (pp. 17–28). Logan, UT: American Reading Forum.

Gambrell, L.B., Dromsky, A.J., & Mazzoni, S.A. (1998). [Middle school students' motivation to read narrative and expository texts]. Unpublished raw data.

Gambrell, L.B., & Marinak, B. (1997). Incentives and intrinsic motivation to read. In J. Guthrie & A. Wigfield (Eds.), *Reading engagement: Motivating readers through integrated instruction* (pp. 205–217). Newark, DE: International Reading Association.

Guthrie, J.T., Alao, S., & Rinehart, J.M. (1997). Engagement in reading for young adolescents. *Journal of Adolescent and Adult Literacy, 40,* 438–446.

Guthrie, J.T., Schafer, W., Wang, Y., & Afflerbach, P. (1993). Influences of instruction on reading engagement: An empirical exploration of a social-cognitive framework of reading activity (Research Report No. 3). Athens, GA: National Reading Research Center.

Harari, O., & Covington, M.V. (1981). Reactions to achievement behavior from a teacher and student perspective: A developmental analysis. *American Educational Research Journal, 18,* 15–28.

Heath, S.B. (1991). The sense of being literate: Historical and cross-cultural features. In R. Barr, M.L. Kamil, P. Mosenthal, & P.D. Pearson (Eds.), *Handbook of reading research* (Vol. 2, pp. 3–25). White Plains, NY: Longman.

Heathington, B. (1979). What to do about reading motivation in the middle school. *Journal of Reading, 22* 709–713.

Iran-Nejad, A. (1990). Active and dynamic self-regulation of learning processes. *Review of Educational Research, 60,* 573–602.

Johnson, D., & Johnson, R. (1985). The internal dynamics of cooperative learning groups. In R. Slavin, S. Sharan, S. Kagan, R. Hertz-Lazarowitz, C. Webb, & R. Schmuck (Eds.), *Learning to cooperate, cooperating to learn* (pp. 103–124). New York: Plenum Press.

Lepper, M.R., & Hodell, M. (1989). Intrinsic motivation in the classroom. In C. Ames & R. Ames (Eds.), *Research in motivation in education* (Vol. 3, pp. 139–186). New York: Academic Press.

McCombs, B.L. (1989). Self-regulated learning and academic achievement: A phenomenological view. In B.J. Zimmerman & D.H. Schunk (Eds.), *Self-regulated learning and achievement: Theory, research, and practice* (pp. 51–82). New York: Springer-Verlag.

———. (1991). Unraveling motivation: New perspectives from research and practice. *Journal of Experimental Education, 60,* 3–88.

Midgley, C. (1993). Motivation and middle level schools. *Advances in motivation and achievement* (Vol. 8, pp. 217–274). Greenwich, CT: JAI Press.

Midgley, C., Feldlaufer, H., & Eccles, J.S. (1989). Change in teacher efficacy and student self- and task-related beliefs during the transition to junior high school. *Journal of Educational Psychology, 81,* 247–258.

Midgley, C., & Urdan, T. (1992). The transition to middle level schools: Making it a good experience for all students. *Middle School Journal, 24,* 5–14.

Mizelle, N.B. (1997). Enhancing young adolescents' motivation for literacy learning. *Middle School Journal, 24*(2), 5–14.

Montaigne, M. (1590/1925). *The essays of Montaigne.* Cambridge, MA: Harvard University Press.

Moos, R.H. (1979). *Evaluating educational environments.* San Fransisco: Jossey-Bass.

Nicholls, J.G. (1986, April). *Adolescents conceptions of ability and intelligence.* Paper presented at the annual meeting of the American Educational Research Association, San Fransisco.

O'Flahavan, J., Gambrell, L.B., Guthrie, J., Stahl, S., & Alvermann, D. (1992, August). Poll results guide activities of research center. *Reading Today*, 12.

Oldfather, P. (1993). What students say about motivating experiences in a whole language classroom. *The Reading Teacher, 46*, 672–681.

———. (1995). Commentary: What's needed to maintain and extend motivation for literacy in the middle grades. *Journal of Reading, 38*, 420–422.

Palmer, B.M., Codling, R.M., & Gambrell, L.B. (1994). In their own words: What elementary children have to say about motivation to read. *The Reading Teacher, 48*, 176–179.

Paris, S.G., & Oka, E.R. (1986). Self-regulated learning among exceptional children. *Exceptional Children, 53*, 103–108.

Pintrich, P.R., & DeGroot, E.V. (1990). Motivational and self-regulated learning components of classroom academic performance. *Journal of Educational Psychology, 82*, 33–40.

Pintrich, P.R., Roeser, R.W., & DeGroot, E.A.M. (1994). Classroom and individual differences in early adolescents' motivation and self-regulated learning. *Journal of Early Adolescence, 14*, 139–161.

Pintrich, P.R., & Schunk, D. (Eds.). (1996). *Motivation in education: Theory, research, and application.* Englewood Cliffs, NJ: Merrill.

Rodin, J., Rennert, K., & Solomon, S. (1980). Intrinsic motivation for control: Fact or fiction. In A. Baum, J.E. Singer, & S. Valios (Eds.), *Advances in environmental psychology II* (pp. 177–186). Hillsdale, NJ: Erlbaum.

Ryan, R.M., & Grolnick, W. (1986). Origins and pawns in the classroom: Self-report and projective assessments of individual differences in children's perceptions. *Journal of Personality and Social Psychology, 50*, 550–558.

Schiefele, U. (1991). Interest, learning, and motivation. *Educational Psychologist, 26*, 299–323.

Slavin, R. (1984). Students motivating students to excel: Cooperative incentives, cooperative tasks, and student achievement. *Elementary School Journal, 84*, 23–63.

Smith-Burke, T.M. (1989). Political and economic dimensions of literacy: Challenges for the 1990s. In S. McCormick & J. Zutell (Eds.), *Cognitive and social perspectives for literacy research and instruction* (pp. 1–18). Chicago: National Reading Conference.

Spaulding, C.L. (1992). The motivation to read and write. In J.W. Irwin & M.A. Doyle (Eds.), *Reading/writing connections: Learning from research* (pp. 177–201). Newark, DE: International Reading Association.

Stipek, D.J. (1988). *Motivation to learn: From theory to practice.* Englewood Cliffs, NJ: Prentice Hall.

Sweeting, L.M., Willower, D.J., & Helsel, A.R. (1978). Teacher-pupil relationships: Black students' perceptions of actual and ideal teacher/pupil control behavior and attitudes toward teachers and school. *Urban Education, 13*, 71–81.

Taylor, B.M., Frye, B.J., & Maruyama, G.M. (1990). Time spent reading and and reading growth. *American Educational Research Journal, 27*, 351–362.

Veenman, S. (1984). Perceived problems of beginning teachers. *Review of Educational Research, 54*(2), 143–178.

Vygotsky, L.S. (1986). *Thought and language.* Cambridge, MA: MIT Press.

Willower, D.J., & Lawrence, J.D. (1979). Teachers' perceptions of student threat to teacher status and teacher–pupil control ideology. *Educational Research, 16*, 586–590.

Wilson, E. (1995). *Reading at the middle and high school levels: Building active readers across the curriculum.* Arlington, VA: Educational Service.

10 "You Want to Read What?"

Giving Students a Voice in Their Own Literacy and in the Literacy Program

TOM LINER
Doughtery County (Georgia) Schools

DEBORAH BUTLER
Wabash College

> *There is little doubt that nothing has so revolutionized the English/Language Arts classroom as the student-centered process approach to writing.*
> —Schweiker-Marra, Broglie, & Plumer, 1997

> *They organize the chaos and agitate the calm.*
>
> —Student

"**M**iz Williams, Miz Williams, I don't know what to write." The hand is up, waving, insistent.

Melissa Moore-Williams, seventh-grade teacher at Merry Acres Middle School, is among her charges, advising and nudging and encouraging, sometimes cajoling, as they begin a new writing assignment.

"What's the problem?"

"I can't get started. I don't know what to write about." This time, Tim is not being difficult; he really is stuck. What he really wants her to do is give him the topic for his paper and tell him how to do it.

"Have you talked to your response group?

He has, and "They are no help. Paul is doing the gang story, and Bobby is writing about war and fighting and stuff. There's no good stuff left for me to write about."

Assuring him there is plenty of good stuff yet unwritten in the class, she leads Tim to a file drawer full of student stories and tells him to pull several writings by the boys and read them. If that fails to spark an original idea, there are several anthologies of student writing lining the chalk trays and prominently displayed on bookshelves around the room. He can browse them. Usually before he gets through even one of the student publications, Tim will find his story idea. If not, he and Melissa will sit down together in a conference about what books he has read so far and what he thinks are the really good parts. And they will look through his class journal for embryonic narratives. When Tim begins sketching out the story, it will be his, not just another school exercise.

In the same way, Tim chooses the books he reads for Melissa. He thinks he can read anything he wants to, as long as he reads. In fact, he reads anything she approves and that his parents allow. Neither she nor they have given up their responsibility. Still, his choices are large. In her classroom alone, there are hundreds of books.

It can be difficult at times to allow students to find their own writing subjects and select their own readings. It can be hard to let them learn from each other and not always be in charge. It takes patience and wisdom, and trust that they will produce for you. That can be scary. Running a reading and writing workshop and working with kids in small groups also take careful planning and confidence in the learning processes of young people. But the difference between reading only assigned texts, writing on only assigned topics, and having real choices and talking to each other about significant topics and issues is dramatic. We have seen some pretty dreary classrooms transformed into exciting and creative places. We can see the difference in the faces of the students and hear it in their voices.

Giving Them a Voice to Find Their Voices

Language arts educators use the term *voice* in at least two different ways. Having a voice in what goes on in the classroom means that I have choices, that I have a say in what is done around here. That, of course, is the point of this chapter. Some of us call that ownership. If I really choose to write a particular story, for example, then it is mine and not just a school exercise. I am much more involved in it; I want it to succeed. I own it, and it is therefore important to me.

Likewise, if I have a voice in program planning, then I have a stake in what goes on in your classroom, in the other classrooms of the teacher team, and, at best, in the daily routine of the school. Teachers who value and honor the opinions of their students on matters of curriculum have more effective curriculums. Workshop approaches, intelligent group work, and significant talk with and among students make it easier to involve them in the directions the teaching curriculum takes as it evolves.

There is also the voice that is distinctive and individually mine when I speak or write. It is echoed in the voice in my head when I read. It is the voice of my creative self, as unique as my fingerprints or DNA. That voice grows, it develops. It becomes more complex, more subtle, capable of nuances, and at times even profound. It is capable of surprising beauty and grating ugliness. And it has another characteristic, which probably is necessary for it to operate at all in the flow of time, but which is also amazing and always surprising: this creative voice we all possess finds out where it is going mostly as it is going there. Writing leads to discovery, and some of the discoveries are wonderful!

In the classroom, giving students real choices—giving them their own voices in what they read and write and view and say and listen to—helps them develop their inner voices, the creative spark within each of them. When I choose the task, it is mine. I become a part of it, and my creative voice grows in strength and subtlety by grappling with the new challenge. The choices you allow me to have are at the core of my learning, and only when I am truly learning this way can I bring my own unique voice to the overall direction of our classroom.

Reading and Writing Workshop

Natasha Colquitt is a woman so energetic and youthful that she easily fits in among her eighth graders. If you get to her classroom when class is starting, bring a book with you because everybody will be reading one, including Natasha, and everyone will be reading a different one. If you forget and don't have a book, some of her students will help you pick one. They know books.

Silent reading will end with a journal response, and soon you will find yourself in a lively discussion, first of what they are reading, and then of the writing. And you will naturally move from there into writing pieces to publish or peer editing or research. You will have to watch closely to see the steps. The reading, talking, writing, and group sharing run into each other easily and comfortably.

We have seen Paul Gainer work the reading and writing workshop with a difficult class of seventh graders, students everyone kept a tight rein on and whose test scores and reading levels were low. Paul was persistent. He put two of the biggest boys in the class in charge of checking out books. He celebrated every success, brought an *Accelerated Reader* computer program into his classroom, and worked with his students to write and publish together. By Christmas, one boy had struggled to read one book, but he read it. One of the girls read 52 novels in the same number of weeks! By the end of the school year they were all readers and all writers. Don't give up.

The main ingredients of the reading and writing workshop are the same ones that Nancy Atwell (1987) described: *choice, time,* and *response.* The principles are simple. Students need a real choice in what they read and what they write. They require time at school to read and write and to work with each other and with their teacher. And they need a genuine, interested response from their teacher and from their peers. You are still in charge. You decide how these essential elements will be played out with your students in the environment you create.

The choice must be real if middle school students are to grow as readers and writers, and, indeed, eventually become scholars and creative and productive citizens. With real choices also comes responsibility. Simply put, you picked the book and told me you would read it and do certain things to share it with me and this class; now do what you promised to do. You decided what you would write and how you would write it; now write it to the standards we agreed on and by the deadline. A lot of educators say that we have a crisis with authority among our young people in our permissive and overabundant society, which is true. It is announced daily in the newspaper and on television. But for many of the students, the crisis is really with taking responsibility and being accountable for their choices. Like it or not, they will learn this lesson at school or not at all. One way to teach responsibility is to give our students responsible choices, but hold them to the decisions they make and high standards we demand.

Risky? Sometimes, because young people do make wrong choices now and then, and the consequences of mistakes are also real, both for them and the class. One of the things school teaches you is that we rarely work alone; others depend on us. If four of us are reading *Somewhere in the Darkness* and have a project due for a class presentation, and I discover too late I do not like the book and do not do my part, well, you know what the results will be for my group, the class, and for me. But that may not be a totally negative experience, for me at least, if you let me suffer the consequences of my choices. That's a part of growing up or, in education jargon, developmentally sound practices.

How do your students know which choices to make, especially if they come from classes where all the choices have been made by the teacher? They need clear instructions about the choices they have in your class, and they need an adult model to show them how. You will need patience as you gradually turn them loose. Don't expect your charges to know instantly what to write (the professionals certainly don't when they start a new book or story). Having lots of student examples in the classroom, as Melissa does, is a big help. Our experience proves that starting with narrative writing is usually a good way to get them going. A lot of journal writing with little threat also instills the habit of writing and choosing their own topics. But the most powerful thing you do is model the writing you want them to do. As Don Graves says, "You write before them and walk in their midst." Peer editing is also part of the formula, as is a lot of reading aloud and sharing in the classroom. Publishing and celebrating the writing is the spice and the motivation. Responsibility comes from deadlines and meeting your standards. It is not an easy way to teach writing, but it grows confident and independent writers.

If students are already fluent readers, they have been choosing their own books for years and will only need you and their peers to introduce them to more titles. But if they are reluctant readers, your work is cut out for you to introduce them to books so interesting that they cannot help but read them. And that takes a little time. Most of students' experiences with books have been prescribed by the teacher in situations in which they probably had no choice at all. No wonder they can't read well. More basal exercises will not improve their reading nor their confidence as learners. What they need is the experience of reading books they choose and the experience of talking to their peers and a trusted adult about those books. That, after all, is what readers do.

Instructions, deadlines, reminders, group reading projects, peer editing, publishing, book talks, rate-a-book lists, sharing, minilessons, author and background research, student-led discussions, writer-to-writer interviews, letters, e-mail—all of these activities in the democratic classroom relate directly to communication. In a sense, the classroom becomes a forum for conversations, sometimes with the whole class, sometimes among group members, and sometimes two people head-to-head (one of the two may or may not be the teacher). The conversations are real because they are important to all the players. These interrelated conversations are the glue that holds it all together. One revealing teaching axiom is "If I do all the planning, researching, and telling, who does the learning?"

Problems and Warnings

What do you do when Thomas will read nothing but *Hardy Boys* mysteries, and Deborah chooses *Lady Chatterly's Lover* for her next book project? We tell Deborah, no, take that one back to the downtown library. It is okay to say no. We have a responsibility to parents and their children. Thomas's case probably will depend on what time of year it is. If it is the third week of school and Thomas is obviously enjoying his new freedom in choosing reading matter, we may let it go after asking him if he doesn't want to try something else this time. All of us indulge in junk-food reading. He probably will get bored with the baby books soon and move on to what the other guys in class are reading. He may also want to see if we really mean what we say. If Halloween has come and gone, however, we may simply tell him to make another choice because we are getting tired of the Hardy Boys. When we give students choices, they do take them. There is an important issue of trust here, but there are also two sides to the conversation.

Some situations can be more serious than others, and there are two related issues you do need to be aware of when students have real choices in reading and writing. Privacy and censorship are almost two sides of the same coin. As Schweiker-Marra, Broglie, and Plumer point out in their article in the *English Journal* (October 1997), the issue of privacy in student writing is one to take seriously and prepare for. Experiences in writing personal narratives such as the memoir or the writing activity "Anatomy of a Memory" are close to the heart of every National Writing Project teacher and every experienced writing process teacher. (The National Writing Project started as the Bay Area Writing Project in San Francisco in 1968. Stressing that writing is taught by writing and that the best teacher trainers are themselves teachers, this project has grown to over 100 sites throughout the United States. Personal writing is part of each National Writing Project institute.) The problem is that the personal narrative can embarrass students and their parents and cause mayhem for well-meaning teachers. Be sensitive and warn students when they choose experiences to write about not to detail anything their mothers would not want talked about at the beauty parlor or at church. Because, however supportive and warm, the classroom is public.

We all have had the experience of a piece of writing taking us where we did not expect, sometimes into uncomfortable and sensitive territory. Student writers are no different, notwithstanding our warnings. The rule of thumb is simple: Allow nothing to go on that will hurt the student or her family.

Censorship, of course, is a better-known danger for reading workshop teachers, and most of us have been singed, if not burned, by "those words" and "those situations" appearing on the pages of the book one of our innocents is reading. Be prepared for these situations.

Good communication with parents—and your common sense—is the best way to avoid either problem. If something your student writes or reads makes you uncomfortable, there is a reason to take another look.

Student Choice, Voice, and Oral Language

We have already talked about many issues with helping students develop a voice and giving students a voice in their writing and reading experiences. Who should have voice? What kind? How much and when? It is really not a question of whether kids should have it or not, but just the logistics. Of course they should be a part of the language arts curriculum and take ownership of their learning—which again means the responsibility for the freedom to decide what to write, read, and say in discussions.

Nowhere in the classroom is this more apparent than with oral language. Sometimes we don't think we have to concern ourselves about giving students voice this way. It seems that middle schoolers come in fully verbal about almost everything—including what they think they should be learning and doing in your classroom. It isn't giving them a voice in their own program so much as it is curbing those voices—or at least some of them. For others, it is getting them to sound out their silent thoughts.

Shaping and Drawing Out Voices: Preparing the Way for Responsible Use of Voice

Just as in reading and writing workshops, there are ways to give students voice in the oral language parts of your day, too. But voicing one's contribution, one's ideas about the partnership in a program, takes responsive and responsible use of one's real voice. And carefully planning kinds of developmental talking experiences in the classroom is one way to help students either gain the confidence to speak or gain the audience skills necessary to be heard.

Like all other parts of the language arts program, all this happens best in unobtrusive ways—if threaded through a good solid meaningful core of reading and writing experiences. What are some those weavable experiences? We remember something about student developmental tasks at this age, and we suggest a constructive approach to encouraging students to use and develop their voices.

Conferencing about Writing

Build students' voices (especially those that need confidence to articulate their thoughts) in one-to-one situations. The best way is over their own writing, where you can be warm, inviting, supportive, yet pushy all at once. We would ask you to try to remember some key principles:

- Who the writing belongs to;
- Being honest and specific;
- Letting the writing establish the need for help and what they want to talk about in each phase of your conferences. (Butler & Liner, 1995, pp. 216–18)

Once students have become comfortable talking with you, or a trusted peer, about their writing, they may be ready for other conversations in smaller groups. (We will talk about small groups in the next section.)

One-to-One Voices and Reading: Book Talks

We call these "End of the Book Conferences with the Teacher" (Butler & Liner, 1995). But really all they are, are outgrowths of a reading workshop, chances to allow students who have finished a book to talk to you or to others about it. These chats can be formal or informal, one to one, with a teacher or friend, or with a small group (more about this later, too). Admittedly, it's not the most original activity, but "it gets the job done" (p. 150). It succeeds in another way, too. It gets every student talking to you or a friend, a partner. Again, students begin opening up, gaining confidence with their voices and literature.

The point behind starting to exercise voice this way is to get everyone's voice up and running over something meaningful, over something they gain confidence from. All the while, students are doing useful writing and reading for their own development, but they are doing it in ways that help them grow the positive power of their oral voices. Their abilities to articulate suggestions or give feedback begins within the safety of book talks with you and a few others.

Progressive Use of Small-Group Strategies

If middle schoolers are going to develop their voices and have a voice in their literacy program, they not only have to build confidence in their voices with you, but within their classroom community too. The best way is through a lot of meaningful small-group conversations and discussions.

One of the hardest things we find that new teachers deal with in student teaching is the instructional planning of and then the management of small-group work. Everybody wants to try it. Everyone is so fired up about cooperative learning and about having students actively involved and learning from one another that they want to jump right in with small groups.

No matter how often we say this, they all have to learn from experience that middle schoolers learn best in small groups if they have been taught how to learn that way. If they are not shown how, they usually do not behave well in the groups.

On the one hand, some students always learn well in groups. They are good students by and large and they do what the teacher asks. But many others spoil the good feeling because they goof off or they just sit. What we worry about is that our young teachers, bolstered unfortunately by some veterans, will say, "Well, another theory out the window; small groups just don't work," or worse, "They just don't work with *these kids.*"

There is an abundance of information that says small groups do work, for many students, in many contexts, for different purposes (Jones, 1990; Johnson, Johnson, Holubec, & Roy, 1984; Sharan & Sharan, 1976; Slavin, 1987). And not only that, but groups are an important strategy for developing voice further because students get to use their voices in different ways, and they hear other voices who share their thoughts, which jog their own, and so on. Sharing in groups improves thinking and can build confidence in one's own voice and its power to carry an influential message.

We think that one of the keys to successful use of group work in the language arts classroom is their progressive use from more simple task groups in which membership is highly structured to more complex task groups in which inquiry dominates and the group's membership may be partially self-chosen or even freely self-chosen. An early model, precooperative learning, came from Gary Gerbrandt's work (1974) with small groups. Gerbrandt described nine types of groups: research and reporting, debating, specific tasks, instructive, interrogative, sequential thinking, digressive, evaluation groups, and teacherlike small groups (pp. 5–7). Many of these types could function within the context of students' reading material and using it for some intellectual product, but many of the group types could also be used to help students orally process issues in society, in the school, or in the classroom itself.

Take, for instance, the simple debating small group in which students take a controversial idea and, within a given time frame, they discuss the pros and cons of the idea and possibly emerge with articulated ideas for and against an idea, or they go beyond that and come to a consensus before finishing the group task. Although we often had our students use this type of group to discuss the merits of a character's decisions in literature, certainly students may also discuss a local issue or the validity of a classroom or school guideline as a way to have intelligent discussion on things that impact them each day (Butler & Liner, 1995, p. 265). Throughout the group continuum, students, when ready, could engage in a longer term inquiry, solving a problem in which they must gather information, process it, and plan a solution based on the best information (sequential thinking small group, somewhat akin to the group investigation in cooperative learning). The more experienced students become with various types of groups and with many subjects or focuses, the more able they become to work with many peers—including best friends or perhaps not-so-good friends—on issues that remain oral, or in reading and writing groups. And this experience is necessary to bring about those good whole-group oral experiences (speeches and drama) in which students also need to exercise their voices. Sources offer similar advice for structuring student learning in groups; a helpful one is *Small Group Learning in the Classroom* (Reid, Foreestal, & Cook, 1989) which lays out five stages in group processing that help with group success.

Moving Along with Reading and Writing Groups

The progression of learning to learn in small groups happens best inside reading and writing workshops, where forming groups for the purpose of sharing writing and reading is a naturally interwoven process of learning to learn in small groups. For example, when students begin to take group work seriously, they can make the best use of the editing group for their own writing, and the best use of literature circles for their own reading.

Editing Groups

We define an editing group as a response group focused on one another's writing. Hopefully, students have begun to learn how to really be helpful as listeners and responders when you have your one-on-one conferences. Then, as always, you are modeling how to respond to writing. But students do need some other kinds of specific teaching to help this go well—at least as an autonomous classroom activity. We would suggest starting overt training by using the "circle within a circle" in which you take several students and model how a writing circle should work, carefully pointing out and teaching what you are doing every step of the way (Butler & Liner, 1995, p. 221). There are some pretty specific rules, too:

1. Papers are always read aloud;
2. The writer speaks first;
3. Everybody in the group responds;
4. Group expectations are clear from the beginning; and
5. Keep the groups to about five people. (pp. 220–21)

This works best for us, and it helps students both speak and share, but to listen critically too, another important development in gaining and using a responsible voice.

Small Groups and Reading Books

Talking about books is traditionally thought of as a post-reading activity, and maybe in too many classrooms only this kind of talk happens. Although the "one-minute book talk" or some other variation has meaning and value as an ending activity in front of the whole class, it does not develop voice; it serves as an outlet for an already developed one. And if it isn't a confident, developed voice delivering that one-minute talk, that moment can be among the scariest minutes of someone's life. At the least these finales should be thought of as small-group possibilities. Some of those structures for "one minutes" can be useful developmentally as part of small-group talk about books when students are partially through with books, when they want to step back and "feel it out" a little. Many "one minutes" follow a structure something like this:

1. Title, author, publisher, year is shared;
2. Short summary of several sentences;

3. Main character description (several words);
4. Theme mentioned in a sentence or two;
5. Short critique of the book (Kuta, 1997, p. 91)

Students can simply share this as part of a group instead of in front of the whole class, or it can be adapted to be used part-way through any book, as a structured way of sharing what the reader thinks and knows so far.

This latter idea hits pretty close to what many teachers call "literature circles," a small group of students discussing and exploring literature selections together in the classroom, either highly structured or less structured, with or without the teacher. In an atmosphere of trust and knowledge of each other and the teacher, many students can come to talk freely, with independence, about connections they make with the book, both personal and with classroom themes, concepts, or other books. These, too, are developmental enterprises; it takes careful observation, careful modeling in whole group discussions and timely interventions by teachers to create situations that prompt everyone's voice to contribute. Kathy Short and Gloria Kauffman (1995) do a good job giving some strategies for setting up such groups that are highly adaptable for middle-grade classrooms. They agree, and we would too, to expect some social talk—and that may not be a bad thing. In fact, it may help students find their focus. Short and Kauffman also suggest ways to move the groups beyond initial talk to more critical explorations of the literature, a use of and development of voice highly necessary for students who will have responsible voices in their literacy programs—all this before too much whole group sounding out of ideas and theories!

The Caveats for Building Voices in Groups

It would be remiss not to take heed of some of the barriers to developing strong voices through group work. It isn't a magic strategy. Elizabeth Cohen's book (1994) is a good handbook to keep around; it is good at helping teachers learn how to build a classroom culture conducive to equity among diverse voices. Some critical group work guides (these do not represent the richness of her discussion!) that we try to live with are the following:

1. Believe yourself that groups are powerful learning situations. Be able to articulate why you think this. By all means, do not give up when they do not go perfectly or even very well for a while.
2. Recognize that groups can and do develop problems; some are potentially inherent, such as status and inequality within the peer group. Educate students and yourself about this and try to avoid the issues.
3. Teach your students cooperative behaviors before you launch into sophisticated groups and tasks.
4. Introduce group work in stages.
5. Make sure everyone has a clear part to play in the group.
6. Make sure those parts play to the strengths of students in the group.

7. Be flexible about your own role, but aim for student independence (do not dominate and do all the talking; you can be surprised what you can learn if you listen more.)

8. Evaluate! (students, groups through peer comments, teacher comments, etc.).

We do not pretend that these conditions, as said before, ensure that groups will always work, but thinking through these points may help you create the conditions for students to keep developing strong voices among their peers, collaboratively and autonomously.

It may be best to move from a tightly structured situation to a more loosely structured classroom. As students show that they learn well and use voice as the medium, loosen up your classroom gradually, toward more autonomy and more responsibility. This is ultimately where they need to operate to be good contributors to their programs. We have to trust them, but they have to earn that trust, too.

Jumping Further into Ownership: Developing Student Voices through Curriculum and Assessments

Reading, writing, and oral work—the classroom strategies we've mentioned so far—are some instructional approaches that can support the development of voices and thus ownership of one's learning. They are prerequisites, we believe, to ownership in programs.

The empowerment of students to be involved responsibly in the literacy program is even more enhanced by affording them choices (and voices) in what they learn and how they will be assessed on that learning. Curricular and assessment choices are part of natural language classrooms, often through self-chosen books in reading workshops, or with an interdisciplinary team of teachers and students, through self-chosen inquiries within thematic, interdisciplinary curriculum and instruction.

For example, as a language arts teacher on a team where interdisciplinary teaming and teaching occurred with seventh and eighth graders, we teachers all witnessed the importance of curricular choice on the development of our students. In several interdisciplinary units, including the City, the Future, and the Environment, students reflected on possible projects that asked them to combine their knowledge and skills with reading and writing; researching; graphing; hypothesizing; researching and testing probable solutions; and formatting and reporting results to various audiences. Once serious choices were made, students truly owned the inquiries and came to school ready to follow their own daily plan of work (self-made schedules of work helping them accomplish their projects).

Many teachers engage their students increasingly in the choices that make up the content of their learning. Elsewhere, we wrote about Pat Bradley's autobiographical books, a project in which students research in-depth their own backgrounds and that of their families. They are given an outline of contents, but must make choices about whom to interview, which events to highlight, which relatives to write about, and which influences are most important in their lives (Butler & Liner, 1995, pp. 368–379). Ross Burkhardt had his students create an end-of-the-year magazine, which was composed of highly personal inquiries by each student and which involved all the disciplines. While he may check the work from time to time, it really is the students' jobs to create the individual magazine and decide who the audience is. These are some of the ways we all think that our students can be freed by their choices and practice the responsibility for them.

In most of these projects, and especially with the interdisciplinary units that our team worked with, responsibility for learning carried with it the responsibility of evaluation—of oneself, of one's peers, and with the teachers. What our team did not do to help our students exercise voice in evaluation was a method popularized eight or ten years later—the portfolio among other kinds of alternative assessments. By definition, alternative assessment (and authentic assessments) are not traditional paper-and-pencil tests, but more than that, they are assessments that often play to students' strengths, learning styles, and multiple intelligences. They are ways of offering students multiple modes by which their learning can be assessed. The more complex, the more choice involved by the students, and the more "voice" students develop in the process of being assessed, the process of learning and showing what they have learned.

A portfolio does these things amply. There are many resources for language arts teachers on portfolios now, and if you are not using a portfolio system yet, we think you will find that it can reinforce the building of student empowerment for meaningful choice. One classroom in Crawfordsville, Indiana, serves as a good model that many sources would support (Butler & Liner, 1995). At the beginning of the school year, the sixth-grade teacher at Tuttle Middle School held a parent workshop to explain to the parents what the portfolio evaluation was all about, what to expect their child to be bringing home, and how they could help their child's reading and writing through responding to the portfolio. Of course, she explained all this to the sixth graders, too. Being very unfamiliar with writing and not liking reading in many cases, they began their year by keeping journals and reading works they liked. They developed drafts from early journal works and kept them in a working portfolio. Slowly, she brought in assessment forms (self-assessment, things for parents to react on, and peer evaluation questions) and she began conferencing with students as writing development and reading occurred. At the end of each grading period, each student and she selected two writings which were placed in another part of the portfolio and evaluated more formally by peers, parents, and teacher. Throughout the year, the minilessons, workshop classroom, and experimentation with ever-more differing and challenging reading and writing consumed their time. At the end of the year, both parents and students proudly exhibited the portfolios of reading and writing progress and accomplishment over the year.

If you are looking for ways to start and continue good portfolio systems, we suggest you check with such resources as the National Middle School Association's journal issue on "Alternative Assessment" (Dickinson, 1993), and especially *Portfolios in Reading/Writing Classrooms* (1992). Both Graves and Sustein's *Portfolio Portraits* (1992) and Yancey's *Portfolios in the Writing Classroom* (1992) also contain good portraits of using portfolios to empower students to make good choices and become stronger language users.

Ultimately, students need to be prepared in every aspect of their learning environment and their programs to make responsible choices, to find voice to do so, and to take responsibility for those choices.

Owning the Whole Show: Teachers and Students and Other Adults

What we have talked about so far is really the support structure within the classroom that we feel needs to exist if you are preparing students to develop and use their own voices and for ownership in their literacy program. But there are certain support structures for this condition that must exist also—and these are outside the classroom situation, although, of course, not entirely separate from it.

1. *The teacher has to be prepared for letting go, and the administrator has to be aware and committed, too.*

Trust is the real issue in giving students choices in their reading, writing, and talking. The plain fact of the matter is it is hard for us to let go. What if they mess up? What if they don't read the right books? What if they write silly things? What if they don't learn enough vocabulary words? What if they don't learn? The answer is that they will mess up. They will read the wrong books, but many of the right ones as well. They will write silly things, but they will also write surprisingly beautiful, thoughtful things. Vocabulary will take care of itself, and they will learn more than lists of words can teach them. They will learn. John Mayher (1990) reminds us that

> it is the process of purposefully using language itself which further develops one's linguistic and communication competence. . . . The process of developing language competence is essentially an indirect and automatic procedure. It depends neither upon deliberately setting out to improve one's "skills" nor upon explicit teaching. It doesn't even require a sequence of experiences, since learners seem to be able to acquire what they need from whatever experiences are available. It does demand a sufficient range of different materials to read and write (or speak or listen to), but this doesn't have to be arranged in any particular order. (p. 207)

In other words, you can trust the process. They will learn when they choose their own books and topics and activities.

The second, and perhaps more compelling question, is, Can you trust them? That answer is not as simple. But it is really not too scary either. After all, you the teacher set the limits of their choices. We are not suggesting that you turn them loose to do anything they want whenever they want. If they are students used to teachers making all their choices for them, as most are, you will want to wean them gradually from an overdependence on your telling them what to do all the time. This much is clear: Responsibility is learned only by practicing it. We encourage students to make real choices in what they write and read and do. We also guide them by example, make our expectations clear, keep up with what they are doing, and carry on a continual, neverending conversation with them about their learning. They take risks, but they have a lot of support.

Trust is also the issue with your principal. Administrators must be informed and involved. Invite them into your classroom often. Tell them what you are doing, and tell them why, and share with them how much your students are involved in their literacy program. Whenever possible, get administrators to help out, to read to your students, to write and publish with them, to enjoy group discussions and research projects with them. Make sure they see the results of the choices your students and you make together. The students' eagerness to learn and what they produce are what will win administrators over to the classroom that empowers student voice, if they need to be convinced at all.

2. *Parents have to be prepared for what students need to develop their literacy.*

Communication with parents is not something that goes on only when Deborah wants to read "that book" or Thomas is stuck in his reading. We talk with and write to parents from the first day of class about the choices their children are being asked to make and why—about how and how much we want these students to become involved in the classroom and its directions. A class syllabus is a very good idea, even when a curriculum guide with clearly outlined procedures is handy. If I cannot put down on paper what I want you to do, then I need to think this over some more until I can. Parents can be demanding and pushy, but they also can be your biggest fans and greatest allies. Clear expectations can make the difference.

Whenever possible, invite them into the classroom. A couple of weeks ago, Melissa's students were writing personal narratives. Parents were invited to come write with them. All of the parents work outside the home, but a few came anyway, taking time off from work to be there. And they did write. The personal narrative (i.e., childhood memory or memoir) was particularly suitable for this setting. Adults could write about their childhood without a lot of introduction to the classroom and its routines. Some of the same parents came back three weeks later for the read-a-round, the celebration of sharing that Melissa has when a big project is completed. The power that experience had on the students whose parents wrote with them and read their writing aloud to their classmates is difficult to describe. Try it with your students' parents. Melissa is not shy about asking parents to come help with response groups, or putting a publication together, or reading to the students. She is in the business of building relationships with parents, as she does with students. Communication is natural, open, helpful. There is a lot of trust there.

Jim Glass, Melissa's principal, also came and wrote with the students. He often reads to them. He knows what is going on in that classroom. None of that happened by accident. Melissa often asks him to come participate with them. Most of the time he is too busy, but she still asks.

Do not be discouraged. If you invite 120 parents and 5 show up, as Melissa experienced, enjoy the ones you have with your students that day. Keep communicating with them any way you can. Yes, they are listening. They are just too busy to take the time to let you know it very often, and their children will not tell you. Be persistent and gently pushy, and ask them to come participate and help out. Especially invite them to the celebrations of your students' work, to read-a-rounds of their published writing, to demonstrations of their research projects, and to their speeches and dramatic productions. Our goal is to see parents at school as often as possible, and not just when there is a problem. Our goal is even more to have parents hear the growth in their own student's personal voices—and to appreciate how important that child's voice is within the community of learners.

Once you have these two "pre-conditions" and the ecology of the classroom's curriculum, assessments, and strategies functioning, trust in the students' voices, their decisions, and their ideas for the broader literacy program pays off in their involvement in the ongoing work of planning the class. Give them voice for choosing program directions through these methods:

1. *Let students know what the program is about—the goals, the directions, the "big picture"—and seek their input.*
Do not wait to do this, or the parts of this that you think your students are ready to do. Do not take our suggestions before this section as a blueprint that has to be accomplished verbatim before you involve students more in the overarching decisions about literacy programs. Do not, however, involve them in too much too quickly, before they are ready. The tricky thing about natural language classrooms is that the teacher uses more judgment than in other classes; classroom design is only as good as what you perceive and what you do about it.

2. *Seek continuous feedback from students on how the class is going, as well as at summative points. Let them see the changes, so they know they truly have an impact on the learning environment.*
In our classes, we try not to wait until the very end of the unit or the lesson sequence, the semester or the year, to get informal feedback from students on how things are going and to make necessary changes. We have developed a use of three quick questions—What things are going well? What things in the class are not going so well for me? and What suggestions do I have that would help things go better?—which yield a very rich set of suggestions for changes in instruction. An important additional question, "What can *I* do to help improve things?" sends the continuing important message that students are a part of the process of successfully managing the instructional environment. A quick conversation by the whole class takes only about twenty minutes and is well worth it.

3. *Become a "kid watcher" yourself. Collect information on how things go in your own journal or log. Watch and record students' unspoken choices. This unspoken voice can tell you lots about how things are going.*
This concept is hardly new and is known to many language arts teachers of younger children. First described by Goodman (1978) in the late seventies, this is the process of purposefully observing students while they read and write in authentic tasks, and observing their products, too. But you need to remember that you must observe students many times in multiple tasks. Cooper (1997) reminds us that the observation must include your background knowledge of development and what expectations are held of students in your teaching/learning contexts. Knowing this, and

observing students' actual work, helps you determine what instruction each needs—more conferencing, more use of peer audiences to test out their writing, reading more widely, and so forth. And, you need to keep track of your observations; some teachers use sticky notes, noting the observation, date, and name of the student (Cooper, 1997), while others will use a chart format.

So What?

As you see, voice is literacy, at least for middle school students. The rudiments of learning to read and write are long behind them. We may want them to be more competent and more sophisticated readers and writers. We may want them to be sensitive and perceptive listeners. We may want them to speak to a group with confidence and speak in a group with consideration. We may want them to think about their literacy experiences and tell us what they think. But the real task at this time in their lives is finding, using, and cultivating their voices, which is, after all, the task of finding out who they really are.

REFERENCES

Atwell, N. (1987). *In the middle: Reading, writing, and learning with adolescents.* Upper Montclair, NJ: Boynton/Cook.

Butler, D., & Liner, T. (1995). *Rooms to grow: Natural language arts in the middle school.* Durham, NC: Carolina Academic Press.

Cohen, E. (1994). *Designing groupwork: Strategies for the heterogeneous classroom* (2nd ed.). New York: Teachers College Press.

Cooper, D.J. (1997). *Literacy: Helping children construct meaning* (3rd ed.). Boston: Houghton Mifflin.

Dickinson, T. (Ed.). (1993). Alternative assessment. *Middle School Journal, 25*(2).

Gerbrandt, G. (1974). *An idea book for acting out and writing language, K–8.* Urbana, IL: National Council of Teachers of English.

Goodman, Y.M. (1978). Kid-watching: An alternative to testing. *National Elementary Principal, 57*(4), 41–45.

Graves, D., & Sustein, B. (Eds.). (1992). *Portfolio portraits.* Portsmouth, NH: Heinemann.

Johnson, D., Johnson, R., Holubec, E., & Roy, P. (1984). *Circles of learning: Cooperation in the classroom.* Washington, DC: Association for Supervision and Curriculum Development.

Jones, G. (1990). Cooperative learning: Developmentally appropriate for middle level students. *Middle School Journal, 22*(1), 12–16.

Kuta, K.W. (1997). *What a novel idea: Projects and activities for young adult literature.* Englewood, CO: Teacher Ideas Press.

Mayher, J. (1990). *Uncommon sense: Theoretical practice in language education.* Portsmouth, NH: Heinemann.

Reid, J., Foreestal, P., & Cook, J. (1989). *Small group learning in the classroom.* Portsmouth, NH: Heinemann.

Schweiker-Marra, K., Broglie, M., & Plumer, E. (1997). Who says so? Authorship and privacy in process writing classrooms. *English Journal, 86*(6), 16–26.

Sharan, S., & Sharan, Y. (1976). *Small group teaching.* Englewood Cliffs, NJ: Educational Technology Publications.

Short, K., & Kauffman, G. (1995). "So what do I do?" The role of the teacher in literature circles. In N. Roser & M. Martinez (Eds.), *Booktalk and beyond: Children and teachers respond to literature* (pp. 140–149). Newark, DE: International Reading Association.

Slavin, R. (1987). *Cooperative learning* (2nd ed.). Washington, DC: National Education Association.

Yancey, K. (Ed.). (1992). *Portfolios in the writing classroom: An introduction.* Urbana, IL: National Council of Teachers of English.

11 Students with Learning Disabilities and Literacy Issues

BOB ALGOZZINE

JOHN BEATTIE

BOB AUDETTE

MONICA LAMBERT

University of North Carolina at Charlotte

Once upon a time, there were no special education classes for students with disabilities. So for many years, students who learned differently spent many unproductive hours in schools without the provision of special services. Their subjects were taught by teachers using instructional methods that did not meet their special learning needs. Recent government figures reflect that more than 5 million students (see Table 11.1), aged 3 to 21, now receive special education services (U.S. Department of Education, 1996); at least 25% are in grades 4 to 6.

Characteristics

Most students with disabilities are included in one of four specific categories (U.S. Department of Education, 1996): learning disabilities (51%), speech/language impairments (21%), mental retardation (12%), or serious emotional disturbance (9%). Students with *learning disabilities* exhibit a disorder in one or more of the basic psychological processes involved in understanding or using spoken or written language. These may be manifested in disorders of listening, thinking, talking, reading, writing, spelling, or arithmetic. Learning disabilities include conditions that have been referred to as perceptual handicaps, brain injury, minimal brain dysfunction, dyslexia, and developmental aphasia. They do not include learning problems that are due primarily to visual, hearing, or motor disabilities; mental retardation; emotional disturbance; or

TABLE 11.1   Children with Disabilities by Age Group

Age	Number of Children		Change		Percentage of Total Aged 3 to 21
	1993–1994	**1994–1995**	**Number**	**Percentage**	
3–5	491,685	524,458	32,773	6.7	9.6
6–11	2,458,924	2,520,863	61,939	2.5	46.4
12–17	2,079,094	2,154,963	75,869	3.6	39.6
18–21	242,144	239,342	−2,802	−1.2	4.4
3–21	**5,271,847**	**5,439,626**	**167,779**	**3.2**	**100**

environmental disadvantage. Students with *speech or language impairments* have difficulty producing sounds (articulation), maintaining rhythm (fluency), and controlling vocal production (voice) when speaking or an inability to apply appropriate words, meanings, grammatical patterns, and sounds when using language. Students with *mental retardation* are those with impaired intellectual and adaptive behaviors and whose development reflects a reduced rate of learning. A student with *serious emotional disturbance* is one who exhibits persistent and consistent severe behavioral disabilities that consequently disrupt his or her own or others' learning processes; the inability to achieve academic progress or satisfactory interpersonal relationships cannot be attributed to physical, sensory, or intellectual deficits.

Students classified with learning disabilities, speech or language impairments, mental retardation, or serious emotional disturbance account for more than 90% of all students with disabilities (U.S. Department of Education, 1996), and they share many characteristics (Hallahan & Kauffman, 1977). For example, students with learning disabilities often have problems with reading comprehension, language development, interpersonal relations, and/or classroom behavioral control (Lerner, 1997). These same characteristics are presented in descriptions of students with speech or language impairments, mental retardation, and serious emotional disturbance (Coleman, 1986; Kauffman, 1997; Lewis & Doorlag, 1991; Robinson & Robinson, 1982) and of many students who are classified with other disabilities (Ysseldyke & Algozzine, 1990, 1994). Because many of their characteristics are not severe and because they overlap in conditions with different names, students with learning disabilities, speech or language impairments, mental retardation, and serious emotional disturbance are sometimes grouped together and called "students with mild disabilities" (Henley, Ramsay, & Algozzine, 1996).

Students with learning disabilities represent more than half of all students receiving special education services. Within mild disabilities, there are more than twice as many students with learning disabilities (55%) as there are students with speech or language impairments (23%), mental retardation (13%), or serious emotional disturbance (9%). Commonly attributed characteristics of these students are presented in Table 11.2.

Clearly, learning disabilities is the largest category of students with special learning needs and literacy skills are their major problem (Bender, 1995; Kaluger & Kolson,

TABLE 11.2 Characteristics of Students with Learning Disabilities

Domain	Elementary School Students	Middle/Secondary School Students
Cognitive	Average or above intellectual test performance; mental processing disorders influence learning and performance	Cumulative deficits in performance evidenced by falling further and further behind, resulting from long-term processing disorders
Academic	Significant performance deficits, limited generalization, work slowly on many tasks	Academic plateau of approximately fifth-grade achievement levels
Adaptive	Sometimes learn to compensate for deficiencies; high dependency needs	On-task and attention problems, passive off-task behavior
Social	Lack social perceptiveness, susceptible to peer influences, demonstrate poor self-esteem	Poor self-concept, poor social skills, poor social relations, lack of motivation
Perceptual-motor	Coordination and orientation problems	Coordination and orientation problems
Language	Receptive, integrative, and expressive language difficulties; poor social communication	Deficits in syntax, semantics, and pragmatic language
General characteristics	Specific learning problems in at least one academic content area; possible concomitant behavior problems	Less than optimal skills for academic success; years of failure manifest in academic plateau around fifth- or sixth-grade level

1978; U.S. Department of Education, 1996; Ysseldyke & Algozzine, 1994). Literacy, or ability to read and write, is critical to success in school. Among the literacy problems of students with learning disabilities are limited word recognition skills and concomitant problems with word, sentence, and passage comprehension as well as an inadequate repertoire of writing skills. These are students who have as much difficulty with oral reading as they do with silent reading. The types of errors they make include omissions of words, incorrect pronunciation of common sight words, long hesitations when encountering unknown words, and a general lack of comprehension of anything read (Bender, 1995). They experience difficulties in printing and handwriting from an early age. Their expressive writing is replete with errors in spelling as well as mistakes in punctuation, capitalization, and other conventions of syntax and grammar. What they write tends to be short, poorly organized, and impoverished in terms of creativity, imagination, and ideas (Lerner, 1997).

Other characteristics of upper elementary school students with learning disabilities also work against successful educational performance. Years of failure in school result in widespread achievement plateaus far below necessary for independence and success in secondary school. These deficits prevent meaningful involvement with many learning tasks and are compounded when the attention, memory, and language problems present in younger students are still present near the end of the elementary school years. They also fail to provide a sound basis for developing positive self-concepts and increase the likelihood that older students with learning disabilities will be social outcasts.

Intervention Perspectives

In 1975, when Public Law 94–142, the Education for All Handicapped Children Act, was enacted (subsequently superseded by the Individuals with Disabilities Education Act [IDEA]), Congress found that the special educational needs of most children and adolescents with disabilities were not being fully met. More than half did not receive appropriate educational services that would enable them to have full equality of opportunity; more than one million were entirely excluded from the public school system. Because of the lack of adequate services within the public school system, families were often forced to find services outside their local schools, often at great distance from their homes and at their own expense.

Since 1975, the act has been amended several times; its purposes, however, have not changed: (1) to ensure that all children, adolescents, and young adults with disabilities have available to them a free appropriate public education that emphasizes special education and related services designed to meet their unique needs; (2) to ensure that the rights of children with disabilities and their parents or guardians are protected; (3) to assist states and localities to provide for the education of all children with disabilities; and (4) to assess and ensure the effectiveness of efforts to educate children with disabilities (U.S. Department of Education, 1996). These four purposes have provided a solid foundation for the widespread delivery of educational services to students with disabilities since 1975.

Special education services are provided in six educational environments. Each involves different degrees of general and special classroom or school placement. Placement in *regular classes* means that students spend the majority of the school day with their general education peers and receive special education and related services outside the general classroom for less than 21% of the school day. Placement in a *resource room* means that students receive special education and related services outside the general classroom for at least 21% but no more than 60% of the school day. Some students receive special education and related services in *separate classes* outside the general class for more than 60% of the school day. *Separate school* includes students who receive special education and related services in a public or private day school for students with disabilities, at public expense, for more than 50% of the school day. *Residential facility* includes students who receive special education in public or private full-time treatment facilities, at public expense, for more than 50% of the school day. *Homebound/hospital* environment includes students placed in and receiving special education at home or in medical treatment facilities as primary service providers.

TABLE 11.3   Students with Disabilities Served in Different Educational Environments

Educational Environments	Age Group		
	6–11	**12–17**	**18–21**
Regular class	53.5	33.3	26.6
Resource room	24.8	35.1	28.1
Separate class	19.3	25.9	30.8
Separate school	1.9	3.7	10.3
Residential facility	0.3	1.1	2.9
Homebound/hospital	0.3	0.8	1.3

Source: U.S. Department of Education, Office of Special Education Programs, Data Analysis System (DANS).

A relatively large percentage of students aged 18 to 21 are served in separate classes and schools. Because general education students typically graduate at age 18, students with disabilities aged 18 to 21 who are still in school do not have same-age peers with whom to interact. Some educators assert that the most natural environments for these students are colleges and universities, work sites, postsecondary vocational training programs, or community-based instructional settings other than secondary schools. Elementary school students with disabilities are more likely than middle and secondary students with disabilities to be taught in regular classes (see Table 11.3). Most (80%) students with learning disabilities are provided special education in regular classes or resource rooms.

Meeting the needs of students with learning disabilities in these different settings has involved a variety of special educational programming options (see Table 11.4). *Full inclusion* and *consultation* keep students with learning disabilities in classes with their natural neighbors and peers. *Skill improvement tutoring* and *basic skills remediation* involve special education personnel more directly in content area teaching. *Functional skill instruction* and *work-study programs* focus on teaching alternative skills to students with learning disabilities. Among the most successful approaches have been those in which *learning strategies* are taught to students with learning disabilities as a means of coping with the demands of the general school curriculum.

Literacy and Learning Strategies Instruction

Early pioneers in educational psychology and the study of learning were interested in how thinking, intellectual skills, literacy, and inner language influenced knowledge, behavior, and development in children and adults. The field of cognitive psychology can be traced to their work and has a bearing on the learning strategies models used to address literacy needs of students with learning disabilities (Bender, 1995; Lerner, 1997). The cognitive model focuses on knowledge, intellectual skills, and inner language

TABLE 11.4   Program Options for Students with Learning Disabilities

Service Delivery Approach	Description	Advantages
Full inclusion	General and special education teachers provide instruction for students with learning disabilities in the same classes as students without disabilities.	Students with disabilities are provided same opportunities for success and failure as students without disabilities.
Consultation	Special education personnel provide assistance to teachers who teach students with disabilities in general education classes.	Students with disabilities remain in classes with neighbors and peers.
Learning strategies	Students with learning disabilities are taught coping skills for meeting the demands of the standard school curriculum.	Students have demonstrated effectiveness across different content areas of instruction and different educational settings.
Skill improvement tutoring	Students with learning disabilities are provided content area tutoring several times a week.	Standard course of study is maintained with assistance provided by trained personnel.
Basic skills remediation	Students with learning disabilities are taught basic skills during special class instructional time independent of instruction in general education classes.	Focus is on improvement of skills assumed necessary for success in standard course of study.
Functional skills instruction	Students with learning disabilities are taught "survival skills" (e.g., completing job applications) in addition to or as an alternative to the traditional school curriculum.	Focus is on skills areas deemed important later in life, not just as appropriate for progress in accepted curriculum.
Work-study programs	Students with learning disabilities are taught job skills and participate in job-related experiences as a part of the school day.	On-the-job experience and training have special relevance and provide motivation for many students.

including simple recall of facts to synthesis and evaluation and their relation to performance. It has bearing on teaching students with learning disabilities because it is a category evidenced by significant difficulties in the acquisition and performance of basic and advanced literacy skills.

An application of metacognitive concepts to the literacy problems of students with learning disabilities was developed and extended at the Kansas Learning Disabilities Institute (Clark, Deshler, Schumaker, Alley, & Warner, 1984; Deshler, Alley, Warner, & Schumaker, 1981; Deshler, Schumaker, Lenz, & Ellis, 1984). Using acronyms to structure inner language and facilitate learning, Deshler and colleagues specified the steps needed to complete common literacy tasks and taught students with learning disabilities how to use them. The *learning strategies* approach specified the steps a person would go through when completing a specific task. The steps formed the basis of an inner language the person could use when completing the task. Strategies have been developed and applied to common literacy tasks such as reading a paragraph, completing a multiple-choice test, and reading a content-specific chapter.

Learning Strategies Approaches

Cognition is how we think. Many children with learning disabilities need to be taught how to think. They need strategies for tasks such as organization, test taking, and remembering facts. They do not think how to approach a task. Some students with learning disabilities think that they will fail before they even attempt a task. If they do perform well, many times these students will attribute it to luck or level of difficulty of the task (e.g., too easy). If they do poorly, they will attribute it to their own lack of ability or effort. Students with learning disabilities need to be taught that they are in control. Reid (1988, p. 88) defines attribution as "children's explanations for their academic performance." Students with learning disabilities need attribution retraining. Some of these students have not been taught how to approach tasks; due to a lack of strategies, they do not know how to develop solutions to problems or tasks and they shut down. It is assumed that they do not care, but they have not been taught the steps to be successful. Teaching these students learning strategies helps them to be successful (Bender, 1995).

Once students are taught strategies and how to use them in various settings, they need to begin developing their own strategies for application in other situations. They need to be taught how to think and approach a task. Once they are successful, they will apply and use new strategies. This approach needs to click for these students. When they are successful, they will attribute this success to effort and continue using strategies they have learned.

Generalization is reached when the learning strategy is applied to various settings and situations. Based on the success of a strategy, students will determine if it is to be used in future situations. They do not always know how to modify a strategy and may need to be taught how to pick and choose pieces of a strategy then generalize. This is the ultimate goal for students with learning disabilities. They often need to be taught how to learn and how to adapt prior strategies to the task or situation at hand. As students find successes, they will begin to generalize strategies to other situations and settings. Many times, they need cues to remind them to use the strategy in their classes.

Learning strategies help students participate more actively in academic tasks. They are generally described as "techniques, principles, or rules that will facilitate the acquisition, manipulation, integration, storage, and retrieval of academic information across situations and settings" (Alley & Deshler, 1979, p. 13). A learning strategies model of instruction is designed to teach students "how to learn" rather than to teach students specific content (Alley & Deshler, 1979, p. 13).

The ultimate goal of learning strategies is to teach students a skill that is needed at the present time and to generalize the skill across situations and settings at various times. The University of Kansas Learning Strategies curriculum was designed to assist children and adolescents with learning disabilities in becoming more independent learners. Learning strategies teach the student a step-by-step process for a learning task, which allows the student to become an active part in the learning process. Learning strategies instruction uses a effective teaching model that proceeds from pretest/description to posttest/generalization stages using demonstration, rehearsal, practice, and feedback as its primary teaching methods (see Table 11.5).

Initially, strategies are learned in a specific context and are used only in that context. After the student is more proficient in strategy usage, he or she can think about the strategies and learn to use them for other tasks. This "conscious access to the routines available to the system is the highest form of mature human intelligence" (Brown, Bransford, Ferrara, & Campione, 1983).

TABLE 11.5   Overview of Learning Strategies Instruction

Step 1: Pretest and commitment	Teacher conducts formal and/or informal assessment to determine present level of functioning and identify appropriate area for strategy use. Teacher and student agree to use learning strategies as method for improving performance.
Step 2: Strategy description	Teacher describes the specific strategy to be used.
Step 3: Strategy demonstration and modeling	After describing strategy, the teacher demonstrates the strategy with specific material. The student observes the model presented by the teacher.
Step 4: Verbal rehearsal	The student, under the supervision of the teacher, rehearses the step-by-step elements of the strategy.
Step 5: Controlled practice and feedback	Teacher provides practice material at or below the student's reading level. The student applies the strategy to the target material while the teacher provides specific and immediate feedback to the student.
Step 6: Content-appropriate practice and feedback	Specific content area material (e.g., social studies) is selected by the teacher. The student(s) applies the strategy to the specific content material. Emphasis is given to using the strategy as previously learned.
Step 7: Posttest and direction for generalization	Data are collected relative to how effectively the student(s) was able to apply the strategy to the content material. Emphasis at this time is given to the application of the strategy to any specific content material.
Step 8: Generalization	Student(s) independently applies the strategy to material in a variety of settings and in a variety of content areas.

Learning Strategies Application

Metacognitive strategies can assist upper elementary school students with learning disabilities in becoming more efficient academic learners. The importance of teaching strategies for improving academic performance stems from the underlying academic deficits included in most definitions of learning disabilities. Students with learning disabilities often have poor organizational and planning skills needed in learning academic content (Englert & Raphael, 1988). They also do not have a plan of action for organizing their thought processes or performing most academic tasks. As a result of these factors, they often have negative attitudes toward learning. Ample evidence exists to support the use of learning strategies, and many are available for improving performance in key areas of literacy.

For example, a word decoding strategy uses the mnemonic DISSECT to assist students in identifying words: **D**iscover the context, **I**solate the prefix, **S**eparate the suffix, **S**ay the stem, **E**xamine the stem, **C**heck with someone, and **T**ry the dictionary. A visual imagery strategy teaches the student to form a mental picture of the events in a reading passage. A self-questioning strategy assists in forming questions about underlying information in a story and helps to answer comprehension questions at the end of the story. A paraphrasing strategy teaches students to paraphrase the main idea and details in each paragraph of the reading passage using the mnemonic RAP: **R**ead a paragraph, **A**sk yourself, "What were the main idea and details in the paragraph?" and **P**ut the main idea and details in your own words. Interpreting visual aids assist students in gaining information from tables, charts, graphs, pictures, maps, and diagrams. Multipass is a strategy to use with textbook chapters. This strategy requires the student to make three passes over the chapter to survey, find key information, and study the key information. Other strategies are focused on improving written language skills. For example, Welch (1992) indicated that students' attitudes toward paragraph writing improved after instruction and successful use of the PLEASE strategy: **P**ick a topic, **L**ist your ideas about it, **E**valuate your list, **A**ctivate a topic sentence, **S**upply supporting sentences, and **E**nd with a concluding sentence and evaluate your work.

An overview of other effective learning strategies to assist students in a variety of literacy areas is presented in Table 11.6. This information provides a quick reference of useful strategies for reading and writing problems commonly associated with learning disabilities. Each uses a structured technique. As described earlier, there are several stages in teaching a strategy to students with learning disabilities. Stage one includes a pretest and requires the student to make a commitment to learn the strategy. Stage two involves the teacher explaining the strategy, telling where to use the strategy, and stating the importance of using it. Stage three includes teacher modeling of the strategy, which allows the teacher to show how the strategy should be utilized. Stage four consists of verbal practice of the strategy steps. It is important for the student to have immediate recall of the strategy steps. Stage five is controlled practice where the student applies the strategy to a level in which they are comfortable working. Stage six involves content-appropriate practice in which the student applies the strategy to grade-level materials. Finally, posttests are used to evaluate competence with the

TABLE 11.6   Selected Learning Strategies with Relevance for Improving Literacy Skills

Reading

Strategies	Author	Practical Illustration
PARS (preview and studying)	Hoover (1989)	Preview Ask questions Review Summarize
SQ3R (content area reading)	Robinson (1961)	Survey. Look at the entire reading assignment for an overview. Question. Self-question using headings. Read. Read to answer questions. Review. Reread text to clarify.
POSSE (comprehension)	Englert and Mariage (1990)	Predict what ideas are in the story. Organize what ideas are in the story. Search for text structure. Summarize in your words. Evaluate.
Question-Answer Relationship (QAR) (comprehension)	Raphael (1986)	1. Right there: Answers are in the story (literal and detail). 2. Think and search: Look for the answer in several places. 3. Author and you: Inferences and conclusions are made. 4. On your own: Answer must come from readers' experience and knowledge.
Critical Thinking Map (comprehension)	Idol (1987)	Include on a story map: 1. Important events 2. Main idea or lesson 3. Other viewpoints and opinions 4. Reader's conclusions 5. Relevance to today

continued

strategy and procedures for generalization into the content area classroom are provided and used.

Each strategy has cue cards to remind students what to do at each of the stages of the instructional model. A student must master one level before progressing to the next. Management charts are kept in folders or posted in the classroom, and the lessons are carefully scripted for the strategy instructor to follow. Research (Deshler & Schumaker, 1986) has shown marked gains in student progress once strategy instruction has been implemented. Student progress is highly related to the strategy instructor's proficiency in the strategy, and the developers of the model want educational agencies to commit to a staff development program to instruct teachers in the strategy usage (Deshler & Schumaker, 1986).

Reading

Strategies	Author	Practical Illustration
Five-Step Reading Comprehension Strategy (comprehension)	Schunk and Rice (1987)	What do I have to do? 1. Read the questions. 2. Read the passage to find out what it is mostly about. 3. Think about what the details have in common. 4. Think about what would make a good title. 5. Reread the story if I do not know the answer to a question.
PENS (for writing sentences)	Sheldon and Schumaker (1985)	**P**ick a formula. **E**xplore words to fit the formula. **N**ote the words. **S**earch and check.
DEFENDS (for writing reason positions)	Ellis and Lenz (1987)	**D**ecide on exact position. **E**xamine the reasons for the position. **F**orm list of points to explain the reasons. **E**xpose position in first sentence. **N**ote each reason and supporting points. **D**rive home position in the last sentence. **S**earch for errors and correct.
TREE (for composing essays)	Graham and Harris (1989)	Note **T**opic sentence. Note **R**easons. **E**xamine reasons. Note **E**nding.
COPS (for monitoring)	Schumaker, Nolan, and Deshler (1985)	**C**apitalization **O**verall appearance **P**unctuation **S**pelling

Source: From *Learning Disabilities* (pp. 266–271), by O'Shea, O'Shea, and Algozzine, 1997, Boston: Allyn and Bacon.

Other Applications

A number of additional metacognitive strategies have been developed and used with students with learning disabilities. Most of these do not rely heavily on self-monitoring or use acronyms to facilitate learning, but each does encourage the use of inner language during the completion of literacy tasks.

KeyWord Method. Inefficient memory process plays a vital role in academic performance of students with learning disabilities. "It has been hypothesized that these memory problems result from failure to approach memory tasks in a strategic manner reflective of metamemorial awareness" (Palincsar & Brown, 1987, p. 66). The key word mnemonic method attempts to provide a way of remembering to facilitate encoding of information for easy retrieval (Mastropieri, Scruggs, Bakken, & Brigham, 1992; Mastropieri, Scruggs, & Levin, 1985). The student is taught to recode, relate, and retrieve information to be remembered. Levin (1983) refers to this process as the "three Rs" of associative mnemonic techniques. The key word technique is a method to remember an unfamiliar item by associating it with a meaningful item in the learners' knowledge base. For example, to learn that *oxalis* is a cloverlike plant, students are taught to think about an ox eating cloverlike plants. Or, to learn that *chiton* means loose garment, they associate a kite made out of loose garments.

Several researchers (Levin, 1983; Mastropieri, Scruggs, & Fulk, 1990; Mastropieri, Scruggs, & Levin, 1985; McLoone, Scruggs, Mastropieri & Zucker, 1986) have found that key word mnemonics are successful in promoting learning of vocabulary words in the content areas. Mnemonic strategies can benefit students with learning disabilities if they are taught how to use the strategy. Mnemonic instruction is an important technique to support the success of students with learning disabilities in upper elementary grades.

Advanced Organizers.   Ausubel, in the 1960s, was the first to present the concept of advanced organizers. Advanced organizers point out to the students what can be expected to occur during the class period. Lenz (1983, p. 12) states that advanced organizers are the activities a teacher does before teaching and include one or more of the following: (1) announcement of the benefits of the advanced organizer, (2) topics and subtopics, (3) physical requirements needed for the learner and instructor to accomplish the task, (4) background information related to new learning, (5) concepts to be learned (specific or general), (6) examples for clarification of concepts to be learned, (7) the organization or sequence in which the new information will be presented, (8) motivational information, (9) relevant vocabulary, and (10) goals or outcomes desired.

Students with learning disabilities profit from being taught how to use advanced organizers. Research has found that advanced organizers can be effective in assisting students with learning disabilities in organizing information (Lenz, 1983). Upper elementary school classroom teachers who use advanced organizers before instruction find they are generally more effective with students with learning disabilities than those who do not.

Working with Parents

The Individuals with Disabilities Education Act directs that an individualized education program (IEP) serves as the foundation for providing free, appropriate special education services to students with disabilities. An IEP includes:

(i) a statement of the child's present levels of educational performance, including—
    (I) how the child's disability affects the child's involvement and progress in the general curriculum; or

(II) for preschool children, as appropriate, how the disability affects the child's participation in appropriate activities;

(ii) a statement of measurable annual goals, including benchmarks or short-term objectives, related to—
    (I) meeting the child's needs that result from the child's disability to enable the child to be involved in and progress in the general curriculum; and
    (II) meeting each of the child's other educational needs that result from the child's disability;

(iii) a statement of the special education and related services and supplementary aids and services to be provided to the child, or on behalf of the child, and a statement of the program modifications or supports for school personnel that will be provided for the child—
    (I) to advance appropriately toward attaining the annual goals;
    (II) to be involved and progress in the general curriculum in accordance with clause (i) and to participate in extracurricular and other nonacademic activities; and
    (III) to be educated and participate with other children with disabilities and nondisabled children in the activities described in this paragraph;

(iv) an explanation of the extent, if any, to which the child will not participate with nondisabled children in the regular class and in the activities described in clause (iii);

(v)   (I) a statement of any individual modifications in the administration of State or districtwide assessments of student achievement that are needed in order for the child to participate in such assessment; and
    (II) if the IEP Team determines that the child will not participate in a particular State or districtwide assessment of student achievement (or part of such an assessment), a statement of—
      (aa) why that assessment is not appropriate for the child; and
      (bb) how the child will be assessed;

(vi) the projected date for the beginning of the services and modifications described in clause (iii), and the anticipated frequency, location, and duration of those services and modifications;

(vii)   (I) beginning at age 14, and updated annually, a statement of the transition service needs of the child under the applicable components of the child's IEP that focuses on the child's courses of study (such as participation in advanced-placement courses or a vocational education program);
    (II) beginning at age 16 (or younger, if determined appropriate by the IEP Team), a statement of needed transition services for the child, including, when appropriate, a statement of the interagency responsibilities or any needed linkages; and

(III) beginning at least one year before the child reaches the age of majority under State law, a statement that the child has been informed of his or her rights under this title, if any, that will transfer to the child on reaching the age of majority under section 615(m); and

(viii) a statement of—
    (I) how the child's progress toward the annual goals described in clause (ii) will be measured; and
    (II) how the child's parents will be regularly informed (by such means as periodic report cards), at least as often as parents are informed of their nondisabled children's progress, of—
        (aa) their child's progress toward the annual goals described in clause (ii); and
        (bb) the extent to which that progress is sufficient to enable the child to achieve the goals by the end of the year.

An "individualized education program team" is responsible for the IEP; this group includes the *parents* of a child with a disability, at least one of the child's general education teachers (if the child is participating in the regular curriculum), at least one special education teacher, and other representatives designated by school personnel and/or the parents (U.S. Department of Education, 1997).

Involving parents has been a continuing interest in special education. Parent groups were instrumental in initiating much of the legislation that governs contemporary practices; recent laws have extended parents' rights and more clearly articulated the extent to which they should be involved in their children's education. Educators also are increasingly aware of the very positive role parents can play in implementing special education programs. Some suggestions for involving parents of children with learning disabilities are as follows:

1. Discuss the specific nature of a child's disability and related literacy problems with his or her parents. Encourage them to discuss the problems and help them talk to their child by participating in an informative meeting with them and their child.
2. Encourage parents to work with school personnel to develop an appropriate plan of action. This might involve arranging screenings and assessments, reviewing test results, and making decisions about classroom placements and teaching approaches. Very often parents provide valuable information for decision making over and above that obtained by working with the child.
3. Encourage parents to work at home with their child even if he or she is receiving special education services. Encourage them to visit their local library frequently and to read to their child every day.
4. Help parents prepare a portfolio of information related to their child's disability. Include copies of school records as well as samples of schoolwork. The information can be a valuable tool in keeping track of progress and useful record to share with new teachers as the child moves along in school.

Perspective on Learning Disabilities and Literacy

Harris and Pressley (1991) indicated three important points in metacognitive strategy instruction. First, strategy instruction is and continues to grow as an area in the field of research. More research needs to be conducted in strategies instruction and how to apply it to the content areas. Strategy instruction needs to be incorporated into the general education classrooms. It will provide an environment for strategy generalization and also assist students without disabilities.

Second, strategy instruction is not a panacea. There are limitations to using strategies. Strategy instruction allows teachers to address the needs of students by providing a step-by-step process for approaching tasks. Strategies should be used when they meet the individual needs of the student, if they assist in remediating the students problem, if they appear to be the best solution, and if teachers are able to teach the strategy effectively (Lerner, 1997).

Third, good strategy instruction is not just memorizing the steps. Good strategy instruction incorporates teaching the students why they are learning a strategy, how it will help, when to use the strategy, and the settings appropriate for the use of the strategy. Students need to be actively involved in all stages of the strategy instruction. The teacher's role is to describe the strategy, model the strategy, provide practice and modify the strategy, and reteach when necessary. Effective teaching uses the following steps when implementing interventions based on the cognitive model:

1. Assess student's strategy usage for a specified task.
2. Teach students a strategy related to the task.
3. Practice using the strategy and evaluate proficiency.
4. Apply strategy in various settings.
5. Evaluate use and modify for application in other settings.
6. Teach students to design their own strategies:
    a. Select a task that needs a strategy.
    b. Break the task into component parts.
    c. Devise a mnemonic or other method to remember steps.
    d. Apply the strategy to the task.
    e. Modify the steps if necessary (include self-monitoring and self-questioning).

Special education serves students with special learning needs. All these students have problems and characteristics that make success in school difficult without special assistance. Students with learning disabilities demonstrate large discrepancies between their abilities and their performance in school. Students with speech or language problems have difficulty communicating with others. Students with mental retardation exhibit subaverage performance on intelligence tests and corresponding adaptive behavior problems. The behavior of students with serious emotional disturbance is characterized by social and emotional problems that inhibit learning. People began providing special education services to these students when it became clear that they were not profiting from the educational menu of experiences provided in regular public school classes.

Early special education services were primarily provided to individuals with mental retardation or serious emotional disturbance. Their educational programs were sometimes characterized as "clearinghouses" or custodial placements that left much to be desired relative to the fundamentals of good instruction and sound educational practices. With the advent of Public Law 94–142 and its subsequent supplements and amendments, more and more students were receiving special education services in public schools. As special education grew, greater concern emerged for the quality of services being provided, and students with disabilities were expected to receive educational services as much like normal as possible.

Today, many types of instructional interventions are included in efforts to provide special education to students with disabilities. Teaching them strategies to use in approaching academic tasks and interpersonal relations has been a popular, effective approach. Similarly, involving parents in their child's education is the method of choice for most children with disabilities. Because most students with mild disabilities receive part of their education in general education classrooms, we end this chapter with a few guidelines for teachers to use in helping children with literacy problems:

1. Sit or stand near children with disabilities when providing instructions or talking with them.
2. Encourage them to answer questions in class, and monitor their answers as a means of checking their learning.
3. Call the child's name before asking a question, and try to ask questions that will elicit a positive response several times during the day.
4. Use activities with time constraints or competitive pressures judiciously.
5. Reward correct responses and avoid punishing incorrect ones.
6. Consider using oral exams rather than written tests.
7. Have students share notes and assignments as a means of encouraging students.
8. Give credit for oral participating in class discussions.
9. Help students organize learning materials and time.

REFERENCES

Alley, G., & Deshler, D. (1979). *Teaching the learning disabled adolescent strategies and methods.* Denver, CO: Love.

Bender, W.N. (1995). *Learning disabilities: Characteristics, identification, and teaching strategies* (2nd ed.). Boston: Allyn and Bacon.

Brown, A.L., Bransford, J.D., Ferrara, R.A., & Campione, J.C. (1982). *Learning, remembering, and understanding.* (Technical Report No. 244). Champaign, IL: Author.

Clark, F.L., Deshler, D.D. Schumaker, J.B., Alley, G.R., & Warner, M.M. (1984). Visual imagery and self-questioning strategies to improve comprehension of written material. *Journal of Learning Disabilities, 17,* 145–149.

Coleman, M. (1986). *Behavior disorders.* Englewood Cliffs, NJ: Prentice Hall.

Deshler, D.D., Alley, G.R., Warner, M.M., & Schumaker, J.G. (1981). Instructional practices for promoting skill acquisition and generalization in severely learning disabled adolescents. *Learning Disabilities Quarterly, 4,* 415–421.

Deshler, D.D., Schumaker, J.G., Lenz, B.K., & Ellis, E.S. (1984). Academic and cognitive interventions for LD adolescents: Part II. *Journal of Learning Disabilities, 17,* 170–187.

Ellis, E.S., & Lenz, B.K. (1987). A component analysis of effective learning strategies for LD students. *Learning Disabilities Focus, 2,* 94–107.

Englert, C.S., & Mariage, T. (1990). Send for the POSSE: Structuring the comprehension dialogue. *Academic Therapy, 25,* 473–487.

Englert, C.S., & Raphael, T.E. (1988). Constructing well-formed prose: Process, structure, and metacognitive knowledge. *Exceptional Children, 54,* 513–520.

Graham, S., & Harris, K.R. (1989). Improving learning disabled students' skills at composing essays: Self-instructional strategy training. *Exceptional Children, 56,* 201–214.

Hallahan, D.D., & Kauffman, J.M. (1977). Labels, categories, behaviors: ED, LD, and EMR reconsidered. *Journal of Special Education, 11,* 139–149.

Harris, K.R. & Pressley, M. (1991). The nature of cognitive strategy instruction: Interactive strategy construction. *Exceptional Children, 57,* 392–404.

Henley, M., Ramsay, R.S., & Algozzine, R.F. (1996). *Characteristics and strategies for teaching students with mild disabilities* (2nd ed.). Boston: Allyn and Bacon.

Hoover, J.J. (1989). Study skills and the education of students with learning disabilities. *Journal of Learning Disabilities, 22,* 452–455.

Idol, L. (1987). A critical thinking map to improve content area comprehension of poor readers. *Remedial and Special Education, 8,* 28–40.

Kaluger, G., & Kolson, C.J. (1978). *Reading and learning disabilities.* Columbus, OH: Merrill.

Kauffman, J.M. (1997). *Characteristics of emotional and behavioral disorders of children and youth.* Columbus, OH: Merrill.

Lenz, K. (1983). Using advanced organizers. *The Pointer, 27,* 11–13.

Lerner, J. (1997). *Learning disabilities* (7th ed.). Boston: Houghton Mifflin.

Levin, J.R. (1983). Pictorial strategies for school learning: Practical illustrations. In M. Pressley & J.R. Levin (Eds.), *Cognitive strategy research: Educational applications* (pp. 213–237). New York: Springer-Verlag.

Lewis, R.B., & Doorlag, D.H. (1991). *Teaching special students in the mainstream* (3rd ed.). Columbus: Merrill.

Mastropieri, M.A., Scruggs, T.E., Bakken, J.P., & Brigham, F.J. (1992). A complex mnemonic strategy for teaching states and their capitals: Comparing forward and backward associations. *Learning Disabilities Research & Practice, 7,* 96–103.

Mastropieri, M.A., Scruggs, T.E., & Fulk, B.J.M. (1990). Teaching abstract vocabulary with the keyword method: Effects on recall and comprehension. *Journal of Learning Disabilities, 23,* 92–96.

Mastropieri, M.A., Scruggs, T.E., & Levin, J.R. (1985). Maximizing what exceptional students can learn: A review of research on the keyword method and related mnemonic techniques. *Remedial and Special Education, 6*(2), 39–45.

McLoone, B.B., Scruggs, T.E., Mastropieri, M.A., & Zucker, S. (1986). Memory strategy instruction with LD adolescents. *Learning Disabilities Research, 2,* 45–53.

Palincsar, A.S., & Brown, D.A. (1987). Enhancing instructional time through attention to metacognition. *Journal of Learning Disabilities, 20,* 66–75.

Raphael, T.E. (1986). Teaching question-answering relationships, revisited. *The Reading Teacher, 39,* 516–523.

Reid, D.K. (1988). *Teaching the learning disabled: A cognitive approach.* Boston: Allyn and Bacon.

Robinson, F.P. (1961). *Effective study.* New York: Harper & Row.

Robinson, N.M., & Robinson, H.B. (1976). *The mentally retarded child* (2nd ed.). New York: McGraw-Hill, 1976.

Schumaker, J.B., Nolan, S.M., & Deshler, D.D. (1985). *The error monitoring strategy.* Lawrence: University of Kansas.

Schunk, D.H., & Rice, J.M. (1987). Enhancing comprehension skill and self-efficacy with strategy value information. *Journal of Reading Behavior, 19,* 285–302.

Sheldon, J. & Schumaker, J.B. (1985). *The sentence writing strategy.* Lawrence, KS: Excel Enterprises.

U.S. Department of Education (1996). *Eighteenth annual report to Congress.* Washington, DC: Author.

U.S. Department of Education. (1997). *Individuals with Disabilities Education Act Amendments of 1997.* Washington, DC: Author.

Welch, M. (1992). The PLEASE Strategy: A metacognitive learning strategy for improving the paragraph writing of students with mild learning disabilities. *Learning Disabilities Quarterly, 15*(2), 119–28.

Ysseldyke, J.E., & Algozzine, B. (1990). *Special education* (2nd ed.). Boston: Houghton Mifflin.

Ysseldyke, J.E., & Algozzine, B. (1994). *Special education* (3rd ed.). Boston: Houghton Mifflin.

12

Exemplary Schooling for Intermediate and Middle School Students Acquiring English

JOSEFINA VILLAMIL TINAJERO

SANDRA HURLEY

University of Texas at El Paso

Erika and Nga are middle school students at Highlands Middle School. Thirteen-year-old Erika and her parents moved to the United States from Mexico eight months ago. She attended school through the fifth grade and is highly literate in her native language, Spanish. Fourteen-year-old Nga moved to the United States from China with his mother and two younger sisters only two months ago. He attended school in his native country for a total of three years. Like Erika, the majority of students at Highlands Middle are Latino, roughly 89%; the others are 1% Asian/Pacific Islanders and 10% other. In the past, the school had a more diverse enrollment and included a greater number of White students. Like many other schools in Texas, Highlands Middle has become increasingly Latino, with a growing Asian/Pacific Islander population. It has also become increasingly non–English speaking. About 28% of students are learning English as their second language. Like Nga, a large number of the limited English proficient (LEP) students at Highlands Middle School are recent immigrants with limited school experiences. Others, like Erika, are highly literate in their native language and have had excellent schooling in their native countries. All bring rich cultural and linguistic backgrounds. Our schools, however, have not been adequately prepared to respond to their needs. Their challenge is to provide equal educational opportunity by involving students acquiring English in the full range of academic possibilities offered to English proficient students while assisting them to develop proficiency in English.

The Challenge

The growing population and diversity of students like Erika and Nga in our schools is of great interest and concern to teachers and administrators. Several recent reports have identified dramatic demographic changes in the United States with particular emphasis on shifts in the ethnic composition of school-age children (Census Bureau, 1993). The increase in the number of students who speak a native language other than English has been dramatic and is expected to remain so (Nieto, 1993). Today, nearly one of every five American students (2.5–3.5 million) entering school knows a language other than English. This number will increase to over 5 million by 2020, and by the 2030s, language minority students are predicted to account for about 40% of the school-age population (Berliner & Biddle, 1995). The LEP student population is present in over 42% of all school districts nationwide, and 15% of all public school teachers have at least one LEP student who is not fluent enough in English to complete most of the assigned work in their classrooms (Development Associates, 1993). The most common languages as reflected by enrollments in bilingual education programs are Spanish (73%), Vietnamese (4%), Hmong (2%), and Cantonese (2%) (Thomma & Cannon, 1995).

The picture presented here of Highlands Middle School and the rest of the country underlines the educational issues and challenges that educators must address quickly, responsibly, and creatively. Finding ways to address the needs of LEP students in our classrooms is an increasing concern, particularly at the intermediate and middle grades, where students like Erika and Nga experience great difficulty understanding concepts and expressing and exploring their thinking in English. In particular, teachers and administrators are grappling with the challenges posed by the linguistic, educational, and socioeconomic differences that students bring to the classroom. These differences include a variety of learning experiences and academic histories as well as a variety of language and literacy proficiencies in both English and other languages.

According to McLeod (1996), "Educating LEP and other minority students to the same high standards that are now expected of all students will be a major challenge for the nation in the next few decades" (p. 2). The challenges are exacerbated at the intermediate and middle school levels where (1) the curriculum is much more cognitively demanding than in the primary grades, requiring high levels of academic language competence and understanding of highly decontextualized concepts and ideas; and (2) teachers must also grapple with the unique needs of adolescents.

Since the late 1960s, educators have developed a wide range of programs to address the needs of LEP students. After much experimentation, U.S. schools now have clear research achievement data that point to the most powerful models and methods of effective schooling for English learners (Thomas & Collier, 1997/1998). Data also exist on exemplary schools that have met the challenge of educating LEP and other language minority students to high standards (McLeod, 1996). This chapter highlights some of these new models and methods from a literacy perspective and challenges schools to implement programs that provide LEP students with access to academic programs of high quality while guiding them toward full mastery of English. This chapter also focuses on pedagogy, on the language of instruction, on methods, and on strategies and techniques that allow students to participate fully in challenging academic work despite their limited English proficiency. It begins with a review of current research and theory and then proceeds to practical curricular, programmatic and hands-on methods and techniques that maximize students' learning opportunities and encourage them to think critically.

The Need for Innovative and Challenging Programs and Curriculum Designs for LEP Students in Grades 4–8

Recall that Erika and Nga, characters from the scenario that opened this chapter, possessed rich resources—their native language and cultural backgrounds and, in Erika's case, literacy in her native language (L1)—that could be supportive of learning to high standards at Highlands Middle School. For too many students in our schools, however, those rich resources remain largely untapped in their classrooms, hidden behind linguistic barriers. Their cultural and linguistic diversity is often perceived by teachers and administrators alike as a problem to be corrected rather than as an asset for classrooms and for society in general (Nieto, 1993; Wiburg, 1998). Students' limited English proficiency is seen as both a barrier to education and a valid criterion for special treatment: remediation, a watered-down curriculum, limited opportunities to interact with proficient English speakers, and endless grammar and vocabulary exercises to the virtual exclusion of more engaging, challenging, and significant content (California Department of Education, 1990, p. 2). Unlike Erika and Nga, most will remain separated from proficient English speakers until they acquire sufficient English. These schools fall short of integrating students in the school community, an important factor in their success. They also fall short of helping students achieve academically to high standards.

Recent interviews with intermediate and middle school teachers and administrators revealed a number of concerns that indicate how some schools fail LEP students. Salient among those concerns were the following:

1. The great majority of students in the middle grades are placed in English as a second language (ESL) pull-out programs in which English acquisition is the sole focus of instruction with no L1 literacy support. This subtractive model eradicates the native language and sends students a strong message that their native language is a barrier to learning, rather than an asset and resource.
2. The majority of students seem to be making appropriate progress in their acquisition of English but lag behind academically. They acquire limited proficiency in English at the expense of a quality education.
3. A large number of LEP students enrolled in bilingual education programs in the elementary grades are exited prematurely, the majority of them at the third- or fourth-grade levels under the assumption that because they know the social lan-

guage, they must know the academic language as well. Serious academic gaps surface in the intermediate and middle grades.

4. Teachers lack a comprehensive, integrated curriculum for grades 7 and 8. Many of them create their own lessons and materials, often borrowing from various programs and sources, including some from the primary grades.

5. A large number of teachers are not comfortable working with LEP students. They lack knowledge, skills, and materials and are in need of extensive staff development.

6. There is a need to align the curriculum both vertically and horizontally because LEP students should not only be the responsibility of ESL teachers but the responsibility of the entire campus. All teachers and administrators in the school should be concerned and knowledgeable about effective instruction for LEP students.

These concerns are indicative of the need for instructional improvement to address the needs of LEP students. They are indicative of the need to implement creative and innovative programs and strategies that will allow LEP students to thrive and excel. The following theoretical framework for language and literacy development and learning will serve as the backdrop for a discussion on these programs and strategies.

Theoretical Framework for Language and Literacy Development and Learning

Beginning in the 1970s, a substantial knowledge base on literacy instruction for nonnative speakers by educators and researchers has been developing. It has yielded information concerning effective program models and excellent instructional practices that teachers can use to meet the needs of intermediate and middle school students like Erika and Nga. To improve instruction for these students, most educators agree that schools must put in place the following:

- Programs that educate LEP students to the same high standards expected of all students by implementing programs and strategies that provide students with access to high-quality teaching (McLeod, 1996)
- Programs that develop high levels of literacy, academic skills, and knowledge (Collier, 1995a) in the L1 and L2
- New and innovative instructional programs and curricula grounded in instructional approaches that consider the students' languages, cultures, and developmental characteristics as valuable sources of knowledge
- Enrichment programs that are intellectually challenging and use students' linguistic and cultural experiences as a resource for interdisciplinary, discovery learning (Chiang 1994; Thomas & Collier 1997)
- Programs that make use of strategies that incorporate the resources available within diverse cultures to build, rather than stifle, student learning (Au, 1993; Wiburg, 1998, p. 272)

■ Innovative scheduling and curriculum models that integrate LEP students into the total school community and make the entire school responsible for them (Emslie, Contreras, & Padilla, 1998).

Exemplary Schooling for Language Minority Students

A recent study of exemplary schooling for LEP students by the National Clearinghouse on Bilingual Education (McLeod, 1996) highlights schools that have successfully met the challenge of providing equal educational opportunities to all students regardless of differences among students in English proficiency and other characteristics. The schools profiled in the report have been able to make education reform work for students who are not yet proficient in English. The study also identifies the features that characterize these exemplary schools as well as the goals that ensure access to high-quality teaching. Findings from the report that relate specifically to language and literacy are as follows. The exemplary schools

1. Provided LEP students with a rich intellectual diet in all areas of the curriculum, including the language arts, not a remedial or basic skills curriculum.
2. Expected LEP students to achieve to high standards in English literacy.
3. Used curriculum approaches and instruction that were congruent with recent education reform trends, emphasizing depth, critical thinking, hands-on learning, relevance, exploration process, and connections across disciplines.
4. Had LEP students engaged in intellectually enriching activities in both English and in their native language in all areas of the curriculum.
5. Focused on delivering a high-quality curriculum in the language arts, and to make it accessible to students, both in their native language and in English.
6. Had comprehensive language development programs for LEP students, designed to help them learn English to a high level of proficiency.
7. Recognized that literacy in students' native language aids them in acquiring English; thus, all schools supported, and where possible provided, instruction in students' native languages.
8. Focused not only on the acquisition of English, but also on the development of mature literacy; thus all the schools attempted to foster in students a deep engagement with reading and writing as processes.
9. Used language arts curricular approaches such as literature-based instruction, readers' theater, readers' workshop, and writers' workshop, commonly used with English-proficient students in many schools, with LEP students.
10. Allowed students to use their native language to ask or answer questions when they are unable to do so in English; thus, students who are not yet fully proficient in English are able to participate using their native language when needed, either with the teacher or with fellow students (McLeod, 1996, pp. 1–15).

Specific strategies observed in the language arts in the exemplary schools (McLeod, 1996, pp. 5–9) included having students

- Discuss various genres of fiction and nonfiction and then work independently writing their own books for an hour at a time (p. 5).
- Work in pairs to read and analyze a work of literature, employing and discussing various reading strategies (p. 5).
- Be involved in writing workshops, reading workshops, and readers' theater approaches to guide them into developing high levels of literacy (p. 6).
- Learn not just to read and write, but to engage in in-depth literary analysis (p. 6).
- Speak, read books, and write in Spanish, with others using English, depending on the stronger language (p. 6).
- Select books to read in either English or Spanish (p. 6).
- Read high-quality literature; write reports, newsletters, and books (p. 6).
- Read authentic literature and conduct literary analyses—exploring plot, character, and theme—rather than simply reading for information or comprehension of facts (p. 9).
- Write journals, news stories, and books, subjecting each to a multistep process of writing, editing, and rewriting (p. 9).
- Be involved not only in understanding story line but also in drawing character maps, writing to compose a persuasive letter, and forming literature discussion groups (p. 9).
- Use laptop computers and Hypercard software to produce multimedia book reports.

In summary, LEP students in exemplary schools included in the study were engaged in challenging academic pursuits in the language arts. Their native language was viewed and used as a resource for learning rather than as an obstacle. Students were allowed to complete assignments and participate in discussions in either English or their native language. The schools' language goal for students was focused on full mastery of English rather than transition from native language to English (McLeod, 1996, p. 9).

Language Development for School

Collier's (1995b) conceptual model of language for school reflects a similar philosophy about the complexity of schooling and the development of literacy skills for LEP students: Language learning cannot be isolated from other educational issues, and the acquisition of English and English literacy should not be the sole concern in educating LEP students. Collier's model helps to explain the many complex interacting factors that the school child experiences when acquiring a second language. The model includes four interdependent and complex components: academic, cognitive, linguistic, and social development.

Collier maintains that all four components are interdependent and that the development of one of the components to the neglect of another may be detrimental to a student's academic success. "The academic, cognitive, and linguistic components must be viewed as developmental, and for the child, adolescent, and young adult still going through the process of formal schooling, development of any one of these three

FIGURE 12.1   Language Acquisition for School

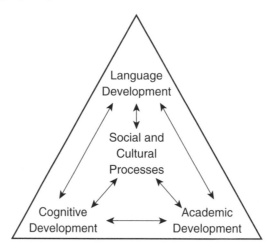

Source: From "Acquiring a Second Language for School" by V.P. Collier, 1995, *Directions in Language and Education, 1*(4), p. 2. Washington, D.C.: National Clearinghouse for Bilingual Education. Reprinted with permission from the author and the National Clearinghouse for Bilingual Education (NCBB), The George Washington University, Washington, D.C.

components depends critically on simultaneous development of the other two, through both first and second languages" (p. 4). Natural language, academic, and cognitive development must be allowed to flourish. Key among the components are the role of the native language, literacy in the native language, and the integration of effective methods and strategies for teaching English. McLeod's study on exemplary schools for LEP students supports Collier's theoretical framework.

Developing Literacy through the First Language

The native language plays a critical role in promoting literacy and, ultimately, in the overall success of LEP students. A number of researchers (Cummins 1989, 1991; Krashen & Biber, 1988; Ramirez, Yuen, & Ramey, 1991) have found that literacy instruction in the native language is the most pedagogically sound way to teach students acquiring English about the relationship between meaning and print in both the native language and English. Literacy in the native language has been found to be the most stable predictor of English literacy. In fact, research shows that those students with high levels of literacy proficiency in the L1 perform better on tasks of academic English than do students with low levels of language and literacy proficiency in their native language (Fischer & Cabello, 1978; Lindholm & Zierlein, 1991; Medina & de la Garza, 1989; Snow, 1990; Krashen, 1995). Thus, "there is good reason to support reading in both first and second language. Free reading in the first language may mean more reading, and hence more literacy development in the second language" (Krashen, 1995, p. 8).

Research has consistently shown that students acquire common underlying literacy skills most efficiently in the primary language and that once these skills are mastered, the students can transfer those skills quite easily to English (Cummins, 1989; Lindholm, 1991; Ramirez, Yuen, & Ramey, 1991; Tinajero & Ada, 1993). Empirical evidence has shown that children who are dominant in a language other than English acquire academic language and literacy skills rapidly and better in both the native language and English when they attain literacy proficiency in the mother tongue. Both on psycholinguistic and sociolinguistic grounds, Cummins (1989) argues strongly that, overall, nondominant speakers of English do better in school, in both their native language and English if they are given ample opportunity to attain literacy proficiency through their native language.

Most recently, a report from the National Research Council (1998) also pointed out the value of the native language in learning to read. The report had several recommendations, including the following concerning LEP students: "If language minority children arrive at school with no proficiency in English but speaking a language for which there are instructional guides, learning materials, and locally available proficient teachers, then these children should be taught how to read in their native language while acquiring proficiency in spoken English, and then subsequently taught to extend their skills to reading in English" (p. 11). Success in learning to read in the primary grades is important to success in reading in the intermediate and middle grades.

Integrating Language Development with Content Learning

To succeed in school, students must develop the cognitive and academic skills required for learning academic subject matter, including the language arts. Students must also acquire high levels of English language proficiency, including the cognitive academic language proficiency needed to manipulate abstract concepts they encounter in the language arts. To achieve these goals, teachers must integrate language development with content teaching, make use of learner's experiences, and focus on higher-level cognitive skills.

The challenge for teachers is to identify effective ways in which language instruction and academic content instruction in the language arts can be successfully combined so as to introduce children to a new language and a new set of cultural experiences simultaneously. The challenges are to adapt the language of instruction without watering down the content and to use materials that follow the core curriculum but that are adapted or supplemented for students acquiring English (Crandall & Willetts, 1986). To meet these challenges, teachers must be knowledgeable and skilled at integrating a variety of strategies and techniques that facilitate language growth across the stages of language acquisition while focusing on teaching the language arts concepts.

Role of Interaction in Language and Concept Development

Classrooms that are highly interactive and that emphasize problem solving and discovery learning facilitate language and concept development (Collier, 1995a; Freeman & Freeman, 1992; Tinajero, Calderon, & Hertz-Lazarowitz, 1993; Wong Fillmore, 1991). Although English acquisition and literacy development are viewed by teachers as primary goals for LEP students, an equally important objective is engaging students in challenging work in cooperative groups in all areas of the curriculum, including the language arts. Cooperative learning activities increase the frequency and variety of second language practice through different types of interaction. Such activities also provide students with opportunities to act as resources for each other and thus assume a more active role in learning. As McLeod (1996) found in his study of exemplary schools, "If a group of students includes a native language mate whose English is more proficient, they can get immediate clarification if they don't understand what is being said. Even if no peer translator is available, LEP students working with other students on a common task are more likely to be able to understand and participate than if they struggled alone to comprehend directions from a teacher or textbook" (p. 16).

Organize Programs and Instruction in Innovative Ways

A number of models, instructional programs, methods and practices, and initiatives have been found to ensure access to high-quality teaching for LEP students, particularly as it relates to literacy. A discussion of some of these models, programs, and methods that show promise for intermediate and middle school LEP students follows.

School Structures and Programs

To build program capacity to support the development of high levels of literacy acquisition for intermediate and middle school students, four initiatives show promise:

1. Change the "quick-exit" mentality of bilingual programs to "late-exit," which gives students the opportunity to develop high levels of proficiency and literacy in both the native language and English before being mainstreamed.
2. Implement more two-way programs in which bilingualism and biliteracy are promoted for all students in grades 4 to 8.
3. Replace traditionally taught ESL-only, pull-out programs at all grade levels with quality programs that integrate state-of-the-art second language practices and subject matter with continuous staff development and that emphasize respect for students' native language and culture (Collier, 1995a).

4. Replace traditional strategies and techniques with those that integrate LEP students into the total school community: interdisciplinary team teaching, block scheduling, cooperative learning, and Sheltered English.

Late-Exit and Two-Way Dual Language Programs

ESL-only and early-exit programs show the highest achievement levels for LEP students as measured by standardized tests in English up to third grade (Ramirez, Yuen, & Ramey, 1991). Those scores begin to fall over the next three years, however. Two-way dual language and late-exit programs were the only programs able to maintain a steady growth in the achievement levels of LEP students. Students in two-way/dual language programs scored at or above the 50th percentile after five to seven years in the programs. Collier (1995a) found similar results. She found that two-way bilingual education at the elementary school level (K–6) was the most promising program model for the long-term academic success of language minority students. As a group, students in this program maintained grade-level skills in their first language at least through sixth grade and reached the 50th percentile or NCE (National Curve Equivalency) in their second language generally after four to five years of schooling in both languages. They also sustain the gains they made when they reach secondary education, unlike students in programs that provide little or no academic support in the first language. Program characteristics include:

- Integrated schooling, with English speakers and language minority students learning academically through each others' languages, including literacy and biliteracy
- Perceptions among staff, students, and parents that it is a "gifted and talented" program, leading to high expectations for student performance
- Equal status of the two languages achieved, to a large extent, creating self-confidence among language minority students
- Closer home–school cooperation by both language minority and language majority parents
- Continuous support for staff development, emphasizing whole language approaches, natural language acquisition through all content areas, cooperative learning, interactive and discovery learning, and cognitive complexity of the curriculum for all proficiency levels

Figure 12.2 summarizes Collier and Thomas's research findings. Collier (1995a) also found that

> the most significant student background variable was the amount of formal schooling students had received in their first language. Across all program treatments, nonnative speakers being schooled in a second language for part or all of the school day typically do reasonably well in the early years of schooling (kindergarten through the second or third grade). But from fourth grade on through middle school and high school, when the academic, cognitive and literacy demands of the curriculum increase rapidly with each succeeding year, students with little or no academic and cognitive development in their first language do less and less well as they move into the upper grades. (pp. 5–6)

FIGURE 12.2   Effectiveness of Bilingual Education Program Models

PATTERNS OF K–12 ENGLISH LEARNERS' LONG-TERM ACHIEVEMENT IN NCEs ON STANDARDIZED TESTS IN ENGLISH READING COMPARED ACROSS SIX PROGRAM MODELS

(Results aggregated from a series of 4–8 year longitudinal studies
from well-implemented, mature programs in five school districts)

Program 1: Two-way developmental bilingual education (BE)
Program 2: One-way developmental BE, including ESL taught through academic content
Program 3: Transitional BE, including ESL taught through academic content
Program 4: Transitional BE, including ESL, both taught traditionally
Program 5: ESL taught through academic content using current approaches
Program 6: ESL pullout—taught traditionally

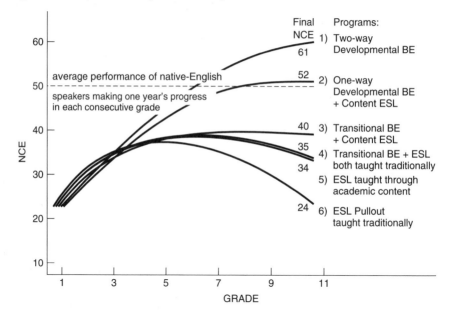

Source: From *School Effectiveness and Language Minority Students* by W.P. Thomas and V. Collier, 1997, p. 53. Washington, D.C.: NCBE Resource Collection Series, 9. Reprinted with permission from the author and the National Clearinghouse for Bilingual Education (NCBE), George Washington University, Washington, D.C.

School-within-a-School Scheduling

Some elementary and middle high schools have integrated a strand of two-way dual language education. One or two sections of each grade, K–6, are designated two-way classrooms so that students can follow this strand as they move up the grades. Similar models are being implemented in middle schools.

Erika and Nga, for example, are 2 of 80 sixth- to eighth-grade students on the

Roadrunner Team heterogeneously grouped by age and language level at Highlands Middle School. The program is for first-year immigrant, non-English-speaking students, organized into a "family" of 50 to 60 students. This structure creates a school-within-a-school that allows students and faculty to create a learning community. The structure reduces isolation and allows Erika and Nga to have a consistent group of faculty members, all subject matter specialists with ESL training. This sheltered English program incorporates a strong ESL component, an integrated curriculum, cooperative learning, and a whole language approach with rich literature-based literacy instruction. The program is implemented by teachers who are specially trained in subject matter, ESL, and sheltered English. The program is supplemented by Spanish language classes. Next year, Erika and Nga will move to the intermediate level, where they will take some sheltered content classes, mainstream classes, an ESL class, and, in the case of Erika, a Spanish language arts class. Before leaving Highlands Middle School, they will be taking mainstream classes while continuing to receive ESL support, and they will thus be ready to meet the challenges of high school.

The program implemented at Highlands Middle School is one of several program models serving intermediate and middle school students. It is also one that integrates a more innovative management and instructional plan. The majority of LEP students in grades 4 to 6, however, are enrolled in self-contained bilingual education programs or ESL pull-out programs. Those in grades 7 to 8 are, for the most part, enrolled in ESL pull-out or sheltered English classrooms.

Block Scheduling/Interdisciplinary Team Teaching

Block scheduling, also referred to as interdisciplinary team teaching, is being used increasingly in middle schools to address the needs of students acquiring English. This type of scheduling involves organizing students in families that allow them to have instructional contact with a small number of staff who deliver core classes, including the language arts, to a small group of students. The Highlands Middle School student body, for example, is organized into eight families: two families at each grade level in grades 6, 7, and 8, and two additional families for newcomer students. Each family has between 125 and 150 students, with the exception of the newcomer families, which have between 50 and 60 students. Students in the newcomer families span the three grade levels at the school but have their mathematics and science classes at the appropriate grade level (Berman, McLaughlin, Minicucci, Nelson, & Woodworth, 1995). The family structure at Highlands creates schools-within-a-school that allow students and faculty to create a learning community and to integrate language and literacy instruction throughout the curriculum. This type of scheduling brings several advantages, such as having a group of teachers interact with a small number of students and students have a consistent group of faculty members who are aware of their language and literacy needs.

The family structure also reduces the isolation students feel in a more impersonal traditional junior high school setting and eases the transition from elementary school to the high school. The family structure lends itself to curriculum coordination across subjects and grade levels, the development of curriculum themes, and team teaching and planning. It has also make it easier for teachers to pursue cooperative learning strategies (Berman et al., pp. 9, 19).

Thematic and Integrated Curriculum/ Interdisciplinary Designs

Block scheduling facilitates the integration of curriculum and thematic units. Some schools have schoolwide themes around which the whole school or whole instructional area or grade level plans its activities. As at Highlands Middle School, themes are used to help teams integrate their curriculum and to provide schoolwide or programwide coherence to the curriculum. Broad-based issues, problems, and themes serve as the organizing element. Teachers determine common generalizations and concepts to be developed across disciplines. For example, at Highlands Middle School,

> the two families for newcomers plan thematic units for the two families. At one point, one family developed an integrated unit on Chile. In social studies, students learned, read and wrote about the historic and continuing tensions between Mexico and New Mexico over the chili crop. In mathematics, students made graphs plotting the relative heat of chilies, studied crop yields in different parts of the world, and computed yield of chilies by acre. Students developed salsa recipes using fractions, adjusting recipe proportions for smaller and larger batches of salsa. In Spanish class, students read literature about the chili god and composed their own stories extending the myth. In science, students studied chilies during the unit on green plants, dissected chilies, and learned about chili seed dispersal. (McLeod, 1996, p. 11)

The language arts curriculum was organized around literary works.

Organizing the Language Arts Curriculum around Literary Works

In exemplary schools identified by McLeod (1996), the curriculum was organized around compelling literary works: prose and poetry, fiction and nonfiction, old favorites and contemporary offerings, and culturally relevant selections. The students read literature pieces related to the theme, wrote in their journals, and wrote expository essays and stories. Quality literature gave students an opportunity to appreciate English in meaningful contexts, to hear the rhythm and intonations of the language, and to become familiar with idiomatic and syntactical structures while gradually gaining an understanding of the text. In short, the literature provided models for language and concept development.

Integrate a Quality ESL Component

At the elementary level, ESL is an important component of bilingual education programs. It is also a stand-alone curriculum model, particularly in the middle school, which focuses on developing high levels of academic English language proficiency by providing comprehensible input—understandable, meaningful instruction. According to Tinajero and Schifini (1993, 1997), ESL methodology experienced dramatic shifts in the 1990s. Exemplary instructional programs and practices for LEP students reflect these shifts, as shown in Figure 12.3.

FIGURE 12.3   Shifts in ESL Impacting Programs and Curriculum Design

From		To
1. Emphasis on survival language and basic communication skills	➡	A focus on building academic language so crucial to success in the mainstream
2. Presentation of language through random topics such as clothing, days	➡	Use of grade-level content as the vehicle for language development
3. Instruction targeted to separate proficiency levels	➡	Content-based instruction with multilevel strategies that include all students
4. Teaching skills in isolation	➡	Teaching skills in the context of purposeful communication
5. Unrelated ESL instruction	➡	Instruction linked to themes and content area concepts
6. Individual student text and workbooks	➡	Wide array of resources relevant to students

Quality ESL programs reflects these shifts and support student learning by:

- Providing students with a rich-language and highly interactive environment
- Using grade-level content as the vehicle for language development and literacy
- Using authentic literature that is connected to grade-level content as the basis for reading and writing activities
- Integrating multilevel teaching strategies to make instruction appropriate and understandable to all students
- Focusing on building academic language proficiency and literacy, not the basic interpersonal communication skills only
- Developing language skills in context
- Using a wide array of materials for hands-on interactive learning
- Integrating strategies and techniques that have proven to be effective with LEP students, such as cognitive mapping, Directed Reading-Thinking Activity (DR-TA), and literature response journals

These strategies and techniques when integrated with teaching content are referred to as sheltered English. ESL and sheltered subject matter integrated with literacy activities provide comprehensible input directly (Krashen, 1995).

Maximizing Achievement in the Language Arts for LEP Students

A number of strategies show promise in supporting student learning and maximizing achievement in the language arts.

Address Students' Learning from Their Cultural Perspective

Like Erika and Nga, each student comes to school with different backgrounds and beliefs. The schools' role is "to validate and affirm students' cultural identity, to instill in students a pride in their heritage and a confidence in their academic ability" (McLeod, 1996, p. 17). Teachers can accomplish these goals by providing LEP and non-LEP students with opportunities to read from a wide selection of culturally relevant literature, to analyze that literature from different cultural perspectives, and to write literature responses from their own points of view. Activities from other cultures should be integrated with language arts themes every day.

Provide Background Knowledge and Personalize Lessons

The more knowledge and experience students have of the language and content of the lesson, the easier it will be for them to understand it. The following strategies will help students access difficult literary pieces:

- Draw examples from the experiences of students as the basis for helping them understand and learn new concepts and to read and write about them.
- Use analogies to relate the teaching of new concepts to experiences in the students' backgrounds, homes, and neighborhoods.
- Personalize the content by using the names of people and places familiar to students.
- Encourage students to explain a character's motive or the main idea of a literature selection to other students with strong command of both languages.
- Elicit experiences and activities relative to the native culture of the students.

Maximize Interaction

Encourage small group work that focuses on cooperative learning to allow for socialization and to build confidence in each student's ability to perform reading and writing tasks successfully. Encourage peer tutoring—students helping students—to facilitate understanding of difficult literature pieces. Try creative classroom arrangements that encourage talking, writing, modeling, and acting out ideas. Use open-ended activities in which students solve real-life problems related to their reading and writing assignments. In short, traditional techniques in which the learner is treated as a passive recipient of knowledge must be replaced with current state-of-the-art approaches that emphasize the participatory nature of language and concept development (Collier, 1995a).

Use of Multilevel Strategies

The level of participation and responses required of students during language arts activities can be tailored to address the specific needs of students who may be at different levels of language proficiency. These strategies are known as multilevel strategies. The unique combination of grade-level content plus multilevel teaching strategies can facilitate access to the language arts core curriculum. For example, students at the preproduction level can be asked to participate in answering questions that require a simple yes/no response, to point to a picture, or to participate in a play which requires little or no verbal response. Students at the early production stages can be asked questions that require short phrase responses or short explanations about a story. Students at the speech emergence level may be asked to provide short explanations, descriptions, or comparisons. On the other hand, students at the intermediate and advanced fluency levels can be asked questions that require the use of higher-order language and that require them to produce language with varied grammatical structures and vocabulary. In this way, LEP students are able to participate in cognitively demanding activities along with students who are proficient in English.

Build on the Strengths and Interests of Adolescents

Middle school students have an intense interest in themselves, in peers, and in social interactions (Vygotsky, 1962; Irvin, 1998). Peer and social relationships are of extreme importance at this age. With physical changes come changes in intellectual capacity and emotional stability. Students this age are restless and active one minute and listless the next. With the advent of formal operational thought comes self-reflection—the ability to think about one's thinking, to reflect on internal events. These are opportunities to capitalize on students' strengths and interests to facilitate learning. These emotional and intellectual changes can be used to help young adolescents become more literate (Irvin, 1998).

Other Strategies for the Intermediate and Middle School Classroom

The success of LEP students in some schools is due in part to a variety of initiatives that support literacy and biliteracy. At one middle school in the Ysleta District in El Paso, Texas, for example, ESL and content area teachers working as a block developed and implemented the following initiatives, which they feel are responsible for their school reaching "recognized" status:

- Weekly writing across the curriculum with emphasis on different modes of writing every six weeks
- Daily sponge activities emphasizing reading, writing, and math skills
- A pull-out tutoring program for "bubble" students designed to provide additional tutoring on the TAAS (state-mandated standardized test) writing, reading, and math objectives
- The creation of an ESL computer lab
- After-school academic tutoring program for both seventh- and eighth-grade LEP students
- Team teaching to enhance language development and literacy

Other services that schools used successfully are counseling services, homework headquarters, computer labs, extended library hours, and accelerated reading programs (literature-based programs with large amounts of time dedicated to independent reading).

Conclusion

The schools' primary task in the language arts is to develop high levels of literacy, which means that teachers must modify instruction to help students participate fully in challenging academic work as they are learning English. Sometimes it means providing instruction in the students' native language. Sometimes it means providing sheltered English instruction while incorporating a variety of strategies and techniques to help students read at a level to access the content area curriculum. Most important, however, is that it means that teachers and principals are committed to implementing unconventional programs, methods, and techniques that provide students equal access to academic programs of high quality.

Intermediate and middle schools face a complicated challenge. Students like Erika and Nga are confronted with difficult academic tasks and face an enormous amount of expectations as they struggle to learn English and master high levels of literacy in the language arts and content courses required for graduation. Key to their success is to offer these students access to an academic program of high quality in the language arts while also helping them acquire high levels of English proficiency. Key also is an attitude and belief among teachers and principals that students are able to participate fully in challenging academic work despite their limited English proficiency. Schools must be willing to reorganize their programs and schedules and the roles of teachers to maximize students' learning opportunities including the language arts (McLeod, 1996). ESL specialists and resource and content teachers who work with these students need to share resources, ideas, and expertise. They need to offer each other important support as they work to offer students the full range of academic possibilities offered to English proficient students.

REFERENCES

Au, K.H. (1993). *Literacy instruction in multicultural settings.* Fort Worth, TX: Harcourt Brace Jovanovich.

Berliner, D.C., & Biddle, B.J. (1995). *The manufactured crisis: Myths, fraud and the attack on America's public schools.* Reading, MA: Addison-Wesley.

Berman, P., McLaughlin, B., Minicucci, C., Nelson, B., & Woodworth, K. (1995). *School reform and student diversity: Volume II Case Studies.* Report submitted to Office of Research/Office of the Assistant Secretary for Educational Research and Improvement, U.S. Department of Education.

California Department of Education. (1990). *Bilingual education handbook: Designing instruction for LEP students.* Sacramento, CA: Bilingual Education Office.

Census Bureau, Population Division, Statistical Information Office. (1993). *Population projections of the United States, by age, sex, race and Hispanic origin: 1993 to 2050.* Washington, D.C.: Author.

Chiang, R.A. (1994). Recognizing strengths and needs of all bilingual learners: A bilingual/multicultural perspective. *NABE News, 17*(4), 11, 22–23.

Collier, V.P. (1995a). Acquiring a second language for school. *Directions in language and education, 1*(4), 1–12.

Collier, V.P. (1995b). *Promoting academic success for ESL students: Understanding second language acquisition for school.* Elizabeth: New Jersey Teachers of English to Speakers of Other Languages-Bilingual Educators.

Crandall, J., & Willetts, K. (1986). Content-based language instruction. *ERIC/CLI News Bulletin, 9*(2), 1, 7.

Cummins, J. (1989). *Empowering minority students.* Sacramento: California Association for Bilingual Education.

Cummins, J. (1991). Interdependence of first- and second-language proficiency in bilingual children. In E. Bialystok (Ed.), *Language processing in bilingual children* (pp. 70–89). Cambridge, England: Cambridge University Press.

Development Associates. (1993). *Descriptive study of services to limited English proficient students* (Vol. 1). Arlington, VA: Author.

Emslie, J.R., Contreras, J.A., & Padilla, V.R. (1998). Transforming high schools to meet the needs of Latinos. In M.L. Gonzalez, A. Huerta-Macias, and J.V. Tinajero (Eds.), *Educating Latino students: A guide to successful practice* (pp. 291–302). Lancaster, PA: Technomics.

Fischer, K., & Cabello, B. (1978). *Predicting student success following transition for bilingual programs.* Los Angeles: Center for the Study of Evaluation.

Freeman, Y.S., & Freeman, D.E. (1992). *Whole language for second language learners.* Portsmouth, NH: Heinemann.

Irvin, J.L. (1998). *Reading the middle school student: Strategies to enhance literacy* (2nd ed.). Boston: Allyn and Bacon.

Krashen, S. (1995, November). Inoculating bilingual education against attack. *NABE News, 7–41.*

Krashen, S., & Biber, D. (1988). *On course: Bilingual education's success in California.* Sacramento: California Association of Bilingual Education.

Lindholm, K.J. (1991). Bilingual proficiency as a bridge to academic achievement: Results from bilingual/immersion programs. *Journal of Education, 173,* 99–113.

Lindholm, K.J. & Zierlein, A. (1991). Bilingual proficiency as a bridge to academic achievement: Results from bilingual/immersion programs. *Journal of Education, 173*(2), 9–20.

McLeod, B. (1996). School reform and student diversity: Exemplary schooling for language minority students. Internet: *NCBE Resource Collection Series.*

Medina, M., Jr., & de la Garza, J.V. (1989). Bilingual instruction and academic gains of Spanish-dominant Mexican American students. *NABE Journal, 13*(2), 113–123.

Nieto, S. (1993). We speak in many tongues: Language diversity and multicultural education. In J. Tinajero & A.F. Ada (Eds.), *The power of two languages: Literacy and biliteracy for Spanish-speaking students* (pp. 37–48). New York: Macmillan.

Ramirez, J.D., Yuen, S.D., & Ramey, E. (1991). *Final report: Longitudinal study of structured English immersion strategy, early-exit and late-exit transitional bilingual education programs for language-minority children* (U.S. Department of Education, Contract No. 300-87-0156). San Mateo, CA: Aguirre International.

Snow, C.E. (1990). Rationales for Native Language Instruction. In A.M. Padilla, H.H. Fairchild, D.M. Valadez (Eds.), *Bilingual education: Issues and strategies* (pp. 60–74). Newbury Park, CA: Sage.

Snow, C.E., Burns, M.S., & Griffiths, P. (Eds.). (1998). *Preventing reading difficulties in young children.* National Reading Council. Washington, D.C.: National Academy Press.

Thomas, W.P., & Collier, V.P. (1997, September 10). *School effectiveness for language minority students.* Washington, D.C.: National Clearinghouse for Bilingual Education.

Thomas, W.P., & Collier, V.P. (December 1997/January 1998). Two languages are better than one. *Educational Leadership, 23–26.*

Thomma, S., & Cannon, A. (1995). Bilingual education is means to an end: Learning English. *LUCE Press Clippings.* St. Paul, MN: Pioneer Press.

Tinajero, J.V., & Ada, A.F. (1993). *The power of two languages: Literacy and biliteracy for Spanish-speaking students.* New York: Macmillan/McGraw-Hill.

Tinajero, J.V., Calderon, M.E., & Hertz-Lazarowitz, R. (1993). Cooperative learning strategies: Bilingual classroom applications. In J.V. Tinajero, and A.F. Ada (Eds.), *The power of two languages: Literacy and biliteracy for Spanish-speaking students.* New York: Macmillan/McGraw-Hill.

Tinajero, J. & Schifini, A. (1993). *ESL theme links program guide.* Carmel, CA: Hampton-Brown Books.

Tinajero, J. & Schifini, A. (1997). *Into English! Teachers guide.* Carmel, CA: Hampton-Brown Books.

Vygotsky, L.S. (1962). *Thought and language.* (E. Hanfmann & G. Vakar, Trans.). Cambridge, MA: MIT Press.

Wiburg, K.M. (1998). Literacy instruction for middle-school Latinos. In M.L. Gonzalez, A. Huerta-Macias, & J.V. Tinajero (Eds.), *Educating Latino students: A guide to successful practice* (pp. 269–287). Lancaster, PA: Technomic.

Wong Fillmore, L. (1991). Second language learning in children: A model of language learning in a social context. In E. Bialystok (Ed.), *Language processing in bilingual children* (pp. 49–60). Cambridge, England: Cambridge University Press.

13 Language Arts Adaptations

Fitting Literacy to Linguistically Gifted Learners

SHELAGH A. GALLAGHER

University of North Carolina at Charlotte

In the poet, then, one sees at work with special clarity the core operations of language. A sensitivity to the meaning of words, whereby an individual appreciates the subtle shades of difference between spilling ink "intentionally," "deliberately," or "on purpose." A sensitivity to the order among words—the capacity to follow rules of grammar, and, on carefully selected occasions, to violate them. At a somewhat more sensory level—a sensitivity to sounds, rhythms, inflections, and meters of words—that ability which can make even poetry in a foreign tongue beautiful to hear. And a sensitivity to the different functions of language—its potential to excite, convince, stimulate, convey information, or simply to please.

—Gardner, 1983, p. 77

$\mathbf{T}$he quotation above immediately invokes memories of favorite poets, the fluidity, originality, and freshness of e. e. cummings, Sylvia Plath, Langston Hughes, Ogden Nash, and many others. As adults, it is easy to recognize and value the contributions of poets, novelists, orators, and essayists, but what were they like as children and adolescents? How did they behave in the classroom? Did their teachers see the seedlings of future creativity? If so, what might they have done to support and enhance their raw ability? Maya Angelo was a seventh-grader once, and so was Pat Conroy. The focus of this chapter is to provide teachers with some background knowledge and fundamental strategies to use with linguistically talented students in the event that the next Pulitzer Prize–winning novelist is in your classroom.

Signs of Verbal Giftedness

Linguistically gifted students share many characteristics with all gifted students: They learn factual information quickly, they show early signs of abstract, conceptual thinking, they are curious and ask many questions, and they like playing with possibilities more than concrete realities (Gallagher & Gallagher, 1994). Even so, the verbally gifted child is often easier to spot than children with other kinds of gifts. With their affinity for language, they love to play with their skills in verbal or written form. Because much of classroom activity centers around oral or written work, their skills naturally emerge. Not many people realize, however, the variety of ways verbal talent can be expressed or how subtly the hints of talent can be expressed. Piirto provides a list of the early indicators of verbal precocity (see Figure 13.1).

Although many people think that having a verbally gifted child in the classroom is a dream come true, that is not always actually the case. Although some of the skills on the list are clearly behaviors teachers love to see (who *does not* like to see parallel structure used well?), others contain the hints of less acceptable behaviors. One important reminders for all teachers is that verbal talent is not always practiced in ways we would approve. Some gifted children's very love of language sometimes gets them into trouble if they "practice" their skills by using their humor at an awkward moment or if they seem "showy" in their use of vocabulary. In fact, verbally talented students sometimes face a greater risk of social ostracism than other gifted students simply because they wear their talent on their sleeves, using a sophisticated vocabulary that their peers simply cannot understand. Other challenges emerge when teachers forget that sometimes the talent is expressed in the context of cultures different from ours. Rap music contains a very restrictive structure and use of rhythm and is just as indicative of verbal talent as the skillful construction of other forms of poetry, if we take time to notice.

FIGURE 13.1   Common Characteristics of Linguistic Giftedness

use of paradox	a feeling of movement
use of parallel structure	uncanny wisdom
use of rhythm	sophisticated syntax
use of visual imagery	prose lyricism
melodic combinations	display of a "natural ear" for language
unusual figure of speech	sense of humor
confidence with reverse structure	philosophical or moral bent
unusual adjectives and adverbs	willingness to play with words

Source: From "Does Writing Prodigy Exist?" by J. Piirto, in N. Colangelo, S.G. Assouline, and D.L. Ambroson (Eds.), *Talent Development* (p. 388), 1992, Unionville, NY: Trillium Press.

Unchallenged Verbal Gifts

Verbally gifted children are not automatically skillful, disciplined, or refined in the use of their gifts. In fact, there are several pitfalls gifted children can face if they do not have appropriate challenges to extend their skills. Four classic examples of the consequences of untrained talent are speed reading, repetitive reading, and limited reading.

Speed Reading

Verbally gifted students are often reinforced for being very fast readers, zipping through more books in a week than everyone else. Fast reading is not, however, necessarily good reading. Without appropriate training, gifted students may become facile readers with no capacity for appreciating the depth of meaning or subtlety of language.

Repetitive Reading

For verbally gifted students, books are often thought of as fond friends. As with any loyal friend, gifted students sometimes want to visit those favorites again and again, rereading a single book any number of times. Without the attention of a teacher's trained eye, these very gifted students may end up with very limited reading experiences, because they have never been encouraged to branch out into new books and genres of reading, writing, and speaking. Even worse is when the books gifted students get "stuck" on are bad literature. Gifted students soak up information like a sponge, and sometimes bad information gets soaked up with the good. Exposure to quality literature is vital for gifted students to learn how to discriminate good literature from bad.

Limited Scope

Linguistically gifted students have the capacity to take on much more challenging reading than their age-mates, and it is important that the reading extend beyond fiction into other genres, including technical readings, essays, and philosophy. If gifted students are to develop their skills to the depth and breadth possible, they need exposure and practice in reading, writing, and discussing the vast variety of forms with which we use language.

What Is the Status of Curriculum for Verbally Gifted Students?

Part of the dilemma of providing verbally gifted students with authentic, meaningful challenge is the lack of ready-made materials suited to their advanced level. This need was recently reinforced in a study conducted by Aldrich and colleagues at Saratoga Board of Cooperative Educational Services in New York (Aldrich & McKim,

1992). They wanted to find out which of the readily available, published basal texts or curriculum units provided opportunities for differentiation for gifted students. The criteria they used to rate the various curriculum were based on both the recognized needs of gifted learners and the common consensus of what constitutes good curriculum for gifted students. Figure 13.2 presents some of the criteria included on the rating scale.

After reviewing the basal texts and several independent units for the gifted, Aldrich and McKim (1992) found that *none* provided adequate challenge for gifted students. Ancillary language arts resource materials fared better, and a few met several of the criteria. Two of the highest rated resource materials were the Junior Great Books and the McGuffy Readers. The Junior Great Books series was praised for its inquiry approach and the inclusion of a variety of levels of reading, including those that would challenge gifted students. McGuffy's Readers scored well on several criteria, missing only varied assessments and multicultural representation in the literature. Another promising resource cited for teachers was the writing course guidelines offered by the Center for Talented Youth at the Johns Hopkins University (Aldrich & McKim, 1992).

FIGURE 13.2   Selected Criteria from the Curriculum Assessment Guide

Curriculum Correlation with Research about Content
for Highly Able Verbal Students

- Uses broad-based issues, problems, and themes
- Uses range of rich, sophisticated literature
- Includes range of genres and writing formats
- Crosses multiple disciplines
- Incorporates sister arts

Curriculum Correlation with Research about Process
for Highly Able Verbal Students

- Uses rigorous techniques, materials, and forms
- Extends existing ideas or produces new ideas
- Uses research and primary-source skills and methods
- Encourages open-ended tasks and experiences
- Requires in-depth work on significant topics
- Uses collaborative engagement
- Requires relationships with varied audiences
- Allows for student creation of assessment tools
- Requires rich opportunities for reflection

Source: Adapted from *The Consumer's Guide to English-language Arts,* by P.W. Aldrich and G. McKim, 1992, New York: Saratoga-Warren Board of Cooperative Educational Services.

Enhancing Literacy in Verbally Gifted Students

Implications of the review of basal texts seems clear: Teachers must find their own ways to create a challenging language arts education for linguistically gifted students, because there are only a few ready-made materials to rely on. The differentiation that does occur will be the result of an individual teacher's resourcefulness and creativity. Fortunately, there are some general guidelines to help stimulate thinking as to how to provide appropriate challenges for verbally gifted students in the regular classroom.

Four Modes of Content Modification

One way to think about adapting the language arts curriculum for linguistically gifted students is to look at the four ways in which curriculum content can be changed and then try to find activities that match the area that is best suited to students' needs and most realistic for your classroom. The four broad modes of differentiation are acceleration, enrichment, novelty, and sophistication (Gallagher & Gallagher, 1994). Most teachers have, at some point, made at least one of these modifications to individualize instruction for their students. The following ideas are offered to help refine the use of each form of content modification.

Acceleration.   Acceleration is the practice of allowing students to work at their own pace of learning. For gifted students, this pace is often more rapid than the traditional scope and sequence organizing our curricula. In one form of content acceleration, students are allowed to demonstrate mastery of the information through a pretest; thus, they can bypass the formal teaching and repeated practice required of other students. This is sometimes called *curriculum compacting* (Reis & Purcell, 1993). Another form of content acceleration simply allows students to self-pace within the material and complete the same work as other students within a much shorter period of time. The time that students "buy" when allowed to accelerate their leaning can be used to provide additional leaning opportunities they might not receive given traditional time constraints.

Example of Acceleration.   Pretest students before beginning a grammar unit and modify the assignment for those students who achieve 90% mastery on the pretest. These students may either move to independent work on writing descriptive paragraphs or analyzing the relationship between grammar and rhythm in the Martin Luther King Jr. "I Have a Dream" speech.

Enrichment.   Content enrichment includes activities and experiences that expand and elaborate on the basic curriculum. Much of what we do for enrichment is appropriate for all students and should include other members of the class as appropriate. The use of enrichment with gifted students is ideal when they have completed their regular classroom work at an accelerated pace and, therefore, have more time to explore and expand on their understandings. Enrichment can be handled independently, in small groups, or, as noted earlier, be designed for the entire class.

Examples of Enrichment.   Gifted students have a capacity to appreciate literature naturally the way we would like all students to learn to appreciate it. One technique that can be helpful in cultivating a love of literature in all children is to have gifted students share their love with their peers. The trick is finding a way for this to happen: Having gifted students lecture about poetry or do a dry reading of poetry will not be any more successful than if you lecture or read. One way is to have the entire class participate in a poetry day in which students select a poem that they will memorize and then stage for students in a local elementary school. On the day of the big performance, students position themselves, complete with costumes and props, in the hallways of the elementary school. Students from lower grades are invited to come and touch a "frozen" poet. The poet then comes to life and recites or acts his or her poem. For gifted students, this is a good opportunity to unveil their own poetry, direct other students, or take on more difficult poetry to memorize and perform (B. Whittenburg, personal communication, October 15, 1997).

A second example of enrichment is the vocabulary web (VanTassel-Baska, Johnson, & Boyce, 1996), which is presented in Figure 13.3. Gifted students' understanding of the language can be deepened through the use of the vocabulary web, because it provides a graphic representation of all the components of the word: its roots, synonyms, antonyms, and usage all at a single glance. As students complete a series of webs, they begin to see the different ways they can sort the words for their similarities and differences. The relationships among words emerge as students complete a series of webs and begin to recognize the ways in which words are similar and different across webs. The web has an added advantage, too: As they look for the information required on the vocabulary web, students begin to look with new eyes at the merits of various dictionaries and learn to prefer a dictionary that gives rich and comprehensive information.

Novelty.   Providing content that is completely different, or novel, is a third way to differentiate. Novelty means providing a learning experience about an area of learning that is not covered in the regular curriculum. Novel information helps to stimulate the gifted child's imagination, opens new career options, and challenges the gifted child to use his or her skills in a new or unique way.

Verbally gifted students love words and enjoy word games, plays on words, word puzzles, crosswords, and the like. How can teachers capitalize on this playfulness? Thompson (1992) gives many examples of word play that are also instructive and challenging. One is called a *mystery sentence,* a technique to encourage students to use grammar to unravel a puzzle. Thompson gives his students a mystery sentence like this:

> A children's story contains a famous compound declarative sentence distinguished by three independent clauses. A coordinating conjunction is used twice to join the three clauses together. Each clause contains a contraction of the first person singular subject pronoun and the helping verb will. The third clause contains a direct object and an adverb. The first two clauses contain only subjects and verbs. What is the sentence? (Thompson, 1992, p. 91)

FIGURE 13.3   Vocabulary Web Model

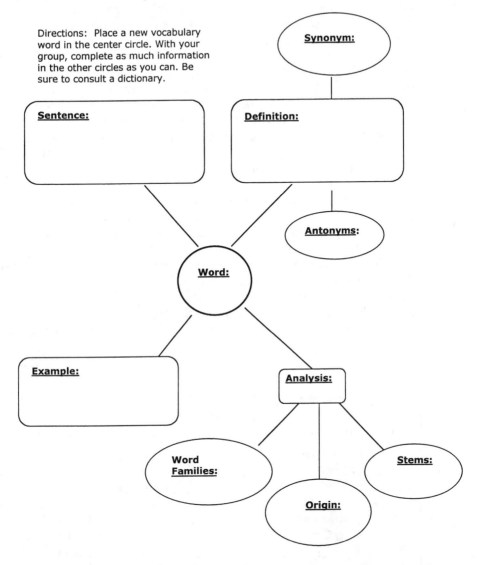

Source: From the Center for Gifted Education, College of William and Mary. Reprinted by permission.

He then sends his students off to find the right famous phrase or passage. Imagine their surprise when it turns out that this grammatically complex line ends up being, "I'll huff, and I'll puff, and I'll blow your house down!" It does not take long for students to come to class actually looking forward to the chance to use their grammar again!

Another example of novelty Thompson encourages is to have students simultaneously develop their extensive vocabularies and their appreciation for poetry. With a good understanding of word roots, suffixes, and prefixes, he asks his students to trans-pose familiar verse into a more complex form, still keeping the intent and the structure of the original verse in place. Figure 13.4 contains a transposition of a familiar children's book a student in his class created.

Sophistication.   Materials that are sophisticated challenge gifted students to see the "big picture" behind an area of study, the abstract concepts behind the content being studied. This could mean learning (1) the laws or principles that govern the different disciplines, such as the rules of grammar or the structure of the novella; (2) the abstract concepts that help organize ideas such as change, systems, patterns, scale, or revolution; or (3) to use thinking skills in a more complex way, especially becoming self-reflective about using metacognitive skills.

Examples of Sophistication.   Students are stretched to understand literature in more depth and complexity when teachers make the curriculum more sophisticated. A good example is the project completed in 1992 at the College of William and Mary. A group of master teachers, curriculum experts, and literary experts joined together to create curriculum units to challenge gifted and talented units. These units were purposefully designed to meet the criteria established in the review of curriculum by Aldrich and McKim discussed earlier in the chapter: The curriculum is conceptually oriented, based on Paul's (1993) model of critical thinking to promote student inquiry, based on rich, complex readings in a variety of genres. Students engage in a systematic, self-

FIGURE 13.4   Example of Novelty

The Querulous Cat

The moon didn't shine out	Neophyte minds
Effulgently bright	That omniscient Cat
So we lay in our beds,	Uttered omnibus kinds
Subjugated all night.	Of retorts and strange malapropisms
When in jumped the Cat	You see, which we
The refractory Cat,	Couldn't repeat, even in soliloquy.
The querulous	Then he gathered up all
Fearless, intractable Cat.	Of the objects with which
"Where's your Mother,"	Our house was replete
He asked,	And he thought he would snitch.
As he jumped through the door	And he made such a face
And he waltzed with effusion	That we found it condign
'Cross the subjacent floor.	When in medias res
To our nonplussed, incredulous	Mom came in from behind.

Source: Copyright © R. Fireworks Publishing Co., Ltd., Unionville, New York. Reprinted with permission.

paced study of grammar and throughout the unit practice writing persuasive essays. Self-assessment is a central component of the assessments in the units. An example of how each of these components is translated into a specific unit is presented in Figure 13.5.

A second form of sophistication is helping students become increasingly self-directed in their own writing goals. Taylor (in Gallagher & Gallagher, 1994) has developed a standard form for her students to use each time they prepare a written assignment in her classes. Figure 13.6 has both the questions to guide students when writing and a statement of philosophy that she shares with her students when they begin the first writing assignment of the year. The brief statement communicates clearly to students that they are to become more and more responsible not only for selecting their goals, but also for articulating the reasons why they were or were not successful in achieving those goals.

FIGURE 13.5   Curriculum Framework for *Literature of the 1940s: A Decade of Change*

Curriculum Characteristics	Application in Unit
Conceptual focus	All activities in the unit illuminate some aspect of the concept *change*.
Readings in a variety of genres	Selections include: Autobiography: *The Diary of Anne Frank* Cartoon/Symbolic: *Maus* Play: *The Member of the Wedding* Nonfiction: *Hiroshima* Poetry: Langston Hughes and Carl Sandburg
Cultivates complex reasoning	Richard Paul's critical thinking model is adapted to enhance depth and complexity of Socratic discussions.
Grammar and writing	Students complete a self-study grammar packet and use the vocabulary web. Unit writings focus on persuasion rather than creative writing.
Interdisciplinary connections	Extension activities include connections to history and art.
Student self-assessment	Assessment rubrics integrated into the unit for student to self-assess writing skills.

Note: Based on *Literature of the 1940s: A Decade of Change,* by College of William and Mary, 1992, Williamsburg, VA.

FIGURE 13.6   Student Self-Assessment of Writing Process

Self-Evaluation of Writing

My evaluation of your work is really a secondary device in service of a primary goal: Like a coach, I urge you on, push you to struggle more, guide you in developing techniques for a more elegant performance. Grades let you know where you are in that process and sometimes they motivate. But the primary goal is self-motivation. I do not want to grade to make you learn. Rather, I want to work with students who have their own learning goals. And if you have your own goals, you need then to assess your own progress. In working for yourself, you have made the critical step toward becoming an independent thinker.

Each time I make a major assignment, I will expect you to have set a goal for yourself. Perhaps, in writing this essay, you wanted mainly to understand better the three words, or perhaps you wanted a clearer understanding of the concept we have been studying. Perhaps you wanted to state a clear and workable thesis. Or maybe you wanted to concentrate on writing unified, coherent paragraphs. For a few of you, the main goal was simply to get the assignment over with. For some of you, setting a personal goal for an assignment will at first be extremely artificial, but at the outset, any new effort is uncomfortable and awkward. By rehearsing the effort, we begin to make it fit us, and in time our performance is nearly natural.

In completing this form, you are beginning a rehearsal of self-evaluation. You will turn in these forms to me, but I will give them back to you. You will add them to your folder of written work.

1. What is your personal reaction to the philosophy of evaluation presented to you here?
2. Is the grade on this essay congruent with the expectations outlined in the assignment sheet? Explain why you believe you have received the grade assigned.
3. What goal did you set for yourself in writing this essay?
4. To what extent were you successful in meeting this goal?

Integrating Affective and Intellectual Needs

All adolescents face difficult challenges in the middle school years; gifted students face some special issues. In an age when peer acceptance is important, gifted adolescents often face censure for being "gifted." Sometimes, gifted students, especially gifted girls, gifted minority students, or gifted disadvantaged students, choose to give up their talent to gain peer approval. Keeping gifted students in tune with their talent requires support, and literature can provide an important source of support. Gifted stu-

FIGURE 13.7   List of Books for Children Featuring Gifted Youth and Adolescents

Blume, J. (1970) *Are you there, God? It's me, Margaret.* New York: Bradbury.

Brooks, B. (1986). *Midnight hour encores.* New York: Harper and Row.

Duncan, L. (1971). *A gift of magic.* Boston: Little, Brown.

Fitzhugh, L. (1964). *Harriet, the spy.* New York: Dell Yearling.

Greene, B. (1974). *Philip Hall likes me. I reckon maybe.* New York: Dial Press.

Hersey, J. (1961). *The child buyer.* New York: Bantam.

Hoffman, M. (1991). *Amazing Grace.* New York: Penguin Books, USA.

Hopkinson, D. (1993). *Sweet Clara and the freedom quilt.* New York: Knopf.

Knowles, J. (1960). *A separate peace.* New York: Macmillan.

Konigsburg, E. L. (1967). *From the mixed-up files of Mrs. Basil E. Frankenweiler.* New York: Yearling Books

L'Engle, M. (1962). *A wrinkle in time.* New York: Farrar, Straus, and Giroux.

O'Neal, Z. (1980). *The language of goldfish.* New York: Viking.

Paulsen, G. (1989). *Hatchet.* New York: Puffin.

Smith, B. (1943). *A tree grows in Brooklyn.* New York: Harper and Row.

Stone, B. (1988). *Been Clever, Forever.* New York: Harper and Row.

Welty, E. (1983). *One writer's beginnings.* New York: Warner Books.

Wojciechowska, M. (1964). *Shadow of a bull.* New York: Atheneum.

Wolff, V. (1991). *The Mozart season.* New York: Holt.

Source: Compiled from Koloff (1996) and Silverman (1993).

dents can learn how others deal with peer and parental pressure and internal conflicts about living with their talent and can learn to take responsibility for creating the adult form of their talent through bibliotherapy. Many excellent authors have included various aspects of being gifted into their stories, not to mention a wealth of autobiographies of real people who had to cope with the often competing advantages and disadvantages of having a special talent. A brief sample of books for or about gifted youth is presented in Figure 13.7; teachers will undoubtedly add to this list over time.

FIGURE 13.8   Alignment of Characteristics of Gifted Students and Strategies for Classroom Differentiation

Characteristic	Challenge	Technique	Example
Fast reader	Students have read the books in the standard curriculum. Students are fast rather than thorough readers.	Content sophistication Content acceleration	Advanced, complex literature Variety of literary genre Discussion based on the principles of good reasoning
Gifted students have a predisposition to use *critical and creative thinking skills.*	Having a talent is different from having a skill. Without training, gifted students are sloppy thinkers, too!	Content novelty Content sophistication Content enrichment	Mystery sentences Self-assessment to enhance metacognition Poetry enrichment
Gifted students love words and have large vocabularies.	Students often only have a surface-level knowledge of their vocabulary.	Content novelty	Vocabulary webs Restructured poetry
Gifted adolescents are adolescents first and gifted second.	They may choose to "underachieve" to seem more acceptable to their peer group.	Bibliotherapy	Provide gifted students the opportunity to read books that portray the experience of gifted people; accompany with journals of their own experiences
Gifted students have the capacity to build more *abstract and complex concepts.*	Without practice, gifted students will not be challenged to see complex or original associations.	Content sophistication	Curriculum based on an abstract theme such as *change.*

Source: From J.J. Gallagher and S.A. Gallagher, *Teaching the Gifted Child,* 1994, Boston: Allyn and Bacon. Reprinted with permission.

Putting the Pieces Together

Each of the examples presented here directly addresses one or more characteristics of gifted students. A synthesis of the alignment between student characteristics, recommended modification, and specific example is presented in Figure 13.8. Needless to say, this list is hardly exhaustive, but it does provide representative examples of the many different directions teachers can go as they seek ideas and materials that will push their linguistically talented students toward new frontiers of learning. Will it be worth the time and effort? Consider the gratitude expressed by one former student:

> In her classroom our speculations ranged the world. She aroused us to book-waving discussions. Every morning we came to her carrying new truths, new facts, new ideas cupped and sheltered in our hands like captured fireflies. When she went away a sadness came over us, but the light did not go out. She left her signature upon us—the literature of the teacher who writes on children's minds.
>
> I've had many teachers who taught us soon forgotten things, but only a few like her who created in me a new thing, a new attitude, a new hunger. I suppose that to a large extent I am the unsigned manuscript of that teacher. What deathless powers lie in the hands for such a person! (Steinbeck, 1995)

REFERENCES

Aldrich, P.W. (1996). Evaluating language arts materials. In J. VanTassel-Baska, D.T. Johnson, & L.N. Boyce (Eds.), *Developing verbal talent: Ideas and strategies for teachers of elementary and middle school students* (pp. 218–239). Boston: Allyn and Bacon.

Aldrich, P.W., & McKim, G. (1992). *The consumer's guide to English-language arts curriculum.* New York: Saratoga-Warren Board of Cooperative Educational Services.

College of William and Mary. (1992). *Literature of the 1940s: A decade of change.* Williamsburg, VA: Author.

Gallagher, J.J., & Gallagher, S.A. (1994). *Teaching the gifted child* (4th ed.) Boston: Allyn and Bacon.

Gardner, H. (1983). *Frames of mind.* New York: Basic Books.

Koloff, P. (1996). Windows and mirrors: Gender and diversity in the literate classroom. In J. VanTassel-Baska, D.T. Johnson, & L.N. Boyce (Eds.), *Developing verbal talent: Ideas and strategies for teachers of elementary and middle school students* (pp. 273–288). Boston: Allyn and Bacon.

Paul, R. (1993). *Critical thinking: What every citizen needs to know in an increasingly complex world.* Sonoma, CA: Sonoma State University.

Piirto, J. (1992). Does writing prodigy exist? In N. Colangelo, S.G. Assouline, & D.L. Ambroson (Eds.), *Talent development* (pp. 387–388). Unionville, NY: Trillium Press.

Reis, S.M., & Purcell, J.H. (1993). An analysis of content elimination and strategies used by elementary classroom teachers and the curriculum compacting process. *Journal for the Education of the Gifted, 16,* 147–170.

Silverman, L.K. (Ed.). (1993). *Counseling the gifted and talented.* Denver, CO: Love.

Steinbeck, J. (1995). "...like captured fireflies." *CTA Journal, 51*(8).

Thompson, M. (1992). *The word within the word* (Vol. 2). Unionville, NY: Trillium.

VanTassel-Baska, J., Johnson, D.T., & Boyce, L.N. (Eds.). (1996). *Developing verbal talent: Ideas and strategies for teachers of elementary and middle school students.* Boston: Allyn and Bacon.

PART THREE

Promoting Literacy in the Classroom: Research into Practice

14 Interdisciplinary Units

An Introduction to Integrated Curriculum in the Intermediate and Middle School

JEANNEINE P. JONES
University of North Carolina at Charlotte

Exhausted, the kids fell back onto the couches, the floor, the desks . . . in short, wherever they happened to be at the moment. The two teachers smiled at each other but groaned at the mess around them. Oh well, who cared? The day had been a shining success. The Superintendent had said so, the principal had told them repeatedly, the parents had echoed the same thought, and even their usually stubborn, too cool to show it, very typical eighth graders had grinned all day. Yes, all in all, the day had gone well; it wasn't hard for them to remember why middle school kids were fun to teach: they were old enough to be responsible but young enough to still play. One more time, it had made for a great day. . . .

"All right, enough of that reveling in the glow-of-the-day stuff. On to the mess," their eyes said to each other, and so they fell into line with the normal banter. "OK guys, break's over. Good job cooking, now let's see a good job cleaning. You know how we are. Come on. Move it, move it. . . ." Their eyes betrayed the serious let's-get-the-cleaning-done-now look, and they finally gave up and laughed. The kids caught on and laughed too, but they also headed in the direction of the tables.

It wasn't hard for the students to get their energy back up as they cleaned. There was, after all, a lot to talk about as they rehashed the last four hours. It had been a great climax to a two-week unit based on Paulsen's Hatchet. *All 58 of them had gotten to school early that day, too excited not to get it started as soon as possible. The bulletin board had gotten them fired up over a week ago: "Wild Foods Fest Friday!" it declared, and so the chatter began. "Now what?" they wondered, for there was one constant about this two-teacher team: They were never boring. That was proven by all of them— yes, all 58 of them—coming to school every day for they were secretly afraid they'd miss something fun if they didn't show up. This was definitely a good place to be.*

This wild foods thing was another piece of evidence. "What in the world did that mean?" they wondered a week ago. Friday brought the answer, and it came in the form of Margo Perkins, a retired math teacher whom they recognized from their earlier years at Western Middle. "Ah, so that's what teachers do when they retire," they laughed. "They go off and learn to cook weeds!" The day's festival was launched. Clover butter, pine-needle tea, dandelion dip . . . they'd respected all the necessary precautions, learned lots about eating in the wild, and then enjoyed actually preparing a feast for themselves and several guests. Always going back to Paulsen's Brian, Mrs. Perkins shared some similarities with the wilds of Canada, and the class speculated ways in which they might have survived had they been the main character. "One thing's for sure," someone laughed, "I could never have lived off of clover butter for two months!"

These kids and these teachers enjoyed each other that day and that year. Lacing their curriculum together with life, literacy, problem solving, and technology through a variety of content connections came easily for these teachers and their young learners. Together they explored, discussed, argued, related, and came to understand in a way that is, frankly, extremely successful and difficult to deny. Deeply grounded in middle school philosophy, given wings by their administration, and holding carte blanche from parents, the two teachers approached each topic of study together through planning, implementation, and assessment. Like the curriculum that resulted, they and their students were integrated across their lives' stories in a powerful and unforgettable way.

Why integrate the curriculum when teaching segregated subjects is so much easier? How does a team of teachers implement that concept once the decision to do so has been made? What are a few examples of instructional strategies that are appropriate for this type of curriculum delivery? This chapter addresses these questions in practical and sequential terms while relying on Gary Paulsen's *Hatchet* (1987) for application.

Why Integrate?

You may not divide the seamless cloak of learning. There is only one subject matter for education and that is Life in all its manifestations.
—Alfred North Whitehead, 1929, p. 10

Why should teams integrate their curriculum, and themselves? The answer is simple: It is the only truly successful approach to teaching early adolescents. These are youngsters who are full of life and all its intrigue. They are naturally curious individuals who want to know absolutely everything about their teachers, their friends, themselves, and their world and who really appreciate good teaching. Failing to bring all of that together in a classroom setting is not only failing to recognize the connections necessary for success in twenty-first-century America, but it is failing to set up the most pleasurable and exciting part of teaching early adolescents.

In response to these kids, their teachers, and the potential for powerful classroom connections, Arnold (1991) called for an integrated middle level curriculum that is "rich in meaning," an approach that embodies three characteristics:

1. It deals with material that is genuinely important and worth knowing.
2. It deals effectively with values.
3. Both its content and methodology relate substantively to the needs and interests of young adolescents. (pp. 8-10)

Likewise, Merenbloom (1988) years ago called for "the creation and implementation of an interdisciplinary, thematic approach to learning," which is necessary if students see "the wholeness of learning, the interrelationships between subjects . . . and . . . the learning needs of the early adolescent learner" (p. 51).

Commissioned by the National Middle School to explore curricular issues, the Middle Level Curriculum Project (McDonough, 1991) similarly defined successful approaches to learning. These participants summarized effective curriculum in terms that manifested the objectives of each individual member of the curriculum camp. This definition suggested that an effective middle school curriculum included everything that the early adolescent experienced during the course of the school day, including "instructional strategies, organizational arrangements, integrated curricular content, and cultural environment" (p. 29). The group continued by noting that this curriculum was actually created by students, teachers, parents, and community that enabled students to seek answers to questions that they had about self and social meaning. Organized in the spring of 1990, this group of teachers, administrators, state department personnel, and university professors pinpointed as its objective a curriculum that is both developmentally responsive and that extends the students' and teachers' worlds to include those things that lie beyond the school doors.

It is indeed difficult to accomplish this goal of a curriculum that is "rich in meaning," a curriculum that is stimulating to even the most reluctant learners and that embraces the wholeness of life in all its consequences, concerns, and celebrations. To meet this objective, the Curriculum Project (McDonough, 1991) first identified a set of specific questions, the answers to which undergird successful integrated curriculum design, including:

1. Who are young adolescents?
2. What questions do they have about themselves and their world?
3. What questions does the world pose for them?
4. In what kind of future world might they live?
5. How can adults help all students learn?
6. What activities should young adolescents engage in at school?

7. How do we design a curriculum that is good for both young adolescents and the adults who share their world?

8. In the school experience, how do we utilize all ways of knowing and all areas of human experience? (pp. 29–30)

Bringing these questions into focus, the project's participants made core recommendations based on successful middle-level education concepts. The basic premise of the curriculum in these schools addresses an adolescent's search for both self and social meaning, for that is generally the early adolescent's most powerful concern. George, Stevenson, Thomason, and Beane (1992) suggested that the sources for this curriculum lie in the evolution of three types of questions, specifically

1. Inquiries that young adolescents generally have about themselves, including self-concept and self-esteem, the future, and personal experiences with developmental changes

2. Questions that they often ask about their own world, including generalities or particulars concerning family units, peer relationships, cultures and societies, and the global community

3. Questions that are not frequently asked by early adolescents, yet that are important because we all live in a common world (for example, issues, problems, and concerns commonly confronted by all people because the world is interdependent: war and peace, human relations, school policies, environmental issues, prejudice, poverty, and others). (p. 93)

The outcomes of this approach are manifold, as was noted by curriculum reformers. For example, Glasser (1992) found that in the "quality school," one never forgets that the desired outcome of curriculum and schooling is not curriculum, but people. Instead, "What we want to develop are students who have the skills to become active contributors to society, who are enthusiastic about what they have learned, and who are aware of how learning can be of use to them in the future" (p. 694).

Finally, the Carnegie Council on Adolescent Development (1989) noted five characteristics that are associated with their vision of the successful twenty-first-century adolescent. They described this child as one who is "an intellectually reflective person, a person en route to a lifetime of meaningful work, a good citizen, a caring and ethical individual, and a healthy person" (p. 15).

In short, perhaps these outcomes, and a plea to participate in their achievement, can best be summarized by noting that an integrated curriculum

is the opportunity to help these students make closer connections with the world in which they live, to construct powerful meanings around their own concerns and those of the larger world, to integrate self and social interests, to gain a sense of personal and social efficacy, to experience learning as a whole and unified activity, to bring knowledge and skill to life in meaningful ways, and to have richer and fuller lives as early adolescents. Isn't this what we should all want for early adolescents and their middle schools? (George, Stevenson, Thomason, & Beane, 1992, p. 103)

Points of Intersection

Our two teachers and their students would certainly argue that the only answer to the previous question is an unconditional yes, that it is worthwhile, and yes, that our young adults do deserve those opportunities and experiences. An integrated curriculum is one that is indeed rich in meaning, for it skillfully weaves together life, literacy, problem solving, technology, and rigorous content connections in such a way that the boundaries are difficult, if not impossible, to define. In short, it embraces the reality of a child's past, present, and future in a seamless and logical way. In doing so, it invites, and receives, genuine participation from each child.

The opening scenario and the illustrations that follow serve as applications of integrated curriculum for a variety of basic reasons. First, this unit in its entirety blurs the boundary lines between subjects as much as possible and at times, witnesses their disappearance all together. Perhaps the best testimony to this are the days when students leave class all excited and proclaiming things like, "Whoa, this is great, Mrs. Thompson. We haven't done science in days!" when the truth is, everything they have done for the past week has been grounded in scientific theory and concepts. Students simply do not realize it because their science lessons have been intertwined with a book they are reading, journal response writing, mathematical computations, a historical perspective, geography lessons, and the like. Again, the lines between those disciplines involved have blurred, often beyond recognition.

Second, the entire experience is grounded in relevant life experiences. For example, and based on Brian's experiences in *Hatchet,* students discuss living through an airplane crash, wilderness survival skills, the importance of believing in oneself, and the emotional fortitude required when one is alone in difficult surroundings for countless days. A secondary tie-back is that Paulsen rarely writes about experiences that he has not had himself, which underscores the importance of basing personal writing on realistic life events; it connects in powerful ways to students who enjoy recording their own encounters and perceptions.

Third, integrated curriculum such as this one celebrates literacy and problem solving as links between content and life's experiences. Many teachers now find themselves reading and writing instructors because, in part, those disciplines provide grounding in the communication skills that young adults must master if they are to become successful citizens in twenty-first-century America. Therefore, it seems only natural that these skills be acknowledged as connectors between content areas. An expansion of these basics includes technology, problem solving, viewing, listening, and speaking skills, each in independent and group settings.

How Do We Accomplish That?

Planning for the Year

Teams do, of course, plan integrated curriculum in a variety of ways, but the point is that they *do* plan for it carefully and deliberately. For example, teachers at Concord Middle School in Concord, North Carolina, picked up a practical strategy from a state conference that they recently attended. They now begin the year with pads of sticky notes and felt-tipped pens. Individuals come to their team's first weekly curriculum meeting armed with topics that each will teach over the coming 10 months listed as one topic per sticky note. They then post the notes on a team chart under their subject heading.

For example, an American history teacher might list the following on individual note pages: exploration and discovery, colonization through Jamestown, colonial period, American Revolution, early government, and so forth. The pages are then arranged sequentially under the social studies heading. Simultaneously, the communication skills teacher is listing things such as writing process, poetry, *Hatchet, The Witch of Blackbird Pond* (Speare, 1958), figurative language, parts of speech, *The Slave Dancer* (Fox, 1973), and short stories. All other content areas represented on the team are doing the same.

Once each teacher has accomplished this task and the chart is filled, the team talks through the arrangement, literally moving the sticky notes around under each subject heading so that they represent an integration of topics as much as possible. This process then begins a year-long discussion that provides the basis for curriculum design and increased integration.

Planning for the Unit

On occasion, this discussion yields a topic or an opportunity that merits a spotlight because of the natural intersections or because, frankly, that particular point in the school year needs a little excitement. When this happens, all disciplines make a concentrated effort to focus their subject matter around a common theme. This instructional example of integrated curriculum is generally referred to as an interdisciplinary unit, which is an excellent introductory step to understanding the attitude and components required of a fully integrated curriculum. Planning this type of instructional unit is fun, energizing, and rewarding for both teachers and students, and the learning that results is deeply ingrained in each because of the powerful personal connections that are made. Basic steps, with illustrations, include the following:

1. Determine the natural intersections for the year's curriculum.
2. Pull out topics or themes that lend themselves well to all disciplines, including both core and exploratory, such as the a novel *Hatchet,* the American colonies, space exploration, recycling, oceanography, a current event, a celebration of cultures, mathematical skills, or the site for a field trip.
3. Brainstorm topics and subtopics that might be covered under that major heading. Use listing, webbing, or another favorite graphic organizer to record initial possibilities. As a result of their introductory brainstorming session, the team that designed the unit based on *Hatchet* came up with the web shown in Figure 14.1.
4. On either individual index cards or sheets of paper, list all content areas that students are taught, such as one card each for mathematics, advisory, social studies, communication skills, guidance, foreign language, science, physical education, and business skills.
5. Divide the subtopics from the list or web in step 3 onto each discipline's card prepared in step 4 (subtopics are represented by the items in capital letters in Figure

FIGURE 14.1 Sample Web

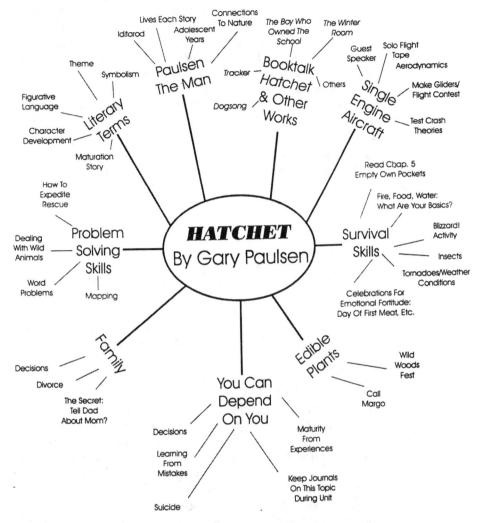

14.1). For example, the science teacher could be primarily responsible for discussing edible plant life, single-engine aircraft, and aspects of both survival skills
and problem solving. (Other members of the team may also blend into the discussions, but the science teacher assumes the lead role.) Each teacher takes the
appropriate card or paper for his or her content area.

6. Set a date for an immediate second meeting, allowing about two days for each
   teacher to work alone compiling major ideas that might fit under the subtopics
   brainstormed. For example, what might you include in a discussion of edible
   plant life? What about a guest speaker? Recipes? A cooking activity? Then on to
   aerodynamics. (Examples of these subtopics are found in lowercase letters in
   Figure 14.1.)

7. At the second meeting, ask each participant to share major ideas and check for both overlap and that all desired methodologies are accounted for. As a team, brainstorm additional ideas and topics and add them to the appropriate content cards. An easy way to do this is to draw a matrix and write each discipline represented across the top. List down the side all major activities that are important to this particular unit. Now fill in the boxes to make certain that, when viewed as a whole, each area to the side is addressed in some way, although perhaps not by every discipline. For example, if the section labeled *use of community resources* were completed with *Hatchet,* one might find blank cells under communication skills and mathematics, but not under social studies, science, or exploratory. On the other hand, all would have contributions to make under *group work.* The first draft of this evolving planning matrix might look like Figure 14.2.

   Again, the idea is not to record details, but rather to log in key words and phrases and to do so throughout the planning and implementation stages. This process will assist with determining intersections and variety while avoiding inappropriate repetition. Finally, note that this technique assumes individual components like content on the selected topic, but aside from that, components are shared with the rest of the team, assessment, and routines.

8. Review the first draft of the matrix. Will there be adequate coverage? Will the unit involve all aspects of integration, including rigorous academics in every subject area? In short, will it be worth the effort required? If not, plan to teach the topic less formally than in a full-team indisciplinary unit. If so, set a date for the third meeting, allowing enough time for all required tasks to be accomplished (step 9). Before dismissal, brainstorm possibilities for introductory and concluding activities that will involve the entire team, thus ensuring a sense of community, students' immediate interests, and regrets that their study is over. One illustration of a culminating activity is the wild foods fest.

9. Prior to the third meeting, individual teachers should first think through such things as individual subtopics, activities, strategies, student responses, and assessment in terms of the major ideas noted in step 6. Second, they should review any standard course of study or other curriculum guidelines required by their schools, districts, or states. These two should then be combined into broad outlines of each day's tentative lesson plan, including objectives, activities, and formative evaluation. Constant conversations among team members must occur throughout this process to ensure as natural an integration of content and methodology as possible. For example, a sampler of activities from individual content areas might include the following:

   ■ *In science and math:* In conjunction with the airplane crash that occurs early in the story, invite the pilot of a single-engine aircraft to speak to the group in terms of personal experiences, aerodynamics, and Chapter 2 in *Hatchet.* In response to this, have each student design and build paper gliders, discussing the most effective geometric shapes. Set up a glider contest outdoors and encourage prediction in various categories: longest flight, best maneuvers, first to crash, most decorative, and longest distance covered. Keep careful records and

FIGURE 14.2   Planning Matrix

	Communication skills	Mathematics	Social studies	Science	Exploratory team
Group work	Reading *Hatchet*, some journal entries; decision making	Some word problems; glider designs	Mapping activities	Wild foods fest cooking groups; insects in Chapter 4	Drama: role play chapters and video to make movie of book; home economics: wild foods fest
Hands-on activities	Chapter 5: survival inventory	Make gliders	Outdoor simulation of Canadian experience, serve as wilderness guides	Glider flights based on aerodynamics	Art: decorative glider contest
Use of community resources			Local libraries and newspaper archives to research recent plane crashes and causes	Speaker: single-engine aircraft and explain Chapter 2; Margo Perkins with wild foods	Health: paramedics to discuss survival in wilderness, first aid; physical education: physical conditioning; guidance: suicide and divorce
Technology	Word processing		Mapping soft-ware; Internet to research plane crashes	Internet to research glider flights	Drama: video role playing groups
Paper, pencil, and textbooks	Read *Hatchet* and discuss, including literary terms	Both simple and complex word problems; estimation; geometric shapes	Canada	Tornadoes and weather; reference movie: *Twister*	Librarian: book talk about books by Paulsen; talk book *Night of the Twisters* (Ruckman, 1984) as companion to science tornadoes

debrief. (Additional connections: problem solving, communication skills, and art.)

- *In language arts:* Use a portion of the fifth chapter to launch a personal survival inventory. Read the pages that highlight Brian's feelings of desolation, which cause him to empty his pockets and inventory everything he has that might help him survive. After reading, have students empty their own pockets or purses, list their contents in a ranked order, and then write about their own chances of survival if they were caught in Brian's situation. A fun addition is to have patterns of large hatchets available, with brown and red paper. Give students time to make hatchets, list the survival items on the handle, and then write a paragraph explaining their uses on the blade. Put these on a bulletin board or hang them from the ceiling. Also, consider discussing the depth of Brian's desolation, which leads to an unsuccessful suicide attempt. (Additional connections: problem solving, art, guidance counselor, advisory, science, and suicide prevention organizations.)

- *In social studies:* As you read the entire novel, ask the students to use an outline of Canada to record clues focusing on Brian's crash and their ideas of his location. After the novel is read, distribute maps of that country and have students pinpoint what they determine his crash location to be. Ask students to debate and justify their ideas. (Additional connections: problem solving, mapping, geography, communications skills, mathematics, and science.)

- *In mathematics:* Have students work in small groups to both design and complete word problems based directly on the day's reading. These could fill an entire period or be spread out as warm-up exercises over the span of the unit. You may want to stress speed, accuracy, and collaboration as a way to ensure interest. For example: Brian lost 17% of his body weight during his ordeal in the Canadian wilderness. How much would you weigh if you lost 17% of your own body weight? Take that answer and add back 6%, which is the amount Brian regained. Would this be physically harmful given your current weight and body type? (Additional connections: problem solving, mathematics, and communication skills.)

- *As a culminating activity:* Contact a wild foods specialist in your area through personal and professional acquaintances, a university, or your city or county's agricultural agency. Ask this person to speak with your class on survival skills and wild foods, particularly those foods found within *Hatchet* and around your school. Give the students an informational cookbook that contains both rules for plant selection and recipes for dishes that they will cook later in the morning. Divide students into groups according to the number of students in class and the number of wild foods necessary for the selected recipes, such as a pine group, a dandelion blossom group, a dandelion leaves group, a plantain group, a clover group (both leaves and flowers), and a wood sorrel group. Following all precautions shared by your wild foods expert, take students on a tour of the school grounds and surrounding area, pointing out different edible plants. Allow the supervised groups time to split off and gather the items for which they are responsible. Return to the classroom workstations, have groups wash their plants well, and then prepare their recipes. Gather all dishes on serving tables and enjoy the feast! Possibilities include such treats as Cream Cheese with Dandelion Blossoms and Wild Cherry Jelly on Crackers, Dandelion Dip with Chips, Canadian Backyard Slaw, Clover Butter on Crackers, and Pine-Needle Tea. After the tasting party, debrief on the day's events. Relate everything back to Brian's experiences in *Hatchet,* reminding them to never eat unidentified plants like the gut cherries in Chapter 6.

10. Bring all outlines to the third team meeting. Determine approximately how long the unit might last, which may be from one day to several weeks, according to content requirements and a predicted lull in students' interests. Rethink the teaching order to ensure as natural an integration of discussions, activities, and content as possible. (Both the sticky note chart and matrix activities apply here as well.) Assign a catchy title. Discuss ways to advertise the coming attraction, like a bulletin board or morning announcements. Generate excitement.

11. Teach and evaluate the unit, considering it a field test. Gather students' suggestions on index cards after each major activity or at regular intervals. Filter out the best of these and store them for the unit's revision next year.

12. Conclude the unit with a final team meeting in which the entire process is discussed and critiqued. Add the teachers' evaluations to those of the students.

It sounds simple enough, doesn't it? The truth is, it does indeed become easier over time. A first experience with designing an interdisciplinary unit may seen awkward, even stilted, and content will probably remain more segregated than integrated, held together by little more than a common theme and some shared activities. The process will smooth out after two or three units, however, and it actually becomes a natural transition into daily integration across content and events in less formal ways.

Words to the Wise

A few words of caution are always appropriate when a very complex task is reduced to a simple listing of steps and illustrations, for the precautions will serve to both clarify initial confusions and flag upcoming concerns. A few initial considerations include:

1. Incorporate interdisciplinary units into a classroom infrastructure that is student centered. Make certain that this classroom is one that is integrated, organized, logical, and alive. Ground it in respect, student responsibility, freedom through choices, and solid decision-making skills. Keep it literacy based, with students both studying authors and then discussing their own contributions to authorship. In short, create a classroom that is an inviting place to be for everyone involved.

2. Select your topic carefully, for it is obviously the basis for everything. Van Til, Vars, and Lounsbury (1967) share a timeless list of selection criteria compiled by their students, which provides an invaluable rule of thumb.

   - The topic should be within our level of understanding.
   - It should be of interest to nearly everyone.

- There should be instructional materials to supply the information we need.
- There should be field trips, experiments, and other student activities.
- The unit should be neither too long nor too short.
- It should be helpful and worthwhile.
- The subject should be one with which we are not already familiar. (p. 261)

3. Remember that once the topic has been chosen, that particular content area returns to its place as being no more important than any others represented. Avoid turf wars. For example, the web discussed in Figure 14.1 is not segregated by disciplines, but rather by a random brainstorming of ideas that could become important and engaging to the unit. Only later are these ideas discussed in terms of content areas and teaching responsibilities. In fact, disciplines should strive for the smooth articulation between daily lessons that ignore turf and eventually give way to a natural flow and order. Only then can boundaries between curriculum, and people, dissolve and true integration occurs.

4. Stress a correlation between content areas and solid teaching rather than a strict adherence to rigid curriculum mandates; stay flexible and remember that we are in the business of teaching children and not simply content.

5. Do not stretch your content to make it fit a certain number of days; you will sacrifice the rigor and integrity of your discipline, and the students will find this a waste of your time and theirs. If your curriculum runs a bit short, pick up a portion of the reading, add a writing activity, or enhance a team member's content by retooling concepts or assignments. If your content simply does not fit beyond a fraction of the unit, the team should scrap the topic for another, leaving the first to be covered in ways less formal than an interdisciplinary unit.

6. Never forget that exploratory teachers are critical to every unit's success. In fact, they are often the spark that brings many at-risk students to school. For example, a student may be a poor math maker but will come to school for art or basketball. Once there, that student will, of course, be part of math class while in route to exploratory courses. Therefore, those teachers must be available though both their content and their personal contributions to the team. It may mean planning at a time aside from a scheduled period during the day, but it is vital to the success of the unit and the students.

7. Infuse a variety of instructional methodologies into the daily activities, a goal that can be monitored through the matrix discussed earlier. For example, consider such things as reading through myriad approaches aside from silent or round robin, learning centers, cooperative learning, experiments, student research based on data collection and analysis, simulations and role playing, readers' theater, discussions, short lectures, scavenger hunts, process writing, brainstorming techniques with graphic organizers, experiences with technology, students as teachers, learning games, use of media, and field trips. In keeping with this, make use of authentic assessment for both formative and summative evaluation.

8. Do integrate your classrooms and your lives constantly, but do not teach more than six formal interdisciplinary units a year, particularly if they average more than one week each. If overdone, they become mundane, and their ability to generate excitement dwindles.

9. Let students help with every aspect of the planning stage, from topic selection to final evaluation of the curriculum. Their contributions will ensure their investment in a mastery of the activities and, therefore, the competencies.
10. Keep parents informed. There is often a tendency to believe that anything this motivating must contain little to no substance. Publicizing the curriculum, activities, and student comments will prove otherwise.

Conclusion

Teaching early adolescents is indeed challenging, for they are perhaps the most stimulated, and stimulating, age group in the whole of education. In tandem with their developmental changes, and, thus, our developmental challenges, are the myriad complexities that loom ahead of them as both adulthood and new experiences appear. Current efforts to teach our children have clearly missed the mark: We live in a fast-paced, highly technological world that has, frankly, left many Americans behind. We cannot afford to allow this to continue, for we are currently teaching not only to our students' futures but to ours as well.

Just as these young adolescents bring their lives' stories into our classrooms, so we must address those rich and vibrant tales in the curriculum and methodology that we support. An integration of life, literacy, problem solving, technology, and an array of rigorous content areas seems only logical, as this approach mirrors the skills necessary for success.

REFERENCES

Arnold, J. (1991). Towards a middle level curriculum rich in meaning. *Middle School Journal, 23*(2), 8–12.

Carnegie Council on Adolescent Development. (1989). *Turning points: Preparing American youth for the 21st century.* New York: Carnegie Corporation.

Fox, P. (1973). *The slave dancer.* New York: Dell Publishing Corporation.

George, P.S., Stevenson, C., Thomason, J., & Beane, J. (1992) *The middle school—and beyond.* Alexandria, VA: Association for Supervision and Curriculum Development.

Glasser, W. (1992). The quality school curriculum. *Phi Delta Kappan, 73,* 690–694.

McDonough, L. (1991). Middle level curriculum: The search for self and social meaning. *Middle School Journal, 23*(2), 29–35.

Merenbloom, E.Y. (1988). *Developing effective middle schools through faculty participation.* Columbus, OH: National Middle School Association.

Paulsen, G. (1987). *Hatchet.* New York: Puffin Books.

Ruckman, I. (1984). *Night of the twisters.* New York: Harper and Row.

Speare, E.G. (1958). *The witch of blackbird pond.* New York: Laureleaf.

Van Til, W., Vars, G.F., & Lounsbury, J. (1967). *Modern education for the junior high school years* (2nd ed.). Indianapolis, IN: Bobbs-Merrill.

Whitehead, A.N. (1929). *The aims of education and other essays.* New York: Macmillian.

15 Integrating Language Arts with the Content Areas

KAREN BROMLEY
Binghamton University

MATT: "See here, the lantern fish has a light on his head! Write that down."

PAULO: "He has funny eyes, too. Let's put that on the chart."

MATT: "It says here he lives at 8,000 feet under the ocean."

PAULO: "Wait, this book shows a picture and see, it has 20,000 feet."

MATT: "One of these must be wrong. Who wrote this book anyway?"

PAULO: "Hold it. What does 'zone' mean? That'll have to go in the report."

MATT: "It looks like the lantern fish lives in one layer of the ocean."

PAULO: "He must have a light on his head because it's dark down there."

MATT: "Let's look him up on the CD-ROM encyclopedia."

PAULO: "Let's check out web sites on oceans and marine life, too."

This excerpt from a discussion between two fourth-grade students shows how they use reading, writing, talking, and viewing to gather, analyze, and interpret information for science reports to their classmates. In this self-contained classroom, Jim, a teacher, and Betty, a reading specialist, collaborate to integrate curriculum and provide students with a two-week marine animal investigation unit. This chapter offers guidelines for sound curriculum integration suggested by research and theory. It describes practices in fourth- through eighth-grade classrooms, like the one above, in which teachers give students a variety of opportunities to become effective language users as they learn in the content areas.

What Is Integrated Curriculum?

The term *integrated curriculum* is often used interchangeably with *integrated instruction, thematic instruction, interdisciplinary instruction, theme immersion, project-based learning,* and *inquiry learning.* These approaches usually organize learning in various content areas around a single theme. They include the language arts: listening, speaking, reading, writing, and viewing. Recently, the importance of viewing or visual literacy has been recognized because of the pervasiveness of electronic media (Pool, 1997). Students need sophisticated viewing skills including navigation strategies and critical thinking for comprehension of electronic text that is accompanied by pictures, animation, and sound (Leu, 1997; Leu & Leu, 1997).

Like Jim, other middle school teachers in self-contained classrooms collaborate with colleagues to integrate curriculum. Integration also occurs when language arts is taught with science or social studies in block schedules to different groups of students. Or, it occurs when language arts teachers collaborate with content area teachers to coordinate instruction in separate classrooms. For all these teachers, one key to successful integration is shared planning time. Without time to collaborate with colleagues, curriculum integration is often hit and miss. But, when planning time is available and wisely used, for example, sixth-grade language arts and social studies teachers can coordinate instruction so when students learn techniques for persuasive writing they can use this knowledge to write about the causes of the Civil War.

How Do You Integrate Language Arts and Content?

There are several ways to plan for integrated instruction. First, you can begin by integrating language arts and one content area, like science or social studies, to do deep and meaningful study. Second, you can alternate curriculum integration with brief focuses on a specific area. You may decide that your students need direct, in-depth instruction in writing reports before it is part of a longer integrated unit, and so you teach a brief unit focused solely on research and expository writing. Or, you can teach an intensive and brief math unit on problem solving, computation, or a concept that you may have limited opportunities to teach within an integrated unit.

There are pitfalls to curriculum integration (Roth, 1994; Shanahan, 1997; Shanahan, Robinson, & Schneider, 1995). For example, when integration focuses on a topic like teddy bears, rather than on a powerful idea or organizing concept, it may lack significance and become a convenient way to organize activities that lack depth and meaning. Or, when curriculum is integrated, you may not have enough time to explore a discipline in the depth needed for learning, and one subject area may take a backseat to another. In addition, integration can lead to a reduction in the amount of language arts instruction that occurs when a content area becomes the focus.

If teachers attend to these pitfalls during planning and implementation, however, integrated units can be beneficial (Shanahan, 1997). With these issues in mind, here are some guidelines to help you integrate language arts and content (Bromley, 1998).

Identify Content First

Decide on a content area to integrate with language arts. Examine your school district or state curriculum guides, the texts available in your classroom, your community or geographic area, and your own special interests and passions. Then, choose a theme or organizing idea of significance. You may want to consider a theme that is important to your students, the community, or society that is broad enough in scope to help them become aware of the interconnectedness of the world (Manning, Manning, & Long, 1994).

Teachers who choose content and themes or organizing ideas find that including student voice and choice in the unit builds ownership and helps students become self-directed learners. Many teachers encourage student input and invite students to shape the direction of their research and study and how they will share it with others. Other teachers use only student-selected units or alternate teacher-selected units with student-selected units. Sharing unit and theme selection with students has several advantages. When students chose a theme, they are often quite interested and excited. Also, the unit may be more relevant or contemporary than mandated curriculum, and it may lead students to social actions that impact their world. For example, one seventh-grade class became personally involved in a study of energy because *they* chose how and what to learn and how to demonstrate their knowledge. As part of their study, they looked at energy use in their school and discovered a new type of costly but energy-efficient light bulb. They calculated the costs to replace existing bulbs with new ones, the resulting energy savings, and the time to recoup the added financial costs, and then they made a proposal to the board of education, which accepted it. These students were given choices and had a personal investment in their study, which resulted in a valuable and memorable learning experience for them.

Identify Goals and Outcomes for Language and Content

Decide on outcomes for learning in both language arts and the content area you have chosen. Be intentional about what you want your students to be able to do and understand as a result of the unit. With students, plan for different ways of understanding content through listening, speaking, reading, writing, and viewing. Examine your school district or state learning standards for the content area and language arts. Standards are a set of guiding principles for planning, instruction, and assessment. They give you and your students goals to attain and help you create teaching and learning experiences that allow students to develop critical language abilities and content area learning.

Jim and Betty selected the marine animals focus for their unit from their state curriculum guide. They examined their state language arts standards and determined that their students needed to learn how to gather information from different sources; analyze, synthesize, and organize this information; write expository reports in their own words; and present their work to classmates. Besides reading multiple print forms, they wanted their students to learn how to use Internet navigation strategies, judge the value of web sites, and access a topic on a CD-ROM encyclopedia. Jim and Betty believe that students should have choices and work cooperatively. They also believe in the active nature of learning and the importance of firsthand experience that make learning meaningful for students (Dewey, 1938).

Provide an Environment Rich with Literature and Resources

A wide array of resources of all types besides classroom texts helps students acquire broad knowledge and understandings. Often, children's literature offers models of language and form, as well as a more personal way than textbooks, to learn and make connections. You will want to gather children's literature in a variety of genres to support your unit, as Betty did.

Betty collected books, including realistic fiction, information, poetry, biography, and picture books as well as videos and magazines from the school library and local libraries. She alerted the library media specialist to the class's unit so that she could support students' research in the library. Jim brought issues of *National Geographic* from home and asked students to bring resources from their homes. They shared books, magazines, posters, Internet addresses, and sources of more information and materials. A video cassette recorder and bank of four computers in Jim's room with two CD-ROM encyclopedias and Internet access provided more resources.

Do not overlook colleagues in your school who can provide specialized knowledge. Like Betty did, you can collaborate with the library media specialist who will provide access to more resources and who can assist students in their research and writing. Work closely with your art, music, and physical education teachers who can help students learn about topics, create projects, and make presentations. Collaborate and coteach with the reading specialist, as Jim and Betty did, and special education teacher to support the learning of students with diverse needs. Send a letter inviting parents not only to share appropriate materials but also to visit your classroom and share related knowledge or interests.

In addition, examine your community to determine which people might provide special insights and knowledge related to your unit. For example, an eighth-grade science class studying the local environment and working in groups of three on a project to develop a local resort facility invited a developer from the area to talk to them. He spoke about the land and real estate issues, such as zoning laws, environmental concerns, and accessibility, that he must consider in choosing an area for development. This visitor provided students with information that helped them create a portfolio including a land assessment and proposal, a topographical map of the area being considered, and a physical model of the resort. The art teacher helped by teaching special lessons on the design of models and guiding the students as they created their models.

Plan for Varied Kinds of Instruction and Learning Experiences

Students need both direct instruction and modeling from you and indirect instruction and guided practice as they learn on their own and with others. Shanahan (1997) reminds us that integration works best when, "within the context of meaning, students are still given opportunities for enough instruction, guidance, and practice to allow them to become accomplished" (p. 18). Routman (1996) specifically calls for direct instruction in skills such as spelling, grammar, punctuation, and handwriting, but within "authentic literacy and literature contexts" (p. 105). Direct and systematic instruction is best imbedded within an integrated curriculum that combines meaningful content and language.

Planning for instruction that includes whole-class, small-group, pairs, and individual work is a good idea because it allows students to become accomplished in a variety of settings. You can use direct instruction with the whole class to teach a new concept or skill and with small groups of students who are ready for a new skill or need one retaught. Of course, you should form groups according to interests, friendships, strengths, and shared purposes as well as skills. Also, do not overlook the use of mixed-ability groups and pairs for reciprocal teaching and learning.

Jim and Betty share Vygotsky's (1978) theory that social interaction forms the basis for learning and language use. They also use Cambourne's (1988) model that suggests learning results when demonstration and immersion are coupled with engagement. They provide opportunities for students to work with partners and in small groups as well as with the entire class to talk, discuss, disagree, refine ideas, and use language to learn content. They believe, as do Wells and Chang-Wells (1994), that when students work and talk together they learn language as they use it to construct meaning, accomplish goals, and get things done. Jim uses heterogeneous groups that include English learners and English speakers because he has seen spoken language grow through purposeful, collaborative talking to learn.

Jim and Betty believe in instruction and learning based on student choice and decision making. They began their unit with an introduction of the collected resources and topic for the research report, marine animals. During an initial discussion with students, Betty used a modified K-W-L chart (Ogle, 1986)—*K,* What I *know; W,* what I *want* to learn; *H, How* I can learn; and *L,* I learned—in which they filled a piece of chart paper labeled *K,* What I *know,* with facts they already knew. This discussion showed Betty their level of knowledge and also uncovered misconceptions. Then Jim and Betty had students examine the resources and think about creatures to study. A few days later, after some initial reading, students brainstormed a list of marine animals, chose partners, and then picked an animal to research. Betty modeled the *W,* What I *want* to learn, and the *H, How* I will learn, using a transparency on the overhead projector (see Figure 15.1). This list gave a purpose to students' investigations and reinforced the variety of ways they could find answers. Then, Matt and Paulo and other pairs of students completed the *W* and *H* on their own K-W-H-L chart about the animal they chose (see Figure 15.2). This allowed students to decide what they wanted to know about their specific animal and where they would go for information. In another whole class lesson, Jim helped students organize a concept map to correspond to the organization of the final report (see Figure 15.3). The web helped students organize their note taking and served as a planning tool for writing.

The class decided on a format for the final sharing shortly after they began their research and created a rubric with Betty. A rubric is a set of criteria for student work that students can use to guide their work and both students and teachers can use to

FIGURE 15.1 Betty modeled a K-W-H-L chart with students to help them set purposes for their investigations and recognize the variety of ways to do research.

Animal's Name ?

K what I know	W What I want to Learn	H How I can learn	L I Learned ..
	Species? Eats? What and how? Where does it live? How fast does it swim? What problems does it have? How big is it? Does it have bones? What zone does it live in?	Read about it in books, encyclopedia, computer, CD, software newspaper Watch movies and videos Discovery channel — TV Trip to zoo, aquarium & internet Library Ask a scientist	

assess the finished product. In a class discussion, they brainstormed the elements of a good presentation and Jim put them into a structured list (see Figure 15.4).

Jim and Betty used pairs for this unit, but there are other ways to organize for instruction. Kagan (1994) provided a variety of cooperative learning structures that work well in classrooms in which teachers integrate curriculum. For example, in a sixth-grade study of Native Americans called Deceit and Broken Promises, students chose books to read in "expert" groups and studied the culture of one tribe. Individual groups read *Indian Summer* (Iroquois) by Barbara Girion (1990), *Thunder Rolling in the Mountains* (Nez Perce) by Scott O'Dell and Elizabeth Hall (1992), *Legend Days* (Northern Plains Indians) by Jamake Highwater (1984), *Ishi, Last of His Tribe* (Yahi) by Theodora Kroeber (1964), and *Sing Down the Moon* (Navajo) and *Island of the Blue Dolphins* (Chumash) by Scott O'Dell. Each group researched its tribe and presented a

FIGURE 15.2   Matt and Paulo documented specifically on their K-W-H-L chart what they wanted to know about the lantern fish and how they would learn it.

Lantern Fish

K what we **know**	W what we **want** to learn	H **How** we can learn	L We **learned**
	How big does it get? What does it eat? What's its enemies? which area does it live in, 'in the ocean? How long does it live? what tempicher of water does it live in? How do they get lights?	Read a book. Aske around. Find out about your animale or (expert) Look in science books. Go to library. Newspaper story about your animale. Go on internet. Look at animale cards.	

dramatization of what they found to the class so everyone could learn about each Native American culture and understand what they had in common.

This teacher could also use "jigsaw" groups for sharing in which new groups form with a representative from each expert group. Then, each student teaches the new group about what he or she learned in the expert group. Jigsaw grouping is a powerful incentive to learn because each student contributes a piece of the puzzle to complete a group's learning.

Planning for instruction can also occur via computers and the Internet. Many teachers use CD-ROM encyclopedias and primary sources on the World Wide Web to find and download information such as historical documents or data from secondary sources like museums or observatories. Teachers examine web sites created for educators to find actual lessons, projects, and units posted by other educators. They borrow

FIGURE 15.3   Jim and the students made a concept map to aid note taking and organizing topics in the research reports.

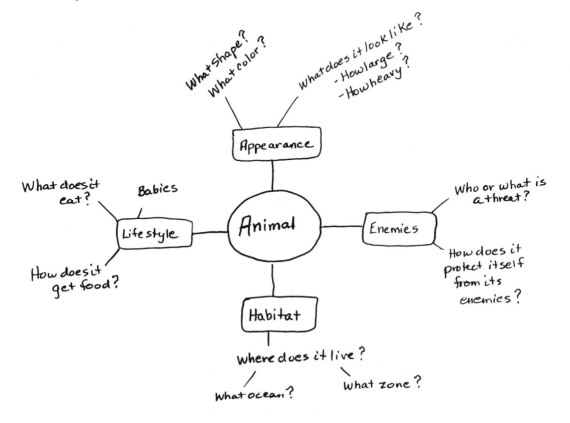

and adapt these lessons and projects and often post their own for others to use. Teachers establish electronic key pal exchanges with classes in other states or countries that can be social or content specific. Classes often take electronic field trips to places around the world to extend learning in a particular content area. Many teachers and students participate in collaborative projects with other schools. The web is a valuable planning and teaching resource, with many sites to help you incorporate technology into your integrated curriculum (see Figure 15.5).

Set Aside Large Blocks of Time

Shanahan (1997) believes that successful integration requires a great deal of attention to the separate disciplines, which requires setting aside large blocks of time each day or several days a week for instruction and student work. Small blocks of time do not allow students to interact fully with the content they are learning and with each other around that content. For example, a sixth-grade teacher and her students undertook

FIGURE 15.4   Students helped Betty decide on the criteria in this rubric.

How Did I Do? Marine Animal Report Self-Assessment Rubric
Each check mark counts as one point. A full score is 20 points.

Title

___ Does it tell which animal I studied?

___ Is it on the cover and first page of the report?

Report

___ Did I describe what the animal looks like?

    ___ Did I include 1 to 2 details?

    ___ Did I include 3 to 4 details?

___ Did I include a diagram of the animal?

___ Are the parts of the animal labeled?

___ Did I describe where the animal lives?

    ___ Did I include 1 to 2 details?

    ___ Did I include 3 to 4 details?

___ Did I include a chart that shows its environment?

___ Did I describe the animal's lifestyle?

    ___ Did I include 1 to 2 details?

    ___ Did I include 3 to 4 details?

___ Did I include a graph that compares the animal with three other animals?

___ Did I describe the main problem my animal has?

___ Did I describe the adaptations the animal uses to solve its problem?

Sources

___ Did I include a list of the books, software, people, or web sites I used for information?

Form

___ Is the report neat and legible?

___ Is all spelling, punctuation, and grammar correct?

___ **Total Points**

FIGURE 15.5   Many web sites exist to help teachers incorporate technology into the integrated curriculum.

Web Sites for Integrating Technology into the Curriculum

1. **CLN WWW Home Page**   http://www.etc.bc.ca/tdebhome/cln.html
   Ideas for integrating technology into the classroom with 3,400 links to other educational sites.

2. **WebTeacher**   http://webteacher.org/index.htm
   Step-by-step tutorial for K–12 teachers for using the web in the classroom.

3. **TechCorps**   http://www.acsa.org/tech/TechCorps.htm/
   A national organization that connects technologically literate volunteers with school districts and teachers who want help using technology in teaching.

4. **Cyber Ed: Rolling into a Twenty-first-Century Education**
   http://www.ustc.org/pressrel/cybered.html
   A volunteer technology organization that provides a classroom in an 18-wheel "big rig" for training teachers and community leaders to use the Internet and technology.

5. **Internet Resources for Staff and Faculty**   http://www.ala.org/ICONN/
   The American Association of School Librarians gives library media specialists, teachers, and students opportunities to learn skills for navigating the web.

6. **Busy Teacher's Web Site**   http://www.kn.pacbell.com/wired/bluewebn/#about.html
   Library of blue-ribbon learning sites organized by subject area with links to K–12 source materials.

7. **Kathy Schrock's Guide for Educators Home Page**   http://www.capecod.net/schrockguide
   Award-winning site of 1,200 classified and annotated links to enhance curriculum and teachers' professional growth. Updated daily.

8. **Judi Harris Activity Structures**   http://lrs.ed.uiuc.edu/Activity-Structures/harris.html
   Contains information collections, information exchanges, telecollaborative projects, electronic publishing, and database creations.

9. **International Curriculum Projects**
   http://owl.qut.edu.au/oz-teachernet/projects/international/international.html
   A calendar of global and U.S. curriculum projects for K–12 teachers and students, such as electronic field trips, interactive projects, experts to interview, and telecollaborative projects.

10. **Thinking Critically about World Wide Web Resources**
    http://www.library.ucla.edu/libraries/college/instruct/critical.htm
    Provides criteria for teachers and students to consider about the validity and reliability of web resources.

---

an in-depth study of Egyptian civilization in conjunction with the art teacher who wanted students to learn about museums and the art displayed in them. Together, the teachers coordinated the study of Egypt's culture in social studies and language arts with the creation of appropriate artifacts in the art room. They visited a local museum to study its displays and hear about the job of the education department there. They learned about archeological excavations and participated in a mock "dig" for artifacts in a sand table in the art room. Students created an in-school museum that contained written descriptions of the objects they created, including papier-mâché animals, collages, paintings, pottery, jewelry, and sculpture to which they invited other classes, family, and visitors. The sixth-grade students acted as museum docents or tour guides, and their tours became mini social studies lessons in which they demonstrated their learning.

Extended periods of time permit integrated whole language learning that combines use of reading, writing, listening, speaking, and viewing as students become competent in a content area or areas. Of course, the more areas you combine in an integrated study, the more time you will usually need to properly accomplish your goals. Effective integration can, however, occur without blocks of extended time. For example, eighth-grade teachers and students launched a cross-curricular study of Charles Dickens's *A Christmas Carol* in their separate classes. They wanted to ensure learning by approaching it from many avenues and through different experiences. In reading class, students read the story and a biographical survey of Dickens. In social studies, they had a minilesson on the Victoria era and the social issues facing the poor from which Dickens drew material for his writing. In a chemistry lesson, the science teacher had students create a foggy London in the classroom with dry ice and carbon dioxide. They also tracked current weather in London via newspapers and the Internet to generate a weather graph. In language arts class, students studied the story elements and Dickens's characterization of Ebenezer's greed. In math class, they learned about British currency then and now and how to calculate the exchange. Students presented their results at a Victorian tea complete with plum pudding and wassail prepared by a home economics class in the cafeteria that was transformed into Fezziwig's Warehouse. Some staff members and students dressed in period costumes for the tea, and at the conclusion of the week's lessons, students visited a local playhouse to see a dramatization of the story.

Typically, it is important to set aside considerable amounts of time for integrated instruction so that meaningful in-depth learning can occur. When large blocks of time are not possible, cross-curricular teaching is a possibility, as is collaboration between two teachers who see natural connections between their curriculums. For example, an eighth-grade special education teacher collaborated with a social studies colleague to coordinate instruction in writing and social studies. Students assumed the roles of the people they were learning about and kept journals in which they wrote entries to demonstrate their learning about pre–Civil War African slave trade (see Figure 15.6).

Many hands-on projects and activities take extended time to complete. Although projects have an important place in the curriculum, Reed (1998) cautions that before including a project, you think carefully about what it is you hope to accomplish. She suggests asking:

- What is it I want students to know?
- Does the project or activity touch on important aspects of the topic?
- Is this the best use of our limited class time?

FIGURE 15.6   In this journal entry, an eighth-grade student took the perspective of a slave to demonstrate his learning about the slave trade.

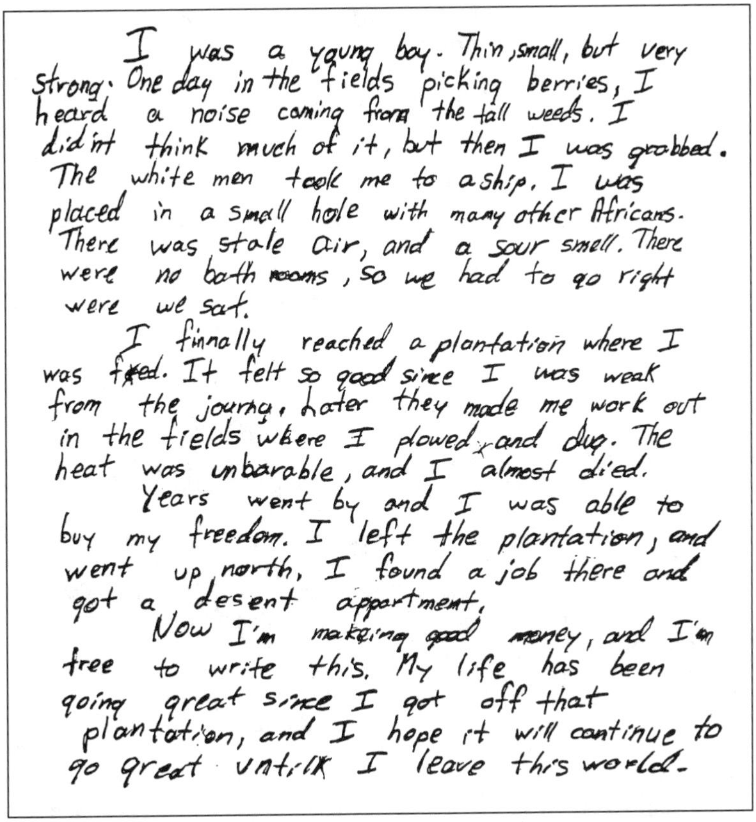

I was a young boy. Thin, small, but very strong. One day in the fields picking berries, I heard a noise coming from the tall weeds. I did'nt think much of it, but then I was grabbed. The white men took me to a ship. I was placed in a small hole with many other Africans. There was stale air, and a sour smell. There were no bath rooms, so we had to go right were we sat.

I finnally reached a plantation where I was feed. It felt so good since I was weak from the journy. Later they made me work out in the fields where I plowed, and dug. The heat was unbarable, and I almost died.

Years went by and I was able to buy my freedom. I left the plantation, and went up north, I found a job there and got a desent appartment.

Now I'm making good money, and I'm free to write this. My life has been going great since I got off that plantation, and I hope it will continue to go great untilk I leave this world.

Making a mobile or a diorama to represent the main idea of a book or story is a hands-on project, but it may take more time than you can afford when there are more effective ways to use time, such as role playing, debates, presentations, creation of timelines, maps, other media, visits from experts, and examination of original documents.

Conclusion

Matt and Paulo's conversation at the beginning of the chapter and descriptions of middle school classrooms included here show what these teachers believe about how students learn. They use demonstration and immersion (Cambourne, 1988) in the content areas accompanied by engagement in listening, speaking, reading, writing, and viewing. They model reading and viewing, interpreting and analyzing data, collaborating together, and the specific behaviors and performances they want their students to acquire. They immerse their students in rich environments and encourage self-directed inquiry and active learning. These teachers provide direct instruction and guided practice within a meaningful context (Shanahan, 1997) to help their students become competent language users and learners. They know there are many ways to achieve effective curriculum integration.

REFERENCES

Bromley, K. (1998). *Language arts: Exploring connections.* Boston: Allyn and Bacon.

Cambourne, B. (1988). *The whole story: Natural learning and the acquisition of literacy in the classroom.* Auckland, New Zealand: Scholastic.

Dewey, J. (1938). *Experience and education.* New York: Macmillan.

Dickens, C. (1997). *A Christmas Carol.* Uhrichsville, OH: Barbour.

Girion, B. (1990). *Indian summer.* New York: Scholastic.

Highwater, J. (1984). *Legend days.* New York: Harper and Row.

Kagan, S. (1994). *Cooperative learning.* San Juan Capistrano, CA: Resources for Learning.

Kroeber, T. (1964). *Ishi, last of his tribe.* New York: Parnassus.

Leu, D.J. (1997). Caity's questions: Literacy as deixis on the Internet. *The Reading Teacher, 51*(1), 62–67.

Leu, D.J., & Leu, D.D. (1997). *Teaching with the Internet: Lessons from the classroom.* Portsmouth, NH: Heinemann.

Manning, M., Manning, G., & Long, R. (1994). *Theme immersion.* Portsmouth, NH: Heinemann.

O'Dell, S. (1960). *Island of the blue dolphins.* New York: Houghton Mifflin.

———. (1970). *Sing down the moon.* New York: Houghton Mifflin.

O'Dell, S., & Hall, E. (1992). *Thunder rolling in the mountains.* New York: Houghton Mifflin.

Ogle, D. (1986). K-W-L: A teaching model that develops active reading of expository text. *The Reading Teacher, 39,* 564–570.

Pool, C.R. (1997). A new digital literacy: A conversation with Paul Gilster. *Educational Leadership, 55*(3), 6–11.

Reed, E.W. (1998). Projects and activities: A means, not an end. *American Educator, 21*(4), 26–27, 48.

Roth, K.J. (1994). Second thoughts about interdisciplinary studies. *American Educator, 18,* 44–52.

Routman, R. (1996). *Literacy at the crossroads.* Portsmouth, NH: Heinemann.

Shanahan, T. (1997). Reading–writing relationships, thematic units, inquiry learning . . . in pursuit of effective integrated literacy instruction. *The Reading Teacher, 51*(1), 12–19.

Shanahan, T., Robinson, B., & Schneider, M. (1995). Avoiding some of the pitfalls of thematic units. *The Reading Teacher, 48*(8), 718–719.

Vygotsky, L. (1978). *Mind in society: The development of higher order psychological processes.* Cambridge, MA: Harvard University Press.

Wells, G., & Chang-Wells, G.L. (1994). *Constructing knowledge together: Classrooms as centers of inquiry and literacy.* Portsmouth, NH: Heinemann.

16 Helping Struggling Learners Read and Write

KAREN D. WOOD

WILLIAM DEE NICHOLS

University of North Carolina at Charlotte

According to recent research, students at risk for educational failure represent the fastest growing segment of our school population (U.S. Department of Education, 1995; Carnegie Foundation, 1995). By 2000, the number of students for whom English is a second language is expected to rise at four times the rate of the general school population (U.S. Department of Education, 1995). Demographic data also indicate that, at present, over 14.5% of our citizens live below the poverty line, and this figure is expected to rise to 26% by 2000 (Carnegie Foundation, 1995). For literacy in the middle school, the statistics are just as bleak. The Carnegie Foundation reports that students' proficiency in science, mathematics, and writing is not adequate enough to keep pace with the higher-level skills required by a global economy. They go on to report that only 28% of eighth-grade students scored at or above the proficiency level in reading in 1994. This rather grim educational outlook means classroom teachers at the middle grades, and all grade levels, can expect to find their jobs more challenging and necessary than ever before.

One of the most valuable attributes of our society is the ability to communicate through the use of written text. People who lack the ability to read and write are severely restricted in their acquisition of knowledge, which becomes most evident when observed in the academic setting where students who lack reading capabilities begin to fail in other areas of academics (Daneman, 1991). Comprehending and understanding what one reads appears to be the highest common denominator for success in our schools. Not only does reading comprehension directly influence learning, but it also has a strong relationship to the development of cognitive skills and reasoning (Stanovich, 1986). Students who are struggling readers are at risk for educational failure and are often unable to undertake even the simplest course assignment due to their inability to read and fully comprehend the textbooks used. Although some of these struggling learners may be identified and served by a resource teacher or inclusionary team, many of these limited readers "fall between the cracks" and receive little or no additional assistance.

Many teachers in the intermediate and middle school grades feel inadequately prepared to teach reading and writing. For some, their most recent experience was one required literacy course as an undergraduate student. Still others, especially at the middle school level, were trained on a secondary model in which knowledge of a specific discipline was paramount to the ability to communicate that knowledge to others.

The remainder of this chapter will focus on several principles expanded from Wood (1998) and Wood and Shea-Bischoff (1992), which have the potential to help struggling learners get the extra scaffolding needed to improve their reading and writing ability.

Principle One: Plan the Daily Curriculum to Be Reading and Writing Intensive

This principle provides the foundation for the remaining principles because providing daily opportunities to practice reading and writing is the only way to improve students' literacy performance. Reading and writing activities must be incorporated into assignments given throughout the day. Such activities may involve engaging in a brief, oral retelling of a science passage with a partner and then together writing down that information in a few sentences. It could involve keeping a journal of responses to a self-selected or teacher assigned trade book in language arts class. Or, it could mean allowing students to work in heterogeneous groups of four or five to jointly write a passage predicting what they will read in their social studies chapter. More detailed examples of the principles to follow regarding specific reading and writing intensive strategies are given throughout.

Principle Two: Ensure That Ample Materials on Varied Levels Are Available

Without materials, the principles to follow are ineffective. Research indicates that many of the students in the intermediate and middle grades are expected to read texts that are too difficult for them to handle (Carnegie Foundation, 1995). Although a problem for all students, it is extremely frustrating for the struggling reader who continues to see the chasm of learning widen beyond their grasp. Consequently, these learners feel frustration when their school day consists of assignments from materials that they can neither read fluently nor understand. It is essential, then, that teachers and administrators have materials available that are written on varied grade levels with an interest level appropriate for pre- and early adolescent learners. This is not to say that struggling readers should receive different content; instead, it is saying that struggling readers should have an opportunity to receive the content through a means appropriate to their instructional reading level. Several publishing companies such as Steck Vaughn,

Cobblestone, and Jamestown Press, to name a few, have addressed this concern by publishing content area text (social studies, science, etc.) that have short passages and related activities using various reading levels. Scholastic also has many trade books (fiction, nonfiction, biographies, etc.) written at the primary level that relate to topics taught in grades 4 to 8. Teachers can seek these materials out at the publishers' exhibits at their state and national conferences. At a minimal cost, a few multiple copies can be purchased to supplement not supplant the classroom instruction.

In addition to purchasing material, teachers should be encouraged to work collaboratively with the media specialist at their school. If notified ahead of time, the media specialist can provide books, videos, and computer software from the school library on various reading levels to supplement the content being covered in class, allowing all of the students in the class to have an opportunity to participate in class discussions. In addition to pulling supplemental material, the media specialist can help the classroom teacher set up a listening center. This way, the teacher can place difficult text on tape so that all students, regardless of their reading level, can have an opportunity to receive the content being covered in class. While using the listening center, the struggling reader should be encouraged to follow along in the book, looking at each word while listening to the spoken word on tape. This practice not only allows students to receive the content, but also to have an opportunity to increase their sight vocabulary.

Principle Three: Use Flexible Grouping to Enable Students to Mutually Benefit from Instruction

Unfortunately, the practice of round robin reading is alive, well, and flourishing not only at the elementary level but at the middle school level as well. The practice of calling on one student at a time to read aloud is both time consuming and an inefficient means of promoting literacy and understanding. Imagine the worst-case scenario, 30 students seated in their straight rows and asked to read in order (or even randomly) from their social studies book. Students who have just read can sit back and not pay attention because it is unlikely that they will be called on again to read. Those who have not read yet may be busy reading ahead and rehearsing their lines, ignoring the words of the person currently reading. Those students in the back of the room are unable to hear the students reading in the front row. The class typically becomes distracted when a struggling learner reads aloud, and struggling learners feel embarrassment and frustration when asked to read aloud as they observe their classmates become restless and bored. About the only time students are on task and focused on the learning is during their own reading. That means that during a typical 30-minute session using this practice, students get to read approximately one minute. One minute is hardly enough time to enhance and improve literacy.

Because round robin reading neither enhances fluency nor comprehension and makes readers feel uncomfortable and frustrated, it is a practice that makes little educational sense. Even average readers in the classroom fail to understand the purpose of reading when this practice is used. Readers who are participants in round robin reading often report that good readers are readers who read fluently, not who comprehend what they read.

To help students improve their literacy, they must have ample time, fully engaged in the reading task (Allington, 1983). One means of engaging students in the literacy act is through the use of flexible grouping, and one method that has proven to be effective is paired reading and retelling. In paired reading and retelling, students can be strategically paired with classmates who can benefit from instruction from one another. Then, instead of calling on students to read individually, the teacher may have the dyads whisper read the first two paragraphs with their partners and afterwards discuss what they recall from their reading. Partners can assist each other with unknown words or concepts, relate what they have read to past experiences, and raise questions to be discussed with the class, and so forth. For the next few paragraphs, the pairs may be asked to read silently and then discuss their reading with their partner. During these reading times, the teacher is free to circulate, monitor, and assist dyads as they are actively engaged in the learning task. Also at this time, the teacher may ask students to read orally after the student has had a chance to practice reading it silently first. At appropriate junctures, the teacher may call for a classwide discussion of the content.

The following discussion occurred in an eighth-grade management school (an alternative school for students expelled from the regular classroom for disciplinary reasons) as they used this strategy to read a North Carolina History chapter on the Civil War.

Teacher: All right class, I want you to get into your teams and read the following pages 319–325 in your text. This section covers several battles that took place near the end of the war. Team 1, you will be responsible for "The Fall of Fort Fisher" pages 319–320, Team 2 will be responsible for "Sherman's Invasion" pages 321–323, Team 3 will be responsible for "Stoneman's Raid" pages 323–324 and Team 4 will be responsible for "Johnston's Surrender" pages 324–325. Remember each team must first read the text silently. Your goal during silent reading is to survey the material and to begin thinking about each section. Once you have completed reading the text silently you must re-read the text orally with your team members. Take turns reading aloud after each paragraph. It is important that during this time the team members who are not reading be good listeners. The listeners should provide assistance when needed. The listener's job is to also retell and summarize what has been read. Make sure you remember key ideas so that you can share with the class. During the retelling make sure you clarify anything that you do not understand. Ask the other members of your team, or ask me if you do not understand key ideas in the text. Once you have completed reading the section write three questions based on your summary. Be sure to provide answers to the questions. You will be addressing your questions to the other teams as well as me. Take your time and remember to do your best, you are the teacher.

Team One's summary and questions are as follows:

Fort Fisher was an L shaped fort that guarded the entrance to the Cape Fear River and was a strong point for the Confederate Army. The walls were constructed of sand and there were 48 long range guns. The Union Army attacked the fort on Christmas Eve, 1864. They used cannon fire from land and from ships and sent in 3,000 men, but were unable to overcome the fort. The Union soldiers attacked again on January 13, 1865. This time they used 8,000 men, 2,000 sailors and marines and two brigades of black union troops, which held off Lee's confederate soldiers. When the union troops finally stormed the fort, they fought the 1500 confederate soldiers for 6 hours using hand to hand combat. In the end the remaining confederate soldiers surrendered.

STUDENT 1: "I'm not really sure what the text is talking about when it states that the 'shot and shell fell like rain.' "

STUDENT 2: "I think that means, like when we were in the Gulf War and we sent in all of our missiles and air attack before sending in the army."

STUDENT 1: "Oh, I remember seeing that on TV. I remember the missiles lighting up the sky, I guess it did look like red rain."

STUDENT 3: "I was not sure what the passage meant when it was talking about hand to hand combat. Is that something like a fight?"

STUDENT 1: I think so. In those days, the soldiers didn't have guns that could shoot a lot of bullets so they would use their guns like clubs in close contact."

STUDENT 2: "Man, that was a long fight. Most heavy weight fights never last more than two hours. The book says that these guys fought for six hours before the confederate soldiers finally surrendered."

Principle Four: Teach Students How to Become Strategic Readers and Read for Information

Reading is often viewed as a process in which the reader constructs meaning through the interaction of stored knowledge and the text information. Skilled readers construct mental representations of the text by using their existing knowledge along with the application of flexible strategies (Rupley & Willson, 1997). When their comprehension breaks down, good readers monitor and change strategies so that comprehension has a better chance of occurring. Struggling readers, however, often do not employ strategies to aid in reading comprehension and need guidance and assistance to use strategies (Jetton, Rupley, & Willson, 1995). One reason that the lack of strategy use may occur among poor readers is that poor readers are unaware of how to use the strategy or they fail to see the importance of it. For a strategy to be selected, it must be perceived as a valuable means toward accomplishing a task (Paris, Newman, & Mcvey, 1982). Teachers can enhance instructional strategy training by combining strategy instruction with flexible grouping and modeling. For example, Robinson's (1961) study strategy, Survey, Question, Read, Recite, and Review (SQ3R) can be combined with flexible grouping to strengthen the learning process. The steps of this strategy are as follows:

Survey. During this time the dyads are encouraged to preview the material in order to develop a general understanding of how the information is organized. They should make predictions about the text and begin associating their previous experiences with the new text.

Question. The readers should begin to raise questions. These questions will serve as a purpose for reading. The students should generate questions based on the information gained from surveying the material. Since flexible grouping is being used the team members could generate questions for each other, or other dyads.

Read. Now that students have activated their background knowledge and have a purpose for reading, the reader should now attempt to answer the questions formulated previously.

Recite. During this stage the two partners can discuss what they have learned and provide answers to the questions they formulated. The teacher can also encourage and participate during this discussion period.

Review/Reflect. During this stage the readers should be encouraged to go back and re-read difficult parts of the text, or parts that seemed ambiguous. During this reflection period students should be encouraged to metacognitively reflect upon the text and determine where and why the text gave them difficulty.

Principle Five: Allow Students Time to Practice Reading for Fluency Using Materials Related to the Topics Under Discussion

If the reading ability of struggling readers is to improve, they must have ample time to practice fluency. Fluency refers to the smoothness of reading, the ability to read material with few interruptions due to inadequate word attack or word recognition problems. It is impossible to improve fluency if the material being read is too difficult for the student. To improve fluency, students must select books that are at their independent/instructional level to ensure that the reading is comfortable and not overly challenging.

Chall (1996) identifies three stages of reading development and maintains that for students to progress to the next stage of reading development, they must successfully pass through the previous stage. Stage 0 is often viewed as the emergent literacy stage in which the student begins to develop an understanding about text and begins to see the connection between the spoken language and the written text. In stage 1, the student begins to break the code of print, develop orthographic knowledge, and build up a sight vocabulary. In stage 2, the student begins to develop fluency using comfortable text. Most intermediate and middle school students are expected to have reached stage 3, which allows them to use reading as a tool for learning. Most struggling readers have not yet reached stage 3, however, and need to be provided with the opportunity to develop fluency.

The importance of developing fluency brings us back to principle 1, which states that instructional material must be available that is appropriate for students reading below grade level. In addition, time must be allotted each day for students to use that material and practice fluent reading. One strategy designed to help students develop fluency was developed by Koskinen and Blum (1986) and is reflected in the form shown in

FIGURE 16.1 Fluency Partner Reading Assessment

Reading #1, 2, 3

How well did you read?

| Score! | Good! | OK | Try Again |

Reading #3

How did your partner's reading improve?

Read more smoothly _____

Knew more words _____

Read with more expression _____

Tell your partner one thing that was better about his or her reading.

_____

_____

_____

Source: Adapted from "Paired Repeated Reading: A Classroom Strategy for Developing Fluent Reading" by P. S. Koskinen & I. H. Blum, 1986, *The Reading Teacher, 40* (1), pp. 70–75.

Figure 16.1. It has been modified here to meet the needs of intermediate and middle grade students functioning below grade level. The procedures are as follows:

1. Preassign the struggling readers to pairs (or a group of three if the number is uneven), making certain that the students are sufficiently similar in ability that they can mutually benefit from instruction. Tell them that the purpose of this assignment is to help them become better readers and that improving ability to read, as with any sport or activity, requires that they practice each day.

2. Provide the students passages that they can read with a minimal amount of assistance. These passages can be taken from the alternative material mentioned

previously (short workbook segments or tradebook excerpts written at the primary level are usually appropriate for the struggling reader). The designated passages should be relatively short (50 to 100 words) so as not to be overwhelming to the students.

3. Students first read their passages silently and then decide who will practice reading first. Students alternate the roles of reader and listener throughout the practice session.

4. When asked to serve as reader, the student reads the passage aloud to the partner three different times. The partner can assist with pronunciation and meaning if needed. Then the reader engages in a self-evaluation answering question, "How well did you read?" When asked to serve as the listener, the student listens to the partner's reading and then notes how the reading improved on the evaluation form shown in the reading and then notes how the reading improved on the evaluation form shown in the figure. The only opportunity given for the partners to evaluate one another requires a positive response, not a negative one.

5. After the third reading, the students switch roles and follow step 3 again. Teachers can then circulate amongst the dyads to provide assistance and to model effective fluent reading for the students.

Principle Six: Help Students Improve Understanding by "Chunking" the Amount of Print They Read at a Given Time

Although developing fluency is critical in the developmental stages of successful reading, it is insignificant if students fail to comprehend the passages to be read. Reading should be viewed as a conversation between the writer and the reader in which the writer of the text is trying to communicate ideas to the reader. For successful communication to take place, the reader must be an active recipient of the information that is being transmitted by the writer. Some students are able to comprehend text on the first reading, whereas others may need numerous opportunities and ample amounts of time to practice comprehension.

One effective means for increasing students' understanding is asking them to engage in a retelling of the content. The act of mentally or vocally rehearsing the content of a selection is a proven means of increasing students' recall and comprehension (Stahl, King, & Henk, 1991). The retelling form shown in Figure 16.2 is adapted from Koskinen, Gambrell, Kapinus, and Heathington (1988) and was originally designed for use with the fluency assessment form shown in Figure 16.1, although it can be used with other strategies and materials as well. As with any learning strategy, the teacher should model or think aloud for the students so they can begin to see the usefulness and value of the strategy being implemented. During the modeling process, the teacher can encourage students to use this form of retelling while engaged in any reading material,

FIGURE 16.2   Comprehension Retelling Reaction Form

Name _____ Date _____

I listened to _____ .

Check one or more things your partner did well:

Narrative (Fiction)	Expository (Nonfiction)
He or she told about the characters.	He or she told about the main ideas.
He or she told about the setting.	He or she told about the details.
He or she told about events in the story.	
His or her story had a beginning.	
His or her story had an ending.	

With the aid of your partner, retell the selection in your own words in the space below.

_____

_____

_____

Source: Adapted from "Retelling: A Strategy for Enhancing Students' Reading Comprehension" by P. S. Koskinen, L. Gambrell, B. Kapinus, & B. Heathington, 1988, *The Reading Teacher, 41* (9), 892–896.

not just the ones selected for fluency practice. Before students select strategies, they need to value the strategy and understand that the strategy can be integrated across the curriculum (Nichols, Rupley, & Mergen, 1998). Listed below are guidlines that can be used during the retelling process:

Guidelines to Use during Retellings
1. Partners can whisper read together, to one another or read a selection silently. For less able readers, these selections should be short and easy to manage, approximately 50 to 100 words.
2. Allow the students to tell each other what they recall about the selection read. With narrative text, the focus is often on the characters, setting, and events of the

story. With expository material, the focus is frequently on the recall of the main ideas and details.

3. Partners can add to and embellish each other's retellings with analogies, anecdotes, and questions about the topic.

4. Last, the partners work together to write their brief retelling in the space provided or use a graphic organizer that allows the students to graphically display the key information that they recall from the text. More than one classwide demonstration and modeling session may be necessary for students to understand how to summarize information.

As with all middle school students who are using reading as a tool for learning, they must learn to implement reading strategies to successfully allow the facilitation of comprehension. Struggling readers especially seem unsuccessful at implementing learning strategies in the context of the classroom. As part of the teacher's duty to empower children in the ability to use reading as a tool for learning, we must begin to model appropriate reading strategies in our classroom instruction. Regardless of the grade level or content that you teach, it is important that we remember that we are all teachers of reading. Not only is it our job to instruct students in the content of our curriculum, but we must also, at the same time, instruct our students in selective strategic learning that empowers them to be responsible for their own comprehension of the text. By becoming a strategic reader, the student is no longer viewed as a passive recipient of learning, but instead they are seen as active participants in the learning process.

One means of helping students become strategic readers is through the use of study or reading guides. Study guides consist of questions or activities that follow the organization of a textbook chapter, enabling students to read and respond to the text in segments or "chunks." This strategy is at variance with the practice of assigning students, regardless of reading proficiency, to read an entire textbook chapter and answer the questions at the end. For many students reading on or below grade level, such an assignment is frustrating, overwhelming, and often unachievable. The study guide provides a "tutor in print form" (Wood, 1994) to guide the students throughout the reading of the text.

A type of study guide described here is the reading road map (Wood, 1994; Wood, Lapp, & Flood, 1992), which enables students to take a "traveling companion" (a preasssigned partner) on a "textbook journey" through a chapter or portion of a text. The reading road map consists of "missions" (interspersed questions and activities), "road signs" (reading rate indicators), and "location signs" (the headings and page or paragraph numbers). The guide shown in Figure 16.3 was designed for use in a seventh-grade science class studying the topic of pollution. Notice how students are asked to engage in a variety of activities along the way, including retellings, recalling, charting, picture analysis, comparing, and predicting. The traveling companions may be asked to read silently, whisper read together, or mumble read and then discuss and assist one another as they decide on the most logical responses. The teacher may intervene at various points during the journey to elaborate, clarify, or request comments from the class as a whole.

FIGURE 16.3   Excerpt from a Reading Road Map

Overall Mission: *You are about to learn how air pollution, water pollution, and pesticides affect our lives.*

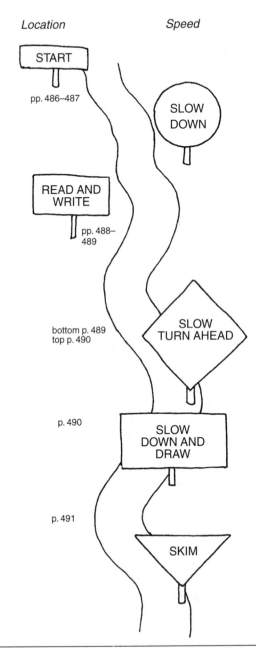

Location   Speed   Mission

AIR POLLUTION

START

pp. 486–487

SLOW DOWN

1. a. What causes the heavy haze we often see in cities?
   b. When and why did this begin?
   c. How is smog produced? How does it make us feel?

READ AND WRITE

pp. 488–489

2. With your partner, draw a chart that shows how auto exhaust affects the ozone layer and releases ultraviolet light.

bottom p. 489
top p. 490

SLOW TURN AHEAD

3. a. Where does carbon dioxide come from?
   b. Explain what happens when there is too much carbon dioxide in the air.

p. 490

SLOW DOWN AND DRAW

4. a. With your partner, write down three steps that can slow down the global warming process.
   b. Explain what Congress has done to reduce pollution.

p. 491

SKIM

5. With your partner, draw a chart that shows the damage done by acid rain.

6. Skim over this page and discuss with your group members what you can do to help the environment.

Principle Seven: Provide Opportunities Each Day for Students to Read Independently in Materials Appropriate to Their Reading and Interest Levels

A most significant means of improving students' reading ability is allowing them to read books of their own choosing. By working closely with the media specialist, teachers can compile classroom libraries of multilevel tradebooks (not to mention magazine articles, newspapers, and brochures) that are topically related to the information under study. In this way, students may select a biography of a famous scientist, fiction or nonfiction about Japan, or an article on lifesaving techniques for health class. Then, they can self-select how they will respond to this reading, through art projects, journal writing, dramatic activities, book talks, and blurbs (sales pitch type summaries), to name a few. Needless to say, keeping track of the individual reading preferences of all the students in a class is a major concern of teachers. One means of addressing this concern is through the use of the reader response form shown in Figure 16.4. This form enables students to see the range of responses from which to choose while simultaneously helping teachers keep a record of their book and response choices.

Principle Eight: Give Students Ample Opportunities to Practice Writing Independently and Communally

All students, regardless of ability level, should be encouraged and expected to write every day (Rhodes & Dudley-Marling, 1996; Routman, 1996; Wood & Shea-Bischoff, 1997). The extant research indicates that there is a reciprocal relationship between reading and writing and that these two processes should be taught and learned together (Tierney & Shanahan, 1991). Research also indicates that the more quality time students spend in meaningful literacy activities, the higher the achievement (Walp & Walmsley, 1995; Wood & Algozzine, 1994). These writing experiences need not be long, sophisticated, or in polished form, but they must be meaningful. Practices such as having struggling learners copy pages from an encyclopedia or copying questions from the end of a textbook chapter to keep them busy are not examples of having students engaged in meaningful writing experiences.

As discussed earlier in the chapter, just as struggling readers need ample time to practice reading to gain control of the reading process, all students need ample time to practice writing in meaningful context to become improved writers. Many of these writing assignments do not need to be graded in the formal sense but instead can be viewed as "practice writing sessions." An analogy can be drawn to the game of basketball in which players practice every day but are only evaluated once or twice a week during the game.

One excellent way of providing writing experiences for students functioning below grade level is through the use of wordless picture books. Wordless picture books

FIGURE 16.4 Sample Reader Response Form

Reader Response Form

Basic Information

Name _____ Class _____ Date _____

Title of Book _____

Author _____ Date of publication _____

I chose this book because _____

Number of pages _____ I read the entire book: _____ Yes _____ No
  If you did not read the entire book, please explain on the back of this form. How much did you read, and why did you decide to stop? (This is important!)

I read the book: _____ at home _____ at school _____ both

Reaction to the book:
(Circle a number):

I liked it very much	5
I liked it	4
It was okay	3
I disliked it	2
I disliked it very much	1

Recommendations about this book:
(Fill out only if you ranked it as a 3 or above)

A friend who'd like it: _____
A teacher who'd like it: _____
Another subject it fits: _____
An author who'd like it: _____

My choice or choices of response:

_____ Book jacket, poster, or picture
_____ Changing one thing about the book
_____ Critical review
_____ Description of favorite parts/ characters
_____ Index card summary and critique
_____ Letter to the author
_____ Linking my own parallel story
_____ Write in my journal

_____ Letter of recommendation
_____ Main character diary
_____ Newspaper article
_____ One-act play
_____ Persuasive essay on an issue
_____ Presentation of a talk show
_____ Rewriting or adding a part
_____ Time line of major events
_____ Writing a song or poem
_____ Make a collage, a mobile
_____ Other

Why did you choose to respond to the book this way?
Briefly explain on the back.

Source: Adapted and revised from Wood (1994). *Practical Strategies for Improving Instruction.* Columbus, OH: National Middle School Association. Reprinted with permission.

provide a perfect model to encourage reluctant writers with an opportunity to create text to coordinate with the rich illustrations. Students who find the printed word intimidating often feel less threatened with wordless picture books. Although wordless picture books provide rich contextual features that encourage language development, they also provide students with story structure and sequence as well as inspiration. Figure 16.5 provides a list of some wordless picture books that are especially appropriate for intermediate- and middle-level students.

Although wordless picture books were traditionally thought of as appropriate only for elementary students, many wordless picture books have appeal for students in the upper grades as well. For example, David Wiesner's (1991) *Tuesday,* a Caldecott Award winner, is an imaginative tale told in pictures where frogs soar through the evening skies on lily pads and invade a sleeping town. Although this text is wonderful for engaging creative writing in literature classes, it could also easily be integrated with units in science dealing with gravity, aerodynamics, or the natural habitat of frogs. In *Time Flies* (Rohmann, 1994), a bird finds shelter from a storm in a dinosaur exhibit at a local museum. While waiting out the storm, the little bird is transported back in time to the Cretaceous period, where it is almost eaten by a hungry *Tyrannosaurus rex. Time Flies* is yet another example of the benefits of using wordless picture books with older students. It provides a nonthreatening vehicle for encouraging struggling writers to write while simultaneously connecting science, history, and language arts.

Another way to integrate reading and writing is through the use of an instructional strategy called story impressions (McGinley & Denner, 1987). Story impressions enable students to activate schemata related to ideas located in the story and actively engage students while at the same time serve as a prewriting activity. Students use a list of clues taken from the story to write a predicted story (see Figure 16.6). As students formulate a written hypothesis of the story, they activate their knowledge of story schema and their own background experiences. The process of writing the prestory improves reading comprehension by using predictions about the text to set a purpose for reading (Bligh, 1995).

Teachers can create story impressions by selecting key words from the chapter or text and listing them in the order in which they occur in the selection. The teacher then helps guide the students in creating their own interpretation of the story based on the key words. Once the predicted story is completed, students read the text and search for comparisons or differences between their predicted story and the author's text. As a postreading and writing activity, students are encouraged to use the story impressions chart to write a retelling or summary of the story to use as a study guide and to strengthen comprehension of what has been read. To ensure that struggling writers will not be left behind, it is recommended that flexible grouping in the form of "communal writing" (Wood, 1994) be employed. In communal writing, students are assigned to heterogeneous groups of four or five and encouraged to "put their heads together" in the composition of a single paragraph(s). They can be assigned specific editing tasks to further "polish" their compositions or the teacher may elect to count this as a practice writing exercise. Figure 16.6 is an example of four students' predictions for a prestory on the selection *Uncle Jed's Barbershop.* For illustrative purposes, the students' names were included in parentheses to indicate their specific contributions.

FIGURE 16.5   Selected Wordless Picture Books for Intermediate and Middle Grade Students

Anno, M. (1977). *Anno's journey.* New York: Collins.

Anno, M. (1978). *Anno's Italy.* New York: Collins.

Anno, M. (1982). *Anno's Britain.* New York: Philomel.

Anno, M. (1983). *Anno's USA.* New York: Philomel.

Bang, M. (1980). *The grey lady and the strawberry snatcher.* New York: Four Winds.

Bonners, S. (1989). *Just in passing.* New York: Lothrop, Lee and Shepard.

Brown, C. (1989). *The patchwork farmer.* New York: Greenwillow.

Cristini, E., & Puricelli, L. (1984). *In the pond.* New York: Picture Book Studio, Simon & Schuster.

Day, A. (1985). *Good dog, Carl.* New York: Simon & Schuster.

dePaola, T. (1979). *Flicks.* New York: Harcourt Brace and Jovanovich.

Dupasquier, P. (1988). *The great escape.* Boston: Houghton Mifflin.

Goodall, J.S. (1979). *An Edwardian holiday.* New York: Atheneum.

Goodall, J.S. (1975). *Creepy castle.* New York: Atheneum.

Goodall, J.S. (1976). *An Edwardian summer.* New York: Atheneum.

Goodall, J.S. (1979). *The story of an English village.* New York: Atheneum.

Goodall, J.S. (1980). *An Edwardian season.* New York: Atheneum.

Goodall, J.S. (1980). *Above and below the stairs.* New York: Atheneum.

Goodall, J.S. (1987). *The story of a high street.* London: Andre Deutsch.

Gross, M. (1971). *He done her wrong.* New York: Dover.

Hoban, T. (1983). *I read signs.* New York: Macmillan/McGraw-Hill.

Hoban, T. (1974). *Circles, triangles and squares.* New York: Macmillan/McGraw-Hill.

Hutchins, P. (1971). *Changes, changes.* New York: Macmillan/McGraw-Hill.

Krahn, F. (1970). *Hildegarde and Maximilian.* New York: Delacorte Press.

Krahn, F. (1977). *The mystery of the giant footprints.* New York: Dutton.

Krahn, F. (1978). *The great ape.* New York: Penguin.

McCully. E.A. (1987). *School.* New York: Harper and Row.

Monro, R. (1987). *The inside-outside book of Washington, D.C.* New York: Dutton.

Rohmann, E. (1994). *Time flies.* New York: Crown.

Spier, P. (1982). *Peter Spier's rain.* New York: Doubleday.

Spier, P. (1982). *Rain.* New York: Delacorte.

Spier, P. (1986). *Dreams.* New York: Doubleday.

Tafuri, N. (1988). *Junglewalk.* New York: Greenwillow.

*Van Allsburg, C. (1984). *The mysteries of Harris Burdick.* Boston: Houghton Mifflin.

Wetherbee, H. (1978). *The wonder ring.* New York: Doubleday.

Wiesner, D. (1988). *Freefall.* New York: Lothrop, Lee and Shepard.

Wiesner, D. (1991). *Tuesday.* New York: Clarion Books.

*Contains some words.

Source: Adapted from Wood, K. D., & Shea-Bischoff, P. (1997). Helping struggling writers write. *Middle School Journal, 28* (4), 50–53. Reprinted with permission.

FIGURE 16.6   Story Impressions: *Uncle Jed's Barbershop* **by Margaree King Mitchell**

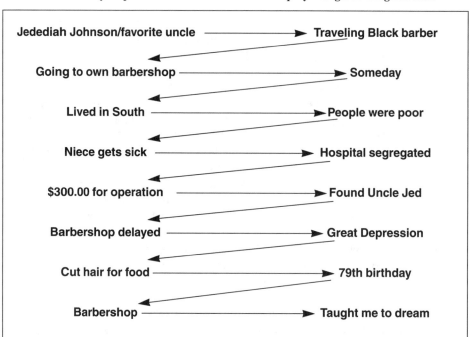

Jedediah Johnson/favorite uncle ⟶ Traveling Black barber

Going to own barbershop ⟶ Someday

Lived in South ⟶ People were poor

Niece gets sick ⟶ Hospital segregated

$300.00 for operation ⟶ Found Uncle Jed

Barbershop delayed ⟶ Great Depression

Cut hair for food ⟶ 79th birthday

Barbershop ⟶ Taught me to dream

I had a favorite uncle named Jedediah Johnson. He was a traveling black barber and he loved to cut people's hair. (Sara) He knew that someday he was going to have his own barbershop and then he would not have to travel from town to town cutting hair. (Rodnico) We all lived in the South and we were all very poor. One day I got very sick and I had to go to the hospital. The hospital was segregated and the doctor wouldn't see me. (Queint) Finally the doctor saw me and he said it would cost $300 for the operation. Well we didn't have that kind of money because we were poor. We had to find Uncle Jed. (Sara) Uncle Jed had to delay his barbershop because he didn't have any money either because it was the Great Depression. He gave me the money for the operation, but it left him broke. (Rodnico) He was so poor after he gave me the money that he had to cut hair just to get food. (Queint) Finally on his 79th birthday we bought him a barbershop for a present. Uncle Jed taught me to dream. (Sara)

Conclusion

As research indicates, students functioning below grade level represent the fastest growing segment of the school population. Consequently, it is imperative that we reevaluate both the methods and the materials used in our teaching, making sure that we give students ample opportunities throughout the school day and across the subject areas to engage in meaningful reading and writing experiences.

REFERENCES

Allington, R. (1983). The reading instruction provided readers of reading abilities. *Elementary School Journal, 83,* 548–559.

Bligh, T. (1995). Using story impressions to improve comprehension. *Reading Horizons, 35,* 287–298.

Carnegie Council on Adolescent Development. (1995). *Draft: Report of the Carnegie Task Force on learning in the primary grades.* New York: Author.

Chall, J.S. (1996). *Stages of reading development.* New York: McGraw-Hill.

Daneman, M. (1991). Individual differences in reading skills. In R. Barr, M. Kamil, P. Mosenthal, & P. Pearson (Eds.), *Handbook of reading research* (vol. 2, pp. 512–538). White Plains, NY: Longman.

Jetton, T., Rupley, W.H., & Willson, V.L. (1995). Comprehension of narrative and expository texts: The role of content, domain, discourse, and strategy knowledge. In K. Hinchman, D.J. Leu, & C.K. Kinzer (Eds.), *Perspectives on literacy research and practice,* 44th Yearbook of the National Reading Conference (197–204). Chicago: National Reading Conference.

Koskinen, P.S., & Blum, I.H. (1986). Paired repeated reading: A classroom strategy for developing fluent reading. *The Reading Teacher, 40*(1), 70–75.

Koskinen, P.S., Gambrell, L., Kapinus, B., & Heathington, B. (1988). Retelling: A strategy for enhancing students' reading comprehension. *The Reading Teacher, 41*(9), 892–896.

McGinley, W., & Denner, P. (1987). Story impressions: A prereading/writing activity. *Journal of Reading, 31,* 248–253.

Nichols, W.D., Rupley, W.H., & Mergen, S. (in press). Improving elementary teachers ability to implement reading strategies in their teaching of science content. In E.G. Sturtevant, J.A. Dugan, P. Linder, & W.M. Linek (Eds.), *Literacy and Community, 20th Yearbook of the College Reading Association* (188–213).

Paris, S.G., Newman, R.S., & Mcvey, K.A. (1982). Learning the functional significance of mnemonic actions: A microgenetic study of strategy acquisition. *Journal of Experimental Child Psychology, 34,* 490–509.

Rhodes, L.K., & Dudley-Marling, C. (1996). *Readers and writers with a difference* (2nd ed.). Portsmouth, NH: Heinemann.

Robinson, F.P. (1961). *Effective reading* (rev. ed.). New York: Harper and Row.

Rohmann, E. (1994). *Time flies.* New York: Crown.

Routmann, R. (1996). *Literacy at the crossroads: Critical talk about reading, writing and other teaching dilemmas.* Portsmouth, NH: Heinemann.

Rupley, W.H., & Willson, V.L. (1997). The relationship of reading comprehension to components of word recognition: Support for developmental shifts. *Journal of Research and Development in Education, 30,* 255–260.

Stahl, N.A., King, J., & Henk, W.A. (1991). Enhancing students' notetaking through training and evaluation. *Journal of Reading, 34,* 614–622.

Stanovich, K.E. (1986). Mathew effects in reading: Some consequences of individual differences in the acquisition of literacy. *Reading Research Quarterly, 21,* 360–407.

Tierney, R.J., & Shanahan, T.J. (1991). Research on the reading-writing relationship: Interaction, transitions and outcome. *Handbook of Reading Research, 2,* 246–280.

U.S. Department of Education, National Center for Education Statistics. (1995). *The Condition of Education.* Washington, DC: Author.

Walp, T.P., & Walmsley, S. (1995). Scoring well on tests or becoming genuinely literate: Rethinking remediations in a small rural school. In R.L. Allington & S.A. Walmsley (Eds.), *No quick fix: Rethinking literacy programs in America's elementary schools* (pp. 177–196). Newark, DE: International Reading Association.

Wiesner, D. (1991). *Tuesday.* New York: Clarion Books.

Wood, K.D. (1994). *Practical strategies for improving instruction.* Columbus, OH: National Middle School Classroom.

Wood, K.D. (1998). Helping struggling readers read. *Middle School Journal, 29*(5), 67–70.

Wood, K.D., & Algozzine, B. (Eds.). (1994). *Teaching reading to high-risk learners: A unified perspective.* Boston: Allyn and Bacon.

Wood, K.D., Lapp, D., & Flood, J. (1992). *Guiding readers through text.* Newark, DE: International Reading Association.

Wood, K.D., & Shea-Bischoff, P. (1997). Helping struggling writers write. *Middle School Journal, 28*(4), 50–53.

17 Using Picture Books with Older Students

MIRIAM MARTINEZ
University of Texas at San Antonio

NANCY L. ROSER
University of Texas at Austin

SUSAN STRECKER
University of Texas at Austin

Learning occurs in classrooms where students are engaged. Although many factors contribute to student engagement, selecting the right materials for instruction is one of the most important considerations (Guthrie, 1996). Because of the potential picture books have for engaging students, promoting literacy, and extending understanding, every upper elementary and middle school teacher should consider them as essential instructional tools.

The Changing World of Picture Books

Upper elementary and middle school teachers all too often overlook picture books as they seek out materials to support their curriculum, assuming that picture books are intended only for young children (Kiefer, 1995a). In earlier decades, children's literature experts would likely have agreed with these teachers. The topics and themes explored in the picture books of years past made them most appropriate for younger children; these topics included family stories, familiar everyday experiences, stories of the country and city, weather and the seasons, realistic animal stories, fanciful animal stories, humorous and fanciful picture books, and picture books of other lands (Huck & Kuhn, 1968; Sutherland & Arbuthnot, 1977). Many of today's picture books continue to explore similar topics, but increasing numbers are dramatically different from the picture books of earlier eras. In particular, many of today's picture books are complex and sophisticated, they explore a wider range of subject matter, and there is a proliferation of picture books across a wider range of genres. As Huck, Hepler, Hickman, and Kiefer (1997) observed, "Picture books are for all ages" (p. 294), with increasing numbers being written for older students.

Complexity and Sophistication

A marked trend in picture books in the 1990s was toward increasing complexity and sophistication. This trend is evident in some of the most widely recognized picture books of the decade. The warning that David Macauley includes on the title page of *Black and White* (1990), winner of the 1991 Caldecott Award as the best illustrated book of the year, hints of the book's complex structure: "This book appears to contain a number of stories that do not necessarily occur at the same time. Then again, it may contain only one story. In any event, careful inspection of both words and pictures is recommended." Jon Scieszka's *The Stinky Cheese Man and Other Fairly Stupid Tales* (1992) is a collection of fairy tale spin-offs that are organized in such a manner as to violate almost every conceivable book convention. Full appreciation of this enormously popular Caldecott Honor book requires an understanding of book conventions as well as familiarity with the original stories on which Scieszka's spoofs are based. The same kinds of expectations are foiled and unraveling required by *Bright and Early Thursday Evening: A Tangled Tale* (1996) "dreamed and imagined" by Audrey Wood. Nancy Willard's *Pish, Posh, Said Hieronymous Bosch* (1991) features wildly imaginative creatures such as might have sprung from the famous painter's imagination. Although some of these sophisticated picture books are appreciated across age levels, the demands of others make them most appropriate for older students.

Wide Range of Subject Matter

Although the picture books of earlier decades tended to highlight the everyday experiences and concerns of young children, the subject matter of today's picture books has broadened considerably. In their listing of topics explored in recent picture books, Huck, Hepler, Hickman, and Kiefer (1997) include appreciating cultural diversity, social and environmental concerns, and war and its aftermath. Some of the particular topics that authors are choosing to explore in picture format include the Holocaust, the bombing of Hiroshima, war-torn Beirut, apartheid, homelessness, alcoholism, AIDS, and suicide. Pictures books addressing topics like these, books such as *Smoky Night* (Bunting, 1994a) and *Hiroshima No Pika* (Maruki, 1980), have stirred considerable controversy in both professional circles and the popular press (Krauthammer, 1995; Sutton, 1996). Yet the controversy appears to arise, in part, from the entrenched belief that picture books, including those addressing serious issues, are intended for young children. When picture books are viewed as being for all ages, however, addressing serious issues in picture book format seems to be not only appropriate but even desirable.

Wider Range of Genres in Picture Book Format

There has been a proliferation of genres in picture book format that, until recent years, appeared primarily as lengthier texts. This trend is especially evident in biographies and historical fiction (Bishop & Hickman, 1992; Temple, Martinez, Yokota, & Naylor, 1998). Diane Stanley and Kathryn Lasky are among the outstanding writers producing biographies in picture book format. Fine writers like Donald Hall, Eve Bunting, Ann Turner, Emily Arnold McCully, and Karen Ackerman have produced historical fiction in picture book format. Although some of the picture books in these genres are appropriate for young children, many are better suited for older students. Biography and historical fiction may be especially well suited to a picture book format because an enormous amount of historical information can be conveyed through a book's illustrations.

These changes in picture books make this genre a valuable tool for upper elementary and middle school teachers. It is true that older students may initially view picture books as "baby books," but if teachers "consider picture books as literature—not children's literature—but as *literature*" (Newkirk, 1992, p.13) and if they share their own genuine enthusiasm for the genre, their students will also come to value the picture books. Then, perhaps, picture books will come to fill a variety of niches (and gulfs) across the curriculum in classrooms that serve older students. In the remainder of this chapter, we explore some of those niches and provide examples of literature that can fill them.

Picture Books in Language Arts/Reading/ English Classrooms

Picture books can fill a host of roles in language arts and reading classrooms. Picture books can provide rich material for literature discussion, serve as models and stimuli for students' writing, provide material for skill and strategy instruction, and serve as material for students' independent reading.

Literature Discussion

In recent years, teachers have increasingly come to value literature discussion. When students are invited to talk about carefully crafted books that explore significant themes, rich and insightful thinking is most likely to occur (Eeds & Wells, 1989; Martinez & Roser, 1995). By no means do only novels have the potential to evoke rich literature discussion. In fact, Carlisle (1992), who has used picture books to engage older students in philosophical thinking, argues that picture books are "an easy place to think" (p. 58). There are a wide variety of picture books that explore significant themes. One example is *The Girl Who Loved Caterpillars* (Merrill, 1992). In this picture book, author Jean Merrill retells a twelfth-century Japanese story of Suzumi, a girl whose passion for learning about caterpillars flies in the face of her society's values. Her parents long for her to develop more conventional interests, but Suzumi steadfastly clings to her passion. Because *The Girl Who Loved Caterpillars* explores issues that still confront many young women, today's students are likely to have a great deal to say in response to this sophisticated picture book. A few examples of the numerous other picture books with the potential to evoke rich conversation are Sherry Garland's (1993)

The Lotus Seed, which explores the importance of intergenerational ties, Patricia Polacco's (1992) *Chicken Sunday,* which looks at the need to reach out across cultural boundaries, and Barbara Cooney's (1982) *Miss Rumphius,* in which a woman seeks a way to make the world a better place.

Relying on picture books for literature discussion offers middle- and upper-grade teachers a genuine advantage when time is considered. While students are reading longer works on their own, the teacher who uses picture books does not have to wait for students to finish a work before engaging them in literature discussion. Typically, a picture book can be read aloud and discussed in a single class session. Thus, students participate in far more literature discussion than in classes where only longer works are discussed. Carlisle (1992) identified yet another advantage to using picture books for literature discussion: By using picture books, teachers can bring more diverse perspectives to bear on a topic than is possible when a single extended work of literature is used to explore the topic. A picture book can be used to introduce an author such as Shakespeare (*Bard of Avon,* Stanley & Vennema [1992]) or Emily Dickinson (*Emily,* Bedard [1992]). The use of multiple picture books in a literature unit also encourages students to make intertextual connections. For example, a unit on social injustices may include *The Bracelet* (Uchida, 1976/1993), *Let the Celebrations Begin!* (Wild, 1991), *How Many Days to America* (Bunting, 1988), and *The Middle Passage: White Ships/ Black Cargo* (Feelings, 1995).

Student Writing

Picture books can make an especially important contribution to the language arts program when they used as writing models. The complexity of novels can make it difficult for students to stand back and see how authors have crafted their work. Further, more extended works may make for less appropriate models because most students are not likely to write extended works of their own. The relative brevity of picture books makes it easier for students to inspect them for structure, form, and the author's use of various literary devices. After inspecting *When I Was Young in the Mountains* (Rylant, 1982) and discovering how Rylant uses repetition to create lyrical language, students might try their own hand at using this technique. Immersing students in literature units structured around sets of picture books can be an especially effective way to help them make discoveries about literary craft (Moss, 1990). For example, reading the picture books of Van Allsburg is likely to heighten students' awareness of the effectiveness of the unexpected twist at the end of a story.

Picture books can support the writing program in yet another way. Quality writing relies on rich experience, and although rich experiences can take many forms, good literature can certainly constitute such experience. Teachers can take advantage of the meaningful experiences offered by well-crafted picture books to foster their students' writing. Of particular note are picture books that feature "universal" experiences or those with novel formats or content.

The subject matter featured in many picture books, if not universal, certainly strikes a responsive chord in many readers. In *My Great-Aunt Arizona* (1992), author Gloria Houston celebrates the life of a beloved older relative. The book is one that could inspire many young writers to write about a person who is significant in their own lives.

Audrey Wood's *Weird Parents* (1990) recounts the embarrassing moments in a boy's life that are caused by his weird parents, a situation with which upper elementary and middle school children readily identify. After reading or listening to Garza's *Family Pictures* (1990), students can make their own family pictures through art and words.

Picture books with novel structures (or story content) can also serve as engaging springboards for students' writing. *The Mysteries of Harris Burdick* (Van Allsburg, 1984) is such a book. It consists of a series of intriguing illustrations with captions that were created to accompany stories. The stories, the author explains, have been lost. Each illustration and accompanying caption serves as an enticing invitation to write. *The Jolly Postman or Other People's Letters* (Ahlberg & Ahlberg, 1986), an equally novel picture book consisting of a series of humorous spin-off letters and postcards written to or by characters from European folklore, begs for older students to write their own spin-offs. For example, an attorney writes to the Big Bad Wolf informing him of a lawsuit the Three Little Pigs plan to bring against him. Jack sends the Giant a postcard, and Goldilocks mails Baby Bear an invitation to her birthday party. In Diane Stanley's *Rumpelstiltskin's Daughter* (1997), the protagonist is so clever that she has no need to call for help when the king asks her to spin straw into gold.

Still other stories leave readers with so much to think about that they are eager to write in response to the story. Who can finish *The Stranger* (Van Allsburg, 1986) without speculating about who this peculiar man was? Readers of Barbara Cooney's *Miss Rumphius* (1982) may want to write about how they envision themselves making the world a better place. After listening to poems in Eve Merriam's (1996) provocative *The Inner City Mother Goose,* students might write about the social problems they see in their world; some may even want to try Merriam's nursery rhyme format.

Skill and Strategy Instruction

Picture books can be excellent vehicles for reading and language arts skill and strategy instruction, especially if they are experienced first for their artistry. Using literature ensures that instruction is done in a meaningful context, and picture books are typically brief enough to be used in the minilessons. Also, it is relatively easy to find picture books that serve as clear-cut examples. For example, the teacher who is targeting cause-and-effect relationships will find that David Macauley's (1995) *Shortcut* provides a humorous context for a lesson. Perspective can be taught through Jeanne Willis's (1988) *Earthlets* or Chris Van Allsburg's (1988) *Two Bad Ants.* It is hard to imagine a better example of irony than Alan Benjamin's adaptation of Somerset Maugham's (1993) *Appointment. Chato's Kitchen* (1995) by Gary Soto is a wonderful vehicle for exploring tone. The language arts teacher who wants to help students understand the way in which language works can turn to Ruth Heller's poetic picture book series on parts of speech, including titles such as *Up, Up and Away* (1991) and *Many Luscious Lollipops* (1989).

Independent Reading

Picture books may be just what the struggling reader in upper elementary or middle school needs for independent reading. Because picture books come in all levels of difficulty and contain texts of varying lengths, there is bound to be a "right fit" for each struggling reader. In fact, struggling readers who have not finished a book in years (or perhaps have never finished one) may be able to do just that when reading picture books. A caution: If picture books are brought into the classroom only for struggling readers to read during independent reading, students may believe there is a stigma attached to reading picture books. If the genre is used to support other facets of the curriculum, however, students will view picture books with new respect and will value the opportunity to read them.

Picture Books in Social Studies Classrooms

Many educators have made a persuasive case for incorporating literature into the social studies curriculum (Steffey & Hood, 1994). Textbooks continue to play an important role in social studies instruction because they typically take a broad overview and thereby provide essential background knowledge. Textbooks, however, tend to be stylistically dry and poorly written (Beck & McKeown, 1991; Freeman & Person, 1998; Tomlinson, Tunnell, & Richgels, 1993). Well-written works of children's literature, both fiction and nonfiction, stand in direct contrast to textbooks. Rather than taking a broad view of a subject, authors of children's literature are more likely to focus on a single subject and examine it in depth. Stylistically, quality works of children's literature are written to engage readers. Writing about history instruction in particular, Tomlinson et al. (1993) argue that readers need historical empathy to develop historical understanding. They hold that readers "must be able to perceive past events and issues as they were experienced by the people at the time" (p. 54). Temple et al. (1998) believe that "helping readers develop historical empathy is what historical fiction does best, by emphasizing human motives and ordinary people" (p. 310).

Children's literature, in general, is an important tool in the social studies curriculum, and picture books, in particular, are valuable resources. Earlier in the chapter we discussed recent shifts in topics and techniques in certain picture books that make them especially (or only) appropriate for use with older students. Some of these same changes underscore their usefulness as resources in the social studies program. Two of those changes are of particular note: the increasing numbers of picture books dealing with cultural diversity and social and environmental concerns and the increasing numbers of historical fiction and biographical picture books. The 1990s have witnessed an unprecedented number of books that highlight diverse cultures both in the United States and other countries. In *Working Cotton* (1992), Sherley Anne Williams writes about the experiences of an African American migrant family. Cross-cultural experiences are the focus of Patricia Polacco's *Chicken Sunday* (1992), Michael's Rosen's *Elijah's Angel* (1992), and Allen Say's *Grandfather's Journey* (1993). In *Days of the Dead* (1994a), Kathryn Lasky writes about the celebration of this important cultural event in Mexico. Florence Parry Heide and Judith Heide Gilliland bring the city of Cairo to life in *The Day of Ahmed's Secret* (1990). This list is, of course, the briefest sampling of titles that celebrate cultural diversity.

Picture book authors are increasingly exploring environmental and social concerns (Steiner & Cobiskey, 1998). Lynne Cherry has explored the human relationship to nature in two beautifully illustrated picture books, *The Great Kapok Tree* (1990) and *A River Ran Wild* (1992). Sheila MacGill-Callahan explores a similar theme in *And Still the Turtle Watched* (1991). In *Amazing Grace* (1991), Mary Hoffman has created a moving account of the way in which racial prejudice affects a child. Eve Bunting uses the picture book format to look at the human side of still other contemporary social issues; she explores homelessness in *Fly Away Home* (1991), aging in *Sunshine Home* (1994b), and immigration in *How Many Days to America* (Bunting, 1988). The Los Angeles riots are the topic of *Smoky Night* (Bunting, 1994a).

The human side of history is increasingly being addressed in historical fiction and biographies in picture book format, many of which are best suited for older students. One of the reasons picture books in these genres can be so valuable to content teaching is that they frequently address facets of history that are not often included in textbooks. For example, the orphan trains are the subject of Eve Bunting's *Train to Somewhere* (1996). Ken Mochizuki's *Baseball Saved Us* (1993) is a fictional account of a Japanese American boy's memories of life in an internment camp during World War II. In *Calico and Tin Horns* (1992), Candace Christiansen writes about the sharecropper rebellion against the wealthy landowners in the Hudson River Valley in the 1840s.

Because of its brevity, historical fiction in picture book format allows the teacher to bring more diverse perspectives into the curriculum. In *Katie's Trunk* (Turner, 1992), the reader meets a Tory family and comes to think about Revolutionary War issues from the perspective of the family. In *Encounter* (1992), Jane Yolen views the arrival of Columbus's ships in America from the perspective of a Taino boy who greeted the explorer. In addition, when historical fiction in picture book format is used in the social studies program, hard-to-imagine historical scenes are brought to life through illustrations. For example, the illustrations in Candace Christiansen's *The Ice Horse* (1993) help readers understand how ice was "harvested" from rivers in the early twentieth century. Illustrations may help readers get a feel for an era in ways that words do not. The illustrations in *Dandelions* (Bunting, 1995) play a critical role in helping readers grasp the loneliness of life on the prairie for early settlers. Kiefer (1995a) has found that illustrations contribute in important ways when picture books dealing with sensitive issues like war, death, and the Holocaust are used as part of classroom studies of these topics. According to Kiefer:

> In *Hiroshima No Pika, Sadako, Sami and the Time of the Troubles,* and *Rose Blanche* the pictures provide more than information, they provide the context for telling of human brutality in ways that do not repel or frighten but that evoke the deepest intellectual and emotional response. (p. 59)

Picture Books in Science Classrooms

Quality informational books in picture book format have proliferated (Elleman, 1992). The wide range of topics in science from plants to animal life to geology to ecology to space and more that are readily available make engaging additions to the science program. Still others address the history of science. In the Caldecott Honor book *Starry Messenger* (Sis, 1996), students can meet Galileo and discover how his scientific explorations changed the way people looked at the galaxy. There are also picture books that help students better understand the scientific process. For example, *Flood Fish* (Eversole, 1995) is an accessible example of the hypothesis-generating process.

As is true of social studies textbooks, science textbooks typically offer broad rather than in-depth coverage. Picture books can be used to amplify, illustrate, and intrigue. For example, although a science text might briefly discuss ecosystems and provide a few short examples, students could turn to Barbara Bash's *Tree of Life: The World of the African Baobab* (1989) for a rich description of the way in which this unusual tree functions as an ecosystem. Still another difficulty with science textbooks is that they have traditionally been stylistically dry and uninteresting, but this is not true of the best of contemporary science picture books. The authors of *Bugs* (Parker & Wright, 1987) use humorous couplets and illustrations to share a wealth of information about insects. The author and illustrator of *And So They Build* (Kitchen, 1993) repeats the phrase "and so they build" to achieve a lyrical effect as he describes the ways in which a variety of creatures construct their homes. Aliki captures the interest of readers from the very beginning of *Wild and Woolly Mammoths* (1977/1996) with an early scene describing the discovery of a mammoth so well-preserved in a glacier for 39,000 years that dogs were able to eat the flesh of the uncovered creature. Picture books like these entice older students in the study of science.

Picture books can fill a variety of needs in the science program. They can serve as important resources for students' research. Equally important, teachers can use picture books to help students discover novel formats for organizing and reporting information for reports. Freeman (1991) notes that well-designed picture books containing features such as headings, indexes, and glossaries serve as wonderful models of well-organized reports. She also identifies some of the most intriguing formats used by picture book authors for reporting information. For example, in *Antler, Bear, Canoe: A Northwoods Alphabet Year* (1991), Betsy Bowen uses an alphabet format to organize information about life in the Northwoods. Andrew Clements uses a counting book format to organize information in *Mother Earth's Counting Book* (1992). In the Magic School Bus series, Joanna Cole uses a mixed-genre format for reporting on a variety of different science topics. In books like *Pond Year* (Lasky, 1995), students can see how information can be reported through narrative nonfiction. These novel formats can spark far more interest in report writing than do traditional reports.

Picture Books in Math Classrooms

Although fewer in number, there are also picture books that the math teacher can incorporate into the curriculum. Some of these picture books address the discipline from a historical perspective. One such picture book is Kathryn Lasky's *The Librarian Who Measured the Earth* (1994b), which features the life and work of the Greek Eratosthenes. Other books explore particular concepts. For example, *Anno's Mysterious Multiplying Jar* (Anno & Anno, 1983) explores factorials. Still other picture books extend opportunities for students to solve problems. Readers of Jon Scieszka's *Math Curse* (1995) are challenged to solve a host of different problems, including problems involving fractions, estimation, binary numbers, and algebraic formulations. Teachers can also use *Math Curse* to challenge their students to generate their own math problems based on their daily lives.

Conclusion

Picture books appropriate for use with older students abound. In this chapter, we have offered only a small sampling of what is currently available in hopes of motivating the reader to seek out still other picture books. We believe that time spent in pursuit of picture books that appeal to older students is time well spent because of the numerous ways in which these books can be incorporated into the curriculum. Alert your librarian to your needs for picture books to support your instruction of middle graders. Publications such as *Book Links* and the *Horn Book* identify picture books for older readers as well. Certainly instructional programs for upper elementary and middle school students cannot be built exclusively around picture books, but we believe that the potential of books in this genre to engage students make them an especially valuable resource for teachers.

REFERENCES

Beck, I.L., & McKeown, M.G. (1991). Research directions: Social studies texts are hard to understand: Mediating some of the difficulties. *Language Arts, 68,* 482–490.

Bishop, R.S., & Hickman, J. (1992). Four or fourteen or forty: Picture books are for everyone. In S. Benedict & L. Carlisle (Eds.), Beyond words: Picture books for older readers and writers (pp. 1–10). Portsmouth, NH: Heinemann.

Bunting, E. (1995). *Dandelions.* Illustrated by Greg Shed. San Diego: Harcourt, Brace.

Carlisle, L.R. (1992). Picture books: An easy place to think. In S. Benedict & L. Carlisle (Eds.), *Beyond words: Picture books for older readers and writers* (pp. 49–58). Portsmouth, NH: Heinemann.

Eeds, M., & Wells, D. (1989). Grand conversations: An exploration of meaning construction in literature study groups. *Research in the Teaching of English, 23,* 4–29.

Elleman, B. (1992). The nonfiction scene: What's happening? In E.B. Freeman & D.G. Person (Eds.), *Using nonfiction trade books in the elementary classroom* (pp. 26–33). Urbana, IL: National Council of Teachers of English.

Freeman, E.B. (1991). Informational books: Models for student report writing. *Language Arts, 68,* 470–473.

Freeman, E.B., & Person, D.G. (1998). *Connecting informational children's books with content area learning.* Boston: Allyn and Bacon.

Guthrie, J.T. (1996). Educational contexts for engagement in literacy. *The Reading Teacher, 49,* 432–445.

Heller, R. (1989). *Many luscious lollipops.* New York: Grosset & Dunlap.

Heller, R. (1991). *Up, up and away.* New York: Grossett & Dunlap.

Huck, C.S., Hepler, S., Hickman, J. & Kiefer, B. (1997). *Children's literature in the elementary school* (6th ed.). Madison, WI: Brown and Benchmark.

Huck, C.S. & Kuhn, D.Y. (1968). *Children's literature in the elementary school* (2nd ed.). New York: Holt, Rinehart and Winston.

Kiefer, B. (1995a). The disturbing image in children's picture books: Fearful or fulfilling? In S. Lehr (Ed.), *Battling dragons: Issues and controversy in children's literature* (pp. 51–62). Portsmouth, NH: Heinemann.

Kiefer, B. (1995b). *The potential of picturebooks: From visual literacy to aesthetic understanding.* Englewood Cliffs, NJ: Merrill.

Krauthammer, C. (1995, March 27). Hiroshima, mon petit. *Time,* 80.

Macaulay, D. (1995). *Shortcut.* Boston: Houghton Mifflin.

Martinez, M., & Roser, N.L. (1995). The books make a difference in story talk. In N.L. Roser & M.G. Martinez (Eds.), *Book talk and beyond: Children and teachers respond to literature* (pp. 32–41). Newark, DE: International Reading Association.

Moss, J.F. (1990). *Focus on literature: A context for literacy learning.* Katonah, NY: Richard C. Owen.

Newkirk, T. (1992). Reasoning around picture books. In S. Benedict & L. Carlisle (Eds.), *Beyond words: Picture books for older readers and writers* (pp. 11–20). Portsmouth, NH: Heinemann.

Steffey, S., & Hood, W.J. (Eds.). (1994). *If this is social studies, why isn't it boring?* York, ME: Stenhouse.

Steiner, S.F., & Cobiskey, L. (1998). Refugees and homeless: Nomads of the world. *Book Links, 7,* 55–62.

Sutherland, Z. & Arbuthnot, M.H. (1977). *Children and books* (5th ed.). Glenview, IL: Scott, Foresman.

Sutton, R. (1996). "Why is this a picture book?" *Horn Book, 72*(4), 390–391.

Temple, C., Martinez, M., Yokota, J., & Naylor, A. (1998). *Children's books in children's hands: An introduction to their literature.* Boston: Allyn and Bacon.

Tomlinson, C.M., Tunnell, M.O., & Richgels, D.J. (1993). The content and writing of history in textbooks and trade books. In M.O. Tunnell & R. Ammon (Eds.), *The story of ourselves: Teaching history through children's literature* (pp. 51–62). Portsmouth, NH: Heinemann.

PICTURE BOOKS FOR OLDER STUDENTS

Ahlberg, Janet, & Ahlberg, Allan. (1986). *The Jolly Postman or Other People's Letters.* Boston: Little, Brown. This book consists of a series of letters written by familiar characters from folklore. The book is a wonderful writing stimulus and can also be used to study different purposes for writing letters.

Aliki. (1977/1996). *Wild and Woolly Mammoths.* New York: HarperCollins. This book contains a wealth of information about mammoths and the ways in which their fate was intertwined with that of man.

Anno, Masaichiro, and Anno, Mitsumasa. (1983). *Anno's Mysterious Multiplying Jar.* New York: Philomel. With minimal text and rich illustrations, the authors help the reader understand factorials.

Bash, Barbara. (1989). *Tree of Life: The World of the African Baobab.* San Francisco: Sierra Club Books. With lyrical language, the author documents the rich ecosystem of the African baobab tree.

Bedard, Michael. (1992). *Emily.* Illustrated by Barbara Cooney. New York: Doubleday. A young girl has an unexpected encounter with her neighbor, the reclusive poet Emily Dickinson.

Bowen, Betsy. (1991). *Antler, Bear, Canoe: A Northwoods Alphabet Year.* Boston: Little, Brown. The alphabet serves as the framework for organizing this informational book about life in the northwoods. Older students can use this as a model of how to creatively report information.

Bunting, Eve. (1988). *How Many Days to America.* Illustrated by Beth Peck. New York: Clarion. Fearing persecution, a family flees their home and journeys by boat to America.

Bunting, Eve. (1991). *Fly Away Home.* Illustrated by Ronald Himler. New York: Clarion. Although they have no home and must live in the airport, a boy and his father do not give up hope.

Bunting, Eve. (1994a). *Smoky Night.* Illustrated by David Diaz. San Diego: Harcourt Brace. When rioters destroy their neighborhood and apartment building, people come together with new understanding.

Bunting, Eve. (1994b). *Sunshine Home.* Illustrated by Diane De Groat. New York: Clarion. When Timmie's grandmother goes into a nursing home, the family must learn to cope with this difficult situation.

Bunting, Eve. (1996). *Train to Somewhere.* Illustrated by Ronald Himler. New York: Clarion. Hoping to be adopted, a girl travels on one of the orphan trains that went west during the 1850s to 1920s in the United States. This book can be integrated into a unit on the westward expansion of our country. It would also be a good book to use for literature discussion.

Cherry, Lynne. (1990). *The Great Kapok Tree.* San Diego: Harcourt Brace Jovanovich. The many different animals that live in a great kapok tree in the Brazilian rain forest try to convince a man with an ax of the importance of not cutting down their home. This book can be used when studying ecosystems.

Cherry, Lynne. (1992). *A River Ran Wild.* San Diego: Harcourt Brace. Six centuries of change and development are depicted in this story of the Nashua River.

Christiansen, Candace. (1992). *Calico and Tin Horns.* Illustrated by Thomas Locker. New York: Dial. A little girl aids sharecroppers who are rebelling against the wealthy landowners in the Hudson River Valley in the 1840s.

Christiansen, Candace. (1993). *The Ice Horse.* Illustrated by Thomas Locker. New York: Dial. Jack witnesses unexpected excitement when he is invited to watch the men harvest ice from the river.

Clements, Andrew. (1992). *Mother Earth's Counting Book.* Illustrated by Lonni Sue Johnson. New York: Picture Book Studio. This informational book about the earth uses a counting book format to organize the information. Students might enjoy trying their hand with this organizational device.

Cooney, Barbara. (1982). *Miss Rumphius.* New York: Puffin Books. Miss Rumphius finds a way of achieving the three goals she sets for herself. This book is likely to evoke reflections.

Eversole, Robyn. (1995). *Flood Fish.* New York: Crown. A boy who lives in the dry outback of Australia wonders why, when the rains finally come, the dry streams that suddenly fill with water are also filled with full-grown fish.

Feelings, Tom. (1995). *The Middle Passage: White Ships/Black Cargo.* New York: Dial. A wordless picture book which captures the agonies of African slaves' journey across the Atlantic.

Garland, Sherry. (1993). *The Lotus Seed.* Illustrated by Tatsuro Kiuchi. San Diego: Harcourt Brace Jovanovich. Before fleeing from Vietnam, a woman takes a seed from the emperor's lotus. This story offers readers the opportunity to explore the importance of intergenerational connections.

Garza, Carmen Lomas. (1990). *Family Pictures.* As told to Harriet Rohmer. Version in Spanish by Rosalma Zubizarreta. Emeryville, CA: Children's Book Press. Artist Carmen Garza portrays scenes from her childhood in a rural Mexican American community in south Texas.

Heide, Florence Parry, & Gilliland, Judith Heide. (1990). *The Day of Ahmed's Secret.* Illustrated by Ted Lewin. New York: Lothrop, Lee and Shepard. As a boy moves through the streets of Cairo doing his work, he looks forward to the evening when he can share his secret with his family—he has learned to write his name.

Hoffman, Mary. (1991). *Amazing Grace.* Illustrated by Caroline Binch. New York: Dial. With the support of a loving mother and grandmother, Grace overcomes thoughtless prejudice and achieves her goal. This book is an excellent example of effective characterization.

Houston, Gloria. (1992). *My Great-Aunt Arizona.* Illustrated by Susan Condie Lamb. New York: Harper. Born in a mountain cabin, Arizona Hughes grew up to become a teacher in the one-room school she attended as a child. Generations of children are inspired by Arizona.

Jeffers, Susan. (1991). *Brother Eagle, Sister Sky.* New York: Dial. This illustrated version of a poetic speech made by a great Native American chief carries an important ecological message. Rich, lyrical language is used.

Kitchen, Bert. (1993). *And So They Build.* Cambridge, MA: Candlewick. This book contains information on ways in which various creatures construct their homes. The phrase "and so they build" is used to introduce each creature. Older students can use this as a model of how to report research in a stylistically engaging manner.

Lasky, Kathryn. (1994a). *Days of the Dead.* Photographs by Christopher G. Knight. New York: Hyperion. Through text and photographs, this book provides extensive information about the in which the Day of the Dead is celebrated in Mexico.

Lasky, Kathryn. (1994b). *The Librarian Who Measured the Earth.* Illustrated by Kevin Hawkes. Little, Brown. This biography tells of the many discoveries and accomplishments of the Greek Erastosthenes including the way in which he measured the circumference of the earth.

Lasky, Kathryn. (1995). *Pond Year.* Illustrated by Mike Bostock. Cambridge, MA: Candlewick. Embedded into this piece of narrative nonfiction is extensive information about changes in the pond over the course of the year. Older students can use this as a model of how to creatively report information.

Macaulay, David. (1990). *Black and White.* Boston: Houghton Mifflin. This is an intriguing four-stories-in-one story in which the episodes from each story are intermingled with those of the other stories. Students will want to read this one repeatedly and perhaps try their own hands using this novel crafting of story line.

MacGill-Callahan, Sheila. (1991). *And Still the Turtle Watched.* Illustrated by Barry Moser. New York: Dial. A turtle carved in rock on a bluff over a river by Indians long ago, watches with sadness the changes man brings over the years. The author uses language effectively to help build tension.

Maruki, Toshi. (1980). *Hiroshima No Pika.* New York: Lothrop. The poignant story of one family's experiences when Hiroshima was bombed. This book can be integrated into a unit on World War II. This book also offers rich fodder for discussion.

Maugham, W. Somerset. (1993). *Appointment.* Adapted by Alan Benjamin. Illustrated by Roger Essley. New York: Green Tiger Press. Death, disguised as an old woman, searches for Abdullah the servant.

This book is the perfect one to use when talking about irony.

Merriam, Eve. (1996). *The Inner City Mother Goose.* Illustrated by David Diaz. New York: Simon and Schuster. These hard-hitting rhymes based on familiar Mother Goose rhymes deal with modern day problems, especially those of the inner city. Students will find a great deal to talk about in this poems.

Merrill, Jean. (1992). *The Girl Who Loved Caterpillars.* Illustrated by Floyd Cooper. New York: Philomel. A young woman in twelfth-century Japan follows her heart rather than the dictates of her culture. Older students will likely have a lot to say in response to this book.

Mochizuki, Ken. (1993). *Baseball Saved Us.* Illustrated by Dom Lee. New York: Lee and Low. A Japanese American boy's memories of life in an internment camp during World War II. This book is perfect for integrating into a unit on this war. It also offers rich discussion possibilities.

Parker, Nancy Winslow, & Wright, Joan Richards. (1987). *Bugs.* Illustrated by Nancy Winslow Parker. New York: Greenwillow. This mixed-genre book contains extensive information about insects. Older students can use this as a model of how to creatively report research.

Polacco, Patricia. (1992). *Chicken Sunday.* New York: Philomel. A group of friends extend a hand of friendship across cultural boundaries. There is a lot worth talking about in this book.

Rosen, Michael J. (1992). *Elijah's Angel.* Illustrated by Aminah Brenda Lynn Robinson. San Diego: Harcourt Brace Jovanovich. When Michael's friend Elijah gives him an angel he has carved, Michael fears that his Jewish parents will view the gift as a "graven image." This book provides rich fodder for discussion.

Rylant, Cynthia. (1982). *When I Was Young in the Mountains.* Illustrated by Diane Goode. New York: Dutton. In lyrical language, a girl tells of her life in the mountains.

Say, Allen. (1993). *Grandfather's Journey.* Boston: Houghton Mifflin. Say describes his family's unique cross-cultural experiences in the United States and Japan.

Scieszka, Jon. (1992). *The Stinky Cheese Man and Other Fairly Stupid Tales.* Illustrated by Lane Smith. New York: Viking. A humorous format is used to present spin-offs of traditional tales.

Scieszka, Jon. (1995). *Math Curse.* Illustrated by Lane Smith. New York: Viking. When the teacher tells her class that they can think of almost everything as a math problem, one student acquires a math anxiety that becomes a real curse. This book offers lots of math problems (of increasing difficulty) to solve and could easily be used to motivate students to write their own experience-based math problems.

Sis, Peter. (1996). *Starry Messenger.* New York: Farrar, Straus, Giroux. This Caldecott Honor book depicts the life of Galileo. Excerpts from Galileo's own writings appear throughout.

Soto, Gary. (1995). *Chato's Kitchen.* Illustrated by Susan Guevara. New York: Putnam. Chato, a low-riding cat from East Los Angeles, invites his new neighbors, a family of mice, to dinner. This humorous barrio tale of a trickster's plan gone awry is perfect for helping students understand "tone."

Stanley, Diane. (1997). *Rumpelstiltskin's Daughter.* New York: Morrow. In this spin-off of the traditional tale, Rumpelstiltskin's daughter is so canny that she has no need to call on others when the king asks her to spin straw into gold.

Stanley, Diane, & Vennema, Peter. (1992). *Bard of Avon: The Story of William Shakespeare.* Illustrated by Diane Stanley. New York: Morrow. This biography brings to life the world and work of William Shakespeare.

Turner, Ann. (1992). *Katie's Trunk.* Illustrated by Ron Himler. New York: Macmillan. Katie and her family are Tories who find themselves surrounded by friends and neighbors who have joined the rebels in the American Revolution.

Uchida, Yoshiko. (1976/1993). *The Bracelet.* Illustrated by Joanna Yardley. New York: Philomel. In 1942 America, a Japanese-American child and her family are sent to an internment camp.

Van Allsburg, Chris. (1984). *The Mysteries of Harris Burdick.* Boston: Houghton Mifflin. A series of mysterious drawings invite students to plot their own stories. Remember that the book's introduction must be read when presenting this book to students.

Van Allsburg, Chris. (1986). *The Stranger.* Boston: Houghton Mifflin. The enigmatic origins of the stranger Farmer Bailey hits with his truck and brings home to recuperate seem to have a mysterious relation to the weather.

Van Allsburg, Chris. (1992). *The Widow's Broom.* Boston: Houghton Mifflin. A broom with special powers brings out the prejudices of the widow's neighbors. This book offers good fodder for discussion.

Wild, Margaret. (1991). *Let the Celebrations Begin!* Illustrated by Julie Vivas. New York: Orchard. A group of women imprisoned in a German concentration camp maintain hope for the future by secretly making stuffed animals for the children in the camp.

Willard, Nancy. (1991). *Pish, Posh, Said Hieronymous Bosch.* Illustrated by Leo & Diane Dillon. San Diego: Harcourt Brace. Strange creatures haunt the housekeeper of Hieronymous Bosch. This beautifully illustrated book can be used to engage students in a discussion about the role of women.

Williams, Sherley Anne. (1992). *Working Cotton.* Illustrated by Carole Byard. San Diego: Harcourt Brace Jovanovich. A young migrant girl's story of picking cotton from sunup to sundown.

Willis, Jeanne. (1988). *Earthlets.* Illustrated by Tony Ross. New York: Dutton. Earth babies are described by aliens. There is no better book to use when studying perspective.

Wood, Audrey. (1990). *Weird Parents.* New York: Dial. A boy tells about the parents he is convinced are the only weird parents in the world. Students will enjoy writing about their own weird parents after listening to this book.

Wood, Audrey. (1996). *Bright and Early Thursday Evening: A Tangled Tale.* Illustrated by Don Wood. San Diego: Harcourt Brace. Verse combines with electronically generated art to create a world of paradoxes and "spectacular contradictions." The challenge will be in inspecting for the weirdness, then matching the style to produce a variant text.

Yolen, Jane. (1992). *Encounter.* Illustrated by David Shannon. San Diego: Harcourt Brace Jovanovich. A Taino boy tries to warn his people of coming destruction when Columbus arrives on their island. This book offers rich fodder for discussion.

18 Spelling in the Middle

CHARLES TEMPLE
Hobart and William Smith Colleges

What's "Middling" about Spelling?

Middle school students stand with one foot in childhood and one foot in adulthood. That image applies to their social development as girls and boys swarm to school dances in separate packs, each conscious for the first time of their appearance to someone in the other pack. It applies to their personality development as they begin to put aside boisterous childhood pastimes and take serious glimpses at their lives in the future. It fits their intellectual development, as they deal more willingly with abstractions like environmental advocacy and racism. It is even true of their spelling.

To justify that last claim, and to see what we can do to help middle school students with the challenges of correct spelling, we have to agree at the beginning on a couple of premises. First, *learning to spell is conceptual*. Learning to spell is more than learning a huge diet of correct spellings. There is some memorizing, true enough, but the essence of the learning that makes students good spellers is a set of concepts and principles about the nature and structure of the English spelling system. Second, *learning to spell is developmental*. Students tend to use certain strategies, and act out of certain understandings about spelling in accordance with their growing awareness of the spelling system of English. In addition, the nature of the words students have to spell changes significantly as students progress through the grades—so spelling development is a sort of mix of rising to the challenges posed by the new sorts of words students are asked to write, and also the changing knowledge students have that enables them to spell these words. The changes in the nature of the words students spell are not always smooth and continuous. Indeed, the most important change in the nature of the words, and in the knowledge needed to spell them, comes right in the middle grades.

In the first section of this chapter, we give a brief overview of spelling development from first grade through middle school, to show why the middle grades host such important changes. Then we describe assessment procedures that reveal how each student is coping with these changes. Finally, we highlight a set of generic instructional approaches that are designed to help students learn best at different stages of development—because certainly not all spellers develop at equal rates, and middle graders find their spelling development spread widely along the spectrum.

A Quick Look at Spelling Development

In this section, we briefly chart the development of children's spelling ability from the early grades through the middle school grades (readers wishing a fuller treatment of this topic are referred to Temple, Nathan, Temple, and Burris, 1994).

Letter-Name Spelling

At about the same time they are beginning to read, kindergarten and first-grade children often write what is called "letter-name" spelling (Read, 1975). They write individual letters as if each were an isolated building block of sound. Following this logic, a precocious four-year-old wrote "Once a lady went fishing and she caught Flipper" this way:

YUTS A LADE YET FEHEG AD HE KOT FLEPR

The child carefully sounded out the phonemes in each word she wanted to write. Then she matched each phoneme with a single letter. To do the matching, she paid attention to the similarity between the *sound of the name of the letter* and the phoneme she wished to spell (a phoneme is the smallest unit of sound in the language, such as the sound of /t/, /b/, and /k/). This "letter-name strategy" results in some bizarre-looking spellings of consonants (such as "Y" for /w/), some unconventional spellings of short vowels (such as "E" for /short-i/), and the omission of the silent letters we conventionally use to mark long vowels. It also leaves some sounds un-spelled, as if they were "covered" in some way by a neighboring letter (as "R" spells -ER and "T" spells -NT).

By the time they reach middle school, students have advanced well past "letter-name" logic in their spelling, but their early spelling behavior is relevant to our discussion in one important way. From their earliest experiences as writers, students use concepts and not just memory as they attempt to spell.

Within-Word Patterns

By second grade, as they do more reading and receive more spelling instruction, young writers are noticing that words are spelled not by individual letters, but by patterns of letters, such as -ack, -it, and -arm and the like. They may confuse the patterns used to spell long and short vowels at first—writing BICK for "bike"—or write them incorrectly—such as LIEK for "like." But the realization has been reached that combinations of letters spell sounds in words at the *phonogram* level (a phonogram is a vowel plus the following consonants that make up a syllable). In this way, their spelling has advanced beyond the earlier "letter-name" strategy.

As they develop as writers, students become able to produce the common letter strings that spell phonogram patterns. By third and fourth grade, students are encountering words that put interesting wrinkles on the challenge of spelling common patterns. For example, we spell the vowel pattern in "may" with -AY, but we spell the vowel pattern in "maid" with -AI. Similarly, we spell the vowel pattern in the second syllable in "money" with -EY, but we spell the vowel pattern in "ceiling" with -EI. There seems to be a rule at work: vowel + I is an allowable spelling in the middle of a syllable, and vowel + Y is the allowable spelling at the end of a syllable. This rule extends to patterns with OY/OI, such as "boy" and "boil," and "toy" and "toil." (There is a similar, though weaker, rule at work in the alternation of vowel patterns ending in U and W.) It's not enough, we see, to learn a string of letters to spell a vowel pattern. Young writers must also pay attention to where that vowel pattern occurs.

A less easily solved problem arises at this point that stays with writers of all ages: *Which* letter combination spells a particular sound pattern? Is the past tense of *teach* spelled TOUGHT or TAUGHT? Is the thing that shows the way the wind blows a weather VAIN or a weather VANE? (Or maybe a weather VEIN)? Their familiarization with spelling patterns will enable young writers to produce letter strings that are reasonable fits here, but they will need the aid of memory to nail down the precise spelling.

Marking Systems and Grammatical Endings

By late second grade, children are coming to grips with the challenge of spelling words of more than one syllable, and words onto which grammatical endings are added. Now they must negotiate the *marking system* of English spelling: the patterns by which we indicate that vowels have their "long" and "short" sounds, and also that some consonants have their "hard" and "soft" sounds. Thus, when the ending -ING is added to "bat," the correct spelling is "batting" and not BATING; unless the T in "bat" is doubled, the I has the effect of marking the A vowel with its long sound. In *bat + ed,* the E in the grammatical ending -ED has this same "lengthening" effect on the A; thus, *bat + ed* should be spelled "batted" and not BATED.

E, I, and Y also have the effect of marking some consonants with their "soft" sounds: so *bag + Y* is spelled "baggy" and not BAGY; otherwise the A would not only be long, but the G would have the sound of G in "cagy."

The challenge of attending to the "marking effects" of vowels in words of more than one syllable stays with many young writers for years. Middle school students writing on the fly often put down BATING for "batting" and HITING for "hitting."

Grammatical endings present one more challenge: Each is pronounced in different ways, but usually has only one spelling. The ending spelled -ED may be pronounced three different ways ("id," "d," and "t"). The ending spelled S may be pronounced "s," "t," or "z." Until they are aware of this, some young writers give us SLODE for "slowed" and HUGZ for "hugs." Unless a student is especially inattentive, however, these problems usually are long past by middle school; most middle school students have added these issues to their spelling competence.

Derivational Spelling

As we said at the outset, young writers' competence as spellers changes and develops for two reasons. One is that the information in their heads is growing more sophisticated. The other is that the words to which they are exposed are growing more challenging, because they are composed differently.

By the middle grades, the vocabulary of writing has grown to include the large store of words derived from Latin and Greek that surround the core vocabulary of Anglo-Saxon words—those words that are mostly used in the lower grades. Thus, in first grade, children spell the Anglo-Saxon word "to see," whereas in fifth and sixth grades they spell the Latin versions of the same word: "vision," "visible," and "visage." At this point, students must come to think about spelling in a new way. No longer is it enough to think of the patterns of spelling within words. To spell correctly and knowledgeably, students must now learn to think of patterns of spelling that are shared by *families* of words. That is, to spell one word, it is often necessary to think of the words to which it is related.

For example, if someone said the word aloud to you, how would you know how to spell "telegraphy"? The word poses several challenges. The vowel in the third syllable is unstressed and indistinctly pronounced: Is it E, I, 0, or A? The vowel in the first syllable is not very clear, either: How should it be spelled? The "f"' sound in the last syllable could be spelled with F or with PH. Which is it? Fortunately, all these questions are easily answered by the writer who relates "telegraphy" to the word from which it was derived, "telegraph." Because the first and last syllables in "telegraph" are stressed, they are easily heard to contain E and A, respectively, and those should be clues to the spellings of the corresponding vowels in "telegraphy." The /f/ sound in "graphy" has to be spelled PH, because it is contained in the stem *graph,* from a Greek word meaning to write. (In words of Greek origin, the /f/ sound is always spelled with PH.)

To spell words like "telegraphy" and "graphic"; "symphony," "phonic," and "sympathy"; and "telepathy" and "pathology" successfully it helps to recognize the family relationships—the common origins, the core of shared meanings, and the shared spellings—that these groups of words have in common.

"Telegraph" and "telegraphy" are both made up of two stems from Greek. *Tele-* means "far," or "at a distance"; and *graph,* as we said, means "to write." Knowing the original meanings of those stems already sheds light on the meanings, in case they were in doubt, of words like "telephone," "telescope" (*scope,* also from Greek, means "to look at"), "graphic," "biography," and "geography" (*bio* and *geo,* both from Greek, mean "life" and "earth," respectively). Recognizing these stems makes their spelling less doubtful, too.

Knowing about word families and origins also helps students spell words with puzzling consonants (sometimes doubled, sometimes not) like "illegal," "commotion," and "connect" and "assure" and "asexual." Most of these words contain some form of the Latin-derived prepositions *ad, a, con,* and *in,* and therein lies the clue to their spelling.

Ad in Latin means, roughly, "to" or "toward." As a prefix in English words, *ad* regularly changes its second letter to agree with the beginning consonant of the stem to which it attaches. Thus, the same prefix is present at the beginning of "ally," "assure," and "accept." "Assure" turns out to be a combination of *ad* plus "sure," with the meaning of "to move in the direction of being sure." Thus, the S has to be doubled in "assure," because the first S is part of the preposition and the second S is part of the word stem.

A, on the other hand, could mean "away from" or "not" in Latin. "Amoral" (not moral), then, is a combination of *a-* and "moral," so the M is not doubled.

Con- comes from the Latin *cum,* which means "with" or "together." Like *ad, con-* changes the final letter to agree with the first consonant of the stem to which it attaches, so "connect," "commotion," and "college" all show variations of *con-*. Some of the stems have grown obscure over the years, but "commotion" shows a combination of *con* plus "motion," with the sense of a lot of people moving around together. (Incidentally, "combine" in the previous sentence is made up of *con* plus *binere,* or "two by two.") "College" combines *con* and *legere* ("to choose"), so a college is a group of people who have chosen, or have been chosen, to study together.

In comes from two different Latin words. One means "not" and the other means "into." Either way, *in* regularly changes its second letter to match the first consonant of the stem to which it is attached. *In* with the sense of "not" shows up in "illegal" (not legal), "innocuous" (*in* plus "-nocuous," or not harmful), "immense" (not measurable, or too big to measure), and "immediate" (*in* plus *mediare,* "to divide in the middle," thus, without delay). *In* also appears in "inactive," or "not active," but because the stem is "active" there is no reason to double the N. *In* with the sense of "inside" or "into" shows up in "innate" (*in* plus *natus,* or "born," thus "born into"), "insert" (*in* plus *serere* "to join," thus "joined into"), and "inscribe" (*in* plus *scribere,* to write, thus "written into").

As these perhaps too detailed examples show, an awareness of word origins forms an essential part of a mature writer's spelling competence. The most immediate advantage shows up as insights that help a writer negotiate puzzling parts of words:

"To double or not to double this consonant?"

"This vowel sounds like 'uh.' How do I spell it?"

"Which letters spell this /f/ sound: F or PH?"

An awareness of word origins, however, also contributes to an educated person's knowledge of what words mean at the same time that they help that person sort out puzzling spellings. For example, the word "decimate" is related to "decimal" and "decade": It comes from the Latin word for the number ten. Its origin goes back to a stern disciplinary measure practiced in the Roman army: Namely, if the troops behaved badly, such as retreating before an enemy, the captain (a word related to "capital," "cattle," and "decapitate"—the root word meaning "the head") would call out every tenth man and kill him. Many people have lost their awareness of the root meaning of that word, though, like the school superintendent who is reported to have said, "I do not intend to *decimate* the teaching staff—just reduce their numbers by 10%."

Spelling Stages and
the Middle-Grade Student

When students learn to spell, they normally progress—sometimes in meandering fashion, to be sure—through the stages of development described previously. Students' strategies for spelling—principles they have in mind about the ways letters represent words, and the features of spelling of which they seem aware—typically progress through the levels we have outlined here: letter-name spelling, within-word patterns, marking systems and grammatical endings, and derivational spelling.

In first and second grade, there is a fair amount of consistency in children's spelling. We can expect to see children using aspects of letter-name spelling and coming to grips with common within-word patterns. By the time students reach the middle grades, however, there is a considerable range of variation in their spelling development. Less confident students will have attached to some common within-word patterns (-ake, -ain, -ight, etc.) but will sometimes use them inappropriately, resulting in spellings like ERTHQUAIK ("earthquake"), SARRY ("sorry"), and COMPLANE ("complain"). Some of the more confident spellers will accurately handle within-word patterns, but not correctly deal with the *marking systems* for vowels and consonants in longer words, yielding spellings like GUNING ("gunning"), DIGING ("digging"), and PLOTES ("plots"). Problems with *grammatical markers* can yield misspellings like HIEKT ("hiked"), EXPOSDE ("exposed"), and WITCHIZ "(witches").

Spelling errors like the above are typical of students who are functioning somewhat below grade level (although to speak of "grade levels" implies that students have had continuous instruction in a systematic spelling curriculum, an assumption that does not currently hold true for all American children). Those students who have progressed normally through the previous stages up to entry into middle school will now be trying to make sense of the derivational phenomena described in the previous section, as the vocabulary they read and write rather suddenly expands to include high proportions of words from Latin and Greek origins. The derivational stage is considered the last stage by most of those who have studied spelling development (Bear et al., 1992; Henderson, 1990; Temple et al., 1993). That is, the issues faced here are the ones faced by most mature spellers. In spelling as in other aspects of development, the middle grades really are in the middle: Children are still dealing with the issues of childhood while trying to embark on the new learnings of adulthood.

What difference does it make to the teacher if students are spread over a wide range of spelling ability? The answer is, possibly a great deal. To explain why, let us explore the idea of *instructional levels in spelling.*

Instructional Levels in Spelling

In reading instruction, we think of the *instructional* level as the level of text a student can read with moderate difficulty, as opposed to two other levels: the level at which the student can read easily and fluently (the *independent* level) and the level at which the difficulties threaten to overwhelm his or her efforts (the *frustration* level).

Reading teachers know that students learn most efficiently when they are given material at their instructional level. Although the temptation to push students into more difficult material is always there (and although some children, given the choice, prefer to read material that is very easy for them), students learn best when faced with a moderate level of challenge.

The concept of reading levels speaks of a relationship between the reading ability of the student and a degree of difficulty in the reading matter. If there were no reliable way of determining the difficulty level of texts, it would be pointless to say that a student had a "third-grade instructional reading level," because we couldn't capitalize on that knowledge by giving the student third-grade level material to read.

In spelling, the same dynamics apply. We have already shown that spelling ability develops through levels or stages. We have also demonstrated that the words students write come to them at escalating levels of complexity as they move through the grades. What we now wish to argue is that for optimal learning to occur, there should be a rough match between a student's level of spelling knowledge and the level of difficulty of the words the student is asked to study.

Quantitatively speaking, if we teach a child to spell seventh-grade level words when her spelling instructional level is fourth grade, the result is likely to be frustration and inefficient learning. *Qualitatively* speaking, if we want a child to learn to spell words at the *derivational* level when she is struggling with words at the *within-word pattern level* he or she will experience confusion at the point where understanding leaves off and will not make adequate sense of the words on the higher level.

Research has shown that greater gains will be made by such a student if we assign the student to studying words right at the level that is the intersection of the known and the unknown, the level at which she or he begins to experience a moderate level of challenge: that is, at the student's *instructional level* (Morris et al., in press). This research also suggests that when students study words on their instructional level, they much more efficiently *transfer* their learning from their spelling instruction to their daily writing.*

What does this mean in practical terms? For a hundred years, educators who have studied this question have agreed that the student's spelling instructional level is the level of spelling words of which the student can spell about 50% correctly without studying (Henderson, 1990). The graded word lists that this placement presupposes are available in most commercial spelling programs (McGraw-Hill, Merrill, Houghton Mifflin, Zaner Bloser, and Scott Foresman are good examples). Writers of such programs have based the choice and the grade assignment of words on what research has shown about students' spelling development. (Indeed, all of these above-named programs were written by students and colleagues of the late Edmund Henderson, a thoughtful researcher of developmental spelling.)

---

*This research finding is significant, since it was the reported lack of transfer from spelling instruction to daily writing that was used by some as a justification for abandoning formal spelling instruction a dozen years ago (see Bean and Bouffler, 1988, for example).

Determining Students' Spelling Instructional Levels

We have shown that it is important to know the level of a student's knowledge of spelling. There are two approaches to finding out what this level is. One way, which we call quantitative assessment, tells us the student's spelling level in terms of grade level spelling lists. The other way, which we call *qualitative assessment* tells us what stage of spelling development a student is in, and can also tell us the patterns and features of spelling at that stage that the student has under control.

Quantitative Spelling Assessment

To determine the students' spelling instructional level in terms of grade level spelling lists, you may construct a spelling inventory consisting of fifteen words drawn at random from each grade level spelling program. For the middle grades, you should choose words from the fourth- through the eighth-grade programs. If you have an alphabetized list of a year's spelling words available, estimate the total number of words in that list and divide by fifteen. Then select every *nth* word, depending on the quotient you come up with. For example, a fifth-grade word list contains a total of 600 words for the year, and 600 divided by 15 is 40: Therefore, you would choose every fortieth word in constructing the fifth-grade list for your spelling inventory.

Ask the students to spell all fifteen words in all of the lists in your inventory. Consider the student's instructional level to be that grade level at which he spells between six and eight of the words in the list correctly. That means that a student who correctly wrote seven of the fifteen words in the fifth-grade list (and, say, twelve of the words on the fourth-grade list and three of the words on the sixth-grade list) should be given words to study throughout the year that were drawn from the fifth grade list.

A word of caution: To be avoided when determining spelling instructional levels are programs based on word frequencies. Such programs assign "gate" to the first grade but "fate" as late as the seventh grade—not only denying students the possibility of seeing patterns in words, but also teaching some words years after they are developmentally challenging or useful.

Qualitative Spelling Assessment

The more adventurous teacher may want to determine students' spelling levels *qualitatively,* and ask them to spell words that pose the sorts of challenges we reviewed in the sections on spelling development. After analyzing a student's errors, the teacher will be able to see not only what stage of spelling a student has attained, but also what features of words are challenging to that student.

Below we present two lists of spelling words to be used in a qualitative spelling assessment with middle-grade students. The first list contains words that test students' control over common phonogram patterns, marking rules, and grammatical endings. The second list tests the students' awareness of derivational principles in words.

The lists can be used in two ways. The simpler way is to count the number of errors and assign the students to a level. The more time-consuming but far more revealing way is to tally the students' spelling of each feature. This latter way gives a more nuanced look at the students' spelling ability.

List 1: Common Patterns

The first list tests students at the level of Common Patterns/Marking Rules/Grammatical Endings. The words assess common spelling patterns, including consonant blends and phonogram patterns. Some of the words assess students' use of the vowel and consonant marking system and their spelling of grammatical endings.

The instructions for administering the list are straightforward. Ask the students to number their papers from 1 to 15. Read the target word once, then pause and read the sentence. Then repeat the target word. Pronounce the target word normally, without exaggerated stress. (One aspect of spelling we want to test is how students represent words to themselves—so we don't sound the words out for them as we call them out.)

Students then mark their answers as you call out the correct spellings. Students who correctly spell nine or fewer of the words in this list probably need spelling instruction that calls their attention to common patterns, marking phenomena, and grammatical endings. These students will benefit from learning and studying words that follow patterns like those in the assessment list.

List 1: Common Patterns

1. claim — **They claim to be millionaires.**
2. proud — **She's proud of her ancestors.**
3. chimes — **The church rang chimes at noon.**
4. release — **They'll release the prisoners tomorrow.**
5. stitched — **She stitched her money into her skirt.**
6. cluster — **There was a cluster of dollars in his hand.**
7. choices — **You have some hard choices to make.**
8. straighter — **This road is straighter than the other.**
9. pane — **Twelve panes of glass were broken by the earthquake.**
10. splitting — **The old woman was splitting firewood.**
11. choked — **He's all choked up with emotion.**
12. chiggers — **The hunter was bitten by chiggers in the woods.**
13. strained — **The player strained her back.**
14. swaggering — **The bully was swaggering and hurling insults.**
15. peeked — **The mouse peeked out of the hiding place.**

For more words for students to study on the appropriate level, teachers can consult the third- through fifth-grade levels of a reputable spelling program.

Analyzing Spellings by Features: Common Patterns

A more finely-tuned assessment can be conducted by examining the errors the student made, asking the following questions. Answers can be plotted on the grid in Figure 18.1.

1. Does the student spell consonant blends (cl, pr, str) and digraphs (ch, tch) correctly?
2. Does the student choose the appropriate common phonogram patterns (aigh, ea, ee) and spell them correctly?
3. Does the student handle the vowel-marking system correctly?

   ■ Consonant doubling
   ■ Long vowel marking

4. Does the student spell grammatical endings (-ed, -s) correctly?

In scoring the words according to this list, for every word spelled correctly, put a check in every blank next to that word. For every word spelled incorrectly, however, you must examine the word and put checks in the blanks corresponding to the features the student *did* spell correctly. If, for example, a student spelled "peeked" as PEEKT, he or she would get checks in the blanks for Phonogram Patterns and Long Vowels, but not for Grammatical Endings. If she spelled "stitched" as STITCHET, she would get two checks in the blank for Consonant Blends, since she spelled both ST and TCH correctly, but no check for Grammatical Endings.

The spellings of all words are marked in this way. Then, reading down the columns of blanks, you count up and tally the number of correct spellings of each feature. This number can be compared to the possible number of spellings of that feature. If a student doesn't spell a feature correctly 75% of the time, she probably can benefit from word study that calls attention to that feature.

As you can see, this scoring procedure yields a lot of interesting information about a student's spelling, but can be onerous. We would recommend that you try marking half a dozen students' spellings in this way. After that, you should be able to make similar judgments about other students' spellings by looking their papers over, without resorting to feature-by-feature scoring.*

---

*Whatever you do, keep this scoring system out of the hands of an overzealous supervisor or assessment committee! It would be awful to be *required* to do this amount of assessment on every student's spelling—especially if you are responsible for more than thirty students.

FIGURE 18.1 Feature Analysis: Common Patterns

	Consonant Blends	Phonogram Patterns	Consonant Doubling	Long Vowels	Grammatical Endings
1. claim	_____			_____	
2. proud	_____	_____			
3. chimes	_____			_____	_____
4. release		_____		_____	
5. stitched	(2)_____				_____
6. cluster	(2)_____				
7. choices	_____				_____
8. straighter	_____	_____		_____	_____
9. panes		_____		_____	_____
10. splitting	_____		_____		_____
11. choked	_____	_____		_____	_____
12. chiggers			_____		_____
13. strained	_____	_____		_____	_____
14. swaggering	_____	_____	_____		_____
15. peeked		_____		_____	_____
Totals:	_____	_____	_____	_____	_____
Possible:	**(10)**	**(9)**	**(3)**	**(8)**	**(11)**

List 2: Derivational Features

The second list will test students at the derivational level. This list should be reserved for those who spell twelve or more of the words on the previous list correctly. The derivational list will test students on their recognition and spelling of common Greek- and Latin-derived stems, on their use of information from one word to spell a related word correctly, and on their spelling of commonly derived endings and prefixes.

List Two: Derivational Spellings

1.	confided	**The convict confided to his cell mate that he knew about three other crimes.**
2.	ignition	**Put the key into the ignition.**
3.	confident	**They're confident they will win.**
4.	symbol	**Our flag is a symbol of our country.**
5.	phonics	**The first grader was practicing phonics.**
6.	immortal	**The gods of ancient Greece were said to be immortal.**
7.	reserve	**Please reserve four seats for my family.**
8.	psychological	**They gave the prisoner a psychological test.**
9.	perspiration	**The player's face was streaming with perspiration.**
10.	resigned	**The police chief abruptly resigned.**
11.	democracy	**The United States is the world's oldest democracy.**
12.	telegraphy	**The invention of telegraphy meant messages could travel long distances in minutes.**
13.	symphony	**My aunt plays first violin in the symphony.**
14.	residence	**There's no one living in that residence.**
15.	democratic	**The United States has a democratic form of government.**
16.	perspiring	**The player was perspiring heavily.**
17.	psychology	**My brother studies psychology in college.**
18.	resided	**The president will reside in Arkansas after he retires from office.**
19.	collision	**No one was hurt in the collision.**
20.	reservation	**We made a reservation for dinner at the restaurant.**

You can score the student's performance on this list in two ways. If you count the number of words spelled correctly, a score of 7 or more out of the 20 would indicate that the student could profit from studying words at the derivational stage.

To find more words for students to study at the derivational level, you could use a reputable spelling program's list for grades 6 through 8.

To take a more finely tuned look at the nature of the student's strengths and needs, you could examine the student's responses to each word, by category or spelling feature. The following chart enables you to tally the student's spelling of different features as they occur in the list of words. As we said before, however, it will usually suffice to do this fine-tuned assessment on half a dozen students. Once you have trained yourself to look for these features, you can scan the other students' papers to see how they have spelled these features, without resorting to feature-by-feature scoring.

Analyzing Spellings by Features: Derivational Spellings

The chart records students' spellings of features of the words in the derivational list. Place a check mark in all the blanks beside a word that is spelled correctly. For those misspelled, place a check mark in the blank for each feature that is spelled

FIGURE 18.2   Feature Analysis: Derivational Spellings

	Derivational Ending	Derivational Prefix	Relating Words	Greek and Latin Stems
confided		_____		
ignition	_____			
confident			_____	
symbol				_____
phonics				_____
immortal		_____		
reserve			_____	
psychological			_____	_____
perspiration			_____	_____
resigned			_____	
democracy			_____	_____
telegraphy			_____	_____
symphony			_____	_____
residence		_____	_____	
democratic			_____	_____
perspiring			_____	_____
psychology			_____	_____
resided			_____	
collision	_____	_____		
reservation	_____			_____
Total:	_____	_____	_____	_____
Possible:	(3)	(4)	(13)	(11)

correctly. Then, reading down the columns, tally a score for the correct spelling of each feature. That score can now be compared to the total possible spellings of that feature.

Students who misspell more than a fourth of the features in each category probably will benefit from practice that calls attention to that feature.

1. **Derivational Endings:** If the student spells the *-tion* ending in *ignition,* the *-sion* in *collision,* and the *-tion* in *reservation* correctly, he or she gets a check in the corresponding blank beside each word.

2. **Derivational Prefixes con-, im-, and col-:** This is a test of appropriate consonant doubling. If the student spells this feature of each word correctly, he or she gets a check in the corresponding blank beside the word.

3. **Relating Words:** Recognizing a feature in one word will make the spelling of a related word easier. The student gets a check in the appropriate blank if he or she correctly spells the unstressed syllables in the words with blanks beside them (the O in "democratic," for example, or the ER in "reservation"), because the spelling list contains words related to those target words, and in these "related words" there are stressed syllables that should shed light on the spellings of the target words. For example, the stressed O in "democracy" should make clear the spelling of the O in "democratic").

4. **Greek and Latin Stems:** Students are given checks in the appropriate blanks if they correctly spell those words that contain Latin and Greek stems.

Spelling Instruction

Three approaches are needed to teach students to spell successfully. One is to have them learn spelling words on the appropriate level. Another is to conduct spelling activities that call students' attention to the patterns and features of spelling that are appropriate to their level of development. The third is to teach them proofreading strategies.

Teaching Spelling Lists

Even though, as we have argued earlier in this chapter, learning to spell is largely a conceptual issue, it still repays the effort to have students memorize lists of spelling words. The best lists arrange words by spelling patterns and features, and also include a hefty diet of the words students write most frequently. Fifteen words a week should be enough to study. We are not trying to teach students all the words they will ever write (we would need to teach tens of thousands of words in that case), but we do want to have them learn plenty of exemplars for the most important spelling patterns and features. Once they have derived the patterns and concepts about spelling from the exemplars, they can generalize the patterns to new words, and, thus, come to spell far more words than we have taught them.*

An astute reader will have recognized a problem: If a class of students is spread over several spelling levels, how do you teach them to spell using weekly lists of words? The procedure recommended by Russell Stauffer (1975) is good advice. Determine each student's instructional grade level in spelling (see "Quantitative Assessment" above), and place each student at that level in a spelling program. When the time comes for a spelling test, assign a number (mix these up, however) to each level list of words you have students working on. Call out a word from list one, list two, list three, and list four (or however many lists of words you have) until you have called fifteen words from each list.

Teaching for Spelling Patterns

There are many kinds of spelling activities that can help make students aware of the patterns and structures of English spelling. All the ones described here are intended to foster an atmosphere of discovery: of boosting students' appreciation for the language they speak, read, and write.

The early activities are appropriate for students who are still learning common patterns, marking systems, and grammatical endings. The later activities are meant for those who are learning words with derivational phenomena.

Word Sorting. Word sorts are grouping activities that call students' attention to spelling patterns and other features words have in common. Word sorts are concrete and active exercises that are intended to help students form inner cognitive categories. In other words, word sorts are an exercise in concept formation.

All word sort activities use spelling words printed on business card–sized pieces of tag board (an index card can be cut into three cards the right size). The words should be within the reading and speaking vocabulary of all the students who participate.

A Predetermined Word Sort. For a predetermined word sort, the teacher works with two to five students. Each person has six to eight cards. The words on the cards share a spelling pattern or phonogram. The words might include:

spite	unite	thought
bright	weight	strait
slightly	mate	eight

Note that it helps if a few do not share the same pattern.

---

*It is also useful to teach high-frequency words, of course, because some 100 of them account for more than half of the words students write, according to some estimates (see, for example, Hillerich, 1978). Nonetheless, those words are usually taught and learned before the end of third grade. In the middle-school grades, you may well want to teach students high-frequency *content words,* drawn from the subject areas of mathematics, social studies, etc. Indeed, many of these words (such as *"bisector," "bicameral," "unanimous,"* and others) are based on the Greek and Latin stems the students will already be studying.

The teacher puts a card on the table, and invites the student to his or her right to put down any word he has in his hand that "goes with" that word. As he does so, the student says what his word has in common with the teacher's word. The person to that student's right is now invited to put down one of his or her words that goes with those two; or if they are unable to, to put down a card that might begin a new category. The play continues until all the cards are discarded. In the process, the group will have distinguished the *-ait* words from the *-eight* words, and the *-ite* words from the *-ight* words, and will have discussed the differences.

An Independent Word Sort. Once the students have become familiar with the way word sorting works, they can do these activities independently. The teacher may prepare packages of cards that contain words having two, three, or four patterns in common. Individuals or pairs of students may be assigned to sort the words into patterns. For follow-up, the students may record the words by pattern in a spelling notebook. Further, they may look through books and magazines for other words that have the same spelling patterns and enter those in the spelling dictionaries, too.

Concentration. For concentration, the teacher writes the list of spelling words on business card–sized cards. Each card is numbered on the back. The teacher puts the cards in a rectangular grid, face down, numbers up. Students take turns turning up pairs of cards. When they find two that arguably share a spelling pattern, they may take them off the table—after first naming the pattern. If winners are desired, students may play in teams and the team with the most cards at the end of the game wins.

Consonant Doubling. For consonant doubling, students sort the following words into those that double the final consonant in the first syllable and those that do not. Then they discuss the reasons for their choices.

manner	setter	dunes	diner	baking
manor	later	gunner	dinner	tacking
trailer	meter	yellow	thanking	taking
teacher	getting	below	backing	sooner

Vowel Alternations. For vowel alternations, students sort these words into two columns. Then they are challenged to find a rule that works in their categorizations.

boy	soil	toil	ray
bay	rail	royal	paid
bail	say	soybean	boil
toy	destroyed	sail	pay

More Vowel Alternations. For these vowel alternations, students sort these words into two columns. Then they are challenged to find a rule that works in their categorizations. They are also asked to find two words that are exceptions to the rule.

now	proud	prow	sow
brow	noun	sound	brown
allow	town	loud	cloud

Word Building with Latin and Greek Stems. For older students, word building is a variation of the concentration game discussed before. Prepare a set of a dozen words with common stems (*-ology, -graph, -scope, -sphere,* etc.). Number these on the back, and place them face down, numbers up, in a rectangular grid. Surround them with prefixes (bound morphemes) (such as *tele-, bio-, micro-, geo-,* etc.). Students take turns turning up word stems in the middle and pairing them with prefixes around the perimeter.

Thinking of Words in Groups. To think of words in groups, students are asked to underline the part of the word in the column on the left that is hard to spell. Then they should circle the part of the word in the column on the right that gives a clue to the spelling of the part they underlined in the word on the right.

photograph	photography
sign	signal
economics	economy
physical	physician
spectacle	spectacular
technical	technique
separate	separation
telegraph	telegraphy
horizontal	horizon
ignorant	ignore
editor	edition
confident	confide
positive	position

Derivational Endings. For derivational endings, students sort pairs into two sets. They are challenged to discover some rules at work here.*

collide	→	collision		attract	→	attraction
act	→	action		decide	→	decision
divide	→	division		collect	→	collection
appreciate	→	appreciation		persuade	→	persuasion

*Hint: The words that end in *-te* add the suffix *-tion,* while the words that end in *-de* add the suffix *-sion.*

Teaching Proofreading Skills

Students must internalize the practice of applying what they are learning in their organized spelling instruction to the spelling they do when they are writing. In essence, we want to teach students the habit of proofreading, and to teach them strategies for correcting their own spelling. We will therefore share some strategies for them to use each time they write, and also do some group exercises to help strengthen their own editing abilities.

Editing Strategies. Encourage students to look over a paper and circle any word with spelling that looks doubtful to them. Have them write the word three different ways, then look up each spelling in a dictionary until they find the correct one.

Daily Edits. For daily edits, the teacher prepares (or asks a group of students to take turns preparing) a sentence or pair of sentences with several of a week's words misspelled in it. The teacher writes the sentences on the board. Volunteers are asked to come to the board one at a time and correct the spelling errors.

The teacher may add punctuation or grammatical errors, too—but takes care not to introduce more than one kind of problem (other than spelling errors) in any one lesson.

A Rotating Spelling Committee. For a rotating spelling committee, before students submit a paper for publication, the teacher has them check their spelling with a spelling committee. The spelling committee should be composed of strong and not-so-strong spellers. Their job will be to look the paper over for words that may be misspelled. The student-writer's job will be to look up in a dictionary any words that are challenged and correct them before submitting the paper for publication. Students should serve limited terms (say, two weeks) on the spelling committee.

Conclusion

The approach taken to spelling instruction here may seem more systematic and rigorous than the more relaxed approaches that are currently in vogue. I hope the reason for this is evident by now. The challenges of spelling accelerate rapidly just as students reach middle school. By sixth grade, students begin to encounter heavy doses of the huge written English vocabulary derived from Latin and Greek. Language arts teachers have the opportunity to help students to get a firm grip on this more sophisticated vocabulary. If you take this challenge seriously, your students will have a real advantage—in writing, reading, and vocabulary—that will serve them through high school and beyond. Indeed, you have the chance to kindle a lifetime fascination for the wonders and traditions of one of the great languages of the world. And it may well be the last chance: Systematic spelling instruction in most school systems in America, and most commercial spelling programs, ends with the eighth grade.

REFERENCES

Bean, W. & Bouffier, C. (1988). *Spell by writing.* Portsmouth, NH: Heinemann.

Bear, D., Invernizzi, M., Templeton, S., & Johnson, F. (1992). *Words their way.* Upper Saddle River, NJ: Merrill.

Henderson, E.H. (1990). *Teaching spelling.* Boston: Houghton Mifflin.

Hillerich, R.L. (1978). *A writing vocabulary of elementary school children.* Springfield, IL: Charles C Thomas.

Morris, D, Nowacek, J., Blanton, L., & Blanton, W.E. (In press). Teaching low achievers at their "instructional level." *Elementary School Journal, 96*(2), 163–178.

Morris, D., Nelson, L., & Perney, J. (1987). Exploring the concept of "spelling instructional level" through the analysis of error types. *Elementary School Journal, 87,* 181–200.

Read, C. (1975). Children's categorization of speech sounds in English. NCTE Committee on Research Report No. 17. Urbana, IL: National Council of Teachers of English.

Temple, C., Nathan, R., Temple, F., & Burris, N. (1993). *The beginnings of writing,* Third Edition. Boston, MA: Allyn and Bacon.

19 Big Words for Big Kids

The Morphology Link to Meaning and Decoding

PATRICIA M. CUNNINGHAM
Wake Forest University

Once students reach the intermediate grades, they meet approximately 10,000 new words—words never before encountered in print—in their school reading each year (Nagy & Anderson, 1984). Most of these words are big words, words of seven or more letters and two or more syllables. What can you do to help children decode and build meaning for 10,000 new words, most of which are going to be big words?

In the past, children were taught a set of syllabication rules and were supposed to apply their phonics knowledge to the syllables once they were successfully divided. Syllabication rules are rarely taught these days because teachers realized and research demonstrates that there is little relationship between knowing the rules and successful reading (Canney & Schreiner, 1977). Even when children can successfully divide words, they often cannot pronounce the word because phonics rules that apply to one-syllable words often do not apply to bigger words.

In the 1970s, instruction in what was called *structural analysis* was a part of most upper elementary reading curriculums. This instruction usually included prefixes, suffixes, and Greek and Latin roots. These word parts were usually taught as clues for determining meanings for words, rather than as clues for pronouncing unfamiliar-in-print words. Often, the word parts emphasized were parts with low utility. *Intra,* for example, was taught as a prefix meaning "within" with the examples of *intramural* and *intrastate.* According to the *American Heritage Dictionary,* 4th edition, only six words, including *intramural* and *intrastate,* begin with the prefix *intra.* The only other words students would be helped to figure out the meaning of from the prefix *intra* were *intravenous, intrauterine, intracellular,* and *intracellularity*! In addition to the lack of utility problem, many of the prefixes taught had as many examples where the prefix did not add to the meaning of the word as those in which it did. *Mis* might help you figure out *misbehave* and *misdeal,* but it does not get you far with the meanings of *miscellaneous* and *mistletoe.*

Instruction about suffixes was often cluttered with grammatical jargon. The suffixes *ance* and *ence* were taught as changing the word from the verb form to the noun form and meaning "the condition or state of." It is doubtful that when students first encountered the word *difference,* they thought of the word *differ* (which is actually lower in frequency that *difference*) and then used *differ* to figure out a meaning for *difference,* "the condition or state of differing"!

Finally, the usefulness of Greek and Latin roots is questionable. Shepard (1974) found that knowledge of Latin roots is not strongly related to knowledge of meanings of words, but that knowledge of stems that are current English words is strongly related to the meaning of related words. Many students know meanings for words such as *collect* and *receive* who do not know anything about the Latin roots *lect* and *ceive,* but students who know the word *sane* have little trouble with the less frequent related word, *sanity.*

For a variety of reasons, this type of structural analysis is seldom found in upper-grade reading curricula today. Later in this chapter, when recommending instructional strategies to help children decode big words, the importance of morphological relationships is highlighted, but it is important to note that the morphologically based instruction supported by research bears little resemblance to the rule-based, low-utility structural analysis done in the past.

What the Research Tells Us about Big Words

In 1984, Nagy and Anderson published a landmark study in which they analyzed a sample from the Carroll, Davies, and Richman's (1971) *Word Frequency Book* to determine the number and relationships of words found in printed school English. Based on a sample of 7,260 words, Nagy and Anderson estimated that there are over 400,000 distinct words (excluding proper nouns, numbers, and foreign words) in "printed school English" (grades 3 to 9). Many of these words, however, are related semantically through their morphology. A child who knows the words *hunt, red, fog,* and *string* will have little difficulty with the meanings of *hunter, redness, foglights,* and *stringy.* Word relationships such as these are defined as semantically transparent. When you group the semantically transparent words together, instead of 400,000 plus words, you have 88,500 word families. For each basic word known, most children would know three or four other words.

Other word relationships exist but are not so readily apparent. Meaning relationships exist between *planet* and *planetarium, vicious* and *vice,* and *apart* and *apartment,* but these will probably not be apparent to most children unless they are pointed out. Nagy and Anderson define these types of meaning relationships as semantically opaque. If readers do, however, understand these more complex morphological relationships, then instead of 88,500 word families, there would be only 54,000 word families. If children knew or learned how to interpret these more morphologically complex relationships, they would know six or seven words for every basic word known.

Excluding proper nouns, numbers, abbreviations, and other "special" words, only 1,000 of the 10,000 new words encountered each year are truly new words, unrelated to other more familiar words.

Nagy and Anderson concluded that students learn most of their word meanings from wide reading and that facility with context and morphological relationships may determine how able they are to take advantage of the opportunities for new word learning presented by wide reading. They suggested that teaching words together as a family will call attention to the morphological relationships and will allow students to take better advantage of these relationships when reading on their own.

A number of studies have demonstrated that poor decoders have a difficult time reading polysyllabic words even when they can read single-syllable words (Just & Carpenter, 1987; Samuels, LaBerge, & Bremer, 1978). Perfetti (1986) concluded that the ability to decode polysyllabic words increases the qualitative differences between good and poor readers. Although the nature of the relationship is not completely clear, there is a strong relationship between reading level and morphological knowledge. Anderson and Davison (1988) concluded that because most longer words are morphologically complex, deficiencies in morphological knowledge may be a cause of poor readers' difficulties with long words. Freyd and Baron (1982) investigated the extent to which readers' use of structural analysis is related to their reading ability. They found a strong relationship and concluded that skilled readers use structural analysis in three ways: to recognize known words more efficiently, to remember the meanings and spellings of partially learned words, and to figure out the meanings and pronunciations of new words.

If we are to teach the word parts that are most useful, we must know what these are. White, Sowell, and Yanagihara (1989) analyzed the words in the Carroll, Davies, and Richman corpus and found that 20 prefixes accounted for 97% of the prefixed words. Four prefixes—*un, re, in* (and *im, ir,* and *il,* meaning "not") and *dis*—accounted for 58% of all prefixed words. The prefixes accounting for the other 39% of the words were *en/em, non, in/im* (meaning "in"), *over, mis, sub, pre, inter, fore, de, trans, super, semi, anti, mid,* and *under.* For suffixes, *s/es, ed,* and *ing* account for 65% of the suffixed words. Add *ly, er/or, ion/tion, ible/able, al, y, ness, ity,* and *ment,* and you account for 87% of the words. The remaining suffixes, each occurring in less than 1% of the words, were *er/est* (comparative), *ic, ous, en, ive, ful,* and *less.*

Because White et al. (1989) were looking at prefixes and suffixes only from the standpoint of helping with the meaning part of big words, they did not include in their count "unpeelable" prefixes and suffixes such as the *con* in *conform* and the *ture* in *signature.* Arguing rightly that few children would be able to figure out the meaning of *conform* or *signature* by peeling away these parts, they deemed them not useful enough to be taught. When you consider not only meaning but also spelling and decoding, however, *con* and *ture* become very useful chunks.

In the remainder of this chapter, three activities—Making Big Words, Word Detectives, and the Nifty Thrifty Fifty—are described. All three of these activities will help students become more mormphologically sophisticated and, thus, cure their morphophobia—fear of encountering big words!

Making Big Words

Making Big Words is a hands-on manipulative activity in which students learn how adding letters and moving letters around create new words. Every Making Big Words lesson has a secret word, a word that can be made with all the letters. Once the words are made, the students sort them into patterns and transfer these patterns to read and spell some new words.

To plan a Making Big Words lesson, we begin with the "secret" word, a word that can be made from all the letters. Using the letters in this word, we choose 15 to 18 words that will give us some easy and harder words, some morphologically related words, and several sets of rhymes. We then decide on the order in which words will be made, beginning with short words and building to longer words. We write these words on index cards to use in the sorting and transferring parts of the lesson. We write the letters on a strip: vowels first, then consonants so as not to give away the secret word.

To begin the lesson, we give students the strips and have them write capital letters on the back and cut or tear them into letters. We place large letter cards with the same letters along the chalk ledge or in a pocket chart. As students make each word, we choose one student to come and make it with the big letters. Here is a sample Making Big Words lesson.

As the lesson begins, the letters A E E U D N R S T V are in the pocket chart. The students have the same letters. The teacher leads them to make words by saying:

"Take three letters and make *due.* Your reports are due Tuesday."

"Add one letter to *due* and you will have *dune.* He slept on the tall sand dune."

"Change the first letter in *dune* to spell *tune.*"

"Let's spell another four-letter word you know—*save.*"

"Change just the first letter and spell *Dave.*"

"Here's another four-letter word you can spell with your letters—*east.*"

"Just change the order of the letters and you can turn the letters in *east* into *seat.*"

"Now spell another four-lettter word—*dent.*"

"Change just the first letter and *dent* becomes *vent.*"

"Now, let's make some five-letter words. Add a letter to *vent* to spell *event.* The annual bike race is a big event in our town."

"Now we are going to six-letter words. Take six letters and spell *avenue.*"

"Let's spell another six-letter word—*nature.*"

"It's time for a seven-letter word—*veteran.*"

"You can spell another seven-letter word—*eastern.* We live in the eastern part of the state."

"Now let's see if you can spell an eight-letter word—*dentures.* My mom has dentures."

"I only have one word left. See if you can figure out the secret word—the word than can be spelled with all your letters. I am coming around to see if I spot the secret word."

If someone figures out *adventures,* let that student come and make it with the big letters. If not, tell them the secret word and have them all make it.

Once all the words are made, lead the students to sort for patterns. For the sorting part of the lesson, we put the words on index cards in the pocket chart or along the chalk ledge. Here are all the words students have made in this lesson:

due	seat	nature
dune	dent	veteran
tune	vent	eastern
save	event	dentures
Dave	avenue	adventures
east		

The first sort is for words with the same prefix, root, or ending. Pull out the words *nature, dentures,* and *adventures* and help students notice the ture spelling and pronunciation. Ask students how they would spell two other words that end in *t-u-r-e,* such as *creature* and *future.* Pull out the word *east* and *eastern* and talk about how they are all related. Ask students how they would spell *western, southern,* and *northern* and what the root word for each word is. The final sort is always for rhyming words. Have students pull out the rhyming words:

due	dune	save	vent
avenue	tune	Dave	dent
			event

When the rhyming words are sorted, we help students see that rhyming words can help them read and spell words. We write two new rhyming words on cards and have them place these words under the rhyming words and use the rhymes to decode them:

prune   prevent

Finally, we say two rhyming words and help them see how the words they made help them spell them:

engrave   clue

Here are the steps for each Making Big Words lesson:

1. Give students the strips and have them write capital letters on the back and cut or tear them into letters. Place large letter cards with the same letters along the chalk ledge or in a pocket chart.

2. Tell students which words to make. Let them know when they just need to add a letter or change the order of letters. Use sentences for words when students might not immediately recognize the meaning.
3. Have one student come and make each word with the big letters. Other students should correct their words if they are not spelled correctly. Keep a brisk pace. Do not wait for everyone to make each word before sending someone up to make it with the big letters.
4. Give students a minute to see if they can come up with the secret word. If no one can figure it out, tell them the word and have them make it.
5. Have students sort the words into patterns. Sort first for words with the same prefix, root, or ending. Have them spell a few words with the same part.
6. Next, sort the words into rhymes and remind the students that rhyming words can help them read and spell words. Write two new rhyming words on cards and have them place these words under the rhyming words and use the rhymes to decode them. Finally, say two rhyming words and help them see how the rhyming words help them spell them. If possible, include some longer rhyming words.

We tie our Making Big Words lessons into the themes or units we are studying. Here are some more example lessons. (For many more lessons, see *Making Big Words* and *Making More Big Words* [Cunningham & Hall, 1994; 1997].)

Letters on strip: A A E I C M N R S
Make: am ram Sam are ace race mace scram cream scream camera racism America Americans

Sort for:	related words:	race, racism
		America, Americans
Spell:		sexism, Mexicans
Sort for:	rhyming words:	ace, race, mace
		cream, scream
		am, ram, Sam, scram
Read and spell:		program steam replace slam

Letters on strip: A E I I O B H N N R T
Make: hit hire tire neat beat hero orbit other nation ration intern inherit inhabit another hibernation

Sort for:	related words:	other, another
	-tion words:	ration, nation, hibernation
Spell:		motion mention
Sort for:	rhyming words:	hire, tire
		neat, beat
		hit, orbit, inherit, inhabit
Read and spell:		armpit retreat wire wheat

Letters on strip: E E I D N P R S S T

Make: dent rent ripe ripen dress press stripe desert dessert pretend present serpent ripened depress presidents

Sort for:	related words:	ripe, ripen, ripened
Spell:		deepen, deepened
Sort for:	rhyming words:	ripe, stripe
		dress, press, depress
		dent rent, present, serpent
Read and spell:		content bless swipe repress

Letters on strip: A E O U M B R R T T

Make: out rot trot name tame team menu trout mount amount nature mature torment ornament tournament

Sort for:	words ending in -ture:	nature, mature
		pasture capture
Spell:	words ending in -ment:	torment, ornament, tournament
Sort for:	rhyming words:	out, trout
		rot, trot
		name, tame
Read and spell:		became scout shame clot

Word Detectives

There are two questions I would like to put into the mouths of every teacher of children from fourth grade through high school:

"Do I know any other words that look and sound like this word?"

"Are any of these look-alike/sound-alike words related to each other?"

The answer to the first question should help students with pronouncing and spelling the word. The answer to the second question should help students discover what, if any, meaning relationships exist between this new word and others in their meaning vocabulary stores. This guideline and these two simple questions could be used by any teacher of any subject area. Imagine that students in a mathematics class encounter the new word:

equation

The teacher demonstrates and gives examples of equations and helps build meaning for the concept. Finally, the teacher asks the students to pronounce *equation* and see if they know any other words that look and sound like *equation*. Students think of

addition, multiplication, nation, vacation, equal, equator

The teacher lists the words, underlining the parts that are the same and having students pronounce the words emphasizing the part that is pronounced the same. The teacher then points out to the students that thinking of a word that looks and sounds the same as a new word will help you quickly remember how to pronounce the new word and will also help you spell the new word.

Next, the teacher explains that words, like people, sometimes look and sound alike but are not related. If this is the first time this analogy is used, the teacher will want to spend some time talking with the students about people with red hair, green eyes, and so on who have some parts that look alike but are not related and others who are.

> "Not all people who look alike are related but some are. This is how words work, too. Words are related if there is something about their meaning that is the same. After we find look-alike, sound-alike words that will help us spell and pronounce new words, we try to think of any ways these words might be in the same meaning family."

With help from the teacher, the children discover that *equal, equator,* and *equation* are related because the meaning of *equal* is in all three.

> "An equation has to have equal quantities on both sides of the equal signs. The equator is an imaginary line which divides the earth into two equal halves."

Imagine that the students who were introduced to equations on Monday during math and were asked to think of look-alike, sound-alike words and consider if any of these words might be "kinfolks" had a science lesson on Tuesday in which they did some experiments with the students using *thermometers* and *barometers.* At the close of the lesson, the teacher pointed to these words and helped them notice that the *meters* chunk was pronounced and spelled the same and asked the students if they thought these words were just look-alikes or were related to one another. The students would probably conclude that you used them both to measure things and that the *meters* chunk must be related to measuring, as in *kilometers.* When asked to think of look-alike, sound-alike words for the first chunk, students thought of *baron* for *barometers* but decided that these two words were probably not related. For *thermometer,* they thought of *thermal* and *thermostat* and decided that all these words had to do with heat or temperature.

Now imagine that this lucky class of students had a social studies lesson on Wednesday during which the teacher pointed out the new word *international* and asked the two critical questions. On Thursday, when they were preparing for a trip to the *symphony,* the music teacher drew their attention to this word and asked the two critical questions. During a tennis lesson on Friday in which they practiced their *forehand* and *backhand* strokes and the teacher asked the two critical questions about these crucial tennis words.

Throughout their school day, children from the intermediate grades up encounter many new words. Because English is such a morphologically related language, most new words can be connected to other words by their spelling and pronunciation, and many new words have meaning-related words already known to the student. Some clever, word-sensitive children become word detectives on their own. They notice the patterns and use these to learn and retrieve words. Others, however, try to learn to pronounce, spell, and associate meaning with each of these words as separate, distinct entities. This difficult task becomes almost impossible as students move through the grades and the number of new words increases each year. Readers do not need to be taught every possible pattern, because the brain is programmed to look for patterns. Some students, however, do not know what the important patterns in words are and that these patterns can help you with pronouncing, spelling, and accessing and remembering meanings for words. Asking the two critical questions for key vocabulary introduced in any content area would add only a few minutes to the introduction of key content vocabulary and would turn many students into word detectives.

The Nifty Thrifty Fifty

To access words from our memory stores that have the same chunks as other words, we must not only be able to read the words but we must also be able to spell them. Many students from the intermediate grades on can read more big words than they can spell. They may be able to read the word *confusion* but be unable to correctly spell *confusion*. Thus, when they see another word that begins with *con* or ends with *sion*, they cannot access *confusion* as a similar word. It would be helpful to older children who are having difficulties decoding, spelling, or accessing meaning for big words to have a store of big words that they could read, could spell, and with which they associated meanings.

I created such a list by deciding which prefixes, suffixes, and spelling changes were most prevalent in the multisyllabic words students might encounter. I included all the prefixes and suffixes determined to be most common in the White et al. (1989) study. Because I wanted to create a list that would provide the maximum help with meaning, spelling, and decoding, I added prefixes and suffixes such as *con/com, per, ex, ture,* and *ian* not included in that study because they were not considered helpful from a meaning standpoint. These prefixes are useful spelling and pronunciation chunks.

Having created the list of "transferable chunks," I then wanted to find the "most-apt-to-be-known" word containing each chunk. I consulted *The Living Word Vocabulary* (Dale & O'Rourke, 1981), which indicates for 44,000 words the grade level at which more than two-thirds of the students tested knew the meaning of the word. Because the test from which it was determined that students knew the meanings also required them to read the word, it can also be inferred that at least two-thirds of the students could decode and pronounce the word. The goal was to find words that two-thirds of fourth-grade students could read and knew at least one meaning for. After much finagling, a list of 50 words that contain all the most useful prefixes, suffixes, and spelling changes was created. All but eight of these words were known by more than two-thirds of fourth-grade students. Seven words—*antifreeze, classify, deodorize, impression, irresponsible, prehistoric* and *semifinal*—were not known by two-thirds of fourth graders but were known by two-thirds of sixth graders. *International,* the most known word containing the prefix *inter,* was known by two-thirds of eighth graders.

Because this list of 50 words is apt to be known by so many intermediate-aged and older students and because it so economically represents all the important big-word parts, I named this list the Nifty Thrifty Fifty.

The Nifty Thrifty Fifty

antifreeze	anti	
beautiful		ful (y-i)
classify		ify
communities	com	es (y-i)
community	com	
composer	com	er
continuous	con	ous
conversation	con	tion
deodorize	de	ize
different		ent
discovery	dis	y
dishonest	dis	
electricity		ity
employee	em	ee
encouragement	en	ment
expensive	ex	ive
forecast	fore	
forgotten		en (doublte t)
governor		or
happiness		ness (y-i)
hopeless		less
illegal	il	
impossible	im	
impression	im	sion
independence	in	ence
international	inter	al
invasion	in	sion
irresponsible	ir	ible
midnight	mid	
misunderstand	mis	
musician		ian
nonliving	non	ing (drop e)
overpower	over	

(continued)

performance	per	ance
prehistoric	pre	ic
prettier		er (y-i)
rearrange	re	
replacement	re	ment
richest		est
semifinal	semi	
signature		ture
submarine	sub	
supermarkets	super	s
swimming		ing (double m)
transportation	trans	tion
underweight	under	
unfinished	un	ed
unfriendly	un	ly
unpleasant	un	ant
valuable		able (drop e)

There are endless possibilities for how the list might be used. First, however, students must learn to spell the words. Teachers might want to start a word wall (Cunningham, 1995) of big words and add five words each week to the wall. They might take a few minutes each day to "chant" the spelling of the words and talk about the parts of the word that could be applied to other words. This talking should be as "nonjargony" as possible. Rather than talking about the root word *freeze* and the prefix *anti*, the discussions should be about how antifreeze keeps a car's engine from freezing up and thus it is protection against freezing. Students should be asked to think of other words that look and sound like *antifreeze* and then decide if the *anti* parts of those words could have anything to do with the notion of "against."

"What is an antibiotic against?"
"What is an antiaircraft weapon?"

For suffixes, the discussion should center around how the suffix changes how the word can be used in a sentence.

"A *musician* makes music. What does a beautician, electrician, physician, magician do?"

"When you need to replace something, you get a replacement. What do you get when someone encourages you?" "What do you call it when you accomplish something?"

Spelling changes should be noticed and applied to similar words.

"*Communities* is the plural of *community.* How would you spell *parties? Candies? Personalities?*"

"When we forget something, we say it was forgotten. How would you spell *bitten? Written?*"

If this list is to become truly useful to students, they need to learn to spell the words gradually over time and they need to be shown how the patterns found in these words can be useful in decoding, spelling, and figuring out meaning for lots of other words. Once all 50 of these words are quickly and fluently spelled and pronounced by the students, there are hundreds of other words they can decode, spell, and infer meanings for. (For activities with the Nifty Thrifty Fifty words, see Cunningham and Hall, 1998.)

Conclusion

Facility with big words is essential for students as they read, write, and learn in all areas of school and life. Many big words occur infrequently, but when they do occur, they carry a lot of the meaning and content of what is being read. English is a language in which many words are related through their morphology. Students who learn to look for patterns in the big new words they meet will be better spellers and decoders. If they learn to look further and consider possible meaning relationships, they will increase the size of their meaning vocabulary stores.

REFERENCES

Anderson, R.C., & Davison, A. (1988). Conceptual and empirical bases of readability formulas. In G. Green & A. Davison (Eds.), *Linguistic complexity and text comprehension* (pp. 23–54). Hillsdale, NJ: Erlbaum.

Canney, G., & Schreiner, R. (1977). A study of the effectiveness of selected syllabication rules and phonogram patterns for word attack. *Reading Research Quarterly, 12,* 102–124.

Carroll, J.B., Davies, P., & Richman, B. (1971). *Word frequency book.* New York: American Heritage.

Cunningham, P.M. (1995). *Phonics they use: Words for reading and writing* (2nd ed.). New York: Harper-Collins.

Cunningham, P.M. & Hall, D.P (1994). *Making big words.* Carthage, IL: Good Apple.

Cunningham, P.M., & Hall, D.P (1997). *Making more big words.* Parsippany, NJ: Good Apple.

Cunningham, P.M. & Hall, D.P. (1998). *Month by month phonics for upper grades: A second chance for struggling readers and students learning English.* Greensboro, NC: Carson-Dellosa.

Dale, E., & O'Rourke, J. (1981). *The living word vocabulary.* Chicago: World Book.

Freyd, P., & Baron, J. (1982). Individual differences in acquisition of derivational morphology. *Journal of Verbal Learning and Verbal Behavior, 21,* 282–295.

Just, M.A., & Carpenter, P.A. (1987). *The psychology of reading and language comprehension.* Boston: Allyn and Bacon.

Nagy, W., & Anderson, R.C. (1984). How many words are there in printed school English? *Reading Research Quarterly, 19,* 304–330.

Perfetti, C.A. (1986). Continuities in reading acquisition, reading skill and reading ability. *Remedial and Special Education, 7,* 11–21.

Samuels, S.J., LaBerge, D., & Bremer, C.D. (1978). Units of word recognition: Evidence for developmental change. *Journal of Verbal Learning and Verbal Behavior, 17,* 715–720.

Shepard, J.F. (1974). Research on the relationship between meanings of morphemes and the meaning of deriv- atives. In P.L. Nacke (Ed.), *23rd N. R. C. Yearbook* (pp. 115–119). Clemson, SC: National Reading Conference.

White, T., Sowell, J., & Yanagihara, A. (1989). Teaching elementary students to use word-part clues. *The Reading Teacher, 42,* 302–308.

20 Literature Circles, Book Clubs, and Literature Discussion Groups

Some Talk about Book Talk

NANCY L. ROSER
University of Texas at Austin

SUSAN STRECKER
University of Texas at Austin

MIRIAM G. MARTINEZ
University of Texas at San Antonio

Our office shelves house a new (and seemingly, expanding) section of professional books. Straddling the space between the textbooks devoted to children's literature and those focused on teaching students to read and write sits a relatively new "genre": professional texts that examine and explain classroom book conversations. The growth of interest in students' talk about books has been both marked and continuous in recent years. Besides the spate of published texts, our professional journals, too, are replete with the discoveries and insights gained from observing, encouraging, planning for, and judging the effects of more and better classroom book conversations. Why this surge of interest, investigation, and teacher-to-teacher sharing about "book talk"? In this chapter, we offer four possible explanations.

Four Explanations for Interest in "Book Talk"

A portion of the current keen interest in what students have to say about books stems from the intense interest in text comprehension that took root in the 1970s, initiating a period of research that contributed to refined theories of how knowledge is accumulated, stored, and retrieved (Pearson, 1985). With better understanding of comprehension came the need to determine what students know and how they bring their experiences to texts. Investigators in this period often used prompts and questions to determine students' understandings, rather than encouraging responsive "book talk."

Perhaps a second explanation for heightened interest in what children have to say about texts is based on a "rediscovery" of sorts. In the 1930s, Rosenblatt (1938/1976), a professor of English education and a literary theorist, described her understanding of reading as a "two-way process" involving a reader and a text interacting in a particular time and circumstance, with both reader and text contributing to meaning. Students, she believed, should be given opportunities to approach literature personally, to reflect upon their responses to it, and then to understand *what* within the work and within themselves contributed to their responses (Farrell & Squire, 1990, Rosenblatt, 1938/1976). In many elementary and middle-grade classrooms, literature discussion groups have begun to do just that: give students opportunity and confidence to reflect upon, to express, and to support their responses to texts.

Still another possible contributor to interest in students' responses to reading may stem from the influence of Vygotsky (1978), who posited that learners, to make sense of their world, must act upon it, "constructing" the sense of it for themselves. Vygotsky considered the vital role that language plays in shaping and clarifying thought. Teachers and researchers who subscribe to a "constructivist" theory provide instructional opportunities that require learners to untangle complexities, problem solve, and hypothesize—that is, to "construct" meanings for themselves. One important "opportunity" teachers provide is good literature, which, by its nature, requires a great deal of "gap filling" (Iser, 1978). Students (sometimes with help) must build the images, patterns, categories, and hypotheses that make the text make sense. They become active, "constructive" readers. When readers act in concert—that is, when they talk over their reactions and interpretations with other readers—their responses can become thicker and richer and more meaningful. Their "socially" constructed meanings (Bakhtin, 1986) can represent the range of experiences, ideas, and backgrounds of the conversants within the conversational setting of book clubs, literature circles, or literature discussion groups.

A fourth explanation for keen interest in classroom book conversations could be a by-product of both the proliferation of fine, "chewable" literature for children and the influx of more "real books" into classrooms and curricula—books not just for literacy instruction but for content study as well. "Literature-based" curriculum, the 90,000 children's titles now in print, and the approximately 6,000 children's books published annually (Huck, Hepler, Hickman, & Kiefer, 1997) mean more impetus both inside and outside the classroom for reading (and talking) about literature.

As with any complex phenomenon, the causes and influences of increased inter-est in book conversations are no doubt multiple and related. Nevertheless, it seems that many kids in middle- and upper-grade classrooms are getting to say *what* they think about books and *why* they think what do.

Why Book Talk Is Important to Literacy and to the Study of Literature

Like the pioneering Rosenblatt, many teachers believe that literature is to be "explored." Given that metaphor, there must be room for both wandering and wonder-ing through a variety of books throughout the classroom day. Even so (and again like Rosenblatt), many teachers also understand that literature has *both* shape and sub-stance; thus, effective "book talk" must consider both the form of the literature as well as its content. To read and talk about a set of folktales without eventually recognizing some of their structural similarities is to miss an opportunity to focus on patterns that aid recognition, understanding, and appreciation. By contrast, to ask readers to notice motifs or to identify literary language without their first having had time to agonize over a character's losses or glory in her victories is to deny them participation in the story world. Classroom book talk *can,* however, move in both directions; it can yield thoughtful expressions of ideas and inquiries as well as in-depth "study" of literature in all its forms. For example, book talk can result in better understanding of informational texts by helping readers shape, confirm, and even modify their individual reactions.

Ensuring Better Book Talk

Whether conversations about books are called literature circles, book clubs, or literary discussion groups, the teachers that offer these special opportunities share some notions about how to best nurture insightful thought and talk in the classroom. See Table 20.1 for some comparisons of the terms.

Good Book Talk Requires a Good Book

Teachers and researchers who value book talk indicate that the better the book, the more gripping its plot, the more gray its choices, the more the ethical dilemmas pull the reader in, the better the book talk. Eeds and Wells (1989), for example, in their bench-mark study of "grand conversations," discovered that fifth- and sixth-grade students, invited to talk about literature, had deeper and richer responses to Babbitt's (1985) *Tuck Everlasting* than to *Harriet the Spy* (Fitzhugh, 1964). *Tuck,* it seems, is the kind of book that demands discussion. There are many others: Lowry's (1993) *The Giver;* Paterson's (1994) *Flip-Flop Girl;* Spinelli's (1990) *Maniac McGee;* Taylor's (1976) *Roll of Thunder, Hear My Cry;* Avi's (1991) *Nothing But the Truth;* Fine's (1992) *Flour Babies;* Staples's (1989) *Shabanu: Daughter of the Wind;* Byar's (1977) *The Pinballs;*

TABLE 20.1   Learning about Conducting Literature Circles, Book Clubs, and Literature Discussion Groups

Terms for Book Conversation Groups	How Defined	Where to Read More
Literature Circles	"A curricular structure to support children in exploring their rough draft understanding of literature with other readers." Readers read independently and think collaboratively. Literature circles are primarily geared toward "encouraging children to become reflective and critical thinkers and readers." (Short, in Hill et al., pp. x–xi)	Hill, B.C., Johnson, N.J., & Schlick Noe, K.L. (1995). *Literature Circles and Response.* Norwood, MA: Christopher-Gordon. Daniels, H. (1994). *Literature Circles: Voice and Choice in the Student-Centered Classroom.* York, ME: Stenhouse. Hanssen, E. (1990). Planning for Literature Circles: Variations in Focus and Structure. In K.G Short & K.M. Pierce, (Eds.), *Talking about Books: Creating Literate Communities* (pp. 199–209). Portsmouth, NH: Heinemann.
Book Clubs	"A group of three to five students who meet to discuss a common reading, including specific chapters from longer books. They share personal responses, clarify confusing aspects of the reading, create interpretations, discuss authors' intent, etc." (McMahon & Raphael, 1997, p. xii)	McMahon, S.I., & Raphael, T.E. (Eds.). (1997). *The Book Club Connection: Literacy Learning and Classroom Talk.* New York: Teachers College Press. Paratore, J.R., & McCormack, R.L. (Eds.). (1997). *Peer Talk in the Classroom: Learning from Research.* Newark: DE: International Reading Association.
Literature Discussion Groups	"Emphasizes the reading and discussing of unabridged . . . literature in small, self-selected groups. It assumes comprehension and relies heavily on open-ended discussions." (Samway & Whang, p.14) Often teacher-guided, with planning for the kinds of literary insights or interpretations that the book provides for. (Eeds & Peterson, 1990)	Eeds, M.A., & Peterson, R. (1990). *Grand Conversations.* New York: Scholastic. Gambrell, L.B., & Almasi, J.F. (Eds.). (1996). *Lively Discussions!* Newark, DE: International Reading Association. Samway, K.D., & Whang, G. (1995). *Literature Study Circles in a Multicultural Classroom.* York, ME: Stenhouse.

Cormier's (1990) *Other Bells for Us to Ring;* Paterson's (1978) *The Great Gilly Hopkins;* and Fenner's (1995) *Yolanda's Genius.* The list is as limitless as the talk can be. Further, our own work has shown different types of books may well move talk in somewhat different directions (Martinez & Roser, 1995).

Good Book Talk Has Agreed-Upon Goals

The more agreed-upon the goals for book talk and the more its procedures are planned and practiced, the better the outcome. Hepler (1991) suggests that the primary goal of literature discussion is to create communities of readers. These communities

> have the advantage of giving children a chance to react to a book in the company of other similarly focused readers. The teacher provides the setting, and in some cases, the direction, and children talk their way through books. (p. 183)

McMahon and Raphael (1997) recommend that teachers and students generate these goals together. Depending on how book talk fits the curriculum—whether as a structure for literature study or as a launch for content units—book talk serves by helping students to think and speak (and even write) more clearly, listen more attentively and respectfully to others' ideas, take turns in conversation, use texts to support their ideas, appreciate the author's craft, and become more immersed in and attuned to the universal themes of literature. Ultimately, it is the teacher's stance toward literature and its centrality that most influences these goals.

Good Book Talk Means a Chance for *Each* Participant to Think and to Talk

Although group discussion can considerably enhance individual "gap filling" (Eeds & Wells, 1989, p. 22), some students may be unduly swayed by others' ideas before their own thoughts have had a chance to germinate. They may require the protective cocoon of a quiet time provided (after reading and prior to book talk) for responding in a reflection journal or literature log—a place to record an idea, a question, or a concern they would like to talk about before that idea is lost. Because students at any level can be silenced by more forceful peers, it is possible that not all novice book talkers will claim the floor unless the group is closely monitored. "Monitoring" may take the form of encouraging students to share from their literature logs—their "preserved" written reactions to the text—and of explicitly teaching roles and responsibilities of group membership, providing models of how to offer ideas, and having a daily group evaluation that includes reviewing each member's participation.

When serving as members of a book discussion group, teachers, too, work hard not to dominate the discussion. They realize that good book talk means judicious use of the imposed question, for example. Researchers who have considered the role of the question (and the questioner) tend to agree that ill-placed, scatter-shot, or rapid-fire questions can interfere with the genuine exchange of ideas that characterizes effective book conversations. Teachers who use fewer questions (Eeds & Wells, 1989), who work themselves to the periphery of the book discussion group (O'Flahavan, Stein, Wiencek, & Marks, 1992; Short & Kauffman, 1995), or who ensure that their contributions are those of a joint respondent support their students' participation in book talk. The teachers are also, however, the most knowledgeable "curator" of the art and the most careful reader of the book. Their contributions to conversations can help to refocus the students' ideas, reinforce and label their literary insights, and, like a curator (see Eeds & Peterson, 1991), help respondents see in new ways.

In the following example of fourth-grade students discussing *Make Way for Sam Houston* (Fritz, 1986), their teacher applied the language of literature study to an insight that Christopher had. Peterson and Eeds (1990) call it shooting "arrows of literary insight at appropriate moments" (p. 62).

> **CHRISTOPHER:**   I think his (Sam Houston's) life is tied together in a big knot and he can't get it untied.
>
> **TEACHER:**   That's a metaphor he just made. Did you hear? He said Sam Houston's life is tied in a knot. Life . . . with a knot. How does life compare with a knot?
>
> **ABBY:**   You can't get out of it.
>
> **ANTOINETTE:**   'Cause you're in trouble and you can't solve it.
>
> **TEACHER:**   What a struggle! You move a little way and you're back into it. What a lovely metaphor. Life . . . and a knot.

As the discussion of Sam Houston continued chapter by chapter over the days that followed, other children returned (in the pages of their journals) to Christopher's metaphor:

- I think his knot is almost undone.
- I think that Sam Houston has gotten half way through the knot in his life.
- I don't think his knot will ever come undone.
- His knot is unraveling.
- In the end, his knot unwravled (*sic*).
- I think his life was finnly (*sic*) out of his knot.

Good Book Talk Depends on a Conversational Setting

As simple as the idea seems, some classrooms are not arranged for good book talk. One teacher we know never asked her students to adjust their chairs or tables so that speakers faced one another for conversation. As a result, talk tended to ricochet for a few turns and then stop short. When she adjusted the classroom seating plan to provide for conversational groups (much like the seating arrangement at kitchen tables), the students adhered to the topic longer, built off others' comments, made eye contact, were more sensitive to dominating the talk, and evaluated the discussion as more effective.

What Good Book Talk Sounds Like

Good book talk is exciting, insightful, and honest exchange. It considers the text as a story world to be lived within, as an "object" that has been crafted by an author, and, often, as "messages" or themes of far-ranging import. It makes reference to the text to support its points. It demonstrates connection with the book experience and the world of literature beyond it.

Fourth-grade students in Ms. Frank's class were talking about *Castle in the Attic* (Winthrop, 1985) when they wondered about the ethics of William, the book's young protagonist, having used a magic charm to shrink his nanny, Miss Phillips, solely to keep her from leaving him:

C1:   I think that's kind of good and kind of bad in a way.

C2:   Not because of his shrinking, but about the way he felt about her.

C3:   She was getting ready to go home and everything.

C2:   And he shrinks her without her permission and everything.

C4:   And then Miss Phillips comes up with a very good idea.

C3:   "I'm not coming out of this room until you come in and get me."

C5:   He can't unless *he* is small.

C2:   I'm really glad because now he understands what he did to Miss Phillips and that wasn't right.

When Ms. Harp's class talked about Jean Fritz's (1986) *Make Way for Sam Houston* as a entrée into their social studies unit on Texas as a young republic, the talk was initially characterized by their involvement with the biography and linkage with Sam, but it moved to the foibles and motivations that were made visible through Fritz's close inspection of a larger-than-life Texas hero:

C1:   I wonder why Sam was so dedicated to doing big things.

C2:   How can he be so intelligent and foolhardy at the same time?

C3:   If Tiana's dead, who's taking care of their children?

C4:   I think Sam needs more . . . get some self control, and self-stopness.

Getting Started with Book Clubs, Literature Circles, or Discussion Groups

From the research on literature discussion groups and book clubs, it becomes clear that rich, cohesive, and insightful book conversations do not simply happen. They take good books (as noted above), and they require a great deal of "practice."

Modeling Book Talk

The best introduction to (and practice for) book conversations seems to occur when good books are read aloud in classrooms daily and teachers and students take time to mull over their reactions. Read-aloud time, then, is not finished with the last page of the day's chapter. That is when the second important phase of read-aloud begins: the talk-about. Whole group discussion, besides providing an open forum for students, permits teachers to model the stance of the questioning, responsive learner. More than one expert recommends that the teachers be thoroughly familiar with the text, open to its possibilities, sensitive to their own initial reactions to it (given they have read it more than once), and aware of the literary elements that can be pointed out or reinforced (such as mood, structure, symbol, theme, extended metaphor). Teachers, according to Peterson and Eeds (1990), float "literary balloons," only some of which are grabbed onto.

Book Selection and Fit

We (and others) have found important variables in the successful organization for book talk: (1) Students need to be given some choice or voice in the selection of the books to be discussed, and (2) the book must be within reach of their reading level. Besides adjusting the levels of books, we have used such "scaffolds" for struggling readers as audiotapes, paired reading, and printed discussion prompts.

Time Management and Class Organization

There is no one plan for organizing for book discussion groups. Smith (1990), for example, gives her fifth- and sixth-grade students approximately five days to read a chapter book such as *Dicey's Song* (Voigt, 1982). The literature group (about six students) meets with her three days the following week (for about 20 minutes each day) to discuss the selection. During the discussion sessions with one group, others are reading in preparation for their discussions (Eeds, Edelsky, Smith, Penka, & Love, n.d.). During the first session, students come together to freely share responses—their thoughts and feelings about the text. In this session, students are likely to skip from one topic to another, with topics not necessarily being explored in any depth. The session ends with students brainstorming topics they think might be interesting to explore in greater depth at subsequent meetings. The group then decides on one or two topics to talk about during the next sessions. With the assignments clarified (and sometimes expanded) by Karen, they delve into the book again in preparation for their discussions, gathering the evidence that supports their thinking. Over time, the discussion grows more connected, focused, and analytic. Karen models how literate readers make connections and offers the language of literature study embedded at relevant points. The third session ends with an evaluation of the discussion and each member's contributions to it.

Other teachers find a safe beginning for literature discussion by initially giving the whole class a copy of the same book and conducting a "giant-sized" book club so that procedures become clear. Still others use the same title, but they organize students into small, concurrent student-led groups (rather than a large teacher-led one). We have worked with three related books being discussed simultaneously in the same classroom (after students have become accustomed to expectations and procedures for book club-bers). Almasi (1995), in her comparison of teacher-led and student-led discussions, noted that students in peer-led groups tended to offer responses that were more elaborate and complex than student-responses in teacher-led discussions. Further, she found that the students explored issues that seemed important to them.

Roles of the Students

Using a nomenclature derived by our colleague, Jim Hoffman, we assigned rotating roles to students new to managing themselves in book clubs. The roles and their responsibilities are printed and passed out to the students each day. A discussion leader checks with each member to make certain the agreed-upon chapters have been read and that each discussant has brought a log to the group with at least one idea for talk. The orator sets the mood for the discussion by reading aloud from a selected passage and then telling why that passage is significant to him or her. The scribe keeps track of the group's important ideas, wonderings, or other notes on language charts. Members of the group are responsible for listening, contributing, and helping to evaluate the effectiveness of each session.

Roles of the Teacher

When teachers choose to provide the direction for book club, they have options. One is to be a guide on the side, to intervene when the talk seriously falters; another is to serve actively as participant, curator, guide, facilitator, interpreter, or literary critic. Rules of participation for teacher are the same as for the rest of the group: Receive each member's contributions, and, without a predetermined destination, entertain the possibilities the text offers.

Chambers (1996), in the book *Tell Me,* offers three easy-to-remember invitations to talk. Labeled as the "three sharings," the invitations are both open-ended and are likely to result in original and unpredictable insights. Students are invited to (1) share

TABLE 20.2 One Plan for Book Talk: The Three "Sharings"

The Sharing of Enthusiasms (enthusiasm for what was noticed in the story)	What did you notice? What parts did you like?
The Sharing of Puzzles (the speculation about meanings, wonderings)	What parts puzzled you?
The Sharing of Connections (the finding of patterns and connections that reflect the core of the book)	Did you notice any patterns? Are you reminded of any other books (or characters) that are similar to this one?

Source: Adapted from *Tell me: Children, reading, and talk,* by Aidan Chambers.

or recall what they most want to talk about, what they noticed or observed in the text; (2) tell what they are puzzled about or uncertain of in the story—their wonderings about the text; and (3) recall what (in the book) they connected with and what they were reminded of, either in their own experiences or in the experiences of other characters and books. Chambers' three invitations, presented in Table 20.2, have given us (and students) a simple, but useful, framework for launching book talk and keeping it afloat.

Good Book Talk Is for Everyone

In classrooms in which children's first language is not English, children become collaborative language learners and meaning makers through book conversations (Battle, 1995; Samway & Whang, 1995; Smith, 1990). In mainstream settings, children who have been referred for special education participate successfully in literature discussion (Goatley, Brock, & Raphael, 1995). Although Wollman-Bonilla (1994) found that struggling readers were so focused on text comprehension that they were hesitant to offer their own ideas for conversation, we have observed many struggling readers succeed in literary conversations when they are matched with appropriately leveled text, when expectations for interpretive thinking are clearly communicated and modeled, and when supported by audiotapes or read-aloud partners. In short, our own experiences with book talk have shown us that book talk works with all children. Christopher, for example, who made the insightful metaphor about Sam Houston, was a child who had been labeled "emotionally disturbed," who spent only a portion of his day in the regular classroom, much of that under his desk.

The books and articles on book talk that crowd our shelves have taught us a great deal. The teachers who provide books and time for thoughtful reading and discussion have taught us, too. Most of all, students have shown us that they are capable of powerful ideas about texts. Their ideas are made more powerful in the presence of others—supportive groups of idea sharers who posit, test, reflect, and often modify their thinking. When good books are made available to students, when the classroom organization provides for groups of book talkers, when literate models show how reflection and support look and sound, there is good reading, good talk, and good learning.

Good book talk is within hearing distance.

REFERENCES

Almasi, J. (1995). The nature of fourth graders' socio-cognitive conflicts in peer-led and teacher-led discussions of literature. *Reading Research Quarterly, 30,* 314–351.

Bakhtin, M.M. (1986). *Speech genres and other late essays.* Austin: University of Texas Press.

Battle, J. (1995). Collaborative story talk in a bilingual kindergarten. In N.L. Roser & M.G. Martinez (Eds.), *Book talk and beyond: Children and teach-* *ers respond to literature* (pp. 157–167). Newark, DE: International Reading Association.

Chambers, A. (1996). *Tell me: Children, reading, and talk.* York, ME: Stenhouse.

Eeds, M., Edelsky, C., Smith, K., Penka, C., & Love, B. (n.d.). *Literature study: Karen Smith's classroom.* Tempe: Center for Establishing Dialogue in Teaching and Learning, Inc., Arizona State University.

Eeds, M., & Peterson, R. (1991). Teacher as curator:

Learning to talk about books. *The Reading Teacher, 45,* 118–126.

Eeds, M., & Wells, D. (1989). Grand conversations: An exploration of meaning construction in literature study groups. *Research in the Teaching of English, 23*(1) 4–29.

Farrell, E.J., & Squire, J.R. (Eds.). (1990). *Transactions with literature: A fifty-year perspective.* Urbana, IL: National Council of Teachers of English.

Goatley, V.J., Brock, C., & Raphael, T.E. (1995). Diverse learners participating in regular education book clubs. *Reading Research Quarterly, 30*(3), 352–380.

Hepler, S. (1991). Talking our way to literacy in the classroom community. *The New Advocate, 4,* 179–190.

Huck, C.S., Hepler, S.,Hickman, J., & Kiefer, B.Z. (1997). *Children's literature in the elementary school.* Madison, WI: Brown and Benchmark.

Iser, W. (1978). *The act of reading: A theory of aesthetic response.* Baltimore, MD: Johns Hopkins University Press.

Martinez, M., & Roser, N.L. (1995). The books make a difference in story talk. In N.L. Roser & M.G. Martinez (Eds.), *Book talk and beyond: Children and teachers respond to literature* (pp. 32–41). Newark, DE: International Reading Association.

McMahon, S.I., & Raphael, T.E. (1997). *The book club connection: Literacy learning and classroom talk.* New York: Teachers College Press.

O'Flahavan, J.F., Stein, C., Wiencek, J., & Marks, T. (1992, December). *Interpretive development in peer discussion about literature: An exploration of the teacher's role.* Paper presented at the 42nd annual meeting of the National Reading Conference, San Antonio, TX.

Paratore, J.R., & McCormack, R.L. (Eds.). (1997). *Peer talk in the classroom: Learning from research.* Newark, DE: International Reading Association.

Pearson, P.D. (1985). *The comprehension revolution: A twenty-year history of progress and practice related to reading comprehension.* Reading Education Report No. 57. Urbana-Champaign, IL: Center for the Study of Reading.

Peterson, R., & Eeds, M.A. (1990). *Grand conversations: Literature groups in action.* New York: Scholastic.

Rosenblatt, L.M. (1938/1976). *Literature as exploration.* New York: Modern Language Association.

Samway, K.D., & Whang, G. (Eds.). (1995). *Literature study circles in a multicultural classroom.* York, ME: Stenhouse.

Short, K.G., & Kauffman, G. (1995). So what do *I* do?: The role of the teacher in literature circles. In N.L. Roser & M.G. Martinez (Eds.), *Book talk and beyond: Children and teachers respond to literature* (pp. 140–149). Newark, DE: International Reading Association.

Smith, K. (1990). Entertaining a text: A reciprocal process. In K.G. Short and K.M. Pierce (Eds.), *Talking about books: Creating literate communities* (pp. 17–31). Portsmouth, NH: Heinemann.

Vygotsky, L.S. (1978). *Mind in society: The development of higher mental psychological processes.* Cambridge, MA: MIT Press.

Wollman-Bonilla, J.E. (1994). Why don't they "just speak"? Attempting literature discussion with more and less able readers. *Research in the Teaching of English, 28,* 231–258.

CHILDREN'S BOOKS CITED

Avi. (1991). *Nothing but the truth.* New York: Orchard.

Babbitt, Natalie. (1985). *Tuck everlasting.* New York: Farrar, Straus and Giroux.

Byars, Betsy. (1977). *The pinballs.* New York: Harper Trophy.

Cormier, Robert. *Other bells for us to ring.* (1990) New York: Dell Yearling

Fenner, Carol. (1995). *Yolanda's genius.* New York: Aladdin.

Fine, Anne. (1992). *Flour babies.* New York: Puffin.

Fitzhugh, Louise (1964). *Harriet the spy.* New York: Harper and Row.

Fritz, Jean. (1986). *Make way for Sam Houston.* New York: G. P. Putnam's.

Lowry, Lois. (1993). *The giver.* Boston: Houghton Mifflin.

Naylor, Phyllis. (1991). *Shiloh.* New York: Atheneum.

Paterson, Katherine. (1978). *The great Gilly Hopkins.* New York: Harper Trophy.

Paterson, Katherine. (1994). *Flip-flop girl.* New York: Lodestar.

Spinelli, Jerry. (1990). *Maniac Mcgee.* Boston: Little, Brown.

Staples, Suzanne Fisher. (1989). *Shabanu: Daughter of the wind.* New York: Knopf.

Taylor, Mildred D. (1976). *Roll of thunder, hear my cry.* New York: Bantam.

Voigt, Cynthia. (1982). *Dicey's song.* New York: Fawcett Juniper.

Winthrop, Elizabeth. (1985). *The castle in the attic.* New York: Bantam-Skylark.

21 Technological Literacy in the Intermediate and Middle Grades

ROBERT J. RICKELMAN
University of North Carolina at Charlotte

ROBERT M. CAPLAN
Tapp Middle School, Powder Springs, Georgia

There are several ways to define technological literacy. Leu (in press) suggested three ways of examining the relationships between the two terms. First, one can examine the effects that technology has on literacy measures (Reinking, in press). In this paradigm, researchers could examine the effects that such activities as e-mail or instructional software have on literacy. A second way of considering technological literacy is to look at the ways that literacy and technology interact with each other, shaping each other over time (Leu et al., in press). HyperCard-based books are a good example of this relationship. At first, books were serially translated to the Hypertext format. As these became more popular, stories began to include branching options and random links. A third, perhaps more intriguing, way of looking at technological literacy is that proposed by Leu (in press), which he calls a deictic relationship; "deictic" comes from *deixis,* a term used by linguists to describe special words whose meanings quickly change. This relationship suggests that "literacy appears to be increasingly deictic: its meaning regularly redefined, not by time or space, but by new technologies and the continuously changing envisionments they initiate for information and communications." This relationship suggests that as technology rapidly develops over short periods of time, the nature of literacy similarly evolves, often faster than its implications for teaching and learning can be adequately measured and reported. This third view suggests that by the time research is collected, written, revised, and published, it could already be outdated as newer technologies further shape the relationship. If this is true, then any published report on research related to technology and literacy might be helpful when looking at past practices, but might not be as helpful in reflecting present practices or for defining future goals.

With this caveat in mind, we begin this chapter by giving a brief report of some of the past theory and research related to technological literacy in the intermediate and middle school setting and conclude by offering several practical suggestions related to ways of thinking about technology in new ways. These suggestions allow the practitioner to take advantage of the deictic relationship between literacy and technology, encouraging teachers to create novel uses for technology that can quickly evolve as the available technology changes in the school classroom.

Background and Research

The 1990s saw the introduction of computers into most intermediate and middle schools. Initially, there was much excitement among teachers and students about how these machines would make teaching easier and more motivating. Soon, however, these machines were wheeled into corners of the classroom as teachers reverted back to more traditional teaching and learning practices. Initial enthusiasm was tempered by the lack of staff development and money to purchase software (Whitaker, 1996). Many were disappointed that the computers did not make teaching easier and, in many cases, made it more confusing and difficult. They looked to the hardware and software to do "something" right out of the box, but when they turned on the equipment, it just sat there. They often struggled with related logistical problems such as, Where will the computer be placed? How should it be used by students? How can I ensure that all students will have access? How do I use one computer with 30 students? How can I control the use of several thousand dollars worth of equipment by untrained 8- and 12-year-olds? How can I teach students to use computer technology when they know more about it than I do? Indeed, in a survey of middle school students, teachers, and administrators conducted by Hollingsworth and Eastman (1997), it was found that students often had more access to a greater variety of technology at home than at school. In addition, students and teachers were using technology in their homes for very different purposes. For instance, students generally used computers to play games, for word processing, and to explore CD-ROM media. Teachers, on the other hand, mainly used computers in their homes for word processing, for e-mail, and for database/spreadsheet uses. When these students and teachers were asked what types of skills they would like to learn most, however, they both put the Internet as their top priority.

Hollingsworth and Eastman's (1997) research implies that when teachers think about technology applications in their classrooms, they have pictures in their heads of what they have traditionally used for years, mainly television and VCRs. A new paradigm, however, a new way of thinking about technological literacy in which unfamiliar technologies must take the place of more familiar, traditional practices is necessary. They concluded, "To successfully integrate computer technologies into classrooms, teachers need to see others beyond the school setting use technologies, and they need to bring what they are familiar with at home to the classroom. They need new models" (p. 51).

Although there has been an abundance of research related to technological literacy in schools (Leu, in press; Reinking & Bridwell-Bowles, 1991), research investigating the benefits of computers specifically at the intermediate and middle schools is sparse. In one study, Seever (1992) investigated the achievement levels of students who were involved in a computer-based magnet school program at a middle school in Kansas City, comparing these students with a matched group who did not use computers. She found mixed results, although she did note a positive trend for improvement for the computer-based group.

Boser and Gallo (1995) discussed the importance of considering learning characteristics of middle school students in planning technology instruction, just as it is considered in other aspects of the curriculum. They suggested ways that hands-on thematic approaches to technology instruction, including student collaborations, could be implemented in the classroom setting.

Typically, published material related to technology at the intermediate and middle school levels falls into two categories. First, some authors discuss how a technology program was implemented at a particular school or school district, with some general suggestions for readers who are in similar settings. For example, Van Dam (1994) discussed how a middle school in Michigan renovated its building to take advantage of technological innovations. The roles that teachers and administrators took is clearly outlined, and a list of 10 potential mistakes similar schools should avoid is included. Even more popular are articles that explore technology issues in general. Buchanan (1997) discussed the social issues related to technology in the classroom, including the cultural, ethical, and professional responsibilities of schools who have integrated technology into the curriculum on a regular basis.

Although there has been a lot written about the uses of technology in the schools, even considering the dearth of data-based research that has been conducted specifically at this level, most practitioners seem to be more interested in practical suggestions for using technology in their day-to-day instruction. The remainder of this chapter explores what several teachers are doing to promote technological literacy with their students to create the new models expressed by Hollingsworth and Eastman (1997) in some very creative ways. Included will be a deitic model of teaching developed by Caplan (1998) in a middle school setting in Georgia in which computers can be used in a literacy program in new ways without relying on extensive staff development or expensive software.

Future Scenario

Imagine a sixth-grade classroom in the year 2010. What looks familiar about this classroom? What looks different? Considering that classrooms have changed little in the past 100 years (Cuban, 1986), will classrooms in the future look at all different from the current settings?

One possible scenario is that there will be little change. Classrooms will be set up much as they were in 1890s, with desks in rows and the teacher as the focus of instruction. Instruction will be delivered mostly through lecture and whole-class discussion. Students will learn about the world mainly from the textbook. The chalkboard will be used on a daily basis, "newer" technologies such as overhead projectors, televisions, and video cassette recorders will be used on occasion, and pull-down charts and maps will be used weekly. Homework assignments will be given daily and will consist of worksheets and papers written with pencil and pen at the kitchen table. Research assignments will heavily involve the encyclopedia as a reference source, with numerous hours spent in the library searching through the card catalog and identifying books and magazines from which to pull information.

Another, very different, scenario could take place in a similar classroom, but the methods and materials used to learn might be vastly different. This classroom will be made up of several learning centers, with no identifiable focus for information delivery. Tables will be placed around the room. The teacher will still provide guidance and facilitate student learning, but the methods will be vastly different. Some students may be in a corner of the room, learning about whales from a multimedia, interactive CD-ROM program. Other students will be linked to the Internet, where in small groups they will search web sites for information and use e-mail to link to people in other countries. Some students may leave the classroom to attend a teleconference with students from other continents and compare and contrast where they live as they learn about diverse world customs. Homework assignments are downloaded into students' portable computers for them to take home, or homework can be accessed from home via the Internet. Students who are absent or who are on vacation can have easy access to work completed throughout the day as well as homework assignments that they missed. They can submit assignments via e-mail or the Internet. The world, via computer links, will be the standard reference. More traditional students might use key word searches to gather relevant information, and issues such as web site censorship and the veracity of Internet information will be discussed in school and home.

Which scenario is the most likely? The answer depends largely on what type of setting we create. Many classrooms now have computer access. Most schools have, at the very least, a computer lab. Many more schools have, or will soon have, dedicated Internet links, either from a lab, the media center, or individual classrooms. Many questions need to be studied, and the answers to these questions will lead us toward one of the scenarios described above or, perhaps, to a unique combination of the two. How comfortable is the teacher in allowing students to work independently? How comfortable are students when working in a self-directed setting? What school policies influence computer use? How do parents feel about Internet access in a "semisupervised" setting? These are all important questions that must be answered, and the answers will determine which scenario the classrooms embrace.

To help decide which type of scenario a school might support, the remainder of this chapter introduces ways in which technology *could* influence the intermediate and middle school classroom setting. Students, teachers, and parents must consider the possibilities and create a comfortable environment in which students will be motivated to learn.

Internet Learning

Recent advances allowing for easy and relatively inexpensive Internet access, along with the resulting implications for classroom use, are both exciting and daunting. Although the Internet offers exciting possibilities, it also has the potential for abuse. As chat room horror stories and pornographic access proliferate, many parents and school administrators are worried about allowing students unlimited access to the Internet, and most school computers have software installed to limit Internet browsing to selected sites. Students who try to access pornographic sites, for example, will be told that access to that web page is restricted. Still, savvy intermediate and middle school students can often find ways to circumvent these restrictions. Parents at many of these schools are asked to sign a waiver to allow their children to have Internet access from school, whereas other parents are reluctant to allow computers with modems in their homes. Although the technology itself is neutral in terms of how it accesses information, human controls are necessary to avoid abuse of the system.

Still, the Internet offers many exciting possibilities for accessing vast amounts of information. Leu and Leu (1999) discussed ways that this medium can be used in a classroom setting. As more schools become "wired," the Internet may soon be the preferred method of quickly sharing information among schools, teachers, parents, and students.

Before students are allowed access to the Internet in a school setting, they must become familiar with methods of locating information in the millions of accessible pages. A new study skill is necessary: the key word search. In the past, students have studied alphabetical order and made decisions about which encyclopedia book to open to find a topic by looking at the beginning and ending guide words printed on the spine. Today, a different type of key word search, both on the Internet and for library online catalogs, is a necessary skill.

A key word search involves identifying a word or number of words to be used as the subject for a search. For instance, let us say that a student is interested in locating information about the economy of Brazil. Using one of the search engines from Figure 21.1, the student can type in the words "South America." The search engine returns with a page that states that 127,945 entries have been found. Obviously, it would be impractical to look at all the pages, because the targeted information may only be found on a few of them. The obvious strategy would be to narrow the search to identify a more manageable number of relevant sites. Most search engines allow only a search of the identified pages by listing additional keywords to narrow the number of available choices to explore further. The student types in the keyword "Brazil." The search engine returns 32,991 sites, still too many to manage, but at least fewer than the original search. The student types in "economy", and the engine returns a list of 1,825 sites. The search is getting better, but there are still too many sites. These sites could include any company that does business in Brazil, which the student is not really interested in finding. By further narrowing a search, typing in the key words "national+economy," which means only those sites that include both the terms national and economy (rather

FIGURE 21.1   Internet Search Engine Addresses

http://digital.altavista.com	**http://www.infoseek.com**
http://www.excite.com	**http://www.lycos.com**
http://www.hotbot.com	**http://www.yahoo.com**

than either word), the student locates 105 sites. This number is still high, but at this point, visiting some of the sites would make sense. Most search engine sites order the list of sites from highest to least probablity that this is what you are searching for, and they also give either a brief summary of the site or else show the first few lines of text on the site to allow the searcher to make decisions about where to further investigate.

One issue related to using the Internet for research purposes is the veracity of the information found on the sites. Many students who use the Internet as a research reference are finding information that lacks serious credibility. Yet they feel that, because it was located on the Internet, it contains truthful information. The problem here is that anyone, regardless of motivation, can put text on a web site. A student, for instance, can locate a web site that "proves" that the Holocaust was a hoax. If students do not question the validity of information found on the web, they can come up with research that actually disputes what most people would accept as mainstream truth. Some professional organizations, such as the American Library Association, are concerned about this issue. Their web site (www.ala.org) contains information about how to evaluate the accuracy of information found on a web site.

For students to use the Internet effectively, either in the classroom or at home, they must be explicitly taught these two skills: key word searches and assessing the accuracy of information found on the web. The teacher might want to use a "gradual release" model for working on these skills. First, the teacher can model several key

FIGURE 21.2   Web Sites That Offer Good Starting Points for Teachers

---

http://curry.edschool.virginia.edu/go/clic/   Content Literacy Consortium offers links to many professional organizations, exemplar lessons, and so forth.

http://www.gsn.org   Global Schoolhouse Network provides information about collaborative learning projects for teachers and students around the world.

http://web66.coled.umn.edu/schools.html   Site of Web66, an international registry of schools that have Internet sites.

http://www.nationalgeographic.com   National Geographic site allows teacher, students, and parents to search a huge information database, including lesson plans.

http://www.geocities.com/Athens/8854/   Leber's K–6 Site contains numerous links to schools, lesson plans, and many other interesting sites.

http://www.lightspan.com   Lightspan offers teachers lesson plans linked to curriculum standards for selected states, as well as exemplary lesson plans and instructional programs across a wide variety of subject areas and grade levels.

http://www. readingonline.org   Online journal of the International Reading Association, updated frequently, contains research, practical articles (with the opportunity to dialog with the authors), and discussion groups related to literacy.

word searches, using the setup described above to walk students through a search by using a topic of interest to the class. The next step is for several student volunteers to complete a key word search, with the teacher talking them through the process. Finally, students can try to search independently, with the teacher available as a troubleshooter. A discussion about the accuracy of web sites can follow a similar format, with the class visiting both accurate and inaccurate sites, comparing the two, and then discussing methods for making decisions about whether to use information found on the web or not. Several good starting points for teachers to consider are shown in Figure 21.2.

New Models of Technological Literacy

One way several teachers are using computers to augment literacy instruction is through the use of the program HyperCard to write cumulative tales (Gillespie, Hemming, & Phang, 1995) with seventh-grade students. This activity began as a collaborative effort between the language arts teacher, who had the content expertise but lacked the technological knowledge, and the computer teacher who knew about computers but had little knowledge about how to teach poetry. HyperCard allows the teacher and students to create individual pages called cards that can be linked together in different ways. In this case, the students first studied cumulative tales, stories with repeated elements. A well-known example of this type of story is *The Gingerbread Boy*. After studying a number of these stories, students wrote their own stories using the cumulative tale framework. After their stories were revised and edited, they were introduced to HyperCard, and the students transferred their stories onto the cards that were then linked. Clip art was incorporated into the stories by students. After the stories were completed, the students invited the kindergarten students to "read" the stories from the computer monitor, and some students printed out their "books" for the younger students to take back to their classroom. Sharing the work in this way was very rewarding to the seventh-grade students, and the kindergarten children's enthusiasm was obvious.

One potential obstacle to this type of collaboration between content teachers and computer teachers involves planning time. Because teachers are often on different schedules, it can be hard to work together except during off-school hours. To be successful, teachers need to make a commitment to meet and work together. If initial efforts are successful, other teachers might become interested in pursuing their own collaborations.

One traditional problem with using computers in the typical classroom setting has been that only several students can use the computer at a time. Teachers have found that two to three students working at each computer is the maximum number that can be accommodated. Sign-up sheets and student checklists are common methods used to ensure that each student receives access to some computer time. A larger question remains, however: How can a teacher effectively use a computer for class instruction when only several students can be actively involved simultaneously?

One of the best ways to establish the use of computers in the intermediate and middle school setting is to go "out of the box." This term means that teachers need to think beyond the computer (the box) and software rather than be at its mercy. Once you begin to think out of the box, creative solutions to common stumbling blocks can begin to take shape. Someone who has taken this approach is Bob Caplan, a teacher at Tapp Middle School and the Microsoft Teacher of the Year for the state of Georgia in both 1997 and 1998. Bob was faced with the problem of having one computer and 30 students, with limited available software. Rather than wait for someone to show him how to use the equipment or for research reports to guide a course of action, he sought to create a new model for his students.

He uses a single computer with two 27-inch high-resolution monitors on portable carts so that all students can see the screen. The computer is wired into the Internet, which allows him to demonstrate web surfing to students as a group. He has also developed several very creative ways to use common software programs to enhance literacy and technology learning for his students.

One of his ideas is what he calls Karaoke Poetry, which is a component of a set of strategies he terms Whole Group Theater™ (copyright © 1999, all rights reserved, Robert M. Caplan). This lesson combines poetry appreciation with a multimedia format for his sixth- through eighth-grade students. This lesson uses the *New Kid on the Block* CD developed by Jack Prelutsky that contains 17 poems that yield over eight hours of classroom instruction. Two to three of these poems can be studied in a typical 50-minute class period. These poems contain text "hot spots," words that can be clicked on to produce an animated sequence. With the sound turned off, students begin the lesson by chorally chanting each page of a given poem out loud, while the yellow highlighted text moves across the television screens. After each karaoke segment, the class locates and discusses all text-animated hot spots for each page of poetry. They discuss the part of speech related to each hot spot as well as why the author decided to make certain words link to hot spots and not others. For example, it would be easy to link an action verb or noun to an animation, but difficult to do so for an article or conjunction. Students are actively involved during this process by taking on different roles. A student scribe, for instance, is assigned the task of tallying the parts of speech used in the hot spots for each page of poetry studied. Guest clickers are invited from the group to click on words selected by the class during the reading to see if it leads to a hot spot. A new guest clicker is chosen for each page of text. At the end of a lesson, all students are asked to write in their journals, discussing the poems and describing their favorite hotspots.

Another idea developed by watching a single student work through a round of the popular software program, *Where in the U.S.A. Is Carmen Sandiego?* As the student worked on tracking down a crook by traveling to different locations, the teacher did a task analysis of the interactions between software and student. By watching one student, a plan was developed to incorporate a whole-class lesson, with each student assigned a specific task during the pursuit of a crook. A 10-student competitive scribe group would be needed to bid against each other concerning the location of the geographic jumps. A correct guess on the first jump would net each student five points. Ten points would be rewarded for a correct second jump, and so on. In addition, a 10-student point scribe group was used to keep track of the score and help decide the winner of each round. A 5-student detective scribe group helped gather evidence to secure a search warrant for the criminal. A fourth group, the research scribes, used the almanac supplied with the software to judge the correctness of the contestants'

FIGURE 21.3   Carmen Sandiego Task Analysis

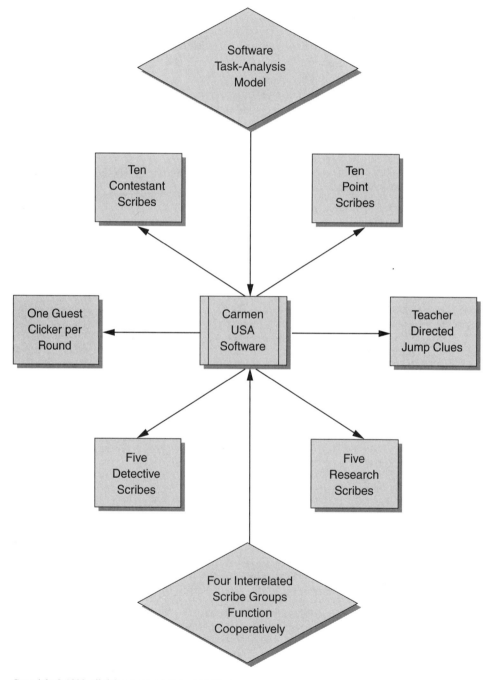

Copyright © 1999, all rights reserved, Robert M. Caplan

destination guesses. Thus, through a simple task analysis, 30 students were involved in reading, writing, and technology activities for an entire class period. Motivation was high as each student completed their "work." Compare this situation with whole-class demonstrations, where most students sit and watch the few students who run the program; the benefits of this approach should be obvious.

In effect, a cooperative learning scheme can be imposed for many different pieces of software to facilitate whole-group interaction as well as instructional goals. Teachers must be willing to go outside the box to view and appreciate the subtleties of this type of whole-group instructional design. Those who expect answers to come from boxes filled with RAM chips and microprocessors, from packaged programs that only include directions for general use in a nonacademic setting, will be sorely disappointed, and the computer will be relegated to the corner of the classroom to collect dust. Teachers who feel empowered to control this technology, on the other hand, can look forward to motivated, involved students who have fun while they are learning. All it takes is the new model, a new way of thinking about instructional technology.

How did Bob come up with these creative, innovative ideas? The solution is actually quite simple. He used a task analysis to watch one student work through a computer program that was available in his classroom. By watching the different activities the student accomplished, he was able to break down the successful navigation of the program into different tasks. Figure 21.3 represents his task analysis for the *Where in the U.S.A. Is Carmen Sandiego?* activity mentioned above.

Through the use of task analysis, by watching students interact with technology individually and in small groups, teachers can take this model and create whole-group learning environments that promote active learning and cooperative learning. Not only is student motivation enhanced, but teacher satisfaction is also promoted. Teachers must feel free to observe, test, and fine-tune lessons based on successes and failures. They must also feel free to share their ideas with others in the hope that a dynamic learning environment can be promoted on a schoolwide level. The key is not to wait for an "expert" for help, because each teacher is empowered to create his or her own technological learning sites. After all, no one knows the students better than the teacher, and only the teacher has the ability to observe firsthand how his or her students learn.

The future of technological literacy holds a lot of promise for teachers and students who are willing to take learning "out of the box," to take risks, and to become their own experts. Only in the hands of these people, however, will a dynamic 2010 be possible.

REFERENCES

Boser, R.A., & Gallo, D. (1995). Pyramids to space stations: Interdisciplinary connections through technology education. *Middle School Journal, 26*(3), 41–46.

Buchanan, E.A. (1997). The social microcosm of the classroom. *T.H.E. Journal, 24*(10), 72–73.

Caplan, R.M. (1998, March). *Technology integration through software task-analysis.* Paper presented at the meeting of the School Technology Exposition, New York.

Cuban, L. (1986). *Teachers and machines: The classroom use of technology since 1920.* New York: Teachers College Press.

Galdone, P. (1975). *The gingerbread boy.* New York: Seabury Press.

Gillespie, J., Hemming, L., & Phang, R. (1995). Cumulative tales: A collaborative computer activity. *Middle School Journal, 26*(3), 26–30.

Hollingsworth, H.L., & Eastman, S.T. (1997). Homes more high tech than schools? *Educational Technology, 37*(6), 46–51.

Leu, D.J. (in press). Continuously changing technologies and envisionings for literacy: Deictic consequences for literacy education in an information age. In R. Barr, M.L. Kamil, P. Mosenthal, and P.D. Pearson (Eds.), *Handbook of reading research* (Vol. III). White Plains, NY: Longman.

Leu, D.J., Hillinger, M., Loseby, P.H., Balcom, M., Dinkin, J., Eckels, M., Johnson, J., Mathews, K., & Raegler, R. (in press). Grounding the design of new technologies for literacy and learning in teachers' instructional needs. In D. Reinking, M. McKenna, L.D. Labbo, & R. Kieffer (Eds.), *Handbook of literacy and technology: Transformations in a post-typographic world.* Mahwah, NJ: Erlbaum.

Leu, D.J., & Leu, D.D. (1999). *Teaching with the Internet: Lessons from the classroom* (2nd ed.). Norwood, MA: Christopher-Gordon.

Reinking, D. (in press). Synthesizing technological transformations of literacy in a post-typographic world. In D. Reinking, M. McKenna, L.D. Labbo, & R. Kieffer (Eds.), *Handbook of literacy and technology: Transformations in a post-typographic world.* Mahwah, NJ: Erlbaum.

Reinking, D., & Bridwell-Bowles, L. (1991). Computers in reading and writing. In R. Barr, M.L. Kamil, P.B. Mosenthal, & P.D. Pearson (Eds.), *Handbook of reading research* (Vol. II, pp. 310–340). New York: Longman.

Seever, M. (1992). *Achievement and enrollment evaluation of the Central Computers Unlimited Magnet Middle School 1990–1991.* Kansas City, MO: Kansas City Public Schools. (ERIC Document Reproduction Service No. ED 348 962)

Van Dam, J.M. (1994). Redesigning schools for the 21st-century technologies: A middle school with the power to improve. *Technology and Learning, 14*(4), 54–61.

Whitaker, T. (1996). Linking technology with the middle school. *Middle School Journal, 27*(7), 8–14.

22 Visual Literacy

Some Important Considerations for Tomorrow's Classrooms

DIANE LAPP

San Diego State University

JAMES FLOOD

San Diego State University

WENDY RANCK-BUHR

San Diego (California) Unified School District

You might be wondering, What is visual literacy? and Why do you need to teach it? Both of these questions certainly need to be addressed before educators can begin to consider how to teach visual literacy. Before we begin to answer these questions, let us look at the visual images that bombard even the very youngest students—preschoolers.

"EXTREME, EXTREME, EXTREME Action Animals!" blares the television commercial.

"Daddy what are they trying to sell us?" asks three-year-old Garrett as he and his Dad view the commercial break in the middle of their favorite cartoon.

"Oh, oh, I know. It is an animal like on my computer game, *Putt-Putt Saves the Zoo.*"

"You're right!" replies Garrett's father as the next commercial, an ad for the latest Disney film, begins playing on the television.

"Daddy look, look! I want to see that movie. C'mon, let's go check out Disney.com. It'll be on there. We can see little movies about that show."

Garrett's father agrees, and the two of them head off to the computer to locate Disney.com on the Internet and begin an entirely new exploration of visual images.

This example illustrates that the development of visual literacy begins at a very young age. By the time the preschooler in this example reaches the middle school level, he will have been exposed to a wide range of visual images delivered to him via print, video, and telecommunications. Realizing this, the educators may need to begin asking how the educational community can help students with a variety of experiences become critical consumers of visual information.

In this chapter, we explore this issue as we discuss the concept of visual literacy and its relative importance to a complete literacy education for *all* students.

What Is Visual Literacy?

In 1991, Carl Kaeslte noted that one of the challenges in studying literacy involves defining the term itself. For example, as recently as 150 years ago, literacy was generally defined (or at least measured) by a person's ability to sign his or her name. Over time, the concept of literacy broadened to include the ability to read longer and more complex tests, to ascertain fact and opinion, and to write persuasive prose. Recent movements in literacy education have extended the definition—defining literacy not only as the ability to read and write at a "functional" level, but also as the ability to speak and listen—to both receive and successfully communicate oral as well as printed messages. Even more recently, educators have suggested that literacy should again be broadened to encompass competence in all the "communicative arts," including the visual arts of drama, art, film, video, television, and other technological innovations.

The call for an expanded definition of literacy derives, in part, from the proliferation of communicative technologies in our society (Alton-Lee, Huthall, & Patrick, 1993; Kubey & Csikszentmihalyi, 1990). It also results from changes in educational philosophy that reflect more constructivists notions. Speaking of links between technological advances and implementation of educational philosophy, Sultan and Jones (1996) explained that, historically, the typical school environment failed to adequately address individual differences among learners. Instruction was delivered primarily through teacher-led lecture. With the advent of filmstrips, overhead projectors, and videos, educators could more ably address issues of learning style and motivation. Sultan and Jones (1996) suggest that now, just as in the past, increased "information diversity—a variety of textual, graphical, audio, video, photographic or animated information from multimedia can help educators further vary their instructional approaches and heighten learned motivation" (p. 96).

Why Teach Visual Literacy?

Although communication technology has become commonplace in U.S. homes, it is less widespread in school. Today, an average home in the United States houses two televisions, six radios, and three telephones (Carey, 1997). Many homes also have at least one personal computer. The ability to operate and communicate with these devices is not only normal, but an expected part of daily life for many Americans. In contrast to the typical American home, the average classroom may have no television, no telephone, no radio, and a limited number of computers (if any). Even when computer technology does exist in classrooms, the issue of access is critical. For example, telephones in classrooms are often intended solely for teacher use, with students rarely using school telephones for academic studies or personal needs. The same is likely true of other technological equipment. One wonders how many classroom students select and load programs on class computers, "surf the net" according to their interest, flip through the educational television channels to preview programs, and so forth.

Beyond the obvious issue of cost, one reason for the dearth of visual media use in classrooms may relate to teacher training and expertise. As Fleming-McCormick, Nyre, Schwager, and Tushnet (1995) found, even in "promising" schools with sufficient equipment, support staff, and active training programs, teachers found it difficult to gain personal expertise with technology and to decide when and where particular interventions "fit" curriculum goals.

Many teachers completed teacher preparation programs long before technology was part of the curriculum. In addition, most in-service education does not accommodate one acquiring this expertise. Recent graduates, however, may be more comfortable and knowledgeable about the use of and curriculum integration of technology. This challenge for teachers is further exacerbated by the ever-changing nature of hypermedia and the Internet (Baule & Lyons, 1996). In addition, DeJean, Miller, and Olson (1995) discovered that even when teachers do implement a particular intervention, students do not always interpret technology tasks in concert with teacher intentions. In their study of a teacher's use of CD-ROM "Talking Books" in third-grade classrooms, DeJean et al. observed that "computers can take on a role that goes beyond their utility and in a class where cooperation was the norm—characteristics of the CD-ROM books seemed to bring out power struggles and selfish behavior" (p. 1).

A second reason for limited visual media use in classrooms may relate simply to the ins and outs of equipment manipulation and operation. What teacher has not planned to show a video in class, wheeled the video cart down the halls from the storage room, and then confronted the frustration of defective equipment? How about the exasperation teachers in "smart" technology classrooms experience when the computer goes "down" and renders an entire presentation useless? Not surprisingly, given limited preparation or training time and negative experiences with equipment, a teacher may decide that it is simply "easier" to delete visual media from his or her lesson.

Although some educators struggle with day-to-day logistics of media and technology access and manipulation, many educators advocate increased use of mass media "texts" to enhance their own teaching and their children's learning. Like Rood (1996), such teachers assert that

> we are now in the age of the visual image. . . . Students must be able to implement a set of skills in order to interpret the content of these visual images, their social impact, and their ownership. Visual literacy involves three abilities: to visualize internally, to create visual images, and to read visual images (Feinsteid, 1993). Within the scholarly debate about the value of visual literacy is the belief that the acquisition of visual literacy bestows the skill of critical viewing. "Learning about visual conventions . . . gives the viewer a foundation for heightened, conscious appreciation of artistry; second, it is a prerequisite for the ability to see through the manipulative uses and ideological implications of visual images (Messaris, 1994, p. 165). (p. 111)

Thus, in some 3,500 classrooms nationwide, we see teachers using not only text-books and trade books in their literacy instruction but extending their resources to include film, video, and computer support (Semali, 1996). Printed and electronic atlases, thesauruses, encyclopedias, and primary source materials are also predominant in more classrooms than in years past, attesting to the view of many teachers that literacy instruction must extend beyond narrow definitions and practices. These teachers believe that a multisource approach to literacy instruction results in a curriculum filled with opportunities for children to make connections across source, becoming conversant with intertextuality and enhancing their own writing skills as they incorporate ideas from multiple sources in their own oral and written expression (Kinder, 1991). Summarizing the view, Semali (1996) writes:

> Because of the dearth of media literacy awareness in classrooms, it is not surprising to find youngsters who study literacy and literature for 12 years and still graduate naive about the techniques and devices used to capture their attention and imagination, about the cultural codes that reflect and shape their thinking in their electronic literature.... Inasmuch as today's children come to school from homes and communities which provide them with wide exposure to nonprint media, it is crucial that literacy education teachers not only draw upon this background, but recognize the students' knowledge and develop the students' critical thinking about nonprint media. (p. 214)

Given some of the pros and cons of media use, a natural result of the push to include media and technology in instruction is the question of whether or not such additions are useful and necessary to instruction. Another even more penetrating question is whether such materials should be included in instruction, not only as add-ons, but as important sources of inquiry in their own right. Already feeling pressed for time to "cover" curriculum and attend to the "basics," some educators question their ability (and the wisdom) in undertaking further curriculum add-ons. They wonder openly about the morality of much available media and suggest that students already spend enough time watching television and playing video games. For educators with this view, a key role of formal education is to encourage the development of more traditional literacy skills: reading the classics and writing cogent research reports and essays.

In contrast to media supporters and detractors, a third group of educators appears ambivalent about the role of media in the classroom. Citing a lack of definitive study into the advantages and disadvantages of extensive incorporation of media into school curricula, these educators appear willing to maintain the status quo until they are "convinced" of the value of media instruction. Such ambivalence is not without precedent among educators, especially those who have taught long enough to recognize the tendency toward "trend swing" within the educational community. It may find further support among those who have seen some currently available CD-ROM materials and found them to be little more than "talking books" with no provisions for student response (Meskill & Swan, 1995). Some teachers may feel that current concern about visual media is simply another trend, something that will provide interesting conversation for a short time and then be relegated to what they see as a long list of relatively unimportant ideas in education. Unfortunately, an inherent danger in ambivalence and its accompanying "I'll wait until I see it" attitude is the lack of active inquiry. If educators all wait for "someone" to discover what works with media in the classroom, such information may be very slow in coming.

The problem seems clear: Outside our classrooms, students live in a world where they are constantly bombarded with visual media in the form of advertisements for products, behaviors, political candidates, and ways of thinking. Given current trends, it is unlikely that such bombardment will decrease. For example, consider the changes that have occurred in the video gaming industry. In the early 1980s, parents and educators had little concern about the visual images shown in video games. Children were playing video games that required very little computer memory and, therefore, resulted in visual images that consisted primarily of geometric shapes. Parents and educators had little concern about these shapes twisting, turning, and breaking apart. These images are in stark contrast to the visual images in video games that children are exposed to today. Current video games can use over 600 megs of memory (6 billion bits of information; 100 thousand times the amount of memory required for early video games). This expanse of computer memory in the video game industry translates into the power to produce games that include a wide range of realistic characters and actions of which the game player is a participate. The scenarios played out in video games have become more complex and assume a certain level of game player sophistication. In a recent interview with the top six video game producers (*Next Generation,* February 1998) Dave Perry stated, "The games are becoming more twisted and weird than they used to be. . . . There's not much in the way of *Mario* clones, but there's a lot of death and mayhem" (p. 58). Another video game producer, Brett Sperry, added:

> The point is to give people the opportunity to do and see things and be in a world that is perhaps socially unacceptable. That's very tempting. People love socially unacceptable behavior in their games. On one level, it might be morbid to go around shooting people in a game, but on another it's a release—a healthy thing. But, as entertainers and as people who create something that's fun, that will always be a rich and exciting area to explore. You have to decide whether or not you want to be socially responsible or even whether that enters into the arts. For some of us who do it for the arts, it's not a question of whether it's socially responsible. That doesn't really enter into the equation. Maybe as realism becomes more and more attainable, that will become a real concern. But today, as realistic as they are, they still have a sort of cartoon aspect that you can't take too seriously. You do begin to glimpse the future, though, and there will come a time when we do brush up against that, and perhaps it will become a serious concern. (p. 59)

Despite the cartoon nature of the modern video games, the industry has already "brushed up against" issues related to controversial characters and situations, as illustrated in the following example. In a letter to the editor of a popular video game magazine, a game player wrote in response to a controversial character in a game who, according to some game players, is offensive because he is too stereotyped, all the way down to the fact that the character speaks in Ebonics. The player stated, "It is just a videogame! Treat it as such" (*Next Generation,* February 1998, p. 127). The game magazine editor replied, "Saying that it doesn't matter if the character is too stereotyped because it is just a videogame ignores the very real power that all forms of entertainment, videogames included, possess" (p. 127). He added, "Videogames are as much of a popular art form as movies or TV and should be open to the same level of criticism. As for the issue of whether or not the character is in fact offensive, in the end, that decision needs to be made by individuals" (p. 128).

Video games are by no means the only area that educators need to consider. Indeed, with the potential expansion of in-school cable programming, students may encounter increased media exposure in the classroom (as well as at home) through such outlets as the Public Broadcasting System (PBS), Children's Television Workshop (CTW), Lightspan, Discovery, and a host of independent cable programming companies. Questions of what our students do and should know about visual literacy lie at the core of democratic ideals. Just as those who do not read become dependent on the verbal and visual input of others as key information sources, so those who do not develop discerning viewing habits may be unwittingly manipulated by the media images that surround them. It is time to rethink not only whether visual literacy should be addressed in our schools, but how we should address it.

How Can Visual Literacy Be Taught?

Historically, the definition of "literacy" has broadened over time, embracing greater numbers of skills and abilities, partly in response to the development of new communication devices and strategies. Recent moves to expand the concept of "literacy" to include notions of visual or media literacy follow this same trend. A challenge inherent in broadening a term like *literacy,* however, involves clarifying what is meant by terms such as *visual literacy* or *media literacy.* Unfortunately, both terms have often been used by communication scholars to refer to the roles of images and media in learning and knowing. Indeed, there seems to be a great deal of confusion in the field about the distinctions between the two. Some scholars use the terms interchangeably, whereas others offer rather precise distinctions, describing media literacy as the understanding and production of messages through physical devices and visual literacy as being limited to a more passive reception of messages through art, drama, television, and film.

The proliferation of different "literacies" does not seem particularly productive as we try to understand how words and images interact both in our comprehension and production of messages. On the contrary, it seems far more productive to broaden our definition of literacy to include word and image and then to focus on the process components of literacy that students need to develop. In this section, we discuss ways teachers have broadened their views of "literacy" and "text."

Extending the Notion of "Literacy"

The idea of expanding the notion of literacy is not new, nor is the movement limited to scholars of a single discipline. Indeed, educators from a variety of fields have suggested that concepts of literacy should be extended to include a number of different ways of representing or conceptualizing knowledge. For example, Eisner (1994) has consistently argued for a conceptualization of literacy that includes multiple forms of knowledge representation, especially forms often seen as more "artistic" or "aesthetic." This argument is, in many ways, closely related to Gardner's (1983) contention that intelligence develops along a number of lines and that various cultures differ in the specific forms of intelligence they value. This contention is nicely demonstrated by considering why members of the Eskimo culture value spatial intelligence, which is so obviously related to their physical survival, whereas educators in the United States have consistently valued and rewarded verbal and logical-mathematical intelligence over other forms, especially with the rise of the information society.

Both Eisner and Gardner contended that school curricula and practices that reward "word" and "number" knowledge over all others have negative effects on students with strengths in other areas and offer unfair advantages to students who conform with system expectations. Such concerns have led many educators to attempt to expand both their definition of literacy and that of the "texts" involved in that literacy instruction.

Extending the Notion of "Text": Four Levels

As educators broaden their personal conceptions of literacy, they seem almost to follow a progression: first of extending the notion of "texts" to include the "classics" and later of expanding the very idea of what a "text" is. We have found it instructive to consider steps toward broadening the definition of text as progression through four levels.

Level 1: Exposure to the "Classics." In efforts to broaden students' exposure to text and thereby encourage greater literacy development, some teachers select "classic" works of literature as reading material for students, believing that contemporary cultural works lack the value of older works. Typical of this view is the *English Language Framework for California Public Schools, K–12,* which states that "classic literature speaks most eloquently to readers and writers" (1986, p. 7). Advocates of this view note the importance of helping students develop the "cultural capital" that results from understanding those works frequently quoted by "educated" members of American society. Ideally, such exposure allows students to become insiders to the references and idioms that permeate Western communication (Bloom, 1987; Hirsch, 1987).

Unfortunately, teachers working from this view often dismiss text from underrepresented cultures and current television programs and related materials as curriculum possibilities. Such dismissal seems ironic given that many "classic" literature pieces began as popular works designed for mass audiences, as was the case with much of Dickens's work (Beach, 1992). Another danger in this practice involves disenfranchisement: despite teacher-identified "classic" content, some "classic" contents texts may be remote and disconnected from students' personal experiences, rendering the concepts difficult to comprehend and therefore making "classic works" unlikely sources of enjoyment. In contrast, current prime-time television programs and contemporary films often arise out of the very issues pertinent to modern life, thus connecting with students immediately. Interestingly, many current programs and movies make use of intertextuality, a practice that can provide helpful links between media developed for "our time" and great literature of the past. Perhaps the question for educators who desire to enhance literacy study with the classics might be helpfully extended to include consideration of how modern-day expression parallels and builds on "classic" themes—working from the present to the past rather than in the opposite direction.

As educators attempt to broaden their conception of "text," we believe that dismissal and oversight of current media productions should be avoided. Not only should debate about the canon of acceptable literary works continue, but it should extend to include works from nonprint sources.

Level Two: Beyond the "Classics."   In many contemporary classrooms, reading and language arts educators have successfully extended the notion of "text" to include works beyond the "classics." Such educators have argued cogently for using picture books, short stories, plays, and nonfiction with students to motivate learning and engage students in meaningful ways. Teachers reflecting this view of literacy believe that by including picture books and other literature in their lessons, they expand and extend the curriculum to address issues salient to their students. They cite animated discussions and thoughtful reader responses as indicators of greater student involvement in literacy instruction.

We applaud the extension of literacy instruction to include a number of print sources. Including primary information sources such as personal diaries, newspapers, and letters in instruction allows a student to develop a greater "feel" for the concepts and concerns of a particular time period or curriculum concept. The question remaining, however, is whether it is desirable to limit students' literacy experiences to printed texts, even including those on computer screens. This question is often addressed by moving to a third level of text expansion and including visual media in literacy instruction.

Level Three: Film/Video and Text Comparisons.   In addition to bringing "classic" literature into the classroom and extending literacy experiences to include numerous sources of print, many teachers embrace a third method of extending "text" in their courses when they ask students to compare a video or film version of a text with the print copy. Students may read a printed text and then view the film and compare the two, or the film may be used as an introduction to the print copy in an effort to motivate students to read the original. An example of this occurred in a middle school classroom in which the teacher had students read Edgar Allan Poe's story "The Tell-Tale Heart" and then view a black-and-white version of the film and compare the text and film versions. Upon completion of the reading and viewing, the students participated in small group discussions about the film and the text and created Venn diagrams, as shown in Figure 22.1, to illustrate the differences that were noted between the two forms.

Classrooms in which such "texts" are extended in this way offer students the opportunity to consider numerous decisions media producers make, such as when to depart from the original text and what to highlight. Still, the exercises may be relatively passive for the students, with them relying more on analysis rather than on active personal production and communication.

Teachers who expand their literacy curricula to embrace video and film are helping to move the educational endeavor beyond an exclusive focus on the printed word. We applaud such steps, for although written language skills are even more important in

FIGURE 22.1   Venn Diagram for Film and Text Versions of "The Tell-Tale Heart"

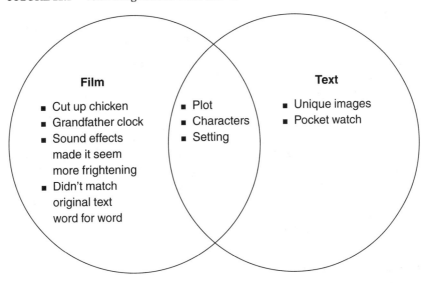

today's world, language is only one symbol system that humans use to express and share meaning. As our understanding of the communication arts has expanded, we have come to recognize that communication is a social, cultural, and contextual phenomenon that involves relationships with many forms of symbolic expression, forms including visual images, sounds, music, dance, and other electronic technology.

As educators embrace television, video, and other visual media in their classrooms, the chance of connecting with students' personal lives is enhanced. As Hobbs (1997) pointed out, we live a society in which media has become the central leisure activity for most people and the most dominant source of information about people and events in the universe. Thus, entering a classroom where visual media is used as a means for extending understanding of print may help students link viewing abilities developed outside of school to forms of communication used within the school. On the other hand, we argue that there is an important difference between using television, computers, video, and film to teach with versus teaching about television, computer, video, and film (Flood, Heath, & Lapp, 1997; Flood & Lapp, 1995, 1997/1998; Lapp & Flood, 1978). We advocate achievement of a fourth level of redefining literacy "texts."

Level Four: Alternative "Texts."   A fourth and even greater extension of the concept of "text" involves the production and use of supplementary and alternative "text." Many educators have produced and continue to produce excellent media presentations (often in the form of videotape) for organizations such as International Reading Association, Association for Supervision and Curriculum Development, National Reading Research Center, and National Council of Teachers of English. Such materials are widely used in university classes to verbally and visually demonstrate a variety of aspects of teaching literacy (see the reference to Presevice Reading Partnership Project, 1997). Other educators have produced materials designed to support specific coursework in K–12 classrooms, materials that, unfortunately, are rarely distributed to others. In addition, numerous authors have focused on greater use of visual images in predominantly print-based media. In fact, pictures in professional journals, books, and teaching manuals have proliferated in recent years. One example of this increased use of visual images appears in a collection on emergent literacy edited by Strickland and Morrow. In preparing the "text," all the authors were convinced that pictures of the two master teachers working with children in their classrooms would significantly enhance efforts to tell the story of how literacy developed in those settings (Roser, Flood, & Lapp, 1989).

As teachers and administrators expand their notions of literacy and "text" to support the concept of visual literacy, they need support and guidance in order to successfully assist children in the development of visual literacy. In the next section, we provide some specific ideas for supporting visual literacy both in the classroom and at the school site.

In Support of the Classroom: How Administrators and Support Personnel Can Help

The following guidelines may be useful to administrators and support personnel in becoming instrumental in supporting visual literacy education:

- *Provide technical support.* Regardless of whether your site has sophisticated technical equipment or just the basics, teachers who are struggling with equipment malfunctions are not able to deliver quality instruction to students.
- *Be a role model.* Include visuals in your presentations to the staff. Be creative in your selections and use a variety of visual media such as video, photos or drawings.
- *Encourage experimentation.* Teachers need support as they expand their knowledge and try new lessons in their classrooms. Be sure to communicate your willingness to support teachers as they learn new ways to support visual literacy.
- *Provide resources.* Developing students' visual literacy is not limited to computers, videos, and television. There are resources in many communities that could provide a wealth of visual input that would promote students' visual literacy. For example, field trips to art museums, plays and performances would all provide rich opportunities for students.

Practical Ideas for Supporting Visual Literacy in the Classroom

Supporting visual literacy in the classroom does not necessarily mean bringing in all sorts of new equipment, watching endless videos, or going on expensive field trips to the latest theatrical performance. It can begin very simply by carefully examining what you already do in your classroom and thinking about it from a visual perspective. Begin by looking carefully at the visual images you have included in your lesson plans and ask yourself these questions:

- Why did I include this image (video, picture book, photograph, web site, etc.)?
- What does this image say about the topic of this lesson?
- What does this image say about different subsections of the population (women, minorities, children)?
- Are there any stereotypes that I need to address or discuss in this image?
- Is there a message in this image? What is it?

Once you have looked at the visual images included in your lesson, you will need to determine which elements of the visual image to address with your students. This selection will be based on the objectives you have for the lesson and the objectives you set for your students in terms of visual literacy. Once you have determined the visual elements of your lesson, some of the ideas that follow may be helpful as you plan instruction to support visual literacy.

Instructional Videos and Films

Many teachers already use instructional videos or films in their classrooms. The value of these instructional materials for enhancing students visual literacy can be increased by making some minor modifications to the typical view then discuss procedure.

- *Use pause and rewind.* Do not save all the discussion of a film or video for the very end. Use pause and rewind as needed to instruct students about important visual elements of the film or video.
- *Encourage discussion.* Allow students to discuss films or videos in small groups. You may even want to assign each group member a specific role such as discussion leader (guides the group), summarizer (summarizes the video or film), content questioner (asks the group questions specifically related to the content of the film), or visual questioner (asks the group questions specifically about the visual images).
- *Ask director's-perspective questions.* Encourage students to think about the director's perspective. Ask them to consider the reasoning behind the director's choice of settings, characters, costume, and color.

Observations

Observations can take many forms. Students may observe an experiment or they may observe an animal in an enclosure at the zoo. Regardless of what they are observing, it is valuable to point out the important visual elements. One method is through the directed viewing activity described here:

1. *Establish background.* Prior to the actual observation, get students involved by calling on their prior knowledge of the subject. It will set the stage for the observation and will allow students to make predictions about what they will see.

2. *Introduce key vocabulary.* Teach students any pertinent vocabulary they will need to discuss what they are seeing or to understand any auditory accompaniment that may be provided with the observation.
3. *Provide springboard questions.* Develop a series of springboard questions to guide students in observing the key content.
4. *Participate in the visual experience.* At this point, students actually participate in the observation.
5. *Follow-up questions.* Follow-up questions are used to check understanding of the visual learning experience and to stimulate interpretative thought. Some follow-up questions may be repeats of the springboard questions, if appropriate.

Print Media

Print media is all around us: in magazines, newspapers, books, and billboards. Many valuable lessons can be taught using a variety of print media. Local newspapers, web sites on the Internet, and magazines are all useful resources in the classroom for lessons such as these.

- *Editor's perspective.* Teach students about the role of editors. Get multiple copies of several different age-appropriate magazines. Divide the students up into groups based on the magazine title they select. Have the students search the magazine for evidence of the values that the magazine editor supports. For example, look for how the magazine portrays families, boys, girls, and so forth.
- *Identify selling techniques.* Teach students about the various propaganda techniques used in advertising. Have students search the newspaper and find ads that use the various techniques. Note: The same activity can be done with television commercials.

Live Performances

Attending a live performance of a dance production, play, opera, or concert is a rich learning experience on many levels. The visual elements of such performances offer an abundance of teaching material. The directed viewing activity described above can be used to help students get the most from this experience. Some helpful springboard or follow-up questions include the following:

- How does the element of a live performance add to this production?
- How does a live performance compare to a prerecorded one?
- Why do you think the director, choreographer, conductor, and so forth selected the costumes and lighting that he or she did?

The ideas presented in this section are just a few of the many things that can be done with visual images in the classroom. Remember, it is most important to start where you are and move forward at a pace that is comfortable to both you and your students.

Some Important Considerations about Visual Literacy Instruction

Although useful and important, efforts to extend the notions of "literacy" and "text" suffer from two major shortcomings. First, at least at present, curriculum changes and extensions tend most often to be made by teachers rather than students. As a result, students continue to function largely as receivers and interpreters of messages rather than as producers and communicators of ideas. Second, the changes often center more on video, film, and print sources rather than those of dance, electronic imaging, and other media forms. If *communicating* is at the heart of literacy, we must consider the value of providing ongoing opportunities for students to devise, express, and communicate ideas through a variety of means.

REFERENCES

Alton-Lee, A., Huthall, G., & Patrick, J. (1993). Reframing classroom research: A lesson from the private world of children. *Harvard Educational Review, 63,* 50–84.

Baule, S.M., & Lyons, S.M. (1996). Using visuals to develop reading vocabulary. In R.E. Griffin, D.G. Beauchamp, J.M. Hunter, & C.B. Schiffman (Eds.), *Eyes on the future: Converging images, ideas, and instruction.* Selected reading from the annual conference of the International Visual Literacy Association (pp. 371–377). New York: The International Visual Literacy Association.

Beach, J.A. (1992, November). New trends in perspective: Literature's place in language arts education. *Language Arts, 69,* 550–556.

Bloom, A. (1987). *The closing of the American mind.* New York: Simon and Schuster.

Carey, J. (1997). Exploring future media. In J. Flood, S.B. Heath, & D. Lapp (Eds.), *A handbook for literacy educators: Research on teaching the communicative and visual arts* (pp. 62–67). New York: Macmillan.

DeJean, J., Miller, L., & Olson, J. (1995, June). *CD-ROM talking books: A case study of promise and practice.* Paper presented at the 23rd annual conference of the Canadian Society for the Study of Education, Montreal, Quebec.

Eisner, E. (1994). *Cognition and Curriculum Reconsidered* (2nd ed.). New York: Teacher's College Press.

English language frameworks for California public schools, K–12. (1986). Sacramento: California State Board of Education.

Fleming-McCormick, T., Nyre, G.F., Schwager, M.T., & Tushnet, N.C. (1995). Final guidelines and procedures for teacher development systems: Integrating technology and instruction. Los Alamitos, CA: Southwest Regional Lab. (ERIC Document Reproduction Service No. ED 388 312)

Flood, J., Heath, D. B., & Lapp, D. (Eds.). (1997). *Handbook of research on teaching literacy through the visual and communicative arts.* New York: Macmillan.

Flood, J., & Lapp, D. (1995). Broadening the lens: Toward an expanded conceptualization of literacy. In K. Hinchman, D. Leu, & C. Kinzer (Eds.), *Perspective on literacy research and practice* (pp. 1–16). Chicago: National Reading Conference.

Flood, J., & Lapp, D. (December 1997/January 1998). Broadening conceptualizations of literacy: The visual and communicative arts. *The Reading Teacher, 51*(4), 342–345.

Gardner, H. (1983). *Frames of mind: The theory of multiple intelligences.* New York: Basic Books.

Hirsch, E.D., Jr. (1987). *Cultural literacy: What every American needs to know.* New York: Houghton Mifflin.

Hobbs, R. (1997). Literacy for the information age. In J. Flood, S.B. Heath, & D. Lapp (Eds.), *A handbook for literacy educators: Research on teaching the communicative and visual arts* (pp. 7–14). New York: Macmillan.

Kaestle, C. (1991). *Literacy in the United States.* New Haven, CN: Yale University Press.

Kinder, J. (1991). *Playing with power in movies, television and video games.* Berkeley: University of California Press.

Kubey, R., & Csikszentmihalyi, M. (1990). *Television and the quality of life: How viewing shapes everyday experience.* Hillsdale, NJ: Erlbaum.

Lapp, D., & Flood, J. (1978). *Teaching reading to every child.* New York: Macmillan.

Meskill, C., & Swan, K. (1995). Roles for multimedia in the response-based literature classroom (Report Series 2.24) Albany, NY: National Research Center on Literature Teaching and Learning. (ERIC Document Reproduction Service No. ED 387 803)

Messaris, P. (1994). *Visual literacy: Image, mind and reality.* Boulder, CO: Westview Press.

Next Generation. (1998, February). A meeting of the minds. *Next Generation, 53*–61.

Poe, E.A. (1970). The tell-tale heart. In G.R. Thompson (Ed.), *Great short works of Edgar Allan Poe* (pp. 384–390). New York: Harper and Row.

Preservice Reading Partnership Project. (1997). *Reading instruction videotapes and observation guides.* San Diego: College of Education, San Diego State University.

Rood, C. (1996). Critical viewing and the significance of the emotional response. In R.E. Griffin, D.G. Beauchamp, J.M. Hunter, & C.B Schiffman (Eds.), *Eyes on the future: Converging images, idea, and instruction. Selected readings from the annual conference of the International Visual Literacy Association* (pp. 111–117). New York: International Visual Literacy Association.

Roser, N., Flood, J., & Lapp, D. (1989). Is it reasonable . . . ? A photo essay. In D.S. Strickland & L.M. Morrow, (Eds.), *Emerging literacy: Young children learn to read and write* (pp. 80–95). Newark, DE: International Reading Association.

Semali, L.M. (1996). Teaching media: English teachers as media and technology critics. In R.E. Griffin, D.G. Beauchamp, J.M. Hunter, & C.B. Schiffman (Eds.), *Eyes on the future: Converging images, idea, and instruction* (pp. 207–215). New York: International Visual Literacy Association.

Sultan, A., & Jones, M. (1996). The effects of computer visual appeal on learners' motivation. In R.E. Griffin, D.G. Beauchamp, J.M. Hunter, & C.B. Schiffman (Eds.), *Eyes on the future: Converging images, idea, and instruction. Selected readings from the annual conference of the International Visual Literacy Association* (pp. 95–100). New York: International Visual Literacy Association.

23 Promoting Independent Study Strategies in the Classrooms of the Twenty-first Century

PAUL CANTÚ VALERIO

JOHN E. READENCE

University of Nevada, Las Vegas

SCENARIO: Maria, a student in this fourth-grade science class, reacting to an assigned text on clouds.

THE FORMATION OF CLOUDS: Air at ground level is denser than air higher up. So as an air parcel rises, it expands and becomes less dense. But expansion cools the air. As it cools, some of the water that is present in the air as vapor (gas) condenses into minuscule droplets that are far too small to be seen with the naked eye alone. Initially, the droplets form around tiny particles in the air (usually dust or pollen) called condensation nuclei. The droplets gather in incalculable numbers to form clouds. A cloud is therefore a big blob of extremely tiny droplets of water, or it can be frozen water in the form of small ice crystals or snowflakes. (Dickinson, 1988, p. 9)

MARIA: This is my first year in the fourth grade, and the teacher wants to give us a test on what clouds are made of on Friday. I know that he wants us to use the big words in the book. We tried reading and talking about this in my group, and Chris said that his sister, Anna, told him that clouds are made out of smoke. Why can't grown-ups use plain words? I heard dad say that when our neighbor's house caught fire last year, you could see the cloud 10 blocks away. Nobody knows what nuclei means. I don't understand the words in the book. Sally says that clouds are made of water when it's hot. When mom cooks she sometimes makes smoke come out of the pot. Is the smoke a cloud?

(The bell signaling the end of the day rings, and the teacher says, "Remember, you have a quiz on Friday. Make sure your books are in your desks, and I'll see you tomorrow.") Maria smiles as she gathers her belongings into her backpack. She thinks, maybe, mom and dad can explain it to me.

As students like Maria advance to the intermediate and middle school levels, they become exposed to a much wider variety of information than they had in earlier years. By the time they leave the primary grades, it is assumed that students have adopted rudimentary knowledge acquisition and retention strategies that they can refine to accommodate this influx of information. These additional demands require students to construct knowledge at more sophisticated levels than they have previously experienced. Needless to say, for students like Maria the ability to employ advanced strategies is necessary for future academic success and survival in the global economy of the next century. Proficiency in the academic areas of reading, writing, listening, speaking, reasoning, and problem solving and in the application of technology are mandated by real-world needs (Texas Education Agency, 1994), but how and where do our students acquire these sophisticated strategies? Perhaps more important, how do teachers support student engagement and independence to promote lifelong learning? In this chapter, we first present a brief discussion on current knowledge construction research, including factors that influence strategy use, followed by some suggestions for teachers to consider as they promote the continued development of independent study strategies for their students in the classrooms of the twenty-first century.

A Look at Some Relevant Research

Knowledge and Knowledge Construction

Current research reveals that knowledge is represented in billions of brain cells called neurons. These neurons, or knowledge capsules, are connected by neural networks, or bridges, of differing strengths. The weaker the connection, the less likely the learner is conscious of the relationship across knowledge capsules. The stronger the connection, the more likely the learner is aware of relationships between knowledge capsules (McCormick & Pressley, 1997). Learners mentally construct representations of knowledge based on their initial and subsequent experiences with new information. They accommodate, modify, manipulate, create, and sometimes reject conflicting information, which suggests that meaning is highly personalized for and by the learner. It also implies that, although stored knowledge is continuously being modified or rejected, the meaning-making act is dependent on the strengths and weaknesses of the connections that link knowledge capsules and not in the knowledge representations themselves. Thus, the stronger the bridge across knowledge representations, the more automatic is constructed knowledge's recall. This process also suggests that learners are more readily able to access mental representations of stored knowledge independently once they recognize the relationships that exist across knowledge structures. It is reasonable to assume that there is a need to foster the meaning-making act—that is, the independent construction of the knowledge bridges—through strategies designed to promote the creation of mental representations.

In addition, a study by Geisler (1990) on the sociocognitive influences of constructing mental models in a philosophical conversation argued that advanced literacy practices are configured by social context; that is, learners' knowledge construction of literacy events is contextually biased. In other words, learners are situationally bound and are less likely to use knowledge construction strategies outside of the classroom (Geisler, 1994). It would seem, then, that some knowledge base—that is, prior knowledge—is an important characteristic of the meaning-making act. Although prior knowledge is an essential enabler to constructing mental models, however, not all prior knowledge is consistent with incorporating new knowledge (Alvermann, Smith, & Readence, 1985; Geisler, 1994). In particular, Geisler (1994) suggested that a resistant dynamic may be responsible for students' rejection of truth as presented in independent text. That is, if students are presented with new knowledge that is not congruent with their prior knowledge or experiences, they may choose to reject the new information in favor of what they believe to be true. It would seem, then, that the teacher must exert the authority and control over classroom cultural activities by providing authentic, meaningful contexts that their students can rehearse over time.

Finally, although results of studies on teacher-directed metacognitive scaffolding suggest that students' self-monitoring strategy use increases with direct instruction, there is evidence to suggest that students do not use these strategies independently once teacher-directed support is withdrawn (Paris, Wasik, & Turner, 1991). Knowledge construction is significantly influenced by an individual's talent for addressing previous experiences and translating that information to new situations (Gilderhus, 1996). If learners do not independently use self-monitoring strategies outside of the classroom culture, however, they may have difficulties incorporating and accommodating the new information without support. This issue may be the most significant factor influencing learners' autonomy, for if students are presented with strategies to foster independent learning and do not use these strategies outside of the classroom, how will educators meet the real-world expectations of their students?

Factors Associated with Strategy Use

Readence, Bean, and Baldwin (1998) described five developmental stages that teachers move through when they accommodate and implement strategies. Their developmental perspective suggests that the stages of awareness, knowledge, simulation, practice, and incorporation are also characteristics of learners' successful strategy use. Learning, thus, is a developmental activity that includes a conception of the learner visualized through the creation of developmentally appropriate activities that tax, demand, and invite a learner to negotiate a learning episode. We advocate an environment conducive to naturalistic, creative inquiry where a teacher's role in the learning episode, although embedded in the cultural activity, is of a more temporary nature. The teacher's presence solidifies as risk manager, partner, and coauthor of the learning episode. Even carefully orchestrated learning environments, however, are significantly influenced by how, when, and why students choose to use learning strategies. Knowledge acquisition is, therefore, dependent on both the source of the knowledge and on its perceived utility to the learner.

Another factor associated with strategy use is that the nature of the classroom—the cultural activity shaped by the cultural capital the students bring to school with them (Bean & Valerio, 1997; Geisler, 1990, 1994)—is often ignored in favor of a didactic, direct teaching approach in the literacy classroom. This assumption ignores the interactive (social and prescribed) dynamics that are embedded in the classroom context (Roe, 1992). This issue can be particularly significant for ethnic and linguistic minorities in that their cultural capital differs from that of mainstream students. Tompkins (1997) identified four ethnic group characteristics that can influence students' classroom cultural activity: avoiding eye contact, cooperation, fear of making mistakes, and the formal classroom environment. Although each of these characteristics may require particular teaching strategies in a diverse classroom that can influence its nature, too often teachers assume an authoritarian stance in the classroom whereby they are the holders of truth and knowledge and decide that, magically, truth (text) can be transmitted directly to all learners. At the other extreme, teachers may decentralize their authority and relinquish all responsibility to the learners, leaving them to construct their own truth, right or wrong. In other words, the teacher as reflective decision maker can, and often does, exert the control and authority that can either limit or maximize learning episodes. Teachers, like learners, must be cognitively aware of their environment, students, and power to influence learning episodes.

Awareness and Cognition

According to Cox and Boyd-Batstone (1997), Vygotsky suggested that learners' cultural cognitive development exists on two planes, social and psychological. In this view, learners' develop cognitively by interacting with the world and with adults who provide them with scaffolding to assist in committing constructed knowledge to long-term memory. In other words, learners must experience new information with assistance when needed in multiple contexts and strengthen linkages across knowledge capsules to make the learning episode meaningful. For example, the word *thirst* in the phrase "man's thirst for knowledge" is meaningful to you because of your social and psychological experiences with the word *thirst* in this context. When nine-year-old Joey is asked what he thinks the word *thirst* means when used in this context, however, he replies, "The man is thirsty and needs to drink something so he could know—Huh?" Left to his own devices, Joey continues to attempt to decipher a correct interpretation of the word *thirst*. His conceptual experience with the word used in this context, however, is limited. Joey's initial reaction is to address his knowledge base of the word *thirst* on a social plane, but he soon finds that he cannot successfully accomplish a viable connection. He becomes frustrated.

At this early stage of Joey's conceptual development, Joey is experiencing frustration similar to that of Maria studying clouds in the vignette at the beginning of this chapter. Although he is aware of the word *thirst,* his experiences with the word used in different contexts is limited. Joey is not able to independently modify and accommodate the knowledge capsule containing the word *thirst* and strengthen the bridge across representations because he has not had the opportunity to simulate, practice, and incorporate the word used in this context. Dyson and Freedman (1991) echoed this view:

> Ways of using both oral and written language are interrelated not only with contexts for using language but also with ways of living—historical and geographical conditions; social and economic resource[s] and opportunities; religious beliefs, values, and motivations. (p. 755)

Although the goal remains that students independently avail themselves of effective study strategies, evidence continues to suggest that students seldom engage these strategies effectively without help (Paris et al., 1991). One method of gauging student success is by monitoring their competency to independently choose effective strategies and actively transfer study techniques to consciously surmount problems they may encounter (Andrews, 1996; Texas Education Agency, 1994). Learners' abilities to analyze a situation and employ a systematic study strategy outside of the school culture, however, are not easily regulated. In addition, evidence suggests that, in many cases, procedural knowledge (i.e., effective use of strategies) may be responsible for increases in student performance (McCormick & Pressley, 1997). Thus, learners' self-efficacy and autonomy may be fostered by an understanding of the learning process and a recognition of the factors associated with the influences of successful independent strategy use. A word of caution from Dyson and Freedman (1991) is appropriate here:

> Efforts to apply the concept of scaffolding to teaching and learning in schools are appealing. However, as Cazden cautions, the scaffolding metaphor is static while the process or teaching and learning is dynamic. The participation of the learner affects the teacher just as the teacher affects the learner, as both move to build a support structure that meets the learner's needs. (p. 768)

We have described promoting learners' needs through the creation of supportive environments that tax, demand, and invite learners to negotiate a learning episode as they move toward independent knowledge construction. We strongly feel that by fostering transferable *organizational* and *mental representation* strategies, learners will engage, extend, and apply these skills throughout their lives. In the next section, we present some of these strategies through vignettes and by weaving in and out of the context of an eighth-grade reading class.

Some Suggestions for Promoting Study Strategies

Now that we have had an opportunity to provide a brief rationale, we should move on to more practical aspects of this chapter: How do I integrate and promote the use of study strategies in the classroom? Which strategies should I focus on? As mentioned previously, teachers exert varying degrees of authority and control in the classroom that can limit or maximize learning episodes. Our suggestion for the successful implementation of the following strategies is that you begin by choosing those strategies with which you are most comfortable. Modify each one you choose to fit both you and your students' needs. Remember, the goal is to foster learners' self-efficacy and independence.

You may want to consider that the study strategy you choose to use, as presented, may not be appropriate for all student and classroom situations. We begin with promoting knowledge organizational strategies by distinguishing the difference between declarative and procedural knowledge illustrated with an example from Joey. In addition, we provide you with specific questions to consider as you move to integrate organizational strategies in your classroom. We then describe mental representations and how one teacher fostered their use in his classroom.

Promoting Knowledge Organizational Strategies

To reiterate, information is stored in knowledge capsules and connected by bridges. The meaning-making process, therefore, is dependent on the strength of the bridge across knowledge capsules. Successful use of study strategies, as expressed by Readence et al. (1998), suggests that learners adopt a systematic process and strategically incorporate this process in their learning. We call this *procedural knowledge,* and it includes knowing how to address and solve a specific problem and just generally knowing how to do things (Reinking, Mealey, & Ridgeway, 1993). For example, when asked to write a description on how to make soup, Joey replies:

> First, you go to the kitchen.
> Then, you take down a can of soup.
> Then, you open the can and pour it in a pot.
> You heat up the pot on the stove.
> Then, you got soup for cold and rainy days!

Joey's example illustrates his conception of making soup based on his cognitive development on both the social and psychological plane. Here he demonstrates procedural knowledge based on production, answering sequentially: first this, then that. In addition, his last statement suggests that he has some conception of *declarative knowledge,* that is, knowing what something is used for, in this case soup. A clearer distinction between declarative and procedural knowledge is the difference between knowing *what* something is and knowing *how* to do something—for example, recognizing what a cloud is—as opposed to knowing how a cloud is formed.

You may have noticed, however, that, in many cases, knowing what something is (declarative knowledge) comes before (and sometimes, not at all) knowing how to do something (procedural knowledge). If we assume that, up to the fourth grade, learners are able to discover learning strategies without assistance, based on their experiences and cognitive development, then experiences are best used to illustrate declarative knowledge such as traffic signals, uses of various forms of writing (cookbooks, newspaper, etc.), adult roles, and so on. The use of procedural knowledge, however, suggests a more sophisticated meaning-making process in that it requires the learner to display a case sequentially. In other words, parts must be organized in a logical pattern that makes sense to the learner.

You may want to begin this process by creating and then modeling a time line for students. Remember, procedural knowledge, at its inception, is dependent on some experience with the content and context of the task. For example, the following is a narrative time line that illustrates a sequence of events that includes progress in a specific activity as a model for students' self-monitoring awareness. This time line was created in response to the question: Describe your first two waking hours this morning, what exactly did you do or accomplish?

> The alarm clock woke me up this morning at 3:00. I put on my slippers and walked the 19 steps to my kitchen to turn the coffee pot on. On the way back to my bedroom, I reached over to the laptop sitting on my kitchen table and flipped on the switch to the computer. I continued through my bedroom and into the bathroom to take a shower. After my shower, I slipped into my pajamas and slippers, walked back to the kitchen, poured a hot cup of coffee, and sat before the computer. I glanced at my kitchen clock, it was 3:20. I spent the next two hours sipping coffee and working on a neverending paper before I got up to stretch and walk back into my bedroom to gently wake my wife. It was now 5:30, and my paper is 5 pages longer!

After sharing this with your students, and as a reflective exercise, you may want to ask your students to document two similar hours of their home life.

Another approach to developing a better understanding of procedural knowledge and its benefits is for the teacher to establish protocols. For example, you may want to have your students create a daily or weekly planner. In other words, begin with fostering time-management skills, including weekly goals. For example, ask students to chart daily and weekly time commitments for (a) sleep, (b) breakfast, (c) lunch, (d) dinner, (e) time spent in class, (f) house chores, (g) sports, (h) television, (i) personal grooming, (j) study time, and (k) other. Have them total up the hours that they have devoted to each activity and begin constructing a time-management plan.

To illustrate, ask students to fold a sheet of paper in half; next ask them to list weekly short-term goals on one side—that is, what they want to do—and list what they need to do on the other. Then, have them refer to the time commitments for the week and have them ask themselves:

> Can I devote more or less time for any of the categories I've listed in my time chart?
>
> What have I left out that I need to devote more time to?
>
> Is there anything in my chart that I can do more effectively if I share the responsibility?

In other words, ask students to identify their priorities. Make this a regular activity for your students. Rehearse and reinforce this practice for, as we have suggested, the use of transferable strategies requires elaboration and simulation. In addition, you may want to consider the following reflective questions for fostering organizational and procedural knowledge:

> Is the content meaningful to the student?
>
> Is the context appropriate?
>
> Am I providing multiple contexts?

Is the task organized, and are protocols established?
Have I elaborated, associated, and modeled the task?
Have we rehearsed the task?

Elaborating and illustrating priorities based on personal goals and commitments empowers learners to visualize and modify their behavior to fit their expectations. The experience of constructing concrete examples and associating these examples in meaningful categories engages learners to review and transfer this management strategy to other areas of their lives. Also, the use of declarative knowledge as well as procedural knowledge, coupled with the use of a systematic process and real-world application, influences memory retention and automaticity of knowledge recall. By providing multiple contexts of this activity, learners are encouraged to apply this strategy outside the classroom cultural activity. In other words, because this activity is highly personalized, learners have a sense of ownership with the activity and are more likely to use this strategy independently, without teacher-directed support. Strategies that foster mental representations, our next topic, can also promote this independence.

Fostering Mental Representations

Graphic organizers, mental models, semantic mapping, and webbing are all examples of topic and thematic representations of relationships. Considering the discussion we had on knowledge and knowledge construction, recall that the mental image you create is a representation of the meaning-making process that, in turn, is dependent on the strength or weakness of the bridge across knowledge capsules. You may now be mentally visualizing a bridge spanning the distance across capsules. If you add a construction crew to each bridge standing by for your directions, you would have a more accurate representation. Each new experience, each different context of the content of each capsule, is like adding a girder of support to the bridge that spans knowledge capsules. The stronger the support, the more accessible the knowledge representations with minimal maintenance; the more accessible the knowledge, the more automatic its recall. In other words, the stronger the link, the less effort required to address relationships across knowledge representations.

Mental representations can be fostered in the classroom by modeling and displaying graphic illustrations of time lines, anticipation guides, story structure charts, Venn diagrams, webs, and maps. Because we want our learners to extend their knowledge construction abilities and transfer these skills outside of the classroom culture, we must give them multiple opportunities to simulate and practice these strategies in different contexts (Readence et al., 1998). For example, let us visit Clark's eighth-grade reading class as he prepares a lesson on word mapping. Clark is an experienced middle school teacher who has worked primarily with seventh- and eighth-grade linguistic minority students. He has often expressed a sincere desire to expose his students to literary activities that take advantage of his students' rich cultural heritage.

Currently, Clark's class has just finished reading a novel about Nat Turner, an escaped slave who led a rebellion in southern Virginia. The class has been alternating their reading assignments, supplementing the novel with short stories about and by

African Americans in celebration of Black history month. Although his class has become used to creating a word list and glossary as they read, including charts of word generalizations and word illustrations, he is concerned that some of his students are not using the vocabulary development strategies they have practiced in class when they read at home. "Well, that's not exactly true," he said. "They are skipping unfamiliar words and, hopefully, searching for context clues in the text. But I see little if any evidence that they are doing anything else besides relying on me to define and pronounce the words for them."

This problem is of great concern to Clark because, aside from his students not using vocabulary strategies independently, they are about to begin a thematic unit introducing works written by Hispanic authors. He is also concerned because the novel he has chosen for his class to read is embedded with many problems, resolutions, and unfamiliar words that they will need to understand to fully appreciate this genre. He wonders what he could do to help his students help themselves and recalls some of the literature he has read. Clark finds, "Teaching students the process of creating word maps not only gives them a strategy for generating word meanings independently, but also fosters self-monitoring and metacognitive thinking" (Brozo & Simpson, 1995, p. 182) on his sister's (who is a secondary school teacher) bookshelf. "Ah-ha," he states, "That's where I'll start!"

As a professional interested in literacy, Clark constructed this lesson based on the following rationale (see Figure 23.1), which he shares with his class:

My reading professors combined effort to educate this *re-planted* military *hand* may have finally bore fruit. They made me realize that, if the learner is unable to expand his/her vocabulary, it is because the strategy he/she uses to *discern* word meaning is limited. It follows that my responsibility is to empower the learner to *utilize* other strategies to *conceptualize*

FIGURE 23.1   Example of a Word Map/Web

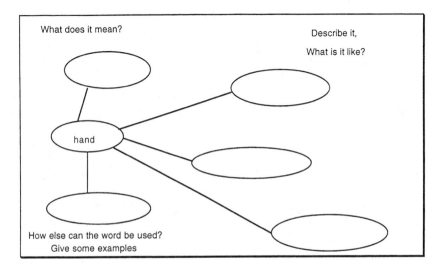

word meaning in context. I believe that an excellent weapon to add to the *arsenal* of the learner's knowledge base is word mapping with the help of context clues.

Clark first models the procedure for his students using an overhead projector and think-alouds for the word *hand*. His students assist him as he completes the word map, and he pauses as he asks himself rhetorical questions about the task. He follows up this lesson by asking his students, seated in heterogeneous groups of four, to construct their own word map of the words he identified in his rationale (*re-planted, discern, conceptualize, utilize,* and *arsenal*). In addition, Clark models the process with think-alouds, explaining that:

> The students need to see that I'm human, that I can make mistakes and it is alright. Mistakes are a way of learning in the real world; we all make them. The ticket is learning from them and, besides, it's fun!

"As teachers talk about their own meaning construction, they help students develop a realistic understanding of their strategy use" (Walker, 1996, p. 290). It would appear that Clark felt that the best way to get his students to identify with the task was to give them a shared experience by verbalizing his inner speech, thus fostering a coauthorship of the task.

One of Clark's goals this year is to foster student engagement. He finds it curious that his school services a community that is over 80% Hispanic, yet none of the literature his class has read this year is written by Hispanic authors. Clark decided to construct a learning unit toward the end of the school year that introduces stories written by Hispanic authors to his class culminating with a Mexican independence day (Cinco de Mayo) celebration. Thus, by introducing a thematic unit on a culturally relevant topic, he feels that he will foster a sense of agency and engagement among his students. Also, because most of Clark's students are unfamiliar with Hispanic authors but have some knowledge of the culture (declarative knowledge), this unit will give him and his class opportunities to extend and accommodate new knowledge as well as opportunities to practice and refine the strategies they are exploring.

The hub of the learning unit in Clark's class is a young adult novel written by Rodolfo Anaya (1972) entitled *Bless Me Ultima.* It is with this novel that Clark begins the process of constructing a story structure chart to compare and contrast with other short stories they read. His objective in using this strategy is for students to explicitly chart similarities and differences in the stories as topics for class and group discussions. As a side effect, the students are also able to monitor their comprehension by identifying and illustrating typical story structure elements. Clark modifies the story structure chart he created, asking his students to identify and write about three events in the current novel they are reading as homework (see Figure 23.2). The novel the class is reading, *Bless Me Ultima,* is the axis to several other short stories written by Hispanic authors. Clark will use the completed charts as discussion directors throughout this unit. In addition, Clark will ask the groups to illustrate the events they have discussed using McConnell's (1993) talking drawings. In this activity, students illustrate

FIGURE 23.2 Juanita's Story Structure Chart

Title	Lupito's Death	Antonio's First Day of School	Florence's Death
State	New Mexico	New Mexico	New Mexico
Author	Rudolfo Anaya	Rudolfo Anaya	Rudolfo Anaya
Illustrator			
Setting	Bridge	Town School	Blue Lake
Characters	Lupito, sheriff, Narciso, Antonio's dad, Antonio, Chavez, Ultima	Antonio, Deborah, Theresa, Miss Maestas, George, Willy	Antonio, Cico, Florence, the rest of their gang
Events (plot)	Lupito kills the sheriff by shooting him in the head. Chavez comes to Antonio's dad to ask him for help.	Antonio, Deborah, and Theresa walk to school. Antonio is in first grade, and his teacher is Miss Maestas.	Cico and Florence were going to tell about the golden carp, but when the gang found them, they were excited.
Other	Antonio's dad and Chavez go to the bridge with the rest of the men. Antonio follows the men trying to kill Lupito. Narcisco tries to stop them, but they kill Lupito as Antonio watches. When Antonio goes home, Ultima gives him some medicine.	Antonio sits by himself; he doesn't know anyone in his class. When it is time for lunch, he has to go outside because he feels uncomfortable in class and meets George and Willy who are like him.	The gang was shouting that Florence had dived into the Blue Lake and not come up yet. And then, finally they got him out and he died.

the mental images evoked by a story or event from which they have some knowledge prior to, and after, a discussion or reading.

Only after his students have had some opportunities to independently practice using the story structure chart does Clark ask them to compare and contrast other short stories they have read during this learning unit on Hispanic authors. "The students seemed to really like this activity. They challenge each other with their comparisons and take a lot of pride in justifying their points." For example, while discussing the conflict between two families (mother's and father's) as they struggle for control of the future of the main character, Antonio (the son), in *Bless Me Ultima,* Beatrice predicts:

> Antonio will become a priest and be well educated because he can fulfill both his mother and father's dream. His mother wants him to become a priest and his father wants him to

travel. Antonio is a curious person; remember when he snuck off to the river. He wants to know things, and he is not afraid of a little adventure.

An additional strategy that students in Clark's class explore is the creation of a story map that is designed much like a flowchart. The story map that the students create provides them with concrete examples of literary essentials, such as, Who are the main characters? What is the setting? What are the major events, problems, and solutions? What is the theme? For example, one of Chris's story maps identifies and resolves an event on the Agua Negra ranch.

> *Problem:* A curse was put on a ghost, and the ghost haunted the Tellez family's house. The ghost was one of three Comanche Indians who used to raid the flocks of Tellez's grandfather. One day the grandfather got tired of it and hung the Indians with some other Mexicans. Three brujas [witches] laid the curse on the Tellez family by awakening the ghosts to do evil.
>
> *Events leading to resolution:* Tellez comes to Gabriel asking for help from Ultima and asks them to come and see for themselves if they don't believe. Gabriel goes to the Tellez ranch to see if what Tellez said about the curse was true. Gabriel comes back telling what he saw and asking Ultima if she will go and help his friend in need.
>
> *Resolution:* Ultima goes with Gabriel and Tony to the Tellez ranch. Ultima blesses it and does some of her magic to get the curse off.

In addition to the story maps, Clark tapes several poster boards on the walls of his class with the following headers: Description(s), Character(s), Problem(s), Resolution(s), and Glossary. Each group is responsible for one poster entry each day. The groups are allowed the freedom of choosing how to represent and organize the knowledge they are constructing. At the end of each week, the groups present what they have constructed to the rest of the class. Clark is pleased to find that, three weeks into the novel, he is running out of wall space. "I think our next project will be to make a big book out of these posters to share at our next open house," he confides. Subsequent interviews with Clark reveal that he is continuously modifying strategies similar to the story structure chart and story maps that now require more extensive independent activities. It is precisely these kind of activities with which Clark wants to involve his students, because he knows how important they are to reinforce their acquisition and retention of new information.

Conclusion

In this chapter, we discussed the use of knowledge organizational and mental representation strategies to help students learn and retain the plethora of information they encounter in classrooms. We have also made the point that experience and simulation are essential components for developing a learner's expertise and independence. Teachers play an obvious and pivotal role in demonstrating and modeling the importance of study strategies. It is only with this support that we can promote students' life-long learning into the twenty-first century.

REFERENCES

Anaya, R. (1972). *Bless me Ultima.* New York: Warner.

Alvermann, D.E., Smith, L.C., & Readence, J. E., (1985). Prior knowledge activation and the comprehension of compatible and incompatible texts. *Reading Research Quarterly, 20,* 420–436.

Andrews, K.Z. (1996). Learning how to learn. *Harvard Business Review, 74,* 12–13.

Bean, T.W., & Valerio, P.C. (1997). Constructing school success in literacy: The pathway to college entrance for minority students. *Reading Research Quarterly, 32,* 320–327.

Brozo, W.G., & Simpson, M. (1995). *Readers, teachers, learners: Expanding literacy in secondary schools* (2nd ed.). Englewood Cliffs, NJ: Prentice Hall.

Cox, C., & Boyd-Batstone, P. (1997). *Crossroads: Literature and language in culturally and linguistically diverse classrooms.* Upper Saddle River, NJ: Prentice Hall.

Dickinson, T. (1988). *Exploring the sky by day: The equinox guide to weather and the atmosphere.* Camden East, Ontario, Canada: Camden House.

Dyson, A.H., & Freedman, S.W. (1991). Writing. In J. Flood, J.M. Jensen, D. Lapp, & J.R. Squire (Eds.), *Handbook of research on teaching the English language arts* (pp. 754–774). New York: Macmillan.

Geisler, C. (1990). Toward a sociocognitive model of literacy: Constructing mental models in a philosophical conversation. In C. Bazerman & J. Paradis (Eds.), *Textual dynamics of the professionals* (pp. 171–190). Madison: University of Wisconsin Press.

Geisler, C. (1994). *Academic literacy and the nature of expertise.* Hillsdale, NJ: Erlbaum.

Gilderhus, M.T. (1996). *History and historians: A historiographical introduction* (3rd ed.). Englewood Cliffs, NJ: Prentice Hall.

McConnell, S. (1993). Talking drawings: A strategy for assisting learners. *Journal of Reading, 36,* 260–269.

McCormick, C.B., & Pressley, M. (1997). *Educational psychology: Learning, instruction, assessment.* New York: Longman.

Paris, S.G., Wasik, B.A., & Turner, J.C. (1991). The development of strategic readers. In R. Barr, M.L. Kamil, P. Mosenthal, & P.D. Pearson (Eds.), *Handbook of reading research* (Vol. II, pp. 609–639). New York: Longman.

Readence, J.E., Bean, T.W., & Baldwin, R.S. (1998). *Content area literacy: An integrated approach* (6th ed.). Dubuque, IA: Kendall/Hunt.

Reinking, D., Mealey, D., & Ridgeway, V.G. (1993). Developing preservice teachers' conditional knowledge of content area reading strategies. *Journal of Reading, 36,* 458–469.

Roe, M.F. (1992). Reading strategy instruction: Complexities and possibilities in middle school. *Journal of Reading. 35,* 190–196.

Texas Education Agency. (1994). *Raising expectations to meet real-world needs: Report of the State Panel on Student Skills and Knowledge to the State Board of Education.* Austin: Author.

Tompkins, G.E. (1997). *Literacy for the twenty-first century: A balanced approach.* Upper Saddle River, NJ: Prentice Hall.

Walker, B. (1996). Discussions that focus on strategies and self-assessment. In L.B. Gambrell & J.F. Almasi (Eds.), *Lively discussions: Fostering engaged readings* (pp. 286–296). Newark, DE: International Reading Association.

CHAPTER

24 Critical Thinking and Discussion

DERA WEAVER

DONNA ALVERMANN
The University of Georgia

Critical thinking is generally seen as one of the principal goals of education; indeed, who could argue convincingly *against* teaching young people to think critically? One might as soon take a stand against morality, or freedom of speech, or a sound economy. As McPeck (1981), however, noted dryly, "It is not at all clear that people mean the same thing by critical thinking, nor that they would all continue to approve of it if they did agree about what it meant. For very often with such matters approval diminishes in inverse proportion to the clarity with which they are perceived" (p. 1).

Clarifying the concept of critical thinking is no simple matter. For Wassermann (1989), the term *critical thinking* is only one in a long list of terms (e.g., lateral thinking, right-brain and left-brain thinking, cognitive processing) that represents the experts' varied conceptions and lack of agreement about what it means to think, much less to think "critically." If, for practical reasons, we try to summarize the wide variety of views on critical thinking into something like "good thinking, connected with rationality and the appeal to reason" (Bailin, 1996), we must take into consideration postmodern world views that challenge the supremacy of reason and rational thought as primary aims of educational practice. Commeyras (1994), for example, suggested that "if rationality is suspect, then so is critical thinking because it is an educational term based on the tradition that individuals should be guided by reason in their search for knowledge and truth" (p. 459).

Even when we can clarify the concept of critical thinking to our satisfaction and view its teaching as a worthy goal, disagreements arise as to how to deliver instruction in the classroom. In the 1980s, for example, a debate raged over the way in which critical thinking should be taught: Ennis (1962, 1987) and like-minded theorists advocated the teaching of critical thinking as "generic skills in separate, free-standing courses" (Lipman, 1991, p. 112), whereas McPeck (1981) called such teaching of critical thinking, unrelated as it was to any particular discipline or subject matter "muddled nonsense" (p. 13).

As teachers and researchers who have long been fascinated by the dynamics of discussions fostered within reading and writing communities, we view classroom talk as one of the most powerful tools available for the development of critical thinking. We, like Helmers (1993), believe that heightened perception and an elevation of the level of discourse in our classrooms "necessarily begin with the ability to discuss subjects with others" (p. 40). Classroom discussions demand no specialized curricular materials or courses, offer flexible opportunities for teacher-designed evaluation and assessment, and tailor themselves to the infinite variety of classroom contexts; in short, talk among classroom peers offers natural, rewarding, and productive opportunities for developing the skills and habits of critical thinking.

In this chapter, we first suggest a "working definition" of critical thinking as it applies to teachers and students in middle school classrooms. Next, we examine two examples of the kinds of critical thinking that may be fostered by classroom discussion. Finally, we offer some principles and techniques that may be helpful for teachers who wish to incorporate discussion into the kinds of classroom communities that support, enhance, and develop critical thinking.

Critical Thinking: A Working Definition

Ennis (1962, 1987) provides a good starting point for consideration of contemporary theories of critical thinking. In 1962, Ennis defined critical thinking as "the correct assessing of statements" (p. 81), a narrow definition, but one consistent with Ennis's background in logic. Over the years Ennis has expanded this early definition, and he now emphasizes the critical thinker's abilities in and dispositions toward "reasonable, rational thinking that helps us decide what to believe and do" (1987, p. 10). Ennis's extensive list of such abilities and dispositions ranges from focusing on a question to interacting with others and, according to Lipman (1991), has enjoyed popularity as a standard definition of critical thinking.

Although Ennis's definition does provide a handy, quotable description of critical thinking, teachers may want to consider two possible limitations to its usefulness in literacy instruction and classroom life: Ennis's dependence on rationality as a descriptor of critical thought and the narrowness of the goals of "believing" and "doing." According to Bailin (1996), challenges to the prevailing views of critical thinking have occupied much current debate: whether or not critical thinking should continue to be seen as the primary educational goal, how the proposal of critical thinking is a culturally biased imposition, and so forth. Such criticisms suggest that rationality has become increasingly suspect as a standard by which to evaluate the quality or efficacy of thought. Commyeras, for example, is troubled by postmodern and feminist views of rationality as a "system of thought that legitimizes a superstructure which excludes, disadvantages and silences certain groups of people" (1994, p. 464). As a solution, she proposes situating critical thinking within broader conceptions of thinking. Commyeras points to Gallo's (1989) writing on empathy and imagination as components of reasoning for one example of the numerous possibilities available to us for finding links and ties among aspects of thinking that have traditionally been seen as oppositional.

Similarly, teachers may want to broaden the goals of critical thinking. Lipman (1991) eloquently contrasts knowledge and wisdom, two intellectual pillars of the ancient world. Knowledge was traditionally seen as

> a body of eternal verities, perennially applicable to an unchanging world. In times of change, however, traditional knowledge was likely to become inapplicable or obsolete. What was emphasized instead were intellectual flexibility and resourcefulness. Wisdom was cultivated, by the Stoics and others, in preparation for whatever might happen, whether for good or for ill. (p. 114)

Lipman translates this ancient notion of wisdom into "good judgment," the major component of critical thinking and one not limited to solutions, decisions, or acquisition of beliefs. For Lipman, critical thinking is "thinking that facilitates judgment because it relies on criteria, is self-correcting, and is sensitive to context" (p. 116). We see this characterization of critical thinking as one of the best working definitions available to teachers and students, descriptive of the kinds of thoughtful inquiry that literacy instruction should call forth. In the next section, we illustrate Lipman's definition through the story of two discussions.

Discussion and Critical Thinking

The students in Dera's eighth-grade English class were reading *To Kill a Mockingbird* as their last class novel of the school year. Much had been made in their class discussions of Atticus's admonition to Scout that "you have to walk around in a man's skin for awhile" to achieve understanding of an individual's actions and reasons for those actions. One rainy Monday morning, children began sharing weekend stories, and one story in particular touched off a lively response: Someone, shopping in the downtown area of this university town, had seen a young man whose arms were covered in tattoos. The following exchange ensued:

CHRIS: That's so gross. I mean, anybody who would do that to themselves is just crazy. All those people downtown with green hair and eighty-five piercings, they ought to be arrested.

MATT: I'm scared to go down there sometimes. There's this one guy, he follows you around and tries to get money and I bet he's really just a college student who oughta be in class.

MARLA: People like that scare me.

Seeing an opportunity to incorporate a theme from the students' reading into their everyday experience, Dera asked, "Can you imagine any reasons why someone, maybe not someone just like you, but a young person with hopes and dreams and a little money to spend, might choose to have a tattoo?"

"Only if they were on drugs, " snorted Jerry. His sentiment was echoed in varying ways around the room until Kate said, "But you know, there are some of the football players who get those little tattoos on their arms, and there was that swimmer in the Olympics who had a little 'USA' or something tattooed on her ankle. I think those tattoos look good, they sorta show you're on a team and you're really proud and stuff."

The resulting discussion incorporated elements of critical thinking in subtle and intricately connected ways. Through their talk, the students established criteria for their judgments (the number of tattoos an individual might sport, for example, was seen as important, even after students agreed that the impulse to get a tattoo might be the same for the spiky-haired "townie" and the clean-cut athlete), corrected their own thinking by listening to each other and to themselves ("I can't believe I just said that! I'm making just as much a stereotype as Chris was!"), and gradually displayed a growing sensitivity for the context in which their judgments were shaped ("When people are pretty much the same as my friends, they don't seem scary and I don't mind if they do something kinda weird").

When asked to relate their discussion back to the book's theme of walking in someone else's shoes, several students immediately brought up the fear that Boo Radley had inspired in the children until they were made to see him as a human being like themselves. Despite Chris's good-natured grumbling ("You were setting us up! I thought we were just talking, and you were making up a lesson!"), the class agreed that examining their own prejudices and beliefs through discussion had made Atticus's words come to life.

The pursuit of critical thinking through classroom discussion is not always simple, however: In Patterson's (1991) description of a discussion she witnessed following a class reading of Harper Lee's *To Kill a Mockingbird,* the students produced a reading that was quite different from the one generated in Dera's room. Instead of finding the novel to be antiracist, the Black students in Patterson's class rejected it for its racist tone. They were not nearly as enamored of Atticus's admonition to Scout as Dera's class had been. In the following excerpt from Patterson's recollection of that discussion, it is clear that a different kind of critical thinking was going on:

> We had just finished reading *To Kill a Mockingbird.* . . . Nice kids from nice homes. The discussion had been lively but generally supportive of the novel's themes. This was in the days when we talked about themes. And authors. When we said things like this: "Harper Lee thinks that people should be more tolerant of others who are different." The tone was white liberal; reasonable, accommodating.
>
> Celine was silent. Her reading journal had picked away at the edges of a barely discernible worry. Now in class she failed to participate. A quiet child . . . she did not speak. And you, Celine, what do you think about the question of race in this novel?
>
> "You wanna know what I think?! I think this book is racist. This class is racist. This discussion is racist. And . . . Harper Lee is racist too." A round of applause from black students in the classroom. Stunned silence from whites. (Patterson, 1991, p. 246)

As Patterson (1991) explained, although it could be argued that the Black students' experiences of racism were different from those of the White students, this is an essentialist argument that categorizes individuals on the basis of group membership as opposed to recognizing individual differences within groups. Like Patterson we prefer to locate Celine's critical interpretation of *To Kill a Mockingbird* in a discursive framework rather than in human essence. That is, if we assume that

> readers may not produce personal interpretations out of their individual experiences so much as produce readings which are positioned by particular sets of values and beliefs, then we can begin to reconceptualize reading as a social practice. It is in this sense that students of different races, different social classes, and different genders may produce reading which challenge dominant or authoritative meanings because they have available to them different sets of values and beliefs. . . . Readers construct readings, not as originators of meaning, but as human subjects positioned through social, political, and economic discursive practices that remain the location of a constant struggle over power. (Patterson, Mellor, & O'Neill, 1994, pp. 65–66)

A critical view of the thinking that goes on in postreading discussions, such as those described above, provides teachers with a foundation for educational practices that are grounded in self-reflection and introspection. By examining our assumptions about the thinking that is generated when readers construct meanings from the social, political, and economic positions afforded them, it is quite likely that those assumptions will not seem as simply "normal" as they once did. In fact, we may find that they are inappropriate and inaccurate, as Patterson (1991) did when she began to question some of her own practices. In her words,

> It took several years of Celines yelling at me, of students refusing to sit in their seats, of silent resistance, of confrontations, of tears and tantrums before I started to ask if there wasn't something not quite right with the way I taught literature. I began to be seriously bothered about the questions my students had been asking me for a long time: Who chooses the literature we're supposed to love? What view of the world do these books promote? Whose reality is this? Finally, I stopped asking, "what is the meaning of this book?" and started asking, "how does this book mean?" (p. 246)

The idea that the language of a book (or any other kind of text) constrains what information is available to readers—in terms of what social, political, and economic positions are available for taking up—adds complexity to Lipman's (1991) definition of critical thinking. In particular, this idea of discursively located readers speaks to Lipman's notion of sensitivity to context. When we no longer assume that readers are the source of their own interpretations of texts, it is possible to entertain the idea that texts position readers in a multitude of ways depending on the context and the particular sets of beliefs and values that are operating within that context.

Critical thinking in discussions where oppositional views such as those expressed by Celine are present is quite different from the critical thinking that takes place in more homogeneous settings. For one thing, the discussions will reflect how different speech communities use language to accord status to some groups and to withhold it from others. For example, in Dera's classroom, the students established criteria for the judgments they made about people who sported tattoos. Some students even changed their thinking as they listened to each other and began to see how contextually bound values and beliefs had influenced their thinking. In Patterson's (1991) class, on the other hand, the status accorded to a mainstream interpretation of *To Kill a Mockingbird* was challenged. Celine's interpretation rested on a different set of beliefs about the main character's motivation. For her, Harper Lee's novel was racist, as was the class and the class discussion of it. This kind of interpretation caused the teacher to reevaluate the criteria she used in selecting literature, a move that eventually led to greater sensitivity to context and to strategies for encouraging students' divergent views.

As these two examples suggest, discussions that encourage critical thinking are lively, exciting, and productive; they are also messy, unpredictable, and even dangerous. There is no easy formula for producing the neatly tied-up and resolved finale of the first example, nor does there exist any early warning system for predicting and deflecting Celine's response. As teachers, we must take comfort and courage from knowing that our willingness to engage students in this kind of talk serves them well and that our commitment to providing classroom opportunities to develop the "good judgment" of which Lipman (1991) speaks can make a difference in the way they perceive themselves and the worlds they will call their own.

Principles for Fostering Classroom Discussion

Several years ago, we participated in a multicase study of middle and high school students' perceptions of their own experience in text-based discussions (Alvermann et al., 1996). By focusing on students' insights into their actions, thoughts, and motives in classroom discussions, we were able to draw three major conclusions: Students are generally aware of the conditions they believe to be conducive to good discussions, students are knowledgeable about the different tasks and topics that influence their participation in a discussion, and students are cognizant of how classroom discussion helps them understand what they read. Students, in other words, have had enough school experience with the various activities that come under the label of "discussion" to know what kinds of discussions are worthwhile to them.

One practical implication of our findings is that teachers should not expect students' viewpoints about conditions, tasks and topics, and the role of discussion in understanding texts to coincide with the teacher's (or any other adult's) viewpoint. For the teacher intent on maintaining control of classroom talk, curriculum, class routine, and learning outcomes, this understanding may present a challenge. For teachers who value critical thinking, student independence, and self-directed learning, however, differing points of view about discussion only serve to enrich the context in which discussion can take place.

We suggest the following principles for fostering an atmosphere of thoughtful discussion (Alvermann et al., 1996):

1. Provide students with frequent opportunities to discuss what they read. A discussion every month or so will not produce the context of thoughtful discussion that allows successful discussions to occur.

2. Develop a sense of community within the classroom. Acknowledge diversity, emphasize common goals, and point out the benefits of cooperation.
3. Be attentive to group dynamics. When group dynamics foster mutual respect and understanding, students will be more likely to try out new ideas, self-correct their own thinking, and be tolerant of others.
4. Be reflective, and encourage students to reflect on their discussions. Spend some class time occasionally in letting students evaluate their own discussions.
5. Moderate; do not dominate. Students can take the lead in directing discussion. Learn to set conversation in motion and then step back.
6. Search for topics that motivate students. Be alert for connections between students' everyday lives and classroom learning, and encourage students to make connections among the various contexts of their daily lives.

In addition to the principles listed above for encouraging discussion, the teacher who wishes to support critical thinking through classroom talk must be cognizant of the different social, political, and economic influences on texts (particularly their authors) and readers. The positions available to readers for taking up in classroom discussions of such texts are frequently limited by teachers' unexamined assumptions about their practices. One way of dealing with this limitation is to support teachers in their learning about themselves and others through the formation of ethnic autobiography clubs (Florio-Ruane, Raphael, Glazier, McVee, & Wallace, 1997).

These clubs, at least as envisioned by Florio-Ruane and her colleagues, serve as the impetus for engaging teachers in peer-led discussions of cultural differences and their relation to schooling, identity building, and literacy learning. As originally conceptualized, the ethnic autobiography clubs included texts written by well-known authors who are recognized as having successfully bridged differences in social, political, and economic backgrounds, such as Vivian Paley's (1979) *White Teacher,* Richard Rodriguez's (1982) *Hunger of Memory: The Education of Richard Rodriguez,* and Mike Rose's (1989) *Lives on the Boundary.* For our purposes, however, we prefer having teachers in our undergraduate and graduate level classes write and share their own autobiographies as a means of building an awareness of how discursively positioned each person is and how such positioning can be resisted or modified.

A classroom within which children can learn to select valid criteria for the evaluation of ideas, to take the risk of being wrong or misunderstood or out of the mainstream, and to value the contexts of others' lives—what better environment could we offer our middle school children for the days they spend with us?

REFERENCES

Alvermann, D.E., Young, J., Weaver, D., Hinchman, K.A., Moore, D.W., Phelps, S.F., Thrash, E.C., & Zalewski, P. (1996). Middle and high school students' perceptions of how they experience text-based discussions: A multicase study. *Reading Research Quarterly, 31,* 244–267.

Bailin, S. (1996). Critical thinking. In J.J. Chambliss (Ed.), *Philosophy of education: An encyclopedia* (pp. 119–122). New York: Garland.

Commeyras, M. (1994). Exploring critical thinking from a feminist standpoint: Limitations and potential. In C.K. Kinzer & D.J. Leu (Eds.), *Multidimensional aspects of literacy research, theory, and practice,* Forty-third yearbook of the National Reading Conference (pp. 459–464). Chicago: National Reading Conference.

Ennis, R. (1962). A concept of critical thinking: A proposed basis for research in the teaching and evaluation of critical thinking ability. *Harvard Educational Review, 32,* 81–111.

————. (1987). A taxonomy of critical thinking dispositions and abilities. In J. Baron & R. Sternberg (Eds.), *Teaching thinking skills: Theory and practice* (pp. 9–26). New York: W.H. Freeman.

Florio-Ruane, S., Raphael, T.E., Glazier, J., McVee, M., & Wallace, S. (1997). Discovering culture in discussion of autobiographical literature: Transforming the education of literacy teachers. In C.K. Kinzer, K.A. Hinchman, & D.J. Leu (Eds.), *Inquiries in literacy theory and practice,* Forty-sixth yearbook of the National Reading Conference (pp. 452–464). Chicago: National Reading Conference.

Gallo, D. (1989). Educating for empathy, reason and imagination. *Journal of Creative Behavior, 23*(2), 98–115.

Helmers, M. (1993). A demand for inspired conversation: Rhetoric and the discussion dilemma. *Writing Instructor, 13*(1), 35–44.

Lipman, M. (1991). *Thinking in education.* New York: Cambridge University Press.

McPeck, J.E. (1981). *Critical thinking and education.* New York: St. Martin's Press.

Paley, V.G. (1979). *White teacher.* Cambridge, MA: Harvard University Press.

Patterson, A. (1991). Power, authority and reader-response. In P. Cormack (Ed.), *Literacy: Making it explicit, making it possible* (pp. 246–252). Adelaide: Australian Reading Association.

Patterson, A., Mellor, B., & O'Neill, M. (1994). In B. Corcoran, M. Hayhoe, & G.M. Pradl (Eds.), *Knowledge in the making* (pp. 61–72). Portsmouth, NH: Boynton/Cook.

Rodriguez, R. (1982). *Hunger of memory: The education of Richard Rodriguez.* New York: Bantam.

Rose, M. (1989) *Lives on the boundary.* New York: Penguin.

Wassermann, S. (1989). Reflections on measuring thinking, while listening to Mozart's Jupiter Symphony. *Phi Delta Kappan, 70,* 365–370.

25 The Enhanced Concerns Framework

A Helpful Heuristic for Working with Middle School Writers

DEBRA BAYLES MARTIN
San Diego State University

JAMES V. HOFFMAN
University of Texas at Austin

The middle school years: For many students and their teachers, they encompass "the best of times" and "the worst of times." This may be, in part, because "young people undergo more rapid and profound personal changes during the years between 10 and 15 than at any other period of their lives" (National Middle School Association, 1995, pp. 5–6). Among the students in any middle school setting, one encounters an overwhelming diversity of social, physical, intellectual, and emotional development. No doubt, middle school teachers agree that one of their greatest challenges is designing developmentally responsive middle school experiences for students who exhibit such dissimilar rates of growth in all areas of development. This situation is particularly true when it comes to helping students grow as writers, given the numerous, often extremely personal, aspects of writing development. Although the variability among adolescents creates numerous challenges for writing instruction, it also portends great promise. By learning about and focusing on differences among student concerns and roles during writing, teachers and students alike can learn not only about the self as writer, but about the self in more general terms.

Over the years, we have found three concepts to be particularly helpful in engaging the adolescent writer in more successful writing ventures: (1) considering how students' prior instructional experiences may impact their current approaches to writing, (2) exploring the notion of "concerns" (Fuller, 1969) to help students (and teachers) identify specific sources of writing challenges through teacher-led conferences, and (3) drawing from Flower's (1981) summary of the roles of a writer to help students discuss and solve writing concerns and challenges through role-play and other related techniques.

Impact of Prior Instructional Experiences on Students' Approaches to Writing

Various iterations of the "writing process" have recently found their way into state and local language arts curricula, especially at the elementary level (see Texas Education Association, 1996, and California Department of Education, 1995). Although these guides frame writing instruction in slightly different ways, it is common for elementary teachers to enact a five-step approach to writing instruction, with students working on a different "stage" each school day: planning/brainstorming on Monday; drafting on Tuesday; revising on Wednesday; editing, proofing, and polishing on Thursday; and publishing and sharing on Friday, for example.

Those responsible for advancing the notions underlying a process approach to writing likely regard five-step (or other structured approaches) as a good idea gone awry. Although the effort to emphasize writing processes is laudable, we believe that for many middle school students, elementary school experience with structured "process" approaches may have ingrained some undesirable or at least inflexible ideas about what writing is and how it is accomplished. For example, how many students encountered difficulty coming up with weekly topics in elementary writing "workshops"? With how many different genres did students gain writing experience? What concerns did students develop about themselves as writers or about particular aspects of writing? How were these concerns addressed? How willing were students to explore various nuances of revising and editing if a completed piece was expected each Friday? How often was peer response accomplished at the teacher's behest, rather than out of a regard for the skills and potential contributions of one's peers? No doubt, many middle school students enter grades 5 to 8 having written more text than students of previous generations, yet numerous questions remain about whether each student author experienced full-faceted support as a developing writer.

In defense of well-intentioned instructional approaches, we acknowledge that it is extremely difficult to operationalize a "process" in a formal educational setting without sacrificing some of its major tenets. Unfortunately, no matter how well-intentioned the pressure to engage in some aspects of the writing "process," perhaps some of our middle school students left their elementary writing experiences unaware of or inexperienced with problem-solving orientations to writing. This may be especially true for students from diverse cultural and linguistic backgrounds who often exhibit more writing problems in their spontaneous writing than other middle school students (Hooper, Swartz, & Montgomery, 1993). Clearly, our efforts to provide culturally responsive middle school education must encompass consideration of our students' past writing experiences, their concerns, and the various roles they assume during the writing process, but how do we represent the writing process to middle school students without encouraging misinterpretations or misapplications similar to those they may have already experienced?

We believe that part of the difficulty in enacting process principles (as in writer's workshop) into instructional programs centers on the images we use to represent an idea, both to ourselves and to our students. Although images can enhance our understanding and help us communicate ideas, they can also distort concepts and mislead teachers and learners. For example, thinking of writing as a single process composed of a series of "stages" or "steps" can help us move beyond a focus on the product and consider other important aspects of authoring. This same image, however, can also encourage us to believe there is "one" writing process comprised of linear, lock-step stages. When this happens, we may overlook the idea of recursiveness in writing (i.e., that writers often loop back into various stages, moving among and between "steps" in endless variations) or the idea of variation in writing approaches. Yet, if we try to remain true to the concept of complex writing processes and introduce students to notions of recursiveness and varied individual writing approaches, we may create an image too complex to be useful.

In contrast to thinking of the writing "process" only as a series of stages or steps, or as a cycle, we find it helpful to consider the writing process through a slightly different lens, derived from concerns theory (Fuller, 1969) and the idea of authoring roles (Flowers, 1981). This enhanced concerns framework has been instrumental to us in designing support systems for adolescent writers. We do not propose the enhanced concerns framework as a *replacement* for writing process stage models, nor do we consider it inherently "better" in the way it represents psychological and social processes associated with writing. Rather, we view it as another way to think about the writing process that may open up some new possibilities for instruction. To share this image, we first describe the roots of concerns theory, then we summarize Flower's (1981) characterization of the roles of an author. Finally, we share how combining these two notions results in the enhanced concerns framework that we use to help adolescent writers enhance their writing skills and learn to "conference" more successfully with others, and with themselves.

Roots of the Concerns Model

In the late 1960s, Frances Fuller undertook a series of studies to explore the processes involved in learning to teach. She interviewed teachers at various points in their careers (preservice, beginning teaching, and in-service levels) in a variety of settings. Fuller noted that at the beginning of their preparation programs, preservice teachers often expressed concerns about themselves and their standing in the eyes of others (e.g., "What kind of grade am I going to get in this methods course?" "Will my supervisor like me?" "Is teaching the kind of career I will be good at?"). She called these concerns *self* concerns. As individuals grew more comfortable with their surroundings and the accompanying expectations, they expressed fewer *self* concerns and focused more on the mechanics of teaching (e.g., "How do I set up cooperative groups?" "How will I distribute materials?" "How can I cover this unit in one week?"). These *task* concerns marked a shift in focus away from the self toward the logistics of teaching, and they often appeared among beginning teachers. In contrast, experienced teachers commented more often about the effect of a particular task or activity on student learning (e.g., "Is this the best method to use with this child?" "Would I get better results if I used more manipulatives?"). Fuller called concerns about student welfare and learning *impact* concerns.

Based on a careful inspection of teachers' comments over time, Fuller formulated a tentative model of teaching development, the concerns model. According to the model, teachers consistently express concerns in the three major areas of *self, task,* and *impact.* High levels of self-concern characterize preservice teachers who worry about how they will be perceived by others and whether their performance will be judged as acceptable. Beginning teachers tend to shift their focus away from themselves toward the task at hand, expressing concern about how to best orchestrate the demands of teaching. Having mastered (to some degree) the managerial aspects of teaching, expert teachers generally express concerns about the impact or value of a task or activity on those involved.

Although a group of teachers (or learners) may be described according to their expressed concerns (e.g., high numbers of *self* concerns likely suggest preservice teachers), it does not mean that teachers in a given stage never express other concerns. Rather, all teachers (regardless of their stage of development) operate with all three concern types at any given point in time. What differentiates groups is not only the number but the *intensity* of the concerns. The beginning teacher, for example, still carries many *self* concerns (e.g., "How will my principal evaluate my teaching?") in addition to high levels of *task* concerns, but the intensity of the self concern is generally much lower than that of other areas.

Over time, teacher concerns usually progress from the self to the task to the impact level. Movement from one stage of concern to the next when concerns at one level are satisfied or reduced. Fuller found, for example, that beginning teachers were generally unable to focus on impact issues until task concerns were resolved. Efforts to push or force teachers from one stage of concern to another (e.g., from task to impact) only led to heightened personal concerns and retarded development. It takes time and experience for a teacher at one stage of concern to address those concerns and move on to other issues.

Many researchers have applied the concerns model to settings beyond teaching, finding similar results with almost any type of change process involving individuals (see Hall & Loucks, 1981). Like preservice teachers, novice learners in any field or endeavor are generally beset with a number of personal or self concerns. As they grow in experience, they tend to focus more on task issues (e.g., the "how-to" aspect of learning). As task concerns are addressed, learners generally move to impact concerns, evaluating the effect of their learning or efforts on others.

In addition to finding parallels between the cycle of teacher concerns and the concerns expressed by individuals in other learning situations, researchers have noted the importance of context in concerns theory. For example, even a career teacher (typically focused on impact concerns) is likely to exhibit self and task concerns when faced with adopting some change (e.g., adjusting teaching practices to be in line with a recently mandated skills testing program). It appears that concerns about self, task, and impact ebb and flow over time, dependent on situational factors as well as one's experiences.

Concerns Theory Applied to the Writing Process

If we were to take a five-step writing process model and consider the five stages/elements (i.e., planning, drafting, revising, editing, and publishing) not as steps along a path, but rather as areas of concern that exist at all times within the writer, we might depict the concerns of an author beginning a project as in Figure 25.1. Note that as the project begins, the author's planning concerns are highest, followed by drafting concerns. Concerns related to revising, editing, and publishing are minimal early in the writing process.

In like manner, the concerns of the same author nearing project completion might look like those in Figure 25.2. Although the writer is still aware of all aspects of the writing process, he or she is now focused most intently (has highest concerns) on revising, editing, and publishing. In this case, what has changed within the writer with respect to a specific project is not necessarily where he or she is along the "steps" or "stages" (because actual writing is recursive and "messy" in nature), but the relative intensity of various areas of concern within the individual. As an idea begins to take shape, planning concerns likely decrease while the author focuses increased attention on revision. Typically, concerns with editing and publishing rise as the writing nears some kind of closure. Thus, as a writer moves through a project, his or her concerns

FIGURE 25.1   Possible Areas of Writing Concern (Beginning a Project)

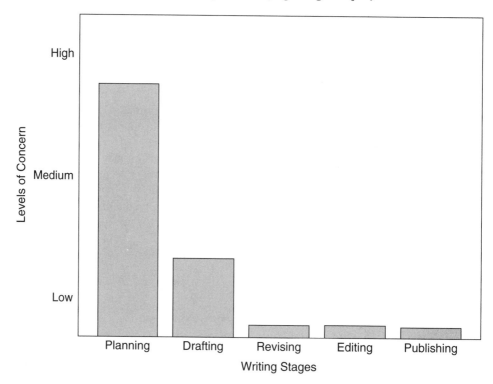

FIGURE 25.2   Possible Areas of Writing Concern (Project Nearing Completion)

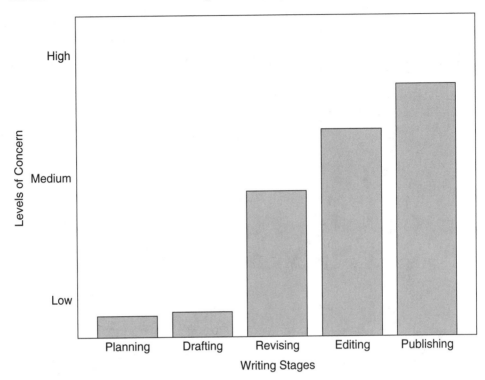

might be predicted as a sort of stair-step progression, with each stage taking its turn as the highest area of concern (moving in a wave pattern).

Admittedly, this analogy may appear somewhat "idealized" and linear in application. Its usefulness becomes more apparent, however, when we consider how to best intervene when students deviate from the expected progression of concerns. Although we believe heightened concern with particular aspects of the writing process is to be expected and even desired as a piece progresses, we have noted that when a writer is "stuck," he or she often exhibits a concerns profile that differs from that described above. These differences often take one of three general patterns. A writer may be "stuck" when experiencing heightened concerns (1) in several areas at once, (2) in non-contiguous areas, or (3) in conflicting areas (i.e., worrying about publishing before planning occurs). Determining which concerns may be competing or out of synch with project progress can help teachers intervene more ably.

Consider, for example, how to best help Shandra, a sixth-grade student who experienced heavy skills emphasis in her elementary school writing projects. When asked to write a short, personal narrative, Shandra freezes, convinced that her spelling and grammar skills will be found wanting. How likely is it that this student will plan and draft freely as long as her editing concern remains this high? A teacher who visualizes Shandra's concerns (as in Figure 25.3) can see at a glance that her worry about editing is both out of synch for the project (e.g., should come later in the process) and unusually high compared with the other, typical concerns. When assured that class members will be given time to help one another edit and correct their drafts *before* submitting them for credit, Shandra is able to turn her attention back to planning and drafting.

Creating the Concerns Framework

If we extend the analogy between Fuller's work with concerns theory and the writing process even further (to reflect elements of writing as well as areas of concern better), we can superimpose concerns of *self, task,* and *impact* on the simple graphs in Figures 25.1 to 25.3 to achieve the *concerns framework* depicted in Figure 25.4. In this framework, concerns with *self* remain labeled as such and appear early in the model, reading from left to right (see the lightly shaded gray area in Figure 25.4). We have divided the notion of *task* to include *content* and *form* to distinguish between the ideas being worked with (content) and the literary structures to be used (form). Initial concerns related to form often operate at the level of genre (e.g., Will I write a story? A poem? A

FIGURE 25.3   Possible Areas of Writing Concern (Competing Stages)

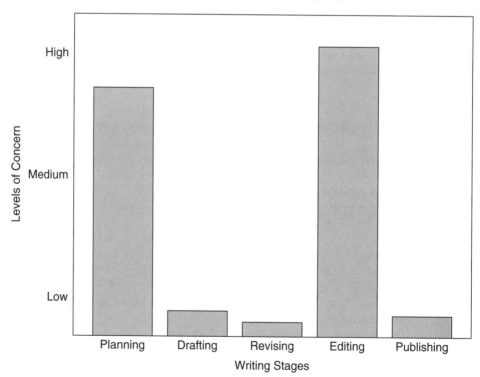

"how-to" piece?). At later stages, the writer becomes more concerned with elements of convention (e.g., Does it need to rhyme? How is my spelling?). Finally, we have relabeled Fuller's notion of *impact* as *audience*. For beginning writers, early notions of *impact/audience* most often center upon the writer himself or herself. Middle school students generally hold a more external notion of audience, often including how they believe peers will respond to their work.

The background in this application of the concerns framework will always stay the same (i.e., the shaded areas of self, content, form, and audience), but the foreground changes based on the status of the writer in relation to the work under way. The skilled teacher, in conducting conferences with students, will listen carefully as students give a status report. Through the status report, the students reveal their concerns. The teacher uses this information to mentally construct the foreground (concerns profile) that can inform decision making about questions, strategies, or activities to move the process along. Based on concerns theory, the guiding principles for conferencing with students are twofold: (1) help the writer reduce the highest-level concerns, and (2) help the writer focus on concerns that are most appropriate to the development of the piece in progress.

FIGURE 25.4   Concerns Framework (Beginning a Project)

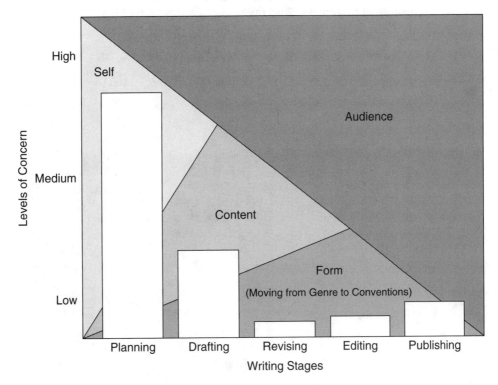

Applying the Concerns Framework

Let us apply the concerns framework to Jarom, a seventh-grade student beginning a tribute to his mother for her birthday. As we approach his desk, Jarom tells us that he is "stuck." If we consider his comments from a traditional writing "stage" perspective, we might assume that Jarom is "stuck" due to insufficient planning and brainstorming for the piece. Before we can suggest further brainstorming questions, however, Jarom spouts, "I *hate* this piece! I want to tell my mom how great she is, since her birthday's coming up. But she likes funny things and this sounds too serious!"

If we attempt to depict Jarom's comments from a concerns perspective, his concerns might look like those in Figure 25.5. Although he still entertains planning and drafting concerns (accompanied by *self* and *content* concerns about how his work will reflect on him), it is clear that Jarom has already engaged in a great deal of planning. Help with planning and brainstorming may not be what Jarom most needs. Rather, beyond the expected planning and drafting concerns Jarom's words suggest a concern of greater intensity: achieving the desired audience response of pleasing his mother. If this concern remains unaddressed, Jarom will probably remain frustrated with his work. Thus, instead of engaging Jarom in additional planning or brainstorming experi-

FIGURE 25.5   Jarom's Concerns Framework (Competing Stages)

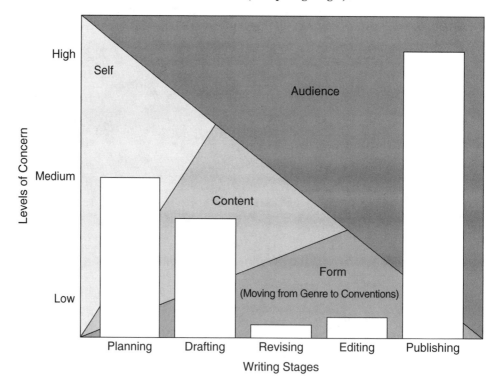

ences, we undertake a discussion about his mother's preferences and responses, perhaps asking such questions as, "Why do you think the piece seems to be assuming a serious tone?" "What do you see in this piece that might lend itself to being funny?" "Does your mom only like funny things?" and "How might she react to a more serious expression of your feelings on a special day like her birthday?" As Jarom considers the possibility that his mother may be open to serious expressions, he is reassured that his focus is potentially rewarding and, thus, overcomes his "block" about the need for humor in this piece.

In applying concerns theory to writers like Jarom and Shandra, we have noticed two frequently recurring patterns of concerns that impede the flow of the writing process. In the first pattern, a student focuses heavily on concern areas not generally associated with typical project progress. Shandra's concerns about her ability to write well without special editing time are a good example of this pattern. Although concerns about editing are normal and desirable, they can impede writing if they arise too early in the process. By examining the shaded areas of the framework that provide background to such concerns (see Figure 25.6), we can see that students exhibiting concern patterns similar to Shandra's likely experience a high degree of concern related to self, content, and audience. Conferencing efforts that fail to acknowledge these

FIGURE 25.6   Concerns about Editing at the Beginning of a Project (Competing Stages)

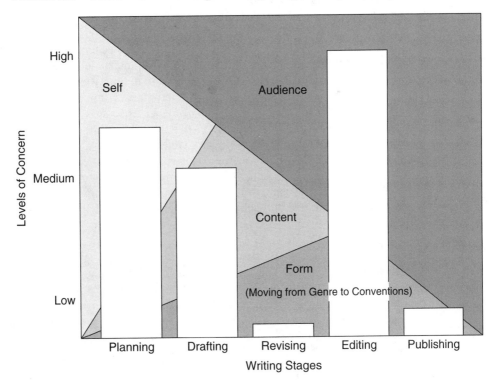

concerns may be less effective, failing to respond to the adolescent writer's affective needs.

A second concern pattern that often impedes writing flow involves not so much the synchrony (or lack of synchrony) of a particular concern with its related writing stage (e.g., Shandra), but rather the overall intensity of particular concerns. For example, in Jarom's case, a concern about audience (which generally rises in intensity during editing and sharing) not only arose early in his work, but it arose with great intensity (i.e., "I *hate* this piece!"). Rather than focusing on planning and drafting, Jarom was absorbed in his negative predictions about the effect of the unwritten piece on his audience (his mother). It was essential for his writing progress that Jarom move away from planning and drafting issues and address the audience concerns plaguing him. Only then could he resume drafting.

Jarom and Shandra's experiences illustrate the "block" in the process that can occur when concerns are extremely intense or arise out of a somewhat "typical" order. If we can determine whether a student's concerns are out of synch with the project's progress or whether the concerns are unusually intense, we can focus our interactions with students on critical issues to help them move smoothly back into the authoring process. We have found that addressing the most intense concern is generally the most productive route for teachers to follow to nudge students back into successful writing. Thinking about the concerns framework helps us decide what kinds of questions to ask and where to place our conferencing emphasis as we work with adolescent students.

Although much of our description of the concerns framework reflects a workshop format (e.g., Calkins, 1980/1996; Atwell, 1987), we also believe that the model may be applied to writing in more focused contexts. In the workshop model, the conference is regarded as one of the most important ways in which teachers can support students as writers, but conferences can occur between teacher and student at any time, in any setting. Conferences can help students move forward in their work with a particular writing project, and they may help students to internalize certain strategies and operations that will guide them toward greater independence as writers. Conferences, of course, are designed for many different purposes (e.g., content, editing) and involve many different interactions (e.g., teacher–student, student–student, student–class). In offering an illustration for how the concerns framework might be applied to instruction, we have focused first on the teacher–student conference and later address the student-to-self conference. It makes no difference in developing our argument whether a conference is student initiated or teacher initiated (e.g., as part of some schedule devised by the teacher).

As teachers conference with students, they can ask them to reflect on where they are with respect to a particular writing project. As we have seen, concerns theory helps predict and reflect the kinds of questions that guide writers as they work to bring a piece to completion. These questions may be explicit in a student's comments or remain implicit, requiring the teacher to infer and make explicit various concerns which may be supporting (or hindering) the writing process. Although not a complete list, the following questions often characterize a specific or heightened area of concern:

Questions Reflecting Self Concern

- Where am I in relation to this piece?
- Where is it coming from?
- How much of an emotional or personal investment do I have in these ideas?
- How close am I to the feelings, experiences, and ideas being expressed?
- How important is the work to me?
- What risks am I exposing myself to through this piece?

Questions Reflecting Task Concern

- What is the informational or experiential base for this piece?
- What are the possibilities for this piece?
- What genre would be best to write in (e.g., poetry)?
- How do I want to (re)structure the piece?
- What materials are necessary to create and publish this piece?
- How long do I have to accomplish this project?

Questions Reflecting Impact Concern

- Who do I foresee as the audience for this writing?
- What kinds of things would this audience expect or like?
- What impact do I hope to have (e.g., entertain, convince)?
- What do I know about this audience?
- Am I (the author) the only audience?

Students do not always express their concerns in the form of a question. We have used questions in these examples because we want to encourage the use of questioning and inquiry in teacher–student interactions. Perhaps when teachers encounter a student statement of concern such as "I can't think of anything to write!" they may want to help students rephrase their statements in the form of a related question to discover the concern underlying their words (e.g., "How can I think of things to write?")

Although many authors suggest the value of holding regular and specific writing conferences with students (cf. Calkins, 1980/1996), we have found that it is rarely productive to engage in a specific content conference (e.g., use of conventions in a particular piece, characteristics of a particular genre, etc.) if other student concerns are elevated. Thus, the concerns framework provides a foundation for addressing the affective needs of adolescent writers, which then allows us to more productively offer other content-based writing support. Unfortunately, the notion of being able to arrive on the scene and ascertain student concerns at the critical moment makes for better dreams than reality. In our busy classrooms (Doyle, 1981), how do we find the time to meet with our students and proffer sensitive feedback whenever it is needed? In addition, even if we could achieve such intervention, is such teacher-centered instruction really our most cherished goal as writing instructors? Although we believe that sensitive instructor–student writing conferences are essential to writers' development (both as models of how to think about writing and as content-based sources of information), we believe that it is even more important to foster in our middle school students the ability and desire to conference "with themselves" as it were, thereby learning to scaffold themselves as writers and provide for their own growth. Beyond sensitive conferencing drawn from the concerns framework, we wondered how to encourage adolescents to "take on" more responsibility for solving their own writing challenges. Flower's depiction of various roles in the writing process provided us with some helpful ideas. In the next section, we describe Flower's ideas and then discuss how they helped us enhance the concerns framework.

Talking to Yourself as Another Self: Exploring Various Roles of a Writer

As mentioned above, we have found that frequent conferences with writers informed by concerns theory help create a responsive atmosphere for encouraging adolescents to write. It is rewarding to help students address specific concerns so they can progress with their writing projects. Still, the question persists: Can sensitive dialogues be taken one step further, so students can learn to address their *own* writing concerns? Our answer to this question is a qualified yes. We draw our support for this view from recent trends encouraging middle school students to take a more active role in their learning (Hackmann, 1997) and from our own experience.

Trends in Student-Led Conferences: What Do They Portend for Writing Instruction?

In a recent summary on student-led parent conferences in the middle school, Hackmann (1997) noted that encouraging students to take the lead in parent conferencing has helped students accept responsibility for their academic performance, learn about the process of self-evaluation, develop organizational and communication skills, and engage in open and honest dialogue. Although at first reading the concept of student-led parent conferences may seem far removed from that of teacher-led or student-led writing conferences, we believe that findings from engaging students in one type of conference may transfer to other conference settings. For example, in implementing student-led parent conferences, middle school teachers have learned that they cannot assume that middle-level students come to them with the requisite communication and organizing skills. Thus, they must prepare students by providing time, practice, and feedback regarding ways to lead a conference. Role playing is one of the techniques teachers call upon to help students prepare for successful conferences (Guyton & Fielstein, 1989). As students explore various conference scenarios with student partners, they are able to "try out" various approaches to conference problems and ascertain their possible effectiveness with minimal personal risk.

We have seen similar results in our efforts to encourage middle school students to take on more responsibility for their writing progress through self-led writer's conferences. After introducing the concepts of the writing process and varying concerns discussed earlier, we spend time engaging in teacher-led writing conferences based on the concerns framework. As students grow familiar with concerns-based interactions, we then introduce the notion of conferencing with oneself as a way of solving writing challenges when concerns are high or when other conferees are unavailable.

Using overhead transparencies or large posters (see Figure 25.7), we introduce Flower's (1981) metaphorical "voices" (depicting various roles of an author) as actual characters with whom students can engage in personal writing conferences. Like our colleagues working with student-led parent conferences, we encourage students to address personal writing concerns through role playing with the Flower characters. We believe that helping students engage in such dialogues and role playing can help them gain greater control over their thinking and their writing.

Figure 25.8 is a replica of an actual handout we use when introducing our students to the notion of various roles an author assumes. After introducing each character (e.g., Madman, Judge, Architect), we engage the students in discussion about the value of each character's contribution to the writing process, and then spend time role playing ways each character might respond to sample pieces of writing and common writing scenarios. When the students seem familiar with the characters and typical responses, we introduce the notion of them assuming each of these roles at appropriate times in their own writing. Often, we map out with the students familiar stages of the writing process and list when each character might be most welcome as well as when he or she would likely hinder the process. Finally (usually on another class day), we discuss what kinds of writing challenges each character might help solve. For example, in addressing the question of what to do if you're having trouble drafting your thoughts, students might respond with ideas such as "You need to invite the Madman in if you're too worried about what you're saying. Let him take over for awhile and just be crazy" or "Kick the judge out for awhile." Once students have defined general solutions for several typical writing problems, we invite them to role play a number of "stuck" authors and one (or more) of the characters we have identified as helpful for a given situation. The last part of this class meeting focuses on asking students how they could apply this knowledge if they were working on their own. Students are generally pleased to discover that if they are "stuck" with a writing problem, they can "take on" the roles of the various characters and consider various problem-solving strategies within themselves, almost as if the characters had actually interacted with them.

Moving from Interactive to Internal Role Play

At this point, we introduce an overhead design (see Figure 25.9) and ask the students to link what they have learned about the writing process, levels of concern that arise within writers, and ways to address those concerns. Students quickly ascertain that the graphic representations of characters appear near the areas where they are generally "welcome guests." In other words, someone with high planning concerns needs to spend time with the Madman, whereas someone with revising concerns should consult the architect and the carpenter. Perhaps you will note, as do our students, the addition of three faces toward the far right of the figure. We have found, in working with Flower's (1981) characters, that students too easily conceive of the negative aspects of audiences rather than the positive. As a result, we added the smiling faces of some

FIGURE 25.7   Summary of Author Roles

Madman: "He's full of ideas, writes crazily and perhaps rather sloppily, gets carried away by enthusiasm or anger, and if really let loose, could turn out ten pages an hour."

energy	ideas	subjective-personal
child	author	eternality
	feeling	air (free-flying)

Judge: "He's been educated and knows a sentence fragment when he sees one. He peers over your shoulder and says 'That's trash!' with such authority that the madman loses his crazy confidence and shrivels up. You know the judge is right—after all, he speaks with the voice of your most imperious English teacher. But for all his sharpness of eye, he can't create anything."

Architect: "She will read the wild scribblings saved from the night before and pick out maybe a tenth of the jottings as relevant or interesting. (You can see immediately that the architect is not sentimental about what the madman wrote; she's not going to save every crumb for posterity.) Her job is simply to select large chunks of material and to arrange them in a pattern that might form an argument. The thinking here is large, organizational, paragraph-level thinking—the architect doesn't worry about sentence structure."

paragraphs	intuition	space
argument	soul	earth (firm grounding)
thinking	subjective-impersonal	

Carpenter: The carpenter "enters after the essay has been hewn into large chunks of related ideas. The carpenter nails these ideas together in a logical sequence, making sure each sentence is clearly written, contributes to the argument of the paragraph, and leads logically and gracefully to the next sentence. When the carpenter finishes, the essay should be smooth and watertight."

sentences	integrity	time
craft	adult	water (smooth sailing)
acting	objective-personal	

Judge: "And then the judge comes around to inspect. Punctuation, spelling, grammar, tone—all the details which result in a polished essay become important only in this last stage. These details are not the concern of the madman who's come up with the ideas, or the architect who's organized them, or the carpenter who's nailed the ideas together, sentence by sentence. Save details for the judge."

mechanics	critical intellect	objective-impersonal
audience	parent	immortality
seeing		fire (thorough cooking)

Source: Excerpts from "Madman, Architect, Carpenter, Judge: Roles and the Writing Process" by B.S. Flower, 1981, *Language Arts, 58* (7), pp. 834–836.

FIGURE 25.8   Enhanced Concerns Framework (Beginning a Project)

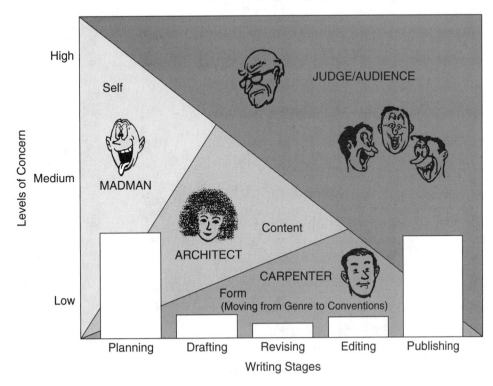

"peers" to remind students that when they write, they should keep in mind not only pleasing the stern judge, but also relishing the kudos of "fans" who will enjoy their work and find it pleasing.

The concept of conferencing with the various "characters" or representations of an author's roles seems to come naturally to our middle school students, just as it does with younger students. For example, students in third grade easily discern the value of inviting a particular character to help them address a writing concern or challenge. For example, when we asked Jose and Ben what to do if the "judge" came in and told them their story was no good, they explained that they would address the judge forcefully:

JOSE: You just go, "Get out of here!" (Pretends to shoot imaginary judge.)

US: Get out of here, huh?

BEN: Get out of my life!

We have found that for middle school students, knowing about and referring to the various author's roles drawn from Flower's characters provides a certain kind of safety, a way of talking about their writing which allows them to open themselves up in

FIGURE 25.9   Possible Areas of Writing Concern Worksheet

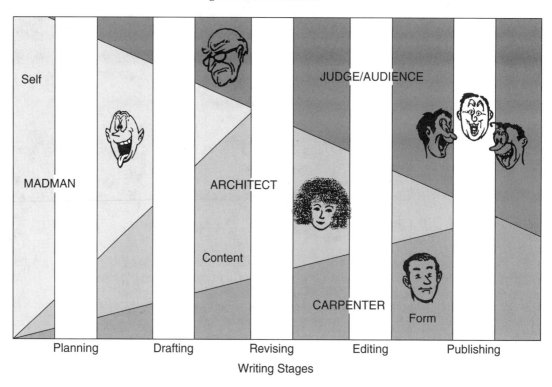

a potentially threatening environment where peer response is powerful. For example, Shandra can refer to her frustration with the "carpenter" rather than say that she is worried about her editing skills. Jarom can ask a peer to read his piece and respond like an "architect." When the peer suggests a change, Jarom can accept it as coming from a neutral third party (the architect) rather than as a direct criticism from a peer.

Depending upon the sophistication of our students, we sometimes introduce the Enhanced Concerns Framework in Figure 25.9 as a tool for them to periodically sketch where they are with a piece, where their concerns focus, and which character they might consult for aid (e.g., which author role they might benefit from emulating). At other times, we pull out one of these sheets during a writing conference and ask a student to help us sketch where he or she is and what the prominent concerns are. We have found that, once introduced to the Enhanced Concerns Framework, teachers find it useful in improving their instruction. We have also found that, given a useful metaphor, students can often assess and address many of their own concerns, concerns that used to backlog teacher conferencing time. Will the day come when teachers implementing a "writers' workshop" will carry on conferences with a notepad in hand, sketching the writer's profile on a grid as they talk with each student? Will the day come when teachers gather together to interpret concerns profiles and discuss the right and wrong kinds of questions to ask? We hope not, in both cases. What we do hope is that the concerns model and its framework will provide teachers another way to envision the writing process that helps in their instructional decision making. We hope that teachers see conferences (at least initially) as a time to listen to the students talk about their writing (status reporting) and to gather insight about student goals and concerns. We hope that teachers will explore the power of questions and inquiries that help the students focus in on self, task, and audience concerns and issues as appropriate to their own work. Finally, we hope that emerging adolescent writers will internalize from these interactions strategies that will nurture their writing independence. By referring to the areas of concern and roles of the author in a concrete way, we have given ourselves and our students new ways to think about ourselves as writers and as individual characters living together in this world.

REFERENCES

Atwell, N. (1987). *In the middle.* Upper Montclair, NJ: Boynton/Cook.

California Department of Education. (1995). Language Arts Framework. Sacramento, CA: Author.

Calkins, L. (1980/1996). *The art of teaching writing.* Portsmouth, NH: Heinemann.

Doyle, W. (1981). Research on classroom contexts. *Journal of Teacher Education, 32*(6) 3–6.

Flower, B.S. (1981). Madman, architect, carpenter, judge: Roles and the writing process. *Language Arts, 58*(7), 834–836.

Fuller, F. (1969). Concerns of teachers: A developmental conceptualization. *American Educational Research Journal, 6*(2), 207–226.

Guyton, J.M., & Fielstein, L.L. (1989). Student-led conferences: A model for teaching responsibility. *Elementary School Guidance and Counseling, 24*(2), 169–172.

Hackmann, D.G. (1997). Student-led conferences at the middle level. *ERIC Digest.* [Eric Document Reproduction Service No. ED 407 171]

Hall, G.E., & Loucks, S.F. (1981). Program definition and adaptation: Implications for inservice. *Journal of Research and Development in Education, 14*(2), 46–58.

Hooper, S.R., Swartz, C.W., & Montgomery, J.W. (1993). Prevalence of writing problems across three middle school samples. *School Psychology Review, 22*(4), 610–622.

National Middle School Association. (1995). *This we believe: Developmentally responsive middle level schools.* Columbus, OH: Author.

Texas Education Association. (1996). *Texas language arts framework.* Austin, Texas.

26 Literacy as Performance

The Power of Creative Drama in the Classroom

PATRICIA DOUVILLE

JANET FINKE

University of North Carolina at Charlotte

At a recent workshop, an elementary teacher confided, "My colleagues are making fun of me, but I just have to tell you—I'm reading entire novels for the first time in my life!" She went on to explain that, as part of an integrated unit, her students had "acted out" each of the chapters in the book *Heidi.* The collaborative experience of working with her students in restructuring each of the previously read book chapters through the medium of creative drama precipitated this teacher's realization that she was capable of constructing the type of images consistent with literacy engagement. Previous to this, the teacher felt she had been incapable of independently completing the narrative structure of a novel as a joyous act of reading. This teacher's experience is an example of how creative drama, such as that of acting out text, can serve as a key for students to unlock potential barriers to reading in a meaningful way.

All teachers are cognizant of the premise that if learning is to be made meaningful, instruction must serve to assist students in making connections with their world of experiences. Creative drama is an effective tool for enhancing learning by creating learning situations in which students are able to make cognitive, emotional, and physical connections between new ideas and what they already know about the world. Using creative drama in the classroom has the potential for helping students go beyond surface knowledge, to knowledge and understanding of "multiple truths and points of view" (Wolf, Edmiston, & Enciso, 1997) that emerge from *living through* ideas. When students are able to take on the roles of explorers, business executives, homeless people, bus drivers, chefs, archaeologists, rain forest animals searching for food, or even molecules or growing plants, they begin to make valuable learning connections that go beyond memorizing facts to understanding and even empathy. Students who engage in creative drama have the opportunity to take on the movements, feelings, and actions of the characters and events about which they have read in ways that allow them to actually enter the "world of the text" (Langer, 1990).

What Is Creative Drama?

The phrase "creative drama" might automatically bring to mind the type of *formal theater* in which parts are memorized and rehearsed, costumes sewn, and elaborate sets created so as to stage a production. Teachers and students who have undertaken such projects are aware of the vast commitment in time and energy necessitated by formal theater productions. *Creative drama,* however, is defined differently. If drama is conceptualized as a continuum with formal theater at one end, creative drama would occupy the opposite end of the continuum. Creative drama is often spontaneous rather than rehearsed, is created by the participants rather than a playwright, is done for the benefit of the participants rather than the benefit of the audience, and focuses on process rather than on a finished product. The Children's Theatre of America has defined creative drama as "an improvisational, nonexhibitional, process-centered form of drama in which participants are guided by a leader to imagine, enact, and reflect upon human experiences" (Davis & Behm, 1978, p. 10).

In describing the many forms creative drama can take in the classroom, Pinciotti (1993) has drawn on the metaphor of "a chameleon poking its head in and out of various curriculum areas" (p. 24) because creative drama is often conceptualized simply as creative teaching. This supposition obscures the notion that creative drama is, in fact, a powerful instructional tool that enables students to draw on personal sensory-rich experiences to learn and apply new ideas in activities such as choral speaking, role playing, reader's theater, and even charades and pantomime.

Why Integrate Creative Drama and Literacy?

Support for teachers' investigating creative drama as an instructional tool is strong. First, creative drama is consistent with reading as a constructivist act. That is, the contemporary notion of reading is that of an active, meaning-making experience in which meaning resides within the reader rather than exclusively within the text (diSibio, 1982; Wittrock, 1988). When students are given the opportunity to construct creative interpretations to text, responses to reading are made rather than found. In merging creative drama with reading and writing activities, teachers provide students with the opportunity not only to *read the lines,* but also to *read between the lines and beyond the lines* in an active construction of meaning.

A number of researchers have found that students who participated in creative drama activities in tandem with reading made significant gains on measures of reading comprehension (Burns, Roe, & Ross, 1988; McCaslin, 1990). In one study, Gray

(1987) found that when sixth-grade students engaged in a postreading creative drama activity, they outperformed students on a comprehension test who had engaged in only postreading discussion of the story. DuPont (1992) also found that when creative drama was integrated with reading literature, fifth-grade remedial readers made significant gains in their reading comprehension scores over students who had either read and discussed the literature or who had received their usual "Chapter 1" instruction.

Paivio's (1986) "theory of dual coding" offers another area of support for the instructional application of creative drama. Paivio explained that learners process information through two mental subsystems. The verbal subsystem allows readers to process the words, phrases and sentences of text. This idea is analogous to the notion of a left-brain, verbal modality function. It is the second, nonverbal, subsystem, however, that allows readers to process images or mental pictures (Sadoski, Paivio, & Goetz, 1991). This notion corresponds to right-brain, or visual-spatial, modality functions. For teachers who are concerned with investigating instructional approaches that serve to engage both mental subsystems in ways that serve to target students' modality or reading-style preferences, integrating reading with creative drama ensures the utilization of verbal, visual, and spatial modalities (Carbo, 1987).

A third area of support is found in the potential creative drama offers for social interaction. Corno and Randi (1997) asserted that when students seek ways to make learning tasks more personally engaging, they work with a peer to create more task interest. Therefore, the very collaborative nature of creative drama is especially appealing for young adolescents because it provides opportunities not only for social interaction but also for physical activities (Albert, 1994). Wolf, Edmiston, and Enciso (1997) also saw the potential for social interaction in their contention that drama in the classroom, to include creative drama, can actually serve to balance the exchange of ideas from those coming primarily from the teacher to a more reciprocal exchange between teachers *and* students. They asserted that drama can serve to bring missing information into the curriculum by fostering communication between the participants, including the teacher. Because drama requires collaboration and cooperation among the members of the group, students emerge from the experience with greater skills in creative problem solving through interdependence.

Finally, creative drama in the classroom guarantees students the opportunity to engage in learning activities geared toward fostering growth in oral language skills. Although oral language is the most frequently used mode of expression, it receives less instructional attention than either reading or writing (Farris, 1997; Stewig & Nordberg, 1995). This observation should represent a valid concern for teachers because the relationships that exist between oral language, reading, and writing are positive ones. Because students' understanding of words comes, in part, through speaking and listening, the correlation between oral language and reading skills can be explained. Providing multiple opportunities for students to gain a greater understanding of words through oral language activities, such as creative drama, leads to an increased ownership of vocabulary that students are then able to bring to reading experiences. In other words, multiple contacts with spoken words facilitate readers' assigning greater meaning to written text. Oral language has also been found to enhance students' writing achievement. When upper elementary students are given experiences in all forms of discourse, including oral language activities, their writing shows greater fluency and awareness of audience (Hennings, 1997) than students not given these options. Because language is best learned through purposeful use, creative drama represents a fertile arena for students to work together in strengthening oral language skills in a collaborative way that is fun for the participants.

How to Get Started

Now that a compelling rationale for incorporating creative drama into classroom instruction has been established, how should the process begin? Venturing into the realm of dramatic interpretation for novice teachers and students can present a daunting challenge. There are, however, a number of introductory, or warm-up, activities that will serve to develop both oral language and imagery skills that can pave the way for more creative dramatic activities. These classroom experiences can all be accomplished in pairs or groups, so all participants are more likely to remain within their individual comfort zones because each end product is the result of group collaboration.

The introductory activities may actually follow a developmental perspective of sorts, beginning with less challenging activities such as choral speaking followed by those that require greater creative independence on the part of the participants such as multisensory activities, pantomime, and charades. Structuring creative drama activities from such a developmental approach allows all participants to build dramatic skills slowly and within a supportive instructional environment.

Choral Speaking

Choral speaking is the oral recitation of text. Although it is appropriate to use any descriptive prose that contains dialogue, poetry is especially suited to choral speaking activities. Teachers may choose to structure choral speaking by dividing students into groups that are then assigned specific sections or lines to recite, or whole classes of students may be kept intact in a unison choral speaking activity.

Bromley (1998) suggested that choral speaking may be structured by refrain or antiphonal activities. In a refrain the leader, who may or may not be the teacher, speaks all the lines with the exception of the refrain which is repeated by the group. Silverstein's "The Unicorn," from the collection *Where the Sidewalk Ends* (1974), is indicative of the type of selection that is especially suited to a refrain activity, with students repeating the final sections of each stanza in which the unicorn is extolled as the loveliest of all the animals on the earth.

In an antiphonal activity, the individual speakers, or groups of speakers, alternate. Bromley suggested that voices can even be grouped according to pitch—for example, male versus female—for added effect. *Joyful Noise: Poems for Two Voices* (Fleischman, 1988) is a wonderful source to use with antiphonal activities. In a preface to this collection, which captures the myriad sounds of insects in nature, Fleischman specifically noted that the poems should be read from top to bottom, with one reader or a group of readers taking the left-hand part and the other taking the right-hand part, in what he calls a "musical duet." Lines at the same horizontal level should be spoken simultaneously. Other exceptionally good sources of text for choral speaking can be found in poetry selections from the following:

The Big Book for Peace (1990), edited by Ann Durell and Marilyn Sachs

The Big Book for Our Planet (1994), edited by Ann Durell, Jean Craighorn George, and Katherine Paterson

Piping Down the Valleys Wild (1968), edited by Nancy Larrick

Celebrate America in Poetry and Art (1995), edited by Nora Panzer

The Dream Keeper and Other Poems (1995), by Langston Hughes

Spirit Walker (1994), by Nancy Wood

While poetry forms are particularly well-suited to antiphonal choral speaking, literature selections may also be adapted for this type of oral language activity. Antiphonal choral reading of selected portions of dialogue creates a specific purpose for repeated readings within the supportive framework of a group. This is particularly beneficial for less capable readers. This type of activity also benefits students by giving them the opportunity to speak and hear the characters' words in ways that enhance the construction of meaningful responses to literature from the multiple viewpoints of different characters.

In *The Gold Cadillac* by Mildred Taylor (1989), two young sisters growing up in Toledo, Ohio, in 1950 are overwhelmed by the sight of the brand new car their father drives home. The conversation the girls have with their father when they first view the magnificent new Cadillac provides an example of how teachers can use narrative text for antiphonal choral speaking. Following Bromley's suggestion of grouping voices by pitch, the following dialogue from *The Gold Cadillac* is structured for girls' and boys' voices.

Girls' Voices	*Boys' Voices*
Daddy, whose Cadillac? Where's our Mercury?	
	Go get your Mother and I'll tell you about it.
Is it ours? Daddy is it ours?	
	Get your Mother! And tell her to hurry!
We got us a Cadillac! We got us a Cadillac! Come on and see!	
	Just off the showroom floor! I just couldn't resist it.
Daddy, are we rich? Daddy, it's ours, isn't it?	
	You like it?
Yes, sir!	
	Then I expect I can't much disappoint my girls, can I? It's ours all right!

Multisensory Imagery Activities

Multisensory imagery activities (Douville, 1998) are those in which students use all their senses—seeing, hearing, smelling, tasting, and feeling—to create the type of elaborated images or visualizations that facilitate both creative drama and engaged reading. The process of teaching multisensory imaging is best accomplished with teachers assuming the greater share of imaging responsibilities in the beginning of each lesson, but gradually releasing responsibility to the students as the lesson progresses. Choosing a topic with which most students will be familiar increases participation because images and visualizations are, for the most part, prior-knowledge dependent. Introducing students to multisensory imaging by taking them on a "mental movie journey," such as the one in the following pizza shop scenario, is representative of one way in which teachers can begin instruction in multisensory imaging.

> (After instructing students to close their eyes and relax their bodies through deep breathing, the mental journey can start.)
>
> *Now that your bodies are relaxed, but you are mentally alert, we can begin. . . . You are walking down the street, and you approach your favorite pizza restaurant. . . . Just seeing the restaurant sign makes your stomach rumble with hunger. . . . You hurry to the door of the restaurant, open it, and go inside. . . . Instantly, you are surrounded by the many delicious smells of baking pizza crusts, bubbling tomato sauce, and melted cheese. . . . You read the menu and order your favorite pizza. . . . While you wait, you listen to the music from the jukebox and you watch the other customers as they eat and chat with one another. . . . You are so hungry. . . . Finally, your pizza is delivered to your table. . . . Now, take a moment and think about how delicious your pizza looks, smells, and tastes. . . .*

After releasing responsiblity to the students to construct individual "pizza images," teachers may choose to conclude the multisensory imagery activity with students describing their constructed images through discussions, writing exercises, or even through artistic representations. Providing multiple opportunities to construct the type of elaborated images consistent with multisensory imaging strengthens students' abilities to make sensory connections between new information and existing knowledge in ways that facilitate revisiting or even reliving prior experiences. For those interested in investigating additional instructional approaches designed to strengthen students' imaging abilities, Ross's *Picture This: Teaching Reading through Visualization* (1989) is an excellent resource.

Pantomime and Charades

Choral speaking provides students with instructional opportunities to develop oral language skills, whereas multisensory imaging activities gives students the experience of mentally structuring or revisiting ideas through engaging multiple modalities. Pantomime and charades, however, introduce students to the importance of *nonverbal* body language and facial gestures in interpreting and communicating ideas.

Pantomime, which uses only gestures and actions to communicate meaning, helps students develop the sense of movement integral to many other creative drama activities. Templeton (1997) asserted that pantomime "helps children turn a conscious lens on past experience in order to analyze it and then form images that they can represent through action" (p. 375). It is suggested that pantomime should begin with all students participating in a warm-up activity designed not only to stretch and relax muscles, but also to set the mood and tone of pantomime exercises (Norton, 1997). Other pantomime activities designed to develop each student's sense of body language and facial communications include:

> *Passing imaginary objects from person to person.* To observe one another, students should be grouped in a circle. Beginning with simple tasks such as passing an imaginary ball from one to another and advancing to more challenging tasks such as passing an extremely hot plate of spaghetti or even a snapping crocodile from one to another, students build body awareness as they physically interpret ideas for others.
>
> *Mirror imaging.* In this classic pantomime activity, pairs of students face each other with one student designated as the actor and the other as the imitator. Beginning with slow, exaggerated movements and progressing to more subtle actions such as facial experessions, the imitator is tasked with "mirroring" the actor's movements, gestures, or expressions. Giving students the opportunity to act as both actor and imitator serves to build not only concentration, but also collaboration skills.
>
> *Emotional reactions.* Creating scenarios in which students pantomime emotions such as fear, joy, amazement, fatigue, sorrow, and confusion provides opportunities for them to merge nonverbal communication skills with multisensory imaging and imagination. As students become more proficient in pantomime, teachers may choose to add an additional element to emotional responses by assigning alternative emotional response perspectives. In this way, students might be tasked with pantomiming the emotion of fear from the perspective of an elderly person versus a baby or the emotion of joy from the perspective of a dog versus a cat.
>
> *Familiar activities.* Activities with which most students are familiar, such as eating an ice-cream cone on a hot day, playing a particular sport, doing the laundry, or flying a kite, are all representative of appropriate pantomimed activities. As with all creative drama activities, teachers may assign pantomime roles to pairs or groups of students, rather than engaging in whole-class activities, as students progressively build creative and interpretive skills.

Charades, like pantomime, requires the "actor" to communicate meaning nonverbally. Unlike pantomime, however, charades includes the additional element of the actor performing for the benefit of an "audience" that is tasked with guessing the action performed. Charades also includes greater reciprocity in communication because the actor is tasked with leading the audience to specific understanding. The audience, in turn, is tasked with communicating understanding through extending guesses to the actor for a specific period of time or until a correct guess is made. Although most of the pantomimed actions discussed earlier may be performed as a charade for the benefit of an audience, charades typically targets more complicated ideas such as titles of books, movies, television shows, songs, or names of famous people. Charades may even be integrated across the curriculum with student actors dramatizing targeted concepts such as "photosynthesis," "equilateral," or "migration." Just as in the traditional game of charades, Bromley (1998) suggested establishing signals for the students to designate whether the targeted idea is a book, song title, famous person, and so forth as well as signals to designate numbers of words or syllables within words. Once students have been given experiences in using their bodies, voices, facial expressions, and mental images in expressing, interpreting, and communicating meaning, the stage is set for those teachers who may wish to move on to more challenging forms of creative drama.

Readers' Theater, Puppetry, and Improvisational Drama

The introductory or warm-up activities of choral speaking, multisensory imaging, and pantomime and charades all serve to benefit students in developing interpretive, communication, and oral language skills. For teachers and students who wish to venture more deeply into the realm of creative drama, however, readers' theater, puppetry, and improvisational drama will assist students in taking even greater control over their thinking as they demonstrate knowledge orally.

Readers' Theatre

Readers' theater is typically defined as an activity in which students read a story script aloud, with individual students reading parts of various characters. A narrator may also be assigned who is responsible for reading sections that supply the setting and actions. Emphasis is placed on oral language skills such as stress, pitch, intonation, and fluency as well as on how effectively the readers interpret their characters' personalities and emotions. Readers' theater involves not just the students who are actively involved in reading their character's dialogue, but also the audience when student observers are tasked with creating their own images from the readers' oral presentations. Although traditional readers' theater reflects students standing or sitting as they read with little incorporation of gestures or body movements, contemporary readers' theater has evolved to include students using not only their voices, but also their bodies in communicating individual character's personalities and story events. Some teachers and students even elect to create simple costumes to add another dimension to character illumination.

In selecting a text appropriate for readers' theater, consideration should be given to potential for student interest as well as to works in which characters reveal thoughts and feelings rather than just actions. Short stories, poems, and excerpts from longer works are all good sources for readers' theater scripts. Selections that document the daily lives of characters such as *Night of the Full Moon* by Gloria Whelan (1994), *Buffalo Gals: Women of the Old West* by Brandon Marie Miller (1996), and *Make Lemonade* by Virginia Euwer Wolff (1994) are all excellent sources for scripts. Picture books may also be scripted for readers' theater. Tom Feelings's *The Middle Passage: White Ships, Black Cargo* (1995) provides powerful pictorial images that students can translate into verbal interpretations.

The best readers' theater scripts are those written by the students. Teachers and students may, however, decide to work together if students have little experience in creating scripts. Teachers might also elect to provide an initial model of a script based on a familiar work to later release students to independence in writing scripts on their own. In creating the script dialogue may be taken directly from the selected text with possible elaborations incorporating the students' own expressions or vernacular. Narrative sections from the text may also be converted to dialogue, or these sections may be assigned to the narrator's role, which can also encompass an introduction, or prologue, that establishes the setting and introduces characters as well as an epilogue to achieve closure. In preparation for presenting the script to an audience, students must be given adequate time for multiple script readings and rehearsals to ensure fluency.

Readers' theater is an instructional approach that is typically used as a *postreading* activity to reinforce and extend text ideas. Recently, however, a fourth-grade teacher chose readers' theater as a *prereading* instructional strategy to provide his students with prior knowledge about the story he later had them read. In the prereading phase of this particular lesson, the teacher gave each of his students a script for the concluding chapters of Roald Dahl's *James and the Giant Peach* (1988). Following a brief silent reading period during which students familiarized themselves with the script vocabulary, each member of the class had the opportunity to read the lines of either the narrator or one of the characters. When all the dialogue and narration had been read, students were released to read the concluding chapters of the book independently for the purpose of completing a "fantasy web." The readers' theater experience the teacher provided for his students ensured their subsequent success with both the independent reading of the chapters and the webbing activity.

Although narrative text naturally lends itself to readers' theater, Young and Vardell (1993) suggested the use of expository text as a way to integrate readers' theater across the curriculum. They asserted that the repeated exposures to the text necessary for performance preparation, as well as the concrete images that are painted for the audience by the readers, serve to enhance students' understanding of content area concepts. Biographies and diary excerpts are excellent sources from which to draw for content area readers' theater. *Only Opal: The Diary of a Young Girl* by Opal Whitely and selected by Jane Boulton (1995), *Anne Frank: Beyond the Diary* by Ruud van der Rol and Rian Verhoeven (1994), *Hiding to Survive: Stories of Jewish Children Rescued from the Holocaust* by Maxine Rosenberg (1995), and *Bull Run* by Paul Fleischman (1994) are representative of texts that are appropriate for the integration of readers' theater across the curriculum.

Puppetry

Like readers' theater, puppetry activities involve students in more creatively challenging ways than the introductory activities of choral speaking, multisensory imaging, and pantomime and charades. Puppetry is also similar to readers' theater in that students may create scripts independently or with the assistance of teachers or peers. What uniquely characterizes puppetry, however, is the process by which students transfer actions and behaviors of the story characters from themselves to the puppet figures. Although this transference can be difficult for some students, other students may be more successful with puppetry than with creative drama activities requiring partici- pants to personify the characters they role play because, for the dramatically reticent student, puppets may actually represent a *support prop*. In other words, student pup- peteers are liberated to construct roles and emotions they might not otherwise feel comfortable assuming since the audience can never be certain who is in control! Tem- pleton (1997) explained that the magic that occurs between students and puppets actu- ally serves to free students to "act out moods and emotions without being personally responsible for them" (p. 379).

In preparation for beginning puppetry activities in the classroom, Norton (1997) suggested that time would be well spent exploring the history of puppets. Researching how puppets are used in different cultures around the world also serves to broaden stu- dents' appreciation for this creative drama art form. In establishing a "community of classroom puppets," students can create figures from simple objects such as folded paper plates, cardboard tubes, paper bags, or socks. Siks (1983), however, extends the caveat that many puppetry projects that are initiated in the classroom are never brought to successful completion because they stop with the making of the puppet. Although more elaborate commercially produced puppets may be used if they are available, Tem- pleton (1997) asserted that it is the act of actually making a puppet that creates the bond between the student and puppet figure that, in turn, enhances the effectiveness of puppetry activities.

As with all creative drama activities, the books from which puppet scripts are adapted should be interesting, should be well liked by the students, and should contain plenty of dialogue. Although Hennings (1997) suggested that students' scripts should be attached to a surface at the back of the puppet stage, Ross (1980) believed that to avoid stilted performances, prewritten scripts should be rejected in favor of students improvising their puppets' lines in a fashion consistent with improvisational drama.

Improvisational Drama

Improvisational drama is that in which students perform without a script. Of all the forms of creative drama discussed to this point, improvisation is the most challenging for students because it offers the least instructional support. Nevertheless, improvisa- tion represents a powerful tool for stimulating students' natural use of language as they create, interpret, and communicate ideas within a purposeful framework.

Moffet and Wagner (1993) suggested an activity that can be used to introduce students to improvisational drama. The activity begins with students writing the names of characters, settings, and problems on slips of paper. The slips are then collected and placed in separate "character," "setting," and "problem" containers. Student groups are formed, and each group then chooses a slip from each of the containers. Each group improvises a skit based on the character, setting, and problem selected. As students become more familiar and comfortable with the process, improvisation activities can be used with literature or, even more creatively, with expository text selections. Because of the high degree of student independence reflected by improvisation, the text ideas on which improvisations are based are understood and appreciated by the participants.

Conclusion

Creative drama represents an effective instructional strategy for providing students with opportunities to develop literacy skills in a purposeful fashion. The cognitive, emotional, and physical connections between new ideas and existing knowledge that students make within a creative drama framework evoke higher-order thinking and problem solving. That creative drama is an instructional approach that is too often neglected in the classroom is especially distressing because when students work together in using their collective imaginations to interpret text ideas, learning becomes not only more meaningful, but also more fun. With an instructional and peer-support network in place, students engaging in creative drama activities will possess the tools necessary to weave a web of senses, feelings, movement, and knowledge in an active interpretation and communication of ideas.

R E F E R E N C E S

Albert, E. (1994, May). Drama in the classroom. *Middle School Journal, 20*–24.

Bromley, K.D. (1998). *Language arts: Exploring connections.* Boston: Allyn and Bacon.

Burns, P.C., Roe, B.D., & Ross, E.P. (1988). *Teaching reading in today's elementary schools.* Boston: Houghton Mifflin.

Carbo, M. (1987, February). Reading styles research: "What works" isn't always phonics. *Phi Delta Kappan,* 431–435.

Corno, L., & Randi, J. (1997). Motivation, volition, and collaborative innovation in classroom literacy. In J.T. Guthrie & A. Wigfield (Eds.), *Reading engagement: Motivating readers through integrated instruction.* Newark, DE: International Reading Association.

Dahl, R. (1988). *James and the giant peach.* New York: Puffin Books.

Davis, J., & Behm, T. (1978). Terminology of drama/theater with and for children: A redefinition. *Children's Theater Review, 27,* 10–11.

diSibio, M. (1982). Memory for connected discourse: A constructivist view. *Review of Educational Research, 52*(2), 149–174.

Douville, P. (1998). *Bringing text to life: The effects of a multisensory imagery strategy on fifth-graders' prose processing and attitude reading.* A research report presented at the 43rd annual meeting of the International Reading Association, Orlando, Florida.

DuPont, S. (1992). The effectiveness of creative drama as an instructional strategy to enhance the reading comprehension skills of fifth-grade remedial readers. *Reading Research and Instruction, 31*(3), 41–52.

Durrell, A., George, J.C., & Paterson, K. (1994). *The big book for our planet.* New York: Dutton Children's Books.

Durrell, A., & Sachs, M. (Eds.). (1990). *The big book for peace.* New York: Dutton Children's Books.

Farris, P. (1997). *Language arts: Process, product, and assessment.* Madison, WI: Brown and Benchmark.

Feelings, T. (1995). *The middle passage: White ships, black cargo.* New York: Dial.

Fleischman, P. (1988). *Joyful noise: Poems for two voices.* New York: Harper Trophy.

Fleischman, P. (1994). *Bull Run.* Glenfield, IL: HarperCollins.

Gray, M.A. (1987). A frill that works: Creative dramatics in the basal reading lesson. *Reading Horizons, 28,* 5–11.

Hennings, D.G. (1997). *Communication in action: Teaching literature-based language arts* (6th ed.). Boston: Houghton Mifflin.

Hughes, L. (1995). *The dream keeper and other poems.* New York: Knopf.

Langer, J.A. (1990). The purpose of understanding: Reading for informative purposes. *Research in the Teaching of English, 24*(3), 229–260.

Larrick, N. (Ed.). (1968). *Piping down the valleys wild.* New York: Dell.

McCaslin, N. (1990). *Creative dramatics in the classroom* (5th ed.). New York: Longman.

Miller, B.M. (1996). *Buffalo gals: Women of the old west.* Minneapolis, MN: Lerner.

Moffatt, J. & Wagner, B. (1993). *Student-centered language arts and reading, K–13: A handbook for teachers.* Boston: Houghton Mifflin.

Norton, D.E. (1997). *The effective teaching of the language arts* (5th ed.). Upper Saddle River, NJ: Merrill/Prentice Hall.

Paivio, A. (1986). *Mental representations: A dual coding approach.* New York: Oxford University Press.

Panzer, N. (1995). *Celebrate America in poetry and art.* New York: Hyperion.

Pinciotti, P. (1993). Creative drama and young children: The dramatic learning connections. *Arts Education Policy Review, 94*(6), 24–28.

Rosenberg, M.B. (1995). *Hiding to survive: Stories of jewish children rescued from the Holocaust.* New York: Clarion.

Ross, L. (1980). *Storyteller* (2nd ed.). Columbus, OH: Merrill.

Ross, L. (1989). *Picture this: Teaching reading through visualization.* Tuscon, AZ: Zephyr Press.

Sadoski, M., Paivio, A., & Goetz, E.T. (1991). Commentary: A critique of schema theory in reading and a dual coding alternative. *Reading Research Quarterly, 26,* 463–484.

Siks, G. (1983). *Drama with children.* New York: Harper and Row.

Silverstein, S. (1974). *Where the sidewalk ends: The poems and drawings of Shel Silverstein.* New York: HarperCollins.

Stewig, J.W., & Nordberg, B. (1995). *Exploring language arts in the elementary classroom.* Albany, NY: Wadsworth.

Taylor, M. (1987). *The gold Cadillac.* New York: Dial.

Templeton, S. (1997). *Teaching the integrated language arts* (2nd ed.). Boston: Houghton Mifflin.

van der Rol, R., & Verhoeven, R. (1994). *Anne Frank: Beyond the diary.* Bergenfield, NJ: Viking/Penguin.

Whelan, G. (1994). *Night of the full moon.* New York: Knopf.

Whitely, O., & Boulton, J. (1995). *Only Opal: The diary of a young girl.* New York: Philomel.

Wittrock, M.C. (1988). A constructive review of research on learning strategies. In C.E. Weinstein, E.T. Goetz, & P.A. Alexander (Eds.), *Learning and study strategies: Issues in assessment, instruction, and evaluation* (pp. 287–298). San Diego: Academic Press.

Wolf, J.L. (1997). Balancing act: Using drama to even the exchange of information in the classroom. In J. Flood, S.B. Heath, & D. Lapp (Eds.), *Research on teaching literacy through the communicative and visual arts* (pp. 68–76). New York: Simon and Schuster/Macmillan.

Wolf, S., Edmiston, B., & Encisco, P. (1997). Drama worlds: Places of the heart, head, voice, and hand in dramatic interpretation. In J. Flood, S.B. Heath, & D. Lapp (Eds.), *Research on teaching literacy through the communicating and visual arts* (pp. 492–505). New York: Simon and Schuster/Macmillan.

Wolff, V.E. (1994). *Make lemonade.* New York: Holt.

Wood, N. (1994). *Spirit walker.* New York: Doubleday.

Young, T.A., & Vardell, S. (1993). Weaving readers theatre and nonfiction into the curriculum. *The Reading Teacher, 46*(5), 396–406.

27 Preparing Intermediate and Middle-Grade Students to Be Document Literate

CATHLEEN D. RAFFERTY

Indiana State University

Why Document Literacy?

Documents pervade all aspects of our lives; just try to imagine a facet of life that does not involve their use. As difficult as this might be, it would probably be easier than trying to list the range and purposes of documents we encounter on a regular basis, documents that we use as individuals, as members of society, and especially in the workplace. In fact, Bassett, Goodman, and Fosegan (1981) identified more than 20 basic functions provided by societal and workplace documents alone.

In the late 1980s and early 1990s, the *Journal of Reading* featured a monthly column by Peter Mosenthal and Irwin Kirsch. Figure 27.1 depicts the types of documents presented and explained in their column. A perusal of document types and specific examples in Figure 27.1 will help the reader better understand that documents really are pervasive. For example, forms—whether used for job application, product registration, census purposes, or the Internal Revenue Service—have ramifications for the workplace, for society as a whole, or for individual citizens. Other specific types of documents such as diagrams or procedural schematics impact individuals either on the job or at home as they assemble a new computer hutch or install new software. Maps, graphs, charts, and lists also support our ability to locate, extract, interpret, and use important information.

Clearly, documents permeate our lives, but how frequently are they used and how frequently is the information properly understood? Unfortunately, there are no wide-scale research studies to answer this question definitively. One study, however, reported that among a range of workers in various occupational groups, reading documents constituted the largest percentage of daily reading time (Guthrie, Seifert, & Kirsch, 1986). More specifically, Figure 27.2, which also serves as an example of a specific kind of

FIGURE 27.1 Types of Documents

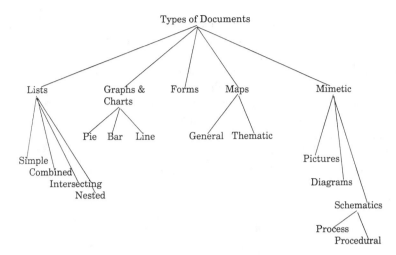

FIGURE 27.2 Occupational Groups and Daily Reading of Documents

Occupational Group	Mean Daily Minutes Spent Reading Documents
Managers/professionals	118
Clerical workers	109
Skilled workers	66
Unskilled workers	25

Source: Adapted from Guthrie, Seifert, & Kirsch, 1986, p. 154.

document known as a combined list (see Kirsch and Mosenthal, 1989), delineates different occupational groups and average minutes spent reading documents. Even unskilled workers interacted daily with documents and given the ever-increasing profusion of knowledge, it is likely that the figures would be even higher for all employment groups and functioning members of our society.

To this point, this chapter has presented insights regarding types of documents, wide-scale use of documents, and frequency of their use, at least in the workplace; but what is known about the nature and quality of individuals' interactions with various types of documents, and how well and how much information is processed? From 1984 to 1986, the National Assessment of Educational Progress (NAEP) assessed the literacy skills of America's young adults (ages 21–25) in three different populations. The Job Training Partnership Act (JTPA) targets economically disadvantaged adults and youths, dislocated workers, and other groups facing serious employment barriers.

Employment Service/Unemployment Insurance (ES/UI) provides job-counseling services and temporary income protection for involuntarily unemployed workers. The final category, young adults, represents a category of individuals who have gainful employment. All three groups were assessed across three dimensions: document literacy, prose literacy, and quantitative literacy. Because the focus of this chapter is document literacy, only related results will be highlighted. For those interested in more detail and/or other literacy aspects, please see Kirsch, Jungeblut, and Campbell, 1992; Kirsch and Mosenthal, 1988 and 1990a; or Sheehan and Mislevy, 1990.

How did these three populations of young adults perform on a NAEP assessment of document literacy? Figure 27.3, an example of a nested list (see Kirsch & Mosenthal, 1990b), reveals that on a five-level scale from 0 to 500, the greatest percentage of young adults, regardless of population, performed at level 3. These types of tasks require that the reader not only locate and integrate information but also match more than two features in more complex displays of information. In fact, extracting and correctly using information according to specific task directives from a display similar to Figure 27.3 would be required for level 3 proficiency.

On a more somber note, however, Kirsch et al. (1992) reported that between 40% and 50% of each of these same three populations who reportedly had a high school education (either diploma or General Education Degree) exhibited competency skills at only levels 1 and 2. Furthermore, these same researchers expressed concern that such large percentages of JTPA and ES/UI populations in particular demonstrated deficiencies in "being able to generate ideas based on what they have read, in attending to multiple features of information contained in complex displays where they may be required to compare and contrast information" (p. 114). Another way to think about this is that between 35% and 45% of these populations who reportedly have a high school diploma or equivalent are successful on tasks that are limited to locating a single piece of information or entering background information on a form. Clearly, there is a mismatch between the prevalence of documents and the ability of many young adults to use them successfully.

A more recent survey of the literacy proficiencies of American adults—that is, those over the age of 16—determined that just over 50% of American adults (nearly 100 million) performed at either level 1 or 2 (National Center for Education Statistics, 1992, p. 4). This U.S. Department of Education project, which used the same document literacy scale reported in Figure 27.3, purports to provide the most detailed portrait ever available on the status of literacy in our country, especially on the unrealized potential of many U.S. citizens. Given that literacy requirements continue to escalate and that two large national studies have determined that tens of millions of our adults lack the literacy proficiencies necessary for the types of jobs that will be prevalent in the twenty-first century, it is obvious that literacy in general and document literacy in particular demand more systematic attention.

Now that the importance of documents and the need for document literacy have been established, it is time to be more precise about the nature of document literacy. The next three sections define and explain document literacy, whereas subsequent sections recommend and illustrate specific approaches and strategies to help develop document literacy proficiency.

FIGURE 27.3   Percentages of Document Literacy Level Performance for JTPA, ES/UI, and Young Adults

Levels	Description of Document Task	Percentage Scoring at Level	
1 0–225	Least demanding tasks. Require reader to locate information based on literal match or to enter information from memory.	JTPA ES/UI Young adults	14.1 13.1 8.0
2 226–275	More varied tasks. Some as described previously but often with several distractors or that require low-level inferences. Information must be integrated.	JTPA ES/UI Young adults	37.3 10.1 24.2
3 276–325	Tasks tend to require the reader to integrate three pieces of information or to cycle through complex tables or graphs that include distractor information.	JTPA ES/UI Young adults	35.4 35.9 39.7
4 326–375	More demanding tasks requiring cycling and integrating of information and multiple-feature matching with increased amounts of inferencing. Conditional information must also be considered.	JTPA ES/UI Young adults	12.2 18.5 24.0
5 376–500	Most difficult tasks, requiring the reader to search complex displays and multiple distractors to make high text-based inferences. Use of specialized knowledge is also required.	JTPA ES/UI Young adults	1.1 2.4 4.1

Note: JTPA = Job Training Partnership Act; ES/UI = Employment Service/Unemployment Insurance.

Source: Adapted from Kirsch, Jungeblut, & Campbell, 1992, p. 46

What Is Document Literacy?

During the mid-1980s, when NAEP began to focus on document literacy, the following definition emerged:

Document literacy involves the knowledge and skills needed to understand and use printed information occurring in a variety of non-prose formats. Non-prose formats include linguistic structures that are not organized in paragraph form. As such, non-prose formats consist of the following: forms, tables, charts, graphs, signs/labels, indexes, lists, schematics, and catalogues. (Kirsch & Jungeblut, 1986)

In many respects, the type of literacy required by documents or nonprose formats may seem both familiar and strange to many individuals. If we consider the traditional approach to literacy development that begins with narrative or story structure and, one hopes, but not always, includes a later focus on expository text, where do document formats and related literacy demands receive attention? In my experience, unfortunately, the answer would be somewhere along a continuum from "nowhere to only in a few select places to on the job training."

Typically, children "learn to read" using narrative text in the early grades, often K–3. Usually around grade 4 a shift to "reading to learn" begins with the use of content area textbooks otherwise known as expository or informational text. Although trends have begun to change (for example, see Freeman & Person, 1998), too often students are still expected to make the shift from narrative to expository text with little or no systematic instruction on the differences, challenges presented, and strategies to use with expository text. Even though both of these text types are forms of prose—that is, in paragraph form—anyone who has examined standardized test scores can recall the marked difference that often occurs between performance on narrative and expository reading sections. There seems to be a connection between the historic trend of more focused instruction on narrative text (learning to read) and less frequent instruction on expository text (reading to learn), and student performance with these two prose structures.

Two additional factors are also warranted when considering student performance and linguistic structure: (1) continued literacy instruction in prose is not a universal feature in middle schools and is basically nonexistent in high schools, and (2) specific instruction in nonprose formats (document literacy) is most certainly an assumption if not an anomaly. Were you, the reader, taught how to read documents? Does your school prepare students to interact with various nonprose formats depicted in Figure 27.1? Regardless, what are some important considerations if we want to prepare students who are document literate or who know how to "read to do"?

"Reading to Do": Document Literacy Tasks

As previously defined, document literacy involves the knowledge and skills necessary to understand and use nonprose information that exists in a variety of formats such as forms, tables, maps, graphs, schedules, schematics, indexes, and catalogs. Because the formats are so varied it would seem that an endless array of skills would be required. In fact, according to the U.S. Department of Labor and NAEP (Kirsch et al., 1992), three broad categories of skills or tasks are required for document literacy. They are locating, cycling, and integrating, all of which may seem at least somewhat familiar given the following descriptions and examples in Figure 27.4.

Locating tasks engage the reader in matching one or more stated-information items with either identical or equivalent information. For example, if a student is given a food advertisement and asked to determine if a particular item is on sale, he or she would be performing a locating task. *Cycling tasks* also involve locating and matching but further involve the reader in a cycle of feature matches as specified in the task. This type of task would require multiple passes, such as determining which items on a grocery list could be purchased at discount according to a supermarket advertisement,

FIGURE 27.4   Document Literacy Skills Examples: Locating, Cycling, and Integrating

SUPER-VALUE FOODS
(Sale Prices Effective 3/10 - 3/17)

Huge Frozen Food Sale!!!
Corn, Green Beans, Lima Beans,
Okra, Spinach, Mixed Vegetables

(Sorry, Peas not included)

Bakery Sale*
Muffins & Bagels (6/$1.50)
Cookies (2 doz./$1.75)(Peanut Butter,
    Sugar, Chocolate Chip, Oatmeal)
Sourdough & Whole Wheat Bread
    (2 loaves/$2.50)

*Stock up on Staples**
All Salad Dressings (2/$3.00)
All Soups (3/$1.50)
Super-Value Dish Detergent (2/$1.75)

Dairy Products
All one-gallon containers 1/3 off!!!!
(Milk, Ice Cream, Frozen Yogurt,
Ice Milk - Regularly $2.50/gal.)

Must purchase minimum number designated to receive sale price.

Grocery List
- 1/2 gal. milk
- whole wheat bread
- spaghetti sauce
- thousand-island dressing
- chocolate chip cookies
- tomato soup
- frozen peas
- dish detergent

Locating Task

Are frozen peas on sale?

Cycling Task

Which items on the grocery list are available at discount (either sale priced or with coupon) at Super-Value Foods?

Integrating Task

If you purchase only the items on your list that are available at discount and buy the minimum number of sale items required, how much money will you spend (pretax dollars)?

through the same information. *Integrating tasks* often demand that the reader compare and contrast information in various parts of a document. An example would be the last question in Figure 27.4 (Kirsch et al., 1992).

On the surface, locating, cycling, and integrating tasks seem fairly straightforward and reminiscent of workbook or end-of-chapter activities in textbooks for classes like mathematics or social studies. Perhaps at the most basic level this situation may be the case, but when we also consider the range of difficulty possible for each task depending on interactions among several task characteristics such as the number of categories to be processed, the number of plausible distractors, the degree of inference required, and the document structure itself, the notion of document literacy becomes more complicated. Additional considerations such as process and performance variables further compound the concept of document literacy. All this serves to underscore the notion that a systematic focus on document literacy instruction is necessary. Combined with previous document literacy performance data from NAEP and the National Center for Education Statistics, the need is even more compelling because too many adults in these sample populations lack adequate document processing abilities. Before identifying some specific instructional approaches recommended to foster document literacy, a brief focus on process and performance variables is warranted.

"Reading to Do": Process and Performance Variables

Beyond the recognition that interaction occurs between the task to be completed and the document used, various research studies have identified procedures that detail the processes involved in performing various tasks that involve use of documents (Fisher, 1981; Guthrie, 1988; Kirsch & Guthrie, 1984; Kirsch & Jungeblut, 1986; Wright, 1980a, 1980b). According to Kirsch and Mosenthal (1988, p. 27), the procedures should:

1. Identify the given and requested information in a directive.
2. Search the document until requested information is located.
3. Make a match between the information identified in the document and the information requested in the document.
4. Determine whether the match adequately meets the criterion of the task.

In addition to these processes (i.e., identifying, searching, matching, and evaluating), Kirsch and Mosenthal (1988) also note that three different variables influence the degree of difficulty of an individual's performance on various document tasks. The first, *degrees of correspondence,* relates to the explicitness or preciseness of the match between what is requested in the task and the corresponding information in the text. In many respects, the type of information processing involved could be equated with the levels on a continuum represented by Raphael's (1982) question-answer-relationships, or ranging from *"right there"* (factual/detail, literal-level, or textually explicit matches) to *"think and search"* (reading between the lines or textually implicit matches) to *"the author and me"* or *"on your own"* (reading beyond the lines or using existing knowledge). Clearly, if the match to be made requires little or no inferencing, it is an easier task to complete. The locating task in Figure 27.4 is a "right there" example because it requires a literal match.

Type of information, the second influencing variable, includes both the type and nature of information required for the task. Task difficulty increases as the number of elements or features to identify or match increases. In other words, if the task calls for matching or identifying several items as opposed to locating or identifying only one item, the task is more difficult. The cycling task in Figure 27.4 is an example of a more difficult task because it requires multiple matches. Also, as noted under degrees of correspondence, literal matches are easier than matches requiring more inferencing.

The third variable that impacts degree of difficulty and, therefore, potentially influences individual performance on various document tasks is *plausibility of distractors.* What comes into play here is similar to, but not totally synonymous with, decisions students make when faced with a well-designed multiple-choice test. That is, they must skim the document and evaluate multiple options to determine the best or most plausible one. This variable is exemplified by the integrating task in Figure 27.4 because decisions must be made between several distractors such as starred items, information in small print, and incongruent container sizes.

This chapter has presented a rationale for the importance of document literacy due to the pervasiveness of documents, identified a variety of document types, defined document literacy according to NAEP, argued for continued literacy instruction for both prose and nonprose formats, and explored various document task characteristics and process and performance variables that can impact an individual's ability to successfully complete tasks requiring use of documents. Next, the focus is on helping students to acquire document literacy proficiency.

Promoting Document Literacy

Generally, much of what has been recommended to promote prose (narrative and expository) literacy, especially in the intermediate and middle grades, can be applied to document literacy. It is important to build on students' prior knowledge; to combine content and process instruction with metacognitive awareness; to employ scaffolded instruction; and to use real-world examples and interdisciplinary and/or thematic approaches, to use various technologies, and to reinforce across multiple grade levels and levels of difficulty. Each is addressed in subsequent sections.

Prior Knowledge

What we already know about something has a significant impact on our ability to learn more (Paris, Wasik, & Turner, 1991). Often known as prior knowledge or previous knowledge, this powerful concept revolutionized not only literacy instruction but content teaching as well. See, for example, a three-part videotape series from the Annenberg/Corporation for Public Broadcasting Math and Science Collection, which examines the power of scientific misconceptions and the types of teaching approaches necessary to help ensure real understanding (Annenberg Foundation/Corporation for Public Broadcasting, 1997). Once we acknowledge that students come not as empty vessels but with previous experiences, thoughts, and ideas, our instructional approaches warrant modification primarily because we must consciously and deliberately elicit and use what our students already know. Previously, it was argued that students first "learn to read" using narrative text and then they "read to learn" using expository text. At a minimum, students will enter the middle grades with a working knowledge of the former and at least a beginning realization that the latter is quite different.

Starting in fourth grade (remember that fourth grade is typically when students shift from narrative to expository and informational text) and continuing throughout the middle grades and beyond, we should help students compare and contrast these two prose formats and their structures. Use of tools like Venn diagrams or feature analysis grids would make explicit and concrete the similarities and differences. Once accomplished, instruction on various types of documents would logically follow. Figure 27.5 provides a concrete example of critical features of narrative and expository text for comparison and analysis. Also, note that the final sections of this chapter provide a scenario that presents additional ideas and suggestions for developing document literacy.

Previous research has shown that a positive relationship exists between students' understanding of expository text structure and comprehension scores (Pearson & Fielding, 1991). It seems reasonable that a similar relationship would exist for docu-

FIGURE 27.5   Comparison/Contrast of Narrative and Expository Text

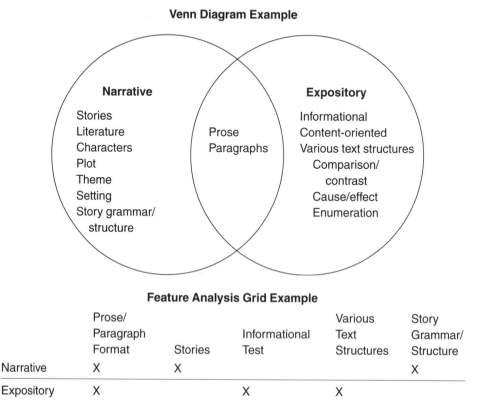

Venn Diagram Example

Narrative	Prose	Expository
Stories	Paragraphs	Informational
Literature		Content-oriented
Characters		Various text structures
Plot		Comparison/contrast
Theme		Cause/effect
Setting		Enumeration
Story grammar/structure		

Feature Analysis Grid Example

	Prose/Paragraph Format	Stories	Informational Test	Various Text Structures	Story Grammar/Structure
Narrative	X	X			X
Expository	X		X	X	

ments and an understanding of their structures as well, but since there is only a moderate correlation (.55) between prose (narrative and expository) and nonprose (document) tasks (Kirsch & Jungeblut, 1986), additional instruction specifically targeting document literacy is imperative.

Metacognition

Although an emphasis on students' prior knowledge is important, it is insufficient. Metacognition, self-monitoring, or "thinking about one's thinking," is another critical instructional consideration. In the preceding paragraph, the relationship between knowledge about text structure and comprehension scores was noted. Metacognition means that a student knows or is aware of what he or she knows or understands when something is confusing, and knows what to do about it. In other words, the student self-monitors the comprehension process and employs "fix-it" strategies when things do not make sense. In the case of document literacy, a student would know or be able to identify various types of documents (e.g., see Figure 27.1), know how to read and interpret the information, know whether he or she was making accurate interpretations of the document's information, and have some strategies available in case he or she realized that the document was not making sense. Of course, this level of metacognitive awareness does not happen by accident (Baker & Brown, 1984; Paris et al., 1991). It must be carefully designed, delivered, and monitored, which leads to an additional critical aspect in literacy instruction.

Scaffolded Instruction

Scaffolding is support provided by teachers to help students learn and carry out a task (Roehler & Duffy, 1991). This type of instruction is multifaceted and ongoing. It incorporates elements such as direct instruction, teacher modeling including use of think-alouds or mental modeling, student practice with an emphasis on self-monitoring (metacognition), teacher coaching and feedback, and a gradual increase in students' responsibility for their own learning. A document literacy example that incorporates previous elements plus several new ones follows.

Real-World Examples, Interdisciplinary and/or Thematic Approaches, Technology Applications, and Reinforcement across Multiple Grade Levels and Levels of Difficulty

Mrs. Apex and Mr. Dix, sixth-grade language arts and social studies teachers at Trailblazer Middle School, want to improve their students' reasoning and inferencing skills, organization and oral presentation skills, familiarity with and use of technology, and document literacy or their ability to use documents such as various types of lists, graphs, and charts. Mrs. Apex and Mr. Dix know from recent curriculum articulation meetings with their fourth- and fifth-grade colleagues (all of whom teach in self-contained classrooms) that the new crop of sixth-grade students have "experience" with all these aspects, but primarily at introductory or awareness levels.

Because Mrs. Apex and Mr. Dix understand that authentic instruction requires real-world connections to help ensure that students see the importance of and application of their knowledge and skills (Newmann, Secada, & Wehlage, 1995), they begin to design a unit to help their students investigate and report about middle-grades students' entertainment preferences. Their working title for this project is "The Trailblazer Middle School Entertainment Choice Awards."

After some preliminary planning, they hope to share their draft unit with other sixth-grade colleagues and later with teachers on various seventh- and eighth-grade teams. In many respects, Mrs. Apex and Mr. Dix think of their draft as a pilot that could ultimately develop into a whole-school project and eventually result in a multiyear survey process whereby students could study and interpret results from previous years to track various trends, develop hypotheses, and then do follow-up investigations. In fact, once their school receives the budgeted computer and Internet connections and upgrades, it would be possible to survey students at schools in other states or even other countries. They have learned, however, that such an ambitious agenda is best developed over time. Their initial ideas follow.

Overall Focus
The Trailblazer Middle School Entertainment Choice Awards

Specific Categories
1. Books and authors
2. Computer and video games
3. Movies
4. Music (artists, CDs, music videos, and songs)
5. Television programs
6. Sports and recreation (participatory, not spectator)

Components
1. Cooperative learning groups or learning teams (LTs) will draw numbers to determine their category for survey development.
2. After designing the surveys, LTs will administer their survey to all sixth-graders at Trailblazer Middle School. (Note: If Mrs. Apex and Mr. Dix have enough time and energy left and *especially* if their sixth-graders express an interest in expanding their database, they might explore its use with sixth-graders at other district middle schools or even beyond. Also, if the technology upgrades have been completed, they could even explore electronic distribution of their surveys.)
3. Once surveys are returned, Mrs. Apex and Mr. Dix will work with their students in the computer lab to create spreadsheets and databases to tally and analyze results. Next, they will help students learn to interpret data and create various types of lists, graphs, and charts to display findings.
4. Finally, LTs will exhibit their work. The exhibitions will include a written paper describing the process used, what LT members learned from the project, individual contributions to the project, and how the LT functioned as a group. In addition, the exhibition will include a poster display of various tables, graphs, and

charts that summarize the analyzed data from the surveys. The final component will be an oral presentation that highlights elements from the written paper, makes connections to the poster display, and makes observations and draws some conclusions about results from the survey. The oral presentations will be video-taped and students will critique themselves and receive feedback from peers so that they can target areas for improvement in the next presentation.

Procedures

A. Mrs. Apex and Mr. Dix begin with a K-W-L (Ogle, 1986) to determine students' prior knowledge of surveys and their experience with survey construction. From the "know" component of K-W-L (know, want to know, learned), they learn that students understand the basic purpose of surveys—to gather information—and that surveys involve writing questions about a particular topic so that others can give you the information you want to know. In fact, as fifth-grade students, most of them had completed a survey distributed by the Trailblazer Middle School guidance office to get their perceptions of issues and concerns about moving to the middle school the following year. Few, if any of their students, however, had experience in designing a survey. As such, Mrs. Apex and Mr. Dix know that they must incorporate elements of scaffolded instruction to help ensure their students' success. They begin with the following concrete example:

"All Learning Teams drew numbers to determine which topic will be the focus for their survey to help us select 'The Trailblazer Middle School Entertainment Choice Awards.' One of the categories—music—has several subsections, so we'll use one of them as an example to help us understand how to create a survey. There are several steps to follow: (1) brainstorm examples from your topic/category to use as options on your survey, (2) group or cluster items to form categories if necessary, (3) write questions that will ask people to give their opinion, (4) try out your survey on classmates to see if directions and questions are clear, and (5) do the final draft and make copies to distribute. Let's practice an example that will take us through these steps together."

1. *Brainstorm examples of your favorite music artists*

   Mrs. Apex and Mr. Dix both conduct a brainstorming session with their sixth-graders regarding their favorite music groups. The following groups emerge through their use of a semantic map.

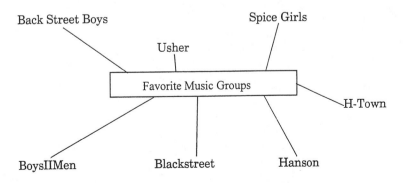

2. *Group/Cluster to form categories if necessary*
   Because there are only seven music groups identified by the class, it is not necessary to cluster or group them for survey purposes. They move on to the next step.

3. *Write questions that will ask people to give their opinion*
   Because the example survey is focusing on favorite music groups, Mrs. Apex and Mr. Dix discuss with students what they would want to know about their peers' choices. During the brainstorming, it was evident that the girls had often identified different groups than the boys (e.g., Spice Girls versus Back Street Boys), but that some groups were the favorite of both genders (e.g., BoysIIMen). From this it was decided that the survey should ask respondents to identify their gender. Also, the students wanted to know the overall top three choices and why students liked particular groups or what it was about the groups that caused their popularity. From this discussion, the following survey was drafted.

Trailblazer Middle School Entertainment Choice Awards

Category: Music Groups

1. Gender   ___ Boy   ___ Girl

2. Rank your top three groups from the following list. (Put a 1 in front of your top choice, a 2 in front of your second choice, and a 3 in front of your third choice.)
   ___ Back Street Boys
   ___ Blackstreet
   ___ BoysIIMen
   ___ Hanson
   ___ H-Town
   ___ Spice Girls
   ___ Usher

3. Why do you like your top three groups? Check (✓) all that apply.
   ___ They are cute.
   ___ I like to listen to their music.
   ___ They are like me.
   ___ I can dance to their music.
   ___ The words (lyrics) mean something.
   ___ Their clothes are cool.
   ___ They are rich.
   ___ Other (please explain).

---

4. *Try out the survey*
   After the survey was drafted, the students tried it out themselves. Mrs. Apex and Mr. Dix timed its administration to ensure that it could be completed during advisory period. They also noted that a few students were confused with item 2 and worked with students to add the directions that appear in parentheses.

5. *Do the final draft and make copies*

Finally, each LT elected a representative to help word process, format, spell-check, and print the survey; take it to be duplicated; and then count, sort, and label the precise number needed by each sixth-grade advisory teacher. These representatives would hand carry the surveys to be administered on the designated day.

B. Now that Learning Teams (LTs) have had some instruction and practice on conducting a survey, each LT now returns to its category (books and authors, computer and video games, movies, music, television programs, sports and recreation) and begins work on its survey. Concurrently, Mrs. Apex and Mr. Dix consult with their sixth-grade colleagues to schedule time during an upcoming advisory period during which various LTs can explain, distribute, administer, and pick up their surveys. Shortly thereafter, word begins to spread about their project, and teachers from seventh- and eighth-grade teams begin to ask questions. Most are interested and very supportive, but a few question the project's importance and wonder if they will also be expected to participate.

C. Once the surveys are administered, Mrs. Apex and Mr. Dix begin to focus on helping the students to organize, tally, input, analyze, and interpret the data. Although these sixth-graders have been "exposed" to reading graphs and charts, primarily in mathematics and social studies, the teachers understood that creating them would require a deeper understanding. To assist the students in making the transition from "reading to creating" graphs and charts, they begin by helping them organize their survey and survey results into various kinds of lists because lists are the building blocks of graphs and charts (Mosenthal & Kirsch, 1990a, 1990b).

The sixth-grade students already understood simple lists, such as grocery lists or lists of spelling or vocabulary words. Hence, Mrs. Apex and Mr. Dix worked from an example they had read in a back issue of the *Journal of Reading* (Kirsch & Mosenthal, 1989) to teach the concept of combined lists, which add together two or more simple lists. Using sample data from their own survey on music groups, they "combined" the rankings list with the list of music groups to create the following combined list.

Rankings of Top Three Music Groups

Ranking	*Music Group*
1	Usher
2	Spice Girls
3	BoysIIMen

Once the sixth-graders saw the results displayed in a combined list, many noted that "their" group was not represented in the top 3 combined list. A few astute students also observed that this list did not display the differences between how boys and girls had voted. This provided Mrs. Apex and Mr. Dix the opportunity to use students' knowledge of television listings to help them better understand how to use and construct intersecting lists (Mosenthal & Kirsch, 1989).

TV Listings Example

Time	7:00 P.M.	7:30 P.M.	8:00 P.M.	8:30 P.M.	9:00 P.M.	10:00 P.M.
Channel 2	*Inside Edition*	*Home Improvement*	Movie Premier: *Jurassic Park* →			
Channel 3	Pregame Show	NBA Basketball →				WGN News
Channel 5	*Wheel of Fortune*	*Frasier:* One Hour Special	*Seinfeld*	*Dateline*		→

Using the above sample, they discussed how the television "intersecting list" was *efficient* because the times and channels were listed only once on the chart. They also constructed several sample practice exercises to reinforce use of these types of lists and to teach the students about different types of skills needed to interact with documents successfully. Several practice exercises are listed below. Refer to the section "Reading to Do": Document Literacy Tasks for a refresher on document literacy skills like locating and cycling.

(Locating task)   1. If you were tuned in to Channel 5 at 8:00 P.M., what would you be watching? (*Seinfeld*)

2. What channel do you need to tune to watch *Home Improvement* at 7:30 P.M.? (Channel 2)

(Cycling task)   3. According to the sample television listing, which channel has the most number of programs between 7:00 P.M. and 10:00 P.M.? (Channel 5)

4. If your parents limit your television viewing to two programs per night and you are not very particular about what you watch, according to the sample television listing, which channel would allow you to watch the most hours of television? (Channel 2 or 3)

Once the sixth-grade students had a basic understanding of intersecting lists, they created some of their own to depict results from the trial survey created and administered during the development phase. In Figure 27.6 the top example shows the actual rankings given by both boys and girls, whereas the bottom example displays the tallies of reasons the top three groups are popular.

Mrs. Apex and Mr. Dix also wanted to involve the students in making databases and generating graphs or charts on the computer to analyze and display data. Unfortunately, Trailblazer Middle School currently lacks updated computer hardware and software for this component. The teachers worked with a colleague to learn enough about Corel Quattro Pro to create a database from their sample survey and to produce the pie chart featured in Figure 27.7 so that the students could see an example of how a spreadsheet program could be used for data

FIGURE 27.6   Top Three Music Group Rankings of Sixth-Grade Boys and Girls (Numbers Designate Actual Ranking Received)

| | Music Group | | | | | | |
Gender	Back Street Boys	Black-street	BoysIIMen	Hanson	H-Town	Spice Girls	Usher
Boys (n=13)	3,1,2,3,2	3,2,3,2,2	2,3,1,2,2, 3,3,3,3,3	2,3	2	1,1,3,1,2,1	1,1,2,2,3 1,1,1,1,1
Girls (n=9)	1,2,3,2,1	3,3	3,2,3	2,2,1,2	1,2,1,3, 1,1,3	2,3,1,1, 3,2	

Tallies of Reasons Top Three Groups Were Selected by Sixth-Grade Boys and Girls

| | Reasons Why Selected | | | | | | | |
Gender	Cute	Listen to Music	Like Me	Can Dance	Words Meaningful	Cool Clothes	Rich	Other
Boys (n=13)	2*	13		6	4	4	3	4
Girls (n=9)	5	7	1	4	5	6	1	4

*Applies to Spice Girls only. Specifically noted on these two boys' surveys.

OTHER
Boys
- I like their music and singing.
- I like their videos and what the background looks like.
- I like their songs.
- The rhythm.

OTHER
Girls
- I can sing to their music.
- I like their music videos.
- They are very talented.
- They have great voices and something I can listen to all day.

Note: The author would like to thank Marylin Leinenbach and her sixth-grade students at Chauncey Rose Middle School in Terre Haute, Indiana, for their assistance with the sample survey.

analysis and presentation of information in various document formats such as graphs, tables, or charts. They hope to expand this aspect of this project in the future so that students can also have this hands-on technology experience.

D. The final component, exhibitions of student work, requires that Mrs. Apex and Mr. Dix continue to refine what their students already know about the writing

FIGURE 27.7   Chart Created on Corel Quattro Pro

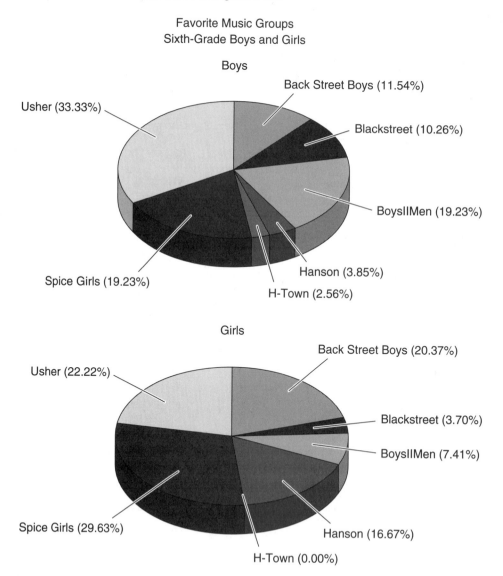

Favorite Music Groups
Sixth-Grade Boys and Girls

Boys

Back Street Boys (11.54%)
Blackstreet (10.26%)
Usher (33.33%)
BoysIIMen (19.23%)
Hanson (3.85%)
H-Town (2.56%)
Spice Girls (19.23%)

Girls

Back Street Boys (20.37%)
Blackstreet (3.70%)
Usher (22.22%)
BoysIIMen (7.41%)
Hanson (16.67%)
Spice Girls (29.63%)
H-Town (0.00%)

process and how to organize information in a paper and in an oral presentation. This component, like others in the project, also requires teamwork and cooperation within the LTs and monitoring by the teachers to ensure that all are contributing and learning from the process. Fortunately, Mrs. Apex and Mr. Dix know that both cooperative learning and the writing process have been emphasized in earlier grades in all the feeder schools. If this were not the case, they recognize that they would have to teach these skills before focusing on the final exhibitions. They are indeed grateful that after reviewing critical components of both, they can concentrate on helping the students with their poster displays and making observations and drawing conclusions from their graphs and charts for both the oral and written presentation modes.

Document Literacy: Next Steps at Trailblazer Middle School

Several weeks have passed, and both Mrs. Apex and Mr. Dix have "recovered" from their inaugural experience with "The Trailblazer Middle School Entertainment Choice Awards." Their principal, Ms. Resh, recently published the results in the school newsletter, which prompted some parents to inquire why their seventh- or eighth-grade students had not been included in the project. Ms. Resh explained that it was a pilot and that the school was considering its future expansion to the upper grades. She also understands, however, that such a project cannot be imposed on either her faculty or the students; they must want to be involved or it stands little chance of being a successful and quality learning experience. She turns to Mrs. Apex, Mr. Dix, and their students for suggestions. More specifically, Ms. Resh wants to know how the students benefitted from the project, what they learned, and how they have continued to apply their knowledge. As she visited with the sixth-graders, this is some of what she heard.

ALEESHA: I learned that there are different kinds of documents but I know more about some of them because we spent more time with some of them.

ROBERT: I learned how to write questions so that I can find out what lots of people think about a certain topic. My group worked on "sports and recreation," and we found out that snowboarding is way cool.

DUSTIN: When I talked to my dad about this project he showed me the types of charts and graphs he uses as work. He's in sales and they make lots of neat graphs to show his boss that he's doing a good job.

MARY: Last year in social studies our book had lots of graphs and charts but I didn't usually understand them much. After making our own, I know more about how to look at them and get stuff out of them.

RYAN: We had to make our charts and graphs by hand, which is O.K., but it's better to do them on the computer like my brother does at the high school or the way Mrs. Apex and Mr. Dix did with their example. Do we ever get some better computers and software for the students to use here?

SHELLEY: It was kind of neat to do something that the older kids aren't doing. My sister's in eighth grade and she was jealous because she thought we were doing something neat rather than boring schoolwork.

DARRYLL: Well, I don't like standing in front of the room talking but because the group was all there we helped each other get it done right. It was fun to see what others thought about music, TV, or movies, even though I didn't agree with some of the choices.

After listening to the students, Ms. Resh asked if they would be willing to present their results in different seventh- and eighth-grade advisories. She thought that after seeing what the sixth-graders had done, both seventh- and eighth-grade teachers and students could then make an informed decision whether to participate. Although a number of the sixth-graders were nervous, they overwhelmingly agreed that they wanted to share their findings and help others understand what they had done with this project.

What If Students Were Document Literate?

The previous scenario need not be fiction. It is vitally important that intermediate- and middle-grades students are literate in all aspects of the word. To achieve success in the twenty-first century, our students must learn to read (narrative), read to learn (expository), and read to do (documents). By combining suggestions from this chapter and others in this handbook, we cannot only promote literacy but can underscore its importance and equip our students with the requisite knowledge, skills, and dispositions to interact with various documents or nonprose formats and narrative and expository texts successfully.

This undertaking will require deliberate and purposeful curriculum planning and collaboration among intermediate, middle grades, and high school faculty members. Just as Mrs. Apex and Mr. Dix built on various literacy and document literacy skills that their intermediate-grades colleagues had taught, they too must work with seventh- and eighth-grade colleagues to develop a coherent sequence of developmentally appropriate instructional activities to lay an appropriate foundation for ongoing development of these skills at the high school level.

As noted in the chapter's introduction, current literacy and document literacy levels of our nation's young adults are inadequate, primarily because development of these skills is not systematically supported in schools. Unquestionably, the demand for highly developed literacy skills—both in society and in the workplace—will continue to increase in the next millennium. The trailblazers among us must work together to find ways to better prepare students for the challenges that await them. Our future depends on it.

REFERENCES

Annenberg Foundation/Corporation for Public Broadcasting. (1997). *Minds of our own* [Videotape series]. (Available from Annenberg/CPB Math and Science Collection, P.O. Box 2345, South Burlington, VT 05407–2345)

Baker, L., & Brown, A.L. (1984). Metacognitive skills and reading. In P.D. Pearson (Ed.), *Handbook of Reading Research* (Vol. 1, pp. 353–394). New York: Longman.

Bassett, E.D., Goodman, D.G., & Fosegan, J.S. (1981). *Business records controls* (5th ed.). Cincinnati, OH: South-Western Publishing.

Fisher, D. (1981). Functional literacy tests. A model of question-answering and an analysis of errors. *Reading Research Quarterly, 16,* 33–43.

Freeman, E.B., & Person, D.G. (1998). *Connecting information children's books with content area learning.* Boston: Allyn and Bacon.

Guthrie, J.T. (1988). Locating information in documents: Examination of a cognitive model. *Reading Research Quarterly, 23,* 178–199.

Guthrie, J.T., Seifert, M., & Kirsch, I.S. (1986). Effects of education, occupation, and setting on reading practices. *American Educational Research Journal, 23*(1), 151–160.

Kirsch, I.S., & Guthrie, J.T. (1984). Prose comprehension and text search as a function of reading volume. *Reading Research Quarterly, 19,* 331–342.

Kirsch, I.S., & Jungeblut, A. (1986). *Literacy: Profiles of America's young adults* (Final Report No. 16-PL-02). Princeton, NJ: NAEP and Educational Testing Service.

Kirsch, I.S., Jungeblut, A., & Campbell, A. (1992). *Beyond the school doors: The literacy needs of job seekers served by the U.S. Department of Labor* (Report No. ISBN-0088685-136–X). Washington, DC: U.S. Department of Labor. (ERIC Document Reproduction Service No. ED 349 460)

Kirsch, I.S., & Mosenthal, P.D. (1988). *Understanding document literacy: Variables underlying the performance of young adults.* (Report No. ETS-RR-88-62). Princeton, NJ: Educational Testing Service. (ERIC Document Reproduction Service No. ED 395 938)

Kirsch, I.S., & Mosenthal, P.D. (1989). Understanding documents: Building documents by combining simple lists. *Journal of Reading, 33*(2), 132–135.

Kirsch, I.S., & Mosenthal, P.D. (1990a). Exploring document literacy: Variables underlying the performance of young adults. *Reading Research Quarterly, 25*(1), 5–30.

Kirsch, I.S., & Mosenthal, P.D. (1990b). Understanding documents: Nested lists. *Journal of Reading, 33*(4), 294–297.

Mosenthal, P.D., & Kirsch, I.S. (1989–1991; 1992–1993). Document strategies and Understanding documents. *Journal of Reading* (Vols. 33, 34, 36).

Mosenthal, P.D., & Kirsch, I.S. (1989). Understanding documents: Intersecting lists. *Journal of Reading, 33*(3), 210–213.

Mosenthal, P.D., & Kirsch, I.S. (1990a). Understanding graphs and charts, Part I. *Journal of Reading, 33*(5), 371–373.

Mosenthal, P.D., & Kirsch, I.S. (1990b). Understanding graphs and charts, Part II. *Journal of Reading, 33*(6), 454–457.

Mosenthal, P.D., & Kirsch, I.S. (1991). Toward an explanatory model of document literacy. *Discourse Processes, 14,* 147–180.

National Center for Education Statistics. (1992). *1992 National adult literacy survey* [On-line]. Available: *http://nces.ed.gov/nadlits/overview.html*

Newmann, F.M., Secada, W.G., & Wehlage, G.G. (1995). *A guide to authentic instruction and assessment: Vision, standards, and scoring.* Madison: Wisconsin Center for Education Research.

Ogle, D. (1986). K-W-L: A teaching model that develops active reading of expository text. *The Reading Teacher, 39,* 564–570.

Paris, S.G., Wasik, B.A., & Turner, J.C. (1991). The development of strategic eaders. In R. Barr, M.L. Kamil, P. Mosenthal, & P.D. Pearson (Eds.), *Handbook of reading research* (Vol. 2, pp. 609–640). New York: Longman.

Pearson, P.D., & Fielding, L. (1991). Comprehension instruction. In R. Barr, M.L. Kamil, P. Mosenthal, & P.D. Pearson (Eds.), *Handbook of reading research* (Vol. 2, pp. 815–860). New York: Longman.

Raphael, T. (1982). Question-answering strategies for children. *The Reading Teacher, 36*(2), 186–190.

Roehler, L.R., & Duffy, G.G. (1991). Teachers' instructional actions. In R. Barr, .L. Kamil, P. Mosenthal, & P.D. Pearson (Eds.), *Handbook of reading research* (Vol. 2, pp. 861–883). New York: Longman.

Sheehan, K., & Mislevy, R.J. (1990). Integrating cognitive and psychometric models to measure document literacy. *Journal of Educational Measurement, 27*(3), 255–272.

Wright, P. (1980a). Strategy and tactics in the design of forms. *Visible Language, 14,* 151–193.

Wright, P. (1980b). Usability: The criterion for designing written information. In P.A. Kilers, M.E. Wrolstad, & H. Bouma (Eds.), *Processing visible language* (Vol. 2, pp. 183–205). New York: Plenum Press.

28 Responding to Research in Grouping

Flexible Grouping in the Middle Grades

JEANNE R. PARATORE
Boston University

RACHEL L. McCORMACK
Plymouth, Massachusetts, Public School

We both spend a good deal of time collaborating with classroom teachers to plan and implement effective instruction in literacy. As we move from school to school talking with teachers about the ways they group children for instruction, we frequently end up in a conversation with at least one teacher that begins something like this:

> I understand that ability grouping is a problem for my poor readers and that they might do better if they were able to work in different groups. But that just doesn't work for my gifted kids. They just need to be challenged and they need a chance to work with other kids like themselves. This heterogeneous grouping stuff just isn't good for them.

Indeed, just three days before sitting down to write this chapter, the conversation occurred once again. As a result, as we began to search and read (or, more often, reread) the studies that have been published in the last several years related to the influence of various grouping practices on children's engagement and achievement in literacy, we did so with particular attention to the effects of various practices on high-achieving students. We asked ourselves over and over again as we read and reviewed published studies: Is it the case that heterogeneous grouping practices are good for some learners but not for all? What do we, in fact, know about grouping practices and about their differential effects on different types of learners, and how can we be certain of what we know?

In this chapter, we begin by sharing with you what we learned from our review of the research in homogeneous and heterogeneous grouping practices in middle grade classrooms and our attempts to answer the questions we raised. Then, in the second part of the chapter, we suggest how one of us (McCormack) put the research to work in her own fifth-grade classroom.

Effects of Ability Grouping

To reexamine the effects of ability grouping on children's performance in literacy, we relied primarily on four published research syntheses. The first two (Good & Marshall, 1984; Slavin, 1990) specifically reviewed studies on heterogeneous versus homogeneous grouping. The third, a metanalysis by Lou, Abrami, Spence, Poulsen, Chambers, and d'Apollonia (1996), reviewed and integrated data from a series of studies on within-class grouping. The fourth, by Hiebert (1983), examined the contexts of different reading groups and the influence of these contexts on children's reading development.

In introducing their review, Good and Marshall (1984) emphasized the complexities that prevent a simple summary of existing studies. They noted, for example, that studies differed in their definitions of the terms heterogeneous and homogeneous and that the range of heterogeneity in any particular study was a factor of the type of school (urban, rural, suburban) in which the study was implemented. Further, they noted that although studies often implemented a single variable approach (i.e., heterogeneous versus homogeneous grouping), several other factors may have confounded the results (e.g., number of groups, class size, age of students, subject matter). Because of such differences in much of the published literature, Good and Marshall focused their review on observational studies in which researchers were explicit in all aspects of their research design and in which they tracked classrooms across a number of different process variables, including peer effects, teacher behavior and attitudes, and instructional content. Beginning first with an examination of such studies examining the effects of tracking, defined as between-class grouping, they concluded that the evidence showed "a consistent pattern of deprivation for low students in schools that practice tracking" (p. 25). They then turned to observational studies of within-class grouping and on the basis of this collection of studies concluded that

> although it is possible to find a few studies that show that elementary students' achievement scores can be increased when students are assigned to higher ability groups (e.g., Dewar, 1963), research that includes systematic observation of instructional process as well as student achievement data has not shown a pattern of achievement gains associated with the assignment of students to ability groups, and indeed, such research has raised questions about the adequacy of instruction that students placed into low groups receive. (p. 29)

In his syntheses, Slavin (1990) examined 27 studies on the effects of ability grouping on the achievement of middle school students, specifically, including only those studies that met the following criteria: (a) ability-grouped classes were compared with heterogeneously grouped classes, (b) achievement data from standardized tests were provided, (c) initial comparability of samples was established, (d) ability grouping had been in place for at least a semester, and (e) at least three ability-grouped and three control classes were involved (p. 538). These studies were generally considered to be between-class grouping studies. He reported that across the 27 studies, "the effects of ability grouping on student achievement are essentially zero" (p. 539). He concluded that

> taken together, studies comparing ability-grouped to heterogeneous placements in the middle grades provide little support for the proposition that high achievers gain from grouping while low achievers lose. (p. 545)

It is important to note that in drawing this conclusion, Slavin drew a clear distinction between the effects of ability grouping and the effects of accelerated learning on high-performing learners. As described by Kulik and Kulik (1984), accelerated learning programs differ from other differentiated grouping programs in that they offer students exposure to content usually taught at a higher grade level and are specifically intended to reduce the time spent by superior students in formal education. The advantages of such programs have been well-documented in a metanalysis conducted by Kulik and Kulik. Slavin, however, dismissed accelerated programs as outside the parameters of ability grouping as it has been defined, because they alter not only the composition of groups, but the curriculum to be studied as well. He has been widely criticized for this viewpoint by proponents of gifted education (e.g., Allan, 1991; Renzulli & Reis, 1991) who argue that the effectiveness of gifted education cannot be judged on the basis of group composition alone, but must also take into consideration the effects of alternative curriculum, class size, resources, and goals. In response to such arguments, Slavin reported in 1991 that a review of existing literature revealed only one carefully controlled study (Mikkelson, 1962) where gifted students were randomly assigned to heterogeneous and gifted education classes, and this study found small differences favoring heterogeneous classes.

Lou et al. (1996) conducted a metanalysis of the effectiveness of within-class grouping on student achievement. In the first of two analyses, these researchers examined the effects of homogeneous, within-class grouping versus heterogeneous, whole-class instruction. Predictably, they found that within-class grouping was better than no grouping and that these effects were strongest for the teaching of reading. The second analysis, however, may be of greater interest in answering the questions posed for this chapter. Here, the researchers examined the effects of the formation of small, homogeneous groups against small, heterogeneous groups. Relying on a small number of studies (12), they aggregated a total of 20 findings. They reported "slight" superiority of homogeneous grouping, but noted a lack of uniformity in this finding across studies. Twelve findings favored homogeneous groups, one found no effect, and six favored heterogeneous groups. Looking at effects across different levels of ability, they found that low-ability students learned more in heterogeneous groups, medium-ability students learned more in homogeneous groups, and there were no differences found for high-ability learners.

Hiebert's (1983) examination of ability grouping differs from the previous three in that she made no attempt to judge the merits of ability grouping versus other organizational schemes. Rather, she sought to understand what happened differently in groups of different levels and what social and instructional effects such differences had on children's opportunities to learn to read. Hiebert's examination focused on studies that were conducted in elementary classrooms through grade 6. Although she reported few definitive findings, she found several trends in the combined data that suggested differences in the quality of instruction offered to students in high- and low-ability groups. For example, when working with children in high- versus low-ability groups, teachers were often (although not always) found to spend more time with children, teachers asked more analytical types of questions, teachers provided students more meaning-based versus graphophonic-based cues, teachers allowed fewer interruptions during the time that they read with students, and teachers assigned more contextual reading.

Hiebert (1983) also examined the effects that placement in different reading-level groups had on students' affective and social development. Citing studies conducted between 1948 and 1980, she reported consistent findings that suggest that children in low-ability groups are generally more self-deprecatory and give lower self-evaluations than their peers in high-ability groups. She also examined studies of ability grouping effects on children's attitudes toward reading and learning to read and found that children in low-ability groups expressed more negative feelings toward reading.

In addition to these four research syntheses, we also reviewed a few individual studies that examined the effects of ability grouping on particular groups of learners and on their subsequent opportunities to learn. In what has become a landmark study, Oakes (1985) studied the nature of instruction in junior high and secondary classrooms. Based on the presentation of her data, it is not possible to separate the junior high classrooms from the secondary classrooms. In relation to this particular aspect of her study, however, she examined 299 English and math classes by reviewing instructional topics and skills teachers taught, the textbooks they used, and copies of sample lesson plans, worksheets, and tests. In addition, teachers were interviewed and asked to indicate the five most important things they wanted their students to learn. In describing the curricula offered students in high- and low-track English classes, Oakes reported that unlike their high-performing peers, students in low-track classes did not read works of great literature and that such works were not read to them nor even shown to them in the form of films. Prominent in the low-ability classes was the teaching of reading skills, generally by means of workbooks and other short-response types of materials. The cognitive tasks expected of them required only simple memory or comprehension, with few opportunities or expectations for application of their learning to new situations. Oakes concluded that

> the types of differences found indicate that, whatever the motives for them, social and educational consequences for students are likely to flow from them. The knowledge to which different groups of students had access differed strikingly in both educationally and socially important ways. (p. 78)

Further, Oakes reported that in the multiracial schools within her sample, minority students were found in disproportionately high percentages in low-track English classes, and the pattern was most consistent in schools where minority students were also poor. Oakes noted that these findings were

> consistent with virtually every study that has considered the distribution of poor and minority students among track levels in schools. In academic tracking, then, poor and minority students are most likely to be placed at the lowest levels of the schools' sorting system. (p. 67)

Braddock and Dawkins (1993) used data from the National Educational Longitudinal Study of 1988 to analyze trends in middle grade and high school tracking and the implications of tracking in the middle grades on the educational aspirations and high school attainments of students. In findings similar to those of Oakes, they reported that African American, Latino, and Native American students were overrepresented in low-ability English classes, participating in such classes at a rate two to two-and-one-half times higher than that of Anglo students. Further, they found that students' high school curricular program placements were strongly affected by ability-group placements in the middle grades, with students from low-ability groups least likely to enter high school academic or college-preparatory programs.

Finally, we chose to include a recent study by Gamoran, Nystrand, Berends, and LePore (1995) particularly because it focused exclusively on the effects of ability grouping in English on the achievement of eighth- and ninth-grade students. In an examination of 92 honors, regular, and remedial classes, Gamoran et al. reported several findings of importance to this review. First, like Oakes and like Braddock and Dawkins, Gameran et al. (1995) found dramatic overrepresentation of poor and minority students in low-track classes. Second, they found different rates of achievement for students in different ability classes, and, more important, statistical analyses led them to conclude that "differences in the nature and effects of classroom instruction constitute an important part of the explanation" (p. 707) for differential achievement.

The combined evidence in ability grouping and its effects on different types of learners led us to draw the following conclusions. When the comparison is made between heterogeneous whole-class instruction and homogeneous small groups, learners of all levels do better within the homogeneous grouping context. In a nutshell, whole-group instruction for long periods of instructional time does not serve any student well. When the comparison is made between heterogeneous small groups and homogeneous small groups, however, the results are quite different and suggest the following:

1. Ability grouping does not have the intended effects on the academic achievement of students. Specifically, students in various levels of ability groups do not achieve the intended academic gains.
2. Ability grouping does not affect the achievement of different levels of learners differentially. That is, despite the widely held belief that high-ability learners "do better" when they work with students like themselves, the evidence does not seem to support the contention. The exception is when high-achieving learners are provided accelerated content that essentially allows them to be instructed in curriculum of a higher grade level.

3. The curriculum offered to students in different levels of ability groups is qualitatively different, providing high-achieving students access to more cognitively challenging, interesting, and motivating material than that given to their lower-achieving peers.
4. Students in different levels of ability groups are provided qualitatively different teaching behaviors, with students in high ability groups more consistently exposed to teaching behaviors that are associated with effective instruction.
5. Students placed in low-achieving groups often experience low self-esteem and negative attitudes toward reading and learning.
6. Students who are poor and who are members of racial and ethnic minority groups are substantially overrepresented in low-achieving groups.

Effects of Alternative Grouping Practices

The negative findings related to ability grouping have led many teachers and researchers to examine alternative practices. Most prevalent among these is the practice of cooperative learning, defined by Johnson and Johnson (1987) as having four basic elements. The first is positive interdependence, the understanding that the success of any individual member of the group is dependent on the success of all members of the group. The second is face-to-face interaction. The third is individual accountability for mastering assigned material. The fourth is the need for students to have and appropriately use interpersonal and small-group skills.

Another grouping practice commonly used is that of peer tutoring or peer dyads. As with ability grouping, to review the body of evidence related to cooperative learning and peer tutoring, we have chosen to rely primarily on data from a series of research syntheses rather than from individual studies.

Cooperative Learning

In 1981, Johnson, Maruyama, Johnson, and Nelson reviewed 122 studies of cooperative, competitive, and individualistic learning and compared the relative effectiveness of each in promoting achievement. Their analysis led them to three major findings: (1) cooperation is considerably more effective than the interpersonal competition and individualistic efforts that characterize traditional instruction, (2) cooperation with intergroup competition is superior to interpersonal competition and individualistic efforts that characterize traditional instruction, and (3) there was no significant difference between interpersonal competition and individual efforts.

Similarly, Slavin (1980) reviewed 28 primary field projects lasting at least two weeks in which cooperative learning methods were used in elementary or secondary classrooms, with the majority of studies being conducted in classrooms at fourth grade or above. He concluded that, in most cases, cooperative learning techniques yielded significantly greater achievement than traditional grouping practices. In addition, he reported that cooperative learning techniques also had strong and consistent effects on race relations, self-esteem, and ability to work cooperatively. In a later article (1990),

Slavin noted that such positive findings are most likely to occur when two particular elements are in place: group goals and individual accountability.

The combined evidence in cooperative learning suggests a few general conclusions:

1. Students of all ability levels who work in cooperative learning groups do better than their peers who work in traditional groups.
2. Students who work in cooperative learning groups have an opportunity to develop strong interpersonal ties and a better understanding of how to develop social relationships.
3. Students who work in cooperative learning groups may develop a stronger sense of self-efficacy.
4. Positive effects are most likely to occur when cooperative learning activities are carefully structured around both group goals and individual responsibility.

The importance of the final point should not be overlooked. A close examination of the evidence indicates that effective implementation of cooperative learning requires not simply physical regrouping of students, but careful selection of the learning task, collaborative planning of the task, and a requirement that every individual display knowledge and understanding upon task completion.

Peer Tutoring

In 1982, Cohen, Kulik, and Kulik conducted a metanalysis of 65 studies of peer tutoring. They included studies that took place in actual elementary or secondary schools, reported on quantitatively measured outcomes in both tutored and untutored groups, and were free of methodological flaws such as differing aptitude levels and teaching of the test to one group. In 45 programs, they found that students who were tutored had higher performance than their peers in a conventional class. In 20 of these cases, the differences in achievement gains were statistically significant, but the effect size was described as modest. In addition, data suggested that in most cases, both tutors and tutees experienced increased achievement gains. The researchers also reported that further analyses suggested that strong effects were consistently associated with certain features, which included highly structured programs, programs of shorter duration, programs that focused on lower-level skills, programs that focused on mathematics rather than reading, and programs that were evaluated on the basis of locally developed rather than nationally standardized achievement tests.

In a further analysis, the researchers identified eight studies that were rigorous in their examination of students' attitudes toward learning and self-concept development. They reported that in all eight studies, researchers found more positive attitudes among students who were tutored and a trend toward improved self-concept than among students who were not tutored. These findings, however, were not statistically significant.

The evidence from the metanalysis led us to conclude that peer tutoring can lead to higher levels of achievement for both members of tutoring dyads, but that such effects are likely to be documented only when the learning task is highly structured and explicit in nature and measured with an instrument highly congruent with the learning activity.

Responding to Research:
Applying the Evidence to the Classroom

As we now shift our attention from studies of the effects of various types of grouping to the particular ways teachers might respond to such evidence, we return first to the question we posed at the start: Is it the case that heterogeneous grouping practices are good for some learners but not for all? The answer to this question, like so many others, seems to be, "It depends." When the choice is whole-class instruction *or* homogeneous small groups, students of all levels generally do better in the latter context. On the other hand, when the choice is homogeneous or heterogeneous small-group instruction, the weight of the evidence firmly supports heterogeneous small-group instruction. Even here, however, there are qualifiers. Close examination of the conditions in which heterogeneous grouping works best suggests that particular learning conditions must be in place. When cooperative learning succeeds, instructional tasks are carefully selected to have shared goals and learning routines require both collaborative and individual responsibility. When these elements are not in place, students typically do less well. In peer tutoring, the tasks that work best are those that are highly structured, explicit in nature, and of a relatively short time duration.

We interpret the evidence to suggest, therefore, that different instructional goals and needs are likely to require the use of different grouping options. The appropriateness of any particular grouping context will depend on the fit between the specific learning task and the chosen grouping strategy; students' preparedness to work within the selected context; and the extent to which teachers monitor, support, and challenge students as they work within any of the grouping options. As described elsewhere (e.g., Paratore, 1994; Radencich, McKay, & Paratore, 1995), we perceive effective classrooms to be those where learning is guided by some basic organizing principles: (1) groups are flexible and changing, with no student functioning as a permanent member of any group; (2) grouping options are selected in response to both individual and curricular needs; (3) the use of different "scaffolds" or types of instructional support are planned and implemented as necessary to increase an individual student's likelihood of success within different grouping frameworks—this ensures that no student is consistently "left-out" of any grouping plan because he or she lacks a specific literacy or social behavior; (4) the "global" plan is characterized by the balanced use of the full range of grouping options.

Sometimes, when such principles are put forth, teachers and administrators respond by noting that although the ideas "look good on paper," in reality, few teachers can make such principles come alive in "real" classrooms with "real" students. There is some empirical evidence to suggest otherwise. For example, in work by the teacher–researcher teams of McMahon and Raphael (1997), Cohen (1991), and

Stevens, Madden, Slavin, and Farnish (1987), students working within classrooms using flexible grouping models have been found to achieve measurable gains in reading, writing, and critical thinking abilities. Like these researchers, one of the authors (McCormack) has put the research to work within her own fifth-grade classroom. The next section of the chapter is written in her voice, as she walks us through exactly what she did and why she did it.

The Classroom Context

There are 21 children—10 boys and 11 girls—in my classroom. The children have a wide range of literacy abilities, achieving on formal tests from three years below grade level to four years above grade level. More important, it was evident to me as I watched them during the first weeks of school that some could read and respond to the regular curriculur materials with ease, whereas others struggled mightily, some because of difficulties at the word level, others because of difficulties in comprehension, and others because of general learning difficulties.

As I began to consider the instructional contexts and strategies that would be most appropriate to this particular group of fifth-graders, I considered many issues. First, as I watched the reluctance with which some of my students, particularly some of the boys, approached the reading task in the early days of school, I was reminded of research that has shown that motivation and interest in reading often diminishes during later elementary school years (Gambrell, Palmer, & Codling, 1996). I was determined to frame instruction in ways that would, in the best circumstance, spark (or respark) my students' interest in reading both in and out of school, and, in the worst circumstance, engage them at least during the time they were in my classroom.

Second, I wanted instruction to reflect what we know as "best practice" in literacy instruction. I planned the classroom instructional routines on the basis of what I understand to be effective practices at all levels of instruction. They are:

1. Students need to read or reread complete text (e.g., story, excerpt, chapter) every day.
2. Students need opportunities to talk to their peers about what they read every day.
3. Students need opportunities to write in response to what they have read and heard every day.
4. Students need opportunities to read something at their comfort level every day.
5. Students need direct instruction in becoming strategic readers and writers every day.

Third, I understood that if students were to develop the comprehension and language knowledge that was essential to advancing their literacy abilities, it was fundamental for all students to have access to high-quality, grade-appropriate text—either through reading or listening—and that all students should be given equal opportunity to respond to that text through writing and language experiences (Cazden, 1992; Fielding & Roller, 1992).

Fourth, I recalled what I knew about grouping practices and set out to devise grouping models that incorporated a variety of grouping configurations: whole-class, peer-led cooperative groups, needs-based groups, peer dyads, and independent. I knew that the students could move from one grouping situation to another, based on both my and their assessment of their needs and interests.

The following section describes three models I have developed as a result of this planning. Although the models share the basic literacy and grouping principles outlined above, each is unique in its focus and each becomes increasingly more demanding in its expectations for student involvement and decision making. Therefore, the models are hierarchical and sequential. To participate effectively in the second model, students must first be accustomed to the literacy and learning strategies of the first; successful participation in the third model assumes familiarity and accomplishment with the second. Because each of the models is used in the classrooms of my fifth-grade colleagues as well as in my own, I often speak of what teachers in general do rather than what I in particular do.

The Take-Five Model

The Take-Five model (Wood, McCormack, Lapp, & Flood, 1997) is presented in Figure 28.1. Designed after Paratore's (1994) flexible grouping prototype, it is largely teacher-directed and intended to provide all students opportunities to learn and practice essential literacy strategies. In addition, it is designed to familiarize all students with various grouping contexts and the types of learning behaviors that are appropriate to each. The same format is carried out each day, allowing students to become knowledgeable about basic instructional routines that will be useful to them as they progress to other, more complex instructional models. The planning sheet displayed in Figure 28.2 is helpful in preparing each day's lesson.

The Take-Five model is so named because of its five daily components: Get Ready, Read, Reread, Respond, and React. In this model, all students read the same high-quality, grade-appropriate text. When the text is a chapter book, one chapter, generally 15 to 20 pages in length, is read every day. When the text is a basal reading anthology, the selection may be divided into two or more sections, depending on length. The procedure for each component follows.

Get Ready.   This part of the lesson helps students get ready to read. Strategic reading is at the center of the design, and there is a great deal of teacher modeling and many opportunities for guided practice. Prereading activities include activating and building background knowledge, developing vocabulary, making predictions, and posing questions. Students, along with the teacher, often do a "quick write"—a short, one-draft prereading writing piece—as a way to motivate them to read the selection for the day. In addition, students are sometimes provided a "minilesson" (Calkins, 1994) on a reading or writing strategy. When reading informational text, students may also be guided to survey the text further by filling in a graphic organizer such as a K-W-L (Ogle, 1986).

FIGURE 28.1   The Take-Five Model

Literature	Content Areas
Get Ready (Whole Class)	
Review previous work	Review previous work
Activate/build background	Activate/build background
Develop vocabulary	Develop vocabulary
Make predictions	Make predictions
Question	Question
Minilesson	Minilesson
Introduce/implement graphic organizers	Introduce/implement graphic organizers
Comprehension monitoring	Survey text
Read (Various Groupings)	
Read with a focus	Read with a focus
Main idea	Main idea
Reread (Various Groupings)	
With a different focus	For detail
For detail	Skim
To identify areas of confusion	Complete graphic organizers
Verbalize/think aloud	K-W-L
Talk/discuss	Answer questions in text orally
Respond (Various Groupings)	
Response journals	Learning logs
Dialogue journals	Response journals
Arts	Convert graphic organizer to connected text
React (Whole-Class or Various Groupings)	
Share journal entries	Share responses or graphic organizers
Teacher-led or peer-led discussions	

Read.   Although the ultimate goal is for all students to read the text independently, in this model the first few pages are read aloud to the whole class, providing them a foundation for successful independent reading. During the read aloud, comprehension monitoring strategies such as reading ahead, visualizing, summarizing, confirming predictions, rereading, and adjusting reading rate are modeled by the teacher, and students are invited to think aloud and think through the strategies as well. Students are then given a focus to continue reading and are asked to read on independently. A small

FIGURE 28.2   Teacher Planning Sheet for the Take-Five Model

Teacher Planning Sheet

Title: _____

Chapter/Pages: _____   Date: _____

Get Ready

   ___ Review

   ___ Build and access background knowledge

   ___ Vocabulary:

         _____

         _____

         _____

   ___ Predict

   ___ Self question

   ___ Minilesson:

   ___ Quick write:

Read

   ___ Read aloud   ___ Silent   ___ Pairs   ___ Other

   ___ Modifications: _____

Reread

   ___ Set new purpose: _____

   ___ Read aloud   ___ Silent   ___ Pairs   ___ Other

Respond

   ___ Discussion prompt:

   ___ Whole class   ___ Groups   ___ Pairs

   ___ Writing prompt:

   ___ Whole class   ___ Groups   ___ Pairs   ___ Individual

React—Share Written Responses

   ___ Whole class   ___ Groups   ___ Pairs   ___ Other

group of students may remain with the teacher to receive additional support. Depending on individual needs, such extra help may take the form of a read aloud of the entire selection, partner reading with the teacher or a peer, or listening to the selection on tape.

Reread.   In this component, students reread the selection in whole or in part for different reasons. It may be necessary, for example, to reread the text or a portion of the text to retrieve specific information from the text, answer a question from the study guide, respond to a prompt, or complete a graphic organizer. For those students who listened to the text on tape or while the teacher was reading aloud, repeated readings of a small section can help build fluency.

Respond.   After the readings, the students respond to a writing prompt. The prompts are recorded in journals. They can be written in groups led by peers or by the teacher or can be composed individually.

React.   Using their journals as prompts, the students meet in small, peer-led groups, or larger, teacher-led groups to share what they wrote in their journals, express reactions to each other's work, or extend their thinking.

The Literature Circles Model

As children acquire autonomy in literacy and learning strategies, they progress to the Literature Circles model. Using strategies suggested by Short (1990) and McMahon and Raphael (1997), the focus of this model is on literacy learning through peer talk. In literature circles, students are provided ample opportunities to interact with their peers, as well as with their teacher, through planning, responding to, and discussing the books they read. They also get many opportunities to practice the reading strategies learned and used during the Take-Five model.

In this model, heterogeneous groups of four to six students join together to read a book they have chosen from a selection of several thematically related titles. Prior to reading, students determine how much they will read each day and who will be the student leader of the day. They use a student planning sheet (Figure 28.3), completed by the group leader prior to the first group meeting, to help structure their activities and interactions. Although some group leaders are able to complete the planning sheet on their own, others require teacher assistance to do so.

Class Meeting.   Literature Circles begin each day with a class meeting. Led by the teacher, students share their groups' plans, ask questions about procedures, and discuss common themes evident throughout the texts. For example, a class reading various texts about the Civil War might benefit from a review of the key incidents surrounding that war, especially if it is part of a thematic unit integrating social studies with literature. In addition, students might be offered a minilesson to introduce or review a skill or strategy of particular importance in understanding the focal texts.

FIGURE 28.3   Student Planning Sheet for Literature Circles

Student Planning Sheet

Title: _____

Chapter/Pages: _____

Date: _____

Student Leader: _____

Get Ready

Say: (1) Let's review.
    (2) Let's make predictions.
    (3) Let's talk about these words: _____
    (4) What questions do we have before reading?

Read

    Let's read.

        ___ In pairs   ___ Alone   ___ In groups

Reread

    Let's think about this while we reread: _____

        ___ In pairs   ___ Alone   ___ In groups

Respond

    Let's respond in our response journals.

React

    What shall we talk about?

Peer-Led Groups.   Next, the students meet in their peer-led groups and the student leader takes over, using the planning sheet as a guide. The students follow procedures they learned in the Take-Five model: They get ready, read, reread, respond in their writing journals, and react through peer-led discussions.

During the peer-led groups, a phase-in, phase-out model is used by the teacher (Lapp, Flood, Ranck-Buhr, Van Dyke, & Spacek, 1997). As the students read and interact, the teacher observes and redirects students as needed. Students having difficulty reading the text are paired with more able peers or with the teacher during the reading segment. If a student leader is unprepared or incapable of managing the group, the teacher temporarily joins that group. Such teacher interventions are brief and relatively rare, particularly as students gain experience and expertise in leading and participating in the groups.

Debriefing.   The whole class reconvenes in a debriefing session to discuss what happened in their groups. Students respond to the themes that tie their groups together, similarities and differences among the books they are reading, and connections to other books they have read individually or as a class. In addition, they sometimes use the debriefing to raise questions about procedures and tasks.

Students' reactions to this model are instructive. They comment that they like working in groups, they like the format, and they like the way everyone in the group gets a chance to be student leader. One student, Jennifer, expressed her approval in this way:

> I really like how we get to work with other people. I really enjoy that. They help you to fix mistakes in your reading and writing. They're there also to tell you that you did a good job.

The students also learn a great deal about themselves after working so closely with their peers. Alison felt that she learned much more than being a better reader; she learned to be part of a group:

> I learned that sometimes I have to open up and do stuff like this because I am shy. I also learned that I am good in a group.

The greatest advantage is that the students learn that reading together helps to enrich their understanding of the text. What is difficult to accomplish alone is often made easier through the interactions with peers. Consider Peter's remarks:

> I have become a better reader. I like to read in groups because you can talk about the books in the groups and ask questions to other group members. It's harder to do that when reading alone.

The Genius Club Model

The Genius Club model was so named after the students did not understand that the original name—Genus Club—meant that they were all reading the same kind of book. It stuck, and the students liked referring to themselves as geniuses. The Genius Club model differs from the Literature Circles model in several ways:

1. As the original name implies, focal texts are related by genre, rather than by theme.
2. Focal texts are differentiated by readability level, enabling lower-performing readers to participate with no teacher or peer support during the reading segment of the lesson.
3. Students pace themselves through the reading of the text, reading as quickly or as slowly as is individually comfortable.
4. Students engage in two separate response groups, first with peers who have read different books, and then with peers who have read the same book.

5. The response groups are not led by a designated student leader, and each member of the group has equal responsibility in achieving a successful discussion.

The model has two phases, phase 1 and phase 2; the procedures for each follow.

To begin the first phase, students meet in heterogeneous groups of five or six. Each group is given the same set of five or six books. Within each text set, the books are characterized by the same genre but represent a variety of reading levels. With the teacher's guidance, each student chooses the book he or she will read.

Class Meeting. Genius Club begins each day with a teacher-led class meeting. During this time, the teacher leads the students in a discussion of the genre being read. They discuss the characteristics of a particular genre and the ways those characteristics might differ among the books that the students are reading. For example, if the genre is biography, the teacher might help students understand the difference between factual and fictionalized biographies. In addition, students discuss the similarities and differences they are encountering in the books they are reading.

Peer-Led Groups. The students then meet in their peer-led groups. For the first 15 or 20 minutes, they read silently. Sometimes they reread what they have read, revisiting parts that they found confusing or that they particularly liked and simply wish to read again. They might also reread and take notes in their journals for discussion later on, recording new or unfamiliar words, jotting down particular ideas, or recording questions they might have.

When children convene to discuss their books, they relate both their general responses and also their thoughts about literary elements and the ways their particular books conformed (or did not) to what they have learned about genre. These discussion groups are more cognitively demanding than those that took place during the Literature Circles model in two ways: The absence of a student leader requires each student to be skilled at entering the discussion in appropriate ways, and the individuality of the text assignments requires students to construct and share their own meaning with little peer support or assistance.

As during literature circles, the teacher circulates around the classroom throughout this time and, when necessary, becomes a participant observer by redirecting students to stay on task, answering with questions, or assisting less capable readers in reading the text.

Debriefing. The class ends with a debriefing session. At this time, groups share what they have learned about literary elements and the particular genre they are studying. They might also share snippets of information about their own books and why they like or do not like them. Teachers comment on and contribute to the students' ideas, and they also share the observations they have made about the ways in which students are interacting in groups.

Phase 1 of the Genius Club model is planned to take approximately two weeks. Because students read at very different rates, some students will finish reading only

FIGURE 28.4   Genius Club Presentation Guide: Biographies

For your presentation, you will need to do the following:

1. Join other students who have read the same biography.

2. Discuss the person you read about. What did you like about the biography? How is this person like you or unlike you? How did the person's accomplishments make you feel? What was the person's greatest contribution?

3. Share your vocabulary notebooks. Choose three new words that you all agree are important or interesting words to teach to the class.

4. Plan your 5- to 10-minute presentation. You need to do the following activities:

   ■ Using your individual summaries as a guide, write a group summary on a five-by-seven-inch index card. Choose someone in your gorup to read it.
   ■ Think of a way to present a main event in that person's life to the rest of the class.
   ■ Think of a way to teach three new words to the rest of the class.

5. Practice your presentation.

one book during this period of time, whereas others may choose to read several. At the end of two weeks, all students should be ready to enter the second phase.

Regrouping.   At the start of the second phase, students are regrouped so that they can join with other students who have read the same book. Now the groups resemble the Literature Circles model. For the next few days, the students meet in their new groups to share their responses to the ideas, characters, events, writing styles, and literary elements of their particular books. The students conclude this phase with a cooperative learning assignment in which they are required to devise a way to present the information they have from their books and their group's discussions to the rest of the class. Figure 28.4 presents a sample assignment sheet for this cooperative activity.

There are many advantages to the Genius Club model. Students read books at their own pace and comfort level, they have an opportunity to discuss the same text from two different perspectives and with two different groups of peers, and they experience multiple texts in a single genre through interaction with their peers.

Students have been predictably enthusiastic about this alternative format. The flexibility of the groups is appealing to them. They like choosing to be with their friends during the first phase of the model, yet they are happy to share what they have read with students who had read the same book in the second phase of the model. They especially like being able to read at their own pace. As one student stated:

> We got to read at our own level and speed. Sometimes when I read, I have to go back and reread something I've read. I could do that without worrying about slowing my group down.

Conclusion

We return once more to the work of Oakes (1985). She wrote:

> Despite the fact that the . . . assumption that students learn more or better in homogeneous groups is almost universally held, it is simply not true. Or, at least, we have virtually mountains of research evidence indicating that homogeneous grouping doesn't consistently help anyone learn better. (p. 7)

We, too, have reviewed the evidence and find ourselves solidly in agreement with Oakes. The alternative models that we have presented, both in published research and in the context of an actual classroom, suggest that there are many ways to respect and support the individual differences that students have without the segregation and sorting that is characteristic of ability grouping as we once knew it. As we continue to work to learn more about effective classroom grouping practices, it is important for us to remember that flexible grouping is an inclusive practice, not an exclusive one; it should be beneficial to all learners. To do it well, we must maintain high expectations for all students and be willing to make substantive modifications for both less and more able students.

REFERENCES

Allan, S.D. (1991). Ability-grouping research reviews: What do they say about grouping and the gifted? *Educational Leadership, 48,* 60–65.

Braddock, J.H., II, & Dawkins, M.P. (1993). Ability grouping, aspirations, and attainments: Evidence from the National Educational Longitudinal Study of 1988. *Journal of Negro Education, 62,* 324–336.

Calkins, L.M. (1994). *The art of teaching writing.* Portsmouth, NH: Heinemann.

Cazden, C.B. (1992). *Whole language plus: Essays on literacy in the United States and New Zealand.* New York: Teachers College Press.

Cohen, E.G. (1991). Teaching in multiculturally heterogeneous classrooms: Findings from a model program. *McGill Journal of Education, 26,* 7–23.

Cohen, P.A., Kulik, J.A., & Kulik, C.L.C. (1982). Educational outcomes of tutoring: A meta-analysis of findings. *American Educational Research Journal, 19,* 237–248.

Fielding, L., & Roller, C. (1992). Making difficult books accessible and easy books acceptable. *The Reading Teacher, 45,* 678–685.

Gambrell, L.B., Palmer, B., & Codling, R.M. (1996). *Elementary students' motivation to read* (Reading Research Report No. 52). Athens, GA: National Reading Research Center, Universities of Georgia and Maryland.

Gamoran, A., Nystrand, M., Berends, M., & LePore, P.C. (1995). An organizational analysis of the effects of ability grouping. *American Educational Research Journal, 32,* 687–715.

Good, T.L., & Marshall, S. (1984). Do students learn more in heterogeneous or homogeneous groups? In P.L. Peterson, L.C. Wilkinson, & M. Hallinan (Eds.), *The social context of instruction: Group organization and group processes* (pp. 15–38). New York: Academic Press.

Hiebert, E.H. (1983). An examination of ability grouping for reading instruction. *Reading Research Quarterly, 18,* 231–255.

Johnson, D.W., & Johnson, R.T. (1987). *Learning together and alone: Cooperative, competitive, and individualistic learning.* Englewood Cliffs, NJ: Prentice Hall.

Johnson, D.W., Maruyama, G., Johnson, R., & Nelson, D. (1981). Effects of cooperative, competitive, and individualistic goal structures on achievement: A metanalysis. *Psychological Bulletin, 89,* 47–62.

Kulik, J.A., & Kulik, C.L.C. (1984). *Effects of accelerated instruction on students. Review of Educational Research, 54,* 409–425.

Lapp, D., Flood, J., Ranck-Buhr, W., Van Dyke, J., & Spacek, S. (1997). Do you really want us to talk about this book? A closer look at book clubs as an instructional tool. In J.R. Paratore & R.L. McCormack (Eds.), *Peer talk in the classroom: Learning from research* (pp. 6–25). Newark, DE: International Reading Association.

Lou, Y., Abrami, P.C., Spence, C., Poulsen, C., Chambers, B., & d'Apollonia, S. (1996). Within-class grouping: A meta-analysis. *Review of Educational Research, 66,* 423–458.

McMahon, S.I., & Raphael, T.E. (Eds.). (1997). *The book club connection: Literacy learning and classroom talk.* Newark, DE: International Reading Association.

Mikkelson, J.E. (1962). *An experimental study of selective grouping and acceleration in junior high school mathematics.* Unpublished doctoral dissertation, University of Michigan.

Oakes, J. (1985). *Keeping track: How schools structure inequality.* New Haven, CT: Yale University Press.

Ogle, D.M. (1986). K-W-L: A teaching model that develops active reading of expository text. *The Reading Teacher, 39,* 564–570.

Paratore, J.R. (1994). Flexible grouping. In A. Purves (Ed.), *Encyclopedia of English studies language arts.* Urbana, IL: National Council of Teachers of English and Scholastic.

Radencich, M.C., McKay, L.J., & Paratore, J.R. (1995). Keeping flexible groups flexible. In M. Radencich & L. McKay (Eds.), *Flexible grouping for literacy in the elementary grades* (pp. 25–41). Boston: Allyn and Bacon.

Renzuli, J.S., & Reis, S.M. (1991). The reform movement and the quiet crisis in gifted education. *Gifted Child Quarterly, 35,* 26–35.

Short, K. (1990). Creating a community of learners. In K. Short & K. Pierce (Eds.), *Talking about books: Creating literate communities* (pp. 33–52). Portsmouth, NH: Heinemann.

Slavin, R.E. (1980). Cooperative learning. *Review of Educational Research, 50,* 315–342.

Slavin, R.E. (1990). Ability grouping in the middle grades: Achievement effects and alternatives. *Review of Educational Research, 60,* 471–499.

Slavin, R.E. (1991). Are cooperative learning and "untracking" harmful to the gifted? Response to Allan. *Educational Leadership, 48,* 68–71.

Stevens, R.J., Madden, N.A., Slavin, R.E., & Farnish, A.M. (1987). Cooperative integrated reading and composition: Two field experiments. *Reading Research Quarterly, 22,* 433–454.

Wood, K.D., McCormack, R.L., Lapp, D., & Flood, J. (1997). Improving young adolescent literacy through collaborative learning. *Middle School Journal, 28,* 26–34.

29 Literacy Assessment

What Should We Use?

ROGER FARR

Indiana University

There are many different literacy assessment instruments and types available to educators today, and the criticisms of (and concerns about) assessment that helped lead to the creation of many of them as alternative assessments have not been clearly resolved. So it is not surprising that many teachers and administrators may well ask, "What am I to do? What should I use?"

There Is No Shortage of Options

Despite a concern about how much classroom time is now dedicated to assessment, the options for selecting literacy assessments to be used in the middle school represent a positive situation. Teachers can choose methodologies and instruments that reflect what they believe about language meaning-making behaviors and how they operate. They can match assessment to their teaching approaches and emphases (Barr, Blackowicz, & Wogman-Sadow, 1995).

Concerns that norm- and criterion-referenced multiple-choice tests do not reflect the way that meaning is constructed from reading, for example, can be allayed by using long-familiar informal assessments, particularly observation, and newer and related alternative assessments like the three major types to be discussed in this chapter:

- Think alongs
- Portfolios
- Performance tests

One of the enduring criticisms of reading tests has been that responding to multiple-choice items is not a valid way to test what theory has described in recent decades as *reading process* (Farr and Tone, 1992; Johnston, 1986; Valencia & Pearson, 1987). Such tests may target a host of subskills traditionally associated with reading using a limited number of items for each. Those multiple-choice items, however, do not reflect behavior that responds to the reader's purpose for reading or actual use of the comprehended text.

Theory-Compatible Alternatives

Language use in general is theorized to be a meaning-making process that links reading to listening and writing to speaking and reading to writing and speaking to listening. Although the focus here (as is often the case) is on reading and writing, all the processes are believed to be nearly identical (Wiggins, 1993). Alternative literacy assessments like those discussed in this chapter reflect that understanding of language use and development. They provide teachers who base their instruction on good theory with assessments that not only can match and enforce their instruction, but that actually can serve as instruction itself.

Score declines in the 1960s into the 1980s on national aptitude tests provoked a great deal of the emphasis on competency testing that has used primarily norm- and criterion-referenced, multiple-choice tests (Calfee, 1987; Hambleton, 1994). There are, of course, important differences between norm-referenced tests and criterion-referenced tests (Farr, 1987), but for the purpose of this discussion, they are usually alike in the way that their items are structured. A few multiple-choice items target each of a host of subskills traditionally believed to add up to reading behavior. The complex issues related to the score declines need not be rehashed here either, but it should be noted that on the National Assessment of Educational Progress (NAEP)—a better measure of national student achievement if undervalued (Calderone, King, & Horkay, 1997; Langer, Campbell, Neuman, Mullis, Persky, & Donahue, 1995; Wirtz & Lapointe, 1982)—scores related to higher levels of thinking (critical thinking) have continued to decline, whereas other performances remained stable or rose slightly (*Results from the NAEP Reading Association—At a Glance,* 1996).

This evidence that U.S. students do not think at higher levels as effectively as we wish or as they did previously has helped sustained demands for accountability testing. As a host of educators, theorists, and writers about assessment have noted, however, alternative forms involve, reveal, and develop thinking much more effectively than multiple-choice items ever can do (e.g., Bartoli, 1985; Marzano, 1988).

Prevailing Traditional Tests

This observation is not intended as an argument that norm- or criterion-referenced tests do not provide particular audiences with some of the information that they desire. It has been charged that teachers and other educators do not understand test and assessment results well enough (Ruddell, 1985). Yet we have entered an age in which teachers, administrators, parents, education critics, and the general public are more exposed to test and alternative assessment results and pressures that high-stake assessments have created than ever before. Promotion, graduation, and teacher salaries and school budgets sometimes depend on test scores these days. The result of this increased exposure is that different assessment audiences are developing new respect for each other's perceived information needs (Farr, 1992).

Many educators would not readily yield to the efficacy of more traditional testing, at least given the high stakes attached to it (Madgic, 1987; Moore, 1983). Yet traditional tests and more familiar assessment reports have prevailed and appear essential in the minds of many of those who want educational accountability (Pearson & Stallman, 1994). State competency mandates have gained stature in recent years. They are accepted as a fact of life by students, parents, teachers, and the public at large. They have survived criticism long leveled at such testing, including the argument that teachers will teach primarily to the tests at the expense of richer and broader curricula. Teaching to the tests has been accepted as a desirable result (Bushweller, 1997). If competency testing can help ensure minimum performance, more power to it. In places like Chicago, tests have been taken up like weapons as part of a get-tough policy (Jones, 1997).

Perhaps one reason that traditional tests have prevailed in accountability testing is that attempts to incorporate alternative assessments in accountability testing have not resulted in dramatic, immediate successes. Several states have worked long and diligently to use portfolios as a major accountability assessment. There are concerns about doing this among some portfolio advocates that are discussed briefly here when describing how portfolio assessment works in the classroom. Nonetheless, numerous states have incorporated alternative assessment as a part of their assessment packages (Valencia, 1994). Some studies that report that nearly every state now has some form of competency testing also report that most include some alternative assessment component or feature (Bond, Roeber, & Braskamp, 1997).

Large-scale portfolio and performance assessment programs are not easily developed and administered. Vermont and New Mexico have given portfolio assessment the time and patience clearly needed to make it a component of their state assessment programs (Dollase, 1996; Statewide Articulated Assessment System, 1995), and Maryland has done that with performance assessment (Kapinus, Collier, & Kruglanski, 1994; Russavage, 1992). Kentucky's struggle to rely on portfolios, however, is another story.

In 1990, the Kentucky legislature mandated portfolio assessment of student writing and other performance indicators in its accountability assessment process designed to promote school reform (Stroble, 1993). Many teachers felt insecure about using the alternative approach, indicating that portfolios did not reflect their teaching emphases. There were papers reporting positive effects (e.g., Kannapel, Coe, Aagaard, & Moore, 1996), but generally the results were slow and invited caution (Winograd, Jones, & Perkins, 1994). There were also rumblings among some teachers (e.g., Guskey, 1994; Harnack, Ellis, & Whitaker, 1994). By 1997, traditional multiple-choice tests had been reinstated as an addition to the state's program, and as reported in the press in early 1998, the state legislature mandated that the program be discarded and completely replaced by 1999.

The Kentucky scenario is indicative of a reinstated faith in more traditional multiple-choice testing among school critics and the public (Kean, 1996). At the same time, in other locales where alternative assessments have not been attempted on such a large scale, administrators, parents, and other audiences have been more receptive to alternative assessments as *additional* sources of information that help them understand student language performance. The ability of performance assessment to inform all assessment audiences to a significant degree, if not primarily, is one probable reason that better understanding of different assessment types is developing across audiences (Anrig, 1992).

So What Is the Teacher to Do?

Administrators can rely on various norm- or criterion-referenced tests to generate information to serve accountability needs, and the same alternative methods and instruments that serve teachers can inform important educational decisions that administrators must make (Farr & Tone, 1998).

Meanwhile, teachers who have gained an understanding of reading and writing as meaning-constructing processes and who have been teaching in accordance with their beliefs should not abandon alternative assessments that fit their teaching approaches and that will enrich the accountability data produced by more traditional tests.

This issue raises concerns that have intensified as the age of educational accountability has materialized: How much classroom time can be invested in assessment? How can the instructional time and other teaching resources we are assessing be protected? Should teachers' concerns about protecting their and their students' high-stakes interests in good test scores tempt them to make assessment even more dominating in the classroom? Studies have shown that developing *test-wise* students can improve scores (Berliner & Casanova, 1986).

Or, will giving students increased opportunities to read and write improve their test performance as well as develop the language behaviors and skills they will need to succeed outside of the classroom? It is hoped that both teachers and educators will decide that this is the case. They will not go back to having students memorize long lists of words out of contexts. They will not skill-drill students on mechanics at the expense of developing the power of expression in their students. They will keep contexts in their teaching that can strengthen thinking abilities as an integral part of language development and use.

In addition, they will look for assessments to use in the classroom that are compatible with these emphases. As the rest of this chapter demonstrates, there are assessment alternatives that will serve these instructional needs; some long-practiced and some newly developed assessment methods and instruments not only do that but that serve as instruction in themselves. Investigating their worth and using them is one obvious solution to concerns about any overemphasis in literacy assessment.

"Kid-Watching": The Basis of Most Alternative Assessment

It is safe to say that all successful teachers use *observation,* every day and consistently in their classrooms. Over the years, particular observational guides, checklists, and formats for recording *anecdotal observations* have been developed to help teachers who wish to systemize their observation of students and to make the practice more diagnostic so as to direct instructional influences (Manzo & Manzo, 1995).

Successful observation, however, need not be overly structured. The master teacher develops an eye and ear for spotting language development in individual students as they apply meaning made from reading and listening as writing and speaking. With practice, the teacher learns to recognize in these behaviors patterns and styles of thinking (Poulson, 1992; Swiderek, 1996). The signs noted will vary from teacher to teacher, class to class, and student to student. The variety of emphases and teacher focuses enrich the guidance a student gets across the grades, and nowhere is the student more ready to grow with good coaching than in the middle school.

An Interactive Investigation.   Good observation is much more interactive than the term may imply. Besides watching and listening to students interacting in classroom discussions and activities, the teacher who observes most usefully engages in conversation with individual students and in small groups, to learn continuously about their interests and how well language is serving—and can better serve—those needs. This aspect of observation is similar to the *conferencing* that is so essential to the success of portfolio assessment.

The conversational exchange that enriches the teacher's observations of a student's behavior can extend beyond the classroom. When the opportunity arises, the teacher can talk with and listen to parents, to learn as much as possible about the student's use of language beyond the classroom.

"How is this *assessment*?" one might ask. Well, it is assessment of the highest, most useful order. Ideally, we would assess how students have developed as language users by following them around to observe and see how effectively they can *use* language. The kind of informal watching, listening, and exchanging suggested here comes about as close to that ideal as we can hope to get. The teacher who observes in this manner is gathering assessment information in a somewhat subjective manner; as we shall observe, however, many of the newer developments in assessment rely to some degree on the educator's professional subjective judgment.

An Ongoing Analysis.   As observational material accrues, some teachers may find it helpful to use some checklist she or he has devised or adopted. Anecdotal records are recommended and are, in effect, just notes on what the teacher has observed. Often possible conclusions are included. There are checklists that the teacher can use in keeping notes or reviewing what has been noted about students. Like the archeologist, the teacher can sort and classify bits of information about a student and then draw conclusions.

It is advisable for the teacher to sit down regularly, perhaps every two weeks or so, to write a paragraph or more about what can be synthesized from observation of each student. As the latest summary is added, the teacher can review what had been entered on the student up to that time. These informal, running records can become very valuable as they develop over time.

Frequently, what the teacher concludes from observing is as practical and instructional as the results of assessment can be: Certain students have revealed particular interests that indicate topics and specific books that should interest them. Some students need help becoming more attentive listeners. Other students avoid committing themselves in front of classmates and need feedback that can build their confidence in their own ideas. A few students' primary strategy to confirm the meanings or spellings of words is to ask someone—the teacher or a classmate; they may need assistance in developing the habit of also consulting the dictionary. The possibilities of clues from such observation range very widely indeed.

It is highly effective and advisable for the teacher to hold a conference with the student over the accruing observation notes on occasion. That creates an opportunity to learn more from the student as he or she reacts to and discusses the teacher's observations. Most important, it helps model ways for the student to become a self-assessor.

Informal Inventories to Inform Placement and Instructional Emphases

There are many procedures, strategies, and devices for informal assessment that are closely related to observation and are as traditionally a part of good teaching as is observation. During the 1960s, when criticisms of and concerns about standardized testing were finding voice, many in language and reading education began collecting and polishing numerous informal assessments. Among these were informal reading inventories (IRIs), which are closely related to observation and are familiar to most teachers (Johns & Lunn, 1983; Johns & VanLeirsburg, 1989; Masztal & Smith, 1984).

Quite simply, IRIs began primarily as assessments to help place students in appropriate levels of instructional—particularly reading—materials. Sometimes, they were simply long word lists that the student was asked to read aloud, but they developed into vocabulary checks that housed target words in sentences. In addition, more specialized IRIs have been developed to reveal potential reading problems or difficulties and that serve diagnosis and instructional decision making. IRIs can be designed with the intention of informing special emphases like language-related thinking behaviors (Manzo, Manzo, & McKenna, 1995). One criticism of these instruments is that they are usually assessments of oral reading, which can be significantly different from and involve reading problems different from silent reading. Another criticism suggests that they are not closely enough reflective of current reading theory (Caldwell, 1985).

A more extensive review of IRIs than can be offered here demonstrates how they grew from word lists read aloud to determine reading placement into instruments for more informative and particular instructional needs (Cheek, 1992) and how they are related to many popular and useful informal assessments and analyses, including *miscue analysis* (see Gunning, 1998, chapter 4).

Three Current Emphases in Literacy Assessment Tend to Link Information Needs

Growing out of observation, as the basic informal assessment methodology, are two newly emphasized alternative literacy assessments with high utility to teachers: These are think alongs and portfolio assessment. A third newly developed assessment methodology is performance assessment, which can serve as a link across assessment audiences (Farr & Tone, 1998, chapter 6).

Think Alongs: A Research Methodology of Instructional Utility

Similar to IRIs and miscue inventories is a new methodology that has been devised to investigate how individual readers process information from texts (Ehlinger & Pritchard, 1994; Robertson, 1995). Various methodologies have attempted to tap students' metacognition activities as they read, which can be done orally, as was the original emphasis, as "think alouds"; but more frequently now it is done as the student reads silently.

The student can be asked to respond orally or in writing to prompts or instructions. When the student responds in writing, it may be in a wide margin left deliberately beside the text. The prompts to get reactions from the student can be used as the student reads, interrupting him or her at particular places in the text or immediately after a text is read. When the latter approach is used, the think along is very similar to a short-essay answer assessment.

An Informal Self-Reporting.   More often than not these days, however, the think along will have the student ruminate in writing about the text being read at regular intervals marked by some symbol. The prompt can be a particular question designed to see if the student is constructing meaning in the most effective or expected way: What do you think of the girl in this story? Have you ever known anyone like her? If the prompt is administered orally by someone sitting beside the reader, an ensuing conversation can build on and clarify the student response.

The student may be asked to pause at the indicated places in the text and simply write what he or she is thinking about at that time. With no more specific prompting than that, the metacognition that may be revealed is undirected, more natural, and a far more dependable look at what the student may be doing with the text. Although there are assessment designers now working on think alongs who ask for more particular responses in an effort to be somewhat diagnostic, the undirected responses that "write what you are thinking about" can be very informative; at the same time, they are much more authentic indications of metacognition.

Process Revealed.   The teacher can look for indications that the student is integrating what is read into his or her experience and personal collection of concepts. One student may be reminded of a personal experience or compare a character with a friend or family member. Another may pause to judge the character's behavior. Still others may analyze why the story or passage is boring, entertaining, informing, or involving them.

What a teacher learns from the synthesis of a series of such comments written while reading one or more texts is necessarily subjective, but it can be very powerful. Subsequent conversations with individual students can seek to clarify student reactions to the text and can reveal more clearly how meaning was being made as it was read.

Sometimes, of course, it will reveal why an expected meaning was not derived. Perhaps, for example, the text's power to evoke feelings was so strong that it overpowered the specifics of the text to change them with the reader's personal recollections. Test makers have always understood the power of passages and stories to do this; thus, they avoid including such prompts on their tests.

Developing Metacognition.   The greatest advantage of using think alongs as informal literacy assessments is that they are very instructional indeed. Quite simply, they encourage and endorse metacognitive self-assessment in readers (Baumann, Jones, & Seifert-Kessell, 1993). Just as teachers will need some practice at interpreting think-along results, students themselves become better at the procedure and more fluent with some experience doing it.

Some teachers gain experience for both by modeling their own metacognition as think alouds. They pick texts to read to the class, pausing as they read, to comment about the text and its contents, about what that text brings to mind, and about their feelings for characters, settings, and ideas. Students are almost invariably fascinated by listening to the teacher do this because it is like getting into the teacher's mind and sensing how it is functioning in reaction to a story, description, essay, or whatever. They find comfort in knowing that some words and phrases, for example, may not be fully clear to an adult, and they can see how the teacher uses contextual clues to solve the problem. They learn that it is not only acceptable, but preferred, that a reader go off the train of text to recall and explore an experience or idea that has been evoked.

After the teacher has modeled a think along with a think aloud several times, students should be encouraged to volunteer to read aloud and report what they are thinking as they read. With that kind of modeling, students will understand quite readily what kind of thoughts are useful in a think along that requires reading silently and writing in the wide margins allowed. They will come to understand reading as an interesting and involving metacognitive activity.

Portfolio Assessment: Effective Literacy Instruction

Portfolio assessment of literacy development is one of the most promising developments in recent years. There is no assessment methodology more closely wedded to instruction than portfolios; they are, in themselves, one of the most effective instructional approaches available to teachers. Portfolios provide a way of seeing how students are *applying* language and at the same time developing the behaviors one would assess (Farr & Tone, 1998; Tierney, Carter, & Desai, 1991).

Portfolio assessment is completely compatible with what we have come to understand about language development over the years: It is the application of the language. It reveals how language serves particular purposes, both of the writers being read and of the students who use it to express themselves. It promotes audience awareness and analysis. It can thoroughly integrate reading, writing, and thinking just as they are integrated in life. It reveals how language use is a thinking process that evolves with widening reading experience and new and revised expression (Deming & Valeri-Gold, 1994).

Portfolio assessment offers impressive instructional benefits, but it creates a considerable amount of work—albeit pleasant work—for a teacher. It cannot go unattended and succeed, and many teachers appreciate considerable assistance and advice in getting it up and running (Arter & Spandel, 1992).

Informing Different Audiences.   Portfolio keeping is all these things; in addition, it has powerful potential to inform a variety of audiences interested in literacy assessment. The teacher can get a vivid, much more complete picture of a student's abilities as a writer, reader, and thinker, and this revelation is displayed as development—almost always some—but not always adequate growth as a language user.

Parents can learn far more about a child's language ability by looking at a portfolio collection of that child's writing and reading than from a letter grade or a score on a multiple-choice test. Many teachers are using portfolio assessment in this way, usually by involving the student. Some plan portfolio back-to-school nights or portfolio parties and have the students explain the collections. Whole collections can be used, or the teacher and student can pull "show portfolios" from their collections to show the parents.

The comments of parents after spending some time looking through their child's portfolio almost always reveal surprise by the extend of language use and of the ideas expressed (Au, 1996). Frequently, they will comment about the amount of misspelling, a traditional indicator in their minds, but they almost invariably are impressed on the whole.

Portfolios can have this same impact on administrators when they are used to mediate decisions or to act as backup and even preferred databases to inform those decisions. Often, decisions that misplace students or deny opportunities to them are made on the basis of test scores. A highly creative, and even articulate, student may have a bad performance day on tests or simply not perform well in the rather esoteric realm of multiple-choice questioning.

When teachers note this situation, they can use students' collections to appeal the decision. Ideally, schools will have such a procedure in place, but even without it, a teacher can take a student's portfolio to a principal or a departmental or district chairperson and say, "Read this, please. It reveals that this student is highly creative and more accomplished as a language user than does the test score that denies her an opportunity to take part in the special course we are planning."

As with parents, reading and writing portfolios can enlighten administrators and others, including educational critics, about the language use of the students who collect them. It is feasible that portfolios can even inform journalists who report on the status of literacy in schools. If such audiences are given the opportunity to examine student portfolios, they may not all agree that all the student writing is as grammatically acceptable as they might wish it to be, but they are very apt to be impressed with the quantity of reading and writing that a majority of students are doing, with their diversity of purposes for using language and the range of ideas involved. The potential of portfolios to serve such information needs is underdeveloped and worthy of educators' attention.

Possible Limitations as Accountability Measures.   As noted earlier here, attempts to use portfolios as large-scale accountability measures have been far from conclusively successful (Bond, 1995). Rating large numbers of the collections is very time consuming, and it is very difficult to get reliability across raters, even when the contents are rather rigidly prescribed. To achieve some rater reliability across the student collections submitted for such assessments, the content may be dictated as a prescribed number of very particular types of writing and written reactions to particular reading. As noted here, these collections are assessment artifacts and not the kind of portfolios that have instructional power (Case, 1994; Irwin-DeVitis, 1996).

Nor do the ratings of large-scale portfolio assessments render scores that will report slight gains or losses in language abilities over time. Descriptive reports on the contents of portfolios across students, schools, districts, and states can be very interesting, but they are not as enlightening as having the parent, administrator, or educational reporter examine true student collections.

Requirements for Successful Portfolio Assessment

Finally, the use of portfolios for large-scale assessment creates what are, actually, less than portfolios. The student loses control of the collection and of the need to self-assess using it. Distinguishing between the kinds of collections that state programs prescribe and the portfolio program that has the potential to serve instruction so effectively becomes clearer when reviewing several of the key factors that make portfolios such effective instruction.

Promoting Self-Assessors.   Portfolios are very powerful promoters of student self-assessment, which will provide a lifelong habit of self-direction in language growth and use. Clearly, self-assessment should be *the* primary goal of all literacy instruction and accompanying assessment.

To achieve this, portfolios must be maintained as *working* collections of student papers and analyses, which are added to, evaluated, and reordered regularly. The sheer quantity of the growing collection forces the kind of student analysis, culling, and structuring that develops self-assessment.

As discussed briefly below, any number of *show portfolios* may be drawn from the contents of the working portfolios for a variety of purposes (including state accountability programs), but to limit the collection to particular papers is, in effect, to do the student's analysis of his or her work for the student: to prejudge what is most important and to classify it with no regard for the individual's purpose for using language.

Ownership: Vital to Student Involvement.   Students must maintain ownership of their collections even though the teacher may require certain organizing tools, such as tables of contents, logs, and analysis sheets. Thus, although the teacher (or even the state) may have some say about what should be in the collections, students can add almost anything they want, can structure the contents from perspectives that are meaningful to them, and can have reasonable control of who will read many of the contents that may relate to personal feelings, beliefs, and reactions.

Students need to be aware of any portfolio contents that may be passed on to some state evaluation team or shown to parents. Along with the teacher's prerogative to add contents and require organizational and analysis features, such inclusions moderate the sense of ownership. Yet becoming aware that certain language behavior and application is required by some elements of society is not a completely negative influence on the student's analysis of his or her work. It can promote an awareness that audience focus is an important part of language use.

Effective portfolioing often involves students in team efforts and partnerships that leads to classmates seeing what is in a student's collection, but the student should have reasonable control over that as well. This concern can affect where the portfolios are kept and who can have access to them. Ideally, they will be easily accessible to the students, who will have optional as well as dedicated times to work with them.

In addition, the students should have a preemptory say about what will be pulled from their working portfolios to create *show portfolios* to serve particular purposes. The teacher can strongly recommend inclusions, but the student should help dictate what work will be seen by

- Their parents
- School administrators or specialists
- Next semester's or next year's teacher
- Other interested outsiders

An Essential Coaching Interaction.   Nonetheless, there are some bottom-line minimums on portfolio inclusions that call for a balance between student ownership and the opportunity to ensure that portfolio assessment is fulfilling its potential. This qualification exists from the initiation of the portfolio when it must be made clear to the student that the teacher will be looking at the contents regularly.

That ongoing interaction is absolutely essential to the instructional and developmental potential of portfolio assessment. The teacher may—and probably will and should—require certain inclusions and should negotiate if necessary with the student to include other papers that the teacher feels are strong indicators of language growth but that have been overlooked by the student.

Features to Promote Analysis of the Contents.   Organizational features, such as tables of contents, reading and writing logs, and sheets to promote regular analysis of new papers added, are vital portfolio contents. They ensure some synthesis of enlarging contents and guide self-analysis. They need to be explained to the student from the outset of portfolioing as requirements and to be used to structure regular student–teacher conferences about the collection.

The logs should require that the students record the titles of texts and the names of authors that they have read and enjoyed as well as the things that they write. It is important that a significant space on the log be allowed for the student to indicate briefly what he or she thinks of what was read or written. These notes can become the seed of subsequent analysis that can help students synthesize what has been read into their understanding of relevant topics. They also direct revision of student writing. Logs are a basic accounting feature of a portfolio that ensure that students add materials regularly and that a significant amount of what is written reacts to something read. The design of such entry lists may vary from classroom to classroom and be designed cooperatively by the teacher and students. They may list writing separately from reading or may combine the two.

Particular organizational guideline sheets can be developed to help students analyze particular pieces of writing, to classify them and evaluate them, and to fit them into the organization of the ideas and interests that the portfolio comes to represent. Reactions from the teacher or fellow students can be included as well along with any revision they promote. These can be written on plain paper or can be facilitated by simple forms and attached to papers in the portfolio.

Ideally, sheets or simple activities of this sort will direct the students to evaluate their work and progress regularly. "How am I doing?" the self-assessor must ask frequently. A sheet, for example, might encourage the students every week or month to select the example of their best writing for the period, to explain why they think that work is their best, and to compare it with pieces they have identified in previous time periods.

Some sheets or procedures presented by the teacher can help students learn to sort and organize the collection into categories that reflect different schemes. Students can organize their collections in a variety of ways that include these basic ones or combinations of them:

- Content: organized by different topics
- Purposes for reading and writing
- Genres and/or audiences
- Stages of development: ideas not yet applied, those used in some way, writing ideas, first drafts, subsequent drafts, writing published
- Favorite or best work and work in need of revision

This kind of analysis should lead to a table of contents that can include brief explanations of why an entry is in the section indicated. The important thing is that students accept the need to revise the contents on a regular basis as materials are added and reorganized after reanalysis. Ideally, students will learn how to create subdivisions within their organizational plans to keep the ever-growing collections in some order that facilitates the very analysis that creates and recreates it.

Classifying and analyzing one's work is admittedly a relatively sophisticated activity. How do middle school children learn to do it (Hansen, 1992)? The analysis sheets can promote and guide such analysis. The teacher can demonstrate to the entire class how to do it, ideally modeling with the portfolio the teacher is keeping.

Student–Teacher Interaction.   Ongoing and regular teacher–student exchanges about portfolio content and what it demonstrates about a student's progress will ensure the self-analysis that is desired. It is this primary element of portfolioing that relates it closely to observation. During class periods that students are allowed to work on their collections, the teacher becomes coach, moving among them, answering and asking questions: "I won't tell you right now, David, whether that story is my favorite. But it is important that you think it is? Why don't you write a note (or use this sheet) to explain why you think it is strong and attach it to it? Where does it go in your organization? Have you added it to your table of contents yet?"

Equally important—and essential to portfolio assessment success—are student–teacher conferences on a regular basis. Because they should be held at least two times a semester or four times a school year, a conference is one of the more demanding aspects of a portfolio program. Most teachers find scheduling the sessions, which should last at least 15 minutes, a primary challenge, but doing so is very important.

In each conference, the student presents his or her collection and explains its organization. The teacher may have provided sheets to allow the student to do this step ahead of time in writing. The conference is scheduled and is understandably a primary motivation for the student to get the portfolio in as good a shape as possible. These are the kinds of points that the conference is apt to focus on:

- The best writing done or revised since the last conference
- Signs of developing language strengths, problems worked on since the last conference, and language goals and objectives that can be the focus of the forthcoming time period
- Plans for what will be read and written in the near future
- Reading that the student has found most interesting and ways that it has been applied or reacted to

Ideally, the teacher does not come to these regular conferences with a prepared checklist, but he or she will let the particular interests, strengths, and needs of the individual student direct where their conversation goes. The idea is to carry on a *conversation* with the student in a manner that generates new awareness and goals and the confidence as a language user to carry them out.

Performance Assessment Is Gaining Acceptance as It Is Better Understood

A third general development in literacy assessment is worthy of particular notice because it answers to our understanding of language use as an integrated meaning-making process directed by a reader's and a writer's purposes. Generally, the test-taker is assigned a purpose for reading a *prompt,* which can be a single text or a combination of texts related to a particular topic. Then, the student responds in writing to the text. Thus, language *performance assessment* is reasonably authentic in that it tests reading and writing ability as a process within an applied use. In performance assessment, the assigned purpose for reading and writing tends to emphasize thinking behavior of a relatively high order.

Equally important, performance testing of literacy answers to some of the needs of all assessment audiences. Because it can be developed with guides to rating the student responses that creates reliability across different raters, it has some of the dependability that gives standardized testing its appeal. Thus, assessment audiences interested in accountability tend to put trust in performance assessment results.

In addition, the measurement of language use as a process appeals to many administrators, some critics of schools, and to the general public, including parents, as a sensible way to focus on language development. One limitation of performance testing's appeal, however, is that it reports student achievement on the test in score ranges from 1 to 3 up to 1 to 6. Nonetheless, administrators and the general public are accepting this newer type of assessment, if only in conjunction with more traditional standardized (normed) and criterion-referenced instruments (Ferrett, 1991). The general result is an increased understanding of literacy as processes not score products.

Two major types of performance assessment are in current and frequent use, and both attempt to lock the comprehension of a passage or story to writing that is based on the text. A passage that is of estimated appropriate difficulty for a particular age or grade level and of interest to students in that group is usually selected from books and articles already in print. Thus, these texts are considered *derivative* and are deemed to be more authentic than texts written specifically for a test. Frequently, the text, called a *prompt* because it is intended to generate student writing, consists of more than one text and more than one type of text on a particular topic. The presentation of the multiple sources on the topic tends to force a synthesis in comprehending them and applying them to the prescribed writing task or tasks, which are also designed to focus on realistic applications of the prompt's content.

Both general types of literacy performance assessment are argued to integrate the comprehension of the prompt (reading) and the application of the comprehension in writing, but the least popular of the two is more "integrated" than the other. In it, the students write just one long response prescribed as a task before they begin reading, and that response is evaluated or rated for both reading and writing (Werner, 1992). Frequently, it is also rated on additional factors or perspectives, often on how well it accomplishes the assigned task. Thus, the student response may be rated with three numbers ranging, say, from 1 to 5.

Possibly because the fully integrated performance test is less familiar than short-answer essay testing formats, the second type separates the student responses into a set to be rated for reading and a longer response to be rated for writing. The reading score is a generalized reaction to four to six questions that focus on comprehension and thinking behaviors appropriate to the particular text. Understandably, synthesizing up to six short essay answers involves a degree of subjectivity; the rater is provided, as we shall see, with adequate help in assigning a score.

The writing task on the second type does not depend on comprehension of the reading prompt, but it is related to it in some thematic way. Thus, the student's performance on this test may result in as few as two scores, one for reading and one for writing. Even more frequently, however, both scores are divided into factors, allowing writing to separate mechanics from organization and content—another appeal to those more comfortable with traditional assessment.

Reliability on the performance test is achieved in two very painstaking ways. First, a *rubric* is devised to describe the kinds of responses that will get a particular score on a particular factor (Arter, 1993). In the fully integrated performance assessment, for example, there may be three factors: *reading, writing,* and *accomplishment of task.* If three such factors are scored in a range from 1 to 3, the rubric table will have nine cells. In each cell, a description of the student response that gets that score on that factor is described.

In addition to the rubric for each prompt or test, the rater is given a booklet of examples of papers (*anchors*) that have received a particular score on each factor. Because writing style and other unique aspects of individual response can create significant differences in papers, two somewhat different responses are presented for each score within each cell in the rubric table. Thus, in rating the response to a prompt on a fully integrated test from 1 to 3 on three factors, the rater would have access to 18 sample anchor papers to assist in assigning scores. There would, for example, be two papers to exemplify a score of 2 on *accomplishment of task,* and so forth.

Usually, these anchor papers are selected from field testing. The results from these tryouts are rated by a panel of raters who subsequently discuss the scores they have assigned in relation to the rubrics, which can be revised in this process if there is much discrepancy across raters. Then, anchor papers are selected from the actual student responses collected in the tryouts and *annotations* explaining what in the sample earned it the particular score it illustrates. This kind of test development attempts to create an instrument with reliability. The judgment in selecting the prompt texts from existing publications and in designing the tasks for applying comprehension of the text is argued to constitute reasonable validity.

Individual teachers or groups of teachers can, of course, develop their own performance tests (Farr et al., 1990). It is an extremely challenging but rewarding task. Think for a minute about the discussions that would be involved as the teachers in one middle school sat down to select prompts that they considered varied and appropriate, tasks that seemed valid for their students, descriptions to represent each score for each factor, and papers from the first administration as a tryout to serve as anchor papers for future administrations. What each teacher involved would learn and clarify about his or her theory about language use and development (and about what one's fellow teachers believe) could constitute a very memorable professional experience. It is the kind of activity that any educator would find valuable.

Meanwhile, more and more published performance literacy tests are available for selection. The selection process could also be a self-defining experience for a teacher. That this is so suggests that the authentic promise of performance testing can be instructional. The student performance on such tests, for example, belongs in the student portfolio, where it can become a part of your overall assessment of the student's literacy performance and the student's own developing ability to self-assess.

Facing Up to the Question

From this relatively brief description of these three new emphases in literacy assessment, a teacher can get a sense of how assessment can be, in itself, highly instructional, thus diminishing the pressures and concerns about the amount of time and energies devoted to assessment. Coupled to one's individually refined methods of observation and to informal assessments that have served the teacher well, a teacher should be able to diagnose for effective individual and group instruction that will incorporate the assessment itself.

The one question remains: Can a teacher be certain that by assessing with think alongs, portfolios, and performance tests, one is preparing students to perform well on the standardized and criterion-referenced tests that will likely yet be a part of the assessment mix? One hopes that an affirmative answer is sure enough that one can invest in assessment methodologies that reflect and strengthen language development by practicing behaviors we believe define literacy as it must be practiced by our students in the real world.

The alternative solution is to drill on skills that tend to be isolated from the full descriptions of those behaviors or, worse yet, on test-taking skills. It is time for teachers, administrators, and other assessment audiences to study and reflect with some respect for each other's information needs. This leaves the teacher in need of assessment that serves instruction.

Each teacher must test the efficacy of what is argued here for himself or herself with the assurance that the newer methodologies for assessing literacy are potentially highly effective instruction *in themselves* and will develop metacognitive language habits in their students that should serve them well outside the classroom.

REFERENCES

Anrig, G. (1992). Testing and accountability. *American School Board Journal, 179*(9), 34–36.

Arter, E. (1992). *The portfolio approach to assessment.* Bloomington, IN: Phi Delta Kappa.

Arter, J. (1993). *Designing scoring rubrics for performance assessments: The heart of the matter.* Paper presented at the annual meeting of the American Educational Research Association, Northwest Regional Educational Lab, Portland, OR.

Arter, J.A., & Spandel, V. (1992). NCME Instructional Module: Using portfolios of student work in instruction and assessment. *Educational Measurement: Issues and Practice, 11*(1), 36–44.

Au, K. (1996). When parents serve as writing critics. *Teaching PreK–8, 27*(2), 61–62.

Barr, R., Blackowicz, C., & Wogman-Sadow, M. (1995). *Reading diagnosis for teachers: an instructional approach* (3rd ed.). Reading, MA: Longman.

Baumann, J.F., Jones, L.A., & Seifert-Kessell, N. (1993). Using think alouds to enhance children's comprehension monitoring abilities. *The Reading Teacher, 47*(3), 184–193.

Bartoli, J.S. (1985). The paradox in reading: Has the solution become the problem? *Journal of Reading, 28*(7), 580–584.

Berliner, D., & Casanova, U. (1986). Should students be made test-wise? *Instructor, 95*(6), 22–23.

Bond, L. (1995). Unintended consequences of performance assessment: Issues of bias and fairness. *Educational Measurement Issues and Practice, 14*(4), 21–24.

Bond, L., Roeber, E., & Braskamp, D. (1997). *Trends in state student assessment programs: Fall 1996 data on statewide student assessment programs.* Washington, DC: Council of Chief State School Officers.

Burns, P.C., & Roe, B.D. (1993). *Burns/Roe informal reading inventory: Preprimer to twelfth grade* (4th ed.). Boston: Houghton Mifflin.

Bushweller, K. (1997). Teaching to the test. *American School Board Journal, 184*(9), 20–25.

Calderone, J., King, L.M., & Horkay, N. (Eds.). (1997). *The NAEP guide: A description of the content and methods of the 1997 and 1998 assessments* (Rev. ed.). Princeton, NJ: National Assessment of Educational Progress.

Caldwell, J. (1985). A new look at the old informal reading inventory. *The Reading Teacher, 39*(2), 168–173.

Calfee, R.C. (1987). The school as a context for assessment of literacy. *The Reading Teacher, 40*(8), 738–743.

Case, S.H. (1994). Will mandating portfolios undermine their value? *Educational Leadership, 52*(2), 46–47.

Cheek, E.H., Jr. (1992). Selecting appropriate informal reading assessment procedures. *Middle School Journal, 24*(1), 33–36.

Deming, M.P., & Valeri-Gold, M. (1994). Portfolio evaluation: Exploring the theoretical base. *Research and Teaching in Developmental Education, 11*(1), 21–29.

Dollase, R.H. (1996). The Vermont experiment in state-mandated portfolio program approval. *Journal of Teacher Education, 47*(2), 85–98.

Ehlinger, J., & Pritchard, R. (1994). Using think alongs in secondary content areas. *Reading Research and Instruction, 33*(3), 187–206.

Farr, R. (1987). New trends in reading assessment: Better tests, better uses. *Curriculum Review, 27*(1), 21–23.

———. (1992). Putting it all together: Solving the reading assessment puzzle. *The Reading Teacher, 46*(1), 26–37.

Farr, R., Lewis, M., Faszhowz, J., Pinski, E., Towle, S., Lipschutz, J., and Faulds, B.P. (1990). Writing in response to reading. *Educational Leadership, 47*(6), 66–69.

Farr, R., & Tone, B. (1992). Theory meets practice in language arts assessment. *ERIC Digest.* Bloomington, IN: Clearinghouse on Reading, English, and Communication.

———. (1998). *Portfolio and performance assessment: Helping students evaluate their progress as readers and writers* (2nd ed.). Fort Worth, TX: Harcourt Brace College.

Ferrett, R.T. (1991). Reading and writing. *Thrust for Educational Leadership, 21*(2) 38–41.

Flynt, E.S., & Cooter, R.B., Jr. (1993). *Flynt–Cooter Reading Inventory for the Classroom* (2nd ed.). Scottsdale, AR: Gorsuch Scarisbrick.

Gunning, T.G. (1998). *Assessing and correcting reading and writing difficulties.* Boston: Allyn and Bacon.

Guskey, T.R. (1994). What you assess may not be what you get. *Educational Leadership, 51*(6), 51–54.

Hambleton, R.K. (1994). The rise and fall of criterion-referenced measurement? *Educational Measurement: Issues and Practice, 13*(4), 21–26.

Hansen, J. (1992). Literacy portfolios emerge. *The Reading Teacher, 45*(8), 604–607.

Harnack, A., Ellis, D., & Whitaker, C. (1994). The impact of Kentucky's Educational Reform Act on writing throughout the commonwealth. *Composition Chronicle: Newsletter for Writing Teachers, 7*(8), 4–7.

Irwin-DeVitis, L. (1996). Teachers' voices: Literacy portfolio in the classroom and beyond. *Reading Research and Instruction, 35*(3), 223–236.

Johns, J.L., & Lunn, M.K. (1983). The informal reading inventory: 1910–1980. *Reading World, 23*(1), 9–19.

Johns, J., & VanLeirsburg, P. (1989). *Informal reading inventories* (Focused Access to Selected Topics No. 39). Bloomington, IN: Clearinghouse on Reading and Communication Skills.

Johnston, P. (1987). Assessing the process, and the process of assessment, in the language arts. In J.R. Squires (Ed.), *The dynamics of language learning: Research in reading and English.* Urbana, IL: National Council of Teachers of English and ERIC Clearinghouse on Reading and Communication Skills, pp. 335–357.

Jones, R. (1997). Getting tough in Chicago. *American School Board Journal, 184*(7), 24–26.

Kannapel, P.J., Coe, P., Aagaard, L., & Moore, B.D. (1996). *I don't give a hoot if somebody is going to pay me $3600: Local school district reactions to Kentucky's high stakes accountability program.* Charleston, WV: Appalacia Educational Lab.

Kapinus, B.A., Collier, G.V., & Kruglanski, H. (1994). The Maryland School Performance Assessment Program: A new view of assessment. In S.W. Valencia, E.H. Hiebert, and P.P. Afflerbach (Eds.), *Authentic reading assessment: Practices and possibilities,* pp. 255–285. Newark, DE: International Reading Association.

Kean, M.H. (1996). Multiple measures: The common-sense approach to education assessment. *School Administrator, 53*(11), 14–16.

Langer, J., Campbell, J.R., Neuman, S.B., Mullis, I.V.S., Persky, H.R., & Donahue, P.L. (1995). *Reading assessment redesigned: Authentic texts and innovative instruments in NAEP's 1992 survey.* Princeton, NJ: Educational Testing Service.

Madgic, R. (1987). Assessment of student learning and school effectiveness: Restoring the focus. *Thrust for Educational Leadership, 16*(4), 38–40.

Manzo, A.V., & Manzo, U.C. (1995). *Teaching children to be literate: A reflective approach.* Fort Worth, TX: Harcourt Brace College.

Manzo, A.V., Manzo, U.C., & McKenna, M.C. (1995). *Informal Reading-Thinking Inventory.* Fort Worth, TX: Harcourt Brace College.

Marzano, R.J. (1988). *Policy constraints to the teaching of thinking.* Aurora, CO: Mid-Continent Regional Educational Lab.

Masztal, N.B., & Smith, L. (1984). Do teachers really administer IRIs? *Reading World, 24*(1), 80–83.

Moore, D.W. (1983). A case for naturalistic assessment of reading comprehension. *Language Arts, 60*(8), 957–969.

Pearson, P.D., & Stallman, A.C. (1994). Resistance, complacency, and reform in reading assessment. In F. Lehr & J. Osborn (Eds.), *Reading, the twenty-first century* (pp. 239–252). Hillsdale, NJ: Erlbaum.

Poulson, L. (1992). Literacy and teacher-assessment at Key Stage 2. *Reading, 26*(3), 6–12.

Results from the NAEP 1994 reading assessment—at a glance. (1996). Washington DC: National Center for Education Statistics.

Robertson, B. (1995). Why think along? Using "think alouds" in the classroom. *State of Reading, 2*(1) 19–22.

Ruddell, R.B. (1985). Knowledge and attitudes toward testing: Field educators and legislators. *The Reading Teacher, 38*(6), 538–543.

Russavage, P.M. (1992). Building credibility for portfolio assessment. In S.F. Clewell, J.F. Almas, and S.A. Wagoner (Eds.), *Literacy: Issues and practices.* Yearbook of the State of Maryland International Reading Association Council, *9,* pp. 19–25.

Statewide Articulated Assessment System. (1995). Sante Fe: New Mexico State Department of Education.

Stroble, E.J. (1993). Kentucky student portfolios: Expectations of success. *Equity and Excellence in Education, 26*(3), 54–59.

Swiderek, B. (1996). Kid-watching (middle school). *Journal of Adolescent & Adult Literacy, 40*(1), 68–69.

Tierney, R.J., Carter, M.A., & Desai, L.E. (1991). *Portfolio assessment in the reading-writing classroom.* Norwood, MA: Christopher-Gordon.

Valencia, S.W. (Ed.). (1994). *Authentic reading assessment: Practices and possibilities.* Newark, DE: International Reading Association.

Valencia, S., & Pearson, P.D. (1987). Reading assessment: Time for a change. *The Reading Teacher, 40*(8), 726–732.

Werner, P.H. (1992). Integrated assessment system. *Journal of Reading, 35*(5), 416–418.

Wiggins, G. (1993). Assessment: Authenticity, context, and validity. *Phi Delta Kappan, 75*(3), 200–208, 210–214.

Winograd, P., Jones, D., & Perkins, F. (1994). The politics of portfolios, performance events and other authentic assessments (Occasional Papers No. 0007). Lexington: Institute on Education Reform, University of Kentucky.

Wirtz, W., & Lapointe, A. (1982). *Measuring the quality of education: A report on assessing educational progress.* New York: Spencer Foundation.

NAME INDEX

SUBJECT INDEX

SUBJECT INDEX